Bantu Historical Linguistics

CSLI Lecture Notes Number 99

Bantu Historical Linguistics

Theoretical and Empirical Perspectives

edited by

Jean-Marie Hombert &
Larry M. Hyman

CSLI Publications *Center for the Study of Language and Information • Stanford, California*

Printed in the United States

03 02 01 00 99   5 4 3 2 1

Library of Congress Cataloging-in-Publication Data

Bantu historical linguistics : theoretical and empirical perspectives /
edited by Jean-Marie Hombert and Larry M. Hyman.
p. cm. – (CSLI lecture notes ; no. 99)
Includes bibliographical references (p.   ) and index.

ISBN 1-57586-203-4 (alk. paper).
ISBN 1-57586-204-2 (paper : alk. paper)

1. Bantu languages–Classification. 2. Bantu languages–Phonology.
3. Bantu languages–Morphology. I. Hombert, Jean-Marie.
II. Hyman, Larry M. III. Series.

PL8025.1.R43 1999
496'.39047–dc21 99-13461
CIP

∞ The acid-free paper used in this book meets the minimum requirements
of the American National Standard for Information Sciences – Permanence
of Paper for Printed Library Materials, ANSI Z39.48-1984.

Contents

3. Comparative and Historical Morphology

Preface

Twenty-two years ago, an important conference entitled "L'Expansion Bantoue", held in Viviers, brought together an impressive array of scholars interested in the comparative and historical study of the Bantu languages and peoples. The proceedings of this colloque, published in three volumes (Hyman and Voorhoeve 1980, Bouquiaux 1980), provide an interdisciplinary synthesis of the history of the Bantu people (linguistic, archeological, and ethnographic).

Since that time there has, of course, continued to be significant historical and descriptive work on Bantu languages. In post-Viviers years, however, much attention has turned to the interaction of Bantu linguistic phenomena with linguistic theory. In the late 1970's and 1980's, for instance, the theoretical study of tone was dominated by the study of African, especially Bantu tone systems. See for example the papers in Clements & Goldsmith (1984) and Hyman & Kisseberth (1998). In syntax as well, Bantu languages were at the center of development of cross-linguistic theories, especially Relational Grammar and Lexical Functional Grammar. See the papers in Mchombo (1993) and references cited therein. In other words, the primarily historical, descriptive, and interdisciplinary goals of Viviers, has, at least in some circles, come to take a back seat to theoretical concerns.

There are several reasons for this. One is personal. Besides Malcolm Guthrie, who passed away in 1972, the post-Viviers period saw the loss of several important Bantuists, most notably A.E. Meeussen, Jan Voorhoeve, and Pierre Alexandre. While their students—and the many scholars who consider themselves their apprentices—continue to work in the comparative and historical tradition which they represented, a number of us have been concerned about the training of subsequent generations to continue this work. It seemed to us that a meeting would be appropriate to discuss what we have learned in the field of Bantu historical linguistics since Viviers and particularly how joint research efforts can coordinated, taking advantage of recent developments in data organization and analysis. We of course thought of organizing a meeting that would be comprehensive and cover most of the important linguistic issues in comparative Bantu. We thought also that this would be an opportune time to present and discuss the various computational tools and lexical data bases that have been recently developed at Berkeley, Lyon, Leiden, Tervuren and elsewhere which have great promise for our future efforts. These products have—and will continue to facilitate the work of established scholars in a major way. Since we deal with about 500 languages within Bantu alone (i.e. not counting Bantoid and further relations), access to this data is crucial. Its availability is in addition an open invitation for others to join us without having to invest a tremendous amount of time in collecting and processing this vast amount of data.

With this in mind, we hosted a "Table Ronde" on Bantu Historical Linguistics at the Université Lumière Lyon2 on May 30-June 1, 1996. This meeting, which was supported in part by a grant from the France-Berkeley Fund, was attended by approximately 60 people. In all, 24 papers were presented or circulated in written form at the conference, of which 18 appear in this volume. In addition, others attended who did not present, but contributed in a significant way to discussions. We are grateful to everyone who participated as well as to their institutions, who provided support for man of them to attend, and to the following contributors to the funding of the meeting: (1) the France-Berkeley Fund; (2) the Université Lumière Lyon2; (3) the Centre National de Recherche Scientifique.

The volume is organized into three parts:

The first deals with issues of classification and linguistic history and includes papers by Derek Nurse (Memorial University, Newfoundland), Christopher Ehret (U.C.L.A.), Yvonne Bastin (Musée Royal de l'Afrique Centrale, Tervuren) & Pascale Piron, Michael Mann (School of Oriental and African Studies, London), and Thomas J. Hinnebusch (U.C.L.A.), "Contact and lexicostatistics in Comparative Bantu studies".

The second part deals with issues in comparative and historical phonology, and includes papers by John M. Stewart (Edinburgh), Larry M. Hyman (U.C. Berkeley), Denis Creissels (Laboratoire Dynamique du Langage (C.N.R.S & Université Lumière Lyon2)), and Catherine Labroussi (Institut National des Langues et Civilisations Orientales, Paris), Thilo C. Schadeberg (University of Leiden), "Katupa's Law in Makhuwa", and Gérard Philippson (Institut National des Langues et Civilisations Orientales, Paris & Laboratoire Dynamique du Langage (C.N.R.S & Université Lumière Lyon2)).

The third part deals with issues in comparative and historical morphology, and includes papers by Claire Grégoire (Musée Royal de l'Afrique Centrale, Tervuren) & Baudouin Janssens (Université Libre de Bruxelles), Pascale Hadermann (Musée Royal de l'Afrique Centrale, Tervuren), Robert Botne (Indiana University), Derek Nurse & Henry Muzale (Memorial University, Newfoundland), and Tom Güldemann (University of Leipzig).

One can see from the table of contents that the issues address are quite varied and are of central concern to Bantuists, whether for historical, comparative, or synchronic purposes. The results reported in this collection represent the accumulation of knowledge over a period of centuries. As we stated at the beginning of this preface, the field of historical and comparative Bantu linguistics has been affected in two ways in recent years. First, it has suffer the loss of several senior scholars. Second, much work in Bantu has been subordinated to theoretical linguistic concerns. One of our hopes in bringing together such a distinguished group of scholars was to produce a conference (and then a volume) that might attract new scholars to the comparative enterprise in Bantu—or perhaps convince some of our theoretical Bantuists to look at the richness of our ca. 500 languages from an historical point of view. What may be most clear is the need to communicate across continents in this effort. More than ever it's important to do joint research efforts, which can be aided by the new computational tools that have been developed at several institutions for comparative work on Bantu.

We would like to thank Suzanne Wertheim for her editorial and formatting assistance in preparing the manuscript for publication, as well as Edmundo Luna for preparing the Language Index.

We hope this volume will inspire present and future scholars in what we feel is, linguistically and otherwise, one of the most exciting comparative areas in the world.

Lyon & Berkeley, October 1998

Towards a Historical Classification of East African Bantu Languages

DEREK NURSE
Memorial University Newfoundland

Preamble

Since its appearance, Guthrie's Comparative Bantu has been the standard referential classification of the Bantu languages. When in doubt, scholars reach for Guthrie's red Volume 2 with its listing of well over four hundred languages/dialects, in which each entry carries a handy tag consisting of letter and number. More recent works list even more languages/dialects. But by Guthrie's own admission, Comparative Bantu was not meant as a statement of the historical development of Bantu languages or the communities speaking them. Comparative linguists and historians have felt the lack of such a statement keenly. Over the two decades following the publication of Comparative Bantu, linguists attempted to fill the gap and these attempts took mainly the form of lexicostatistical assessments of similarity, hence alleged degree of relatedness, between various Bantu languages or sets of Bantu languages[1]. While these assessments were in

---

I would like to thank Thilo Schadeberg for extensive comments on this essay, and for all the cartographic work, and also thank David Odden for his help.

[1] Not all attempts at historically oriented statements were based on lexicostatistics. Some have used shared lexical innovations, others

many cases a better approximation of a historical scenario, they were also not perfect. Participating in, and observing, this activity, I—and other scholars in the area—developed some ideas on what the next stage of a 'historical classification' would look like and how it might be achieved. I present these ideas here.

Archaeology now provides a good general historical background for such a classification. During the last half of the first millenium BC, Bantu-speaking communities spread slowly east and south from the rainforests, gradually becoming the predominant linguistic population of most of subequatorial Africa. At some times and places this spread was rapid, at others it was slow. It involved much interaction with previous non-Bantu populations and often assimilation of them. It also involved interaction and assimilation between Bantu groups. These events continued over the first millenium of our era and into the current millenium. A proper historical linguistic statement will reflect the divergence *and* the convergence involved in these movements. Over time and space, communities and their languages expand and split up continuously. Comparative linguistics ought to be able to group together languages which share a common ancestor, or a series of common ancestors at different levels. At the same time, historical linguistics should be able to detect the traces of contact and assimilation between communities. It should be able to distinguish shared features resulting from common inheritance from those resulting from contact. We ought to aim to provide an outline that will reflect inheritance and indicate significant contact.

The linguistic procedure followed here has two steps. The first step, Part 1, identifies low level subgroups of Bantu languages in East Africa. The second, Part 2, arranges these lower level groupings into higher groups on the basis of the geographical distribution of a small set of phonological features. Part 2.1 discusses some general methodological considerations. A large set of some thirty possible diagnostic features is displayed in 2.2, and three are selected as useful. 2.3 lays out the higher groups that result from the application of the three features.

The treatment of each language group in Part 1 follows the same format. After the group name and its alternatives, (a) provides subgrouping, insofar as it is available, and the basis/bases and major references for the grouping and the subgrouping. Subsection (b) presents an assessment of the general reliability of the grouping, any problematic members, problematic methodology, and any known significant contacts during the last two millenia.

I have also deliberately departed from Guthrie's numerical listing because it is so closely tied to his nonhistorical classification.

The linguistic procedure followed has two steps. The first step, Part 1,

---

strands. It is not my purpose here to evaluate these (see Nurse 1994-5).

identifies low level subgroups of Bantu languages in East Africa. The second, Part 2, arranges tch group, the italicized label and abbreviation are then used in the text.

1. Immediate groupings

The subgroups set out below are widely accepted and I have only modified the received wisdom in a few details. The subgroups, which by and large are obvious to linguists, are based on some combination of: relative mutual intelligibility, lexical innovations, lexicostatistical similarity, and various nonlexical innovations. To arrive at these subgroups I have synthesized available work and evaluated conclusions. Most of these conclusions are not based on considering all possible data and in many cases the data used as a basis for one subgroup is not that for another subgroup. This inevitably means that some parts of the area are better covered than others, and that some statements are better founded than others. Despite this, I think any comparative linguist familiar with the languages of the area would agree with most of Part 1.

A question mark then inevitably arises about the genetic reliability of these groupings (and of course also those in Part 2). It is not only that they are based on data of different kinds, quality, and quantity, it is also that the rules of the game have changed in recent decades. Linguistic change is seen not just as endless binary splitting but rather as something more akin to a kaleidescope, with splitting and merging, diverging and converging. It is not a total kaleidescope because the units that act like this are ultimately connected and had a common origin. This change of perspective can be seen even in this volume. On the one hand scholars who operate basically synchronically, such as Odden, accept labels such as Rutara and "P" (= Rufiji-Ruvuma below)[2], which are certainly labels for typological if not low level genetic groupings. On the other hand, we have Creissels who doubts that Zone S is valid, Donnelly concerned with tonal and other phonological transfer phenomena in southern Africa, and Labroussi charting

[2]List of abbreviations and labels used often in the text:

CK = Central Kenya (E.60+)
GL = Great Lakes (roughly Zone J)
Kilombero = G.50
KT = Kilimanjaro-Taita (E.60, part of E.70)
Mara = E.40 less Logooli
NEC = North-East Coast (E.71-2-3, G.10, G.20, G.30, G.40)
NM = North Mozambique (old P.30)
RR = Rufiji-Ruvuma (Rufiji N.10, P.10, Ruvuma P.20)
S = Zone S
STH = Southern Tanzania Highlands (G.60)
Suguti = E.25+
SWT = Southwest Tanzania (M.10, M.20)
WT = West Tanzania (roughly Zone F)

the spread of Spirantisation through single languages and across sets of languages in southern Tanzania.

In subsection (b) of each group below I try to make clear how genetically reliable I think it is.

1.1. Central Kenya (CK) = Thagicu = Guthrie's E.50 (Kenya, except Sonjo and Daiso in Tanzania)

(a) Northern CK = Meru, Tharaka, Cuka (E.53, 54)
Southern CK = Sonjo (E.46), Gikuyu, Embu, Kamba, Daisu (E.51, 52, 55, 56). This first divides into Eastern SCK (Kamba, Daisu) vs West SCK, then Sonjo vs Gikuyu/Embu, then Kamba vs Daisu.

The most creative thinking about this group has come from P. Bennett, with several published works (1967, 1969, 1983), and an unpublished 1200 item reconstructed lexicon (1981). These deal with various aspects of phonology, verb systems, and the lexicon. Other authors have based Central Kenya on shared loan words: for Cushitic loans in particular, Ehret (1974: 78, 85), Ehret et al (1989), Nurse (1979: 511-523, 1986, 1988). For Nilotic loans, Ehret (1971). For all loans, Ehret (in press). For Sonjo (spoken near Lake Natron in Tanzania), Nurse & Rottland (1991-2, 1993). For Daiso (spoken 50 miles northwest of Tanga, in Tanzania), Nurse (in press). For lexicostatistics, Nurse & Philippson (1980), Nurse (1988: 97), Nurse & Rottland (1991-2).

(b) The grouping and the subdivisions are reliable, and there are no obvious linguistic problems. There was some light early contact with various Cushitic- (extinct) and Nilotic-speaking groups (see Nurse & Rottland 1991-2 for references) and later with Maasai. Sonjo and Daiso, both spoken by fairly small communities, separate from the main group for centuries, and surrounded by other language communities, are the most disparate members of the group, which is otherwise fairly homogenous and conservative (7 vowels, vowel length retained, no Spirantization, Dahl's Law). There are some problems reconciling the linguistic with nonlinguistic scenario: 1. the Kamba, Meru, Gikuyu have oral traditions of having "come from" different places, Kamba from the south around Kilimanjaro, Meru fom the Tana River, Gikuyu from northeast of where they live today. Although the linguistic evidence sees this clearly as a divergent, not a convergent group, and is thus unsympathetic to the picture presented by these traditions, nevertheless the discrepancy between them and the linguistic picture needs further investigating. 2. Did the proto-CK drop the Sonjo off while migrating from Lake Victoria to Central Kenya, or did the early Sonjo migrate separately from Ugikuyu to Lake Natron later? Related to this, why does Sonjo bear certain strong similarities to the languages of eastern Lake Victoria, especially Gusii?

Ehret (various) and the lexicostatistical study behind Vansina (1995) both suggest a genetic link between CK and Kilimanjaro-Taita. I are sceptical about these, as all other lexicostatistically or lexically based claims, until nonlexical support is forthcoming.

1.2. Kilimanjaro-Taita (KT) = E.60, E.74

(a) Taita (Kenya) = Davida and Kasigau vs Saghala
Kilimanjaro (Tanzania) = Gweno vs Chaga proper (= West Kilimanjaro, Central Kilimanjaro, Rombo)

The bases for this group are a set of nonlexical innovations (Nurse 1981), lexical innovations (Ehret 1971, 1974, in press, Nurse 1979, Philippson 1984), and lexicostatistical unity (Nurse & Philippson 1980, Nurse 1988:96, Winter 1980). Philippson (1989), Hinnebusch & Nurse (1981) treat certain parts of this groups's phonological development, for which the data is also outlined in Nurse (1979: 393-403). For Taita see Ehret & Nurse (1981).

(b) The group itself is solid, as is the division into Taita vs Kilimanjaro. To what extent the tripartite division of Chaga itself, and the distinction of Chaga vs Gweno, result from initial early developments as opposed to later lateral spread across contiguous Chaga dialects is less clear. Chaga is usually called one "language" with several "dialects", whereas the Central Kenya group above is usually referred to as consisting of several "languages". This way of labelling reflects ethnic feeling rather than linguistic divisions as Kilimanjaro-Taita is less homogenous than the heartland Central Kenya "languages": beside having undergone Spirantization, 7 > 5 reduction, Dahl's Law, loss of distinctive vowel length, and a number of other common innovations, individual members or subsets of Kilimanjaro-Taita have undergone numerous other changes.

Kilimanjaro and Taita, collectively (early) and separately (later), shows signs of contact with various Cushitic (extinct) and Nilotic communities, and recently with Maasai.

The status of Saghala, and thus the unity of Taita, are problematical. Saghala shows many linguistic signs that point to a Miji Kenda language (see North-East Coast, following): is it originally a Taita language with input from a Miji Kenda language, or vice versa ? This needs to be resolved. Even the lexicostatistical cohesion of Taita is low.

1.3. North-East Coast (NEC) = some E.71-2-3, G.10, G.20, G.30, G.40

(a) Sabaki = Ilwana (northeast Kenya), Swahili (coast of Somalia, Kenya, Tanzania), and certain isolated remnants in Mozambique versus Pokomo (northeast Kenya), Miji Kenda (southeast Kenya), and Comorian (Comoro Islands).
Seuta (northeast Tanzania) = Shambala, Bondei, Zigula, Ngulu.

Ruvu (east, northeast, and centraleast Tanzania = Gogo, Kaguru, Sagala, Luguru, Zaramo, Kami, Kutu, Vidunda, Doe, Kwere (for subdivisions, see Nurse & Philippson 1980).
Pare-Taveta (northeast Tanzania, adjacent Kenya) = Asu, Taveta (also called Tuveta).

The term "North-East Coast" Bantu (upper or lower case) has been used for decades with variable reference. As Guthrie's numbers above imply, he did not identify it as a single group. Its current, precise, complete, linguistic reference started in the 1970s and the details were clarified by the 1980s. The group rests on a combination of lexical innovation, lexicostatistical solidarity, and nonlexical innovations. Despite the likelihood that the protolanguage of this group dates to some two millenia ago, the set of early lexical and nonlexical innovations is relatively small.

Nurse & Phillipson (1980) was the most comprehensive early lexicostatistical assessment; Hinnebusch (1981) is lexicostatistical and phonological; Moehlig (1981) is phonological; Ehret (1971, 1974, in press) sets out loan sets. Nurse & Hinnebusch (1993) deals with lexical, phonological, morphological innovation, besides lexicostatistics. Since it is the most complete statement and refers to all previous work, readers should consult its Bibliography.

(b) This is a solid grouping. The group extends 300 kms from the eastern coast inland to the Gogo speaking area, and along the coast from Brava in Somalia 1500 kms south into Mozambique—although this statement of north-south spread gives an exaggerated picture of the size of the group because it includes isolated members at the ends of the Swahili continuum. The list above in (a) includes over 20 "languages" and some of them have considerable dialect variation. Given this geographical and linguistic spread, and the two millenia since the protolanguage, there is considerable divergence, especially at its edges, where contact with other languages (Cushitic in the north, Bantu elsewhere) has altered the configuration of some members. Historically, earlier stages of languages of this group were in contact with and/or absorbed speakers of Cushitic languages, now mostly extinct.

The work on this group has raised wider methodological problems. One arises from the small Swahili-like languages along the Mozambique coast. These languages show an opaque mixture of features from Swahili and local languages: what were the circumstances that led to this mixture, and how are these languages to be classified (e.g. Schadeberg 1994)? A second has to do with the relationship between features in contemporary languages and assumable features in an ancestral language. All NEC languages today have undergone Spirantization. All the larger, better known, members, and a majority of all members, have undergone 7 > 5 reduction, neutralized the vowel length distinction, weakened **b* before labial vowels, and have no verbal preprefix. But one geographically peripheral language (Ilwana) still has 7 vowels; two (Ilwana, Mwiini) still keep the inherited vowel length distinction and several show signs of having given it up only recently; a few (e.g. Mwiini, Bajuni, Pare, Gogo) have not weakened **b* before back vowels; and several have an active preprefix. One lesson here is that the evidence from minor or peripheral languages is important for making statements about earlier stages for all. Another lesson is that 7 > 5 reduction, length neutralization, b-lenition, and loss of the preprefix are processes that can apparently spread across adjacent and related languages.

A third problem derives from the statement above that "the set of early lexical and nonlexical innovations is relatively small." It is not too hard to explain this: the protoperiod was probably short, allowing little time for the development of innovations, whereas two thousand years have passed since that period, allowing much divergence. It should be said that NEC can also be defined negatively, as in Hinnebusch (1981) and Moehlig (1981). That is, the adjoining groups (CK, KT, West Tanzania, Southern Tanzania Highlands, Kilombero, Rufiji-Ruvuma) show various innovations that have not penetrated NEC.

A final and intriguing issue is the relationship of Spirantization to 7 > 5 reduction. They are clearly linked and Spirantization precedes 7 > 5 (Schadeberg 1994/5). Since proto-NEC had not undergone 7 > 5, had it undergone Spirantization? Although all NEC members today have spirantized, the linguistic equation suggests that PNEC had not yet spirantized, and this is supported by certain loans from Cushitic which are not spirantized in Central Kenya languages but are spirantized in NEC (Nurse & Hinnebusch 1993: 125-133).

1.4. Great Lakes (GL) = Lacustrine = Interlacustrine = D.40, D.50, D.60, E.10-40 = Zone J.

(a) The exact membership of this large group is controversial. If we take the notion of "Zone J" as a working hypothesis, then the fullest statement of its membership is in Schoenbrun (1990), from which what follows is taken[3]. I repeat all his detail, including the internal ordering and labels. That

[3]Guthrie's historical assessment of this area is not quite complete. The fit between Guthrie's zone and the new zone J (Bastin (1978)) is as follows (ignoring small details):

Guthrie	Bastin
E.10	J.10
E.20	J.20
E.30	J.30
E.40	?
D.40	J.40
D.50	J.50
D.60	J.60

"J" suffers from two drawbacks: (1) it does not recognize that E.20 contains E.21-2-3 and E24-5, which are each part of two different subgroups (Rutara,

should not be taken to mean that I necessarily accept them! Perusal of Tucker & Bryan (1957) and Ladefoged et al. (1971) suggests Schoenbrun may have a few very minor omissions.

(i) Luhya = E.30 plus Logooli (Kenya): this most likely divides into three (Bennett 1973): northern dialects (Gisu, Bukusu), southern dialects (Logooli, Idaxo, Isuxa), and central (all the intervening dialects).

(ii) Gungu (single language: no Guthrie number, spoken at the northern tip of the Nyoro area, at the northeast end of Lake Albert = Rwitanzige, south of the Nile).

(iii) West Nyanza
North Nyanza = E.15-7 = Ganda, Soga, Gwere, Syan (Uganda).
Rutara = parts of E.10 and E.20 = Nyooro, Tooro, Chiga. Nyankore (Uganda), Haya, Nyambo, Zinza, Kerewe (Tanzania).

(iv) Western Lakes
Rwenzori = D.40 = Konzo, Nande, etc (Uganda, Zaire)
Kivu = D.60 and D.50. D.60 = West Highlands = Rwanda, Rundi, Shubi, Hangaza, Ha, Vinza (Tanzania, Burundi, Rwanda)
D.50 = Forest = Tembo, Hunde, Haavu, Mashi, Fuliiru (D.63), Viira (D.32) (Zaire)
Kabwari = D.56 (single language) (Zaire)

(v) East Nyanza
Suguti = E.20 = Regi, Ruri, Kwaya, Jita (Tanzania)

Suguti) within the whole, and (2) it does not recognize E.40=Mara at all. Most E.40 languages belong with the rest of Great Lakes, at least typologically, if not historically.

In terms of comparative linguistic procedure, Schoenbrun is open to two criticisms. One is that he tacitly assumes the validity of Great Lakes and simply offers proof for it. Great Lakes is not compared to other East African groups and its status is not objectively discussed. Second, though he stresses more than once the desirability of using lexical and nonlexical criteria, in the end the external and internal validity of Great Lakes rest on using lexicostatistics and lexical innovations.

The status of both Great Lakes and its subgroups could be further determined by considering the status and exact geographical distribution of firstly, additional nonlexical verbal features such as *-aga* vs *-anga*, the distribution of [laa] vs [naa] Far Future, specific shape of *-ile*, specific shape of the 1pl (*tu-*, *ku-*, *ki-*), range of markers of 3sg (*a-*, *y-*, *w-/u-*, *k-*), whether the language has 1sg negative si-, and the specific shape of negative markers, and secondly, nonlexical, nonverbal features such as the inversion of auxiliary and lexical verb, shape of nominal preprefixes, consistent lowering of augment vowels, expression of locative, presence of vowel harmony from stem into affixes, the Luyia Law (Mould 1981: 194-195), and 7 vs. 5 vowels. Additionally, for the languages for which we have so far little or no data, we need to know about Spirantization, Dahl's Law, and Meinhof's Law (see 2.2.1, 2.2.3).

Mara = E.40 less Logooli = Gusii, Suba, Kuria, Ngurimi, Simbiti, Zanaki, Shashi, Nata (Kenya, Tanzania)

The assumption of the validity of this group quietly grew from Meeussen's suggestions in the 1950's until it was widely accepted two decades or so later. There is really no substantive evidence for it: lexical innovation and loan words (Schoenbrun 1990, Ehret 1971, 1974, in press) and lexicostatistics (Nurse & Philippson 1980, Schoenbrun 1990). It seems almost churlish to say this because the archaeological, palaeoecological, cultural, and other evidence (Sutton 1994-5: 263-315 is a summary) suggests a unified and steady peopling of this area by a population likely Bantu-speaking, starting in the last half of the first millenium BC at the forest edge and spreading to the western side of Lake Victoria, then around it to the east by the early centuries of our era. This working hypothesis has led to really fruitful historical work. The expansion included contact with groups speaking Cushitic, Sudanic (both now extinct), and Nilotic.

Such nonlexical studies as have been done do not cover the whole group nor even substantial parts of it. (Mould 1981, Bennett 1973, 1983, Nurse & Muzale (this volume).

The introduction of the label "J" represents historical reality better than what went before but also suffers from the limitations mentioned in footnote 3. Schoenbrun's outline, by omitting all numbers, cuts neatly through the labelling problem. But there are also more substantial content difficulties. As might be expected of a group which is almost 700 kms north to south and similar east to west, it is quite diverse internally. Schoenbrun's (1990: 361) lexicostatistical picture is not quite as convincing as it looks. We know from other studies that the southern boundaries are firm enough but in the west, where large parts of his Western Lakes subgroup adjoin other languages, there are no figures which would permit us to judge the real boundary. The phonology suggests a discrepancy between evidence from lexicostatistics and phonology (see discussion in 2.1, below).

(b) While nonlinguists assume the historical unity of the communities speaking Great Lakes languages, there is little solid linguistic proof so far that these communities derived from a single ancestor, nor of the linguistic features of any putative proto-Great Lakes.

I see the genetic affiliation of Gusii, Kuria, and maybe Suba as particularly contentious. Are they "Great Lakes" languages which had lengthy and significant contact with some Central Kenya language? Or did the speakers of some Central Kenya language once live along the eastern shores, only to be submerged by early Gusii and Kuria? Or is there a particular older genetic link between ancestral Great Lakes and Central Kenya? (cf Whiteley 1960, Nurse & Rottland 1991-2, hinted at in Mould 1981). This is discussed in more detail in section 5.

That southern Luhya, adjacent Mara languages, and a few nonadjacent Ugandan languages (cf 2.3 for details) have not undergone Spirantization or 7 > 5 raises the same methodological issues as we saw in NEC, above (also elsewhere in Bantu, e.g. Shona, group 7 and others below). These isoglosses split not only Luhya but also nearby Suba (Rottland 1993, Rottland & Okombo 1986). What does this linguistic evidence say about the genesis of an ethnic group? Suba is known to result from communities having undergone language shift—but "Luhya"?

At an early point, and at points thereafter, Great Lakes communities were affected by contact with communities speaking Cushitic, Nilotic, and Sudanic languages. During the second millenium AD, communities to the east and northeast of Lake Victoria were heavily affected by contact with Luo (Dimmendaal forthcoming).

1.5. West Tanzania (WT) = Takama = Zone F less some members (all Tanzania)

(a) Sukuma/Nyamwezi (F.21-22: these are dialects of one language) Kimbu (F.24), Nilyamba (F.31), Nyaturu (F.32).

Most scholars have followed Guthrie and assumed the unity of this group. It is often touted as being one of the few of Guthrie's groupings to have historical validity but it at least needs reshaping. As Central Kenya, this is a phonologically conservative group, and most of the obvious phonological features shared by this group are retentions (e.g. 7 vowels, vowel length distinction, little or no Spirantization, class 5 prefix (see Nurse 1988: 34-35)), generally acknowledged to be of limited use for classification. Some of the few innovatory features diagnostic elsewhere for defining groups actually split WT down the middle, dividing Sukuma/Nyamwezi from the other three (Bantu Spirantization, Dahl's Law, lenition of **p*, see sections 2.2.2 and 2.2.2, below). I suggest below that this is because Dahl's Law ceased to operate in Kimbu/Nyaturu/Nilyamba, and because *p*-lenition and some components of Bantu Spirantization entered Sukuma/Nyamwezi (maybe from adjacent members of other groups today sitting to the west or north). The only real evidence for the unity of this group so far is lexical and lexicostatistical. A new supporting set of shared innovations needs drawing up. Ehret (1971, 1974, 1984, in press) has sets of loans.

(b) The core group of West Tanzania (as in 1.5a) is generally accepted and probably valid but needs better documentation of shared innovations.

Several languages usually included in the group are doubtful to different degrees and should be excised:

The F.10 languages, Tongwe and Bende, are very similar to each other but quite different from the main West Tanzania languages and from other neighboring languages in significant ways (for a brief discussion, see Nurse 1988: 58-59). They do not belong here but then it is not clear where they do belong.

Similarly, Bungu (F.25) does not obviously belong here but its affiliation is unclear (Nurse 1988: 33-34, 50, 59, and Labroussi (this volume)).

Sumbwa (F.23) shows some obvious similarities to Sukuma/Nyamwezi and the Sukuma/Nyamwezi refer to it as the "western" tongue, dialects of Nyamwezi constituting the "southern" tongue, and Sukuma dialects the "eastern" and "northern" tongues. But it differs from Sukuma/Nyamwezi in significant ways (it has full blown Spirantization and 7 > 5, whereas they don't) and shows massive lexical and similarities with J.60 languages and Haya/Zinza. Is Sumbwa a West Tanzanian language heavily affected by its neighbors, or vice versa?

Finally, although Langi (F.33) and Mbu(g)we (F.34)—very similar to each other—have traditionally been assigned to this group on lexicostatistical grounds, that affiliation needs more examination. Lexicostatistically, they only just belong to West Tanzania (inheritance or borrowing?) (Nurse & Philippson 1980). Lexically, they show some quite different vocabulary (Ehret in press), and consideration of the main phonological features of West Tanzania (Nurse 1979: 420-423, 1988: 34-35) shows unexplained differences. Conversely, comparison of phonological features with Pare and Chaga, across the Maasai Steppe, shows certain unexplained similarities (Nurse 1979: 393-395, 404-405, 420-423, 1981: 178): what was the settlement pattern of Bantu communities in the Maasai Steppe before the irruption of the Maasai a few centuries ago?

Again, all this raises general questions. One is about how Spirantization starts. In Sukuma/Nyamwezi there are some pairs of words in which one member shows Spirantization, the other not. Are some of them loan words (where from?)? Is Sukuma/Nyamwezi Spirantizing even now? How does Spirantization spread?

The West Tanzania area is the only place in Africa where representatives of the continent's four language families are still spoken. Khoisan communities have probably been present for many millenia, Cushitic and Bantu since the first millenium BC, and the current Nilotic community for just a few centuries. This melting pot has not been well examined linguistically, but West Tanzanian languages show at least lexical influence from all three, and probably phonological and morphological from Cushitic (and Khoisan?), possibly from Nilotic.

Analysts, using lexical or lexicostatistical methods, do not agree on WT's external affiliations. Some favor a connection to GL, others to NEC (and Southern Tanzania Highlands).

1.6. Langi and Mbugwe = F.33, 34 (Tanzania)

(a-c) Although little public information is available on Langi and almost none for Mbugwe, data collected for Mbugwe by M. Mous and for Langi by Nurse and Philippson suggests that they are overwhelmingly similar. Guthrie and Ehret 1974 agree, although their data sources are unclear. Once Langi and Mbugwe are detached from West Tanzania, they are not obviously unambiguously related to any other East African group. See 1.5b preceding.

1.7. Southern Tanzania Highlands (STH) = Southern Highlands = G.60 plus Manda (N11) (Tanzania)

(a) This is a fairly homogenous group. While there are internal isoglosses at the usual levels (including 7 vs 5 vowels), they do not form convincing bundles, so any subdivision is avoided here. This might be expected from the physical configuration of the group (Nurse 1988a: 13).

Lexicostatistical figures can be seen in Nurse & Phillipson (1980) and in Nurse (1988a: 92). Phonological and lexical features are implied rather than formally set out at various points in Nurse (1979: 440-442) and (1988a: 40-43, 102, etc). Lexical borrowings are in Ehret (1974: 79-80), in press, and Nurse (1988b). For some tentative lexical reconstructions for this group and the following groups, see Nurse (1988a: 108-115). Labroussi (this volume) discusses features shared by STH, Wungu, Bemba, and groups 10, 11 below.

(b) All observers are agreed on the unity of this group.

The group was quite strongly affected, at least lexically, by a now extinct S. Cushitic community (Ehret 1974). In more recent times various member languages have had interactions with neighbors: Kisi and Manda have been affected by Nyakyusa, Bena and Hehe have interacted strongly with NEC languages, especially Gogo, to their north, and southern members, especially Manda, have been influenced by Rufiji-Ruvuma languages to the south and east.

In fact, Manda appears in Guthrie not as a member of this group but of N10, a branch of Rufiji-Ruvuma (see 1.9, below). For reasons for regarding it as a original member of STH influenced by N10, rather than vice versa, see Nurse (1988a: 46-48).

1.8. Kilombero = G.50 (Tanzania)

a, b, c. Despite the misimpression given by Nurse (1988a: 95), this is a two member group (Pogoro, Ndamba). The position of Mbunga vis-a-vis Pogoro and Ndamba is similar to several situations reviewed already: Mbunga is similar on the one hand in certain ways to Pogoro/Ndamba and on the other hand to adjacent Rufiji-Ruvuma languages. This is discussed in Nurse (1988a: 36-40) and resolved by regarding Mbunga as an original member of Kilombero heavily influenced by eastern Rufuji-Ruvuma languages. These are small communities, pulled linguistically in different directions by their larger neighbors (STH, Rufiji-Ruvuma, and Ruvu languages to the north), and thus do not form a very cohesive group. Nonetheless, the lexicostatistical (Nurse and Philippson 1980) and phonological evidence (Nurse 1988a) supports this group.

1.9. Rufiji-Ruvuma (RR) = N.10 less Manda, P.10 (both Tanzania), P.20 (Tanzania and Mozambique)

(a) Rufiji = Mbinga = Ngoni (west), Matengo, Mpoto, (Ndendeule), (Ngindo) (Mbunga) (centre), Ndengereko, Rufiji, Matumbi (east)

Ruvuma (P20) = Yao, Mwera$_1$, Makonde, ? others in Mozambique

This is not a group in Comparative Bantu but widely accepted in recent decades. Its bases and subdivisions are phonological (Moehlig 1981: maps, Nurse 1988a: 43-49, 103, 1979: 442-446, Ngonyani forthcoming), lexical (Ehret in press), and lexicostatistical (Nurse 1988a: 93-94).

'Makonde' has much dialect variation. A first draft of this paper included reference to Ndonde and Maviha, but Schadeberg pointed out that Maviha is not an acceptable label, and that there is no reason to highlight only the Ndonde dialect, as it is one of several.

While some of the members here are robust (Makonde, Yao), others (Ndengereko, Rufiji) are ailing.

(b) This is a fairly disparate group, some of whose peripheral members have been heavily influenced by neighbors, sometimes to the point where their original affiliation is hard to see (e.g. see discussion of Mbunga (and Manda) above). Despite this, Rufiji-Ruvuma is a convincing group. Earlier Cushitic settlement seems to have stopped at the Rufiji as there is little sign of older, shared, Cushitic loan material here.

Throughout parts of southern Tanzania, people draw attention with pride to the historical presence of Nguni, from southern Africa. The only group in the area to carry on the ethnonym, the Ngoni, seem to have abandonned the language in the nineteenth century in favor of the local language (Moser 1983, Nurse 1985, Ngonyani forthcoming).

1.10. Nyakyusa = M30 (Tanzania)

(a) This consists of Nyakyusa, Ndali, Nkonde, and other "varieties" of Nyakyusa. Little is known of the nature of variation within Nykayusa or indeed of Nyakyusa in general. Park (1988:135) says that "the manifest political destiny of the Nyakyusa was to incorporate all weaker neighbouring communities into their distinctive political culture," and he describes this as having happened in recent centuries for Ndali, Kukwe, and Selya (Konde?). Lexical loan material (at least) from Nyakyusa has visibly also entered Manda, Lambya, and Kisi. The implication here is that Nyakyusa in earlier centuries was politically and linguistically (Nurse 1988a: 54) expansionist but itself relatively resistant to outside influence. It would be interesting to investigate this further.

The basis for this small group is lexicostatistical, phonological, and some possible lexical innovation (Nurse 1988a: 54-55, 91, 106, 108-115).

(b) There are traces of Cushitic loan material in Nyakyusa.

This group highlights the possibility that languages grow more alike because of political developments and geographical adjacency.

1.11. SW Tanzania (SWT) = Corridor = Nyika-Mwika = M.10, M.20

(a) Nyika = Lambya, Tambo, Nyiha, Malela, Safwa (M.10, M.20) (Tanzania).

Mwika = Pimbwe vs Rungwa, Fipa, Rungu, Mambwe, Wanda, Namwanga, Iwa (and others in Zambia?) (M.10, M.20) (Tanzania, Zambia)

Mwika-Nyika, collectively and separately, are quite homogenous phonologically, somewhat less so lexically. The bases here are lexicostatistical and phonological (Nurse 1988a: 49-53, 91, 104-105, also Labroussi, this volume).

Kashoki & Mann (1978) suggest lexicostatistical similarity between these SW Tanzanian languages and those of Zambia but a rapid phonological survey (Nurse 1988a: 56-58) doesn't really support this. Moehlig (1981: map 22) suggests the nearest affiliations of most of these Zambian languages are to be sought in Zaire.

(b) There is little doubt that this is a solid genetic group.

As a group consisting of mostly smallish communities, it is again not surprising that individual members show signs of contact with their neighbors. Nyika, and to a lesser extent Mwika, have absorbed lexicon from a now extinct S. Cushitic community. There is also nonBantu vocabulary of unidentified origin, and at least one Khoisan word ('giraffe') in Nyika.

1.12. North Mozambique (NM) = P.30 = Makua, Lomwe, Chuabo, Marendje, (also Koti?), (Mozambique)

(a) Guthrie combines this with parts of Rufiji-Ruvuma as Zone P. The bases for this current grouping and for its separation from Rufiji-Ruvuma are phonological and lexical. Although this is not discussed exhaustively (e.g., Hinnebusch 1981, Moehlig 1981, Nurse 1988a), there is general agreement that the phonological characteristics of North Mozambique are quite distinctive and warrant its excision from the languages to the north.

Independently of each other, Janson (1991-2), on phonological grounds, and Ehret (in press), on lexical grounds, propose that NM's nearest genetic affiliation is not with the languages to its north but with languages of Zone S, particularly with Sotho.

(b) This is a reliable grouping. In demographic terms, it is large, having over 5 million of Mozambique's population of over 11 million. It is likely that lexical and phonological interaction with RR members was heavy.

1.13. Other groups further south

It is often suggested that the groupings below are valid. These suggestions are, as usual, lexically or lexicostatistically based.

(a) N.20 (Tumbuka) N.30 (Cewa, Nyanja), N.40 (Nsenga, Kunda, Nyungwe, Sena, etc) (Malawi, Mozambique, Zambia, Zimbabwe)
(b) M.40 (Bemba, etc) and M.50 (Biisa, etc) (Zaire, Zambia)
(c) M.60 (Lenje, Tonga, etc) (Zambia)
(d) Zone S (Botswana, Lesotho, Mozambique, South Africa, Zimbabwe)

I have no specialized knowledge of these groups and am loth to say much about them. At this point I do not want to comment on the validity of N.20-30-40, M.40-50, or M.60 but in Part 2, following, I consider the geographical distribution of the general diagnostic features and the possible implications of their distribution in these languages.

A succession of scholars, before, including, and after Guthrie, held the Zone S languages to be a safe grouping. Recently, this view has come under fire (e.g. Creissels (this volume), Ehret in press, Schadeberg p.c). Can Shona really be attached to a putative proto-S (Huffman & Herbert 1994-5)? Sotho—in contrast to the others—has not Spirantized and strongly resembles Makua in its phonological development (Janson 1991-2). Ehret (in press, lexically based) considers Makua, Shona, the rest of S, N.20-30-40, and M.60 as five coordinate members of a large southern grouping. Zone S languages are not further treated here.

2. Larger groupings

2.1. Larger groupings: methodological considerations

Arranging these smaller groups into larger sets is harder and more controversial. While Guthrie managed to subsume the languages above under seven zones (D, E, F, G, M, N, P) the preceding scenario has twelve groups, and this does not include dozens of other languages in some of the seven zones not considered here. This is clearly splitting, not lumping: once you break thin ice, the more likely it is to crack and splinter. From a taxonomic view point, Guthrie's arrangement is more economical. But the target here is not economy of statement but a classification that reflects historical development. Is it possible to combine these twelve groups in a way that reflects a smaller number of original communities slowly splitting and increasing over a period which started in the mid or late first millenium BC, and becoming more or less established in their present pattern by the end of the first millenium AD? How would these low level groups fit together at higher levels within the classic tree diagram model? Would they be more or less coordinate or more or less subordinate? Is it even desirable to fit them together in this conventional way?

Historical linguistic classifications have correlates in models of history. The classic tree diagram representation of the development of Bantu languages, with their usual binary (occasionally ternary) splits and increasing subordination, corresponded to a historical model which saw an initial Bantu wave rolling inexorably across east and south Africa, breaking as it went into smaller and ever smaller waves. Recently, that historical model has fallen into disfavor, outside Africa and within (Vansina 1995, Ehret in press), and is being replaced by two alternatives. One sees little spread of people but a spread of technology carrying language with it. The other—at least for East Africa—sees a small number of quick early longer movements, sowing a thin Bantu-speaking population over scattered parts of the area, followed by many later small local movements. This latter historical model would correspond to a contemporary linguistic picture with a large number of coordinate groups. This is not the place to discuss the pros and cons of these historical models. Only time will tell whether this change of view is a swing of the historical pendulum or a major shift of historical paradigm. I seek here rather to develop the linguistic possibilities (fairly) independently of historical correlates.

Two main kinds of linguistic data have been used as evidence for classifying Bantu languages and for interpreting Bantu history: lexical and phonological/morphonological[4]. Lexical data consists either of sets of loans (from Cushitic, Nilotic, Sudanic, Khoisan, or neighboring Bantu) or of internal lexical or semantic innovations. The main providers of this kind of data have been Bennett (1967, 1969, 1973, 1981), Ehret (1971, 1973, 1974, 1980, 1984, in press), Ehret & Nurse (1981), Nurse (1979, 1985, 1988a, 1988b), Nurse & Hinnebusch 1993), and Philippson (1984). Data and detailed discussion of (morpho)phonological processes and features in the area under consideration can be found in Bastin (1983), Bennett, Guthrie (1967-71), Hinnebusch (1981), Hinnebusch & Nurse (1981, 1993), Moehlig (1981), Mould (1981), Nurse (1979, 1981, 1988), and Philippson (1989).

It is acknowledged that lexical data, borrowed or otherwise innovated, has to be used carefully. The dangers of not so doing can be illustrated by considering just one word, the word for 'milk' that in Standard (= Southern) Swahili appears as *ma-ziwa* . Guthrie (1971, 2: 125) gives this as a proto item **-diba* HL, class 5, 6, with geographical distribution limited to northeastern Bantu. Ehret (1974) improves on this by proposing that the limited distribution results, not from descent from an inherited item, but rather from a transfer from a Southern Cushitic form **iliba.* This item then forms part of a lexical set used as a basis for making statements about the Southern Cushitic role in earlier East African history. From a historical viewpoint, that explanation is an advance over Guthrie's taxonomic display. Reflexes of this lexeme, as one or the only word for 'milk' occur in Central Kenya (typical shape *i-ria)*, Kilimanjaro-Taita (typical shape *ma-ruBa)*, the North-East Coast groups (e.g. Swahili Spirantized *ma-ziwa)*, and a set of languages down to Rufiji-Ruvuma and SW Tanzania (see Ehret 1974:19, Map 1). But this distribution is flawed because in all the southern languages it is not cognate (Nurse 1988a: 102-108) and visibly a recent transfer, probably from Swahili. Its real distribution, that is, its occurrence in cognate form, is restricted to just CK, KT, and NEC. And what does even this restricted distribution mean? It might mean that all three groups had a single common ancestor which took over this word from Cushitic just once. Or it might mean that it was taken over early in the Bantu presence in East Africa, where the recipient languages were so similar that they treated it

[4]Occasional approaches have tried to incorporate morphology (e.g. Mould 1981, Nurse and Muzale, this volume) or morphosyntax (Güldemann 1996). These approaches are in their infancy.

identically (and early NEC later Spirantized the initial consonant). Or it might mean that just one of the three early groups took it from Cushitic but then passed it to the others. So it certainly implies the ancestral groups were adjacent but it does not necessarily mean there was just one group ancestral to CK, KT, and NEC.

It has long been recognized that vocabulary is the linguistic component which travels most easily from dialect to dialect, from one related adjacent language to another, and from one genetically distant or unrelated adjacent language to another[5]. To have real historical value, a map or list indicating the geographical distribution of lexemes has to be accompanied by an statement of which are cognate and which are not, which derive from a proto-item and which are merely the result of recent or not-so-recent transfer. We have to treat the geographical distribution of lexemes with great care and to be slightly suspicious of historical claims based solely on lexical data. Most maps showing linguistic relatedness on the basis of shared vocabulary, either inherited or innovated, also indicate that the communities affected are adjacent. That is, these assessments of similarity and relatedness seem to reflect earlier history *and* more recent geography and history.

All this seems to be leading to the suggestion that nonlexical features are more reliable as indicators of shared origin. I do not think this is necessarily true. Since Labov and his colleagues started their painstaking and detailed studies of how change spreads across contemporary communities, historical linguists have been revising their thinking about change. Current texts on historical linguistics increasingly foreground change, and move the more traditional concerns of comparative linguistics such as reconstruction into the background. Out of this work—in general and also in Africa—has risen a recognition that phonemic units, phonological processes, phonological patterning, morphophonology, derivational and inflectional morphemes, morphological patterns, morphosemantic and morphosyntactic categories can also slide easily across dialect and language boundaries, whether of the same or a different family. This has been demonstrated in individual cases and can be suspected in others by just looking at the geographical distribution of such features. As with vocabulary, these features show a disturbing tendency to occur in adjacent Bantu languages and groups. While these are often adjacent because they descend from a common ancestral form, this is not always the case. Conversely, even genetic subgroupings which are widely accepted—as in Part 1 above—are often bisected by the distribution of nonlexical features. All the nonlexical analyses mentioned above assume, inter alia, that languages which share features do so because they have inherited them from a single common ancestor. But it is obvious from considering the geographical distribution of the features that many of them are not always coterminous with genetic boundaries and must have crossed them.

---

[5]Twentieth century technology has expanded this list.

Which such features are relatively reliable indicators of common origin? The main nonlexical analyses mentioned above (Bastin, Bennett, Hinnebusch, Moehlig, Mould, Nurse), if put together, contain long lists of nonlexical features. Different writers attach different degrees of historical importance to these features, they interpret them differently, and the historical classifications and scenarios that emerge are different, sometimes radically. A major cause for disagreement is whether the contemporary distribution of a feature results from shared inheritance, or from transfer across group boundaries, or from independent innovation. These features are combined and conflated below, and a few more added. They are arranged in four rough sets (2.2.1-4). A proper treatment of these decisions underlying these four categories would take much justification, which for reasons of space is not possible here, so some claims may seem arbitrary. In each section, the features are in rough order of frequency, with the most frequent first, and features of minor value for the area are omitted (Nurse 1987). Judgements of frequency and usefulness are based on the East Africa area.

We sorely need a good study of how all the processes below work and specifically how or whether they spread, phonologically and geographically.

Six considerations underlie claims about the diagnostic value of the geographical distribution of these features. The first is to look at their contemporary distribution but also to take into account what might be reasonably assumed about about their presence in the protoform of the different groups (from here on, protogroups will be indicated by p-). For example, Dahl's Law is found today in active form (i.e. in prefixes) or as widespread traces in stems (e.g. *-iguta* < **-ikuta* 'be satiated', or *maguta /mavuta* < **makuta* 'oil') in many or all[6] member languages of Central Kenya, Kilimanjaro-Taita, and Great Lakes. It is found only in some member languages and some phonetic contexts in West Tanzania (Sukuma/Nyamwezi, Sumbwa), Northeast Coast (Ruvu, Seuta, Pare), and Southern Tanzania Highlands (e.g some STH languages have *-ikuta* , others *-iguta* , some have *mbepo* 'cold', others have *mepo* < **m-pepo*).While a few isolated lexemes carrying lexicalized Dahl's law might be borrowed, I take the general position here that loss of Dahl's Law is more likely than the opposite. Dahl's Law does not operate actively today in Kamba nor in one dialect of Ha (H. Muzale, personal communication), yet we know that Kamba and the Ha dialect, as members of CK and J.60, respectively, must have had Dahl's Law at one point, which is born out by their retaining frozen lexical forms. Presumably Dahl's Law can stop functioning at any time, including at an early point, which latter case would leave no traces. So I take it that Dahl's Law was once operative in all WT, NEC, and STH, thus in the ancestral forms of, for example, Swahili, Nilyamba, Kimbu, Nyaturu, and Sangu, where it does not operate or has not left traces today.

---

[6]In a few cases I am not sure that Dahl's Law (or any other feature) is present in every eligible context in every eligible word in every eligible language.

A second consideration is that linguistic features do not jump across geographical gaps. They have to be carried across the gaps, either by bodies of people migrating from place to place or by constant and otherwise attested contact between individuals from linguistic groups. In East Africa, certain linguistic communities seem to have been geographically isolated for a long time and to have had little contact with Bantu-speaking neighbours: Nyakyusa, Rwanda/Rundi, Langi-Mbugwe, Chaga, and the core CK communities. The evidence suggests that some of these have often been donors rather than recipients: Nyakyusa, Rwanda/Rundi, and the core CK communities. The situation of the latter is particularly striking as the main Central Kenya languages are nowhere adjacent to other Bantu communities. In the west, CK has been cut off from contact with the Lake Victoria Bantu communities by the Maasai for the last four centuries or so. It is likely that this isolation on the west has in fact obtained for the last two millenia (T. Spear, personal communication), as the Maasai replaced other earlier nonBantu communities. To the southeast and east, the evidence is that members of CK have exported some of their influence during the second millenium, but the traffic has not been two way. To the south, although the southern limits of the Kamba community are not far from northeastern Chaga, that has not resulted in much linguistic contact (Nurse 1979: 339, 352). In these situations, features shared by communities long isolated are of particular interest. If isolates share features with neighbors or others, there is a better than average chance that they result from common inheritance.

The third consideration concerns the general axiom in historical linguistics that related languages which share an innovated feature today are more likely to have inherited it from a single ancestor than to have innovated it independently and later. This underlies much of the work written by the authors above and in general is valid. But I think it needs tempering by positing a correlation between phonetic naturalness of any process and the likelihood that it will occur more than once. If a process is natural and phonetically simple, it is likely to occur often or can be transferred as a process between adjacent communities. Thus, palatalization of velars, loss of nasal before voiceless spirant, voicing of stop after nasal, replacement of accent by tone, 7 > 5, spirant devoicing, and some kinds of lenition, seem to have occurred independently and more than once. They also apparently cross genetic boundaries easily. On the other hand, the phenomena known as Dahl's Law, Bantu Spirantization, probably lenition of **p*, and probably the Ganda/Meinhof's Law, although their results are present in many languages today, have occurred once or a limited number of times historically.

The fourth is an axiom that says that where lexical and phonological indices are at odds, lexical similarity is more likely to indicate recent events (contact), while phonological similarity more likely points to an older underlying connection. This is not always correct because it rests on the misconception that vocabulary is always more easily transferred than other linguistic components, which is often but not always true. But certainly, if lexical and phonological indices are at odds, that is cause for serious pause. It is true for Daiso, some Western Lakes languages, Langi-Mbugwe, Manda, Mbunga, Mwani, Ndamba, Saghala, Sonjo, Sumbwa, and others.

The fifth concerns the possibility of reversing processes by contact. Some processes can apparently be 'reversed', others not. So, if a language which once had a contrast between voiced and voiceless stops following homorganic nasals (**nd* vs. **nt*) merges the two (e.g as nd), then it clearly cannot separate them again later, even under conditions of heavy contact. By contrast, linguistically salient features such as palatalization or details of the morphophonology of class prefixes can easily be undone by speakers who are bilingual in a language without the features.

The sixth and final consideration concerns the time framework. Archaeological information now makes it clear that Bantu communities first entered East Africa about 2500 years ago, emerging out of the rain forest just west of the Great Lakes[7]. At first there were a few major movements of people and communities, while later there was much local movement. The linguistic evidence suggests that the first period was quite short and what followed was far longer. This is because, of the many isoglosses that bisect East (and South) Africa, few are really major and clear, whereas many crisscross, or are local, and present an opaque picture, suggesting much shifting and accumulation of linguistic features over the last two millenia or so, largely obscuring what much have been a initially simpler picture. The Bantu community or communities that first entered East Africa had linguistic variation but not much.

2.2. Phonological and other nonlexical changes

2.2.1. Shared features whose current distribution appears to result mainly from older shared inheritance

These features—few in number—are shared by whole sets of groups. I would not claim that these features never cross language boundaries but rather that they are more likely to be inherited in our languages from an early stage of common development and thus historically diagnostic for the early period. In the current state of our knowledge, this is a statement of relative probability. They are:

Dahl's Law, which characterized p-Central Kenya, p-Kilimanjaro-Taita, p-Great Lakes, p-NEC (Nurse and Hinnebusch 1993: 466), p-WT, and p-STH, that is, a fairly tight group of languages in the northeast of the Bantu-speaking area (Davy & Nurse 1982). Within East Africa, it is not found

---

[7]This seemingly simple claim masks as much as it reveals. For instance, it is not clear whether one or several early communities entered just west of the Great Lakes. Early Bantu communities may also have entered East Africa at other times and places.

south of this area, nor, as far as I know, to the west. These groups could share it for any of four reasons: single common origin, single origin but spread across groups adjacent at an early stage, independent innovation up to six times, later intergroup transfer. Since the first two groups are today geographically discrete and likely have been for nearly two millenia, that makes the fourth reason implausible, at least for some of the groups. The third reason is unlikely and uneconomical. I assume the first or the second reason and see no way of distinguishing them. Both presuppose that the early ancestors of these six groups lived together. An educated guess would put that on, or west of, Lake Victoria in the second half of the first millenium BC.

Bantu Spirantization. As a glance at the relevant maps in Guthrie or Moehlig (1981) will show, this covers a huge area and has affected many Bantu languages (Schadeberg 1994-5). Most of the languages not affected are contiguous and spoken in the rain forest, in Guthrie's zones A, B, C, and D. With very few exceptions, all Bantu languages south and east of the rain forest have been affected. Aside from NM and Sotho, most of the exceptions are dotted around the northern parts of East Africa. They are: all CK, parts of WT (Kimbu /Nyaturu/Nyilamba are not affected, Sumbwa now affected, the evidence from Sukuma/Nyamwezi is ambiguous), and some members of GL. The latter pose a particular problem of interpretation addressed below in B3. Although the details of the geographical distribution are not quite the same as for Dahl (or Meinhof), this again separates a small northeastern from a large southern set of East African languages.

Since this process is so widely attested in Bantu, it would seem to have occurred early. The seeds of Spirantization would seem to have been planted at least by the time early Bantu communities left the rain forest, as nearly all—but not quite all—non-forest languages are affected by it. As Hinnebusch (1981: 41) says, "..Spirantization has its source in a complex mix of genetic and diffusional mechanisms." While admitting we need to know more about the details of how Bantu Spirantization spread phonetically and geographically, it poses a particular problem for those who posit a split of non-rain forest languages into Eastern and Western Bantu. That it occurs in the majority of Eastern and Western languages could be accounted for by positing that Spirantization preceded any East-West split but then its nonoccurrence in p-CK, p-WT, some Great Lakes languages, NM, and Sotho—"Eastern" languages for most scholars—would be hard to deal with.

But how early is early? What is the chronology of Spirantization versus that of Dahl's Law? The geographical facts of distribution—Dahl's Law limited to the northeast, Spirantization much more widespread—suggest the latter preceded the former. But consideration of linguistic logic suggests the opposite. We have just seen that Dahl's Law would be best explained by supposing that the groups affected by it had a single common origin, or were at least adjacent at an early stage, in some place preceding their current locations, and that the process affected them during their protoperiods or earlier. On the other hand, Spirantization can be shown to have affected the languages of at least one group above (NEC) after its protoperiod (Nurse & Hinnebusch 1993: 125) and within East Africa. The same linguistic logic suggests that Spirantization affected some, many, or all of the other groups similarly. In other words, while the seeds of Spirantization might have been planted early, they didn't sprout until after the protoperiod of current groups, and in or near their current location.

P-lenition*. Lenition of the voiced series **b, d, g* has proved relatively hard to interpret: for example, for **b*, what was its original value ? what are today's exact facts? And how best to interpret movement along a line of reflexes that includes *ɓ, b, β, v, w,* and *Ø*? The facts of lenition of the voiceless stops (p, t, k*) are clearer, easier to interpret, and, as befits stronger segments, lenition has affected the voiceless stops less. **P*-lenition is the earliest lenition affecting the voiceless stops. Within Bantu Africa as a whole, it has a fairly clean distribution, affecting most languages, the major exception being a solid block of languages centred on southern Tanzania, Mozambique (NM behaves differently, as usual), Malawi, and Zambia, with a smaller block based on Zone R and part of H. In East Africa it is useful because it (again) divides northern and southern languages. In the north, it affected early p-Central Kenya, p-Kilimanjaro-Taita, p-Great Lakes, p-Langi, and p-F.10. Later it spread across much of NEC and part of WT (Sumbwa, Nyaturu: Sukuma and Nyamwezi data ambiguous)). This gives the impression of being part inherited (CK, KT, GL, Langi), part diffusional (adjacent parts of NEC and WT).

In Comorian, much of Luhya, NM, and much of S, lenition of **p* is part of a wider lenition of voiceless stops.

Linguistic logic dictates that, where both Bantu Spirantization and *p*-lenition have occurred, *p*-lenition follows spirantization (Hinnebusch 1981: 64). Despite this, there are language groups (CK, parts of WT and GL) where lenition of voiceless stops, including **p*, has occurred, but with no sign yet of Bantu Spirantization.[8]

2.2.2. Features whose distribution in East Africa can result from shared inheritance or later geographical spread

Available evidence suggests these have happened quite often and/or travel easily. They are many.

- palatalization of velars (at least some members of nearly every group have a form of this, and it is transferrable and reversible. For details and general scenario, see Hyman and Moxley 1996).

---

[8]Does lenition of stops tend to bleed and thus inhibit Spirantization? In this area p-lenition only cooccurs with Spirantization in two whole groups, GL and KT, and also in parts of two other and adjacent groups, NEC and WT. They also occur elsewhere, e.g. in southern Africa.

- reduction of class 5 **li-* to *i-* or zero in regular stems (nearly all except STH, Kilombero, RR, and part of GL (eastern side of Lake Victoria). Hinnebusch (1981: 66) thinks this a very early change. In any case the innovating languages are so numerous and otherwise heterogenous that this is not useful and not used in B3 below.
- 7 > 5 vowels (all KT, Kilombero, NM: none of CK, WT (except Sumbwa), Langi: most other groups have some members with 7, and other with 5). 7 > 5 also throughout N.20-30-40, M.40-50-60, and all S except Sotho.
- voicing of voiceless stop after homorganic nasal (all Luhya, Nyakyusa, Bungu, most of KT and RR, part of CK and Kilombero)
- instability of nasal before fricative : a situation which varies from subgroup to subgroup, and which depends phonetically on factors such as the voicing of the fricative.
- lenition of **B* (the reflexes of **B* are many, the facts are not always clear, details of the process are not always clear, and the different reflexes can be altered by contact)
- loss of inherited vowel length distinction (all KT, Kilombero, NM, N.20-30-40, all of S, M.60, most of NEC, parts of RR and SWT, Manda)
- lenition of **g* (nearly all groups have at least some members with a fricative, and lost in parts of CK, Kilimanjaro, NEC, WT, Langi, RR, NM, Nyakyusa, SWT, Bungu). Completely lost in M.40-50-60.
- spirant devoicing (RR, Chaga, Luhya, SH, Nyakyusa, F.10, NM, (Kilombero), M.40, M.60. It is possible that spirant-devoicing is closely linked to general obstruent devoicing, which removes the voicing contrast in obstruents. This may be further linked to postnasal phenomena—all of which remove the voicing contrast in stops after homorganic nasal. This needs more work.
- replacement of prefixal locatives (Classes 16, 17, 18) by a single suffixal *-(i)ni*. KT, most of CK, Sabaki only within NEC, S except Shona.
- tones > penultimate stress, a crude criterion but a well defined path has not so far been fleshed out[9]. This can apparently occur independently (Nyakyusa, Langi) but can also cross group boundaries: a continuous area covering most Swahili, adjacent parts of East Ruvu, Mbunga, and Kilombero). Tone loss or reduction of tonal contrasts also occur in N.20-30-40.

---

[9]T. Schadeberg has suggested that one of the intermediate steps might be, for example, shift of a high tone one syllable to the right. This has occurred in some or all of CK, KT, WT, and NEC. I am reluctant to use this until we are sure of its significance and distribution.

2.2.3. Processes for which it is hard to determine the reasons for their current distribution.

These are few.

- treatment of nasal plus homorganic voiceless stop *(*mp, nk, nk)* (nasal devoicing, stop aspiration, etc). These behave in one of three ways. They are retained *(mp)*, or the stop is voiced (**mp > mb*: see 2.2.2, above), or a range of other probably related changes occurs. The latter include aspiration, devoicing of the nasal, loss of the stop, and combinations of these. These are hard to use, because neither the facts nor the correlations between them are well established. They occur in all STH and NM, in parts of NEC, WT, and widely elsewhere in Bantu.
- loss of nominal preprefix. The geographical distribution of the preprefix is easy enough to establish. It appears in some form in all of GL (not D30), Nyakyusa, SWT, Bungu, and widely elsewhere in Bantu, historically probably in p-WT, -NEC, and -STH, and not at all in CK (although one Meru dialect is reported to have traces), KT, or other minor languages. The difficulty is in explaining how and why it disappears. In Greenberg's classic sequence for demonstratives being grammaticalized as class markers, the penultimate stage is the "nongeneric article", where it occurs with nouns in most or all contexts and is so redundant. At this point, it can fuse with the noun, or it can delete. The geographical distribution of this suggests that what happens in neighboring languages also plays a role. Greenberg's hypothesis is not based on East African languages and we have few field examinations of East African facts. What does the current distribution mean?
- Meinhof's Law. This is hard to judge because it takes different forms in different languages and the eligible sequences are not frequent. In active morphophonological form, it only occurs in most (?) CK and GL languages in forms such as 'tongue (sg.)' *lu-limi* , (pl.) *nnimi* or *nimi*. But it occurs in a few lexical items in languages across KT, WT, NEC, STH, Rufiji, Kilombero, Mwika, and Nyakyusa (typical words are *ng'ombe* 'cow, *ng'oma* 'drum' < **ngombe*, **ngoma*). Guthrie's data shows it at least as far south as Bemba. In a sketchy geographical overview, Herbert (1977: 367) states there are traces or historical remnants in Zone L and "most Western Bantu zones, especially C", but no signs in N or S. In a word list even as long as 1000 items, few eligible words are found, and the evidence is often contradictory, some words showing it, others not, some having it in one context but not another. How does it come to be in these languages? Geographically, how far does it extend? Are the few lexical forms frozen relics or have they diffused by contact? For these reasons, this feature has often been dismissed as of little diagnostic significance (Hinnebusch 1981: 75). My guesses are that, because it is not common crosslinguistically, it is diagnostically useful, and, following Meeussen and Herbert, that the most likely explanation for a geographical distribution from northern

East Africa south to Zambia and up west to an indeterminate point in the rain forest languages is inheritance from PB rather than lexical diffusion. Because it is kept in active form in the northeast again makes it tempting to use in section 2.2.1 above, but this should only be done only after our data base expands.[10] (Meeussen 1963, Herbert 1977, Johnson 1979, Schadeberg 1987)

2.2.4. Minor processes

These are processes which are apparently useful because the outcome is much contemporary variation. In fact they turn out to have limited use either because they are of limited and local distribution and thus not diagnostic on a broad scale, or because it is hard to interpret the phonetic details.

- spirantization of class 5 **li-* to *zi-* or *ri-* before vowel stems (NEC (and maybe Cewa etc))
- loss of **d* (*l* > zero: parts of CK, KT, NEC, Nyaturu)
- reduction of voiceless spirants to h to zero (RR, NM, a few adjacent languages)
- lenition of *t *(*t > d > r* : parts of KT and NEC, Luhya, Nyaturu, S except Shona)
- lenition of **k* (**k > x*, **k > h*: parts of Luhya, parts of WT, STH, Nyika, parts of S))
- split of **d* into /l/ and /r/ before nontense vowels (scattered languages).
- lenition of **b, d, and g* (small parts of CK, KT, others)
- lenition of **p, t, and* k (Comorian, Luhya, NM, parts of S (Janson 1991-2: 90-95))
- devoicing of **g* (Luhya, Pangwa, parts of J.50, D.30, D.50) or of stops in general.
- **d > r* before tense vowels (KT, Langi)
- two forms of Class 10 as plural of Class 11 (KT, Langi)
- unusual results from Bantu Spirantization (e.g. **tu/du > su/zu* rather than *fu/vu*: parts of Seuta, Kinga, SWT, Langi, Sukuma/Nyamwezi/Sumbwa)

2.3. Larger groupings: a tentative set

This section treats mainly the larger groups, as evidence from small groups with one or two members is suspect. Evidence for some processes above often comes from just a few lexemes which in a small group might all be loans.

The distribution of Dahl's Law suggests that the following groups shared a single ancestor, or at least that their ancestral communities were adjacent, in East Africa: WT, CK, GL, KT, NEC, and probably STH. (The

---

[10] The significance of the presence of Meinhof's Law in e.g. Bemba (M.42) and elsewhere has to be considered more fully when a detailed historical classification of languages outside East Africa is carried out.

distribution of Meinhof's Law suggests the same grouping, without, or with a question mark next to, STH—see footnote 10).

P-lenition supports this conclusion for CK, GL, and KT. Its presence in Langi, and parts of WT and NEC, can be explained by later diffusion across communities in their present positions.

The facts of Dahl's Law can be reconciled with those of *p*-lenition by positing that p-CK, p-KT, p-GL, p-WT, p-NEC, p-STH were part of an early dialect chain in which p-CK, p-KT, and p-GL were necessarily adjacent, a chain probably spoken somewhere in the area of current GL languages.

Thus the split between the early form(s) of these six groups and those of the other groups south and west is the major division within East African Bantu languages.

It can be noted that Meinhof's Law is kept in active form only among GL and CK languages, with fairly clear and numerous traces among the other Dahl's Law/*p*-lenition languages, and lesser traces outside the area. But whereas Dahl's Law is innovation, Meinhof's is retention.

The distribution of Bantu Spirantization is harder to understand and lends itself to two main possible interpretations (or some combination thereof). Either all today's Spirantizing languages (nearly all outside the rain forest, some inside) derive from a single ancestor or from a small chain of early adjacent ancestral communities. Or the seeds (whatever that means in phonetic terms) were sown in the rain forest at an early point but came to maturity as early Bantu communities spread out of the rain forest in time and space. It is possible, but is as yet unproved, that geographical diffusion, not just of the details, but of the process of Spirantization, also played a role in at least the second scenario. In either case the ancestors of GL, KT, NEC, STH, RR, SWT, Nyakyusa, Kilombero, and many others further south and west, were different or separate from those of CK, WT, Langi, and NM. Historically, this would mean that the protos of the latter were on the periphery of the dialect chain or that the chain had split.

These groupings are impossible to represent on a conventional tree diagram because the isoglosses involved are crosscutting. In general they divide the Bantu languages of East Africa into northern and southern sets. Individual groups thereafter, both in the north and south, are then defined by other innovations.

Central Kenya languages are phonologically conservative and, beside the innovations above, share only lenition of **b* (and loss of preprefix?) and new locative -(i)ni.

Beside being part of the Spirantizing group above, *Kilimanjaro-Taita* underwent 7 > 5, voicing of stop after nasal, loss of distinctive vowel length, loss of preprefix, spirant-devoicing, split of **d* into *l* and *r*, new locative -(i)ni, and, sometimes after the protolanguage, lenition of **t*. There is of course no way of dating the 7 > 5 change, so both p-KT and p-GL might have had 7 vowels, with 7 > 5 occurring or spreading after the protoperiod.

Generalizations about what can be assumed for *p-NEC* are bedevilled by the existence of Ilwana. Sitting isolated up the Tana River, it has been immune from change sweeping over other Bantu languages and serves a a methodological warning beacon[11]. It keeps 7 vowels and distinctive vowel length, for instance. Besides being part of the Spirantizing group above, p-NEC is then only defined by the new Spirantized class 5 prefix before vowel stems (but see Nurse & Hinnebusch 1993 for some verbal innovations). Other analysts (Hinnebusch 1981, Moehlig 1981) found NEC equally hard to define.

Great Lakes presents one well known classificatory problem and some minor ones. Lexicostatistically it adheres well enough (Nurse & Philippson 1980, Mould 1981, Schoenbrun 1990). But as pointed out above, this may well be because these studies only consider putative GL languages and not the adjacent languages to the west. Also, use of the few major phonological criteria above divides any possible GL at places. The most obvious crack is on the eastern side of Lake Victoria, where a block consisting of Luhya, especially southern Luhya, Mara, and Suguti, behaves conservatively, and differently from most other Great Lakes languages. This can be presented thus and it can be seen that southern Luhya and Mara are at the core of the deviant block:

Feature	Great Lakes in general	NLuhya	SLuhya	Mara	Suguti
Bantu Spirantization	yes	yes	no	no	yes
7 > 5	(yes)	yes	no	no	yes
Class 5 only *li-/ri-*(retention)	no	yes	yes	yes	yes
Spirant-devoicing	no	yes	yes	?[12]	yes
nasal + stop [-vd][13]	[-vd]	[+vd]	[+vd][-vd]	[-vd]	[-vd]

The current state of affairs can be explained by one of two scenarios (see also Mould 1981: 233). In one, Bantu Spirantization, 7 > 5, and reduction of Class 5 li- were not features of p-GL, but started after GL communities became established in more or less their present locations. They started at some point not east of Lake Victoria and diffused, carried by sociolinguistic

[11]For an analysis of Ilwana, see Nurse (in press).

[12]Mara languages have no coherent fricative set as they didn't undergo Spirantization. Luhya, especially southern Luhya, Mara, and Suguti make either no or minimal voicing contrasts in obstruents in general. So the fact that Mara does not specifically devoice fricatives is not important.

[13]Voicing of stops after nasal is one of a bundle of features defining Luhya. See Bennett 1973 and Mould 1981.

factors, but never reached the areas east of the Lake, so these eastern communities were conservative outliers. Other innovations, such as spirant-devoicing, the neutralization of voice after nasals in Luhya, and the other Luhya features alluded to in footnote 12, diffused along the eastern side of the Lake.

The second scenario starts with the observation that the absence of features such as Spirantization and the 7 > 5 change does not just distinguish these languages from other Lacustrine languages but also links them to CK languages, across the Rift valley to the east. This would be explained by saying that the ancestors of certain east Lake Victoria languages were originally part of the same group as CK: southern Luhya and (especially northern) Mara are obvious candidates. They separated and isolated early from core CK and the rump languages along the east Lake were influenced by their new GL neighbors and became increasingly like them over two thousand years.

I favor the second scenario and would put Gusii at the center of these east Lake languages. It has other similarities to CK which are impossible to explain by diffusion, as Gusii and CK have likely not been adjacent for some two millenia. An example is the verbal suffix -iite, found in this whole northern area only in CK and Gusii[14].

In Schoenbrun's expanded version of J, it is not just these eastern Lake Victoria languages which do not Spirantize or undergo 7 > 5 or even have no traces of Dahl's Law. Several GL languages have no or few visible traces of Dahl's Law but since Dahl's Law can be undone in its early stages, that is not an insuperable difficulty. However, Schoenbrun shows Gungu, Konzo, Nande, and Syan with 7 vowels and no Spirantization or Dahl's Law: Tucker and Bryan have Bwisi with 7 vowels and no Spirantization: some sources (Schoenbrun) show Gwere with 7 vowels, some with 5, yet others with 6 (Nurse and Philippson 1980): data in Tucker and Bryan (1957: 17-18, footnotes) suggests northern Soga has not undergone Spirantization. The Rwenzori languages (Konzo, Nande) can be dealt with by saying that it is simply unproved that they belong to GL and need more work: the lexicostatistical correlates to the west are not clear, and the lexicostatistical and phonological evidence are at odds. Gungu, Bwisi, northern Soga, Gwere, and Syan are not so easily dismissed. All are at the northern edge of the Bantu area in Uganda and we have little data for them. Is the extant data reliable? Are they outliers, remnants of some Forest group to the west? Is Spirantization (and therefore 7 > 5) something which did not occur in p-GL but started to diffuse later and never reached the far north? Three approaches are possible: we say Spirantization and 7 > 5 were not features of p-GL and

[14]Several authors have been struck by these similarities. For a short list of authors and similarities, see Nurse and Rottland 1991-2.The suffix *-ite* exists as an allomorph or the main allomorph of *-ile*, or in some kind of variation with *-ile*, across southern Tanzania in at least Rufuji-Ruvuma, Kilombero, and Southern Tanzania Highlands.

have diffused meanwhile (which wouldn't upset the scenario at the start of this section too much), or we say they are remnants of some other group, or we say the data does not yet allow us to make a sound judgement. I prefer the last approach. After all, this is work in progress, not a final judgement.

If we exclude the eastern Lake languages, the Rwenzori languages, and these northern outliers, we are left with a slightly reduced GL but one that is easier to classify. GL would be initially defined by having all three major features above, and later by 7 > 5 reduction. The paucity of defining features is not an obstacle, even when compared to the multitude of local innovations in the interim. The archaeology suggests that p-, or early, GL communities were in one place for only a short period in the second half of the first millenium BC, during which they acquired, or had acquired, their few defining characteristics. They then edged their way east, south, and north, and spent two thousand years diverging.

West Tanzania is not defined by any of the phonological innovations above other than the two general areal ones mentioned. It is so phonologically conservative that p-WT must have looked like a late version of proto-Bantu. It is always harder to find innovations shared by larger than smaller sets of languages, es can be seen by comparing WT with Langi/Mbugwe, following.

Langi-Mbugwe presents an interesting methodological problem. They are physically isolated from all other Bantu communities but adjacent to a range of several non-Bantu communities. Apart from *p*-lenition, Langi-Mbugwe is not defined by any of the larger reliable isoglosses above, but can be defined by a set of the smaller ones and others such as **t* > *c* before high vowels, *g*-loss, loss of **b* before round vowels and **b* > *v* elsewhere, **p* > *f* before tense vowels (but no Spirantization otherwise), and **d* > *r* before tense vowels but **d* > *l* and *r* before nontense vowels. This is an opaque set in that various parts of it are shared with various neighboring languages. It shares the largest subset with Pare and with Chaga, across the Maasai Steppe. In Nurse & Philippson (1980) Langi's closest lexicostatistical connection is to WT, but only by a small margin over Pare. Since Langi's lexical similarity to WT might be explained by lengthy proximity, that places more weight on the phonological similarity to Pare. Keeping in mind the axiom that where lexical and phonological indices are at odds, lexical similarity is more likely to indicate recent events (contact), while phonological similarity more likely points to an older underlying connection, we might tentatively posit a connection between Langi/Mbugwe and Pare/Taveta or Chaga, but this needs more thought as they do not share the major features such as Bantu Spirantization in general, or Dahl's Law.

F.10, another member of the Spirantizing/*p*-lenition group, later devoiced spirants, palatalized velars, and lost the preprefix.

Southern Tanzania Highlands , apart from belonging to the Dahl's Law and Spirantizing group above, is defined by rather distinctively turning inherited nasal plus voiceless stop into aspirated nasal, by spirant devoicing, and by retaining li- in all Class 5 contexts. My estimate here is that the first of these is the most significant, as spirant devoicing is shared by several neighbors (see below) and can probably diffuse, and Class 5 li- is a retention and diagnostically less useful.

Kilombero is a part of the large group defined by at least some of the major features above, and is further affected by 7 > 5, loss of vowel length, loss of preprefix, replacement of tone by penultimate stress, and retention of class 5 li- in all contexts. Kilombero consists of two fairly small language communities, known to have had heavy and regular contact with the various groups (West Ruvu, RR, STH) around them. Not one of these minor features is unique to Kilombero, all may result from diffusion. At this point, we can only say that Kilombero is defined lexically and by the major features above.

Rufiji-Ruvuma is a large member of the Spirantizing group. Besides li-retention, it is distinguished by spirant-devoicing, and spirant-reduction and loss (see Nurse 1981: 43-45 for discussion and further possible features). Since spirant-devoicing precedes reduction and loss, it is likely to be of considerable age in RR. Although individual developments postdating the protoperiod outnumber these early shared processes affecting spirants, the latter had a major effect, at least on consonant inventories.

Nyakyusa, part of the Spirantizing group, further underwent voicing of stops after nasals, replacement of tones by penultimate stress, and spirant-devoicing. While the latter may be the result of areal diffusion, the first two are specific in the area to Nyakyusa.

Southwest Tanzania, also part of the Spirantizing group, further underwent palatalization of velars, and palatalization (?) of **l* and *t* before tense **u* through *v/f* to *z/s*.

North Mozambique is widely acknowledged to be so deviant as to cause observers to posit that it was settled at a different time and from a different source than its northern neighbors. It is not affected by Bantu Spirantization, Dahl's, or Meinhof's Law and **p* has lenited but as part of a much more general lenition affecting all voiceless and most voiced stops. Nasal and voiceless stops have lost the nasal and aspirated, nasal and voiced stop have devoiced and lost the nasal, the Class 5 nominal prefix behaves in an idiosyncratic way, there is no distinctive vowel length, 7 > 5, spirants have devoiced, tones are replaced by stress, **d* splits into *l* and *r*, **b* has deleted, and **c* and **j* have become dental. Many of these are shared with some or all of core S.

All members of *N.20-30-40* , part of the Spirantizing group, share 7 > 5, palatalization of velars, loss of vowel length distinction, loss of preprefix, and at least reduction of tonal contrasts.

All members of *M.40-50* , further Spirantizing languages, share 7 > 5, *g*-lenition, and probably Meinhof's Law. *M.60* shares the same changes (except different in details of Spirantization), plus loss of inherited vowel length.

Summary

This chapter has sketched a nonlexically based historical classification of East African Bantu languages. By 'historical classification' is meant a classification that reflects the divergence, and acknowledges the convergence, processes of the last two millenia or longer, and implicitly reflects a historical scenario in which the ancestors of some, many, maybe even all, of today's language communities emerged from the rainforest during the early or mid first millenium BC. 'Nonlexically based' means that it is based on a set of phonological and morphophonological innovations, deemed to have diagnostic value (Part 2.2). It is the geographical distribution of these innovations more than their linguistic evolution that forms the basis of the classification. A distinction is made between major and minor innovations.

At the lower level, smaller, tighter, groups emerge that in general are not controversial (Part 1). Working out the likely historical relationship between them is harder.

The picture that emerges does not lend itself well to representation via tree diagrams. Two of the three major innovations (Bantu Spirantization, Dahl's Law) and many of the minor ones have affected only or mainly languages outside the rainforest and are therefore assumed to have occurred outside and after the rainforest period. Dahl's Law occurs only in East Africa and its distribution suggests that p-WT, p-CK, p-GL, p-KT, p-NEC, and probably p-STH have a single origin or were part of a dialect chain, probably spoken somewhere in the area of today's GL languages. The distribution of *p*-lenition—which in fact might be older as it occurs widely across Bantu—confirms this for p-CK, GL, and KT. The fact that some adjacent groups are partly affected by these phenomena points to later diffusion. Bantu Spirantization suggests a single origin or proximity of ancestral communities for: GL, KT, NEC, STH, RR, SWT, Nyakyusa, Kilombero, M40-50, M60, N20-30-40, most of S, and many others further west. CK, WT, Langi, and NM/Sotho are separate: historically, this presumably means that their protos were on the periphery of the dialect chain or that the chain had split. For most of these groups—the obvious exceptions are WT and CK, and maybe SWT—the few shared early innovations are outnumbered by later changes, which are often areal. This suggests a short shared early period and a longer later one. It does not support the idea of a single large wave constantly undergoing binary splits into clearly demarcated successors. Just like lexical distribution, it suggests constant divergence *and* convergence.

This study has its limitations. One is that it covers only a somewhat arbitrarily defined part of the Bantu area. Hence it does not examine seriously the widely posited splits of Eastern vs Western Bantu[15], or Eastern vs Central vs Western, other than suggesting that Bantu Spirantization tends to support a division of forest vs non-forest languages, but not Eastern vs Western. It has not seriously examined Zone S languages. Another is that its concentration on larger groups means that it pays little attention to the smaller marginal groups. A third is that its phonological criteria are arbitrarily asserted rather than properly discussed.

This study suggests some directions for future work. One would investigate what processes can be demonstrated to spread or have spread by diffusion. A second would refine the set of criteria. A third would look more carefully at the historical and methodological significance of the smaller, marginal groups: F.10, Langi-Mbugwe, Kilombero, Gungu, Bwisi, Syan, the Rwenzori languages, and isolates such as $Mwera_2$ (Mbamba Bay on Lake Tanganyika in SW Tanzania) and Wungu (Nurse 1988:51-53, Labroussi this volume). A fourth would expand this kind of classification to cover more or all of the Bantu area, initially the languages in southern Africa, then languages to the west and southwest. A fifth would compare these results with those from lexically-based overviews: a brief comparison with Ehret in press (especially) and Vansina (1995) for East Africa shows broad similarity but also differences. A final area would be to examine closely the overlap between linguistic and ethnic boundaries: how have "the Chaga" come to regard themselves as a unit, but not the communities speaking CK languages, when the linguistic differences between Chaga dialects visibly exceed those within CK? What happened on the eastern side of Victoria, where "the Luhya" (and the Suba) speak of themselves as one group, but their dialect area is split by what linguists would consider major differences? Does an ethnolinguistic group, such as "the Ilwana", ever have long enough folk memories to justify saying that another group, such as "the Swahili", are really their siblings who have just forgotten their origins?

References

Bastin, Yves. 1983. Statistique grammaticale et classification des languages bantoues, *Africana Linguistica* 9: 17-37.

Bennett, Patrick R. 1967. Dahl's Law in Thagicu, *ALS* 8: 127-159.

Bennett, Patrick R. 1969. A comparative study of four Thagicu verbal systems. (Unpublished Ph.D thesis, SOAS.)

Bennett, Patrick R. 1973. A phonologic history of NE Victoria Bantu. (Unpublished MS. Cyclostyled.)

Bennett, Patrick R. 1981. Proto-Thagicu lexical reconstructions. (Unpublished MS).

Bennett, Patrick R. 1983. Patterns in linguistic geography and the Bantu origins controversy, *History in Africa* 10: 35-51

---

[15] A new version of this appears in Huffman and Herbert 1994-5.

Davy, James I. M. & Derek Nurse. 1982. The synchronic forms of Dahl's Law, a dissimilation process, in Central and Lacustrine Bantu languages of Kenya, *JALL* 4: 157-195.

Dimmendaal, G. forthcoming. Language shift and morphological convergence in the Nilotic area, *SUGIA* 14.

Ehret, Christopher E. 1971. *Southern Nilotic History.* Evanston: Northwestern University Press.

Ehret, Christopher E. 1973. Patterns of Bantu and Central Sudanic settlement in Central and Southern Africa, *TJH* 3, 1-2.

Ehret, Christopher E. 1974. *Ethiopians and East Africans.* Nairobi: East African Publishing House.

Ehret, Christopher E. 1980. *The Historical Reconstruction of Southern Cushitic Phonology and Vocabulary.* Berlin: Reimer.

Ehret, Christopher E. 1984. Between the Coast and the Great Lakes, in D.J.Niane (ed), *UNESCO General History of Africa, Africa from the 12th to the 16th Century.* Berkeley: University of California Press. 1: 481-497.

Ehret, Christopher E. in press. *Eastern Africa in the Early Iron Age: Explorations in History, 1000 B.C. to A.D. 300.*

Ehret, Chris & Derek Nurse. 1981. The Taita Cushites, *SUGIA* 3: 125-168.

Ehret, Chris, Edward P. Elderkin & Derek Nurse. 1989. Dahalo lexis and its sources, *AAP* 18: 5-49.

Greenberg, Joseph H. 1978. How does a language acquire gender markers?, in Greenberg (ed.). Universals of Human Language. Cambridge, Mass.: The MIT Press, 3: 41-82.

Güldemann, Tom. 1996. *Verbalmorphologie und Nebenpraedikationen im Bantu: eine Studie zur motivierten Genese eines konjugationalen Subsystems.* Bochum: Brockmeyer.

Guthrie, Malcolm. 1967-71. *Comparative Bantu.* Farnborough: Gregg International Publishers Ltd.

Herbert, Robert K. 1977. Phonetic analysis in phonological description: prenasalized consonants and Meinhof's Rule, *Lingua* 43: 339-373.

Hinnebusch, Thomas H. 1981. Northeast Coastal Bantu, in Hinnebusch T.H & D.Nurse & M. Mould (eds), 21- 125.

Hinnebusch, Thomas H, Derek Nurse & Martin Mould (eds). 1981. *Studies in the Classification of Eastern Bantu Languages.* Hamburg: Helmut Buske Verlag.

Hinnebusch, T.H., Derek Nurse. 1981. Spirantization in Chaga, *SUGIA* 3: 51-78.

Huffman, Thomas N. & Robert K.Herbert. 1994-5. New perspectives on Eastern Bantu, *Azania* 29-30: 27-36.

Hyman, Lawrence M. & Jeri Moxley. 1996. The morpheme in phonological change: velar palatalization in Bantu, *Diachronica* 13,2: 259-282.

Janson, Torre. 1991-2. Southern Bantu and Makua, *SUGIA* 12-13: 63-106.

Johnson, Marion R. 1979. The natural history of Meinhof's Law in Bantu, *SAL* 10,3: 261-271.

Kashoki, M.E. & Michael Mann. 1978. A General Sketch of the Bantu Languages of Zambia, in Ohannessian, Salome, M.E. Kashoki (eds.), *Language in Zambia.* London: International Africa Institute, 47-100.

Labroussi, Catherine. 1998. Vowel Systems and Spirantization in S.W.Tanzania, this volume.

Ladefoged, Peter, Ruth Glick & Clive Criper. 1972. *Language in Uganda.* London: Oxford University Press.

Meeussen, A.E. 1963. Meinhof's Rule in Bantu, *ALS* 3: 25-29.

Moehlig, Wilhelm J.G. 1981. Stratification in the history of the Bantu languages, *SUGIA* 3: 251-319.

Moser, Manfred. 1983. *Aspekte der Kulturgeschichte der Ngoni in der Mkoa wa Ruvuma, Tansania.* Vienna. Afro-Pub.

Mould, Martin. 1981. Greater Luyia, in Hinnebusch, T. H., D. Nurse, M. Mould (eds), 181-236.

Ngonyani, Deogratias. forthcoming. The evolution of Tanzanian Ngoni, *SUGIA* 14.

Nurse, Derek. 1979. *Classification of the Chaga Dialects.* Hamburg: Helmut Buske Verlag.

Nurse, Derek. 1981. Chaga-Taita, in Hinnebusch. Thomas H., Derek Nurse, Martin Mould (eds.), 127-180.

Nurse, Derek. 1985. Review of Moser 1983. *JALL* 7: 207-211.

Nurse, Derek. 1986. Reconstruction of Dahalo history through evidence from loanwords, *SUGIA* 7,2: 267-305.

Nurse, Derek. 1987. Towards a typology of diachronic linguistic change in Bantu languages. *Journal of the Atlantic Provinces Linguistic Association* 9: 100-122.

Nurse, Derek. 1988a. The diachronic background to the language communities of SW Tanzania, *SUGIA* 9: 15-115.

Nurse, Derek. 1988b. Extinct Southern Cushitic Communities in East Africa, in Marianne Bechhaus-Gerst, Fritz Serzisko (eds.), *Cushitic-Omotic.* Hamburg: Helmut Buske, 93-104.

Nurse, Derek. in press. *Inheritance, Contact, and Change in Two East African Languages.* Cologne: Ruediger Koeppe.

Nurse, Derek, Thomas Hinnebusch. 1993. *Swahili and Sabaki: a Linguistic History.* Berkeley: University of California Press.

Nurse, Derek & Henry Muzale. 1998. Tense and Aspect in Great Lakes Bantu Languages, this volume.

Nurse, Derek & Gerard Philippson. 1980. The Bantu Languages of East Africa: a Lexicostatistical Survey, in Polome, Edgar C, Christoper P.Hill (eds), *Language in Tanzania.* Oxford: Oxford University Press, 26-67.

Nurse, Derek & Franz Rottland. 1991-2. Sonjo: description, classification, history, *SUGIA* 12-13: 171-289.

Nurse, Derek & Franz Rottland. 1993. A linguists' view of the history of Sonjo and Engaruka, *Azania* 28:1-5.

Park, George. 1988. Evolution of a regional culture in East Africa, *SUGIA* 9: 117-204.

Philippson, Gerard. 1984. *Gens des Bananeraies*. Paris: Editions Recherche sur les Civilisations.

Philippson, Gerard. 1989. Essai de phonologie compareé des dialectes Chaga de Tanzanie, in Rombi, Marie-Francoise (ed.), *Etudes sur le Bantu Oriental*. Paris: SELAF.

Rottland, Franz. 1993. 'Suba': searching for linguistic correlates to an ethnic notion, *AAP* 33: 7-36.

Rottland, F, D. & Okoth Okombo. 1986. The Suba of Kenya: growing ethnicity and receding language competence, *AAP* 7: 115-126.

Schadeberg, Thilo C. 1987. Silbenanlautgesetze im Bantu, *Afrika und Uebersee* 70: 1-18.

Schadeberg, Thilo C. 1994. Kimwani at the Southern Fringe of Kiswahili, in Bakker, Peter, Maarten Mous (eds.), *Mixed Languages*. Amsterdam: IFOTT, 239-244.

Schadeberg, Thilo C. 1994-5. Spirantization and the 7-to-5 Vowel Merger in Bantu, in Dominicy, Michel, Didier Demolin (eds.), *Sound Change*, special issue of the *Belgian Journal of Linguistics* 9: 72-84.

Schoenbrun, David L. 1990. Early history in Eastern Africa's Great Lakes region. (Unpublished Ph.D thesis, UCLA.)

Vansina, Jan. 1995. New linguistic evidence and 'The Bantu Expansion', *JAH* 36, 2: 173-195.

Whiteley, Wilfred H. 1960. *The Tense System of Gusii*. Kampala: East African Institute of Social Research.

Winter, Christoph W. 1980. Internal classifications of Kilimanjaro Bantu compared: towards an East African dialectometry, in Guarisma, Gladys, Suzanne Platiel (eds), *Dialectologiue en Afrique Noire*. Paris:SELAF, 101-132.

Appendix: Maps

Great Lakes languages covered in this article

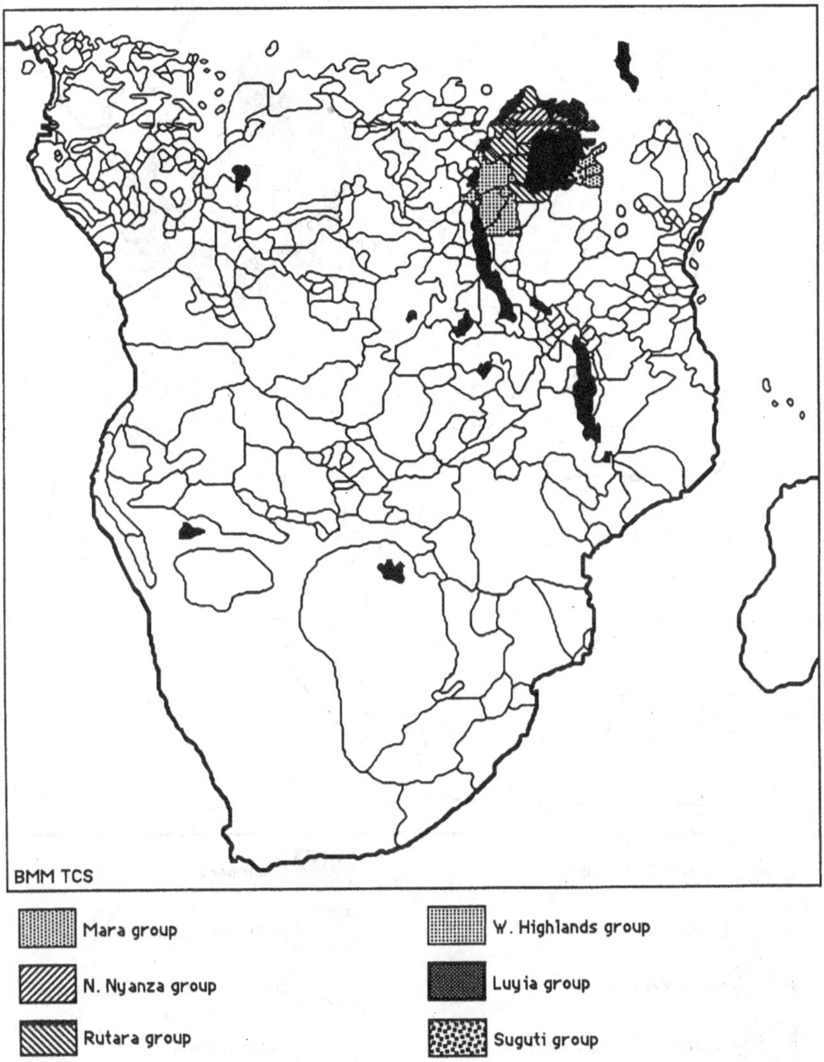

Map 1: Bantu language subgroups of eastern Africa

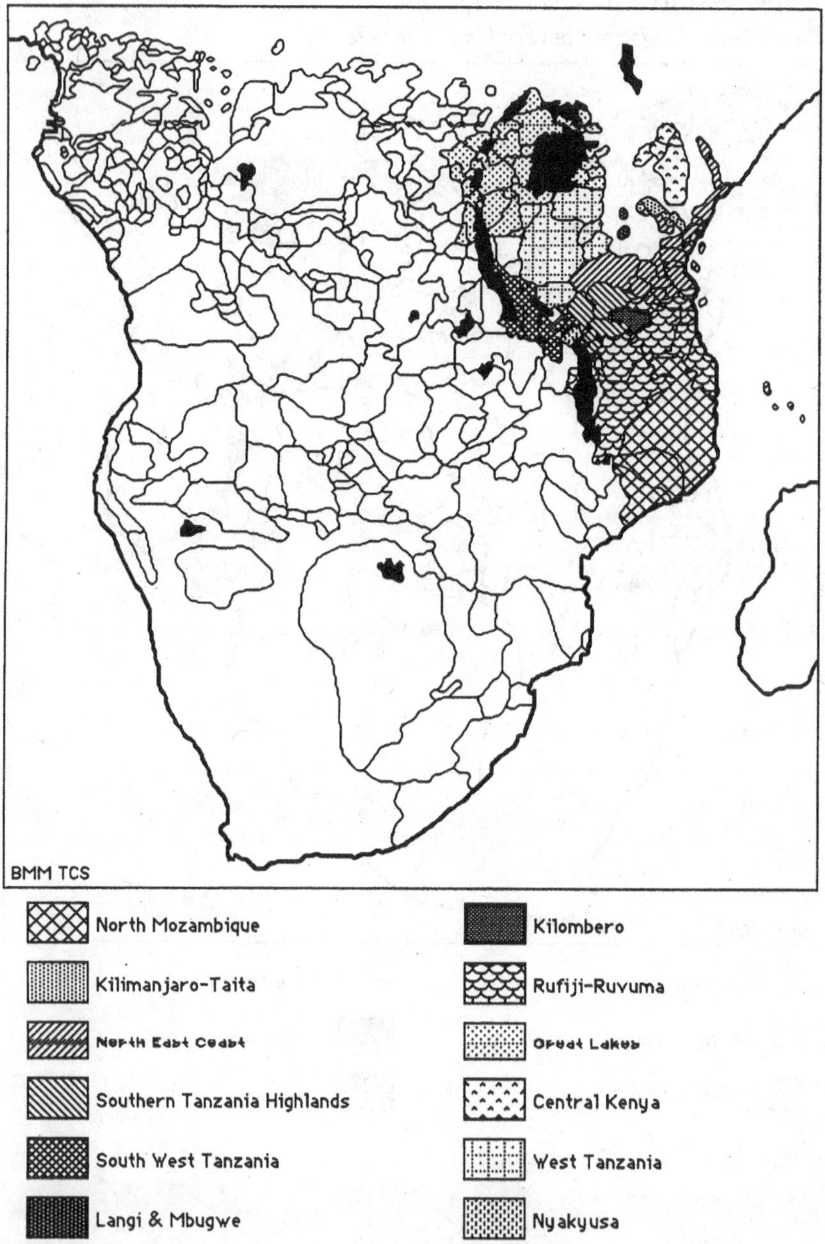

Map 2: Subgroups in whose ancestors Dahl's Law was probably active

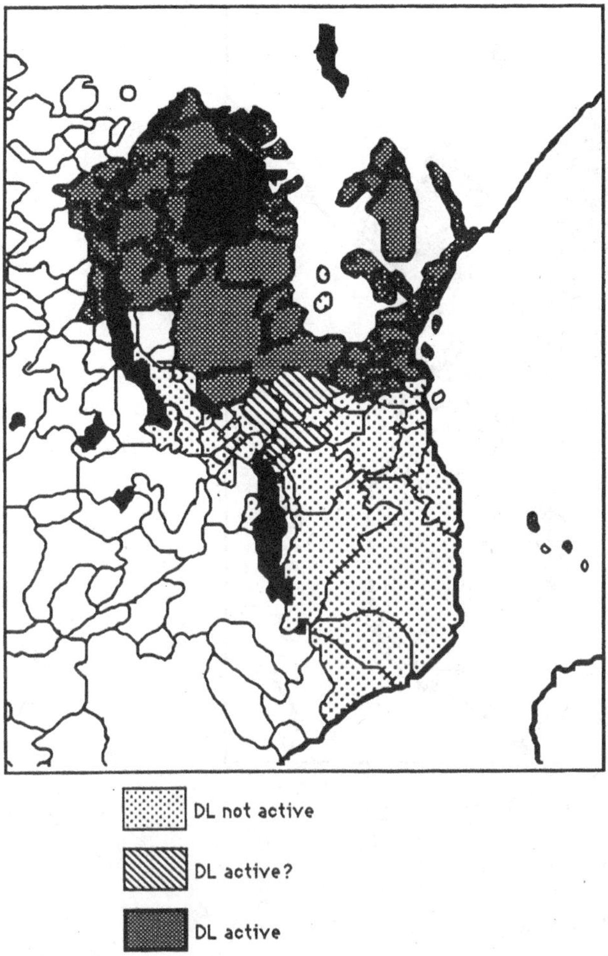

Map 3: Subgroups in whose ancestors p-lenition had probably occurred

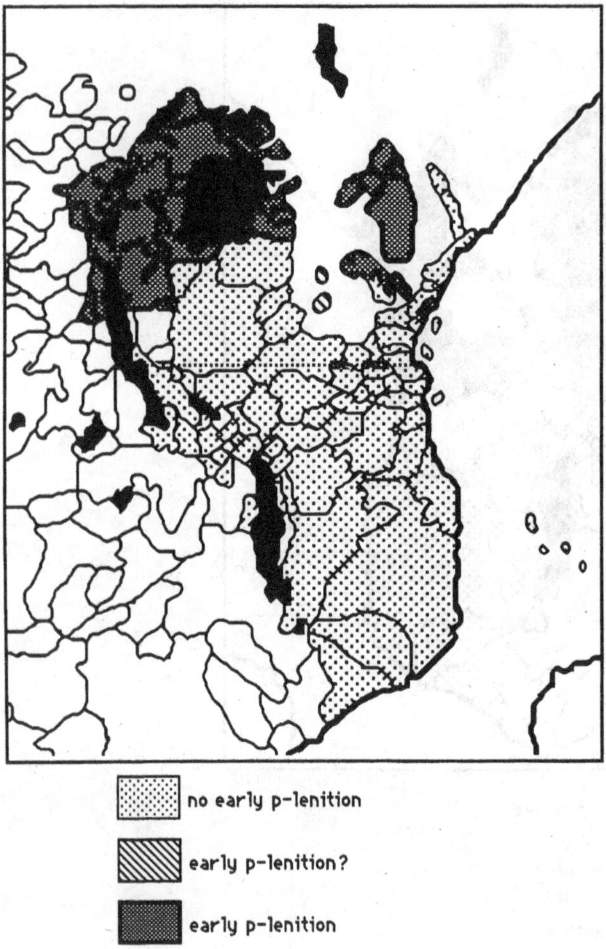

Map 4: *Subgroups whose ancestors were early affected by Bantu Spirantization*

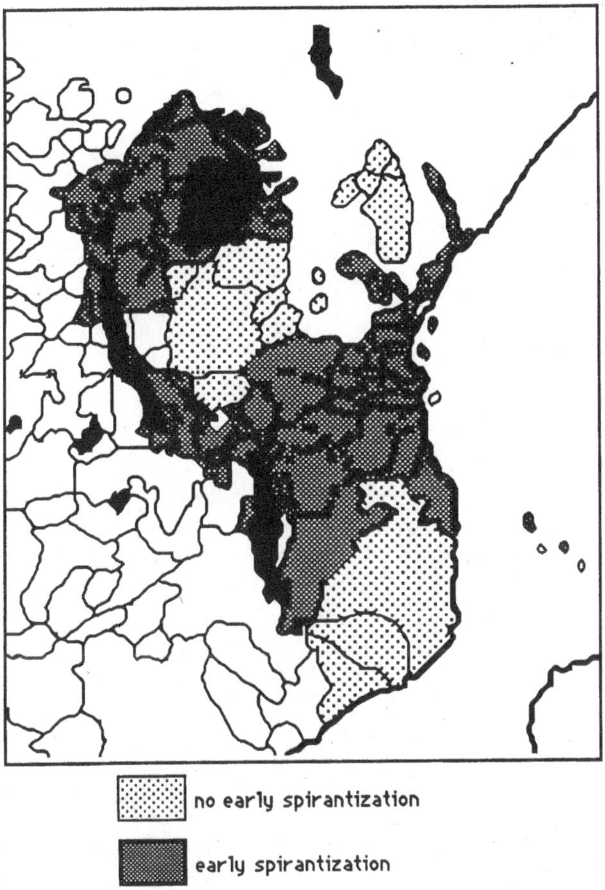

Subclassifying Bantu: The Evidence of Stem Morpheme Innovations

CHRISTOPHER EHRET
University of California, Los Angeles

1. Establishing a subclassification of Bantu

This article begins the process of putting the subclassification of the Bantu language group on a more solid basis than that provided so far by lexicostatistical calculations alone. To this end, the core of the work, in sections 2-5, focuses on charting the evidence of stem-morpheme-innovation histories for Bantu subgrouping and on laying out the Savanna division of Bantu substantiated by those data. A short presentation of several old Bantu sound shift rules, the distributions of which corroborate the key features of the resulting subclassification, then follows in the section 6. The text concludes with a survey in section 7 of the human historical implications of the classification. A tabling of data and argument closes out the work. Other scholars in future, it is hoped, will build on this classificatory effort by applying similar approaches to the history of affixal morphology in Bantu and by investigating systematically and systemically the phonological histories of Bantu languages.

The power of lexicostatistical methods in the subclassification of language families should not be downplayed. Consistently, with much less effort, they provide the same results as the laborious traditional methods of subgrouping, as long as the divisions within the wider language group are relatively clear-cut ones. Even where long-term dialect chaining has accompanied the expansion and diversification of the language group, the underlying genetic breakdown of the group still remains mostly discoverable from the lexicostatistical figures, simply because dialect chaining leaves its own characteristic numerical distributions.

Nevertheless, for two reasons, the establishment of a generally accepted subclassification of the Bantu languages will require that we go beyond lexicostatistical approaches. One reason is an artifact of current fashions and interests in the field: despite the repeatedly demonstrated utility of lexicostatistical methods, at least where the conditions are suitable, many linguists feel a generic skepticism about this shortcut and need to be reassured by extensive corroboratory arguments from the direct evidence of shared innovation. The second reason, however, is particular to Bantu. The lexicostatistical figures for the Bantu languages have not only been deeply and recurrently skewed by long-term dialect borrowing; they have also been significantly distorted in numerous instances by word-borrowings that have resulted from subsequent reëxpansions of Bantu languages across areas previously the territories of other Bantu languages. This situation is amply attested in the already available archeology and the linguistic historical studies from several regions (e.g., Phillipson 1977, Ownby 1986, Huffman 1989, Ahmed 1996, and Ehret 1998a). Especially in eastern-central Africa, as will emerge below, this latter effect leads to thoroughly misleading results if lexicostatistical method only is relied upon.

There is one other recurrent problem in the lexicostatistical efforts so far undertaken for the Bantu group. Almost none of these studies have taken the essential first step, of attempting rigorously to identify loanwords—admittedly an often difficult matter in Bantu—and to remove them from consideration before counting up the apparent true cognates in their word lists. As has been demonstrated in the literature of lexicostatistical method (Ehret 1971, 1980; Embleton 1986), any loanwords from non-related languages that appear in one or both of two related languages *lower* the expected percentage of shared cognation of those two languages in direct proportion to the percentage occurrence of loanwords in their counted word lists. This effect is most strongly evident in a number of northern East African and southeastern African Bantu languages, whose "uncalibrated" rates of cognation with languages of more westerly-lying Bantu regions, and with other eastern languages, have been skewed significantly lower by their very extensive word-borrowing from non-Bantu languages. The Southeast-Bantu subgroup, which includes Nguni, and the Chaga dialects of Tanzania, provide particularly notable examples.

Undetected loanwords that have passed from one of two related languages into the other of course have an opposite effect: they *raise* the apparent cognation between those two by exactly the number of undetected loans involved. This consequence is especially evident in the more recent global calculations of Bantu cognation, where the criteria and approaches used have, if anything, accentuated the upward-skewing effects of intra-Bantu borrowing on the apparent cognation, especially in the western areas and in parts of south-central Africa, thus increasing the blurring of the lines of relationship among such language subgroupings and making them often appear more closely related than may truly be the case. In using lexicostatistical method, it is far better to err on the side of skepticism, applying neogrammarian criteria with absolute rigor and ruling out every even slightly suspect candidate for cognation. In the case of Bantu it may be essential to follow that tack, so pervasive have been the effects of intra-Bantu borrowing.

2. Shared innovation as a tool for subclassification

What categories of innovation are grist for the classificatory mill? The most solid and discretely definable items of data fall into two categories, morphemic and phonological. By morphemic, we mean data comprised of individual meaning-bearing units of utterance, either stems (i.e., roots, in the parlance of reconstruction) or affixes.

The use of morphemic evidence in much previous language classification work has suffered from an often unrecognized theoretical weakness. Rather than restate the problem anew, the arguments in Chapter 4 of the writer's historical-comparative reconstruction of the Nilo-Saharan language family can be cited here (Ehret, forthcoming, Chapter 4):

> The single substantive basis for the subgrouping of languages is the identification in them of shared innovations [that are unlikely to be due to borrowing]. ... But the chief practical consequence of this principle is rarely recognized or, if recognized, tends to be worked around rather than confronted and directly dealt with. To wit, a linguistic item or usage—a stem or affix morpheme, a phoneme or allophone, or a syntactical or morphological rule—can be identified as an innovation only if we can give probable identification to the item or usage it displaced or supplemented, that is, to the item or usage it was an innovation in place of or supplementary to. The non-presence of an item or usage in a language is not negative evidence; it is not evidence one way or the other. There are two possible reasons for an element to be lacking in a language: (1) it may never have been present at any time in the language's ancestry, or (2) it may once have been in the language but have been dropped from use at some point in the evolution of that language. The presence of an element in two related languages and its lack in a third thus does not by itself choose between the two possibilities. Alone, it tells us nothing whatsoever about the subgrouping among the three.
>
> Linguists try to get around this problem by accumulating sets of cases involving the presence versus non-presence in languages of linguistic items and usages, drawing isogloss maps of presence-versus-non-presence distributions, and so forth. This is nothing more than a counting up of shared retentions. The retentions may include shared innovations, but such innovations are countable because they are present or elicitable now or in earlier written forms from a language. Their countability has no necessary connection to how or when they originally came into use in their

> languages. If similar amounts of overall change have taken place, *as is typical in the limited portion of a language called core or basic vocabulary*, then the results of counting will be roughly in line with genetic linguistic reality. [Emphasis is added here, to point up the real utility of lexicostatistics, a matter adverted to in the previous section of this article.] But everywhere else in a language, the amounts of change that can take place over any given period of time can vary immensely. Counts of shared isoglosses might just as well reflect the relative conservatism, or its opposite, in the languages being compared.
>
> Middle English is the outstanding well-known example of this fact. By the sixteenth century English had lost most of its distinctively Germanic and Indo-European morphology and greatly reshaped its vocabulary through word-borrowing. Its count of items other than vocabulary uniquely shared with other Germanic languages is relatively quite small. Nevertheless, despite the lesson of English, efforts at Indo-European subclassification still mostly fail to confront this problem adequately, and scholarly arguments still too often are based on counting and mapping of what, for all we are told, may well be just patterns of random shared retention. ...
>
> The failure to develop methods for distinguishing innovations and probable innovations from shared features that cannot be so identified is a fundamental weakness of historical-comparative theory that we need not continue to tolerate. (Why the problem has not been enunciated more clearly and confronted systematically is also rather difficult to understand, but need not divert us here.) Three approaches to this problem show promise: (1) ordered sound-shift histories (as in Ehret 1980); (2) lexical replacement histories in basic vocabulary (Ehret and Ali 1984; also Ehret and Kinsman 1981); and (3) pan-familial semantic histories. ...

The approach followed here draws on the ideas of both lexical replacement and semantic histories. It defines each of its genetic subgroupings of Bantu languages by identifying the set of innovated stems (roots) that are restricted to that particular subgroup. A stem morpheme can be identified as an innovation because it meets one or more of the following conditions:

(a) it demonstrably displaced wholly *or partially* from use another, earlier Bantu stem; and/or

(b) it previously bore a different meaning from which its innovated meaning logically derives; and/or

(c) it was derived by morphological addition (or rarely deletion, i.e., back-formation) to an earlier Bantu stem; and/or

(d) it underwent an individualized sound shift through the operation of analogy or assimilation-dissimilation processes.

In applying all four kinds of inference, two kinds of distributions are particularly strong diagnostic criteria of the correctness of identifying one stem as the earlier bearer of a particular meaning, or one form of the stem as the earlier morpheme shape:

(i) the earlier stem (or stem-shape) appears in Bantu languages outside the subgroup in question and also in a relict distribution in a few languages of the subgroup, especially in languages at its geographical peripheries; and/or

(ii) the earlier stem occurs both outside the subgroup and in related Niger-Congo languages outside of "Narrow" Bantu as a whole.

The second criterion is the most usually cited in this kind of work and the one best understood by non-specialists. But the first criterion is an equally powerful indicator, because it takes account of the practical reality of how the displacement of one term for a meaning by another term takes place. Normally a new word comes into use initially as a synonym for the existing word for that meaning. For an indeterminate period the two words coexist in use. Eventually one of the two, usually but not always the newer term, becomes the preferred item and gradually drives the other out of use among the speakers of the language. If, however, this kind of change is taking place during a period of dialect differentiation in a language, the new term may indeed displace the old one in a majority of the emerging dialects, but the old word may hang on in use in a few areas, especially though not necessarily only among the geographically more peripheral dialects. In later times, the older term will thus be retained in a relict scatter of languages that derive from those emergent dialects, whereas the innovated term will occur much more widely among the descendant languages.

In a very few instances, the older morpheme may widely continue in use for a long time alongside the innovated item. The use of the terminology, "wholly or partially" displacing from use, in the statement of condition (a) above is meant to account for this possibility.

An additional consideration comes into play in identifying cases of condition (b), namely, the matter of deciding which is the later and which is the earlier meaning or function of a morpheme. Two criteria (as given in Ehret, forthcoming, Chapter 4) have most commonly been applied in resolving this kind of issue:

(iii) A concrete meaning is historically prior to an abstract, metaphorical, symbolic, euphemistic, descriptive, or attributive meaning for a root.

(iv) A non-technical meaning for a root is normally prior to a culturally, economically, or technologically specific meaning.

3. Results: A subclassification of the Savanna-Bantu group

From the distributional analysis of stem morphemes, undertaken in accordance with the conditions and criteria described above, a historical sequence of successively narrower Bantu subgroups can be depicted.

The deepest genetic group established in this initial stage of investigation can be called "Savanna-Bantu" (see Table 1 for the supporting stem morpheme innovations). It is a grouping of immensely wide geographical spread, covering three-quarters or more of the Bantu-speaking territories of Africa. It comprises, beginning from the west, the languages of Guthrie's zones H.20 (and possibly H.40), R, K, L, M, D.20-60, E, F, G,

N, P, and S. (A substitute, post-Guthriean, J zone is widely recognized by scholars; it combines D.40-60 and E.10-40 and forms the Lakes subgroup of Schoenbrun 1990.) The H.40 group, Mbala, is provisionally included in Savanna-Bantu, but its inclusion remains debatable because of the paucity of citable evidence. The zone H.10 languages, which include Kongo and Vili, do *not* belong, according to the evidence developed here, to Savanna-Bantu, and the Yaka group (H.30) probably does not belong either.

In the classification of Klieman (1997), the Savanna-Bantu languages, despite their vast geographical spread, form just one of a number of deep-level genetic branchings of Narrow Bantu, all the rest of which are confined to the northwestern portions of the Bantu field. In her reckoning, it forms one subgroup of one sub-sub-branch of one of the primary branches of Narrow Bantu. The preliminary indications of the stem morpheme innovation histories seem to support this picture. The names, Nzadi-Kwa and Ṣangha-Kwa, which are used in the data tables at the end of this article, refer to Klieman's proposed next two successively deeper branchings of Narrow Bantu prior to the Savanna-Bantu stage (see Klieman 1997 for more on these branchings). They identify sets of earlier stem morphemes that appear provisionally attributable to those two prior stages of Bantu history. But a fuller investigation of these indicators must await a later study.

Savanna-Bantu in turn divides into two primary branches of its own, Western-Savanna (the evidence for which appears in Table 2) and Eastern-Savanna (for which see Table 3). According to a lexicostatistical study done two decades ago by the writer and two of his students (reported in Papstein 1978), the Western-Savanna branch itself diverged originally into a horseshoe-shaped dialect chain of six equidistantly related subgroups:

A. Western-Savanna
1. Luyana-Southwest-Bantu (including Nkoya in the Luyana subgroup and Yeyi as an outside member: Guthrie's zones K.30, L.60, and R.20-40);
2. Lwena (K.10);
3. Lunda (L.50, including both Ndembu and Ruund);
4. Pende (L.10);
5. Kimbundu (H.20); and
6. Ovimbundu (R.10).

The Mbala group (H.40) possibly also belongs in the larger Savanna-Bantu division, but whether or not they fit in the Western-Savanna branch remains to be seen.

The Eastern-Savanna branch, which contains the remainder of the Savanna-Bantu languages, is comprised of one geographically extensive group in eastern Africa, Mashariki (formerly "Eastern Bantu"), and several less widely spread groups in the central areas of the southern savanna belt of Africa. Mashariki consists of the languages of zones J (D.40-60 and E.10-

40), E.50-70, F, G, M.10-30, N (except for N.41), P, and S (along with K.21, a nineteenth-century creole of an S.30 language). The remaining Savanna-Bantu tongues form the Luban (L.20-L.40), Lega (D.20), Sabi (M.40-50 and N.41), and Botatwe (M.60 and K.40) groups:

B. Eastern-Savanna
1. Lega
2. Luban
3. Botatwe
4. Sabi
5. Mashariki

It is possible that the Botatwe and Sabi groups are slightly closer related to Mashariki, but the stem-morpheme evidence for this position can also be explained as a deriving from Mashariki substrata in each of them (see discussion in next section).

Finally, the evidence of stem-morpheme innovation identifies a further two-way division of Mashariki into a northern, Kaskazi group (seen in Table 5), and a southern, Kusi group (seen in Table 6). Kaskazi comprises nine subgroups, and Kusi four subgroups:

5. Mashariki
a. Kaskazi
1. Lakes (zone J [D.40-60 and E.10-40]);
2. Upland (E.50-60 and E.74a);
3. Langi (F.33-34);
4. Takama (F, except for F.33-34);
5. Northeast-Coastal (E.70, except for E.74a, and G.10-40);
6. Njombe (G.60);
7. Kilombero (G.50 and P.15);
8. Rufiji-Ruvuma (N.10 and P.10-20, except for P.15);
9. Mwika-Rungwe (M.10-30).
b. Kusi
1. Nyasa (N.20-40, except for N.41, which belongs to Sabi, for which see Eastern-Savanna B.4 above);
2. Makua (P.30);
3. Shona (S.10);
4. Southeast-Bantu (S.20-60 and K.21).

Significant additional bodies of stem-morpheme innovations, supportive both of the narrow Mashariki group and of its Kaskazi and Kusi subgroups, are published in Ehret (1998). These data are identifiable as innovations on somewhat different grounds than those cited in this article. For one, these morphemes all entered the early Mashariki dialects as loanwords from several non-Bantu languages formerly spoken in parts of eastern Africa. Often, too, they name elements of culture or environment that were not part of the Bantu experience before the divergence of the ancestral Mashariki language out of its earlier Eastern-Savanna ancestry. Very few of these items turn up in Tables 4-6; for the most part they constitute a separate corroborative corpus of stem-morpheme evidence for this subclassification, additional to what appears here.

4. Factoring out areal influences in the data

The mapping of innovations suffers, as does basic word-counting, from the effects of lexical diffusion, but in ways that show more sharply the stigmata of the diffusionary origins of portions of a corpus. We need to take a look at these indications before moving on to sum up the subclassification proposed here.

In the case of the Mashariki group, for example, a major set of root innovations define the grouping by being restricted to just Mashariki languages, while at the same time appearing in languages scattered all across and/or at the far extremes of the Mashariki field (Table 4, Section A). Several lesser sets of Mashariki root innovations have the same kind of distribution, but with one difference: They also have one or more reflexes in certain other Eastern-Savanna or Western-Savanna languages that are spoken today geographically adjacent to undoubted Mashariki languages. More often than not, the overlapping spreads cannot certainly be demonstrated on phonological criteria alone to be due to word borrowing (although some of them can indeed be so shown). Their suspect histories thus will often not be self-evident in lexicostatistical counts. But when mapped, their occurrences—widely in Mashariki, but narrowly overlapping into a single language or a very few adjacent languages of the Luban, Lega, or Western-Savanna groups—immediately reveal their suspect status. They have, in other words, just the kind of distributional overlap typical of their having entered the language only after it had diverged from its nearest relatives and after it had, in addition, come to be spoken in areas of contact with Mashariki languages. Similar cases can be found farther west, most notably the instances of Savanna-Bantu stem morphemes whose distributions overlap from the Luban or Lega speech areas into Tetela or from the Luban areas into Kuba. The stem morphemes having such distributions—and because of the long historical prevalence of intra-Bantu contacts, they are common—are included in separate sections of the relevant tables, lettered "B", "C", "D", etc. "Section A" in each instance is reserved, of course, for the innovations restricted to the genetic grouping they properly define.

Two problematic cases of this kind are the Sabi and Botatwe groups, the languages of each of which contain a large number of stem innovations that elsewhere occur only in "narrow" Mashariki and sometimes only in the Kaskazi branch of Mashariki (Table 4, sections B-D, and Table 5, sections E-G). Two explanations of these data are possible. One is that many of the items are borrowings from Mashariki languages into Sabi and Botatwe, but that others derive from a common ancestor, a proto-"Wide"-Mashariki dialect of the proto-Eastern-Savanna language. The alternative answer is that all are borrowings, reflective of Mashariki substrata in Sabi and Botatwe.

Close studies of the southeastern Central African region (Ahmed 1996; Ehret 1998) reveal a history characterized over the past 2000-plus years by repeatedly cross-cutting layers of language shift. A marked set of phonologically demonstrable loanwords from an extinct "narrow" Mashariki language, apparently of the Kaskazi group, occur in the Botatwe languages (Ehret 1998), indicating that, before the spread of Botatwe settlement across parts of southern Zambia, starting late in the first millennium A.D. (Ahmed 1996, combining archeological and linguistic evidence), Kaskazi peoples inhabited parts of the region. Similar arguments can be made for eastern Zambia, namely, that a Kaskazi substratum underlies the Sabi languages today spoken across the region. The initial Sabi expansion is to be correlated with the spread of the Lwangwa archeological tradition since about 1000 A.D. This tradition overlays the Kalambo culture of the previous thousand years, which can be attributed to Mwika-Rungwe or other peoples of Kaskazi affiliations (Ahmed 1996). The farthest direct extension of this earlier Mashariki impact, dating to the first half of the first millennium A.D. reached the eastern side of the Zambezi floodplain in far southwestern Zambia, where it had repercussions for the development of the early Luyana-Southwest peoples farther west (see Table 4, sections F-H, and Table 5, section I).

During the past 1000 years, new layers of language shift, as well as growing trade contacts along the Zambezi and its tributaries, left a more uneven and variegated distribution of stem morphemes. The Sabi expansion had a major cultural impact on the Nyanja-Chewa speakers of the Nyasa group in the first half of the present millennium, as is apparent in the archeology of the Malawi region and in their oral traditions. A small part of the impact of this history on Nyanja-Chewa vocabulary can be seen in Table 7. Sabi influences also were strong on some of the Botatwe languages, mostly notably Lenje; and Botatwe influences also flowed the other direction to some extent. The Lamba language of the Sabi group in particular seems to have adopted a significant number of words from a Botatwe dialect (for an example, see *-kèndè in Table 4, Section D). The stem morphemes spread by this process of course include items belonging to sets otherwise restricted, for instance, to Botatwe and the Kaskazi branch of "narrow" Mashariki.

Language shift at the beginning of the millennium in Zimbabwe probably accounts for another strong set of cross-cutting lexical influences, apparently from a Nyasa-related language, on the central Shona dialects (a very small sampling of this influence appears in the data dealt with in this study; it is cited in Table 8). And a wide zone of multidirectional cultural interaction took shape at uncertain dates among the peoples of the lands on both sides of the middle stretches of the Zambezi. Table 9 identifies a specific set of such words, but a number of others can be recognized in the distributional descriptions in Tables 4-6. A key descriptive phrase to look for in such a case is the abbreviation, "mid-Zamb. areal." In addition, many of the less widespread stem morphemes included in Table 6, sections C-D, may actually come, too, from this same long-term set of cultural interactions.

So varied and complex, then, were these interactions that they may indeed be enough to explain, as substrata effects, all the overlapping distributions of Mashariki stem-morpheme innovations into the Sabi and Botatwe languages. Nevertheless, it still cannot be entirely ruled out that some of these morphemes might remain from a period of shared Sabi, Botatwe, and Mashariki ancestry in a proto-"Wide"-Mashariki dialect of proto-Eastern-Savanna Bantu.

A few other sets of stem morphemes indicative of wide areal interactions need also to be factored out in interpreting the data. One notable sphere of cultural diffusion involved the more westerly members of the Lakes subgroup of Kaskazi and early Sabi and sometimes Luban speakers. The data on these contacts are biased toward subsistence culture, suggesting that the evidence for the most part reflects the diffusion of new features of economy (Table 9: sorghum, hamper, ram) that we know from other evidence to date to around 2000-1500 years ago. A second sphere of interaction apparently extended across the northern edge of the Kalahari. Again some of the components of this data set (Table 11) may reflect the early spread of subsistence knowledge, e.g., of sorghum or bulrush millet and of sheep, about 2000-1500 years ago. But the set as a whole is more heterogeneous and probably includes items reflective as well of later interactions of Kusi peoples with the Luyana, Southwest-Bantu, and Yeyi groups to their northwest.

Another zone where various layerings of Bantu settlement apparently have taken shape over the past 2000 years lay to the immediate west of Lake Nyasa (Lake Malawi) and to the north and northeast of the lake. Here there seems to have been a history of recurrent language shifts involving southerly Kaskazi groups on one hand and northerly Kusi groups on the other. A Kaskazi substratum has been argued (Ehret 1998) to underlie the Nyasa group's settlement in parts of Malawi (see Table 5, section C, for some of the proposed evidence), while an earlier Kusi population may have preceded Kaskazi peoples in some parts of Tanzania to the northeast of the Lake (Table 6, section B, contains evidence that seems to support this inference; some of the data in Table 13 may also reflect that history).

To the east of the Corridor Region, in what is today northern Mozambique, a less variegated history of contact between Kaskazi and Kusi groups seems indicated. There long-term interactions between Rufiji-Ruvuma groups on the north and Makua peoples to their south appear also to have made their effects apparent in the data studied here (see Table 5, section B, for proposed examples).

5. Summing up the subclassification

Taking into account these various effects, we can now combine our proposals into the following overall classification of Savanna-Bantu:

A. Western-Savanna
 1. Luyana-SW Bantu (K.30, L.60, R.20-40)
 2. Lwena (K.10)
 3. Lunda (L.50)
 4. Pende (L.10)
 5. Mbundu (H.20)
 6. Ovimbundu (R.11)

B. Eastern-Savanna
 1. Luban (L.20-40, 60)
 2. Lega (D.20)
 3. Botatwe (M.60 and K.40)
 4. Sabi (M.40-50)
 5. Mashariki
  a. Kaskazi
   1. Lakes (zone J [D.40-60 and E.10-40]);
   2. Upland (E.50-60 and E.74a);
   3. Langi (F.33-34);
   4. Takama (F, except for F.33-34);
   5. Northeast-Coastal (G.10-40 and E.70, except E.74a);
   6. Njombe (G.60);
   7. Kilombero (G.50 and P.15);
   8. Rufiji-Ruvuma (N.10 and P.10-20, except for P.15);
   9. Mwika-Rungwe (M.10-30).
  b. Kusi
   1. Nyasa (N.20-40, except for N.41, a Sabi language)
   2. Makua (P.30);
   3. Shona (S.10);
   4. Southeast-Bantu (S.20-60 and K.21).

C. Mbala (H.40): possible third branch of Savanna-Bantu?

As traced out here, Savanna-Bantu does not include any of the languages of zones A, B, C, D.10 and D.30, and H.10. The Yaka group, H.30, probably stands outside the Savanna branching; the position of Mbala, H.40, is uncertain. These languages, the evidence indicates, belong to a variety of branchings of Bantu, related at several deeper levels to the Savanna group.

6. Corroborative evidence from Bantu phonological history

Bantu phonological history can be seen, even in the current preliminary stage of our knowledge of the topic, to provide a few strong, individual corroborations of the main historical stages of this classification.

In many cases, identifying the phonological innovations diagnostic of wider subgroupings in Bantu is going to be an immensely difficult enterprise. So often an invaluable tool in subgrouping other language families, phonological change is a major problem area for Bantu subclassification, simply because, time and again, linguistic drift has brought about the same or similar sound shifts separately across large portions of the Bantu field. I refer here especially to the recurrent spirantizing effects in the Savanna-Bantu languages of the super-high vowels *į and *ų on preceding consonants. It is clear in repeated instances that these shifts have taken place independently and at sharply different times in the past in different Savanna subgroups, even when they have repeatedly produced identical outcomes (such as *k > *f* /_ *ų*)) To get anything useful out of these data, it will probably be essential for investigators to try to establish the differing details of spirantization and the differing courses of ordered sound shift that lie behind the modern surface similarities of phonology in different subgroups, and even that effort may often turn out to be inconclusive in its results.

The most telling evidence for subgrouping is provided by sound shifts whose environments differ from those that trigger linguistic drift effects in Bantu and which are individual in their characteristics and not widely paralleled elsewhere in language history. Five shifts that meet these criteria can be identified right now, each matching up with one of the key nodes of the classification proposed here. Two of them, shifts 1 and 4, have long been well known to Bantuists. Shifts 1, 2, 4, and 5 are strong and consistent in their indications; shift 3 is a more provisional postulation.

(l) Dahl's Law. This phonological rule is diagnostic of the Kaskazi branch of Mashariki. In its original form, it voiced the first of two voiceless consonants in the same word. The evidence of its former or current productivity is found in every subgroup that makes up the Kaskazi group as defined here, and only in those subgroups. The only exception may be the Mwika-Rungwe subgroup (according to Nurse 1979), but the writer's own survey has turned up a few apparent fossil occurrences even there. In a minority of the Kaskazi languages it has remained productive down to the present. Everywhere else it eventually dropped from use, although normally leaving behind scattered relics of its former presence in the form of skewed pronunciations of certain words—cases, for example, where original *k should have gone back to being pronounced /k/ after the dropping of the rule, but has instead remained /g/.

(2) *g > *j /ị -_. This sound shift rule is diagnostic of the Kusi branch of Mashariki. It involves palatalization, a common kind of shift among the world's languages. What makes it unusual, both inside Bantu and outside of it, is its environment: palatalization here affected the consonant that followed the governing vowel but not, as is usually the case, the consonant that preceded the vowel.

A striking and especially clear example of this shift is provided by *i̧-jànà '100', cited in Table 6. Another example involving a *g-initial stem, where the governing environment is provided by the class 5 prefix *(l)i̧-*, is *+lì̧-gèmbè, originally 'blade' (rather than specifically 'hoe' or 'ax' as is usually presumed). All the Kaskazi reflexes of this root can be referred to an original form containing *g. (The apparent exceptions in the Sabaki subgroup of Northeast-Coastal Bantu can be attributed to a proto-Sabaki stem with irregular *g loss; i.e., Swahili *jembe* , pl. *majembe* 'hoe' reveals underlying *j-embe, pl. *ma-j-embe, with Swahili regular *j-* reflex of the class 5 prefix plus stem *-embe, and regular *ma-j- class 5/6 plural prefixation of vowel-initial stems with class 5 singulars.) The Kusi reflexes, in keeping with the postulated Kusi sound shift, produced a proto-Kusi stem shape *-jèmbè. (The spread of this stem shape westward, with the meaning 'ax', to the Sabi and Lunda languages is thus presumptive evidence for the Early Iron Age diffusion of the word and therefore of the tool it named, the iron ax, from early Kusi peoples to their western neighbors.)

A notable stem-medial example of the shift *g > *j /i̧-_ can be seen in the Shona reflex *twiza* of proto-Mashariki *-tùi̧gà 'giraffe'. (Guthrie gives *-tùigà as the general reconstruction, but the evidence from the Lakes and Shona subgroups shows that *-tùi̧gà was the original shape and that *-tùigà arose only later, through a vowel-height assimilation that spread to several proto-Kaskazi dialects after Kaskazi differentiation was already getting underway.)

(3) *n > *l /#-Ci̧ _ -(a)#, where C is a labial stop (examples of *p and *m are known so far). This shift is diagnostic of the Mashariki group as a whole. It appears in four roots presented here, three in Table 4 and one in Table 5: proto-Mashariki *-mì̧l - 'to blow nose', *-mì̧là 'snot', *-mì̧l-'to swallow', and *-pí̧là 'pus.' The shape *-pí̧là is attested in one language of the Botatwe group, and the shape *-mì̧l- 'to swallow' in one language of the Sabi group. But those are clearly isolated borrowings, since the other Botatwe and Sabi languages maintain the same roots without this sound shift. The rule thus appears to be consistently lacking in Savanna-Bantu outside of Mashariki. On the other hand, the rule does rest on a less strong foundation than shifts 1, 2, 4, and 5, and this is because small inconsistencies appear in its verb-stem-final outcomes within the Kusi subgroup the Mashariki. In particular, several Kusi languages show conflicting reflexes, sometimes with expected *n > *l in the appurtenant environment, but other times preserving *n. The older *n also recurs in the Nyanja (Nyasa subgroup) reflex of *-mì̧là 'snot', but this particular item is most probably a Sabi loanword.

(4) Meinhof's law: *NC > NN / _VNC, where both C are voiced (*NN is structurally realized as [N] in most modern-day languages because of their general lack of long or geminate consonants). This law is attested in all languages of the proposed Eastern-Savanna branch of Savanna-Bantu and, with three exceptions, only in those languages. The three apparent

exceptions are all Western-Savanna languages spoken in areas long contiguous to Eastern-Savanna speech areas, and at least two, Luyana and Yeyi, evince very strong Eastern-Savanna influences in their vocabularies. The third, Ndembu, shows contradictory outcomes for sequences of *NCVNC, so it is possible that its cases of *NVNC, as opposed to its *NCVNC reflexes, may have originated as loanwords. Because the rule is no longer productive in many of the languages that once had it, NCVNC outcomes have also sometimes arisen in Eastern Savanna languages after the rule disappeared, in cases where an earlier class 3, 5, or 7 singular marker of a *-CVNCV stem was replaced with the class 9 singular, *N-.

(5) Vowel height harmony of a certain type in verb extensions. This phonological rule has been noted by Larry Hyman to largely coincide in its distribution with the Savanna-Bantu group identified in this article. For its formulation and the argument, the reader should turn to Hyman's article in this volume.

7. Implications of the subclassification for human history

This genetic subclassification has some strong geographical and demographic implications as to how Bantu languages got to the eastern side of Africa. It implies a history not quite like any other recently proposed by scholars.

The clear overall implication of the later distributions of Savanna-Bantu societies—provided the classification proposed here is correct—is that the territories of the proto-Savanna-Bantu people lay close to the Kwa-Kasai-Congo confluence. The first divergence of that people into daughter sets of communities produced a proto-Western-Savanna society, the descendant languages of which are spread far southward, southwestward, and southeastward from the Kwa-Kasai-Congo confluence region; a proto-Eastern-Savanna society, the descendants of which extend eastward from those areas; and possibly a third branch, ancestral to the Mbala group of languages, still spoken today just south of the Kwa-Kasai confluence.

The subsequent divergence of the proto-Eastern-Savanna people gave rise to a series of societies—proto-Luban, proto-Sabi, proto-Botatwe, proto-Lega, and proto-Mashariki—stretched out along the southern edge of the equatorial rainforest and northern edge of the woodland savanna just south of the forest. It is hard to avoid concluding that the Sankuru River, which flows almost directly westward across this zone to the Kwa-Kasai confluence, provided the main access for the eastward advance of Eastern-Savanna Bantu communities. The Luban societies of later times extended from the middle Sankuru River southward through the Kwilu region and parts of Shaba. The more easterly centers of gravity of the proto-Sabi and proto-Botatwe lands show that they derived from Eastern-Savanna communities located to the east of the proto-Lubans. Their ancestors could have moved southward from the upper Sankuru country into their later territories by following respectively the Lubilashi and Lomami rivers into west-central and central Shaba (Ahmed 1996). The proto-Lega and proto-Mashariki would have formed the eastern outliers of this chain of expansion, with the proto-Mashariki communities moving the farthest east, right into the highland areas all along the western edge of the great West Rift. From that region in a subsequent era of history, the Kaskazi- and Kusi-speaking descendants of the proto-Mashariki would have scattered out across much of the eastern side of the continent.

Far to the west, the proto-Western-Savanna society can be proposed to have expanded at first contemporaneously in two directions from the Kasai-Kwa-Congo confluence region (Papstein 1978): (1) south and southeastward through the woodland savannas of the Kwilu watershed and into the upper Zambezi country, and (2) more directly southward, up the Kasai watershed as far as the Benguela highlands. The easterly of these two expansions gave rise to the later Lunda and Lwena subgroups; its farthest extension south was the proto-Luyana-Southwest people, who initially settled, it would appear, on the wet soils of the Zambezi floodplain. The Southwest-Bantu form a subsequent Luyana-Southwest offshoot, which spread west from the floodplain, across the northern Kalahari fringes and into the Kunene River areas. There they came into close contacts with the other arm of Western-Savanna expansion, the far south extension of which comprised the Ovimbundu subgroup of the Benguela interior. It also seems probable, from the overlapping distributions of stem morphemes between the Kimbundu and Kongo groups (discussed above), that the areas around and just south of the mouth of the Congo River were once part, too, of the lands of the Western-Savanna peoples—that the initial stages of Western-Savanna Bantu expansion included those areas.

References

Ahmed, Christine. 1996. Before Eve was Eve: 2200 years of gendered history in East Central Africa. [Doctoral dissertation, University of California at Los Angeles.

Ehret, Christopher. 1971. *Southern Nilotic history: Linguistic approaches to the study of the past.* Evanston: Northwestern University Press.

Ehret, Christopher. 1974. Agricultural history in Central and Southern Africa, c.1000 B.C. to A.D. 500, *Transafrican Journal of* History 4: 1-25.

Ehret, Christopher. 1980. *The historical reconstruction of Southern Cushitic phonology and vocabulary.* (Kölner Beiträge zur Afrikanistik 5.) Berlin: Reimer.

Ehret, Christopher. 1995/96. The establishment of iron-working in Eastern, Central, and Southern Africa: Linguistic inferences on technological history, *Sprache und Geschichte in Afrika* 16/17.

Ehret, Christopher. 1998. *An African classical age: Eastern and Southern Africa in world history, 1000 B.C. to A.D. 400.* Charlottesville: University Press of Virginia.

Ehret, Christopher. Forthcoming. *The historical-comparative reconstruction of Nilo-Saharan.*

Ehret, Christopher & Mohamed Nuuh Ali. 1984. Soomaali subclassification, in: T. Labahn (ed.), *Proceedings of the of the Second International Congress of Somali Studies*, Vol. 1, pp. 201-270. Hamburg: Buske.

Ehret, Christopher & Margaret Kinsman. 1981. The dialect classification of Shona and its implications for Iron Age history in Southern Africa, *International Journal of African Historical Studies* 14.3: 401-443.

Embleton, Sheila. 1986. *Statistics in historical linguistics.* Bochum: Brockmeyer.

Huffman, T. N. 1989. *Iron Age migrations: The ceramic sequence in Southern Zambia: Excavations at Gundu and Ndonde.* Johannesburg: Witwatersrand University Press.

Klieman, Kairn. 1997. Peoples of the Western Equatorial rainforest: A history of society and economy, from ca. 3000 B.C. to 1890. [Doctoral dissertation, University of California at Los Angeles.]

Nurse, Derek. 1979. Description of Sample Bantu Languages of Tanzania, *African Languages/Langues Africaines* 5.1:1-150.

Ownby, Carolan. 1985. Early Nguni history: The linguistic evidence and its correlation with archaeology and oral tradition. [Doctoral dissertation, University of California at Los Angeles.]

Papstein, Robert. 1978. The Upper Zambezi: A history of the Luvale people, 1000-1900. [Doctoral dissertation, University of California at Los Angeles.]

Phillipson, David. 1977. *The later prehistory of Eastern and Southern Africa.* London: Heinemann.

Schoenbrun, David. 1990. Early History in Eastern Africa's Great Lakes region: Linguistic, ecological, and archaeological approaches, ca. 500 B.C. to ca. 1000 A.D. [Doctoral dissertation, University of California at Los Angeles.]

Appendix: Tables

Representing the data in the tables

The tables of innovations are arranged in three columns. In the first column of each, the stem morpheme and its meaning are listed. The second column gives the known distribution of the item with that meaning, and the third presents the arguments as to why the stem in that meaning and/or shape is to be considered an innovation.

Several different notations introduce the arguments in the third column. Three different phrases focus attention on the earlier uses of a stem. (1) The words "Morphological innovation" indicate that the stem in question can be derived from another, earlier Bantu stem by morphological addition, deletion, or substitution. (2) "Semantic innovation" denotes the stem as having had previously in Bantu language history a different meaning from which the proposed innovated meaning can be derived, while (3) "Phonological innovation" signals an innovatory sound shift particular to the stem, either analogical, assimilatory, or dissimilatory in origin. A fourth notation, "Displaced," introduces the stem morpheme, along with its distribution, that was previously used to express the same meaning as the innovated stem. (Rarely, where the older stem continued to maintain wide currency long after the innovated term was put in use, the alternative introductory phrases "Partially displaced" or "Competed with" may be employed.) In a large number of cases, both kinds of argument—a derivation of the stem, prefaced by phrases (1), (2), or (3), and the identification of an earlier stem displaced wholly or partially from use by it—can be offered.

In representing the stems in the tables, I have followed the lead of Michael Mann in reconstructing PB (proto-Bantu) *s where Guthrie has *c. I have also continued to find *l, as used by earlier scholars, a more satisfactory reconstruction of the consonant given by Guthrie as *d, at least back to the proto-Savanna-Bantu node. For ease of reference, however, the order of presentation follows Guthrie's alphabetization, with *b thus immediately preceding *s (Guthrie's *c), and *s preceding *l (Guthrie's *d). In many cases, I have also not recognized Guthrie's *y as a stem-initial consonant, preferring to reconstruct vowel-initial stems in such instances, with the surface occurrence in some languages of [y] reflexes understood to be attributable to morpheme structure rules (as yet undefined). Again, whether or not a stem-initial *y has been represented in the data as presented here, such items have been alphabetized as in Guthrie and thus appear following the stems that begin in *t.

For reasons of insufficient space, the distribution of a particular morpheme is usually not given exhaustively, but in a manner that is representative of the known overall geographical extent of its occurrence. A morpheme cited for a single language in a tightly related subgroup may occur within the subgroup only in that language, but usually that item can be expected to occur in some other dialects or languages of the group also.

Non-Savanna languages of occurrence are also named when they contain a stem that, from its distribution or its phonology, can be argued to be a probable loanword from a contiguous Savanna subgroup. Because Guthrie's H.10 is a heterogeneous collection of subgroups, the presence of a stem in either the Kongo or Vili groupings is usually cited, too, by language or subgroup name. Outside of those instances, the non-Savanna occurrences of a stem are normally identified simply by their zone, either A, B, C, or D. This procedure simplifies data presentation for this study, in which the fact of a stem morpheme's wider presence outside of Savanna-Bantu matters, but a more detailed subclassification of the Bantu languages of the A-D zones is not at issue.

It should be noted that, in the tabling of data, the notation "D zone" refers only to the D.10 and D.30 of Guthrie. His other D zone groups all belong to Savanna-Bantu as defined here, and thus stem occurrences in D.20 and D.40-60 are cited by subgroup or language name: as Lega or Holoholo

(D.20), as Konjo (D.40), as Forest subgroup or Bembe (D.50), and as Rundi, Rwanda, or Ha (D.60).

Abbreviations used in the tables

Central-Tanz. areal	Central Tanzania areal set of stems
ESav	Eastern-Savanna Bantu
Kask	Kaskazi
Luba-Sh	Luba-Shaba
mid-Zamb. areal	Middle Zambezi areal set of stems
NE-Coastal	Northeast-Coastal Bantu (Kaskazi subgroup)
PB	proto-Bantu
PCS	proto-Central Sudanic (Nilo-Saharan branch)
PM	proto-Mashariki
PNS	proto-Nilo-Saharan
SavB	Savanna-Bantu
SE-Bantu	Southeast-Bantu
SW-Bantu	Southwest-Bantu (R.13-14, R.20-30)
Nzadi-Kwa	branching of Bantu (after Klieman 1997), consisting provisionally of Savanna-Bantu plus B.30-80, C.30, C.60-80, H.10, and possibly H.30
Sangha-Kwa	branching of Bantu (after Klieman 1997), consisting provisionally of Nzadi-Kwa plus B.20, C.10-20, and A.80
WSav	Western-Savanna Bantu

List of tables

Table 1: Stem morpheme innovations defining the Savanna-Bantu group

Root <u>*innovation*</u>	<u>*Distribution*</u>	*Root wholly or partially displaced by innovated root;* <u>*additional explanations and commentary*</u>
*-bàbá 'wing'	WSav; Luban; Botatwe; relict Mashariki (Kask: NE-Coastal, Rundi; Kusi: SE-Bantu [Chopi])	Displaced PB *-pàpá, found outside Narrow Bantu and in AB zones, relict SavB (Luban: W.Luba; Mashariki: Kask [Lakes]; Kusi [Venda]; also a few languages in loanword shapes).
*-bálá 'baldness'	WSav (Lwena); Luban; Botatwe	Probable derivation from same root seen also in SavB *-bálà 'spot, speckle; wound, scar,' i.e., bare spot.
*-bàlʊ̀ 'rib; side of body'	WSav (Lunda); Sabi; Mashariki (general Kask.; Kusi: Shona area [Shona,Venda]), also in Holoholo; also isolated in A zone (Bulu)	Displaced PB *-bànji´, found in ABC zones, and Kongo. Isolated *-bàlʊ̀ in one A-zone language as 'rib' implies PB presence of this root, but probably in collective meaning 'side of body,' with 'rib' in the A zone as an independent parallel innovation of that meaning; this proposal needs investigation.
*-bánd- 'to split (tr.)'	WSav (Ovimbundu in extended shape); Sabi; Mashariki 'to chop wood' (Kask: Upland; SE-Bantu: Sotho)	Displaced PB *-pánd- and *-yát-: see *-pànd- 'to split' below in this table
*-bánd- 'to flatten' (+ ext. > 'lie flat')	WSav (SW-Bantu); Mashariki (Kask: Lakes, Takama; Kusi: Nyasa, Shona ['lie flat'], SE-Bantu)	Semantic innovation: < PB *-bánd- 'to put low,' found in A ('hold down'), B ('throw down') zones.

*-bèlek- 'to carry child on back'	WSav (Ovimbundu, Lwena, SW-Bantu), and relict Mashariki (Kask: Rufiji-Ruvuma, NE-Coastal; Kusi	Partially displaced PB *-pààp-, found outside Narrow Bantu and in B zone (Guthrie cites only a loanword instance) and relict SavB (Zambian areal: SE-Bantu, Sabi, Kaonde; also Matengo of Rufiji-Ruvuma; also > Central Tanz. areal: 'bear child': Gogo, Rimi)
*-bų́ 'soil, earth'	WSav (Ovimbundu, Pende, SW-Bantu, Yeyi, Luyana, Lwena); Botatwe; relict Mashariki (Kusi: SE-Bantu); also in Soko (C zone)	Proposed semantic innovation: < proposed pre-PB *-bų́ 'dust,' attested separately in PB *-bų́ 'ashes' (found in AB zones and Mashariki: widespread in Kask). Displaced PB *-lòbá 'soil, earth,' found in A zone, relict WSav (Ovimbundu, SW-Bantu), Luban, Holoholo, Sabi, Botatwe, and relict Mashariki (Kask: some Lakes).
*-sàk- 'to desire, want'	WSav (Lwena); Luban; Sabi; Mashariki (Kask: NE-Coastal; Kusi: Venda [n. 'desire'])	Semantic innovation: < PB *-sàk- 'to search for.' Displaced Sangha- Kwa *-kúnd- 'to desire, want,' found in BC zones and relict SavB (Lega, Sabi, and relict Kask [Lakes, NE-Coastal].
*-sák(ul)- 'to comb'	WSav (Lwena); Luban; Sabi; Botatwe; relict Mashariki (Kask: Takama)	Displaced Sangha-Kwa *-sàn-, found in BC zones, Kongo, Lega, and relict Mashariki (Lakes: Ganda (extended shape *-sànilil-], NE-Coastal).
*-sàkul- 'to choose'	WSav (Lwena, Lunda, Herero ['guess']; relict Mashariki (Kask: Ngazija, Kilombero)	Morphological innovation: < PB *-sàk- 'to search for.' Displaced Sangha-Kwa *-sóól-, found in BC zones and Kongo. Partially displaced Nzadi-Kwa *-sàl-, found in B zone, Kongo, and SavB (WSav, Luban, Mid-Zamb. areal [Kaonde, Botatwe, Nsenga, Shona, Venda]).

*-sángal- 'to be pleased'	WSav (Ovimbundu); Luban; Sabi; Mashariki (Kask: Lakes)	Morphological innovation: < Sangha-Kwa *-sáng- 'to be pleased,' found in C zone, Kongo, relict Mashariki (Kusi: Sotho [as *-sángil-]).
*-séngò 'horn'	Mbala; WSav (Lunda, Nkoya); Luban; Sabi; relict Mashariki (Yao)	Displaced PB *-í̀gá, found in AC zones and relict SavB (WSav: Luyana, SW-Bantu; Botatwe; and Mashariki: Kask: Luyia).
*-sì̧ngà 'strand, fiber'	WSav (Ovimbundu 'hair'); Mashariki (various meanings: 'fiber,' 'straight hair,' 'sinew thread'): Kask (Lakes, Takama, NE-Coastal); Kusi (SE-Bantu)	Semantic innovation: < PB *-sì̧ngà '(fiber) string,' found in ABC zones, Kongo, and relict ESavB (Luba; SE-Bantu).
*-sʊ́á 'termite'	WSav (Lwena, Lunda, Luyana-SW Bantu); Luban; Sabi; Botatwe; Mashariki (Kask: Lakes, Takama, NE-Coastal; Kusi: Nyasa, SE-Bantu)	Semantic inovation: < PB *-sʊ́á, possibly 'flying stage of termite,' as found in A zone. Displaced PB *-sélèlí or *-sélìlí, found in ABC zones and Kongo.
*-làm- 'to look after'	WSav (Lwena); Luban; Sabi; relict Mashariki (Upland *-lamat- 'to be guardian of'); also Tetela	Displaced PB *-sùng-, found in AC zones, Kongo, and relict SavB (WSav: SW-Bantu; Sabi; Mashariki: Kask [NE-Coastal], Kusi [Nyasa: overlap from Sabi?]).
*-làmat- 'to stick (intr.)'	WSav (Lwena); Luban; relict Mashariki (Lakes)	Semantic cum morphological innovation: < Sangha-Kwa *-lam- 'to stick (tr.),' found in C zone, Kongo, and relict SavB (WSav: Ovimbundu; Sabi: Nsenga).
*-lél(uk)- 'to become light in weight'	WSav (Ovimbundu, Lwena, Lunda); Mashariki (Kusi: Nyasa, SE-Bantu); meaning implies intermediate shift 'glide, float')	Semantic innovation: < PB *-lél- 'to swing (suspended)' (see Table 3 for distribution).

*-léét- 'to bring'	WSav (Lunda; SW-Bantu); Sabi; Botatwe; Mashariki (Kask: Lakes, NE-Coastal; Kusi: SE-Bantu)	Displaced PB *-bèg-, found in ABC zones, and Kongo, and retained in relict Mashariki with meaning shift to 'to set before' (e.g., Ganda, Sotho).
*-lɪ́ó 'right hand'	WSav (Ovimbundu, Lwena, SW-Bantu); Luban (Hemba); Sabi; Mashariki (Kask: Lakes, Takama, Rufiji-Ruvuma; Kusi: Shona)	Morphological innovation: < PB *-lí- 'to eat,' found outside Narrow Bantu and generally across Narrow Bantu.
*-lɪ̧́mbà 'body'	WSav (Lwena, Lunda); relict Mashariki (Kask: Kilombero [Pogolo]; Kusi: SE-Bantu [Nguni])	Displaced PB *-yútù ~ -jútù, found outside Narrow Bantu and in ABC zones, Kongo, and relict WSav (Luyana, Nkoya; loanword in Herero).
*-lɪ̧̀ul- 'to pull up'; AND *-lɪ̧̀uk- 'to revive'	WSav (Lwena, SW-Bantu); Luban; Sabi; Botatwe; Mashariki (Kask: Lakes, Takama, NE-Coastal; Kusi: Nyasa, Shona); AND WSav (Pende); Luban (general); Mashariki (Kask: Lakes, Upland, Takama, NE-Coastal, Rufiji-Ruvuma; Kusi: Nyasa, SE-Bantu)	Morphological innovation: < PB *-lɪ̧̀- 'to go down' (seen also in PB -lɪ̧̀al- 'to sit; dwell' [found in AC zones] and PB *-lɪ̧̀am- 'to sink' [found in AB zones, Kongo, WSav (SW-Bantu), and relict Mashariki (Kask: Lakes, NE- Coastal; Kusi: Nyasa]), by addition respectively of *-ul-, *-uk- extensions containing PB conversive.
*-lòndà 'sore'	WSav (Lwena, SW-Bantu); Luban; Sabi; Botatwe; Mashariki (Kask: Lakes, Upland, Takama, Rufiji-Ruvuma; Kusi: Nyasa, Shona, SE-Bantu)	Displaced PB *-pútá 'wound, sore,' found in ABC zones, Kongo, and relict SavB (Luban; Mashariki: Lakes [Nkore 'wound'].

*-lòngà 'river'	WSav (Ovimbundu, Lwena, Lunda, SW-Bantu); Luban (Sanga only); Subiya; Sabi; Botatwe; Mashariki (Kusi only: Nyasa [Tumbuka], Shona, SE-Bantu)	Semantic derivation: < Nzadi-Kwa *-lòngà 'low-lying wet ground,' seen in B zone ('valley'; 'channel'). Probably displaced Sangha-Kwa *-jálé 'river,' found in BCD zones and Kongo. Partially displaced competing Sangha-Kwa root *lu-ị́jì 'river,' found in C zone, Kongo, Vili, and WSav (Kimbundu, Ovimbundu; SW-Bantu 'waterhole'), Luban, and Mashariki (Kask: Lakes, Langi, Upland, Rufiji- Ruvuma, Mwika-Rungwe; relict Kusi: SE-Bantu [Venda 'waterhole'])
*-lóótà 'dream'	WSav (Lwena); Luban (W.Luba); relict Mashariki (Kask: Lakes; Kusi: Makua, Sena)	Morphological innovation: < PB *-lóót- 'to dream,' found in BC zones, A zone (in derived nouns), Kongo, WSav, Luban, and Mashariki. Displaced PB *-lóótó, found in AC zones and relict SavB (WSav: Herero; Luban: W.Luba; Sabi (Bemba). Note also *-lóótị̀, found in a few A zone and one Mashariki cases (Takama): probable independent parallel formations.
*-lùnd- 'to add to'	WSav (Pende); Sabi; relict Mashariki (N'n Mozambique areal: Yao, Makua)	Semantic innovation: < Sangha-Kwa 'to gather up, store up,' found in C zone, Kongo, and relict SavB (WSav: Lwena; Mashariki: Takama).
*-lúndù 'hill'	WSav (Kimbundu, Pende, Ovimbundu, Lwena, SW-Bantu); Sabi; Botatwe	Displaced PB *-gùlù, found outside Narrow Bantu and in B zone and relict SavB (WSav: Ovimbundu; Luban: Luba-Sh; Lega; isolated Mashariki: Kask (Lakes: Bembe: areal spread < Lega?).

*-gùè 'stone'	WSav; relict Mashariki (some Takama); also in Enya (D.10)	Displaced PB *-tálè, found in ABC zones, Kongo, and isolated WSav (Ovimbundu [Kongo areal influence?]); Lega; isolated instances in Lakes, Takama of Kask; *-tálè narrowed its application in ESav to 'stone for making tools' (Ehret 1995/96)
*-gùlùbè 'bushpig'	WSav; Luban; Sabi; Botatwe; Mashariki: Kask: Upland, NE-Coastal, Rufiji-Ruvuma, Takama; Kusi: Nyasa, Makua, Shona, SE-Bantu; also Holoholo	Displaced PB *-gùyá, found in ABC zones.
*-gʊ́ɪ́ 'arrow'	WSav (Lwena; SW-Bantu); Subiya; Lega; Mashariki (Kask: Lakes, Upland, Sabaki of NE-Coastal; Kusi: Nyasa, Makua [Chuabo]) SE-Bantu	Displaced PB *-bànjí, found outside Narrow Bantu and in ABC zones and Kongo (as *-bànjà).
*-kélik- 'to strain, filter'	WSav (Lwena); Luban; Sabi; relict Mashariki (Upland, Lakes [Luyia])	Morphological innovation: < Nzadi-Kwa *-kél-, found in B zone, Kongo, and derived SavB noun *-kélè 'salt' (filtered from ash of salt-producing reed)
*-kɪ̀pà 'tendon, vein'	WSav (Kimbundu, Ovimbundu, Lwena, SW-Bantu); Luban (Kaonde); Sabi; Mashariki (Kask: Upland, NE-Coastal, Rufiji-Ruvuma; Kusi: SE-Bantu)	Displaced PB *-tɪ́ngà 'vein' (see Table 1, section B) and PB *-sɪ̀ɪ̀sá 'tendon,' found in ABC zones and relict SavB (WSav: Lwena; Botatwe; relict Mashariki: Lakes [Ganda]).
*-kókul- 'to clear away	WSav (Ovimbundu); Mashariki (Kask: Lakes, NE-Coastal, Rufiji-Ruvuma; Kusi: Nyasa, Shona)	Morphological innovation: < PB *-kók- 'to pull,' found in AB zones, Kongo, WSav (Ovimbundu, Lwena, SW-Bantu), Luban, Botatwe, and Mashariki (Kusi: Nyasa, SE-Bantu).

*-kúá 'inhabitant'	WSav (Ovimbundu); Luban; relict Mashariki (Kusi: Nguni 'lineage'); also in Kongo	Displaced Sangha-Kwa *-sí, found in BC zones, Kongo group, and relict SavB (Luban: Songye).
*-náni̧ 'who?'	WSav (Pende); Mashariki (Kask: NE-Coastal, Rufiji-Ruvuma, Takama, Njombe; also Kongo; also in Kuba	Displaced PB *-náà, found outside Narrow Bantu and in B zone and Kongo.
*-nùngu 'porcupine'	WSav (SW-Bantu); Luban; Sabi (as *-nùngɪ́); Mashariki (Kask: Takama, NE-Coastal; Kusi: Nyasa, Shona, SE-Bantu); also as Sabi loanword in Ndembu (WSav)	Displaced PB *-gùmba, found in ABC zones and Kongo.
*-nụnk- 'to smell (intr.)'	WSav (Ovimbundu, Lwena); Luban; Sabi; Botatwe; Mashariki (Kask: Lakes, Takama, NE-Coastal, Rufiji-Ruvuma; Kusi: Nyasa, SE-Bantu); also in loan shape (*-nụ̀ụk-) in Kongo and Luyana-SW-Bantu (of WSav)	Displaced PB *-lụ̀mb-, found in Kongo and relict SavB (Ila; Mashariki: SE-Bantu), and seen also in PB *-lụ̀mbá 'smell (n.),' found in A zone, Kongo, and SavB (WSav, Luban, and widely in Mashariki).
*-nyí̧ngà 'blood'	WSav (Kimbundu; Lwena; Luyana); relict Mashariki (Takama; Lakes [Gusii])	Morphological innovation: < earlier Nzadi-Kwa *-í̧ngà, seen in Kongo. Displaced PB *-gì̧lá, found in ABCD zones.
*-pálà 'forehead'	WSav (Kimbundu, Ovimbundu, Lunda, Lwena, Luyana, SW-Bantu); Luban; Holoholo	Displaced PB *-bómbó, found in ABCD zones, Kongo ('nose'), Yaka, and relict Mashariki : Kusi (SE-Bantu only [Chopi 'forehead'; Sotho, Nguni 'bridge of nose']).

*-pák- 'to pack'	WSav (Lwena, SW-Bantu); Luban; Sabi; relict Mashariki (Kask: Lakes; Kusi: SE-Bantu)	Semantic innovation: < Nzadi-Kwa 'to put (in),' found in Kongo and relict Mashariki (Kusi: Sotho 'pour in') and implied in SavB *-pákul- see below).
*-pákat- 'to hold (on shoulder, etc.)'	WSav (Ovimbundu); Luban; Sabi; Mashariki (Kask: Lakes, NE-Coastal, Rufiji-Ruvuma; Kusi: Nyasa, Shona)	Morphological innovation: < *-pák- 'to pack' plus *-at- extension as durative.
*-pákul- 'to take out; to castrate'	WSav (Herero 'put aside'); Luvale 'castrate'); Luban; Sabi ('take out'); Mashariki (Kask: Lakes, Upland, NE-Coastal, Rufiji-Ruvuma; Kusi: SE-Bantu)	Morphological innovation: < pre-SavB *-pák- 'to put in' plus *-ul- reversive extension.
*-pànd- 'to split (tr.)'	WSav (Lwena); Luban; Botatwe; relict Mashariki (Shona 'to separate')	Displaced PB *-pánd-, found in ABC zones. Also displaced PB *-yát-, found in ABCD zones, Kongo, and SavB (relict Mashariki only: Kask [Lakes]; Kusi [Nguni]; in extended shape *-yátul- in WSav: Luyana group; Mashariki (relict Kask: Lakes, Upland, NE-Coastal).
*-pápat- 'to touch, grope'	WSav (Ovimbundu); Mashariki (Kask: Lakes, NE-Coastal, Rufiji-Ruvuma; Kusi: Nyasa, Shona)	Morphological innovation: < PB *-pát- 'to hold' (found in AC zones, WSav (SW-Bantu), and Mashariki (Kask: NE-Coastal, Njombe; Kusi: Makua, SE-Bantu) by partial reduplication.
*-pí́áng- 'to sweep'	WSav (SW-Bantu), Lega (Guha); Sabi	Partially displaced PB *-kómb-, found in ABC zones, Kongo, WSav (Ovimbundu, Lwena, SW-Bantu), and Luban.

*-tálá 'section of village'	WSav (Lunda 'house'); Sabi (Bemba 'neighboring village'); Mashariki (Lakes: Konjo, Luyia 'homestead'; NE-Coastal (Swahili 'ward of town')	Displaced Sangha-Kwa *-gàndá 'ward, section of village,' found in BC zones (in various meanings: 'quarter of village,' 'village,' 'chief's section of village,' 'fishing camp,' etc.), Kongo group ('village,' 'chief's section of village'), and relict occurrence or, more probably, cultural diffusion in SavB (Lwena 'chief's village'). Arguments for this reconstructed meaning of *-gàndá are made in Ehret 1998.
*-téndé 'foot'	WSav (Ovimbundu 'foot'); Luban (LubaSh 'leg'); Botatwe 'foot'); Mashariki 'heel' (see Table 4)	Semantic innovation: < prePB meaning 'point, tip' (in this case, foot as the tip of the leg), implied also in ABC zone reflex, *-téndé 'thorn.'
*-tį́ká 'wet season'	WSav (Lwena, Lunda); Luban; Mashariki (Kask: NE-Coastal, Rufiji-Ruvuma; Kusi: SE-Bantu; originally clearly meant 'wet season,' but in some more southerly languages > 'cold (n.)' or 'cold season'	Morphological innovation: < Sangha-Kwa *-tį́k- 'to flow' (Guthrie 'to go downstream'), found as verb in C zone and Kongo and in its derived noun in lefthand column.
*-túb-, *-túbul- 'to pierce'	WSav (Lwena, Lunda, SW-Bantu); Luban; Lega; Mashariki (Kask: Njombe, Mwika-Rungwe; Kusi: SE-Bantu *-túba 'hole, opening'); Kongo alternate shape *-tubul-* is probable WSav loanword	Phonological innovation: < Nzadi-Kwa *-tób- by irregular *u > o /_b-. Displaced PB *-tų́ų̀b- 'to pierce,' found in ABC zones. Also displaced Nzadi-Kwa *-túl-, found in B zone and relict SavB (Holoholo; Sabi; Botatwe; Kask: Upland).
*-tùndà 'hump'	WSav (Lwena, Lunda, SW-Bantu); Botatwe; Mashariki (Kask: Lakes [Rundi], Rufiji-Ruvuma; Kusi: Nyasa, SE-Bantu	Morphological innovation: < Nzadi-Kwa *-túnd- 'to swell.'

*-tùndù 'tribe'	WSav (Pende); Luban; Sabi; Mashariki (Kask: Takama; Kusi: Nyanja)	Displaced PB *-lùngù, found in AB zones and relict SavB (Luban: Songye; Mashariki: Sotho).
*-yàbuk- 'to cross river' AND *-jàbuk- 'to cross river'	WSav (SW-Bantu); Luban; Sabi; also in in Kongo; AND WSav (Ovimbundu, Pende, Lwena), Botatwe, and relict Mashariki (Kask: Lakes); also in Holoholo	Displaced Nzadi-Kwa *-sabuk-, found in BC (*-sapuk-) zones and relict SavB (Luba). Morphological innovation: < Kongo, SavB*-yàbú 'crossing place' plus *-Vk- extension.
*-ku-élì̧ 'moon'	WSav (Lwena, Lunda, Luyana-SW-Bantu); Luban (Luba-Sh); relict Mashariki (Lakes; SE-Bantu)	Morphological innovation: < PB *mu-élì̧ 'moonlight' (found in ACD zones, Kongo, and relict SavB [WSav: Ovimbundu, Lwena; Luban: Luba-Sh; Kask: Yao (Nyasa loan?); Kusi: Nyasa, Nguni]), by substitution of *ku- 'place of' ('moon' as 'moonlight-place') prefix for original *mu-/*mi- class markers. Displaced PB *-gòndè, found in ABC zones, Kongo, and relict SavB (Lunda; W.Luba). Also displaced Sangha-Kwa *-súngí or *-súngé, found in BCD zones, Kongo, and relict SavB (W.Luba).
*-yèp- 'to avoid, get out of way'	WSav (Ovimbundu; Lwena, Lunda: *-yèpuk-); Luban; Mashariki (Kask: Upland, NE-Coastal, Mwika-Rungwe; Kusi: SE-Bantu); also in Kongo (in WSav shape); also in Kuba (in W.Luba shape)	Partially displaced PB *-dég-, found in AC zones and relict SavB (WSav: Ovimbundu; Luban: Hemba; areal Mid-Zamb: Sabi, Botatwe, Nyanja, Shona)
*-ígà 'thorn'	WSav (Kimbundu, Pende, Lunda, SW-Bantu, Yeyi, Subiya; relict Mashariki (as *-íngà, with progressive nasal assimilation: see Table 4, Section B)	Displaced PB *-téndé ~ *-séndé, found in ABC zones and Kongo.

*-ìná 'pit'	WSav (Lwena, SW-Bantu); Luban; Sabi; Botatwe; relict Mashariki (Kask: Lakes, Upland, Takama]; also in Holoholo	Displaced PB *-bílá, found outside Narrow Bantu (e.g., Nkim 'grave'), and in ABC zone, Kongo, and relict WSav (Lunda). Tone *and* vowel differences suggest SavB *-bí́ílà 'grave,' of WSav (Kimbundu, Ovimbundu, SW-Bantu) and relict Mashariki (Upland, NE- Coastal), to be a chance resemblance. Use of *-bílá for 'grave' in Kongo and some B zone languages thus may reflect WSav semantic influence from *-bí́ílà.
*-į́lìmà 'darkness'	WSav (Ovimbundu, Lunda, Lwena, Luyana); Luban; relict Mashariki (Kask: Lakes, Upland; Kusi: SE-Bantu)	Morphological innovation: < PB *-į́l- 'to get dark,' found outside Narrow Bantu and in BC zones, WSav (Lwena), Luban, Lega, and relict Mashariki (Kask: Lakes; Kusi: Nyasa). Partially displaced Sangha-Kwa *-pį̀pį́ 'darkness,' found in BC zones and relict SavB (WSav: Lwena; Sabi; Kask: Lakes [Bembe: areal spread < C zone?]; Kusi: Makua, Venda).
*-į́gų- 'to hear'	WSav (Pende, Hungu, Lwena); Mashariki (Kask: Upland, Takama, NE-Coastal, Rufiji-Ruvuma; Kusi, Makua, SE Bantu	Phonological innovation: reduction of *#-yu to *#-į in SavB *-yúgų- (which see just below).
*-į́kut- 'to become satiated'	WSav (Pende, Lwena, SW-Bantu); Luban; Sabi; Botatwe; Mashariki (Kask: Lakes, Upland, Takama, NE-Coastal, Rufiji-Ruvuma, Mwika-Rungwe; Kusi: Nyasa, SE-Bantu)	Displaced PB *-kų́t-, found in ABC zones

*ma-į́má 'water'	Mbala; WSav (Lwena, Lunda); Luban; Lega, itself derived by reanalyzing PB *ma-lį́bá 'water' (found outside Narrow Bantu and in ABC zones and isolated Mashariki occurrence [Konjo only] as the plural of a regular singular *l-į́bá (*lį-/*malį- paired sing./pl. 5/6 class prefixes of vowel-initial stems plus this stem reanalyzed as underlying *-į́ba).	Phonological innovation: progressive nasal assimilation of early Bantu *ma-į́bá, found in AB zones and WSav (Kimbundu, Ovimbundu, Lwena, SW-Bantu)
*-áį́nk- 'to give'	WSav: Ovimbundu, Lunda; relict Mashariki: Sn Kask areal (Takama, NE-Coastal, Rufiji-Ruvuma); also in Kuba (C zone).	Competed with PB *-pé- 'to give,' found in ABC zones, WSav, Luban, Sabi, Botatwe, and widely in Mashariki
*-į̀pik- 'to cook'	WSav (Lwena; Ovimbundu); Luban; Sabi; Botatwe; Mashariki (relict Kask: NE-Coastal, Upland; Kusi: Nyasa, Shona, SE-Bantu)	Displaced PB *-lámb-, found outside Narrow Bantu and in ABC zones, Kongo, and relict SavB (Mbala; Luban: W.Luba).
*-į̀pag- 'to kill'	WSav (see Table 2); Luban; Lega; Sabi; Botatwe; isolated Kaskazi occurrence: in western fringe languages (Bembe of Forest subgroup of Lakes; Tongwe: both possible overlap from Lega); Lower Zamb. areal spread: Nyasa (irreg. *g > Ø), Makua (irreg. *g > Ø), Shona, Tonga (of Rufiji-Ruvuma); also in Enya (D10)	Displaced Sangha-Kwa *-į́t-, found in C zone (Soko group) and relict Mashariki (Kask: Lakes)

*óbé 'you (sing., pron.)'	WSav (Lwena, SW-Bantu); relict ESav: Luban (Luba-Sh); Sabi (in poss. formation); relict Mashariki (Kask: Njombe)	Morphological innovation: < PB *-bé 'you (sing., bound).' Other separate derivations of independent pronouns from this bound root appear in Kaskazi (e.g., *bébé: Swahili, Takama, etc.; *ɪ̨́bé: Luyia; etc.).
*-yúgʊ̨- 'to hear'	WSav (Luyana-SW-Bantu, Nkoya); relict Mashariki (Kask: Rufiji-Ruvuma)	Morphological innovation: PB *-yúg- (found outside Narrow Bantu and in ABC zones and Kongo) plus *-ʊ̨- extension (proposed old venitive see *-niʊ̨́- 'to drink' under *-nì- 'to rain' in Table 4).

Table 2: Stem morpheme innovations defining the Western-Savanna branch of Savanna-Bantu

Root <u>*innovation*</u>	<u>*Distribution*</u>	*Root wholly or partially displaced by innovated root;* <u>*additional explanations and commentary*</u>
*-bàgàlà 'male, man'	Kimbundu, Pende, Lwena; also in loanword shape in Kongo and adjoining B zone languages	Displaced PB *-lúmè, found outside Narrow Bantu and in ABC zones, Kongo, relict WSav (Ovimbundu, SW-Bantu), Luban, Sabi, Botatwe, and Mashariki (Kask: general; Kusi: Shona).
*-bìnd- 'to plait'	Ovimbundu, Lwena, Lunda; also apparent overlap northward into Kongo, Nzebi (far southern B zone)	Displaced Sangha-Kwa *-lùk-, found in BC zones, Luban, Holoholo, Sabi, Botatwe, and Mashariki (Kask: Lakes, Takama, NE-Coastal, Rufiji-Ruvuma; Kusi: Nyasa, Shona, SE-Bantu).
*-bìngà 'horn'	Kimbundu, Ovimbundu, Pende, Lwena, SW-Bantu	Displaced SavB *-séngò, for which see Table 1 above (relict area occurrence in Ndembu and Luvale of WSav, and Nkoya of Luban).
*-bį́lò 'dirt'	Lwena, Lunda, SW-Bantu; also, probably by separate parallel meaning extension, in Kele (C.55) and in Rundi, GiTonga, and Makua (Mashariki)	Semantic innovation: < Nzadi-Kwa *-bį́lò 'soot' (see *-kį́lį̀ 'soot,' Table 4, Section A for distribution). Displaced PB *-bį́ndo 'dirt', found in ABC zones, Kongo, and isolated SavB (W. Luba).

*-séké 'sand'	Ovimbundu, Lwena, Luyana-SW-Bantu, Lunda ('sandy soil'); also isolated cases of root as 'sand' in several scattered regions (some A zone languages; Holoholo, Lega; Chopi [of Kusi]; isolated occurrence suggests them to be separate semantic innovations	Semantic innovation: < PB *-séké, *-ségé 'grains, particles, dregs,' found in ABC zones, Kongo, and relict SavB (Lega). Displaced Sangha-Kwa *-sèngà, found in A zone (as 'gravel,' 'pebble'), BC zones, Vili, Luban, Sabi, Botatwe, and relict Kask (Rundi), and in loanword shape in Nyanja (Kusi: loan < Sabi?).
*-sí 'fish'	Ovimbundu, Lunda, Lwena, Luyana-SW-Bantu, Nkoya; also apparent isolated parallel assimilation shift in Tetela group and in Bolia (C.30 group)	Phonological innovation: diphthong simplification of PB *-sų̀í, found outside Narrow Bantu and in ABC zones, relic WSav (Pende; Yeyi), Luban, Botatwe, and Mashariki (Kask: Lakes [Nata, Ha], NE-Coastal, Rungwe, also loanword shape in Takama).
*-lànd- 'to buy'	Ovimbundu, Pende (in n. for 'trade'), Lwena, SW-Bantu; presumed separate innovation of this meaning in two contiguous A zone subgroups	Displaced PB *-súmb- 'to buy' (see *-gùl- 'to buy' in Table 3 for distribution)
*-làpò 'paddle'	Ovimbundu; Luyana; loanword shapes in Lwena, Lunda; also in Subiya; also in Kaonde	Displaced PB *-kápɪ̨́ 'paddle,' found in ABCD zones, Kongo, Luban, Holoholo, Sabi, Botatwe, and relict Mashariki (Kask: Lakes, NE-Coastal; Kusi: Nyasa)
*-lùndik- 'to add to'	Ovimbundu, Lunda, Lwena; also in Sabi (Nsenga only?)	Morphological innovation: addition of *-k- ext. to SavB *-lùnd- 'to add to' (see Table 1); Nsenga is probable independent innovation.
*-lų̀mbò 'lip'	Kimbundu, Lwena; also in Subiya subgroup	Phonological or morphological innovation: < PB *-lų̀mbų̀ 'mouth,' seen in AB zones.

*-gɪ̨́là 'bird'	Kimbundu, Ovimbundu, Pende, Lunda, Lwena, SW-Bantu	Displaced PB *-ònɪ̨̀, *-ùnɪ̨̀ found outside Narrow Bantu and in ABD zones, Luban, Lega, Sabi, Botatwe, and Mashariki (Kask: Lakes, Upland, Takama, Rufiji-Ruvuma; Kusi: Nyasa [Tumbuka], SE-Bantu).
*-jàmbá 'elephant'	Kimbundu, Ovimbundu, Pende, Lwena, SW-Bantu; also as alternate term in Kongo	Displaced PB *-jògʊ̨̀ (isolated occurrences in Luyana and one SW-Bantu case: probable examples of north Kalahari areal spreads from Mashariki as for stems in Table 11)
*-jɪ̨̀pag- 'to kill'	Kimbundu, Ovimbundu, SW-Bantu, Lwena; Lunda (in skewed shape); also in Nkoya, borrowed shape in Tetela group?	Phonological innovation: < SavB *-ɪ̨̀pag- (see Table 1) by *-(y)ɪ̨̀- > *-jɪ̨̀- (Guthrie reconstructs *g instead).
*-jòlil- 'to be pleased'	Ovimbundu, Lwena	Morphological innovation: < PB *-jòl- 'to laugh,' found outside Narrow Bantu and in ABCD zones and WSav. Displaced Sangha-Kwa *-sèpil-, found in C zone and Luban (Luba-Sh).
*-kómbò 'goat'	Kimbundu, Ovimbundu, Pende, SW-Bantu; also in Mbala; also in Yaka; also in Kongo group	Displaced PB *-búlɪ̨̀ (see *-pènɛ́ 'goat,' Table 5, Section A). Separate root *-pèmbè 'goat' appears in Lwena and Lunda of WSav.
*-mónò 'castor-bean'	Kimbundu, Ovimbundu, SW-Bantu, Lwena; overlap into mid-Zamb. areal (Shona, Sabi)	Phonological innovation: regressive nasal nasal assimilation of PB *-bónò (*b > m /_VnV).

*-tı̨́ı̨́tú 'meat'	Kimbundu, Ovimbundu, Lwena; also in Poto (C zone: probable separate parallel shift)	Semantic innovation: < PB *-tı̨́ı̨́tú 'animal,' found in AB zones, WSav (Pende, Lwena), and Luban (Songye group). Displaced PB *ny-àmà, found in ABC zones, Kongo, and relict WSav (Lwena: Luvale; SW-Bantu: Herero), Luban, Holoholo, and Mashariki (general).
*-tuba 'testicle'	Kimbundu, Luyana	Displaced Sangha-Kwa Bantu *-kàtà (see *-kèndè in Table 4, Section B).
*-àníá 'day(light)'	Kimbundu, Pende group; also Nkoya (*-àná, with *ni > ny > n /a_a)	Phonological innovation: irregular vowel shift in PB *-ı̨̀níá, found in A zone and ESavB (Luban).

Table 3: Stem morpheme innovations defining the Eastern-Savanna branch of Savanna-Bantu

Section A

Root innovation	*Distribution*	*Root wholly or partially displaced by innovated root; additional explanations and commentary*
*-bég- 'to cut hair'	Luban (W.Luba); Lega; Sabi; relict Mashariki (Lakes; SE-Bantu)	Semantic innovation: added meaning for PB *-bég- 'to break, snap (off)' (see *-bégú 'seed,' Table 4, Section A).
*-béng- 'to dislike'	Luban (W.Luba); Mashariki (relict Kask: Lakes ['avoid out of aversion to'], Rufiji-Ruvuma; Kusi: Nyasa, Shona, SE-Bantu)	Displaced PB *-bèl-, found in ABC zones, Kongo, and relict Mashariki (Kask: loanword shape in NE-Coastal [Seuta])
*-bìlì 'body'	Luban; Sabi; Botatwe; Mashariki (Kask: Lakes, Upland, Takama, NE-Coastal, Njombe; Kusi: Makua, Shona, SE-Bantu; also spread to Yeyi (WSav)	Displaced SavB *-lį́mbà (see Table 1).
*-bìlí 'two'	Luban; Lega; Sabi; Botatwe; Mashariki (general); also in Luyana, Nkoya; also in loanword shape in Yeyi of WSav; isolated in a few C zone languages: presumed independent assimilation shift?	Phonological innovation: regressive vowel assimilation < PB *-bàlí found outside Narrow Bantu and in ABC zones, Kongo, and WSav; also preserved as alternate shape, coexisting with reflex of *-bìlí, in Luba-Sh.
*-bólò 'penis'	Luban; Kask: Lakes, Takama, NE-Coastal, Rufiji-Ruvuma; Kusi: Makua, Nyasa, Shona, SE-Bantu	Semantic innovation: < earlier different, possibly more general application to genitals: e.g., Botatwe 'testicles'; Lingala (C zone) 'vagina.' Displaced PB *-suka, found outside Narrow Bantu and in ACD zones and SW Lega

*-bùè 'stone'	Luban; Sabi; Botatwe; Mashariki: Kask: Takama, NE-Coastal, Rufiji-Ruvuma, Mwika-Rungwe; Kusi: Nyasa (Tumbuka), Shona, SE-Bantu	Phonological innovation: < SavB *-gùè (see Table 1) by *g > *b /-[wV] (irregular shift?).
*-búlù 'monitor lizard'	Luban; Sabi; Botatwe (loanword shape?); Mashariki (Kask: Lakes, Takama, NE-Coastal, Rufiji-Ruvuma; Kusi: SE-Bantu; also in Lunda (areal overlap from Luba)	Displaced Sangha-Kwa *-bámbè, found in BC zones, Kongo, and relict Luban (retained with meaning shift in Luba-Shaba to 'crocodile')
*-búng- 'to gather up'	Luban; Botatwe; Holoholo; Mashariki (Kask: Lakes, NE-Coastal; Kusi: Nyasa, SE-Bantu)	Displaced Nzadi-Kwa *-kúng-, found in B zone, Kongo, WSav (Lunda, Lwena); retained in ESav with meaning shift to intr. 'assemble' (Luban: Luba-Sh; Kask: NE-Coastal).
*-ìlò 'fire'	Luban; Sabi; Botatwe; relict Mashariki: Kask (Lakes); Kusi (peripheral Shona, SE-Bantu); also in Luyana-SW of WSav (Yeyi, Luyana, SW-Bantu: probable case of north Kalahari area spread, as for stems in Table 11)	Displaced PB *-pí à, found in ACD zones, Kongo, SavB (WSav: Kimbundu, Pende, Lwena, some SW-Bantu), Luban (W.Luba), and relict Mashariki (Kask [Luyia]; Kusi [Chopi]).
*-làndá 'poor person; poverty'	Luban; Sabi; Mashariki (Kask: Yao; Kusi: Shona ('slave'), SE-Bantu (Venda 'poverty,' Sotho 'foreigner')	Morphological innovation: < PB *-lànd- 'to pay (something owed)' (see Table 5, Section D, *-làndú 'debt' for this reconstruction). This root and *-làndú 'debt' both imply semantic shift as well at ESav stage to meaning 'to owe (and not yet have paid) for.'

*-lél- 'to glide, float'	Luban; Sabi; Mashariki (Kask: Upland, Takama; Kusi: SE-Bantu)	Semantic innovation: < PB *-lél- 'to swing (suspended),' found in BC zones, Kongo, and relict SavB (Botatwe).
*-lúái̧lé 'illness'	Luban; Sabi; Mashariki: Kask (Lakes, Takama, NE-Coastal [Comoro], Rufiji-Ruvuma; Kusi: SE-Bantu [Venda] Shona, SE-Bantu).	Morphological innovation: irregular formation from Nzadi-Kwa *-lúál- 'to become ill,' found in B zone, Kongo, Sabi, and Mashariki (Kask: Lakes, Upland, Takama, NE-Coastal, Rufiji-Ruvuma; Kusi: Nyasa, Shona, SE-Bantu).
*-gàbò 'shield'	Luban; Sabi; Mashariki (Kask: Lakes, Upland, NE-Coastal; Kusi: SE-Bantu [Tsonga]); also in Tetela (Luban loan?)	Displaced PB *-gʋ̀bà, found in ABC zones, WSav (in shape *-gʋ̀bò with progressive vowel assimilation), and relict Mashariki (Gusii, Kuria); also WSav loanword shape in Kongo
*-gúé 'you (sing., indep. pron.)'	Luban (W.Luba); Botatwe; Sabi; Mashariki: Kask (Lakes, NE-Coastal [Ruvu], Rungwe, Rufiji-Ruvuma; Kusi: SE-Bantu [Chopi])	Displaced SavB *óbé (Table 1 above).
*-gùl- 'to buy'	Luban (W.Luba); Botatwe; Mashariki: Kask (Lakes, Takama, Upland, NE-Coastal, Mwika-Rungwe); Kusi (Nyasa); also loanword shape in Holoholo; also in Luyana	Semantic innovation: < PB *-gùl- proposed here to have originally meant 'to sell,' found outside Narrow Bantu and in ABC zones (three isolated occurrences in meaning 'to buy' are cited by Guthrie). Displaced PB *-súmb- 'to buy,' found in ABC zones, Kongo, and isolated SavB (Luban: W.Luba).

*-kálì̧ 'woman'	Luban; Botatwe; Mashariki (relict Kask: Lakes; Kusi: Nyasa, Shona, SE-Bantu; also in Holoholo; also in isolated BC zone instances and isolated in Kimbundu	Semantic innovation: < PB *-kálì̧ 'wife' (see Table 5, Section F, *-káyɪ̧ 'wife' for distribution of this root). Displaced PB *-káyɪ̧́-ntù 'woman,' found in ABC zones, Kongo, WSav (Kimbundu, Pende, SW-Bantu, Lwena), and isolated ESav case (Botatwe: loan < WSav?) (but there as separate meaning exension, as shown by common co-occurrence as synonym for *-káyɪ̧́-ntù: e.g., in Kimbundu and Tsogo citations in Guthrie)
*-kólù̧ 'scar'	Luban; Sabi; Mashariki: Kask: Lakes, NE-Coastal; Kusi: Shona; also as Sabi loanword in Botatwe	Partially displaced SavB *-bálì̧ 'scar' (found in WSav [SW-Bantu] and relict Mashariki [Lakes: Luyia; Rufiji-Ruvuma; Kusi: SE-Bantu), earlier sense 'spot, bare place,' seen in BC zones, Kongo, and SavB reflexes (Guthrie CS #26-28).
*-kó 'dirt'	Luban; Sabi; relict Mashariki (Kask: Lakes, Takama, Upland)	Semantic innovation: < Sangha-Kwa *-kó 'blemish, dirty spot,' found in C zone and WSav (Herero 'body spots caused by fire'). Displaced PB *-bì̧ndò 'dirt,' found in ABC zones, Kongo, and relict SavB (W. Luba].
*-kùàlɪ́ 'partridge'	Luban; relict Kask: Lakes; Kusi: Nyasa, SE-Bantu; loanword shape in Makua	Displaced PB *-gùàlɪ́, found in ABC zones, Kongo, and WSav (Lwena, Lunda, SW-Bantu). Phonological innovation: irregular devoicing of PB root.
*-mì̧n- 'to blow nose'; *-mì̧na 'snot'	relict Mashariki (Kusi: Nyasa, Shona; SE-Bantu; AND Luban; Sabi; Botatwe; relict Mashariki (Kusi: Nyasa, SE-Bantu)	Displaced PB *-pémb-, found in ABC zones, Kongo, WSav (Ovimbundu, Lwena, Luyana), and Luban; also in loanword shapes with MidZamb. areal occurrence (Botatwe, Shona, Venda).

*-nìànt- 'to tread'	Luban; Lega; relict Mashariki (Kusi: SE-Bantu *-nìàntil-)	Phonological innovation: < PB *-nìat- (found in ABC zones, Kongo [in derived form *-nyatakan-* 'be trampled'], Holoholo, and isolated Mashariki occurence [Kask: Lakes: Bembe: loan < C zone language?]), by progressive nasal assimilation. Also displaced PB *-lìat-, found in ABC zones, Kongo, WSav (Lwena, SW-Bantu), Luban, and Botatwe.
*ki-ntù 'thing'	Luban; Sabi; Botatwe; Mashariki (general, except Mwika-Rungwe)	Semantic cum morphological innovation: < PB *mu-ntù 'person' by prefix substitution. Displaced PB *-ʊ́mà, found outside Narrow Bantu and in ABC zones, Kongo, WSav (general), and relict ESav (Luban: W. Luba; Mashariki: Kask: Mwika-Rungwe).
*-pàkà 'boundary'	Luban; Sabi; Kask: Upland, NE-Coastal Mwika-Rungwe; also in loanword shape in Tetela (loan < Luban?); also loanword in Lunda (< Luba)	Displaced PB *-lìlà, found in ABC zones, WSav (Ovimbundu), and isolated Mashariki occurrence (Lakes: Forest subgroup, as probable loan spread from C group languages).
*-pènɪ̧ 'lightning'	Luban; Kask: Lakes, Upland, NE-Coastal; Kusi: Shona	Morphological innovation: < PB *-pèn- 'to flash,' found in Luba-Sh and Sabi and in extended shapes *-pènɪ̧- (WSav: Pende, Lwena, Luyana; Luban; Mashariki: Kask [Upland], Kusi [Shona]) and *-pèlɪ̧m-, with nasal dissimilation (A zone, Kongo, and relict ESav [Sabi; also Nyasa *-pènɪ̧m-). Displaced Sangha-Kwa *-jàlɪ̧́ 'lightning,' found in BC zones, Kongo, WSav (Lwena, SW-Bantu), and relict ESav (Luba; Kusi: SE-Bantu; also loanword shape in Yao [Kask]).

*-pònd- 'to pound'	Luban; Sabi; Mashariki: Kask (Lakes, NE-Coastal, Rufiji-Ruvuma, Corridor areal 'to forge'; relict Kusi: Shona)	Displaced PB *-tú-, found in ABCD zones, Kongo, WSav (Ovimbundu, Lwena), Luban, Holoholo, and relict Mashariki (Kask: NE-Coastal; Kusi: Shona, Venda ['hit']).
*-tų́mò 'spear'	Luban; Lega; Kask: Lakes, Upland, NE-Coastal, Mwika-Rungwe; Kusi: Shona, SE-Bantu; also in Sabi; also in Botatwe (in Mwika-Rungwe loanword shape); also in D zone (Enya: probably reflects westward spread of iron spears)	Morphological innovation: < PB *-tų́m- 'to stab' (also 'to sew'), found in ABC zones, Luban, Lega, and Mashariki (Kask: Lakes, NE- Coastal). Displaced PB *-gòngá, found outside Narrow Bantu and in ABC zones and WSav (Kimbundu, Lunda, Lwena, SW-Bantu), and in specialized meaning in Botatwe
*-tų́ng- 'to tie up'	Luban; Sabi; Botatwe; Kask: Upland, NE-Coastal, Takama, Rufiji-Ruvuma; Kusi: Nyasa only	Probable semantic innovation: < Sangha-Kwa *-tų́ng- 'to tighten,' found in C zone and SavB (WSav: Luyana; Luban; Sabi; Botatwe; and Mashariki: Kask (Upland, Takama, NE-Coastal, Njombe, Rufiji-Ruvuma); areal north fringe Kusi: Nyanja, Makua; also loanword, probably < Nyanja, in Shona). Displaced PB *-gàng-, found in ABC zones, Kongo, and relict SavB (Botatwe; Sabi: Nsenga; relict Mashariki Kask: Lakes: Bembe; NE-Coastal; Kusi: SE-Bantu: Ronga]).
*-ánį̀ 'leaf'	Luban; Mashariki (Kask: Lakes, Upland, NE-Coastal; Kusi: Nyasa; also in Subiya also in Holoholo; also isolated parallel derivations in A zone	Semantic innovation: < PB *-ánį̀ 'grass' (see Table 4, Section A, *-súa 'grass,' for distribution). Displaced PB *-káyá 'leaf,' found in ABC zones and Kongo and in skewed shape *-kányá in WSav (Lwena) and Luban (W.Luba).

*ku-ápà 'armpit'	Luban (*lį- pref. for *ku- in W.Luba); Lega group (*bu- pref. for *ku- in some languages of group); Sabi; relict Mashariki (Lakes: Rundi: areal spread < Lega?)	Displaced PB *-kápì̧, found in A zone and relict SavB (Kusi: SE-Bantu).
*-àyò 'sole (of foot)'	Luban; Sabi (Nsenga); Kask (NE-Coastal, Mwika-Rungwe; Kusi: Makua, Shona, SE-Bantu); also loanword in Holoholo	Eastern Sahelian loanword (Ehret 1998). Displaced PB *-támbí, found in ABC zones (A: 'shoe'), Kongo; retained in Mashariki with meaning shift (Kask: Upland 'thigh').
*mu-èndá 'nine'	Sabi (Bisa); relict Mashariki (Lakes only)	Displaced PB *-bų̀á, found in ABCD zones, Mbala, and WSav (Pende, Kimbundu, Lunda [*-bų̀], Lwena, SW-Bantu [Nkumbi]).
*-ɨ̀k- 'to descend'	Luban; Sabi; Mashariki: Kask (Lakes, Takama, Njombe); Kusi (SE-Bantu [Nguni])	Semantic innovation: < PB *-ì̧k- 'to sit (?),' seen in A.10 group ('to live, be') and in derived Nzadi-Kwa root *-ì̧kal- 'to sit; dwell,' found in Kongo, WSav (Ovimbundu, SW-Bantu), Luban, and Mashariki (general); also in Tetela (Luban loan?).
*-ɨ̀mb- 'to dig'	Luban (W.Luba); Sabi; relict Mashariki: Kask (Rundi); Kusi: SE-Bantu	Displaced PB *-tį́m-, found in ABC zones, Kongo, Yaka, WSav (SW-Bantu), and relict Mashariki (Lakes; SE-Bantu: Nguni 'cultivated field'). Also displaced PB *-tį́mb-, found in A zone and relict Mashariki (Lakes, NE-Coastal [Ruvu]; SE-Bantu [Nguni in extended shape]).

*-ɪ́nik- 'to name'	Luban; Sabi; relict Mashariki (Kask: Takama)	Morphological innovation: < PB *-ɪ́nà 'name,' found in ABCD zones, WSav (SW-Bantu), Luban, Botatwe, and Mashariki (Kask: Lakes, Upland, Takama, NE-Coastal, Rufiji-Ruvuma; Kusi: Nyasa [loanword shape?], SE-Bantu [GiTonga]). Displaced Sangha-Kwa *-lùk-, found in BC zones, Kongo, WSav (Pende, Ovimbundu, Lwena, SW-Bantu), and relict ESav (Sabi: Nsenga; Kask: Lakes [Rutara]).
*-ɪ́pulɪ- 'to ask'	Luban; Sabi; Holoholo; isolated Mashariki occurrence (Lakes: Nkore with tone skewing)	Morphological innovation: < PB *-ɪ́pul- found in A zone (*-ɪ́pʊl-), WSav (Pende, Lunda, Lwena, Luyana group), and relict Mashariki (SE-Bantu: Chopi 'to talk').
*-úmà 'belongings'	Luban; Sabi; Botatwe; relict Mashariki: Kusi only: Nyasa, SE-Bantu (Chopi)	Semantic innovation: < PB *-úmà 'thing (in general),' found outside Narrow Bantu and in ABC zones, Kongo, and WSav (Lwena, Nkoya).

Section B — Innovation linking Western and Central Savanna against Mashariki

*-sùm- 'to bite'	WSav (Kimbundu, Lwena, SW-Bantu); Luban; Sabi; also in Holoholo; also loanword shape in Kuba	Displaced PB *-lùm- found outside Narrow Bantu and in ABC zones and Mashariki (general).

Section C — Innovations ambiguously linking some Western and Central Savanna

*-kúábó 'other'	WSav (Ovimbundu; Lwena; SW-Bantu); Luban	Coexisted with (or displaced) SavB *-ngɪ́ in two WSav subgroups (areal spread from Luban source).
*ámé, *ámɪ́ 'I'	WSav (Ovimbundu; Lwena; SW-Bantu); Luban (Luba-Sh)	Displaced PB *mé, *mɪ́ (see Table 4, Section C, *-ɪ́né).

Table 4: Stem morpheme innovations defining the Mashariki subbranch of Eastern-Savanna

Section A — Innovations restricted to Mashariki group

Root innovation	*Distribution*	*Root wholly or partially displaced by innovated root; additional explanations and commentary*
*-bèg- 'to set (out)'	Kask: Lakes: Ganda ('to serve food'); Kusi: SE-Bantu (Sotho 'to set')	Semantic innovation: < PB *-bèg- 'to bring' (see Table 1 for PB attestation of this root).
*-bégú 'seed, part of plant replanted for new crop'	Kusi: Nyasa, Shona, SE-Bantu; relict Kask: Lakes (Ha), Upland, Takama, some NE-Coastal; possible isolated occurrence in one B zone subgroup	Morphological innovation: < PB *-bég- 'to break, snap off,' i.e., snap off pieces of plant for planting new crop. Displaced PB *-bútò, found outside Narrow Bantu and in BC zones, WSav (general), Holoholo, Botatwe, Sabi, and isolated Mashariki occurrence (Lakes: Rundi).
*-búlag- 'to kill'	Kask: Upland, Takama, NE-Coastal (irregular Swahili reflex *-u-*, with unexpected *g loss), Langi (*contra* Guthrie, reflex is regular), Rufiji-Ruvuma; Kusi: Shona, SE-Bantu	Morphological innovation: < PB *-búl- 'to hit, smash, break,' found in ABC zones, Kongo, and SavB (Luban; Lega); sense 'to kill' was independently added to unextended root in several A zone languages. Displaced SavB *-ìpag- (see Table 1).
*-bùgà 'threshing floor'	Kask: Lakes, Takama, NE-Coastal (Ruvu: Gogo), Njombe, Rufiji-Ruvuma; Kusi: Shona, SE-Bantu (loanword in Nguni)	Semantic innovation: < PB *-bùgà 'open space,' found in AB zones, Kongo, WSav (SW-Bantu), and relict Mashariki (Kusi: Makua).

*-bų́nj- 'to break, snap'	Kask: Lakes, NE-Coastal, Mwika-Rungwe; Kusi: SE-Bantu	Displaced PB *-bų́n-, found outside Narrow Bantu and in ABC zones, Sabi, and relict Mashariki (Kask: Lakes, Takama, Upland; Kusi: Shona).
*-sàà̀gul- 'to choose'	Kask: NE-Coastal, Takama, Rufiji-Ruvuma; relict Kusi: SE-Bantu (Sotho, Tsonga). Displaced earlier SavB *-sàkul- (see Table 1). Note that SavB root is a chance resemblance to *-sàà̀gul-.	Semantic innovation: < pre-PM tangible sense 'to separate,' still preserved in Nyakyusa (Kask) reflex and second Sotho (Kusi) meaning.
*-sèkil- 'to be pleased'	Kask: NE-Coastal; Kusi: Nyasa; also in Sabi; also in Sanga (Luban)	Morphological innovation: < PB *-sèk- 'to laugh,' found outside Narrow Bantu and in BC zones, Luban, Sabi, Botatwe, and Mashariki (general). Displaced Sangha-Kwa *-sèpil- 'to be pleased,' found in C zone and SavB (Luban: Luba-Sh).
*-sínj- 'to butcher'	Kask: Upland, Sabaki, Takama; Kusi: SE-Bantu; also as loanword in Makua, presumably < early Rufiji-Ruvuma	Semantic innovation: < earlier Bantu with more general meaning 'to cut up' (e.g., ESav: Holoholo 'to fell tree'; also in Nyoro (Lakes of Mashariki as 'to cut horn of cow').
*-sòòs- 'to poke (and ram) in'	Kask: NW-Coastal; Kusi: SE-Bantu	Displaced PB *-sòk-, found in A zone, Kongo, WSav, Luban, and relict Mashariki (Kask: Lakes, Takama).

*-sòn- 'to sew'	Kask: Lakes, Takama, NE-Coastal, Njombe, Mwika-Rungwe, Rufiji-Ruvuma; Kusi: Nyasa, Shona; loanword in Bemba (Sabi); also in Kaonde (overlap < Sabi)	Partially displaced PB *-tų́m-, found in ABC zones, Kongo, Luban, Holoholo, and Mashariki (Kask: Upland, Takama, NE-Coastal, Mwika-Rungwe; Kusi: Shona).
*-súá 'grass'	Kask: Takama, Upland; Kusi: Shona, SE-Bantu	Semantic innovation: < Nzadi-Kwa *-súá 'low (under)growth' (Kongo 'grassy place'; WSav: Herero 'undergrowth,' Kwanyama 'shrub'; ESav: Lega 'garden'; relict Mashariki : Lakes (Luyia 'grassland'). Displaced PB *-ánį̀, found in ABC zones, Luban, Sabi, Botatwe, and relict Mashariki (Kask: Lakes [Bembe: spread from C zone language?], NE-Coastal; Kusi: SE-Bantu.
*-sùùj- 'to strain, filter'	Kask: Sabaki; Kusi: Nyasa; SE-Bantu	Displaced SavB or Nzadi-Kwa *-sùùs-, found in Kongo, WSav, Sabi, and relict Mashariki (Shona areal: Sena, Shona, Venda). Also displaced SavB *-kélik- (see Table 1).
*-súngù 'bitterness'	Relict Kask: NE-Coastal; relict Kusi: SE-Bantu	Displaced Sangha-Kwa *-lùlù, found in BC zones, Kongo, WSav, Luban, Sabi, and relict Mashariki (Kask: Upland, Takama).
*-làgul- 'to divine'	Kask: Lakes, Upland, Takama, NE-Coastal; Kusi: Nyasa, SE-Bantu (Sotho)	Displaced PB *-búk-, found outside Narrow Bantu and in WSav (Lwena, SW-Bantu), Luban, and relict Mashariki (Shona). Morphological innovation: < Sangha-Kwa *-làg- 'to show' found in BC zones, WSav, Holoholo, Sabi, and relict Mashariki (Kask: Lakes; Kusi: SE-Bantu).

*-lèmil- 'to become heavy'	Kask: Lakes, Yao; Kusi: Nyasa, SE-Bantu	Morphological innovation without semantic effect: Sangha-Kwa had simple *-lèm- 'to become heavy,' found in BC zones, Kongo, WSav, Luban, Sabi, Botatwe, and relict Mashariki (Kask: Rundi; Kusi: Shona).
*-lìbal- 'to forget'	Kask: NE-Coastal, Rufiji-Ruvuma; Kusi: Nyasa, Makua, SE-Bantu	Morphological innovation: addition of *-al- verb extension to Nzadi-Kwa *-lìb- 'to become unused,' found in B zone and relict Mashariki (Lakes: Ganda 'be obsolete'). Displaced Sangha-Kwa *-lį́mb- 'to forget,' found in ABC zones and SavB (Luban: W.Luba).
*-lìmìlà 'Pleiades'	Kask: Upland, Rufiji-Ruvuma, NE-Coastal; Kusi: SE-Bantu	Morphological innovation: < Sangha-Kwa *-lìm- 'to cultivate,' found in BC zones, Kongo, WSav, Luban, Sabi, Botatwe, and Mashariki.
*-lį́ų́ng- 'to wander'	Kask: Upland, NE-Coastal, Rufiji-Ruvuma; Kusi: Nyasa, SE-Bantu	Semantic innovation: < Sangha-Kwa *-lį́ų́ng- 'to turn round (intr.),' found in BC zones, Kongo, WSav (SW-Bantu), and relict Mashariki (Kask: Lakes).
*-lɔ́ɔ́tò 'dream'	Kask: Lakes, Upland, NE-Coastal; Kusi: Nyanja, Shona, SE-Bantu	Morphological innovation: < PB *-lɔ́ɔ́t- 'to dream' by addition of *-o deverbative suffix. Displaced PB *-lɔ́ɔ́tó and SavB *-lɔ́ɔ́tà (see Table 1).
*-lúmik- 'to bleed (cup)'	Kask: Lakes, NE-Coastal, Rufiji-Ruvuma; Kusi: Nyasa, Shona, SE-Bantu	Displaced earlier Bantu *-sų́mik-, found in Kongo, WSav, Luban, and Botatwe.

*-gàlį́ 'blood'	Kask: Takama, Mwika-Rungwe; Kusi: Nyasa, SE-Bantu	Together with *-lòpà, displaced SavB *-nyį́ngà (see in Table 1; see also *-lòpà in Section E below. Also see Kaskazi innovated shape *-àlį́ 'blood,' in Table 5 with common Kaskazi deletion of medial *g.
*(l)į-gànà 'hundred'	Kask: Lakes, Upland, Takama, NE-Coastal, Rufiji-Ruvuma; Kusi (see *(l)į-jànà, Table 6, Section A, below)	Displaced PB *-kámá, found in ABC zones, Kongo, Luban, and Holoholo.
*-kálįng- 'to fry, roast'	Kusi: Nyasa, Makua, SE-Bantu; relict Kask: NE-Coastal (Seuta), Mwika-Rungwe (Nyakyusa)	Displaced PB *-kàng-, found in ABC zones, Kongo, WSav (Ovimbundu, Lwena), Luban, Sabi, and isolated Mashariki occurrence (Shona; other examples in Guthrie are cases of *-kálang-, Table 5, Section F).
*-kį́lį̀ 'soot'	Kask: Upland, NE-Coastal; Kusi: Nyasa, SE-Bantu	Displaced PB *-bį́lò, found in BC zones, Kongo, WSav (SW-Bantu), and relict Mashariki (Kask: Upland, Lakes; Kusi: SE-Bantu).
*-kómbè 'ladle' (> 'spoon, cup')	Kask: Upland, NE-Coastal, Rufiji-Ruvuma; Kusi: Nyasa, Makua, Shona, SE-Bantu	Semantic cum morphological innovation: < PB *-kómb- 'to scrape (out),' found outside Narrow Bantu and in ABC zones, Kongo, and relict Mashariki (Kask: NE-Coastal).
*-kúél- 'to go up'	Kask: NE-Coastal, Rufiji-Ruvuma, Mwika-Rungwe; Kusi: Makua, Nyasa, SE-Bantu	Phonological innovation: vowel height dissimilation of SavB *-kúíl-, found in C zone and relict Mashariki (Kask: NE-Coastal [Seuta]; Kusi: Nyasa [Sena], Shona).

*-kùngú 'fog'	relict Kask: NE-Coastal; Kusi: Nyasa, SE-Bantu	Semantic innovation: < SavB *-kùngú 'dust' (via sense 'cloud of dust'), found in WSav (Lwena, Lunda), Lega, Sabi, and relict Mashariki (Lakes [Konjo], Upland).
*-kų́nd- 'to tie knot'	Kask: Upland; Kusi: Shona, SE-Bantu	Displaced PB *-lį́t-, found in AC zones, Kongo, WSav (Ovimbundu, SW-Bantu, Pende, Lwena), Luban, and relict Mashariki (Kask: Lakes [Rundi]).
*-mį̀l- 'to swallow'	Kask: Lakes, Takama, Njombe, Rufiji-Ruvuma; Kusi: SE-Bantu; also in loanword	Phonological innovation: nasal dissimilation of PB *-mį̀n- found in ABC zones, Kongo, WSav (Lwena, SW-Bantu), Luban, Holoholo, Sabi, and Botatwe; *n preserved in Mashariki only in old PB extended root shape *-mį̀nį- (Kusi: SE-Bantu).
*-mį̀l- 'to blow nose'; *-mį̀là 'snot'	Kask: Lakes, Upland, Takama, Rufiji-Ruvuma; Kusi: Shona, SE-Bantu	Phonological innovation: nasal dissimilation of SavB *-mį̀n- (in Table 1); same PM rule, *n > l / #-m[+high/+vocalic]_, as in *-mį́l- 'to swallow,' preceding, carried to completion in Kaskazi but yielding *n ~ *l alternance verb-stem-final in early Kusi (see soundshift rule #3 in text).
*-mù- 'to shave'	Kask: Lakes, Mwika-Rungwe; PM *-mùò 'razor' (see Section B; Guthrie has *-mò-)	Displaced PM *-bég- (see Section D below).
*-náį́nk- 'to give'	Kask: Lakes, Upland, NE-Coastal, Mwika-Rungwe; Kusi: Nyasa, SE-Bantu	Phonological innovation: nasal insertion in SavB *-áį́nk- (see Table 1).

*-ángú 'my'	Kask: NE-Coastal, Njombe, Rungwe; Kusi: Shona	Displaced PB *-ángáį́, found in AC zones, WSav (Lwena, SW-Bantu), and relict Mashariki (Kusi: SE-Bantu, Makua; Kask: Lakes). Displaced alternate possessive *-ámé/í, found ABC zones, Kongo, WSav (Lwena), Luban (Luba-Sh), and relict Mashariki (Kusi: SE-Bantu).
*-nì- 'to rain'	Kask: NE-Coastal (Swahili), Rufiji-Ruvuma; Kusi: Shona, SE-Bantu	Semantic innovation: < old NC root *-nì- 'to seep, flow, spill,' seen also in PB *-nį̀- 'to defecate' (< *-nì- + PB *-į-causative) and PB *-nių́- (*-nyų́-) 'to drink' (< *-nì- + *-ų-extension [probable old venitive: cf. *-yúgų- 'to hear' in Table 1. Displaced PB *-nók- ~ *-lǫ́k-, found outside Narrow Bantu as *-nók-) and in ABC zones, Kongo, WSav, Luban, Sabi, and isolated Mashariki occurrence (Lakes: Forest subgroup: probable loan spread from neighboring C group language).
*-nòòl- 'to sharpen'	Kask: Upland, Takama, NE-Coastal, Rufiji-Ruvuma; Kusi: SE-Bantu (Nguni *-lòòl-, with regressive liquid assimition of *-nòòl-); also in loanword shape in Bisa (Sabi)	Phonological innovation: progressive nasal dissimilation of ESav *-nòòn-, found in Luban, Sabi, and relict Mashariki (Kusi: Makua)
*-pànd- 'to plant'	Kask: Upland, NE-Coastal, Rufiji-Ruvuma; relict Kusi: implied in SE-Bantu (Sotho *-fatǫl-* 'to dig up,' stem + conversive ext.)	Semantic innovation: < SavB *-pànd- 'to split (tr.)'. (see Table 1). Displaced PB *-kún-, found in ABC zones, Kongo, WSav (Ovimbundu, SW-Bantu), and Sabi.

*-pémb- 'to light fire'	Kask: Lakes, NE-Coastal, Mwika-Rungwe; Kusi: Nyasa, SE-Bantu (Nguni)	Semantic innovation: transitive reapplication of Nzadi-Kwa *-pémb- 'to shine,' found in B zone, WSav, and relict Mashariki (Sotho), from still earlier pre-PB *-pémb- 'to be bright, alight, white' seen in the derived Nzadi-Kwa noun *-pémbà 'white clay' (found in B zone, Kongo, WSav, Luban, Botatwe, and relict Mashariki [Kusi: Shona, SE-Bantu]), and in PB noun *-pémbé 'white clay' (found outside Narrow Bantu and in ABC zones and Kongo group).
*-pémbè 'horn'	Kask Lakes, Takama, NE-Coastal, Rufiji-Ruvuma, Mwika-Rungwe; indirectly attested in Kusi reflexes of PM *-pémbè-lè 'rhinoceros' (Nyanja, Shona, SE-Bantu), literally 'having or characterized by a *-pémbè,' i.e., a horn	Displaced SavB *-séngò, for which see Table 1 above.
*-pókų 'eland'	Kask: Takama, NE-Coastal; Kusi: Nyasa (Nyanja), Shona, SE-Bantu Lunda)	Displaced SavB *-sèCų́ (C = *p, *t, or *k), found in WSav (Lwena, Luban, Sabi, Botatwe, and relict Mashariki (Kask: Rufiji-Ruvuma; also as loanword in Nyanja of Kusi).
*-tàkà 'soil'	Kask: Lakes, Rufiji-Ruvuma; Kusi: Nyasa, Makua, Shona	Semantic innovation: < Nzadi-Kwa 'wet ground,' seen in Kongo, WSav (Ovimbundu 'marsh'), and relict Mashariki as 'mud': Kask: Kamba; Kusi: Chopi 'potting clay'; also in loanwords for 'mud' in Venda, Sotho. Displaced SavB *-bų́ and PB *-lòbá 'soil' (Table 1)

*-támbò 'string (of snare trap)'	Kask: NE-Coastal (Sabaki); Kusi 'string', (for which see Table 6, Section C)	Semantic innovation: < PB *-támbò 'snare trap,' found in ABC zones, Kongo, and relict Mashariki (Kask: Sabaki of NE-Coastal, Rufiji-Ruvuma; Kusi: Nguni of SE-Bantu).
*-tándàtú 'six'	Kask: Upland, Takama, NE-Coastal; Kusi: SE-Bantu, peripheral Shona	Displaced Nzadi-Kwa *-sààmànò, *-sàmbànò, found in B zone, Kongo, WSav (Lwena, Pende, SW-Bantu), Luban (Songye), and also in Kuba (areal < Luban?) and Fang (areal < B zone languages?).
*-tétil- 'to cackle'	Kask; Kusi	Displaced Nzadi-Kwa *-kókul-, found in Kongo, WSav (SW-Bantu), Botatwe, and relict Mashariki (Kask: Lakes; Kusi: SE-Bantu).
*-tòpè 'mud'	Kask: NE-Coastal, Rufiji-Ruvuma; Kusi: Nyasa, Shona, SE-Bantu	Displaced earliest Mashariki *-tàkà 'mud' (which see under *-tàkà 'soil' above). Nilo-Saharan loanword (Ehret 1998).
*-tùmbò 'belly'	Kask [Sn Kask areal]: NE-Coastal, Rufiji-Ruvuma, Njombe; Kusi: Nyasa, SE-Bantu	Morphological innovation: < SavB *-tùmb- 'to swell.' Displaced PB *-bụmó, found in ABC zones, Kongo, WSav, Luban, Sabi, and Botatwe. PB *-làà, found outside Narrow Bantu and widely in Narrow Bantu, probably referred originally to the abdominal cavity or its organs though in a number of speech regions it applies to 'belly' today.

*-tų́ 'cloud'	relict occurrence: Kaskazi: Lakes, Upland; Kusi: SE-Bantu	Semantic innovation: < Nzadi-Kwa *-tų́ 'dust,' found in C zone (Tetela) and relict Mashariki (Kusi: Nyasa [Sena]). Displaced SavB *-lų̀ndè, found in WSav (Ovimbundu) and areal Mashariki occurrence (Sn Kask areal: Takama, NE-Coastal, Njombe, Rufiji-Ruvuma; Kusi: Makua only: presumed areal spread < Rufiji-Ruvuma).
*-ágí 'egg'	Kusi: Nyasa, Shona, SE-Bantu; > Kask *-áyí (see Table 5 below)	Phonological innovation: voicing of medial *k of Nzadi-Kwa *-ákí, found B zone, Kongo, and WSav (Kimbundu group, Lwena). Competed with PB *-gèyį (*-géyí, *-gį̀yé [metathesis: AC zones], *-gį̀yį́, *-gé, *-gí, etc.), found outside Narrow Bantu and in ABC zones, Kongo, WSav, Luban, Sabi, Botatwe, and relict Mashariki (Kask: Lakes, Takama, NE-Coastal; Kusi: N.Sotho).
*-àmbuk- 'to cross	Kask: Lakes; Mwika-Rungwe; Kusi: Mid-Zamb. areal (Nyasa, Shona, Venda)	Displaced Nzadi-Kwa *-yàbuk-, found in Kongo, WSav (Ovimbundu, SW-Bantu, Lwena), WSav (general), and relict Mashariki (Lakes, as *-jàbuk-) and also in Holoholo.
*ny-élèlį́ 'star'; AND *ny-ényèlį́ 'star' ($C_1VC_2VC_2$ > $C_1VC_1VC_2$)	relict Kask: Gogo; Kusi: Nyasa, SE-Bantu relict Kask: Lakes (E. Nyanza, Luyia), NE-Coastal (Sabaki); Kusi: Nyasa, Shona	Morphological innovation: < PB *-él- 'to shine, be bright, become white,' found in BC zones, WSav, Luban, Lega, and relict Mashariki (Lakes, Takama), seen also in PB *-élį̀ 'moonlight' (see Table 1). Displaced Nzadi-Kwa *-nyényè, found in relict occurrence in Kongo, Luban (Nkoya), and Mashariki (Ganda).

*-ı́t- 'to name'	Kask: Lakes (Rundi), Upland, Takama; Kusi: SE-Bantu	Semantic innovation: < Sangha-Kwa *-ı́t- 'to call,' found in C zone, Vili, Luban, Sabi, Botatwe, and Kask (Lakes, Upland, Takama, NE- Coastal, Mwika-Rungwe). Displaced ESav *-ı̧́nik- (see Table 3).
*-ı̧̀p- 'to clear away'	Kask: Lakes, Upland, Mwika-Rungwe; Kusi: SE-Bantu	Partially displaced SavB *-kókul- (see Table 2) and Nzadi-Kwa *-kúkul- found in Kongo, Sabi, Botatwe, and Mashariki (Kusi only: Nyasa, Shona, SE-Bantu).
*-òng(el)- 'to add (to)'	Kask: Lakes, Takama, Upland, NE-Coastal; Kusi: Nyasa, SE-Bantu	Semantic innovation: < PB *-òng- 'to gather up (tr.),' seen in A zone (Duala 'to heap up') and WSav (Kwanyama 'to gather'). Displaced SavB *-lùnd- (see Table 1).

<u>*Section B — Innovations found in Mashariki, Sabi, and Botatwe*</u>

Root <u>*innovation*</u>	<u>*Distribution*</u>	*Root wholly or partially displaced by innovated root;* <u>*additional explanations and commentary*</u>
*-bàìjò 'adze'	Kask: Lakes, NE-Coastal, Rufiji-Ruvuma; Kusi: Makua, Shona, SE-Bantu; also in Sabi; also in Botatwe; also in Luyana	Morphological innovation: < Nzadi-Kwa *-bàìj- 'to work wood.' Displaced PB *-bàgò 'adze' (see Ehret 1995/96 for reconstruction of this meaning; Guthrie gloss 'hoe'), found in AB zones (variously as 'hoe,' 'adze,' or 'ax'), C zone (as 'knife'), Kask (Luyia 'hoe(handle)', and Rufiji-Ruvuma (variously as 'ax' or sometimes 'adze').

*-bèlé 'grain (gen.), bulrush millet'	Kask: Lakes, Upland, Takama, NE-Coastal; Njombe; Kusi: Nyasa, SE-Bantu; also in Sabi; also in Botatwe; also in SW-Bantu; in loanword shape in Luba	Nilo-Saharan loanword in PM (see Ehret 1998).
*-buulį- 'to ask'	Kask: Lakes, Upland, Takama, NE-Coastal, Rufiji-Ruvuma, Kusi: SE-Bantu; also in Sabi; also in Botatwe; also in Lega	Displaced ESav *-į́pul- (see Table 2 for distribution).
*-sàmb- 'to wash'	Kask: Upland, Swahili ('wash after defecating'); Kusi: Nyasa, Shona, SE-Bantu; also in Sabi; also in Botatwe	Displaced PB *-sų̀k-, *-sùk-, found in ABC zones and relict Mashariki (Malawi areal [Yao, Nyasa]; also Bembe [Forest subgroup of Lakes: probable overlap from C zone); also preserved, but with specialized meanings, in Luban, Sabi, and some Mashariki (Kask: Upland; Kusi: Shona); also general meaning 'to wash' was recreated by addition of extensions to the root in various SavB languages. Semantic innovation: < earlier Bantu *-sàmb- with some such meaning as 'to immerse' or 'to be immersed,' as indicated in the derived SE-Bantu noun *-sàmbį̀ 'fish.'
*-lìp- 'to pay'	Kask: Lakes, Upland, Takama, NE-Coastal, Rufiji-Ruvuma; Kusi: Makua, Nyasa, Shona, SE-Bantu; also in Sabi; also in Botatwe; also in Kaonde; also in Lega	Displaced Sangha-Kwa *-pų́t-, found in BC zones, Kongo, WSav (SW-Bantu, Ovimbundu), Luban, and Sabi

*-kóndò 'war'	Kask: NE-Coastal, Rufiji-Ruvuma; Kusi: Makua, Nyasa, Shona; also in Sabi; also in Kaonde	Displaced PB *-tá, found outside Narrow Bantu and in ABCD zones, Kongo, WSav (Ovimbundu, Lwena, SW-Bantu), Luban, Sabi, and relict Mashariki (Kask: Upland, NE-Coastal, Takama; Kusi: SE-Bantu 'enemy').
*-kúnd- 'to copulate'	Kask: Lakes (Luyia); Kusi: SE-Bantu; also in Sabi (in specialized meaning); also in Botatwe	Semantic innovation: < Sangha-Kwa *-kúnd- 'to desire, want,' found in BC zones, Lega, Sabi, and relict Mashariki (Kask: Lakes, NE-Coastal). Displaced Sangha-Kwa *-tòmb-, found in C zone and relict ESav (Sabi; Kask: NE-Coastal, Rufiji-Ruvuma; elsewhere, ESav meaning shift to 'be receptive to copulation,' reflected in Luba-Sh (Luban) 'vulva,'. Sotho 'become in heat,' Nguni 'reach puberty').
*-pél- 'to be finished, come to an end'	Kask: Lakes, NE-Coastal; Kusi: Makua, Shona, SE-Bantu; also in Sabi; also in Botatwe (Ila); also in Kaonde (Luban)	Semantic innovation: < PB *-pél-, probably 'to be used up, no longer be present,' reflected in A zone (Bulu 'to dry up') and relict Lakes (Konjo 'to get lost') examples. Displaced PB *-súg-, found in AC zones and Kongo.
*-ákúé 'his, her'	Kask: Upland, Takama, NE-Coastal, Rufiji-Ruvuma; Kusi: Makua, SE-Bantu (Sotho); also in Sabi; also in Botatwe	Displaced PB *-ándé, *-ándí, found in BCD zones, Kongo, WSav (Lwena), and Luban; meaning shift to 'other' in Lakes, Takama of Kask. As alternant for PB *-áké, found in AC zones and retained in Lega and many Mashariki languages (Kask: Upland, NE-Coastal, Rungwe; Kusi: Nyasa, Shona, SE-Bantu [Nguni]).

*mu-élį̀ 'moon'	Kask: Lakes, Upland, Takama, NE-Coastal, Mwika-Rungwe, Rufiji-Ruvuma; Kusi: Makua, Nyasa, Shona, SE-Bantu; also in Sabi; also in Botatwe; also in Holoholo; also in SW-Bantu	Semantic innovation: < PB *mu-élį̀ 'moonlight.' Displaced SavB *-ku-élį̀ (see Table 1).

<u>*Section C — Innovations found in Mashariki and in Sabi*</u>

Root <u>*innovation*</u>	<u>*Distribution*</u>	*Root wholly or partially displaced by innovated root;* <u>*additional explanations and commentary*</u>
*-bèlek- 'to bear (child)'	Kask: NE-Coastal; Rufiji-Ruvuma; Kusi: Nyasa, Shona, SE-Bantu; also in Sabi; also in Luyana	Semantic innovation: < SavB *-bèlek- 'to carry (child) on back' (see Table 1). Competed with PB *-bí́ál-, found widely all through Bantu.
*-bí́ál- 'to plant'	Kask: Lakes, NE-Coastal, Njombe; Kusi: Nyasa, SE-Bantu; loanword shape in Shona; also in Sabi; also in Kaonde	Displaced PB *-kún- (see *-pànd- 'to plant' above in Section A).
*-bí́g- 'to fence'	Kask: Rufiji-Ruvuma; also derived NE-Coastal, Takama, Rufiji-Ruvuma noun *-bigo 'thorn-hedge'; Kusi: Nyasa, SE-Bantu; also spread to Lamba (Sabi)	Displaced Sangha-Kwa *-gùmb-, found in BC zones and WSav (Pende, Ovimbundu, SW-Bantu).

*-bóp- 'to bind'	Kask: Lakes, Upland, NE-Coastal; Kusi: SE-Bantu; also in Sabi	Displaced Nzadi-Kwa *-kút- 'to bind,' found in B zone, Kongo, WSav (Ovimbundu, SW-Bantu), Luban (as 'wrap up'), and relict Mashariki (Kask: Rufiji-Ruvuma; Kusi: Nyanja 'to wrap': Luban influence?).
*-sáánò 'five'	Kask: NE-Coastal, Langi, Njombe; relict Kusi: Ndau (Shona); also in Sabi	Morphological innovation: generalization of *Cį- prefixed allomorph of PB *-táánò, found outside Narrow Bantu and in ABC zones, Kongo, WSav, Luban, Lega, and relict Mashariki (Kask: Lakes, Upland).
*-sátù, *-sátò 'python'	Kask: Lakes (Rundi), Upland, NE-Coastal, Takama; Kusi: Nyasa, SE-Bantu; also in Sabi; also isolated in Ila of Botatwe	Displaced PB *-bòmà, found in ABC zones, Kongo, WSav (Lunda, Lwena, SW-Bantu), and Botatwe
*-súngù 'poison'	Kask: Lakes, Takama, NE-Coastal; Kusi: SE-Bantu; also in Sabi; also in Hemba (Luban); also in Lwena (loan diffusion?)	Semantic innovation: < PM *-súngù 'bitterness' (Table 4, Section A).
*-láá 'louse'	Kask: Lakes, Upland, Takama, NE-Coastal (Seuta), some Rufiji-Ruvuma; Kusi: Nyasa, Shona, SE-Bantu; also in Sabi	Displaced Nzadi-Kwa *-gina, found in B zone, WSav (Lwena, SW- Bantu), Botatwe, and relict Mashariki: Kask (Ruvu, Zigula; also Lakes [Ganda 'nit']).
*-lámb- 'to lick'	Kask: Lakes, Takama, Upland, NE-Coastal, Rufiji-Ruvuma; Kusi: SE-Bantu (Sotho); also in Sabi	Displaced Sangha-Kwa (?) *-léét-, found in BC zones.

*-(g)ų́ílí 'hair'	Kask: Lakes, NE-Coastal, N.Njombe; Corridor regional *-ų́ílí (Mwika-Rungwe, Takama, S. Njombe [Kinga]; northern regional *-jų́ílí (Lakes [Konjo], Upland, Langi, Seuta [Upland loanword]; Sabaki, Nyiha [Mwika-Rungwe] *-ų́élé: separate loans < languages in which PB *i > [e]; relict Kusi: SE-Bantu (Nguni *-nų́élé: loan < language with PB *i > [e]); also in Sabi; also in Holoholo (apparent Mwika-Rungwe loan; also in Lega (W.Lakes loanword shape); also in Luba-Sh, Hemba (loanword in shape seen in Nyiha)	Displaced PB *-sų̀kí, *-sùkí (2nd shape was created early in Bantu history < 1st shape by regressive vowel height assimilation), found in ABC zones, Kongo, WSav (SW-Bantu, Luyana, Nkoya), Luban, and Botatwe. Separate root *-sų̀í 'hair' postulated by Guthrie (CS 428) is not viable; all reflexes but one are referable to *-sų̀kí, *-sùkí root; the one exception (cited for E.41) is a reflex of a different root found in several northerly Kaskazi languages.
*-kų́bà 'chest'	Kask: Lakes, Takama, NE-Coastal, Rufiji-Ruvuma; Kusi: Nyasa, Shona, SE-Bantu; also in Sabi; also in Lega; also loanword shape in Subiya	Displaced PB *-túlò, found in ABC zones, Kongo, WSav (Ovimbundu, Pende, Lwena, SW-Bantu), and Luban (Songye); retained in some Mashariki, but with meaning shift to 'shoulder.'
*-kų́ndò 'knot'	Kask: Lakes, Upland, NE-Coastal, Rufiji-Ruvuma; Kusi: Nyasa, Shona, SE-Bantu; also in Sabi	Morphological innovation: < PM *-kų́nd- 'to tie knot' (see Section A above). Displaced Nzadi-Kwa *-lį́tà, found in zone, Kongo, WSav (SW-Bantu), and Luban (W. Luba).

*-pálá 'baldness'	Kask: Lakes, Upland, NE-Coastal, Rufiji-Rufiji-Ruvuma; Kusi: Nyasa, Shona; also in Sabi	Morphological innovation: < Sangha-Kwa *-pál- 'to scrape,' found in BC zones, Kongo, WSav (Luyana-SW, Lunda), Luban (E. Luba), Sabi, and Mashariki (Kask: Lakes, Upland, NE-Coastal, Rufiji-Ruvuma; Kusi: Nyasa, Shona, SE-Bantu); semantics: scrape off, i.e., leave bare, hence bare surface. Displaced SavB *-bálá (see Table 1, Section A); not 'osculant' pair with *-pálá because clear separate derivation for each.
*-pàndé 'piece'	Kask: Lakes, NE-Coastal; Kusi: Nyasa, Shona; also in Sabi	Morphological innovation: < SavB *-pànd- 'to split' (see Table 1).
*-pumi 'forehead'	Kask: Lakes; Kusi: Nyasa; also in Sabi	Displaced SavB *-pálà (see Table 1).
*-pų̀kò 'mole'	Kask: Lakers, Upland, NE-Coastal, Rufiji-Ruvuma; Kusi: Nyasa, SE-Bantu; also in Sabi; also as apparent loanword in Luba-Sh	Morphological innovation: < PB *-pų̀k- 'to dig up, fling up (earth),' found in AC zones (A in extended form *-pų̀kul-) and relict SavB (WSav: Lwena; Sabi; Kask: Rufiji-Ruvuma); see also *-pų̀kul- in Section E below.
*-téndé 'heel'	Kask: Mijikenda, Rufiji-Ruvuma; Kusi: Nyasa, Shona, SE-Bantu; also in Sabi	Semantic innovation: < SavB *-téndé 'foot' (see Table 1). Displaced PB *-tį́ndį́ 'heel,' found in ABC zones, Lega (as 'leg'), and Nkoya and Botatwe areal (as *-tį́ndí).

*-tị̀kɪ́ 'stump (of tree)'	Kask: Lakes, Takama, NE-Coastal, Rufiji-Ruvuma; Kusi: Shona; also in Sabi; also in Luba-Sh	Displaced Sangha-Kwa *-kɪ̀gɪ́, found in C zone (Soko), WSav (SW-Bantu), Luban (Songye), and Botatwe. Probable Eastern Sahelian loanword: < PESah *ṭīk' 'pole, log' (< earlier PNS *ṭīŋk').
*-tɪ̧́ngà '(tendon) bowstring'	relict Kask: NE-Coastal, Rufiji-Ruvuma; Kusi: Nyasa (Tete), SE-Bantu; also in Sabi	Semantic innovation: < PB *-tɪ̧́ngà 'vein, tendon,' found in A zone, WSav (Ovimbundu), and relict Mashariki (Kusi: Makua, Venda).
*-tùnd- 'to urinate'	Kask: Takama, Rufiji-Ruvuma; Kusi: Shona, SE-Bantu; also Sabi (Nsenga)	Displaced Nzadi-Kwa *-sʊ̧̀b-, found in B zone, Kongo, and Botatwe.
*-àlɪ̧m- 'to borrow'	Kask: NE-Coastal, Rufiji-Ruvuma; Kusi; SE-Bantu; also in Sabi; also in Luba-Sh	Displaced Sangha-Kwa *-sòmb-, found in BC zones, Kongo, and Luban (W.Luba).
*-àmb- 'to begin'	relict Kask: Upland; Kusi: Nyanja, Shona; also in Sabi	Semantic innovation: < Sangha-Kwa *-àmb-, exact meaning uncertain, but also present in Bobangi derived verb *-ambọl-* 'to begin.' Displaced PB *-táátik-, found in AC zones, Kongo, WSav (Lunda), Sabi.
*ɪ̧́né 'I (indep. pron.)'	Kask: Lakes, Takama, and Njombe (redup.); Kusi: Nyasa, SE-Bantu (Venda); also in Sabi (Tabwa redup.; Bemba); also in Lega	Displaced PB *mé ~ *mɪ́, found in ABC (AB *mé, C *emɪ́) zones, Kongo, Lega group, and relict Mashariki (Kask: NE-Coastal [Swahili *mimi, Mijikenda *imi, etc.]; Kusi *mɪ́: Makua, SE-Bantu [Tsonga]).
*-ɪ́ngà 'thorn'	Kask: Upland (Chaga), Mwika-Rungwe; Kusi: Nyasa, SE-Bantu (Xhosa); also in Sabi; also in Luyana	Phonological innovation: progressive nasal assim. of SavB *-ɪ́gà (*mu-ɪ́gà > *mu-ɪ́ngà), for which see Table 1.

Section D— Innovations found in Mashariki and Botatwe

Root innovation	*Distribution*	*Root wholly or partially displaced by innovated root; additional explanations and commentary*
*-bèlè 'front'	Kask: Lakes (Rundi), Upland, Sabaki: Kusi: SE-Bantu (Venda 'female genitals'); also in Botatwe; also as alternate shape in Holoholo	Phonological innovation: progressive vowel assimilation of SavB *-bèlì, found in WSav (as 'first-born'), Luban (Songye; Luba 'firstborn,' also 'front'), Holoholo, Sabi ('first-born'), and relict Mashariki : Kask (Lakes: Ganda; NE-Coastal: Ngazija); Kusi (Shona).
*-bɪ́lʉ- 'to be cooked'	Kask: NE-Coastal, Mwika-Rungwe; Kusi: SE-Bantu; also in Botatwe	Morphological innovation, < PB *-bɪ́l-, found in ABC zones, by addition of old *-ʉ- extension (as, for example, in 'to hear,' Table 1, Section A.2), probably a venitive.
*-bón- 'to see'	Kask: Lakes (Rundi), Upland, Takama, NE-Coastal, Njombe; Kusi: Nyasa, Shona, SE-Bantu; also in Botatwe; note also set of *-bón- with Ubangi confluence areal occurrence (BC zones)	Phonological innovation: regressive nasal dissimilation of Nzadi-Kwa *-món-, found in B zone, Kongo, WSav (Ovimbundu, SW-Bantu, Lwena), Luban, Sabi, and relict Mashariki (Lakes: in Luyia n. 'eyes').
*-búy- 'to return, come/go back'	Kask: NE-Coastal, Rufiji-Ruvuma; Kusi: SE-Bantu, Shona ('come'); loanword shape in Botatwe	Displaced PB *-bʉ́t-, found in ABC zones, Kongo, and WSav (Pende).
*-bùyú 'baobab'	Kask: Sabaki; Kusi: Shona areal (Shona, Tete, Venda); also in Botatwe	Semantic innovation: original Bantu application to different tree because word occurs in languages where baobab never was present (e.g., Kongo as 'mahogany').

*-sùlį̀ 'broth'	Kask: Takama, NE-Coastal, Rufiji-Ruvuma; Kusi: Nyasa, SE-Bantu; also in Botatwe	Phonological innovation: < SavB *-sòlį̀ by vowel raising (*o > *u /_Cį), found in WSav (Lwena, Lunda), Luban (W.Luba), and relict Mashariki (Kask: Upland, Takama, NE-Coastal).
*-súkù 'cupping horn'	Kask: NE-Coastal; Kusi: Nyasa, SE-Bantu; also in Botatwe	Displaced SavB *-sų́mò; *-súkù as 'hemp pipe' in Luba-Sh reflects distinct development from that seen in Kaskazi.
*-làlá 'Hyphaene palm'	Kask: NE-Coastal; Kusi: Makua, Nyasa, SE-Bantu; also in Botatwe (Ila)	Semantic innovation: earlier Bantu 'palm frond,' found in Kongo, Luban, Botatwe (Ila) and in relict Mashariki (Yao).
*-làndú 'debt'	Kask: Upland, Takama, NE-Coastal (Miji-Kenda), Mwika-Rungwe; Kusi: Makua, Shona, SE-Bantu; also in Botatwe	Morphological innovation: < PB *-lànd- 'to pay (something owed),' noted by Guthrie in A zone (in two contiguous subgroups in which it displaced PB *-súmb- for 'to buy') and WSav (separately shifted in meaning to 'to buy': see Table 2), and attested also in ESav *-làndá 'poor person; poverty' (Table 3).
*-lèm- 'to become too difficult for'	Kask: Lakes, Upland, Yao; Kusi: Shona; also in Botatwe	Semantic innovation [as for *-lèm- 'to become tired,' above].
*-lìnd- 'to wait'	Kask: Lakes, NE-Coastal, Rufiji-Ruvuma; Kusi: Makua, Nyasa, SE-Bantu; also in Botatwe.	Semantic innovation: < Sangha-Kwa *-lìnd- 'to watch,' found in BC zones and relict Mashariki (Kask: Lakes, NE-Coastal; Kusi: Shona). Displaced Sangha-Kwa *-lį̀l-, found BC zones, Kongo, and relict ESav (Botatwe).

*-lìndì 'pit'	Kask: NE-Coastal, Langi, Njombe; Kusi: Shona, SE-Bantu; also in Botatwe; also in SW-Bantu (Herero)	Displaced SavB *-ìná (see Table 1).
*-lòpà 'blood'	Relict Kask: NE-Coastal (W.Ruvu), Mwika-Rungwe (Nyakyusa: loan < Nyasa?); Kusi: Nyasa, Shona, SE-Bantu; also in Botatwe; also in Totela; also in Lega	Together with PM *-gàlį́ displaced SavB *-nyį́ngà (see *-gàlį́ in Section A above for evidence and arguments).
*-lų́lí 'shadow'	Kask: NE-Coastal; also Mid-Zamb. areal: Shona, Botatwe, Nsenga (Sabi)	Displaced Sangha-Kwa *-lį́lį́, found in BC zones, Kongo, and relict Mashariki (SE-Bantu 'dimness').
*-góyì, *-góyè '(fiber) string'	Kask: Lakes, Takama, NE-Coastal, Rufiji-Ruvuma; Kusi: Shona; also in Botatwe (Lenje)	Proposed semantic innovation: < PB *-góyì '(bark?) fiber,' seen also in AB zone areal *-góyį 'cloth.' Displaced PB *-gòlį́, found in ABC zones, Kongo, WSav (SW-Bantu, Lwena, Luyana), Luban, Lega, Holoholo, Botatwe (Ila), Sabi and relict Mashariki (Kask: Lakes, NE-Coastal; Kusi areal: Shona, with Chopi and Tswa of SE-Bantu).
*-gùènà 'crocodile'	Kask: Lakes, NE-Coastal, Rufiji-Ruvuma; Kusi: Shona, SE-Bantu (*-gùènyà); also in Sabi; also in Botatwe; also in Luba-Sh; in both Sabi and Luba-Sh this root coexists with the PB root and thus is suspect as borrowed word	Semantic innovation (?): seeming earlier Bantu application to different reptile (e.g., Kongo *lungwena* 'chameleon'). Displaced PB *-gàndú, found in ABC zones, Kongo, WSav, Luban, Lega, and Sabi.

*-kèndè 'testicle'	relict Kask: NE-Coastal; Kusi: Makua, Nyasa, Shona, SE-Bantu; also in Botatwe; also in Sabi (Lala-Lamba only: probable Botatwe loan)	Displaced Sangha-Kwa *-kàtà, found in BC zones, Kongo, and SavB (Luban)
*-kéng- 'to deceive'	Kask: Lakes (Luyia 'bewitch'), NE-Coastal; Kusi: Shona; also in Botatwe ('skill')	Semantic innovation: < PB *-kéng- 'to be clever (?),' seen in AB zones and SavB (as *-kengel- 'to use one's wits': Lega 'think'; Ganda 'scrutinize'; Mid-Zamb. areal 'to be clever,' etc.). Displaced PB *-lì̧mb-, found in ABC zones, Kongo, and relict SavB (Lakes, with tonal skew; also in loanword shape in W.Luba).
*-kónò 'forearm'	Kask: Lakes, Upland, Takama, NE-Coastal, Mwika-Rungwe, Rufiji-Ruvuma; Kusi: Nyasa, Makua, SE-Bantu; also in Botatwe	Semantic innovation: < SavB *-kónò 'lower part of leg,' found in WSav (Lwena 'leg'; Lunda 'lower part of leg'), Luban (W.Luba 'paw'; Luba-Sh 'hoof'), and relict Mashariki (Kusi: SE-Bantu 'foreleg').
*-kúápà 'armpit'	Kask: Lakes, NE-Coastal, Njombe, Rufiji-Ruvuma; Kusi: Nyasa, Shona, SE-Bantu; also in Botatwe; also in Kaonde; also in SW-Bantu	Morphological innovation: < ESav *ku-ápà by amalgamation of class prefix into stem.
*-mát- 'to (daub) plaster'	Kask: Takama, Rufiji-Ruvuma; Kusi: Makua, Nyasa, SE-Bantu; also in Botatwe; also in Lwena (WSav)	Semantic innovation: < ESav *-mát- 'to be sticky,' found in Luban (W. Luba 'to drip') and relict Mashariki (Kask: Upland 'become viscous'; Rundi 'to stick to'). Displaced PB (?) *-bùg- 'to plaster,' found in AC zones?

*-pólų̀ 'foam'	Kask: Lakes, NE-Coastal; Kusi: Makua, Nyasa; also in Botatwe	Phonological innovation: vowel metathesis of Nzadi-Kwa *-pų́lò, found in B zone, Kongo, WSav (Lwena as *-pų́lù, with progressive vowel assimilation), and relict Mashariki (Kask: Lakes, Takama, Rufiji-Ruvuma; Kusi: Shona, SE-Bantu). AC zones *-pų́lù: separate noun derivation < common underlying PB verb *-pų́l- 'to froth.'
*-pòngó 'he-goat'	Kask: Upland (Chaga), Langi 'jackass,' Njombe, Mwika-Rungwe, Rufiji-Ruvuma; Kusi: Nyasa, SE-Bantu; also in Botatwe ('goat, generic'); also in Luyana, Nkoya as 'goat' (probable areal spread < Botatwe)	Displaced Sangha-Kwa *-boko, found in C zone, Kongo, and relict Mashariki (Kusi only: Nyasa, in loanword shape in Xhosa, other SE-Bantu 'bull').
*-tų́ 'flour'	Kask: Lakes, Upland, Rufiji-Ruvuma; Kusi: Shona; also in Botatwe; also in Holoholo	Semantic innovation: < Sangha-Kwa *-tų́ 'dust'; see -tų́ 'cloud,' also derived < this root, via sense 'cloud of dust,' in Section A for more information. Displaced SavB or very early PM root *-ùngà, found in areal southern savanna distribution (Lwena; Lunda; Sabi), relict Mashariki (Kask: NE-Coastal only), and Lega.
*-énjé 'cockroach'	Kask: Lakes, Upland, NE-Coastal; Kusi: Shona; also in Botatwe (Mid-Zamb. areal?)	Semantic innovation: < Sangha-Kwa *-énjé 'kind of cricket,' found in C zone, Kongo, Luban (W.Luba), and relict Mashariki (Kask: Upland, NE-Coastal; Kusi: Nyasa, SE-Banu). Displaced Sangha-Kwa *-pénjų̀, found in BC zones, WSav (Lunda *-pénjį̀) and Luban.

*-į́gų̀à 'thorn'	Kask: Lakes, Upland, Takama, Njombe, Mwika-Rungwe, Rufiji-Ruvuma; Kusi: Shona, SE-Bantu; also in Botatwe (as *-į́ngų̀à)	Phonological inovation: progressive labial assimilation plus vowel-raising of SavB *-ígà (*mu-ígà > *mu-į́gų̀à), for which see Table 1.
*-į́nò 'salt'	relict occurrence: Kaskazi: Ganda, Gogo; Kusi: Venda; also in Botatwe (Ila)	Morphological innovation: < PB *-į́n- 'to dip,' descriptive of method of obtaining salt at earliest Mashariki period, i.e., from salt ponds such as at Katwe and Kisaka. Displaced Nzadi-Kwa *-ùngúá, found in B zones, Kongo, and WSav (Kimbundu, Ovimbundu, Lwena, Lunda, SW-Bantu), itself derived from PB *-ùgúá (found in AC zones) by progressive nasal assimilation (*mu-ùgúá > *mu-ùngúá).
*-(į́)nyù 'salt'	Kask: Lakes, Upland, Takama, Rufiji-Ruvuma, NE-Coastal, Njombe; Kusi: Nyasa, Shona, SE-Bantu (Zulu 'acidity'); also in Botatwe (Lenje)	Phonological innovation: progressive assimilatory raising of V_2 of original Mashariki *-į́nò (see preceding entry) with accompanying palatalizing shift, *n > *ny / *-į __.
*-òyò 'heart (physical)'	Kask: Lakes, Takama, NE-Coastal; Kusi: Mid-Zamb. areal: Shona and Botatwe; also in Kongo (presumed separate semantic derivation)	Semantic innovation: < Nzadi-Kwa *-òyò 'stomach; life (as symbolized by stomach),' found in zone B, Kongo, WSav (Luyana), Luban (W.Luba), and relict Mashariki (Kask: Lakes, Upland; Kusi: Shona). Partially displaced PB *-tímà 'heart,' found in ABC zones, Kongo, WSav, Luban, Holoholo, and some Mashariki (Kask: Lakes, Upland, some NE Coastal, Rufiji-Ruvuma; Kusi: Nyasa, Makua: areal spread < Kask ?).

Section E — Innovations found in Mashariki and in Central or Eastern Luban

Root innovation	*Distribution*	*Root wholly or partially displaced by innovated root; additional explanations and commentary*
*-sàyá 'jaw'	Kask: NE-Coastal, Mwika-Rungwe (Nyakyusa 'cheek'); Kusi 'cheek': Nyasa (Nyanja), SE-Bantu (Sotho); also in Hemba ('lower jaw')	Displaced Sangha-Kwa *-bángá, found in BC zones, Kongo, Luban, and Holoholo (Guthrie glosses *-sàyá as 'cheek.').
*-lúlį́ 'whistling'	Kask: Upland, Takama, NE-Coastal, Rufiji-Ruvuma; Kusi: Nyasa, Shona, SE-Bantu; also in Luba-Sh	Displaced Nzadi-Kwa *-lòòlį̀ or *-lòògį̀, found in Kongo, WSav, Botatwe, and relict Mashariki (Kask: Lakes, Rufiji-Ruvuma; Kusi: Nyasa)
*-kúlù 'big'	Kask: Lakes, Takama, NE-Coastal, Rufiji-Ruvuma; Kusi: Nyasa, Shona, SE-Bantu; also in Luba-Sh	Semantic innovation: < PB *-kúlù 'mature, grown-up,' found in A zone, WSav (SW-Bantu), Luban, Sabi, and relict Mashariki (Kask: Lakes; Kusi: Shona). Displaced PB *-nénè, found in ABC zones, Kongo, WSav (Lwena, Lunda, SW-Bantu; loanword shape in Ovimbundu), Luban (W.Luba), Botatwe, and relict Mashariki (Kask: Lakes, Upland; also retained, but with meaning shifts in Swahili ['fat'], Nguni ['right (hand)'], Chopi ['good']).
*-tèngá 'feather'	Kusi: Nyasa, Shona, SE-Bantu; relict Kask: Rufiji-Ruvuma; also in Luba-Sh	Displaced PB *-sálá, found in ABC zones, Kongo, WSav (as 'feather headdress'), Luban (W.Luba; Kaonde), and isolated Mashariki occurrence (W.Lakes: Bembe, as probable areal spread from C zone).

*-į́bà 'thorn'	Kask: NE-Coastal; Kusi: Makua, SE-Bantu; also Luba-Sh; other Luban *-eba indicate a probable spread to Luban by borrowing	Irregularly sound-shifted form of PM *-į́gṷà (*gṷa > *ba), for which see Section A above.

Additional roots cited previously: in Section B, *-bèlé 'sorghum' (loanword shape in Luba: PM *-bèlé 'grain (gen.), bulrush millet'); *-gùènà 'crocodile'; *-(g)ṷ́ílí 'hair'; and *-úmà 'object of value'; in Section C, *-súngù 'poison'; *-pṷ̀kò 'mole' (loanword shape in Luba-Sh); *-tį̀kí 'stump (of tree)'; and *-àlįm- 'to borrow'; in Section D: *-mùò 'razor.'

<u>Section F — Innovations found in Mashariki and in Kaonde</u>

Root innovation	*Distribution*	*Root wholly or partially displaced by innovated root; additional explanations and commentary*
*-káán- 'to deny'	Kask: Upland, NE-Coastal, Rufiji-Ruvuma; Kusi: Nyasa, SE-Bantu; also in Kaonde	Semantic innovation: < Sangha-Kwa *-káán- 'to refuse (to do),' found in BC zones, WSav (Lwena), and scattered Mashariki (Kask: NE-Coastal, Yao, Rungwe; Kusi: Nyasa, SE-Bantu). Displaced PB *-tún-, found outside Narrow Bantu and in BC zones, Kongo, Luban, Holoholo, and relict Mashariki (Kusi: Makua).

Additional roots cited previously: in Section A, *-sòn- 'to sew'; in Section B, *-lìp- 'to pay'; *-kóndò 'war'; and *-pél- 'to become finished'; in Section C, *-bíál- 'to plant'; in Section D, *-kúápà 'armpit.'

<u>Section G — Innovations found in Mashariki and in Luyana</u>

Root innovation	*Distribution*	*Root wholly or partially displaced by innovated root; additional explanations and commentary*
*-į́nsí 'day(time)'	Kask: Lakes (Rundi), Upland, Langi, Rufiji-Ruvuma, NE-Coastal, Mwika-Rungwe; Kusi: Shona, Venda (Shona loan); in Luyana (loanword shape); also in Lega (loanword shape)	Phonological innovation: progressive nasal assimilation of PB *mu-į́sí *mu-ísí, found in AC zones, Kongo (> 'night'), Luban (W.Luba 'morning'), and isolated Mashariki occurrence (Lakes: Forest subgroup: probable spread from C zone).

*ma-ɪ́jɪ̀ 'water'	Kask: Lakes, Upland, Takama, NE-Coastal, Rufiji-Ruvuma; Kusi: Makua, Nyasa, SE-Bantu; also in Luyana. (Scatter of cases in Bobangi, Lega group, and Mbole are probable parallel separate derivations)	Semantic cum morphological innovation: < Sangha-Kwa *lu-ɪ́jɪ̀ 'river' (see Table 1, *-lòngà 'river') by class prefix switch. Displaced SavB *-ɪ́má 'water' (see Table 1).
*-úmà 'bead'	Kask: Lakes (Luyia), Upland, Takama, Rufiji-Ruvuma; Kusi: Shona; also in Luyana	Semantic innovation: < ESav *-úmà 'belongings' (see Table 1). Displaced PB *-sángá, found in AB zones, Kongo, WSav (Lwena, Lunda, SW-Bantu), Luban, and relict Mashariki (Kask: Takama, loanword shape in Kamba [Upland] and Sabaki [NE-Coastal]; Kusi: Tete [Swahili trade word?]).

Additional roots cited previously: in Table 3, *-lìlò 'fire' and *ki-ntù 'thing'; in Section B of Table 4, *-bèlek- 'to bear (child)'; *-bàìjò 'adze'; and *-íngà 'thorn.'

Section H — Innovations found in Mashariki and in Southwest-Bantu

Root innovation	*Distribution*	*Root wholly or partially displaced by innovated root; additional explanations and commentary*
*-pépò 'wind'	Mashariki (Kask: Lakes, Upland, NE-Coastal, Njombe, Rufiji-Ruvuma; Kusi: Nyasa, Makua, Shona, SE-Bantu); also N'n Kalahari areal (Luvale, Luyana, SW-Bantu); also Tetela group; also outside Narrow Bantu but presumed be a separate derivation there	Semantic innovation: < PB *-pépò 'cold (n., of wind),' found in A zone, Kongo, WSav (Luyana), Luban (Hemba), Sabi, Botatwe, and Mashariki (Kask: Lakes, Upland, NE-Coastal, Takama, Rufiji-Ruvuma; Kusi: Nyasa, Shona, SE-Bantu), itself a morphological innovation: < PB *-pép- 'to blow (*in* the wind),' found outside Narrow Bantu and in AB zones, WSav, Sabi, and relict Mashariki (Kask: NE-Coastal, Rufiji- Ruvuma). Displaced Sangha-Kwa *-pùùpò ~ *-pùùpù 'wind,' found in CD zones, Kongo, WSav, Luban, Sabi, and Botatwe, itself a mophological innovation < Sangha-Kwa *-pùùp- 'to blow (*of* wind),' found in BC zones, Kongo, Luban, Sabi, and relict Mashariki (Kask: Lakes, Upland, Takama). Root *-pùùpò ~ *-pùùpù earlier partially displaced PB *-pèèpè 'wind,' found in ABC zones, Kongo, and relict SavB (WSav: Ovimbundu, Pende; Lega; Mashariki: Kask: Rufiji-Ruvuma) and derived < PB *-pèèp- 'to blow (*of* wind),' found outside Narrow Bantu and in ABC zones, Kongo, Luban, and relict Mashariki (Kask: NE-Coastal; Kusi: Nyasa).

*-pítì̧ 'spotted hyena'	Kask: Lakes; Kusi: SE-Bantu; also in Ovambo subgroup of SW-Bantu	Displaced SavB *-mbúí̧, found in WSav (Lwena), Luban (general), Holoholo, and relict Mashariki (Gogo; Mwika-Rungwe; also Tumbuka *ci-mbwe*).
*-àtí̧ 'grass'	Kask: Lakes, Takama, NE-Coastal, Rufiji-Ruvuma; Kusi: Nyasa, SE-Bantu; also in Herero	Along with *-súá (Section A above), displaced PB *-ánì̧ (see entry for *-súá for more information).

Additional roots cited previously: in Table 3, *-lìlò 'fire'; in Section B, *-bèlé 'grain (gen.), bulrush millet' and *mu-élì̧ 'moon'; in Section D, *-lìndì 'pit' and *-kúápà 'armpit.'

<u>*Section I — Innovations found in Mashariki and in Lega group*</u>

Root innovation	*Distribution*	*Root wholly or partially displaced by innovated root; additional explanations and commentary*
*-lį̀kò 'country'	Relict Kask: Lakes (Forest subgroup), Upland (Chaga *-rų̀kò, with common Chaga shift: *-lį̀ > *-rų̀ /_CV#); Kusi: Makua, SE-Bantu (regular in Tsonga; Tsonga loan in GiTonga); also in Lega	Alternative explanation of Lakes reflex: loan to Forest subgroup from Lega. Probably displaced PB *-sɪ́ 'country; ground' found in meaning 'country' in ABC zones, Kongo, Botatwe, and restricted Mashariki (Kask only: Lakes, Upland, Takama, NE-Coastal).
*-ùmbá 'house'	Kask: Lakes, Upland, Takama, NE-Coastal, Mwika-Rungwe, Rufiji-Ruvuma; Kusi: Nyasa, Makua, Shona, SE-Bantu; also loanword in Lega; also in Tetela (in specialized meaning)	Displaced PB *-jú(b)ò 'house,' found in ABC zones, Kongo, WSav (Ovimbundu, Pende, SW-Bantu, Luyana), Luban, and relict Mashariki (Kask: Lakes; Kusi: SE-Bantu).

Additional roots cited previously: in Section B, *-buulį- 'to ask'; *-lìp- 'to pay'; *-(g)ų́ílí 'hair' (separately borrowed by Lega and Holoholo); and *mu-élį̀ 'moon'; in Section C, *-kų́bà 'chest' and *į́né 'I (indep. pron.)'; in Section D, *-bèlè 'front' (as alternate shape in Holoholo along with *-bèlì); *-lòpà 'blood'; and *-tų́ 'flour'; in Section G, *-í nsí 'day(time).'

Section J — Innovations found in Mashariki and in Tetela

Root innovation	*Distribution*	*Root wholly or partially displaced by innovated root; additional explanations and commentary*
*-bụ́n- 'to harvest'	Kask: Lakes, NE-Coastal, Rufiji-Ruvuma; Kusi: Nyasa, Shona, SE-Bantu; also in Tetela	Semantic innovation: PB meaning 'to break, snap (tr.),' found outside Narrow Bantu and in ABC zones and relict Mashariki (Kask: Lakes, Upland, Langi). This action is descriptive of manner of reaping grain in eastern Africa — hence the innovation here is a meaning extension by the proto-Mashariki to describe an activity of cultivation new to them

Additional root cited previously: in Section I, *-ùmbá 'house.'

Table 5: Stem morpheme innovations defining the Kaskazi subgroup of Masharik

Section A — Innovations restricted to Kaskazi languages

Root innovation	*Distribution*	*Root wholly or partially displaced by innovated root; additional explanations and commentary*
*-béyú 'seed'	Upland, NE-Coastal, Takama, Rufiji-Ruvuma	Phonological innovation: deletion of medial *g in PM *-bégú (see Table 4, Section A above; this shift turns up unevenly in Kaskazi, presumably reflecting an old alternance).
*-sàngà 'sand'	Upland, NE-Coastal, Njombe, Mwika-Rungwe; also isolated in Luban: Songye group: separate semantic innovation?	Semantic innovation: < PB *-sàngà 'particle, grain,' found outside Narrow Bantu and in C zone and relict SavB (Luban: W.Luba). Note also probable related PB *-sàngà 'island' (see *-lʊ́á 'island,' Section C below). Displaced Sangha-Kwa *-sèngà (see *-séké 'sand' : Table 2).
*-lìmà 'hill'	Upland, NE-Coastal; also in Lakes (Ha)	Displaced SavB *-lúndù (see Table 2).
*-lìbat- 'to tread'	Lakes, NE-Coastal, Rufiji-Ruvuma	Displaced ESav *-nìànt- (see Table 3).
*-ló 'night'	Lakes, Upland (Chaga), Njombe, Mwika-Rungwe, Rufiji-Ruvuma	Semantic innovation: < PB *-ló 'sleep' (n.), found in ABCD zones, Kongo, WSav, Luban, Sabi, Botatwe, and relict Mashariki (Kask: Lakes, Takama; Kusi: Nyasa). Partially displaced PB *-tʲ́kù, *-tʊ́kù, found outside Narrow Bantu and in ACD zones, WSav, Luban, Lega, and Mashariki.

*-kóbà 'leather strap'	Lakes, Takama, NE-Coastal, Njombe	Semantic innovation: < PB *-kóbà 'skin, hide.' Along with *-kándà (see Section H below), displaced SavB *-bi´á, found in WSav (Mbangala; Ovimbundu; SW-Bantu), Luban (Hemba), and relict Mashariki.
*kèndá (< *ka-èndá) 'nine'	Lakes (Western subgroup), Upland, Takama, NE-Coastal, Njombe, Mwika-Rungwe	Morphological innovation: < ESav *mu-èndá (for which see Table 3) by substitution of *ka- noun class prefix for original *mu- (see Table 3).
*-kùngúgú 'fog'	[Kati:] NE-Coastal, Takama, Njombe; also in Rundi as 'dust' (i.e., dust kicked up into the air)	Phonological innovation: partial reduplication of PM *-kùngú 'fog.'
*-mèlò 'gullet'	Lakes (Konjo), Upland, NE-Coastal (Ruvu)	Morphological innovation: < PB *-mèl- 'to swallow,' found outside Narrow Bantu and in ABC zones and Mashariki (Kask: Lakes, Upland, NE-Coastal; Kusi: Nyasa, Shona, SE-Bantu). Displaced PB *-kòlò (see also *-mį̀lò 'gullet' in Section B following).
*-mòòg- 'to shave'	[Sn Kask areal:] Takama, NE-Coastal (W. Ruvu), Rufiji-Ruvuma	Displaced PM *-mù- (see Table 4, Section A); probable derivation from it by addition of *-ag- extension (< *-mù-ag- > *-mòòg-).
*-mùlì 'torch'; AND *-mùlik- 'to shine'	Lakes, Upland, Takama, Njombe, Rufiji-Ruvuma; AND Lakes, Takama, NE-Coastal, Njombe, Rufiji-Ruvuma, Mwika-Rungwe)	Phonological innovation: nasal dissimilation of SavB *-mùnì, found in Luban (W.Luba) and isolated Mashariki occurrence (Kusi: Nyasa: Sabi loan?), and of Sabi *-mùnik- 'to shine,' found in WSav (SW-Bantu, Lwena), Luban, Sabi (Bemba), and isolated Mashariki occurrence (Kusi: Nyasa: Sabi loan?).

*-pèné 'goat'	Lakes, NE-Coastal, Mwika-Rungwe; also isolated in Yeyi and Subiya; also loanword shape in Lega	Semantic innovation: < PM *-pèné 'steinbock,' retained only in SE-Bantu? Partially displaced PB *-búlì̧, found outside Narrow Bantu and ABCD zones, Luban, Holoholo, Sabi, and Mashariki (Kask: Lakes, Upland, Takama, NE-Coastal, Rufiji-Ruvuma; Kusi: Makua, Nyasa, Shona, SE-Bantu).
*-pʉ́ngàté, *-pʉ́ngàtí 'seven'	[Sn Nyanza areal:] Lakes (E.Nyanza), Upland, Takama, NE-Coastal, Njombe, Mwika-Rungwe	Southern Cushitic loanword. Displaced Sangha-Kwa *-sàmbù, 'seven,' found in BC zones, Kongo, WSav (Lwena 'six'), and relict Mashariki (Kask: Lakes *-sàmbʉ̀.
*-tónj̧- 'to rain'	[Sn Nyanza areal:] NNE-Coastal, Mwika-Rungwe, Rufiji-Ruvuma	Morphological innovation: < Sangha-Kwa *-tón- 'to drip,' found in C zone, Sabi, and relict Mashariki (Kask: Takama, NE-Coastal). Displaced PM *-nì- 'to rain' (see Table 4, Section A).
*-áyí 'egg'	Lakes (Forest group), NE-Coastal (Swahili, Rufiji-Ruvuma)	Phonological innovation: shift of medial *g to *y or nil (as in 'seed' above) in PM *-ágí: see Table 4.
*-òyá 'feather'	Lakes, Upland, NE-Coastal, Takama	Semantic innovation: < Nzadi-Kwa *-òyá 'fur,' found in Kongo, Luban, Kusi of Mashariki, and relict Kaskazi (Lakes, Sukuma, Swahili). Displaced PM *-tèngá (see Table 4, Section B).
*-(ʉ́)nyʉ̀ 'salt'	Lakes, NE-Coastal, Mwika-Rungwe	Phonological innovation: rounding assimilation of PM *-į́nyù (see Table 4, Section D above).

Section B — Innovations found in Kaskazi and in Makua of Kusi group

Root innovation	*Distribution*	*Root wholly or partially displaced by innovated root; additional explanations and commentary*
*-sáálè 'arrow'	Lakes, NE-Coastal, Rufiji-Ruvuma; also in Makua	Displaced SavB *-gʊ̨́í̧, which see in Table 1 above.
*-sese 'four'	Rufiji-Ruvuma; also in Makua	Displaced PB *-nàyɪ́ 'four,' found outside Narrow Bantu and throughout Bantu.
*-sí̧mb- 'to dig'	[Sn Kask areal:] NE-Coastal, Takama, Rufiji-Ruvuma; also in Makua	Phonological innovation: irregular spirantization of PB *-tí̧mb-. Displaced PB *-tí̧m- and ESav *-ì̧mb- (see Table 3 for distributions of these three roots).
*-mì̧lò 'gullet'	Lakes, Upland, Takama, NE-Coastal, Njombe, Mwika-Rungwe; also in Makua	Morphological innovation: < PM *-mì̧l- 'to swallow' (see Table 4). Displaced PM *-kòlò (relict only: Kask: NE-Coastal; Kusi: SE-Bantu). Formation influenced by *-mèlò 'gullet' (see Section A).
*-pùlà 'nose'	NE-Coastal, Langi, Rufiji-Ruvuma, Mwika-Rungwe; also in Makua	Displaced PB *-úlù, found in ABC zones, Kongo, WSav, Luban, and relict Mashariki (Kask: Lakes, Takama, Upland).
*-tápik- 'to vomit'	Upland, NE-Coastal, Rufiji-Ruvuma, Mwika-Rungwe; also in Nyasa (Sena), Makua	Morphological innovation: < PB *-táp- 'to draw water.' Displaced SavB *-sànj- and PB *-lúk- (see Table 1, Section A).

*-tóndùà 'star'	[Sn Kask areal:] NE-Coastal (*-tòndò, *-tòndùè), Njombe *-tòndùè), Rufiji-Ruvuma, Mwika-Rungwe; also in Makua; also in Nyasa	Morphological innovation: < hypothesized underlying verb root *-tóndu- 'to be scintillating' or the like.
*mu-óto 'fire'	Takama, NE-Coastal, Mwika-Rungwe, Rufiji-Ruvuma; also in Makua; also in Nyasa; also in Central Shona (displaced proto-Shona *-lìlò)	Morphological cum semantic innovation: < Sangha-Kwa *ki-ótò 'fireplace' (found in BC zones (> 'fire' in Tsogo), WSav, Luban, and relict Mashariki [Lakes: N.Nyanza; Kusi: Shona]), by switch of noun class prefixes. Displaced PM *-lìlò (see Table 4, Section D above).
*-úmà 'iron'	Lakes, Takama, NE-Coastal, Njombe; also in Makua; also in Tumbuka of Nyasa; also spread to Luban and Lega as word for particular kinds of items made from iron	Semantic innovation: < ESav *-úmà 'belongings' (see Table 1, Section A.2)

Section C — Innovations found in Kaskazi and in Nyasa subgroup of Kusi group

Root innovation	*Distribution*	*Root wholly or partially displaced by innovated root; additional explanations and commentary*
*-bànò 'arrowshaft'	Lakes; Takama; Upland; NE-Coastal; also in Nyasa (Nyanja)	Displaced PM *-tulu (see Ehret 1998 for this root).
*-bìngù 'cloud'	[Sn Kask areal:] NE-Coastal, Mwika-Rungwe; also in Nyasa (Tumbuka, Sena)	Displaced PM *-tų́ (see Table 4, Section A).
*-sàná 'day(light)';	Kask: Lakes, Takama, NE-Coastal, Rufiji-Ruvuma; Kusi: Nyasa (Nyanja); also in Lwena; AND	Displaced PB *-ì̧nı́á (see Table 2, *-ànı́á above). 2nd shape, *-sànı́á, may reflect phonological influence of the displaced root.
*-sànı́á 'day(light)'	Kask: Upland (*-sènyá), Mwika-Rungwe; also in Nyasa (Tumbuka)	
*-sób- 'to lack'	[Sn Kask areal:] NE-Coastal, Rufiji-Ruvuma; also Nyasa (Nyanja)	Semantic innovation: < PM *-sób- 'to not do, not function' (writer's inference from Guthrie data).
*-sòm- 'to pierce'	[Sn Kask areal:] NE-Coastal, Rufiji-Ruvuma; also in Nyasa (Nyanja)	Semantic innovation: < PB *-sòm- 'to poke into,' found in ABC zones, Kongo, WSav, Luban, and relict Mashariki (Kask: some Rufiji-Ruvuma; Kusi: SE-Bantu). Displaced SavB *-tóbol-, *-túbul- (see Table 1).
*-kómb- 'to lick (food) with finger'	Kask: Lakes, Upland, Takama, NE-Coastal, Rufiji-Ruvuma; also in Nyasa; also in Botatwe; also in Sabi	Semantic innovation: < PB *-kómb- 'to scrape (out)' (see PM *-kómbè 'ladle' (Section A above).

*-làm- 'to get well'	Lakes, Takama, Rufiji-Ruvuma; also in Nyasa (Nyanja)	Semantic innovation: < Nzadi-Kwa *-làm- 'to endure, last,' retained in B zone. Displaced early PM *-pón- (see Table 4, Section A).
*-lèm- 'to become tired'	Kask: Sabaki, Lakes; Kusi: Nyasa; also in Botatwe	Semantic innovation: < Sangha-Kwa *-lèm- 'to become heavy,' found in BC zones, Kongo, WSav, Luban, and relict Mashariki (Kask: Rundi; Kusi: Shona).
*-lúá 'island'	Kask: Lakes, Rufiji-Ruvuma; Kusi: Nyasa; also in Botatwe	Displaced PB *-sàngà, found in ABCD zones, Kongo, WSav (Kimbundu: loan < Kongo?), and Luban and retained but with shifted meaning in some Mashariki (e.g., Sukuma 'foreshore of lake').
*-kólò 'lower trunk and tap root'	Lakes (N.Nyanza), NE-Coastal, Rufiji-Ruvuma; also in Nyasa (Nyanja)	Semantic innovation: < Nzadi-Kwa *-kólò probably meaning 'stem' (Kongo 'origin'; Luban 'leg'). Displaced PB *-tį́nà, found outside Narrow Bantu and in ABC zones, Kongo, WSav, Luban, and relict Mashariki (Kask: Lakes, Upland, Njombe).
*-kòj- 'to urinate'	Sn Kask: NE-Coastal; also in Nyasa	Partially displaced PM *-tùnd- (see Table 4, Section A).
*-mùò 'razor'	Kask: Lakes (Luyia), NE-Coastal; Kusi: Nyasa; also in Botatwe; also in Sabi (only Lamba ?); also in Luba-Sh	Morphological innovation: < PM *-mù- 'to shave' (see Table 4, Section A).
*-nį̀ò 'anus'	Kask: Lakes, Upland; Kusi: Nyasa; also in Botatwe	Morphological innovation: < PB *-nį̀- 'to defecate.' Displaced PB *-kúndú, found in AC zones, Kongo, WSav, and relict Mashariki (Kask: NE-Coastal, Rufiji-Ruvuma; Kusi: Nyasa).

*-négin- 'to speak'	Kask: Upland, Mwika, NE-Coastal (loanword into Sabaki); also loanword shape in Nyasa (Nyanja); also in Luba-Sh	Displaced PB *-gàmb-, found in ABC zones, Kongo, WSav (Lwena), Luban (W.Luba), and relict Mashariki (Kask: Lakes, NE-Coastal; Kusi: Nyasa, SE-Bantu [Venda]).
*-nòkų̀ 'flesh'	Kask: Lakes, NE-Coastal, Rufiji-Ruvuma; also in Nyasa (Nyanja); also in Sabi; also in Holoholo; also loanword in Luba-Sh	Displaced PB *-sùnį̀, found in ABC zones, Kongo, WSav (Lwena), Luban, Lega (in skewed shape *-sùnà), and relict Mashariki (Lakes).
*-pàndé 'piece'	Kask: Lakes; Upland; NE-Coastal; Kusi: Shona; also in loanword in GiTonga (< Shona); also in Sabi	Morphological innovation: < SavB *-pànd- 'to split (tr.)' (see Table 1).
*-pį́tį̀ 'hyena'	Lakes, Takama, Upland, NE-Coastal, Mwika-Rungwe; also in Nyasa (Nyanja)	Phonological innovation: regressive vowel assimilation of PM *-pítį̀ (see Table 4, Section G).
*-pòk- 'to receive'	Lakes, NE-Coastal, Ruvuma; also in Nyasa; also in Sabi	Displaced Nzadi-Kwa *-tóól-, found in B zone, Kongo, Tetela, Lega, Botatwe, and Mashariki (Kusi: Shona, SE-Bantu; relict Kask: Lakes).
*-pùàgul- 'to pound'	Takama, Rufiji-Ruvuma; also in Nyasa (Nyanja)	Morphological innovation: < PM *-pùàg- 'to strike,' found in Kask (NE-Coastal 'to pound') and Kusi (SE-Bantu: Nguni).
*-pų̀kul- 'to dig up (earth)'	Kask: Lakes, Upland, NE-Coastal, Rufiji-Coastal, Rufiji-Ruvuma; also in Nyasa (Nyanja); also in Luba-Sh	Morphological innovation: < PB *-pų̀k- by addition of -Vl extension, but without semantic shift; parallel addition of this extension appears in an A-zone reflex (see *-pų̀k- in Table 4, Section C).

*-tándik- 'to begin'	Kask: Lakes, Rufiji-Ruvuma; also in Nyasa (Nyanja)	Displaced PM *-àmb- (see Table 4, Section C).
*-tántàtú 'six'	Kask: Lakes (only RR), Upland, some Njombe; also in Nyasa (some Nyanja); also in Central Shona	Phonological innovation: devoicing assimilation of PM *-tándàtú (see Table 4, Section A).
*-tų́mbí 'egg'	Upland, Rufiji-Ruvuma, Mwika-Rungwe; also in Nyasa (Tumbuka)	Displaced Mashariki *-ágí, found in Kusi (Nyasa, Shona, SE-Bantu [Sotho], and in relict occurrence in Kaskazi, with medial *g-deletion, as *-áyí (see Section A above).
*ki-álá 'finger'	Lakes, Upland, NE-Coastal, Rufiji-Ruvuma; also Nyasa (Nyanja)	Morphological cum semantic innovation: < PB *-álá 'nail' (in Mashariki sense 'nail' was preserved for root via noun prefix shift to classes 11/10. Displaced PB *-nùè, found in A zone, WSav, Luban, Sabi, Botatwe, Kusi (Makua, Shona, SE-Bantu) and relict Kask (Lakes).

Additional roots previously cited in Section B preceding: *-tápik- 'to vomit'; *-tóndùà 'star'; *mu-ótò 'fire'; and *-úmà 'iron.'

<u>*Section D — Innovations found in Kaskazi and in Lega group*</u>

Root innovation	*Distribution*	*Root wholly or partially displaced by innovated root; additional explanations and commentary*
*-lòl- 'to look, look at'	Lakes, Upland, Takama, NE-Coastal, Njombe, Mwika-Rungwe, Rufiji-Ruvuma; also in Kaonde; also in Holoholo	Semantic innovation: < SavB *-lòl- 'to face towards,' meaning seen in Sabi and as additional sense in some Lakes, Upland, and Rufiji-Ruvuma reflexes. Along with *-láng- (see Section G below), displaced Sangha-Kwa *-tál- found in BC zones, Kongo, WSav (Ovimbundu, Lwena, SW-Bantu), and Luban.
*-lṳ́g- 'to cook'	Lakes, Upland, Takama, NE-Coastal, Rufiji-Ruvuma, Mwika-Rungwe; also in Lega	Semantic innovation: < PB *-lṳ́g- 'to paddle,' found outside Narrow Bantu and in ABC zones, WSav, Luban, and relict Mashariki (Kask: Lakes; Kusi: Shona [Ndau]). Semantics: 'to paddle' > 'to stir food with cooking paddle' > 'to cook.' Displaced SavB, PM *-ḭ̀pik- (see Table 1, Section A).
*-pḭ́ágil- 'to sweep'	[Sn Nyanza areal:] Upland, Langi, NE-Coastal; also in Holoholo	Phonological innovation: irregular vowel raising in diphthong, < PM *-pí́ágil- (see Table 4, Section A).
*-àlḭ́ 'blood'	[Sn Kask areal:] NE-Coastal, Rufiji-Ruvuma; Mwika-Rungwe; also as loanword in Luban; also as loanword in Holoholo	Phonological innovation: deletion of medial *g (as in other Kask instances) in PM *-gàlḭ́ (see Table 4 above).

Additional roots previously cited: in Table 3, *-gùl- 'to buy'; in Section A above, *-pèné 'goat'; in Section B, *-úmà 'iron'; in Section C, *-nòkṵ̀ 'flesh' (in Holoholo, but counterindicated for Lega).

Section E — Innovations found in Kaskazi, Sabi, and Botatwe

Root innovation	*Distribution*	*Root wholly or partially displaced by innovated root; additional explanations and commentary*
*ma-bį́ 'faeces'	Kask: Lakes, Upland, NE-Coastal, Rufiji-Ruvuma; also in Sabi; also in Botatwe	Morphological innovation: substitution of *ma- (class 6) noun prefix for original *tu- (class 13) in PB *tu-bį́, found in AC zones, Kongo; WSav, Luban, and Holoholo
*-súúl- 'to dislike'	Kask: Upland; also in Sabi; also in Botatwe	Semantic innovation: < SavB root seen in Lwena (WSav) *-súúl- 'to sulk.' Displaced ESav *-béng- (see Table 3).
*-gàndá 'house'	Kask: Lakes, Takama, Upland ('temporary shelter'), NE-Coastal (Ruvu only), Mwika-Rungwe; also in Sabi; also in Botatwe; isolated case of meaning shift to 'house' in Bongili (C zone)	Semantic innovation: < Sangha-Kwa *-gàndá 'ward, section of village' (see under *-tálá, Table 1; the reasons for reconstructing this meaning for *-gàndá can be seen there; for further arguments on this issue, see Ehret 1998). Competed with PM *-ùmbá 'house' to displace PB *-jú(b)ò (for both of which, see Table 4, Section 4).
*-kùàlé 'partridge'	Kask: Lakes, Upland, Takama, NE-Coastal; Mid-Zamb. areal (Tete, Sabi, Manyika of Shona, Botatwe)	Irregular phonological shift: < ESav *-kùàlí (see Table 3).
*ma-(į́)njì 'water'	Kask: Upland, Takama, NE-Coastal (Ruvu), Mwika-Rungwe; also in Sabi; also in Botatwe	Phonological innovation: < PM *ma-(į́)jì, by nasal insertion (a recurrent tendency in Bantu *-įs-/*-įj- stems: e.g., *-į́nsí 'day(light)' in Table 4, Section 5)

Additional root previously cited in Section C, *-mùò 'razor.'

Section F — Innovations found in Kaskazi and in Sabi

Root innovation	*Distribution*	*Root wholly or partially displaced by innovated root; additional explanations and commentary*
*-bı̧̀mb- 'to thatch'	Lakes, NE-Coastal, Rufiji-Ruvuma; also in Sabi; also in Kaonde	Semantic innovation: < PM or ESav *-bı̧̀mb- 'to put under cover' (Kusi: Xhosa 'to store away,' Sotho 'to hide'; also Botatwe 'to hide').
*-kálang- 'to fry, roast'	Kask: Lakes, Upland, Takama, NE-Coastal, Rufiji-Ruvuma; also in Sabi	Displaced PM *-kálı̧ng- (see Table 4, Section A).
*-káyı̧́ 'wife'	Kask: Lakes, Upland, Takama, NE-Coastal, Mwika-Rungwe; also in Sabi (in Mwika-Rungwe shape); also in Sanga (Luban), with Sabi shape	Semantic innovation: < pre-PB root *-káyı̧́, probably 'female,' seen also in PB compound noun *-káyı̧́-ntù 'woman' (PB *-ntù 'person'; see Table 3, *-kálı̧̀ 'woman,' for distribution). Displaced PB *-kálı̧̀ 'wife,' found outside Narrow Bantu and in ABC zones, Kongo, WSav (Kimbundu, Luyana), Luban, Botatwe, and Mashariki (Kusi: Nyasa, Shona, SE-Bantu [GiTonga; implied in Sotho meaning 'marriage']; also relict Kask: Lakes).
*-kóp- 'to borrow'	Kask: Upland, NE-Coastal; also in Sabi	Semantic innovation: < proposed SavB 'to seek to acquire' (cf. Herero 'become avaricious'). Displaced PM *-àlı̧m- (see Table 4, Section B).

*-kų́ndik- 'to tie knot'	Lakes, Upland, NE-Coastal; also in Sabi	Morphological innovation: < PM *-kų́nd- (see Table 4, Section A).

Additional roots previously cited: in Section C, *-kómb- 'to lick (food) with finger'; *-nòkų̀ 'flesh'; *-pàndé 'piece'; and *-pòk- 'to take, receive'; in Section D, *-lòl- 'to look at.'

<u>*Sectionn G — Innovations found in Kaskazi and Botatwe*</u>

Root innovation	*Distribution*	*Root wholly or partially displaced by innovated root; additional explanations and commentary*
*-ba 'yard of homestead'	relict Kask: NE-Coastal, Takama; also in Botatwe	Central Sudanic loanword (PCS *ɓa 'homestead')
*-sèlel- 'to descend'	Kask: Upland, NE-Coastal, Rufiji-Ruvuma; also in Subiya (Botatwe); also in Lwena (Mbunda: northern Kalahari areal, as in Table 11?)	Morphological innovation: < Sangha- Kwa *-sèl- 'to slip' (found in BC zones, WSav (SW-Bantu), Luban, Lega, and relict Mashariki (Kusi: Nyasa, Shona; also in Yao: probable Nyanja loan?). Displaced Nzadi-Kwa *-túúluk-, found in B zone, Kongo, WSav (Ovimbundu, SW-Bantu, Lwena), Luban, and relict Mashariki (Kusi: Shona; Kask: loanword in Yao).
*-láng- 'to look, look at'	Kask: Lakes, Central Tanz. areal (Langi, Gogo); also in Botatwe	Semantic innovation: detrans. of Nzadi-Kwa *-láng- 'to show,' found in Kongo, Luban, Holoholo ('teach'), Sabi, and relict Mashariki (Kask: Lakes [Ganda 'announce'], NE-Coastal [Pokomo]; Kusi: Nyasa [Nyanja 'to reprove']). Along with *-lòl-, displaced Sangha-Kwa *-tál- (for both these roots, see Section D above).
*-lí́là 'umbilicus'	Kask: Lakes, Takama, Upland; also in Botatwe	Probable borrowing of PSC *del- 'umbilicus.'

*-jóbé 'situtunga, marshbuck'	Kaskazi: Lakes 'situtunga, marshbuck'; Kati 'donkey'; also Botatwe 'situtunga'	Displaced early Bantu *-bṳ́lį́, attested in ABC zones (e.g., Bobangi *mbúli*´ 'water antelope'), Kongo *vudi* ('an antelope'); WSav (Ndembu *mbudi*, Luvale *vuli* 'situtunga'); Guthrie gives *-bṳ̀lį̀, improbably glossed as 'kudu,' but balance of evidence favors meaning given here.
*-pį́là 'pus'	Kask: Lakes, Upland, Takama, Rufiji-Ruma, Mwika-Rungwe, Njombe; Kusi: Nyasa (Tumbuka); also in Botatwe (Ila); also in Soko-Kele group (C zone), presumably by parallel, but independent sound shift	Phonological innovation: < PB *-pį́nà, found in AC zones, Kongo, WSav (Lwena), Luban, Sabi, and Botatwe (Lenje), by PM sound shift *n > *l /#-[+labial/-cont][+front/+vocalic]_-, < PB *-pį́n- 'to squeeze (with finger),' via sense 'to squeeze pus (from boil, sore).' Also displaced PB *-pį́nyà, found in ABC zones, Kongo, and relict Mashariki (Nyasa: Nyanja), derived from alternate PB verb shape *-pį́nį- 'to squeeze,' attested in A zone, Kongo, Luban, and Mashariki (Kaskazi: Lakes, Upland, NE-Coastal, Rufiji-Ruvuma; also Nyasa).
*-inie 'liver'	Kask: Lakes, NE-Coastal, Rungwe (Nyakyusa); also in Botatwe	Central Sudanic loanword (PCS *-nye).

Additional roots previously cited: in Table 4, Section D, *-bèlè 'front'; in Section C above, *-lèm- 'to become tired'; *-lúá 'island'; *-kòjó 'urine'; and *-nį̀ò 'anus'; in Section E, *-gàndá 'house'; in Section F, *-kómb- 'to lick with finger.'

Section H — Innovations found in Kaskazi and in Central or Eastern Luban

Root innovation	*Distribution*	*Root wholly or partially displaced by innovated root; additional explanations and commentary*
*-kándà 'strap'	Kask: Lakes, NE-Coastal, Rufiji-Ruvuma; also in Luba-Sh; also in A zone (but separately derived by addition of class 14/4 class prefixes to already prefixed noun)	Semantic innovation: < PB *-kándà 'skin,' found in B zone, Kongo, Luban, Sabi, Botawe, and Mashariki (Kask: Lakes, Takama, Upland, NE-Coastal, Rufiji-Ruvuma; Kusi: Shona, also Shona loan in Venda). Along with *-kóbà (see Section A above), displaced SavB *-bɪ́á.
*-pòkel- 'to receive'	Kask: NE-Coastal, Rufiji-Ruvuma; also in Hemba	Morphological innovation: < Kask *-pòk- (see Section C above).

Additional roots previously cited: in Section B, *-úmà 'iron wire'; in Section C, *-mùò 'razor'; *-négin- 'to speak'; *-nòkʉ̀ 'flesh'; and *-pʉ̀kul- 'to dig up, fling up (earth)'; in Section D, *-àlɪ̀ 'blood'; in Section E, *-làl- 'to crack.'

<u>*Section I — Innovations found in Kaskazi and in Lwena or Yeyi or Luyana or Herero*</u>

Root innovation	*Distribution*	*Root wholly or partially displaced by innovated root; additional explanations and commentary*
*-lòngò 'ten (in multiples of ten)'	Kask: Lakes, Upland, NE-Coastal, Rufiji-Ruvuma, Mwika-Rungwe; also in SW-Bantu (Herero)	Semantic innovation: < PB *-lòngò 'line of objects,' found in ABC zones, WSav (Lwena, SW-Bantu), Luban, Holoholo, Sabi, Botatwe, and relict Mashariki (Kask: Lakes, NE-Coastal; Kusi: Nyanja, Shona). Displaced PB *-kúmɪ̀ 'ten' in this function.
*-tènd- 'to act, do'	Kask (Sn Kask areal): Takama, NE-Coastal, Rufiji-Ruvuma; also in Luyana	Displaced PB *-gìl-, found outside Narrow Bantu and in AC zones, WSav (Lunda), Holoholo, Sabi, and relict Mashariki (Kask: Lakes; Kusi: SE-Bantu).

Additional roots previously cited: in Section A, *-pèné 'goat'; in Section C, *-sàná 'day(light).'

Table 6: Stem morpheme innovations defining the Kusi subgroup of Mashariki

Section A — Innovations restricted to Kusi

Root innovation	*Distribution*	*Root wholly or partially displaced by innovated root; additional explanations and commentary*
*-ɓáb- 'to become bitter'	Nyasa, Makua, Shona, SE-Bantu; also in Yao (presumed Nyanja loan)	Semantic innovation: < Nzadi-Kwa *-ɓáb- 'to sting, smart,' found in B zone, Kongo, Botatwe, Sabi, and Mashariki (Kask: Lakes, Takama, NE-Coastal; Kusi: Nyasa, Shona, SE-Bantu).
*-sáánù 'five'	Nyasa, Makua, Shona, SE-Bantu; also Mabia (Rufiji-Ruvuma) of Kask (loan < Makua); also in Botatwe (loan < Shona?)	Phonological innovation: irregular *o > *u /_# in PM *-sáánò (see Table 4, Section B, above), resulting from counting-sequence influence of the structurally parallel, preceding number 'three,' PM *-sàtù ~ *-tàtù, in which final *u is the regular outcome.
*-sèbè 'arrow'	Nyasa, Shona, SE-Bantu	Displaced SavB *-gʊ̨i´ (see Table 1). Nilo-Saharan loanword (Ehret 1998).
*-sínj- 'to pound'	Nyasa, SE-Bantu (Sotho); Shona (loanword shape?)	Displaced ESav *-pònd- (see under *-tú- 'to pound' in Table 3).
*(l)ị-jànà 'hundred'	Nyasa, Shona, SE-Bantu	Phonological innovation: palatalization of *g of PM *(l)ị-gànà (which see in Table 4, Section A above) in environment of preceding *ị

*-kàmbà 'tortoise'	Nyasa, Shona, SE-Bantu	Semantic innovation: < PM *-kàmbà 'shell,' seen, e.g., in Swahili ***kamba*** 'lobster,' ***mkamba*** 'large sea crab.' Displaced PB *-kúlù̧, found outside Narrow Bantu and in ABC zones, Kongo, WSav (SW-Bantu), Luban, Sabi, Botatwe, and Mashariki (Kask: Lakes, Upland, NE-Coastal [in compound *-kụlụgobe]; relict Kusi: some SE-Bantu).
*-káp- 'to bail (water)'	Nyasa, Shona, SE-Bantu (in derived forms); also in Yao (presumed Nyanja loanword)	Semantic innovation: < pre-PB verb *-káp- 'to move (?) water,' seen in derived PB noun *-kápį́ 'paddle' (see Table 2, *-làpò 'paddle').
*-kí́á 'stump'	Makua, Nyanja, Shona, SE-Bantu	Semantic innovation: < Nzadi-Kwa *-kí́á 'stumbling block [i.e., piece of plant, etc, sticking up in path],' noted by Guthrie in B zone and Kongo. Displaced PM *-tį̀kí́ (see Table 4, Section C).
*-nyàngá 'horn'	Makua, Nyasa, Shona, SE-Bantu	Displaced SavB *-séngò (for which see Table 1, Section A.1). Also Zambian areal spread in meaning 'ivory' to Yao, Bisa (Sabi), Lwena (WSav), presumably during era of ivory trade
*-túndį̀ 'shadow'	Makua, Nyasa, SE-Bantu	Displaced PM *-lú̧lí́ (for which see Table 4, Section A above).
*-į́ngụ- 'to hear'	Nyasa, Shona, SE-Bantu	Phonological innovation: SavB *-į́gụ- (see Table 1, Section A.2), with irregular nasal insertion.
*-òl- 'to gather up'	Nyasa, SE-Bantu	Displaced ESav *-búng- (see Table 3).

Section B — Root innovations of Kusi found also in far southern Kaskazi

Root innovation	*Distribution*	*Root wholly or partially displaced by innovated root; additional explanations and commentary*
*-sómbá 'fish'	Nyasa, Shona; Sn Kask: Rufiji-Ruvuma, Njombe, Sn Takama (Nyamwezi), Ruvu (southernmost NE-Coastal subgroup)	Displaced PB *-sụ́í (for which see Table 2, *-sí 'fish').
*-pìkò 'wing'	Nyasa, SE-Bantu; Sn Kask: Njombe; also in Sabi; also in Comoro (via old Makua influence?)	Displaced PB *-pàpá (and SavB alternant *-bàbá (see Table 1).
*-tòb- 'to hit, smash'	Kusi: SE-Bantu ('break, smash'); Sn Kask ('hit'): Gogo, Njombe, Rufiji-Ruvuma (Mpoto); also in Sabi ('break, smash')	Probable loanword from Nilo-Saharan (Ehret 1998).
*-tùmbù 'belly'	Kusi: Shona, SE-Bantu; Sn Kask: Sn Njombe, also Yao	Phonological innovation: progressive vowel assimilation of PM *-tùmbò (see Table 4).

Section C — Root innovations found in Kusi and in Sabi

Root innovation	*Distribution*	*Root wholly or partially displaced by innovated root; additional explanations and commentary*
*-sánà 'back'	Makua; Nyasa; Shona; SE-Bantu; also in Sabi; also in Kaonde; also in Totela with Shona meaning 'back-bone': presumed Mid-Zamb. areal spread)	Displaced PB *-gòngò, found in ABC zones, WSav, Luban, Lega, Botatwe, and Mashariki (Kaskazi: general; in Tumbuka of Kusi as probable areal influence from Mwika-Rungwe of Kaskazi).
*-ŋà 'crack'	Nyasa, Shona, SE-Bantu; also in Botatwe; also in Sabi	Phonological innovation: < earlier Bantu *-gà, found in C zone and Kaskazi of Mashariki (Lakes, NE-Coastal, Takama, Rufiji-Ruvuma).
*-pùnò 'nose'	Makua (Chuabo), Nyasa, Shona (*-pı̀nò with rounding dissimilation); also in Sabi	Displaced PB *-yúlù, which see under *-pùlà 'nose' in Table 5, Section B.
*-tı̧́tı̧̀, *-sı̧́tı̧̀ 'hair'	Nyasa (Nyanja *-sı̧́sı̧̀), SE-Bantu (Tsonga, Sotho); also in Sabi; also in Yeyi; also in Sanga (Luban, adjacent to Sabi group)	Displaced PM *-(g)ʋ̧́ílí (see Table 4, Section C). Possible derivation < same root as that cited by Guthrie for Bulu (A.74) 'hair.'

Additional roots previously cited in Section B, *-pı̀kò 'wing' and *-tòb- 'to hit, smash.'

Section D — Root innovations found in Kusi and in Botatwe

Root innovation	*Distribution*	*Root wholly or partially displaced by innovated root; additional explanations and commentary*
*-kèt- 'to choose'	Nyasa, SE-Bantu; also in Botatwe	Semantic innovation: < Sangha-Kwa *-kèt- 'to cut' (reflexes cited by Guthrie for BC zones and relict SavB [WSav: Lunda; Mashariki: Kask [Rutara]; Kusi [Nyanja]); proposed semantics: to cut off > separate out, hence 'choose.' Displaced PM *-sààgul- (Table 4, Section A).
*-kúng- 'to tie up'	Nyasa, Shona, SE-Bantu; also Manda (Rufiji-Ruvuma: probable spread < Nyasa); also in Botatwe	Semantic innovation: < Sangha-Kwa *-kúng- 'to connect, put together,' seen in Guthrie CS 1226-27. Displaced PM *-túng- (see Table 3).
*-pìịp- 'to become black'	Nyasa, Shona, SE-Bantu (in secondary derived shapes); also in Botatwe	Morphological innovation: back-formation < Sangha-Kwa *-pìịpí 'darkness' (found in BC zones and relict SavB: Lwena [WSav], Sabi, and relict Mashariki [Kask: Bembe of Lakes: areal spread < C zone (?); Kusi: Makua, SE-Bantu]), as per arguments of Guthrie.

Section E — Root innovation found in Kusi and in Kaonde

Root innovation	*Distribution*	*Root wholly or partially displaced by innovated root; additional explanations and commentary*
*-támbò 'fiber string'	Nyasa, SE-Bantu; loanword in Shona; also in Kaonde	Semantic innovation: generalization of PM *-támbò 'string of snare trap.' Displaced PM *-gòyì, *-gòyè (see Table 4, Section A for these).

Additional root previously cited in Section C, *-sánà 'back.'

<u>*Section F — Root innovations found in Kusi and in Luyana-SW-Bantu*</u>

Root innovation	*Distribution*	*Root wholly or partially displaced by innovated root; additional explanations and commentary*
*-lı̭̀lı̭l- 'to become cold (of person)'	Kusi: Nyasa, Makua, SE-Bantu; also in Herero	Morphological innovation: < Sangha-Kwa *-lı̭̀lı̭̀ 'cold (n., of person),' found in BC zones and Kongo and in derived Sangha-Kwa root *-lı̭̀lim- 'to become cold, shiver.' Displaced *-lı̭̀lim-, found in BC zones, Kongo, and SavB (WSav: SW-Bantu; Sabi; Mashariki: Kask [NE-Coastal, Rufiji-Ruvuma]).
*-tùbı̭́ 'faeces'	Kusi: Nyasa, Shona, SE-Bantu; also in SW-Bantu	Morphological innovation: addition of *ma- (class 6) noun prefix to PB word *tù-bı̭́, class 13 prefix plus stem (see Table 4, Section E, *ma-bı̭́ 'faeces,' above), with fossilized prefix *tu- as part of new stem; separate parallel developments took place in three other languages (in Swahili with class 9 prefix added, and in two C zone languages, Bobangi with class 1a prefix and Ngombe with class 11 prefix).

Additional root previously cited in Section C, *-tı̭́tı̭̀, *-sı̭́tı̭̀ 'hair.'

Table 7: Sabi-Nyanja stem morpheme sharings

Root innovation	*Distribution*	*Root wholly or partially displaced by innovated root; additional explanations and commentary*
*-bàndà 'manifestation of spirit'	Nyanja; Sabi; Kaonde	Semantic innovation: < Nzadi-Kwa *-bàndà 'supernatural danger.'
*-sángalal- 'to be pleased'	Nyanja; Sabi; also in Yao; also in W.Luba	Morphological innovation: doubling of *-al- extension of SavB *-sángal- (see Table 2).

Additional roots previously cited in Table 4, Section A: *-sèCų́ 'eland' (loanword in Nyanja) and *-làm- 'to look after.'

Table 8: Nyanja-Central Shona stem morpheme sharings

Root innovation	*Distribution*	*Root wholly or partially displaced by innovated root; additional explanations and commentary*
*-tántàtú 'six'	[see Table 5, Section C]	Phonological innovation: devoicing assimilation of PM *-tándàtú (see Table 4, Section A).

Additional root previously cited in Table 5, Section B: *mu-ótò 'fire'

Table 9: West Lakes-Luban-Sabi stem morpheme sharings

Root <u>innovation</u>	<u>Distribution</u>	*Root wholly or partially displaced by innovated root;* <u>additional explanations and commentary</u>
*-sàká 'sorghum'	W.Lakes; Sabi	This term probably reflects the initial diffusion of sorghum southwestward from northern East Africa.
*-sèkè 'hamper'	W.Lakes; Sabi	This term may reflect the diffusionary spread of the particular item named.
*-kúmù 'thumb'	Lakes 'finger'; W.Lakes: Konjo, Rwanda-Rundi; also Rutara 'thumb'; *-kúmò: Luba-Sh 'big toe'; Sabi 'thumb'	Morphological innovation: < SavB *-kúm- 'to touch,' found in WSav (SW-Bantu), Luban ('bump against'), Sabi, and relict Mashariki (Lakes); also in Holoholo; also loanword shape in Tetela (C group). Semantics shows that Lakes 'finger' must be original sense; > 'thumb' only in areal western Lakes distribution, implying loan spread in that meaning to Luba-Sh and Sabi.
*-kʊ́lùe 'tortoise'	W.Lakes (Rundi); Takama; Sabi; also in Botatwe	Phonological innovation: irregular diphthongization in PB *-kʊ́lʊ̀ (see *-kàmbà 'tortoise,' Table 5).
*-pángá 'ram'	W.Lakes; Luba; also in Sabi, Kuba, Luchazi as 'sheep'	No earlier term because evidence indicates sheep were new introduction to Bantu of southern Congo Basin around 2000 B.P. (Ehret 1974). Distribution of term probably reflects initial sheep diffusion from Western Rift zone west & southwestward across basin into upper Zambezi region.
*-àlò 'country'	Lakes; also in Holoholo; also in Sabi; also in Nyanja [probable areal overlap < Sabi]	Semantic derivation: < PM *-àlò 'bare or open ground,' seen in Kask: Takama (Sukuma 'landing beach'), Upland (Kamba 'rock outcrop'), NE-Coastal (Seuta 'sugarcane field'); Kusi: SE-Bantu (Venda 'grave')
*-ʊ́ngʊ- 'to hear'	W.Lakes, Luba, Sabi; also Lega (*-úngʊ-)	[see Table 1, Section A.2]

Table 10: Stem morphemes of middle Zambezi areal spread

Root <u>*innovation*</u>	<u>*Distribution*</u>	*Root wholly or partially displaced by innovated root;* <u>*additional explanations and commentary*</u>
*-sàndul- 'to alter (tr.)'	Nyanja; Shona; Botatwe	Semantic innovation: < Nzadi-Kwa *-sàndul- 'to turn over,' found in Kongo, Botatwe, and relict Mashariki (Kusi: Shona).
*-sànó 'principal wife'	Nyanja; Yao; Sabi; Lunda, Lwena	Probably reflects cultural influences spreading since the beginning of Luangwa era in the archeology of the region (since c. 1000 A.D.)
*-lụ́lí 'shadow'	Shona, Botatwe, Nsenga (Sabi) [see Table 4, Section D]	
*-lùngù 'bead'	Venda; Sabi; Botatwe	Displaced PM *-úmà (see Table 4, Section G); diffusionary spread via spread of long-distance trade inland?
*-kùàlé 'partridge'	Tete, Shona (Manyika); Sabi [see Table 5, Section F]	Displaced ESavB *-kùàlí (see Table 3). Borrowing from Bantu language in which PB *i > [e].
*-kúmbil- 'to ask for'	Tete, Shona, Botatwe; also loanword shape in Tswa (SE-Bantu)	Displaced PB *-lómb-, found in ABC zones, Kongo, WSav, Luban, Holoholo, Sabi, Botatwe, and Mashariki (Kask: NE-Coastal; Kusi: Nyasa, SE-Bantu. Morphological innovation: < Sangha-Kwa *-kúmb- 'to call out,' seen in Guthrie's *-kúmbó 'name,' *-kúmbul- 'to answer,' and Herero (WSav) *-kumb-* 'to ask for.'

*-pàndul- 'to split'	Sena, Shona, Venda; Sabi; Botatwe also Yao (probable Nyanja loan)	Morphological innovation: < SavB *-pànd- 'to split' (see Table 1), but without surface semantic effect.
*-pátà 'valley'	Nyanja, Shona; Sabi; also Yao (probable Nyanja group loan)	
*-pémvù 'cockroach'	Nyanja; Sabi; also loanword shape in Luba-Sh; also in Yao (probable Nyanja loan)	Phonological innovation: spread of unexplained irregular outcome of Sangha-Kwa *-pénjų̀ (see Table 4, Section D, *-énjé 'cockroach').
*-pìlì 'hill'	Nyanja; Sabi; Kaonde; Nkoya; Lunda, Lwena; also in loanword shape in Botatwe	Displaced SavB *-lúndù (see Table 1).
*-pómb- 'to bind'	Nyanja, Shona; as Shona loanword in Venda; Sabi; also in Luba-Sh	Displaced PM *-bóp- (see Table 4, Section C).
*-tóngé 'cotton'	Nyanja, Yao; Sabi; Botatwe; Kaonde	Diffusionary spread with the spread of cotton-weaving in Later Iron Age?

Table 11: Stem morphemes of northern Kalahari areal spread

Root <u>*innovation*</u>	<u>*Distribution*</u>	*Root wholly or partially displaced by innovated root;* <u>*additional explanations and commentary*</u>
*-bèlé 'grain (gen.)'	Mashariki; SW-Bantu	[see Table 4, Section B]
*-sánsè 'spark'	Botatwe; SW-Bantu	Phonological innovation: nasal insertion in Sangha-Kwa *-sásè, *-sásì, found in C zone, WSav (Lwena), Luban, Sabi, and Mashariki (Kask: Lakes, Takama; Kusi: Shona, SE-Bantu).
*-ìlo, 'fire'	Mashariki; SW-Bantu [see Table 4, Section D]	
*-ìndì 'pit'	Mashariki; SW-Bantu [see Table 4, Section D]	
*-lį́án- 'to dance'	Shona; Botatwe; SW-Bantu; loanword shape in GiTonga (SE-Bantu); also in Lega (presumed separate innovation of same meaning)	Semantic innovation: from PM *-lį́án- 'to play.'
*-lùbí 'brain'	Shona, Venda; Nkoya; Luyana, SW-Bantu	Displaced PB *-òngó, found in ABC zones, WSav (Lwena, Lunda), Luban, Botatwe, and Mashariki (Kask: Lakes, Upland, NE-Coastal, Rufiji-Ruvuma; Kusi: Nyasa, SE-Bantu).

*-gų́ 'sheep'	SE-Bantu; SW-Bantu, Luyana (as *-gú); [Yeyi *-ꝁú is a separate loanword from undetermined Khwe source]	Khoikhoi loanword in Bantu; loan diffusion westward via Luyana is implied by Luyana shape; Yeyi form is a separate borrowing from Khwe (Khoisan) language; distribution of this root probably reflects initial diffusion of sheep to SW-Bantu.
*-máng- 'to bind'	Nyanja, Shona; Luyana, SW-Bantu	Displaced PM *-bóp- (see Table 4, Section C).
*-nùn- 'to become fat'	[see Table 4, Section C]	
*-pepo- 'wind'	[see Table 4, Section H]	
*-píù 'red'	Nyanja; Botatwe; Yao (probable Nyanja loanword); also in Herero (SW-Bantu)	
*-pítį̀ 'hyena'	Mashariki; Ovambo subgroup of SW-Bantu [see Table 4, Section H]	

Table 12: Stem morphemes of Luban-Sabi-Lwena or Luban-Sabi-SW-Bantu areal spread

Root <u>*innovation*</u>	<u>*Distribution*</u>	*Root wholly or partially displaced by innovated root;* <u>*additional explanations and commentary*</u>
*-kásù 'hoe'	Mwika; Nyanja; Sabi; also some so'n Lega; also in Luba-Sh; also in Lunda; also in Luyana	Distribution may partly mark the original diffusion of iron hoes in early Iron Age to the southwest and west of Lake Tanganyika and partly reflect later trade and ethnic interactions.
*-ì̧nà 'inhabitant'	WSav (SW-Bantu); Luban; Sabi	[see *-kʊ́á 'inhabitant' above]; semantic innovation: < PB *-ì̧nà 'mother,' i.e., those belonging to the same matrilineage or matriclan (those who inhabit the same kin-owned land); but this is surely a regional cultural spread of the last 1500 years (Ahmed 1996).
*-ùngà 'flour'	[see Table 4, Section D, *-tʊ̧́]	This may be a SavB root, but its block distribution across portions of the southern savanna belt makes it suspect as a very early loanword spread accompanying the first adoption of grain cultivation.

Table 13: Stem morphemes of Greater-Corridor areal spread

Root <u>*innovation*</u>	<u>*Distribution*</u>	*Root wholly or partially displaced by innovated root;* <u>*additional explanations and commentary*</u>
*-gʊ̀ìnà 'crocodile'	Takama; Nyakyusa; Matengo	Phonological innovation: < PM *-gʊ̀ènà by progressive vowel height assimilation.
*-tándà 'six'	Mwika-Rungwe, Njombe, some Ruvu (NE-Coastal), probably by loan spread < Njombe; also Sabi; also Holoholo	See Table 4, Section A, *-tándàtʊ́, for earlier roots for 'six.'

Classifications lexicostatistiques: bantou, bantou et bantoïde: de l'intérêt des "groupes flottants"

YVONNE BASTIN ET PASCALE PIRON
Musée Royal de l'Afrique Centrale, Tervuren
et Université Libre de Bruxelles

1. Introduction

Les classifications lexicostatistiques sont un outil parmi d'autres pour approcher la classification généalogique des langues sans tradition écrite ancienne. Elles permettent d'obtenir à moindre frais une classification préliminaire dont les résultats devront ensuite être précisés et validés par d'autres approches.

La classification lexicostatistique dont il est question ici fait suite à l'enquête portant sur 214 relevés et publiée en 1983. Elle est due à l'initiative d'A. Coupez qui a recueilli auprès de nombreux chercheurs et, de manière directe ou indirecte d'informateurs, un total de 542 relevés comprenant une liste de 92 mots du vocabulaire de base.[1]

Les correspondances pour chacun des items concernés ont été établies au Centre pour l'Etude des Langues africaines à Tervuren avant

[1] La liste reprenant le vocabulaire concerné figurera dans la publication que prépare M. Mann (SOAS, Londres). On y trouvera également le nom de tous les collaborateurs qui ont accepté de participer à ce travail d'équipe et des indications relatives à la localisation du relevé des lexèmes.

d'être transmises à M. Mann (SOAS) qui, au moyen de traitements informatiques sophistiqués, en a retiré une série d'arbres, dont deux sont classiques, le "Group Average" et le "Branch Average". Les autres qu'il qualifie de "Variable Neighbourliness" (VN) se différencient entre eux selon le seuil de voisinage exigé comme condition de rattachement de deux groupes. En considérant par exemple deux groupes comprenant respectivement 5 et 6 relevés, on obtient 5 x 6 = 30 indices de ressemblance. On peut dès lors imaginer réunir les deux groupes au niveau d'un cinquième des indices les plus élevés (VN20), d'un tiers (VN33), de la moitié (VN50) ou de n'importe quel pourcentage. On remarque que les arbres obtenus aux deux extrêmes de cette méthode, VN0 et VN100, sont équivalents au "Nearest Neighbour" et au "Furthest Neighbour" classiques. M. Mann suggère que les arbres à seuil bas sont plus accessibles aux influences latérales tandis que les arbres obtenus à partir de seuils plus élevés rendent davantage compte de liens historiques. On observe aussi que les analyses à seuil haut, comme le "Branch Average" tendent à produire des embranchements compensés et équilibrés alors que les branches isolées tendent à se multiplier dans les analyses à seuil bas.[2]

Le grand nombre de relevés et la complexité des calculs statistiques effectués par M. Mann fournit un base de réflexions dont il faut tirer des conclusions sur deux plans:

- Il faut interpréter les arbres de manière à en extraire une vue générale, en ignorant les problèmes de détails sur la manière dont s'organisent les langues bantoues. Il faut ensuite dégager, autant que faire se peut, la signification historique des embranchements.
- Dans le détail, la diversité des arbres permet de situer les groupes stables et d'identifier les langues ou les groupes problématiques, que P. Piron (1996, 1997) appelle "flottants" parce que leur articulation varie en fonction du type de calcul effectué.

Dans le cadre limité de cette étude, nous avons exclu les arbres basés sur les seuils extrêmes et choisi de prendre en considération les deux arbres "classiques" que sont "Branch Average" et "Group Average", ainsi que l'arbre central (VN50) et deux arbres issus de seuils de calcul inférieurs. Ce choix devrait permettre d'apercevoir certaines interférences entre filiation historique et influences latérales sans toutefois donner un poids trop conséquent à ces dernières.

---

[2] Voir aussi l'article de M. Mann dans le présent volume. Je remercie M. Mann pour son aide, en particulier pour sa contribution dans la rédaction de la présentation des modèles statistiques.

2. L'organisation globale des langues bantoues et l'articulation bantou/bantoïde

2.1. Organisation globale des langues bantoues

De manière très schématique, en ne retenant que les premiers embranchements, une comparaison basée sur cinq arbres permet d'établir quatre groupes principaux tels qu'ils sont présentés dans la carte réalisée à l'aide du programme Bantu Map Maker 3 de J. Lowe et Th. Schadeberg (1996) ci-dessous. Les langues "marginales" (partie des groupes C.40 et D.10, D.20 chez Guthrie, 1970) ont été écartées provisoirement car elles sont très marquées par l'impact de langues non bantoues, ce qui augmente l'écart par rapport à la filiation généalogique et explique qu'elles forment des embranchements périphériques. Il faudra les traiter avec des procédés spécifiques permettant d'écarter les distorsions liées aux influences latérales externes au bantou pour les situer correctement dans les embranchements généalogiques. Il faut souligner que leur étude est indispensable pour obtenir une vue cohérente sur la totalité de l'aire bantoue et notamment pour établir la clef de la dispersion est-sud des langues bantoues.

L'observation des embranchements supérieurs présentés dans les schémas ci-dessous (1) montre que l'agencement des groupements supérieurs diffère selon le type de calcul. C'est à ce niveau que l'interprétation est importante puisqu'elle a des implications historiques. On peut déjà remarquer que l'unité observée dans la partie orientale du domaine bantou rejoint le point de vue de plusieurs archéologues (O. Gosselain, P. Lavachery: communications personnelles, 1996) et que les tables de similarité montrent que la différenciation linguistique y est globalement moins accentuée que dans le reste du domaine bantou. Une présentation plus exhaustive des résultats sera publiée par l'auteur des calculs dans un avenir proche.

Certains groupes de langues sont flottants même au niveau des embranchements supérieurs (A.50, B.20, K/R) et méritent donc une attention toute particulière.

La réunion des zones K et R (centre-ouest) avec l'est-sud dans un seul arbre, l'arbre "20" peut être attribuée aux influences latérales. Le type de calcul qui aboutit à cet arbre favorise en effet l'impact de la diffusion. Les déclassements et reclassements successifs entre des langues telles que le pheende ou le ruund témoignent d'ailleurs de manière indirecte de l'observation d'interférences entre des langues de la zone L et de la zone K.

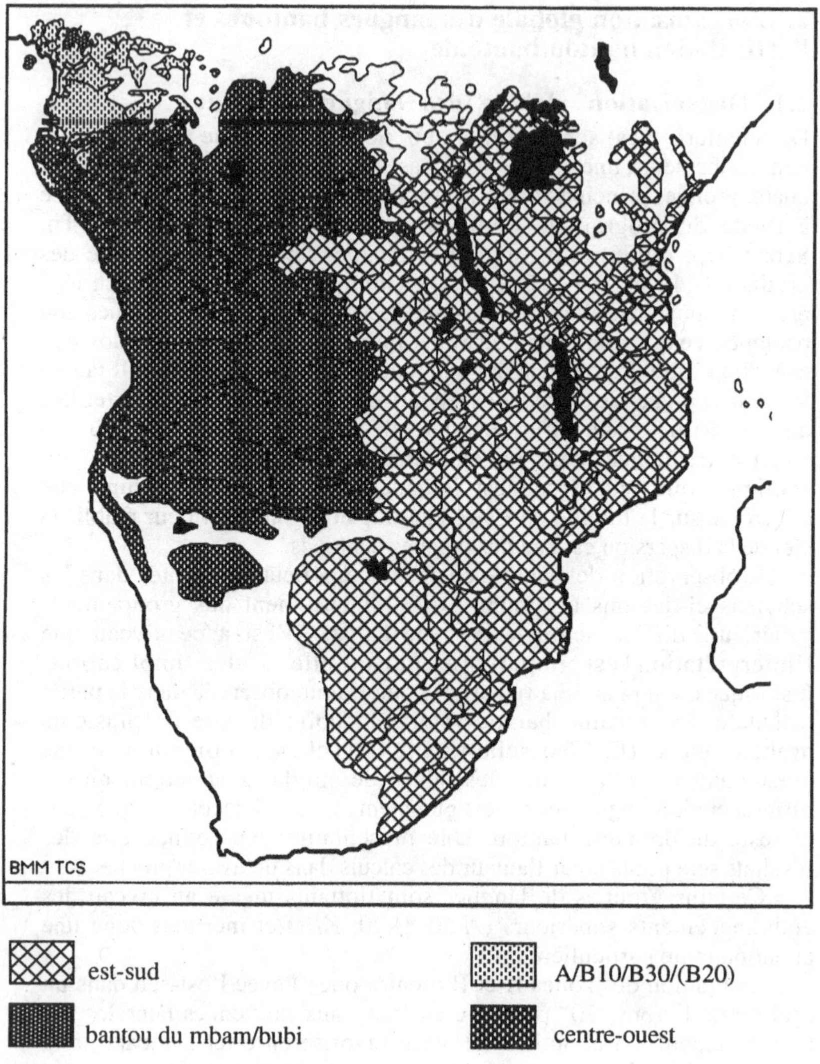

Map 1. Les grandes divisions du bantou

Le positionnement instable du groupe A.50 (langues bafia), qui tantôt s'associe au bantou du Mbam,[3] tantôt au reste de la zone A, doit retenir l'attention en raison d'une part de sa situation géographique et d'autre part du rôle que la place "historique" de ce groupe peut jouer dans

3 Appellation reprise à M. Dieu (1983).

l'interprétation de l'articulation bantou/bantoïde. Il serait donc très utile d'axer une étude comparative approfondie sur les langues bafia. Par contre, la solidarité entre les langues "bantoues du Mbam" est reconnue depuis longtemps: rappelons que le rapport privilégié entre les langues classées en A.60 et le nen avait déjà été remarqué en 1977 par L. Hyman et J. Voorhoeve ainsi que par L. Bouquiaux au colloque de Viviers (voir Bouquiaux, 1980). En revanche l'inclusion du A.31 bubi dans ce groupe est plus aléatoire et pourrait être liée à un regroupement "par défaut": cette langue apparaît en effet dans l'état actuel des connaissances comme un isolat dont la filiation historique devrait faire l'objet d'une étude spécifique. Le problème posé par les langues classées en B.20 sera traité sommairement au point 3.

(1) Organisation des embranchements dans les cinq arbres:

A50 et l'organisation du nord-ouest:

Group average/Branch average/20

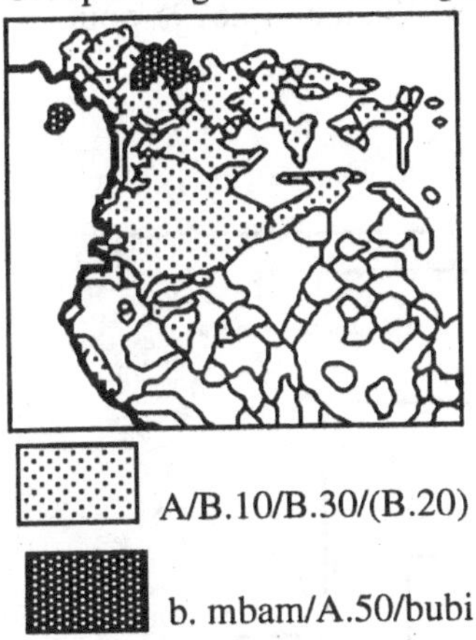

50/33

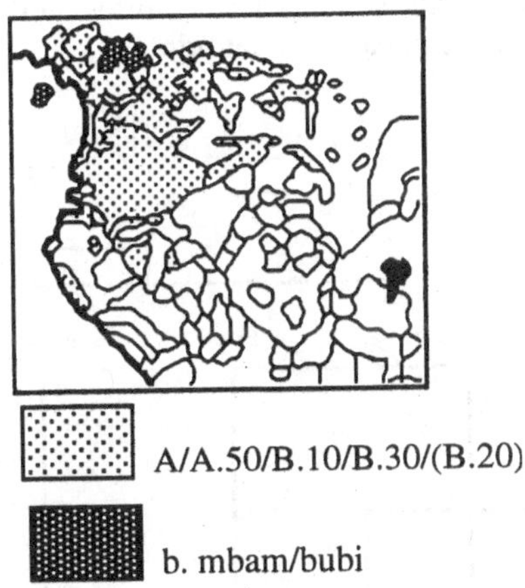

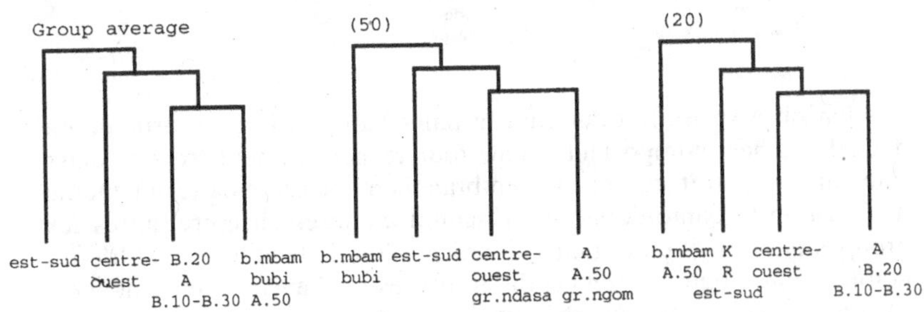

Branch average

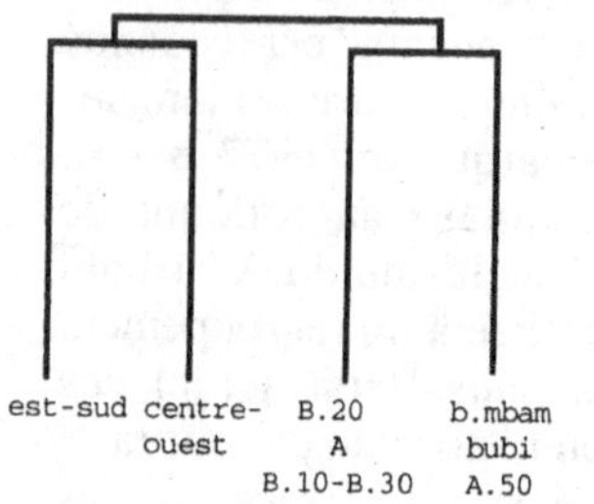

(33)

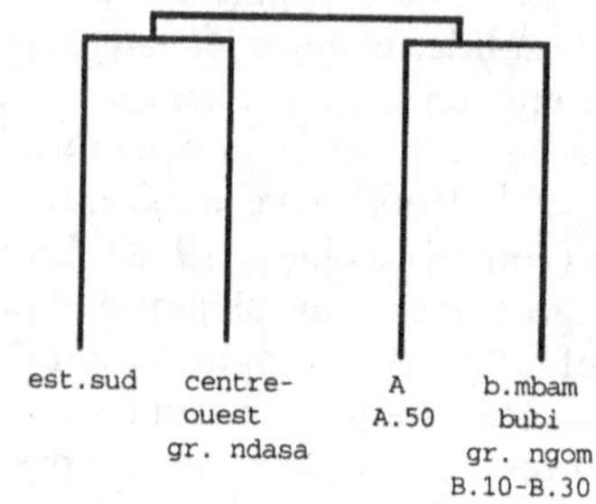

2.2. L'organisation bantou-bantoïde

La classification de P. Piron (1996) obtenue par le calcul de la "moyenne de groupe" du programme Lexistat de Th. Schadeberg fournit les résultats schématisés comme suit (2) par l'auteur (p.629) pour l'articulation bantou-bantoïde:

(2)

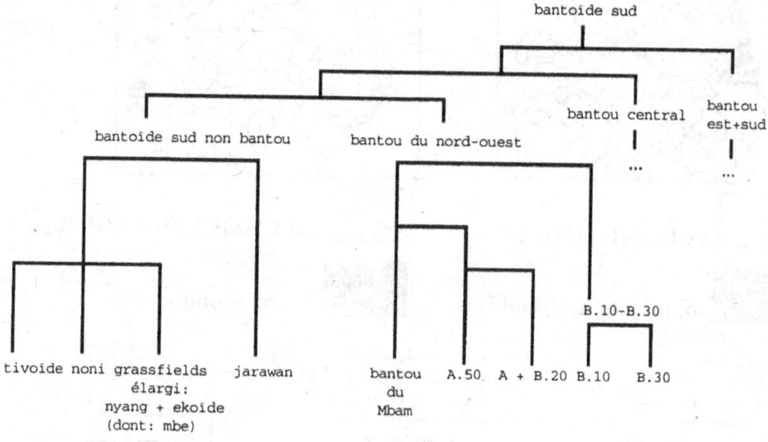

On observe un fait curieux: le bantou du nord-ouest, articulé en deux branches, comportant à leur tour respectivement trois et deux rameaux, apparaît comme un embranchement secondaire au même niveau que le bantoïde sud non bantou comprenant entre autres les groupes jarawan et Grassfields. L'articulation du bantou central (défini comme centre-ouest en 2.1) et du groupe est-sud avec cet ensemble est identique à celle que l'on observe dans le même arbre lorsqu'on traite uniquement du bantou: voir (1) Group average.

On a donc une classification originale qui n'est pas opposée aux résultats présentés pour le bantou stricto sensu; on y remarque que l'est-sud se retrouve dans un embranchement distinct.
Dans un arbre (3) basé sur la technique du "voisin le plus éloigné" (p.628) , on retrouve le bantou du Mbam et les parlers A.50 dans un sous-groupe de l'ensemble du bantoïde non bantou, ensemble auquel vient ensuite se rattacher un embranchement comprenant le reste du bantou.

(3)

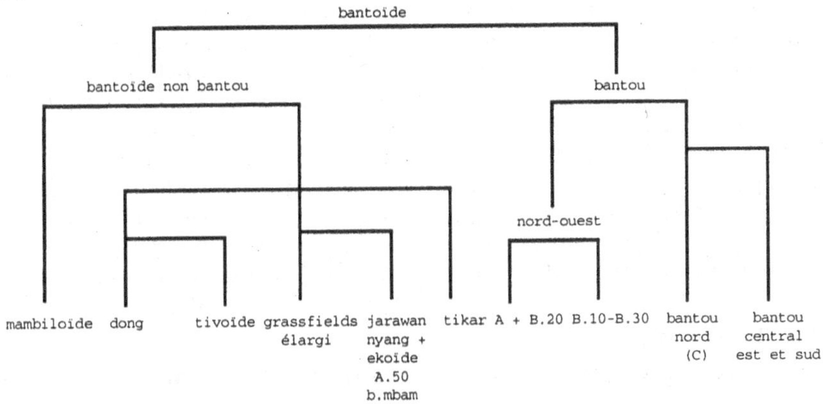

Tout ceci confirme que la clef de l'articulation entre bantou et bantoïde se situe dans le bantou du Mbam qui tantôt attire le reste de la zone A et B.10, 20, 30 vers le bantoïde, tantôt est associé, avec le seul A.50, à un embranchement bantoïde non bantou. La position fluctuante du groupe A.50 bafia qui avait été observée dans les classifications limitées au bantou se retrouve dans les différentes classifications qui associent le bantou traditionnel au bantoïde. On ne peut donc qu'insister sur l'intérêt de dégager ce qui relève d'une classification généalogique et ce qui est lié aux influences latérales. La position géographique des langues bafia, coincées entre différents groupes du bantoïde et le bantou du Mbam, dont les relations premières avec le bantoïde sont moins problématiques, pourraient opacifier quelque peu des relations diachroniques plus étroites avec le reste de la zone A.

3. Problèmes particuliers

3.1. La position des groupes B.10 et B.30

Quel que soit le type de calcul effectué par P. Piron et par M. Mann, les langues B.10 myene (nkomi, galwa, pongwe) et B.30 (tsogo, pinji, himba, pove) forment ensemble un premier embranchement: il y a donc deux sous-groupes stables qui constituent un groupe également bien établi. Cet embranchement rejoint, avec des modalités qui peuvent différer, le reste de la zone A dont il faut exclure le bantou du Mbam et parfois les langues du groupe A.50 bafia. L'affinité entre des langues du groupe B.10 et la zone A a été remarquée par plusieurs bantouïstes, parmi lesquels B. Janssens (1993:326) qui cite plusieurs traits morphologiques et phonologiques communs aux langues bantoues du Mbam, le nen en particulier, et le nkomi. Dans les approches lexicostatistiques, l'ensemble B.10/B.30 ne paraît pas se rattacher à un sous-groupe particulier de la zone A, ce qui permet de situer cet embranchement après celui du bantou du Mbam (et A.50), et avant la fourche qui comprend le reste de la zone A. On peut confirmer cette position en faisant appel, avec toutes les réserves qui s'imposent, à quelques distributions innovantes. Ainsi les langues B.10/B.30 ne participent pas à des innovations comme *-pìcí 7/8 'os' qui figurent en zone A, à l'exception du bantou du Mbam, comme dans les zones B, C et H. L'ensemble B.10/B.30 ne participe pas non plus à des innovations qui épargnent la zone A mais sont présentes dans le reste de la zone B telles que *-kúmbú 9 'nom'. On notera encore que la position du noeud B.10/B.30 indique une scission relativement précoce des deux sous-groupes. Ces quelques observations remettent en cause la classification de Guthrie et suscitent plus de questions qu'elles n'apportent de réponses.

3.2 Scission et flottement: les langues du groupe B20

Un des avantages de la lexicostatisque, au niveau des sous-groupements instables, est de poser les problèmes afin de susciter l'intérêt des chercheurs plus spécialisés dans les études régionales, et qui de ce fait sont plus compétents pour trouver les solutions. Dans ce cadre, il faudra aussi comparer les résultats engendrés par la lexicostatistique avec ceux qui ont été acquis ou qui seront proposés par d'autres chercheurs sur des groupes de langues déterminés. Dès à présent, il est clair qu'il faudra procéder à des études plus pointues pour établir la filiation généalogique de certaines langues et de certains groupes de langues. Dans le cadre de la lexicostatistique, on dispose du modèle méthodologique conçu par Th. Schadeberg (1992, 1995) pour démontrer la filiation généalogique de P.311 (e)koti[4] avec le P.31 makua ou du G.401 mwani avec le P.23 makonde.

Le problème des groupes flottants peut être illustré par les langues classées en B.20 par M. Guthrie (1970) dont il faut d'abord exclure le B.21 sekiyani qui est "isolé" et se rattache toujours très haut dans l'arbre. P. Ondo-Mebiame (1986) note que les "Bedenyi et les Mbiki de Guinée Equatoriale parleraient une/des langue(s) proche(s) du sekiyani". Il faut donc vérifier si cette position isolée n'est pas liée à l'absence de

4 Cette numérotation en trois chiffres pour les langues qui ne sont pas citées par Guthrie est reprise à Th. Schadeberg (BMM 3, 1996).

documents sur les parlers concernés dans l'étude lexicostatistique. La carte de migration supposée des Sekiyani qui figure dans le mémoire de P. Ondo-Mebiame oriente les recherches vers A.80/A.90. A l'appui de cette hypothèse, on relèvera que le sekiyani ne participe pas à l'aire d'innovation *-kúmbú "nom" caractérisant la zone B. Par contre, il partage avec la zone A (sans le bantou du Mbam) *-pìcí 7/8 'os' et *-kų́bà 9/10 'poule'.

Les autres langues du groupe B.20 qui figurent dans l'étude lexicostatistique ont une organisation identique: elles forment deux groupes stables bien distincts, l'un comprend le ndasa, le wumbvu, le kota et le mahongwe-shama; l'autre le ngom, le mbangwe et le sake. Chacun des groupes est "flottant", comme le montrent les arbres ci-dessous (4) qui reprennent l'embranchement le plus proche pour chaque groupe. De plus lorsqu'on reprend la classification générale (1), on voit que le rattachement aux embranchements supérieurs est lui aussi flottant.

(4)

B.20 groupe 1 ndasa: ndasa, wumbvu, kota, mahongwe-shama
groupe 1 ngom: ngom, mbangwe, sake

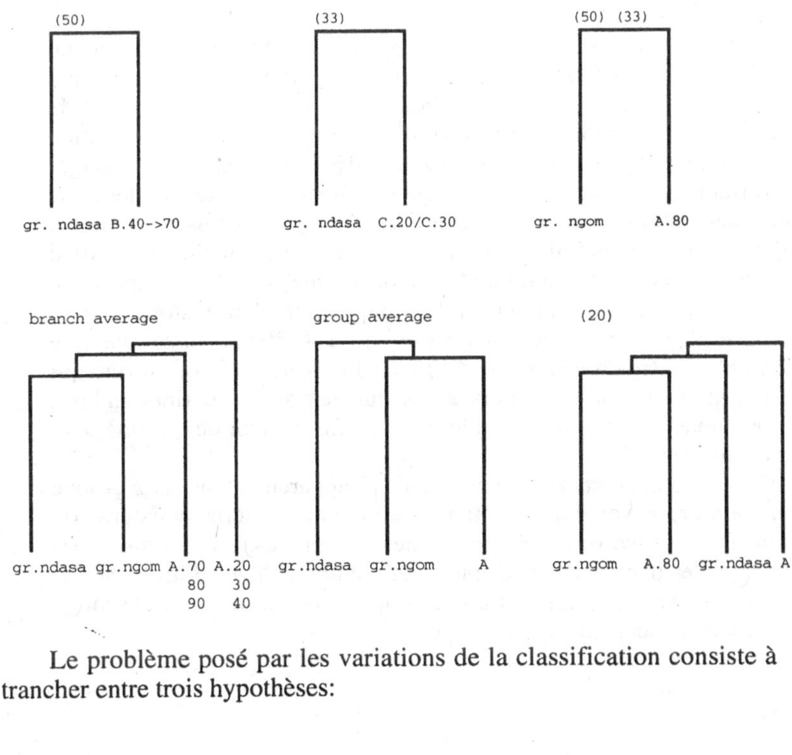

Le problème posé par les variations de la classification consiste à trancher entre trois hypothèses:

- On pose un ensemble généalogique B.20: plusieurs des langues issues de ce noeud sont très marquées par les influences de A, principalement A.80, ce qui explique l'attirance vers A.
- On pose un ensemble généalogique AX, dont les descendants sont marqués inégalement par les influences de B (et accessoirement de C.20/30). Cette influence est prépondérante dans le groupe ndasa, faible sur les langues de l'autre groupe.
- On pose un groupe B.20 et un groupe AX(A.80bis), ce dernier étant très marqué par les contacts avec B.20 (ndasa).

L'interprétation qui paraît plausible au premier abord est que les trois langues ngom, mbangwe et sake sont généalogiquement apparentées au groupe A.80. Leur situation géographique actuelle explique les interférences avec B.20 à proprement parler. A son tour, B.20 (kota, mahongwe-shama, ndasa, wumbvu) est attiré vers A en raison de l'impact qu'il a eu sur les langues du groupe ngom. Pour ce dernier, l'hypothèse avancée rejoint l'opinion de Vansina, dont les critères sont plus historiques que linguistiques. On observe que l'innovation *-pìcí 7/8 'os' est attestée partout, ce qui peut confirmer l'embranchement supérieur mais ne fournit aucun élément pour l'embranchement suivant. Si l'on considère la distribution de thèmes caractéristiques de la zone B tels que *-kúmbú 9/10 'nom', on note que celui-ci figure en ndasa et comme variante en wumbvu, à côté du thème protobantou *-jį́nà 5/6, dont les réflexes sont attestés dans les autres langues considérées ici. Cette distribution fait penser à une diffusion de l'innovation en relation avec la position géographique: elle est présente dans les parlers les plus méridionaux. Par déduction, on peut envisager une influence très marquée des langues B sud sur des parlers qui historiquement pourraient appartenir à la zone A. Mais l'usage des aires de dispersion ne conduit pas toujours aux mêmes conclusions. Ainsi quand on observe la distribution d'un mot comme 'viande', l'impression qui incite à poser que les langues du groupe ngom sont historiquement apparentées à la zone A, en particulier à A.80, subsiste puisque l'ensemble atteste un réflexe de *-tį́tú 9/10 < *-tį́tú 3 'forêt', forme qui figure également en B.25 kota alors que les autres parlers (ndasa, wumbvu, mahongwe-shama) ont le réflexe conservateur de *-ɲàmà 9/10 'viande, animal'.

On notera donc provisoirement que si l'apparentement A.80/groupe ngom paraît relativement bien établi, l'articulation interne et externe du groupe B.20 ndasa pose des problèmes complexes, dans lesquels on perçoit que les phénomènes de contact et d'embranchement historique se superposent. Selon l'angle d'observation, on note à travers l'ensemble des résultats lexicostatistiques que ces langues soit

- s'écartent progressivement de B pour se rapprocher de A: 1. kota, 2. mahongwe-shama, 3. wumbvu, 4. ndasa;
- quittent A pour se rapprocher de B, dans l'ordre inverse: 1. ndasa, 2. wumbvu, 3 mahongwe-shama, 4. kota

Il n'est d'ailleurs pas évident que la filiation historique soit identique pour chacune des langues de ce sous-groupe et il ne faudra pas négliger le rapprochement avec C.20/30 qui apparaît dans l' arbre 33 (4) pour résoudre ce problème. Une étude qui inclurait toutes les langues (avec leurs variations dialectales) classées en groupe "B.20", dont les locuteurs sont dispersés au Gabon et au Congo, pourrait contribuer à fournir la clef historique.

3.3. Variations dialectales et influences latérales: le cas de B44 lumbu-bwisi

Les difficultés engendrées par la superposition de la filiation généalogique et des influences latérales sont transparentes dans quelques cas où leur mise en évidence est assurée par les variations dialectales. Ce point peut être illustré à l'aide des cinq relevés dont on dispose pour le B.44 lumbu-bwisi:

- Gabon (enquêteur: Marchal-Nasse)
  1: entre la zone punu et la mer, au nord de Mayumba: "lumbu côtier"
  2: estuaire Libreville (localité d'origine de l'informateur?)
- Congo
  3: Nkola (Kouilou), enquêteur Ndamba
  4: Banda (Niari), enquêteur Elounga
  5: bwisi: Loubetsi (Niari), enquêteurs Ndamba et Baka

L'articulation des parlers du groupe peut être schématisée comme suit (5):

(5)

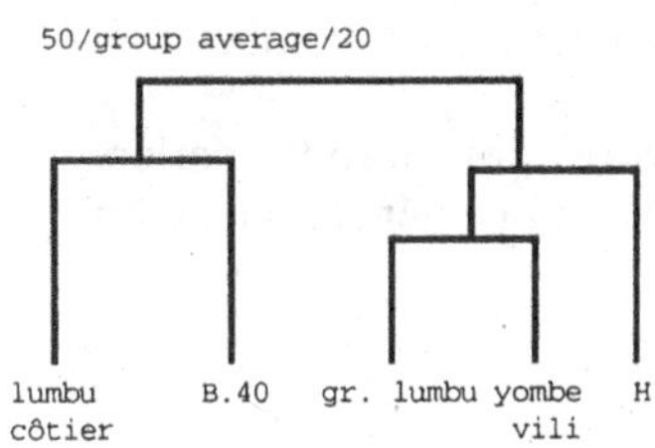

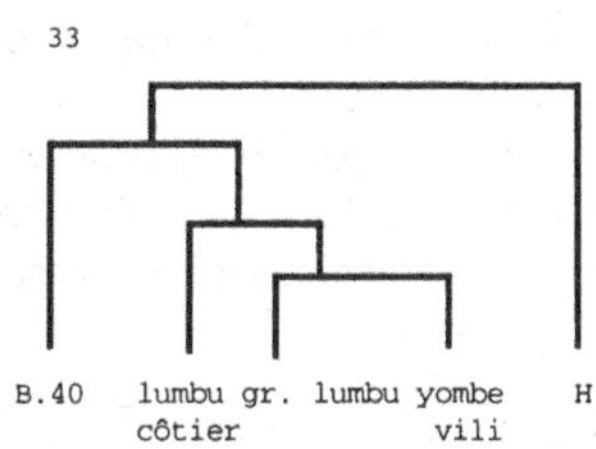

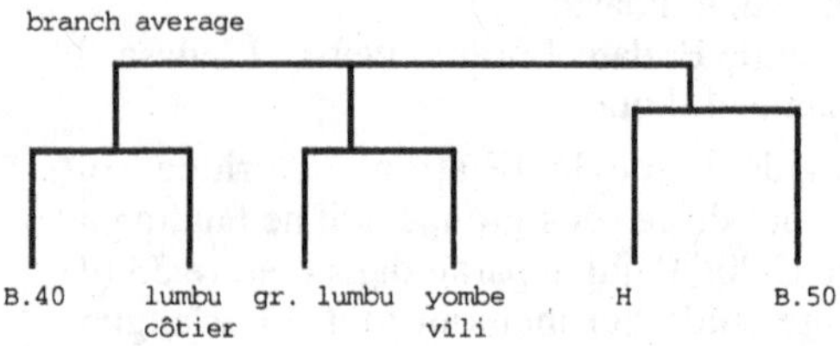

On observe que:

- le lumbu côtier est le seul qui se rattache nettement au groupe B.40 punu-sangu, mais il est aussi celui qui en est géographiquement le plus proche;
- les autres parlers lumbu-bwisi[5] sont solidaires du yombe-vili et, par ce noeud intermédiaire, de la zone H;
- le lien entre le lumbu côtier et les autres parlers, tel qu'il apparaît dans l'arbre "33", est moins étroit que le lien entre ces parlers et le yombe-vili.

De plus, il est curieux de constater que les langues classées en B.40 forment toujours leur premier embranchement avec la zone H, ce lien particulier a déjà été observé par plusieurs auteurs dont A.E. Meeussen qui avait souligné cette proximité à maintes reprises. En ce qui concerne le lumbu et le bwisi, les auteurs de l'Atlas linguistique du Congo (1987, p.38) notent que "cette classification (en zone B), est contestée par les locuteurs-natifs et est contradictoire avec leurs traditions orales. L'appartenance au groupe koongo (H.10) est revendiquée".

Cette situation et ces observations engendrent deux questions:

- le lumbu côtier est-il marqué par des apports de langues contiguës du groupe B.40 et généalogiquement apparenté au yombe-vili ou, au contraire, les parlers lumbu appartiennent-ils généalogiquement au groupe B.40 punu-sangu, ce qui implique que certaines variétés soient profondément marquées par l'impact des parlers yombe et/ou vili ?
- les affinités qui apparaissent dans la classification entre les parlers classés en B.40 et la zone H reflètent-elles un lien généalogique ou sont-elles liées aux aires de contact?

---

5 Le bwisi est toujours—et logiquement si l'on considère sa position géographique—très étroitement relié au lumbu de Banda (Niari).

3.4. L'impact des langues véhiculaires et des influences latérales: le E.64a dawida et E.74b saghala.

Un autre difficulté est liée à la superposition d'une langue véhiculaire, le swahili en particulier, principalement lorsque son utilisation tend à supplanter les langues locales.

Ce problème peut s'ajouter à celui des influences latérales et rendre plus complexe encore l'interprétation des arbres. Ce point peut être illustré par deux langues orientales, le E.74a dawida et le E.74b saghala. Dans l'ouvrage consacré aux langues de Tanzanie, Nurse et Philippson (1980, p.39 et 52) notent que les parlers dawida et saghala se sont influencés mutuellement alors que le dawida est historiquement apparenté au groupe E.60 caga et le saghala aux langues de la zone G. Dans cette hypothèse, les arbres montrent que l'influence du saghala prédomine puisque le rattachement ne se fait jamais avec le groupe. E.60. L'impact du saghala doit être suffisant pour attirer les deux langues dans le groupe G.20, mais l'écart historique du dawida augmente sans doute la distance du rattachement. L'embranchement généalogique différent de chacune des langues repose sur un faisceau d'indices, notamment sur les différences importantes dans les réflexes des segments. On remarque en outre que les deux langues ne font pas les mêmes emprunts au swahili, mais on observe parfois des faits curieux: ainsi le réflexe de *-bókò "'bras' est attesté en E.60 et en saghala alors que le dawida, le swahili et toutes les langues de la zone G comprises dans l'enquête, à l'exception du kinga, ont un réflexe de *-kónò dont le sens premier est 'avant-bras' (Guthrie 1970, CS 1142). De plus, chacune des langues atteste des lexèmes isolés et différents, empruntés à des langues non bantoues (Ehret and Nurse, 1981). Cette superposition d'influences latérales diverses associées à l'impact différencié d'une langue véhiculaire accentue sans doute la distance observée pour le noeud qui relie ces deux langues l'une à l'autre d'une part, et pour celui qui les relie à des ensembles plus étendus d'autre part. Ces interférences multiples opacifient également les liens généalogiques. Dans ce cas aussi, on observe que la lexicostatistique est un marqueur qui permet de situer les problèmes sans apporter de réponse définitive.

4. Conclusions

L'apport de la lexicostatistique n'est pas négligeable et sa validité relative découle du fait que les indications concernant les classifications généalogiques des langues sans tradition écrite ancienne obtenues par la lexicostatistique sont souvent confirmées à posteriori par d'autres études. La performance des outils statistiques dont on dispose aujourd'hui permet de pondérer les résultats tout en fournissant une vue générale sur les embranchements.

D'un autre côté, la multiplicité des arbres permet de repérer les problèmes et incite à rechercher dans chaque cas les causes des divergences dans la hiérarchisation des groupes de langues. Il faut alors procéder à des recherches poussées pour établir le rapprochement généalogique le plus plausible, ce qui implique une documentation suffisante. Il est également possible d'affiner les calculs statistiques en y intégrant d'autres variables ou en modifiant celles-ci. Il peut être intéressant par exemple de comparer les résultats obtenus en traitant l'ensemble du vocabulaire de base à ceux qui résulteraient d'une étude ne retenant que les rétentions du protobantou d'une part et les innovations d'autre part. Il n'est dépourvu d'intérêt d'observer les embranchements formés en excluant les langues suspectes d'impact sur un parler posant problème ou encore pondérer les réflexes d'un même étymon en fonction de différences phonétiques, phonologiques ou morphologiques. L'interprétation des différences et des constantes obtenues dans les arbres devrait permettre d'aboutir à des démonstrations fiables dans une majorité de cas surtout si l'on y associe une étude comparative exhaustive.

Références

Bastin, Yvonne, André Coupez & B. de Halleux. 1983. Classification lexicostatistique des langues bantoues (214 relevés). Bruxelles. Académie royale des Sciences d'Outre-Mer, *Bulletin des Séances* 27, 2: 173-199.

Bouquiaux, Luc (ed.). 1980. *L'expansion bantoue*. Actes du Colloque international du CNRS Viviers (France), 4-16 avril 1977. Paris, SELAF, numéro spécial 9, vols 2-3, pp 290-848.

CELCO. 1987. *Atlas Linguistique du Congo. Inventaire préliminaire.* ACCT, CERDOTOLA, Equipe nationale du Congo.

Dieu, Michel & Patrick Renaud. 1983. Atlas linguistique de l'Afrique Centrale (ALAC): *Situation linguistique en Afrique Centrale. Inventaire préliminaire: Le Cameroun.* Paris, ACCT; Yaounde, CERDOTOLA et DGRST.

Ehret, Christopher & Derek Nurse. 1981. The Taita Cushites, *Sprache und Geschichte in Afrika* 3: 125-168.

Guthrie, Malcolm. 1970. *Comparative Bantu.* Vols. 3-4. Farnborough: Gregg International Publishers.

Janssens, Baudouin. 1992-1993. Doubles réflexes consonantiques: quatre études sur le bantou de zone A (bubi, nen, bafia, ewondo). [thèse non publiée, Université Libre de Bruxelles].

Lowe, John B. & Thilo Schadeberg. 1996. *Bantu Map Maker 3 (programme informatique).* Leiden, Rijksuniversiteit te Leiden.

Nurse, Derek & Gérard Philippson. 1980. The Bantu Languages of East Africa: lexicostatistical survey, in: Polome, Edgar C. & Christopher

P.Hill (eds), *Language in Tanzania*. Oxford: Oxford University Press, 26-67.

Ondo-Mebiame, Pierre. 1986. *Esquisse phonologique et morphologique du Seki.* [Mémoire non publié, Université Omar Bongo, Libreville.]

Piron, Pascale. 1996. Identification lexicostatistique des groupes bantoïdes stables. *The Journal of West African Languages* 25, 2: 3-30

Piron, Pascale. 1997. *Classification interne du groupe bantoïde*. München-Newcastle (Lincom). Studies in African Linguistics, Volumes 11-12.

Schadeberg, Thilo. 1985. *Lexistat (programme informatique)*. Leiden, Rijksuniversiteit te Leiden.

Schadeberg, Thilo. 1992. Kimwani: Historical language contact at the Southern fringe of Swahili. Communication, Tervuren, Séminaire MRAC.

Schadeberg, Thilo. 1995. De Swahili-talen van Mozambique. Communicatie: KNAW.

A Note on Historical and Geographical Relations Among the Bantu Languages

MICHAEL MANN
School of Oriental and African Studies, London

Reference has been made in this Round Table (Nurse, this volume, Bastin and Piron, this volume) and elsewhere (Vansina 1995) to classifications based on a 92-word vocabulary sampled over 542 Bantu language varieties. Classifications made were of two kinds: hierarchical (inviting historical interpretation), and geographical (reflecting areal influences). Hierarchical classifications producing tree-diagrams were produced according to two well-known methods (Branch Average and Group Average) for comparison with previous more limited analyses, but also according to a series of seven graded approaches (VN0–17–33–50–67–83–100)[1] by attaching different weights to the conflicting requirements of connectivity and exclusivity—and generally finding the resultant trees wanting.

In the ideal world imagined by the tree model, we should expect that all the languages within any group or branch would be more closely related to one another than any of them was to any language outside, but in the real

[1] Five "variable neighbourliness" analyses were made first (VN0–33–50–67–100); these together with Branch Average and Group Average were the seven analyses available to Vansina (1995). Subsequently VN20 and VN25 were produced experimentally, but for presentation it was decided to use VN17 and VN83 to produce the series of analyses listed above.

world the groups that we claim to detect often fail in connectivity (the relationship between perhaps extreme members of the group is feeble) or in exclusivity (some members of the group display ambiguous relationships with other languages outside it). The graded approach described here affords a formal measure of connectivity and exclusivity.

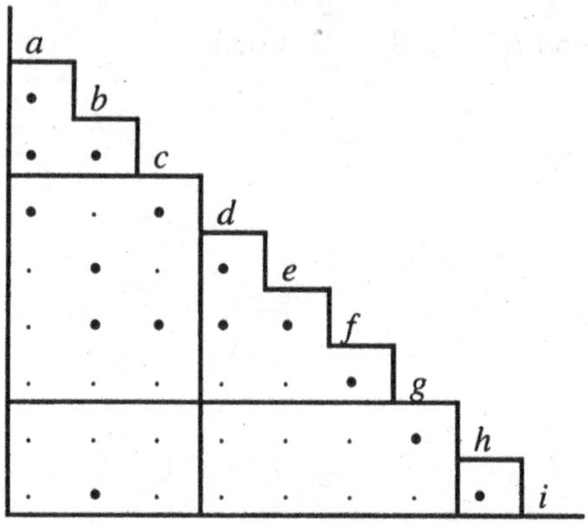

Figure 1. Connectivity and exclusivity

All the analyses referred to above rest on a count of shared vocabulary for each pair of languages in the sample, set out conventionally in a triangular matrix as in Figure 1. In this case instead of using actual figures, we have imagined a stage in the analysis in which *abc*, *defg* and *hi* have been established as groups above a particular level of similarity, and that all figures above this value are represented by a heavy blob and all below by a lighter blob. Group *abc* is fully connected at this level—all the blobs in the top jagged triangle are black—and so trivially is *hi*. But group *defg* is only 4/6 connected ("67% connectivity"), since the similarities *dg* and *eg* are below the current level. At the same time, group *defg* shows only limited (40%) exclusivity, since of the 10 similarities above the current level involving languages of the group, 6 are external (*ad, cd, be, bf, cf, gh*) and only 4 are internal (*de, df, ef, fg*).

By what criteria is it decided when to allow two groups to be merged into a larger group, e.g. to make a new group *abcdefg* out of *abc* and *defg*? Some traditional methods (Group Average, Branch Average) do computations on the similarities involved (the 12 figures in the upper rectangle of Figure 1). The VN approach uses the median and related statistical concepts. The median of a set of figures is a value such that there is equal number of figures above and below this value; this is our VN50, with 50% of the figures above the current value used as a minimum condition for merging two groups. But we can set this threshold at any value, insisting that only a third be higher (VN33) or that a full five-sixths should be higher (VN83). Of the two extreme cases, VN0 (requiring only a single linkage between two groups) is equivalent to the traditional Nearest Neighbour, and VN100 (requiring all links to be at or above the current value) is equivalent to Furthest Neighbour or Complete Linkage.[2] VN0 guarantees exclusivity (at the expense of connectivity, since groups are formed with only minimal linkage), while VN100 guarantees connectivity at the sometimes massive expense of exclusivity. Intermediate approaches compromise. Trees drawn according to these methods are accompanied by miniature pie-diagrams on each stem measuring the connectivity and exclusivity of the groups they represent.

It appears informally that analyses that insist least on connectivity reflect recent and generally apparent influences, while analyses most strict on connectivity and consequently lax on exclusivity plausibly reflect more distant relationships (Jan Vansina commented that of the original five trees (VN0–33–50–67–100), only VN100—equivalent to Furthest Neighbour—made any sort of sense of the remoter relationships). It is possible therefore that the series of intermediate trees will give insights into intermediate time-depths, but always with much caution in interpretation since the distortions are patent and measurable.

While the hierarchical classifications referred to above are based on the entire 146611 pair-by-pair similarities between the 542 languages, the geographical classification presented in Figure 2 considers the relationship of each language with its geographical neighbours only (some 1611 measurements in all), and has been conceived to highlight the location of

---

2 For hierarchical classification methods in general see e.g. Jardine & Sibson (1968) or Everitt (1974). I did not find what I have called "Variable Neighbourliness" defined precisely in the literature, although it is related to a series of hierarchical methods which vary in the precise criterion used for forming a cluster, and is unlikely to be wholly original. The sheer volume of close to 150,000 inter-language comparisons was too great to hold in computer memory, so they were first sorted and processed in turn from the most similar to the least, and a method adopted which considered the number of links already seen (and therefore above the current level) between two clusters rather than their actual numerical values. In the case considered above, where there are twelve similarities to be considered between groups *abc* and *defg*, according to the threshold of neighbourliness adopted the two groups will form a new cluster after 1 (VN0), 2 (VN17), 4 (VN33), 6 (VN50), 8 (VN67), 10 (VN83) or 12 (VN100) links have been seen. The idea of measuring the distortion (or "stress") involved in constructing a tree or sub-tree is also well-established, though the forced order of processing again dictated the precise measure used.

When I was subsequently asked to produce conventional Group Average and Branch Average classifications of the data for comparison, I succeeded by reducing all measures of similarity to the nearest 0.4%, so that individual values could be stored in the memory space required for a single character; I made no attempt to calculate stresses for such approximate data.

marked geolinguistic discontinuity. Each language is associated with a point on the map (corresponding in principle to the provenance of the linguistic informant), suggested here by the convergence of the grey background lines that represent the pairs of languages whose similarity has been considered. Wherever this similarity is feeble—less than 50%—a "boundary" has been drawn in by a black line between the triangles on either side. It does indeed show some isolated languages and groups—Ndebele (1), Chaga (2), Thagicu (3) and the relative isolation of Shona (4) and other Southern Bantu languages (5). But almost everywhere the boundaries "leak", and there is a chain of connecting similarities from the Swahili of southern Somalia (6) to Herero in the South West (7) and by sometimes narrow funnels far into the recesses of the North-West (8, 9). The overwhelming impression is of a "maze" of relationships (French "labyrinthe").[3]

In contrast Figure 3 brings us back to the artificial world of hierarchy. The heavy lines here represent the boundaries between groups of languages constituted at a level of 50% similarity according to the VN17 analysis. All boundaries are here continuous except where we run off the edge of the map. In the grey background are shown not the entirety of inter-neighbour links, but only those that are closer than 50% (the converse of the boundaries of Figure 2). Inspection will show numerous places where black boundaries cut through grey links (e.g. 10): failures in exclusivity exacted by the hierarchical method; less apparent perhaps are grey connections missing within a group (e.g. 11)—weak links representing failures of connectivity.

The lexicostatistical study that is briefly reported here has a long history and has enjoyed the contributions of many scholars, to be fully acknowledged in the full presentation now being prepared; the most recent work represents a collaboration with Yvonne Bastin and André Coupez of Tervuren, who have been responsible for data collation and cognation judgements, and with Jan Vansina in Wisconsin, who has been a chief animator and advocate. Publication is planned to include schematic maps for each gloss, a series of heteroglossic maps like Figure 2 at different levels of similarity, and documentation and discussion of the different hierarchical analyses.

---

3 The heteroglossic maps described and illustrated here were inspired by straight-line maps in Kurath 1972, but the precise methodology I worked out for myself. Inevitably I was re-inventing the wheel: it appears that the triangular network and associated polygons are known to some mathematical geographers as Thiessen or Voroni polygons, but I only recently found reference in Laurini & Thompson (1992: 246). I am unaware of any previous use of these diagrams in linguistics, other than in theses of my own students.

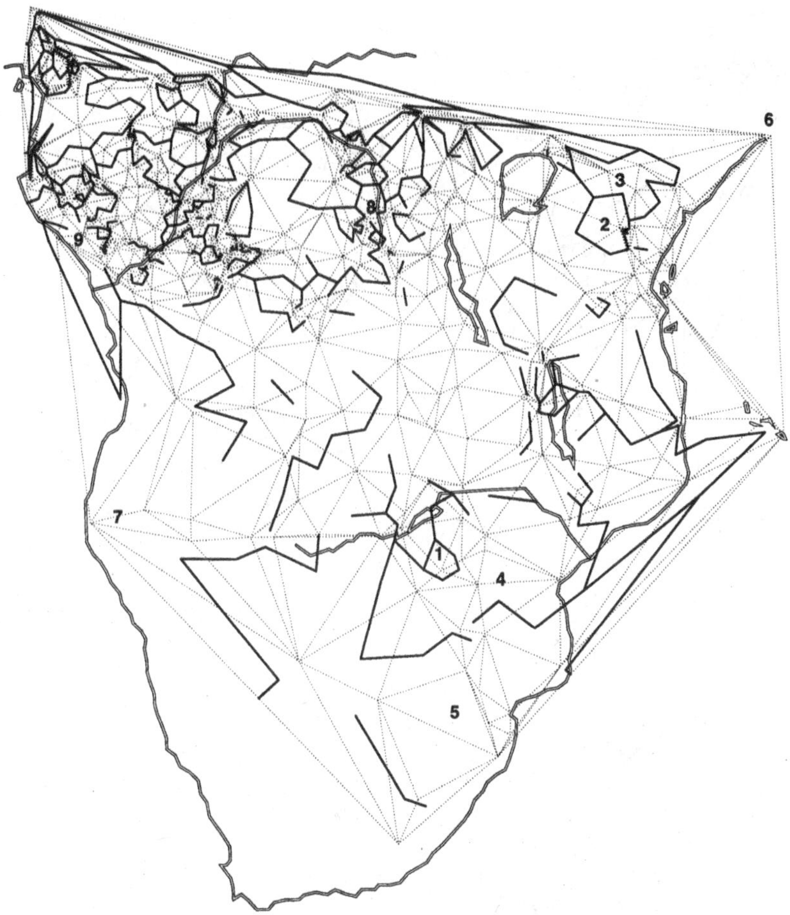

Figure 2. Discontinuities among Bantu languages

Figure 3. Groups formed by VN17 tree sliced at 50% compared with actual similarities over 50%

References

Everitt, Brian. 1974. *Cluster analysis.* London: Heinemann Educational Books for Social Science Research Council.

Jardine, Nicholas & Robin Sibson. 1968. The construction of hierarchic and non-hierarchic classifications, *Computer Journal* 11: 117-184.

Kurath, Hans. 1972. *Studies in area linguistics.* Bloomington: Indiana University Press.

Laurini, Robert & Derek Thompson. 1992. Fundamentals of spatial information systems. San Diego: Academic Press.

Vansina, Jan. 1995. New linguistic evidence and 'the Bantu expansion', *Journal of African History* 36: 173-195.

Contact and Lexicostatistics in Comparative Bantu studies*

THOMAS J. HINNEBUSCH
University of California, Los Angeles

1. Introduction

This paper sets as its course a discussion and demonstration of the potential a commonly applied methodology in Bantu comparative linguistic studies—lexicostatistics and, only incidentally, the Comparative Method—have in detecting contact situations among Bantu languages. Lexicostatistics (henceforth LS) and the Comparative Method have both played roles in producing genetic classifications of Bantu languages and in subgrouping

*A version of this paper was first presented at the 1st World Congress of African Linguistics, Kwaluseni, Swaziland, July 18-22, 1994. I wish to thank the organizers of that conference, Professor Bob Herbert and Professor Euphrase Kunene, for their generous assistance in supporting my participation. I would also like to acknowledge my debt to my colleague Derek Nurse for his substantive contributions to this paper not to mention the ideas I've honed over the years about methodology and comparative/historical Bantu through our discussions and debates about Bantu. Derek is responsible for the lexicostatistical analysis of the Sabaki languages on which some of this paper is based and which has been published in our book on Sabaki. The present views and interpretation of that analysis are my own. I would also like to thank Professors Larry Hyman and Jean-Marie Hombert for their suggestions and help in making this a better paper.

them. Their role in identifying contact situations is only recently gaining some attention (Nurse and Walsh 1992, Hinnebusch 1992). This paper is a contribution to that discussion.

For purposes of discussion here, by lexicostatistics we mean any statistical study of a limited set of vocabulary items of a group or groups of languages which result in numerical indices of similarity and are then analyzed to yield a classification, in some cases genetic, in others, not.[1] This would include, for example, Swadesh-type studies (see Embleton 1986) which use word lists of basic lexical items (e.g. Heine 1973; Nurse and Philippson 1975, Mann 1980, Coupez et al. 1975, Bastin et al. 1979, 1983); Henrici's (1973) study of Guthrie's Test Languages, and dialectometrical studies (Möhlig's 1980d, 1986a; Möhlig et al. 1980), etc. For some scholars, e.g., Teeter (1963),[2] glottochronology—essentially hypotheses about rates of linguistic change, rates of loss of basic vocabulary, and the relation of these to a time depth (see Embleton 1986:2)—is part of LS. Most scholars using LS in African studies distinguish LS and glottochronology and eschew the latter. This study like most others in the Comparative Bantu field ignores glottochronology, the attempt to assign specific dates to successive splits among genetic groups.

The Comparative Method is the procedure by which form-meaning elements of related or potentially relateable languages are matched in sets of correspondences in order to establish their genetic relatedness and to reconstruct the proto-language from which they descend (Hoenigswald 1960, Anttila 1989). Guthrie's work on the Bantu languages is still the preeminent example of the methodology as applied in Bantu comparative studies. Other examples includes Meeussen's work (1980 [1969]) and that of other scholars from the Tervuren school.

By contact, I have in mind the widest possible understanding of contact-induced phenomena that occur when two or more languages interfere with one another for whatever reason, be it geographical proximity, cultural and historical intrusion, etc. For a wide-ranging discussion of the topic see Thomason and Kaufman (1988).

2. The function of LS in Comparative Bantu studies

After early work in the 50s by Meeussen (1956), Coupez (1956), and Olmsted (1957),[3] soon after the development of the methodology by

---

[1]For a useful, up-to-date, discussion of LS see Embleton 1986.

[2]Teeter's definition (1963:638): "...the statistical manipulation of lexical similarities for the purpose of making inferences as to genetic relationship and subrelationship among languages, including the attempts, known as glottochronological studies, to fix the dates of so-called language splits."

[3]While Greenberg's work (1957, 1963) is not avowedly lexicostatistical in the Swadesh sense, his methodology of "mass comparison" had profound implications for the classification of Bantu, and thus his work should be

Swadesh and colleagues and its application in American comparative studies, LS hardly played a role in Bantu studies. It was ignored by Guthrie.[4] It wasn't until the late 60s that scholars began to take another look at the methodology. Its revival was due to several events. First, there were the African country language and linguistic surveys that were being done in eastern and central Africa sponsored by the Ford foundation and mostly published in the 70s (Ladefoged, Glick, and Criper 1972, Whiteley 1974, Bender et al. 1976, Ohannessian and Kashoki 1978, Polomé and Hill 1980). Ladefoged used LS to measure mutual intelligibility in Uganda (Ladefoged, Glick, and Criper 1972) and Nurse and Philippson (1980a) used it to work out a classification of Tanzanian languages for practical purposes related to education and literacy; they were also motivated to provide historians with evidence for the interpretation of prehistory (Nurse and Philippson 1980b:685). Kashoki and Mann (1978) looked at lexical similarity percentages in connection with a discussion of dialect and language differences in Zambian Bantu languages. Lehmann (1978) included a LS study in his discussion of the languages of the Kafue Basin in Zambia.

While this work was going on, Heine and associates (Heine 1973, Heine, Hoff, and Vossen 1977), using a selected but balanced sample of languages, were busy in Cologne doing a classification of all of Bantu as a contribution to the debate that was then raging about Bantu origins and expansion. Henrici in London was taking another look at Guthrie's test language data and applying statistical methodology to reinterpret the data or, at least, present results using techniques that were accepted methodology in other disciplines (Henrici 1973; see also Mann 1980).[5] Möhlig was also working in East Africa and applying testable methodologies to subgroup Central Kenyan Bantu languages, using a methodology from European dialectology known as dialectometry (e.g., see Möhlig 1986a and b; Winter 1980; Möhlig et al. 1980). In Nurse's dissertation (1979), the research for which was done in the late 60s and early 70s, LS is used to work out intermediate subgroupings; other studies with similar intentions include Williams (1973), Hinnebusch (1976a and b), Gerhardt (1980), Batibo (1989), etc. Linguists in Tervuren were also active (Coupez, Evrard, and Vansina 1975, Bastin 1979, 1983; Bastin, Coupez, and de Halleux 1979, 1983), producing to date the most ambitious and comprehensive studies.

---

mentioned here. His method is broadly statistical in nature, although I am not aware of Greenberg ever publishing numerical similarity measures.

[4]Guthrie developed his own statistical approach in his comparative study and developed several measures: a coefficient of Bantuness, indices of relationship, and modulus of dispersion (Guthrie 1967-71, Vol. I:96-110. I've not made a special study of his methods for this paper.

[5]See Flight (1988) for a different and interesting effort to reinterpret Guthrie's data.

These, in turn, generated others (e.g., Bennett 1975-1976; Gregersen 1975-1976; Schadeberg 1986) which began to look critically at the methodology, just as similar studies in American Indian linguistic studies had induced close scrutiny (e.g., Bergsland and Vogt 1962; see Embleton 1986 for some discussion).

Wonderful claims have been made for LS, and in some cases Africanists have uncritically used the methodology, or simply glossed over the inherent problems connected with it. Many studies have presented their results assuming that they were outlining a picture of genetic development. Here I want to simply acknowledge the literature that does exist on the subject (e.g., Bergsland and Vogt 1962; Hoijer 1956; Hymes 1960 a, b; Fodor 1961; Teeter 1963).

Criticism in some cases has been mild, but an especially strong stance was taken by Teeter (1963:648):

> ...faith in lexicostatistics as a possible shortcut in the determination of questions of genetic relationship is misguided, and... allows none but the grossest sort of inference as to genetic relationship or sub relationship, and certainly gives us no dates of split or divergence.... [S]ince lexicostatistics provides no way of going beyond lexical similarity, it can be no more than a first step in studying genetic relationship. Its proper use is in the study of lexical and cultural change.

Teeter also (1963:645) argues bluntly for the Comparative Method against LS:

> We do not draw... genetic conclusions by collecting lexical items and reshuffling them by techniques which are at bottom statistical. It is only on the basis of correspondences, validated by the reconstruction of grammatical systems and their comparison, that we can arrive at statements of genetic relationship and its details.

In the face of similar persuasive opposition we in the African field have hidden behind the claim that we are merely exploring the methodology in order to present hypotheses of possible genetic classification that could then be later proven by more traditional and testable methodologies; by this, the Comparative Method is usually meant.

3. Lexicostatistics and contact

In spite of the shortcomings of LS methodology, most of us would argue that within the field it has been a valuable and practical tool and agree with Heine's assessment that LS can provide us with testable hypotheses of genetic relationships.[6] But there is another dimension that I would like to

---

[6]Heine wrote that LS was useful (1) in discovering genetic relationships, but not probably in offering proof of genetic relationships which require the Comparative Method; (2) in subgrouping related languages; and 3) in providing a foundation for the Comparative Method, that is, LS can show where the Comparative Method is likely to bring results ("the application of the

introduce now, that of the potential LS has for providing evidence of contact. The operative assumption here is that similarities which are measured by LS are more than an indication of genetic transmission, that such similarities are of multiple origins. This point was forcefully argued by Teeter (1963:640); lexical similarities can be inherited from a proto-language, but they can also derive through chance (English *egg* and Luganda *eggi* [ejji]), universal symbolism (words like *mama* 'mother'), and from borrowing through contact. Teeter (1963:641) says:

> Lexical similarities and dissimilarities do not come about in any one simple way, and any mechanical method of counting lexical similarities cannot separate those due to chance, universals, diffusion, and common origin. Lexical change is the result of many factors, and all are scrambled together in the final result.

Others working in the African field have been explicit about this characteristic as well. The literature, both in American and African comparative studies, is replete with observations that contact and other variables (e.g. geography) can skew the results of a LS study.[7] I will make reference to a few of them here. Nurse (1979:61) discusses such phenomena in his study of Chaga; Heine (1974:17) cites two cases, both of which I repeat here in detail; Heine points out:

> The Nilotic languages Samburu and Nandi share 9.9 percent lexical resemblances on the basis of the 200-word list. The percentage between Masai and Nandi, on the other hand, amounts to 15.7. These two languages have been in close contact over the last few centuries (cf. Ehret, 1971). It seems reasonable to assume that the difference of 5.8 percent between Samburu/Nandi and Masai/Nandi is a result of the process of borrowing which took place between Masai and Nandi.

A second case, a comparison between Tepes and Nyang'i (part of the Kuliak group which also includes Ik (Teuso) and "Dorobo") on the one hand and Kalenjin languages (Southern Nilotic) on the other, is also outlined by Heine; in a 200-word list the following percentages obtain, as given in Figure 1:

Comparative Method is likely to be unsuccessful if the languages compared share less than 10 percent of basic vocabulary resemblances, and... even if the percentage is under 20...." (1974:18).

[7]Elmendorf (1969) first brought to my attention the effect of geography on lexicostatistic subgrouping. His article was the beginning of my view of LS as a source of evidence for both genetic relationships and contact networks.

Kuliak		Kalenjin	
Nyang'i	-	Nandi	8.2
Tepes	-	Nandi	13.5

Figure 1. Kuliak - Kalenjin Comparisons

Heine makes the following observation about these figures:

> The difference of 5.3 percent between the closely related languages Nyang'i and Tepes is due to the intensive contact between Tepes and Kalenjin (especially Pokot), which resulted in Tepes borrowing many words from Kalenjin. This process did not affect Nyang'i. (1974:17-18).

Thus in two cases we find skewings in the range of 5 to 6 percent due to intimate borrowing of basic vocabulary. Heine suggests that this or even higher percentages may not be unusual for the borrowing of basic vocabulary. Below, where I discuss skewing in LS tables, it is often the case that skewed figures are in this range or higher, confirming Heine's observations.

Bastin, Coupez, and de Halleux (1979:383) point out that in trees which are derived from LS: "la diffusion tend à effacer les frontières généalogiques et elle procède de manière variable en ce sens que chacun de ses phénomènes tend à occuper une aire géographique différente." They also state that genetic facts cannot be distinguished from those due to diffusion (1979:385).

Bennett, in contrasting LS- and Comparative Method-type classifications of a number of Central Kenyan Bantu dialects, concluded that the different subgroups, deriving from the different methodologies, result from events that are "of recent origin and due to geographic proximity of those dialects" (1976:156). He further (1976:157) says:

> ...differences between statistical and innovative groupings can validly be used to reveal contacts occurring well after a split between dialects. The oft-noted tendency of lexicostatistics results to reflect geography (especially apparent in statistical studies of Bantu thus far) can similarly aid the historical linguist. Cases where lexical relationships do not match geography may often indicate past movements or lines of communication.[8]

The theoretical position to which we can all agree is clear: LS similarities measure genetic and non-genetic variables alike. This is apparently true even in cases where the researcher sets out at the beginning to eliminate borrowing by only counting cognates, that is, he has already applied the Comparative Method. So the practical problem becomes one of how we take a table of figures (for example, the table of similarity indices in Appendix 1) and unscramble it to provide an analysis that yields information on both

---

[8]Similar views are expressed in Möhlig's work (see references to his work in the Bibliography).

genetic variables and contact variables. Techniques and statistical applications exist for interpreting such a table in terms of a genetic classification and rendering the results in the form of a tree (e.g., Henrici's application of "group averaging" but see Flight's (1988) critique of these techniques; also see Embleton 1986 for others). I want to show how we might begin interpreting a table of lexicostatistical similarity measures to yield information on contact.

4. Properties of LS similarity measures

LS tables have certain properties when we look at the array of similarity indices that constitute them. Here I will discuss two of them though there are undoubtedly more.[9] The first characteristic is that the LS figures which define the internal relationships of the members of a group are very similar. The second is that LS figures for individual languages/dialects of any given group have similar lexicostatistical relationships to the languages/dialects of other groups. My working assumption is that both characteristics should be true if an array of figures is measuring genetic relationships among the languages being compared in this way. Where these percentages are not in balance we have reason to look for other nongenetic variables. (Nurse and Philippson 1975), following Bender (1971), talked about some of these properties of LS groups in terms of "strong" and "weak" groups.)

4.1. Internal consistency and low dissimilarity

The first property speaks to the notion of internal consistency and dissimilarity within groups. Members of well-defined and closely related groups of languages as judged by other criteria (e.g., testimony by native speakers, phonological evidence, the Comparative Method, etc.) have higher similarity measures to each other than to any other language/dialect of the sample. For example, in Nurse's LS analysis of the Sabaki languages (Nurse and Hinnebusch 1993:271-285) we find several groups that demonstrate both internal consistency and low dissimilarity (the cognate percentages on which that analysis is based are repeated in Appendix 1 of the present study). Internal averages and ranges are illustrated in Figure 2 for several major Sabaki subgroups: Lamu Archipelago Swahili (Tikuu, Siu, Pate, Amu), Mombasa area Swahili dialects (Mvita, Chifundi, Vumba), Zanzibar Island Swahili dialects (Pemba, Tumbatu, Makunduchi and

---

[9] Another property which I will not discuss further is that groups of languages tend to be clearly distinct from other groups, even and especially from their nearest neighbors by similar margins. Thus in the table in Appendix 1 we see, for example, that the Lamu dialect cluster (Amu, Siu, Pate, and Tikuu) is bounded by a fall in the figures to the left of the Tikuu column of figures of at least 7% and an average of 8%, and below the Amu line by a fall of some 9%. Pokomo, Mijikenda, Comorian are similarly defined as is all of Swahili vis-à-vis Pokomo, Mijikenda, and Comorian, but not Mwani.

Unguja), Northern Mijikenda (Chonyi, Giryama, Duruma),[10] Mijikenda (Giriama, Chonyi, Duruma, Digo), and Comorian (Ngazija, Mwali, Nzwani, Maore). (See Appendix 1 Sabaki Subgroups).

What do these numbers in Figure 2 signify?

	Internal Average	Highest internal range	Average internal range
Lamu	89	5	2.7
Mombasa	78	5	2.18
Zanzibar	72	6	2.4
NMK	79	4	2.5
MK	73	15	7.5
Com	81	6	2.7

Figure 2. Sabaki internal averages and ranges

For example, the Lamu dialect cluster of Swahili forms a very cohesive group with little internal lexical dissimilarity, as the high group average cognation index indicates; moreover, the internal relationships of the members of the group, compared one to another within the group, are similar and symmetrical, thus for the Lamu Cluster the greatest internal difference is 5% with an average difference between members of 2.7%.[11] Such differences are referred to as ranges in this study. A range can be thought of as an expression of how dissimilar the members of a group are internally, or conversely how cohesive the members of a group are. The smaller the range the more cohesive the group is internally—the more alike its members are; the higher the range the more diffuse it is. Comorian is similarly cohesive lexically (81 group average; 2.7 average difference and a range not greater than 6). Northern Mijikenda is similar (79 group average; 2.5 average difference and range not greater than 4). I presume here that high group averages and low range indices correlate to lexical similarity, cohesiveness, and low lexical diversity within a particular group. Low range indices indicate symmetry in the pair-wise comparisons and a low level of skewing, where skewing as a term is used to indicate asymmetry in the pair-wise comparisons. Also, it is predicted that such high group averages and low range indices should also correlate with other evidence indicating high levels of mutual intelligibility, genetic descent, and other markers of

[10]The inclusion of other Mijikenda dialects, excluding Digo, makes little difference to this figure. For reference, all figures cited in this section were computed using the LS table in the appendix.

[11]A highest "internal difference" refers to the figure gotten for the highest comparison (e.g., 91% between Pate and Siu or Pate and Amu in ND) less the lowest comparison (for example, 86% cognation rate between Tikuu and Siu in ND), thus 91 - 86 = 5; the "average difference" is the average of all such pair-wise comparisons.

cohesion (see Ladefoged, Gluck and Criper 1972 and Winter 1980). Equally important, of course, is that there should be a correlation with criteria that support a genetic classification.[12]

In contrast to the northern most Swahili dialects of Lamu, as also seen in Figure 2,[13] the cluster of Swahili dialects spoken on the coastal strip centered on Mombasa and the cluster spoken on Zanzibar and Pemba are progressively more differentiated lexically with lower internal group averages.

The Mijikenda and Northern Mijikenda examples, in Figure 3, are also illustrative. Percentages for selected pairs of Mijikenda languages are given with range figures for each of those pair comparisons, first without Digo and then with Digo. For Northern Mijikenda the group average is high and the ranges are low. When percentages of cognation for Digo are added to the equation, the internal average for all of Mijikenda drops to 73 with a corresponding jump in ranges. The presence of Digo skews the internal balance of figures that numerically represents Mijikenda. The working assumption here is that the figures defining a "genetic" group should be in balance and in proportion. We've known for sometime—coming from work I did in the early 70s (1973, 1976)—that the Digo are more culturally assimilated to Swahili than their Mijikenda neighbors and that some basic core vocabulary of Digo that would otherwise define it as Mijikenda has been eroded away through intense contact with Swahili. Some examples of core vocabulary loaning from Swahili into Digo are given in Figure 4. I maintain that such differences in both the internal averages of groups and differences in ranges, especially the lack of symmetry, involving one member of a group, can be taken as evidence that nongenetic variables may be operative. Other examples are possible. The low internal average for all of Swahili together is indicative of a low level of internal consistency and high diversity. I maintain that such skewing, or lack of symmetry, involving one member of a group can be taken as evidence that nongenetic variables may be operative.

---

[12]I will not demonstrate such correlation in this paper. In general, however, it is the case that these highly cohesive Sabaki LS subgroups with high internal averages and low ranges correlate with phonological and morphological innovations.

[13]I figured group averages and give only the highest range figure for the Mombasa cluster and Zanzibar/Pemba cluster, but not the average range difference. Average range difference is computed by taking each figure with every other figure in turn and averaging the difference.

Northern MK range averages

Chonyi		Giryama		Duruma	
Ch-Gi	81	Gi-Ch	81	Du-Ch	78
Ch-Du	78	Gi-Du	77	Du-Gi	77
Range	3	Range	4	Range	1

Group average: 79 (81 + 78 + 77 ÷ 3)

Average internal range: 2.5 (Ch, Gi and Du—3 + 4 + 1 ÷ 3)

Northern MK and Digo range averages

Chonyi		Giryama		Duruma		Digo	
Ch-Gi	81	Gi-Ch	81	Du-Ch	78	Di-Gi	66
Ch-Du	78	Gi-Du	77	Du-Gi	77	Di-Ch	68
Ch-Di	68	Gi-Di	66	Du-Di	70	Di-Du	70
Range	11.5	Range	12.5	Range	7.5	Range	2.5

Group average: 73 (81 + 78 + 77 + 70 + 68 + 66 ÷ 5)

Range average: 10.5 (Ch, Gi and Du with Digo)

Figure 3. Mijikenda Range Averages

Digo		Other MK
-ɓaya	'bad'	-ii
ɗamu	'blood'	milatso
mfuβa	'bone'	musoza
-pika	'cook'	-gita or jita
-zee	'old'	-ţœumia
nyota	'star'	nyenyezi
yai	'egg'	iji ~ tumbi
-ema	'good'	-dzo
-refu	'long'	-re
-fupi	'short'	-fuhi ~ -futi
mguru cl. 3	'leg'	gulu cl. 5 ~ 7

Figure 4. Swahili loans in Digo

In intermediate level groups, we do not find the same level of cohesion. A good example is "Coastal Sabaki", a group which consists of the Swahili cluster (including the Zanzibar, Mombasa, and Lamu clusters), Mwiini,

Comorian, and Mwani.[14] When we contrast this large group with Pokomo and Mijikenda, both hinterland Sabaki groups, we find the following. Coastal Sabaki has a group average of 64 with a very high internal range difference of 33 (Tumbatu - Mwali 58 versus Pate - Siu 91) so it is not a very cohesive group. This should not be surprising when we look at the geographic distribution of the groups involved, nor should we forget the function of time: presumably all of the constituents of Coastal Sabaki have been "distinct" for some time. In contrast, both the Pokomo group (Lower Pokomo + Upper Pokomo) and the Mijikenda group have group averages of 73, with low ranges: Pokomo with all of Sabaki has a range average of just under 3 with the highest range difference of 7 (with Digo). Mijikenda with all of Sabaki has a range average of 6 with several high ranges of 10 (all involving Digo). Thus, Pokomo and Mijikenda are fairly cohesive groups in contrast to Coastal Sabaki which is less so. Pokomo is consistent in having symmetrical ranges with other Sabaki languages, but Mijikenda is skewed by Digo. Coastal Sabaki with the remaining Sabaki languages of Pokomo, Mijikenda and Elwana has relatively high skews, ranging from a low of 7 to a high of 11. Figure 5 below shows these ranges as well as the numerical relationship of Coastal Sabaki with other Sabaki subgroups:

	Coastal Sabaki	Range			
El	56	10	Mak 51	-	Pa 61[15]
LP	60	9	Mak 58	-	Pa 67
UP	62	11	Mak 58	-	Pa 69
Ch	61	7	Tu 58	-	Jo 65
Gi	61	7	Tu 58	-	Chi 65
Du	60	7	Mak 57	-	Pa 64
Di	50	10	Ung 50	-	Pa 60

Figure 5. Coastal Sabaki ranges

What this means is that Coastal Sabaki has the lowest group average of all the Sabaki groups and considerably more skewing than others. This is so, our hypothesis holds, because it is not only genetic relatedness that is being measured by lexical similarity indices. The ranges in Figure 5 point to the source of the skewing: the Zanzibar cluster of Swahili on Zanzibar,

[14]This Sabaki subgroup is based on a LS analysis presented in Nurse and Hinnebusch 1993:279-281 where Coastal Sabaki is more or less in a coordinate relationship with each of the other Sabaki subgroups: Elwana, Pokomo, and Mijikenda.

[15]The ranges here are arrived at by looking at the columns for each of the non-Coastal Sabaki languages and its figures for the languages which are members of the Coastal Sabaki group.

having the lowest cognate percentages with other Sabaki languages, is the focus. On the high side it is the northern cluster of Swahili located on the Lamu archipelago. Below we will discuss the implications of skewing further.

4.2. Numerical symmetry

Of more interest perhaps is the second property of LS tables. Languages which group together lexicostatistically will tend to have a numerical symmetry with other noncontiguous languages in the comparison set if in fact the grouped languages form a genetic group. This is a working assumption that needs to be independently verified.[16] I illustrate the claim by outlining three case studies, from Comorian, Mwiini, and Nguni.

4.2.1. The Comorian case study

The dialects of the Comorian cluster, Ngazija, Mwali, Nzuani and Maore, are spoken on the islands of Grande Comore, Moheli, Anjouan, and Mayotte, respectively. The islands are located in the Mozambique Channel about midway between the Mozambique coast and the northern end of Madagascar. The nearest Sabaki sister dialect is Mwani, located about 300 kilometers across the channel to the west, so the present-day Comorian dialects are not in immediate geographic proximity to other Sabaki languages. All four are closely related, mutually intelligible dialects, derived from the same intermediate proto-language (Nurse and Hinnebusch 1993). The relevant LS figures are given in Figure 6, as extracted from the LS table in Appendix 1.

	Ng	Mh	Nz	Ma	Range
EL	57	55	54	57	3
UP	61	58	59	59	3
LP	56	54	55	56	2
Ch	59	60	59	59	1
Gi	60	58	59	60	2
Du	60	58	58	59	2
Di	56	54	56	59	[5]
Mw	64	65	65	66	2
Ti	70	70	72	71	2
Si	69	69	71	70	2
Pa	70	71	72	72	2
Am	70	71	72	72	2
	Ng	Mh	Nz	Ma	

[16]For this paper I will not attempt to do this other than informally.

	Ng	Mh	Nz	Ma	Range
Jo	66	66	68	67	2
Mv	65	65	67	68	3
Chi	65	65	67	65	2
Vu	65	66	67	68	3
Mt	64	64	66	66	2
NPe	61	60	61	63	2
SPe	60	60	62	64	[4]
Ung	61	60	61	62	2
Tu	61	58	59	60	3
Mak	63	62	63	64	2
Mn	60	60	61	61	1
	Ng	Mh	Nz	Ma	

Figure 6. Comorian-Sabaki similarity indices and ranges

For each horizontal comparison in Figure 6 with each of the other Sabaki dialects we find a consistency in lexical similarity between the Comorian cluster and the other Sabaki languages as indicated by the low range indices (with two exceptions placed in square brackets). Each member of Comorian has, within a range of Ø to 3, a balanced numerical relationship to other members of the comparison set.[17] This is what we should expect to see if indeed Comorian is a cohesive genetic group. The two exceptions of Digo and Southern Pemba have range indices higher than 3. We've discussed the Digo skewing already. For Southern Pemba, Maore is apparently the focus of the skewing here since it has the highest similarity figures with the Zanzibar cluster dialects except for Tumbatu.

4.2.2. The Mwiini case study

Another example is provided by comparisons involving Mwiini. If we look at Sabaki subgroup ranges with Mwiini in Figure 7 we find that except for the skewing caused by Digo, and an elevated range for the range index for

[17]The range index figure in Figure 6 is the difference between the highest and lowest figure in the horizontal set; it is not an average. I have somewhat arbitrarily set the upper limit of a consistent symmetrical numerical relationship at 3%. In all the comparisons I've done within Sabaki the normal ranges seem to be in the neighborhood of 2%. Any figure over 3% I consider skewed. Selecting 4% as exceeding the norm has the practical consequence of isolating glitches in the numerical symmetries expected for genetic groups, whereas a cut-off at 3% does not. I rather suspect also that ranges may differ somewhat on a sliding scale depending on the languages being compared, but I would like to stress that this and the determination of the notion "skewed" are empirical questions.

the Mombasa cluster of Swahili, the relationship of the Sabaki subgroups (Mijikenda, Comorian, the Lamu and Zanzibar clusters of Swahili) with Mwiini is uniform and what we expect.

	UP	LP				Pokomo	Range
Mw	62	61					1
	Ch	Gi	Du	Di		Mijikenda	1/[4]
Mw	59	59	58	55			
	Ng	Mh	Nz	Ma		Comorian	2
Mw	64	65	65	66			
	Ti	Si	Pa	Am		Lamu	2
Mw	79	79	81	80			
	Jo	Mv	Chi	Vu	Mt	Mombasa	[6]
Mw	71	69	67	66	65		
	NPe	Spe	Ung	Tu	Mak	Zanzibar	3
Mw	62	60	61	59	60		

Figure 7. Mwiini-Sabaki similarity indices and ranges

Now, if we look just at the details of the relationship of all of Swahili to Mwiini we find in Figure 8 below that the similarity indices show a highly skewed situation. Here we have a clear example of skewing caused, at least partially, by geographical proximity. The skewing is highlighted by the high numbers for "highest range" and "average range". As is well known, Swahili extends along 1000 miles of East Africa coastline. At the northern extremity is Mwiini, spoken in the town of Brava on the southern Somali coast. The most northerly located modern Swahili community with which Mwiini speakers are in immediate contact is the Lamu cluster of Tikuu, Siu, Pate and Amu; the next but not immediately proximate community is the group centered on Mombasa (Mvita, Jomvu, Chifundi, Vumba and Mtang'ata), and then the group located on the islands of Zanzibar and Pemba. As can be seen in Figures 8 and 9, Mwiini has the highest similarity index with the Lamu cluster (80), and the lowest with the more remote Zanzibar group (60) and an intermediate figure (68) with the centrally located Mombasa cluster. If we look beyond the averages at the actual numbers themselves for the central and southern clusters, which are geographically closer than either is to the northerly cluster, we see the numbers decreasing in small increments from a high figure of 81 to a low of 59. The chain of numbers, either as averages or not, including the range numbers, and the geographical chain itself are in striking accord (see Figure 9). LS tables, in addition to measuring genetic relationships, also reflect geographical dialect chain relationships (cf. Elmendorf 1969).

	Ti	Si	Pa	Am
Mw	79	79	81	80

80 average

	Jo	Mv	Chi	Vu	Mt
Mw	71	69	67	66	65

68 average

	NPe	Spe	Ung	Tu	Mak
Mw	62	60	61	59	60

60 average

Highest range: 22 (81-59=22)

Highest average range: 13 (12+20+8=40 ÷ 3)[18]

Figure 8. Swahili - Mwiini similarity indices

But note that Mwiini has a bit higher similarity index with Comorian (Figure 9), a dialect cluster which is located further south at a greater distance than the more southerly Swahili group in the data set, yet has a higher figure by 6 than the lower figure in the Zanzibar Swahili set (59). With the Pokomo cluster the figure is 61 average and with Mijikenda 58 average, yet both these dialect clusters are located closer geographically and we would expect higher figures if they were in a geographical-lexicostatistical chain relationship with Mwiini as Swahili seems to be. Thus, Comorian, Pokomo, and Mijikenda break the chain. We know of course that Mwiini and Comorian are part of the Coastal Sabaki network of contact that exceeded the coastal-hinterland contact relationship in intensity.

What then is the "real", if you will, genetic, linguistic relationship of Mwiini to Swahili in terms of LS figures? Do the figures for Mwiini with the Lamu Swahili dialects represent the norm, or do the figures with the Mombasa and Zanzibar dialects? The elevated figure of Mwiini with the Lamu Swahili dialects is suspect because of the close geographical proximity of the languages. If the similarity figure for Mwiini and the Mombasa cluster is the norm (the figure of 68 is almost the same as the average of Mwiini with the whole Swahili group : 80 + 68 + 60 = 208 ÷ 3 = 69), then the Comorian figure of 65 may be a genetic norm as well, especially if Comorian is "Swahili". Then we would see that the ranges for Zanzibar-Mwiini, Mombasa-Mwiini, and Comorian-Mwiini (all hovering in the 60s) are the norm and the high range for Mwiini-Amu the aberrant one.

---

[18]The average range figure here is based on the Mwiini - Swahili group averages of 80, 68, and 60.

El	60	Ilwana
UP	62	Pokomo
LP	61	61.5 average
Ch	59	
Gi	59	Mijikenda
Du	58	57.75 average
Di	55	
Ng	64	
Mh	65	Comorian
Nz	65	65 average
Ma	66	
Ti	79	
Si	79	Lamu Swahili
Pa	81	80 average
Am	80	
Jo	71	
Mv	69	Mombasa Swahili
Chi	67	68 average
Vu	66	
Mt	65	
Npe	62	
SPe	60	Zanzibar Swahili
Ung	61	60 average
Tu	59	
Mak	60	
Mn	61	Mwani

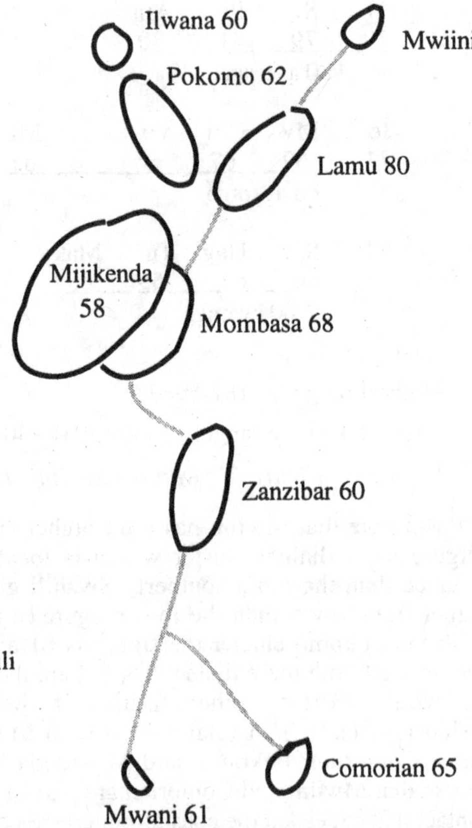

Map is stylized and not necessarily drawn to scale; language positions are approximate and intended only to show relation of one language to another.

Figure 9. Mwiini-Sabaki chain relationship

In addition to the geographical chain, there exists a cultural continuity here as well which reinforces the impression that the figures for Mwiini and Swahili represent a nongenetic situation: The Mwiini and the Swahili share a common mercantile, seafaring, urbanized culture, as do the Comorian (and the Mwani). If the Comorian-Mwiini similarity index, which is higher than the index with Zanzibar Swahili, is not a reflection of a genetic relationship, then the figure may point to stronger historical links between the two than between Mwiini and the dialect cluster on Pemba and Zanzibar. Other variables, which are not immediately apparent, may be at work as well. There could be internal variables peculiar to the sets of the comparison. The more northerly dialects as well as Comorian may independently retain more common lexis, while the more southerly Swahili cluster has lost common lexis thus lowering its figure. Clearly we need to go beyond the figures. But for the moment geography seems to be the likely explanation and the point is made: skewed figures in a LS set point to nongenetic variables.

4.2.3. The Nguni case study

A final example is provided by Southeastern Bantu languages, based on a study by Tunks (1993).[19] In Figure 10 we see that Zulu, Xhosa and Swati (hereafter Nguni), which form a close-knit cluster and are linguistically considered as dialects of the same language and thus reflexes of the same proto language, have a consistent lexicostatistical relationship with the noncontiguous, less closely related, southern Bantu languages of Venda and Shona. With Shona, the Nguni languages share an average similarity index of 41 with just a range difference of 2. With Venda, the average is a bit higher with an index of 47 and a 2 for range difference. In each case the relationship is symmetrical and the range differences are small. In contrast, however, is Nguni's relationship to Sotho. Here the average is 44, midway between the 41 and 47 of the other two comparisons, but the low of 41 for Zulu and the high of 48 for Swati gives a range of difference of 7 which is significantly higher than the 2 of the other two comparisons. What might account for this skewed range? We must suspect geographical contiguity. Sotho is in contact with Nguni languages along a long front. If we knew the dialect of Sotho on which Tunks based her study, we might be able to be more specific about the skewing.[20] If a northern variant, than the high figure with Swati and the low figure with Zulu would make sense since Swati is in contact with northern Sotho. In any case, whatever the specifics of the facts, contact provides a ready explanation for the difference.

[19]Tunks used the techniques for counting similarities suggested by Blount and Curley (1970) in their study of Luo.

[20]Tunks used Christeller's (1961) Sotho dictionary which does not specify the dialect of Sotho on which the dictionary is based.

						Range
Zulu	-					
Xhosa	91	-				
Swati	85	75	-			10
Sotho	41	44	48	-		7
Venda	48	46	47	50	-	2
Shona	42	40	40	42	62	2
	Zulu	Xhosa	Swati	Sotho	Venda	

Figure 10. Southern Bantu similarity indices and ranges

Another example is provided by the same table. If we compare the figures in Figure 10 for the highly mutually intelligible Nguni subgroup of Swati, Zulu and Xhosa (84% internal average), the low figure of 75 for Xhosa-Swati and the high figure of 91 for Xhosa-Zulu are notable; moreover, the ranges are in sharp contrast (16 for Xhosa-Zulu and Xhosa-Swati, 10 for Swati-Zulu and Swati-Xhosa, and 6 for Zulu-Swati and Zulu-Xhosa). We should expect more balance for a genetic group which surely, by all other criteria, Nguni is. That there isn't points to a complex of nonlinguistic variables, which are not easily teased apart by simply looking at the numbers. For now I will only offer the following observations: Xhosa, Zulu, and Swati are in a geographic-chain relationship running from south to north. Swati, nearly surrounded by adjacent Zulu dialects, has been, until recently, dominated by the superior numbers of the majority Zulu in he region. Moreover, it is distantly removed from the Xhosa, and the two languages have never been in contact. Finally the Zulu and Xhosa have adamantly maintained cultural distinctiveness for at least the last several centuries. If we compare the ranges with the internal average of 84%,[21] all are skewed, using the range measure of about 3-4% that we've seen earlier in the other test cases. Thus the high figure of 91 for Xhosa and Zulu may be too high and may well mask interdialectal borrowing. The 85 for Zulu and Swati may also be too high, even though it comes close to the internal average. The lower figure of 75 for Xhosa and Swati, which are at either ends of the dialect continuum and less likely to have been in a borrowing situation, may be a more accurate measure and reflection of genetic relatedness than either of the other figures since neither are in contact. The point to be emphasized here is that the skewing we find calls for a close examination of the actual lexis. This could provide more precise information on the sources of the skewing.[22]

---

[21] The internal average, of course, is a function of the three numbers and, in itself, may indicate a process of dialect leveling through interdialectal borrowing.

[22] From a 100 word list this would be difficult to determine, but a study of a larger corpus—say a 1000 word list—might reveal the extent to which interdialectal borrowing has occurred.

5. Skewing and noncontact variables

A skewing, or imbalance, in LS figures does not always indicate contact. As we know, there are other factors that affect lexical similarity. Lexicostatistics, at least as it has been applied in Bantu studies, does not discriminate between similarity that has different sources, e.g. similar retentions from a proto-period, shared innovations, undetected shared borrowings, drift leading to convergence,[23] and so on. Where skewed figures correlate with geographic proximity there is the reasonable assumption that the skewing is due to diffusion related to contact between speakers. However, where geographic contiguity is not a likely explanation, other causes must be investigated. A nice example is found in Bennett (1976). In that study he provides a LS classification of a set of Thagicu, or Central Kenyan Bantu, dialects consisting of two Kamba dialects (Kilungu and Machakos), two Mwimbi dialects (Upper and Lower), Imenti, and Embu. He uses several different techniques for counting similarities, ranging from a rough measure of cognacy (Figure 11) to ones which attempt to take into account skewing (i.e., where one or more features of a comparison of obviously similar, possibly cognate, items do not correspond and are thus weighted differently) and innovation (where a shared innovation is given greater weight). In each case the subgrouping results are the same. But he also quantifies phonological innovations and expresses these in a lexicostatistical type of array as in Figure 12.

Mach	-					
Kil	96	-				
Emb	70	68	-			
UMw	76	74	88	-		
LMw	68	66	86	90	-	
Ime	70	68	72	74	72	-
	Mach	Kil	Emb	UMw	LMw	Ime

Figure 11. Similarity rates based on rough cognacy

Mach	-					
Kil	120	-				
Emb	98	98	-			
UMw	85	85	89	-		
LMw	80	80	89	112	-	
Ime	83	83	92	100	105	-
	Mach	Kil	Emb	UMw	LMw	Ime

Figure 12. Similarity rates (phonological history)

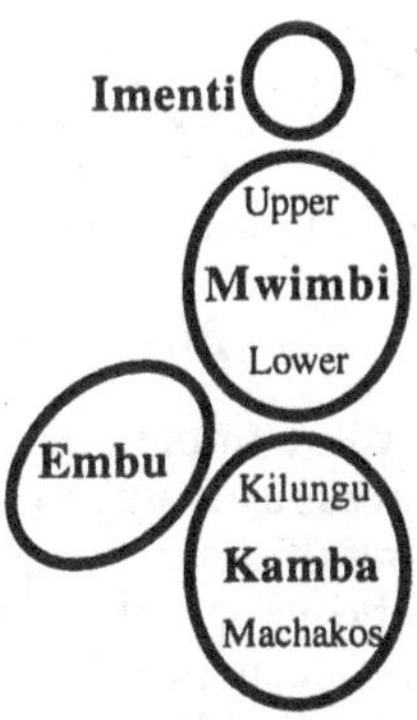

Relative geographical position of the CK dialects

---

[23] Drift (Sapir 1921) refers to independent change that occurs because languages share common typological structures albeit because of common descent from the same proto language; e.g., a certain set of changes may occur in languages that have noun class morphologies, or certain kinds of phonological structures.

In both classifications the two Kamba dialects (Machakos and Kilungu) and two Mwimbi dialects (Upper and Lower) form close-knit groups. But, as Bennett points out, Embu is treated differently: in one subgrouping it falls in with Mwimbi and in the other with Kamba. The second classification is independently based on a analysis of common phonological and morphological innovations arrived at by applying the Comparative Method and reflects, for Bennett, genetic history, while the first classification, which shows the lexical similarity of Embu with Mwimbi, is of recent origin and due to the geographic proximity of those dialects, thus due to contact. In Figure 13 the conflicting classifications are given in the forms of corresponding trees. Note the position of Embu in each.

But let us go a step further. If we compare the two statistical tables on which Bennett bases his conclusions we find the following: In the first LS table (Figure 11), we find that both the Kamba and Mwimbi dialects have a symmetrical set of figures with Embu and Imenti as we would expect if both sets of dialects are genetic groupings. In the course of examining and comparing Bennett's classifications for patterns of symmetry and asymmetry, however, something else quite interesting showed up in the figures.

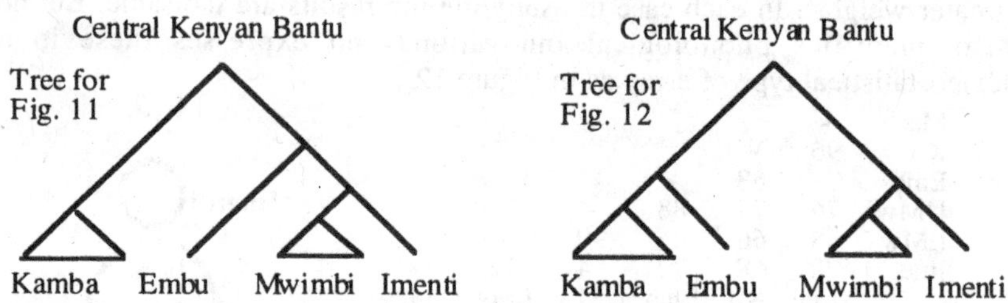

Figure 13. Central Kenya Bantu relationships

When we compare the figures for both Mwimbi dialects with the noncontiguous Kamba dialects we find that Upper Mwimbi is the dialect that is out of scale on the high side. What is the reason for this skewing? It cannot be geography since Upper Mwimbi is not contiguous with the Kamba dialects (see map adjacent to Figures 11 and 12). Bennett's data and analysis provide a possible answer. For each set of given lexical comparisons (a total of 50) he gives information on the compared lexis and indicates if an item is a retention, innovation, or loan. It turns out that Upper Mwimbi shares three retentions with Kamba that the other two dialects of its group (Lower Mwimbi and Imenti) do not, because they have either replaced the items in question with loans or have innovated and replaced them. The higher figure with Kamba reflects this fact: retentions are counted as similarities thus elevating the figures. The difference of three plus or minus the scaled values in his computations accounts for the rough difference of 6 in the range (in a set of 50 comparisons 50 x 2 = 100 and 3 x 2 = 6).

6. Borrowing and nonskewing

While there are many examples of contact induced skewing in LS tables, and given the nature of contact phenomena and the nature of LS methodology—it does not yield discrete results in measuring just one variable, it should be clear that not all contact situations will be detected in a LS exercise. One illustration of this can found again in Sabaki. The Zanzibar dialect of Unguja has undergone extensive influence from one of the northern Swahili dialects, most probably a Lamu area dialect given the nature of the evidence. The main evidence comes from the Comparative Method in the form of correspondence sets as given in Figure 14:

PSA/CB :	ND :	SD	PSA/CB :	ND :	SD
*c	t̪	c	*fy/fi	s(i)	fy/fi
*nj	nd̪	nj	*vy/vi	~z(i) ð+i)	vy/vi
*g	Ø	g	*ly	l	ly

Figure 14. CB / Proto-Sabaki (PSA) : ND : SD regular correspondences[24]

A major linguistic distinction between the northern Lamu (ND) and southern Zanzibar dialects (SD) is seen in the reflexes of Proto Sabaki **c, *nj, *g, *fi ~ *fy-, *vy ~ *vi*, and **ly*.[25] ND dialects typically have as reflexes of these the phonemes /t̪, nd̪, Ø, s(i), z(i) ~ ð (i), and l/, while SD, including Unguja, typically have /c, nj, g, fi ~ fy, and vi ~ vy/ respectively (the colon in the figure means "corresponds to").

Thus, we know that words in Unguja, and consequently Standard Swahili, which do not correspond with the expected shape, but whose shape closely matches those in ND must have entered the language through borrowing. For example, the future tense marker (PSA **-ca-* < **-cak-* 'want') in Unguja/Standard Swahili is *-ta-*, but this is a skewed shape; the regular shape would be *-ca-* as still attested in Makunduchi and Vumba; it is *-t̪a-* in northern dialects and when borrowed into Unguja the dental stop was reinterpreted as alveolar; like-wise when northern forms with any dental entered the southern dialects, they were reformed as alveolars because the SD phonologies did not have the dental series (*t̪* > *t* and *nd̪* > *nd*). A list of such loans is given in Figure 15.

---

[24]The supporting data for the comparative data is drawn from Nurse and Hinnebusch (1993: Appendix 2, pp. 577-655; also see pp. 297-299, 442-444, 563-566 relevant to the ND/SD contact interface.

[25]The Proto-Sabaki vowels **i* and **u* in Figure 15 are the superclose Bantu vowels which Guthrie marks in his works with a subscript cedilla. For the nonclose vowels I use **ɩ* and **ʋ* in this paper.

This sample illustrates the wide ranging categories of lexis in Unguja from animals to cultural terms and even vocabulary in the "basic" category (e.g. skin, black, eat, kill, old, that, I, and you) whose source is clearly a northern dialect. One would expect that the lexicostatistics should reflect this level of intimate borrowing. It does not unequivocally do so.

PSA	*Unguja*	*SD Shape*	*ND Shape*	*Gloss*
*-caka	-taka	-caka (Mak)	-t̪aka	'want'
*-cana	kitana	kitana ~ canuo	-t̪ana	'comb' (n./ v.)
*-celo	uteo	uceo'cleared area'	ut̪eo	'winnowing'
*-cunzya	-tunza	-cunza (Pe)	-t̪ud̪aa	'take care of'
*njovu	ndovu	njovu (Vu)	nd̪ovu	'elephant'
*menje	mende	nyenje'cricket'	nyend̪e	'cockroach'
*-penj-	-penda	-penja (Pe)	-pend̪a	'like, love'
*-Winja	-winda	-winja (Pe,Mak,etc.)	-wind̪a	'hunt'
*-Wulaga	-ua	-uaga (Vu,Mt)	-ua	'kill'
*iWɩga	bia	biga (Mt)	ubia	'pot'
*Wʊgɩmbɩ	wimbi	ugimbi'beer'	wimbi	'millet...'
*-fyokoca	-sokota	-fyokoca	-sokot̪a	'twist, etc.'
*-pofya	-posa	-pofya (Vu)	-posa	'arrange marriage'
*-fyom-	-soma	-fyoma (Pe)	-soma	'read'
*kifyu	kisu	kifyu (Vu,Pe)	kisu	'knife'
*-ilʊ + ifi	-eusi	-eufi (Mt,Vu)	-eusi	'(very) black'
*mwivi	mwizi	mwivi (Pe,Vu,Mt)	mwizi	'thief'
*ngovi	ngozi	ngovi (Vu,Chi)	ngozi	'skin'
*-vyal-	-zaa	-vyaa (Mt,Mak)	-zaa	'give birth'
*-vyele	-zee	-vyele (Vu)	-zee	'old'
*-lya	-le	-lya (Mak,Pe)	-le	'that'
*-lya	-la	-lya (Mak,Vu,Tu)	-la	'eat'
*mi	mimi	miye (Mak,Pe,Tu)	mimi	'I'
*we	wewe	weye (Mak,Pe,Tu)	wewe	'you'

For a list of abbreviations see Appendix 1; items in the'ND Shape' column are mostly from Amu, though other dialects of the Lamu cluster are represented; glosses are approximations. In Unguja both mwizi and mwivi'thief' are attested. Unmarked items in the middle column are attested in Unguja.

Figure 15. Northern Swahili loans in Unguja

The lexicostatistical figures for Unguja (see Figure 16), the locus for all these loans, with Amu or Siu, the likely source of the loans, are within the expected ranges, and in line with what we find for the other Zanzibar dialects of Pemba, Makunduchi, and Tumbatu. Unguja is only about 2-3% closer to the Lamu dialects than the others.

NPe	68	69	70	70
SPe	68	69	70	70
Ung	70	71	72	72
Tu	66	67	68	68
Mak	67	68	69	69
	Ti	Si	Pa	Am

Figure 16. Northern and Southern Swahili similarity indices

Furthermore, Vumba, Chifundi and Mtang'ata (See Appendix 1) whose phonologies are conservative and retain older forms from presumably a proto stage prior to the period of massive influence from the north, show higher LS figures with Lamu area dialects than the dialect that was most affected. As a group, whose geographic position is as distant from Lamu as the Zanzibar/Pemba dialects, they have an average cognation rate of 77 versus the 71 average of Unguja with the Lamu dialects. There is a viable explanation and it clearly has to do with the nature of the borrowing process. First, identifiable northern Swahili forms are found in all of the Sabaki dialects. Then, when we actually take a look at the 100 wordlist upon which the LS figures are based, we find that the non-Unguja dialects in the south are also affected by borrowing but not to the same extent. In the 100 wordlist, 8 percent of Unguja lexis is identifiable northern lexis; Makunduchi, Tumbatu and Vumba each have 4 (but not necessarily the same lexis); Southern Pemba has 5.[26] Of the others, Northern Pemba and Mtang'ata each have 2 and Chifundi has 3.[27] So all the dialects show some borrowing and this may have evened out any skewings that might have showed up otherwise.[28] So, while it may be true that the average 2-3%

---

[26]The southern Pemba area came under the sway of the 19th and 20th century Zanzibari Omani plantation cultural sphere and the dialects in the area were affected accordingly; thus the slightly higher figure may reflect recent loan history via Unguja/Standard Swahili rather than from the period responsible for the massive loaning of northern material into Unguja. Unguja may, as well, be the immediate source of all northern lexis in the environs of Zanzibar Town, the center of Omani power and influence.

[27]The northern lexis that shows up in all these dialects is more or less the same set of basic vocabulary that makes up the 8% in Unguja, but it is distributed differently in the others which suggests that the influence postdated the split of the proto-dialect community.

higher figure for Unguja that we see in Figure 15 with the Lamu area dialects vís a vís its closest neighbors may reflect the borrowing process, the LS figures themselves are not skewed in the way we have been using the term until now. So, here, in this example it was the Comparative Method that allowed us to detect the borrowing and eliminate it as a factor.

But let us not forget the chain of geo-lexicostatistical Swahili dialects ranging from north to south where Swahili dialects increase their percentages with Lamu dialects as we move north (Appendix 1). We find that the Mombasa area dialects which include Vumba, Chifundi, and Mtang'ata have higher figures with Lamu area dialects, but not particularly higher percentages of identifiable northern loans. Thus, assuming that more northerly location means higher figures which means more contact opportunities, then we have to conclude that there is more loan material in these dialects than can be identified at this moment either by LS skewing or the Comparative Method. We have seen in this section that (1) not all contact situations will lead to lexicostatistical skewing (Unguja) in a 100 word list[29] and that (2) we cannot necessarily identify the lexis that is responsible for the skewing (Mombasa area dialects such as Chifundi).

7. Conclusion

Bennett (1976:151) makes the point that borrowing and other types of areal interaction among Bantu languages are often difficult to detect:

> Contiguous forms of Bantu are generally so similar in basic areas of lexicon as to be nearly mutually intelligible and phonologic differences are rarely so great that regular correspondences are not transparent to the native speaker. For example, Swahili items in Nyankore borrowed through Luganda frequently show 'regular' Nyankore-Luganda correspondences rather than simply phonetic approximation. A natural consequence is a very high degree of 'intimate borrowing' and areally directed evolution that can only rarely be detected.

While I certainly agree with this view on the difficulty of detecting evidence of contact among closely related Bantu languages, we have seen that a careful inspection of skewing in LS tables can frequently lead to evidence for areal interaction. Lexicostatistics has value beyond creating

---

[28] Remember that the counting process carried out by Nurse (Nurse and Hinnebusch 1993) took into account known borrowings as revealed by the Comparative Method, thus eliminating the borrowing factor, but not all borrowing can be identified by means of the Comparative Method (see Bennett 1976:151 quoted in the concluding section of this paper).

[29] In this paper I have not explored in detail what implications larger lists (200, 400, or 1000 words) might have for understanding skewing and contact. On the face of it, it would seem that the larger the list the less basic it becomes and thus more vulnerable to borrowing so skewing from contact might show up better on larger lists.

trees of genetic relationships. Instead of bemoaning the deficiencies of the methodology for doing genetic classification—something I have done myself—we should take advantage of them in ways suggested in this paper and mine the methodology for the historical information that can be uncovered.

Through studying skewing we can be led into intriguing and interesting studies of the lexis of Bantu languages. Skewed figures for Digo focused us on the specific sociocultural-linguistic reason for the lack of balance in the Mijikenda figures. Likewise, using LS in tandem with the Comparative Method in Swahili studies provided a most interesting array of evidence for interdialectal borrowing. Rich areas of inquiry into the nature of lexical change, cultural change, and history can be potentially catalogued. These are the kinds of endeavors that add to the inherently interesting and enjoyable nature of comparative work. We can do worse than do linguistic archaeology.

What's left to do? As always there's never an end to what is possible, but I do have a few suggestions for scholars who are interested in pursuing these ideas further. For example, I did not look at Bastin and Coupez's work. Given, I assume, the consistent application of the methodology in their work, for large numbers of Bantu languages, it would seem a most fruitful exercise to study their tables using the techniques discussed here. Because we now have explicit LS classifications, and we have a good beginning on reconstruction using the Comparative Method, I do not think it is premature to begin reexamining what we now have and begin cataloguing the evidence for contact. In the beginning, we may have to take a taxonomic approach and do just cataloguing—comparable to Guthrie's Common Bantu—before we can work out an elaborate well-considered reconstruction of linguistic interactions that result from contact. And even prior to that we should probably do more case studies in areas that are well-known to see, for instance, if ranges of 2%-3% are the norm for genetic comparisons. The southern Bantu languages with the area's long tradition of comparative study, good descriptive studies, a solid understanding of the phonetic and phonological structures of Bantu languages would be a good field for further studies.

We also need to see what different kinds of lists might show. Do large lists yield more evidence of skewing than 100-word lists? Further, do the different counting procedures used by researchers (e.g., counting only cognates, or using scaling) make a difference? Is skewing eliminated if we only count cognates? Bennett's (1976) work, discussed earlier in the paper, indicates that the answer is no. The results of Sabaki LS studies (Nurse and Hinnebusch 1993) also support this view. But other studies need to be checked. I would suspect that eliminating lexical similarities which are demonstrably non-cognates would lower ranges in pair-wise sets of comparisons, so if our goal were to highlight skewed ranges or yield skewed ranges then we might just want to count similarities whatever their nature.

What do we value more highly? Complete or partial similarity? Most LS studies and investigations into the nature of the methodology have focused on how to go about eliminating the effect of contact because the goal of LS studies was always genetic classifications. Should we perhaps begin moving in the other direction?

Finally, we can add the caution in the spirit of Teeter's remarks (1963:648) that the proper use of LS is the study of lexical and cultural change, and that LS can only be a first step in studying contact situations, albeit, an important one. There will be no substitute, however, for detailed lexical studies that can only be possible with the kind of power the Comparative Method provides us.

References

Anttila, Raimo. 1989. Historical and Comparative Linguistics. (2nd revised edition.) Amsterdam, Philadelphia: John Benjamins.

Bastin, Yvonne. 1979. Statistique grammaticale et classification des langues bantoues, *Linguistics in Belgium* 2, Bruxelles, 17-37.

Bastin, Yvonne. 1983. Essai de classification de quatre-vingts langues bantoues par la statistique grammaticale, *Africana Linguistica* 9:11-108.

Bastin, Yvonne, André Coupez & B. de Halleux. 1979. Statistiques lexicale et grammaticale pour la classification historique des langues bantoues, *Bulletin des séances de l'Académie Royale de Sciences d'Outre Mer* 3:375-387.

Bastin, Yvonne, André Coupez & B. de Halleux. 1983. Classification lexicostatistique des langues bantoues, *Bulletin des séances de l'Académie Royale de Sciences d'Outre Mer* 27.2:173-199.

Bastin, Yvonne, André Coupez & B. de Halleux. 1989. Position lexicostatistique du bantu G42 swahili, in: Marie-Françoise Rombi (ed.), 143-148.

Batibo, Herman. 1989. Les parlers ruraux de Zanzibar: 'dialectes' swahilis? Premiers résultats d'une enquête lexicostatistique, in: Marie-Françoise Rombi (ed.), 63-68.

Bender, Marvin Lionel et al. 1976. *Language in Ethiopia*. London: Oxford University Press.

Bennett, Patrick R. 1975/6. Some problems of Bantu Lexicostatistics, in: Isidore Dyen, G. Jucquois, 147-173.

Bergsland, K. & H. Vogt. 1962. On the validity of glottochronology, *Current Anthropology* 3.2:115-152.

Blount, Ben & Richard T. Curley. 1970. The Southern Luo languages: a glottochronological reconstruction, *Journal of African Linguistics* 9.1:1-18.

Bouquiaux, Luc (ed.). 1980. *L'Expansion Bantoue* Vols. 2-3. Paris: Société d'Etudes Linguistiques et Anthropologiques de France.

Brenzinger, Matthias (ed.). 1992. *Language Death: Factual and Theoretical Explorations (with special reference to East Africa)*. Berlin and New York: Mouton de Gruyter.

Coupez, André. 1956. Application de la lexicostatistique au mongo et au rwanda, *Aequatoria* 19:85-87.

Coupez, André, E. Evrard & Jan Vansina. 1975. Classification d'un échantillon de langues bantoues d'après la lexicostatistique, *Africana Linguistica* 6:133-158.

Dyen, Isidore. 1962. The lexicostatistically determined relationship of a language group, *International Journal of American Linguistics* 28:153-161.

Dyen, Isidore. 1963. Lexicostatistically determined borrowing and taboo, *Language* 39:60-66.

Dyen, Isidore & G. Jucquois (eds.). 1975/76. Lexicostatistics in Genetic Linguistics II, Proceeding of the Montreal Conference, Centres de Recherches Mathématiques Université de Montréal, May 19-20, 1973. *Cahiers de l'Institut de Linguistique de Louvan* 3:5-6.

Ehret, Christopher. 1971. *Southern Nilotic History. Linguistic Approaches to the Study of the Past.* Evanston: Illinois.

Ehret, Christopher, et al. 1972. Outlining Southern African History: a re-evaluation A.D. 100-1500, *Ufahamu* 3.1:9-27.

Elmendorf, William W. 1969. Geographic ordering, subgrouping, and Olympic Salish, *International Journal of American Linguistics* 35.3:220-225.

Embleton, Sheila M. 1986. Statistics in Historical Linguistics. Bochum: Brockmeyer.

Flight, Colin. 1988. Bantu trees and some wider ramifications, *African Languages and Cultures* 1.1:25-43.

Fodor, Istvan. 1961. The validity of glottochronology on the basis of the Slavonic languages, *Studia Slavic* 7:295-346.

Gerhardt, Ludwig. 1980. An attempt at a lexicostatistic classification of some Bantu and some not-so-Bantu languages, in: Luc Bouquiaux, Vol. 2, 341-350.

Greenberg, Joseph H. 1957. *Essays in Linguistics.* Chicago: University of Chicago Press.

Greenberg, Joseph H. 1963. The Languages of Africa. The Hague: Mouton; *International Journal of American Linguistics* 29.1. (Publication 25 of the Indiana University Research Center in Anthropology, Folklore and Linguistics.) Bloomington: Indiana University Press.

Gregersen, Edgar A. 1975/6. The glottochronological performance of African Languages, in: Isidore Dyen, G. Jucquois (eds), 107-147.

Guarisma, Gladys & Wilhelm J. G. Möhlig (eds.). 1986. La Méthode Dialectométrique Appliquée aux Langues Africaines. Berlin: Dietrich Reimer.

Guarisma, Gladys & Suzy Platiel (eds.). 1980. Dialectologie et Comparatisme en Afrique Noire, *Actes des journées d'étude tenues au Centre de Recherche Pluridisciplinaire du CNRS,* Ivry (France) , 2-5 juin 1980. Paris: Société d'Etudes Linguistiques et Anthropologiques de France.

Heine, Bernd. 1973. *Zur genetischen Gliederung der Bantu-sprachen.* Afrika und Übersee 56:164-184.

Heine, Bernd. 1974. Historical linguistics and lexicostatistics in Africa, *Journal of African Linguistics* 11.3:7-20.

Heine, Bernd. 1980a. Methods in Comparative Bantu linguistics, in: Luc Bouquiaux (ed.), 295-308.

Heine, Bernd, H. Hoff & R. Vossen. 1977. Neuere ergebnisse zur territorialgeschischte der Bantu, in: Wilhelm J. G. Möhlig, Franz Rottland & Bernd Heine, pp. 57-72.

Heine, Bernd & Wilhelm J. G. Möhlig. 1980. *Geographical and Historical Introduction, Language and Society, Selected Bibliography.* (Language and Dialect Atlas of Kenya I.) Berlin: Dietrich Reimer.

Henrici, Alick. 1973. Numerical classification of Bantu languages, *African Language Studies* 14:82-104.

Hinnebusch, Thomas J. 1976a. The Shungwaya hypothesis: a linguistic reappraisal, in: Joseph T. Gallagher (ed.) East African Cultural History, 1-41. Syracuse, NY: Maxwell School of Citizenship and Public Affairs, Syracuse University.

Hinnebusch, Thomas J. 1976b. Swahili: genetic affiliations and evidence, in Larry M. Hyman, Leon Jacobsen, Russell G. Schuh (eds), *Papers in African Linguistics, in Honor of W. E. Welmers*, 95-108. Studies in African Linguistics, Supplement 6.

Hinnebusch, Thomas J. 1979. Eastern Bantu subgrouping: areas of interaction, Paper delivered at the 22nd Annual Meeting of the African Studies Association, Los Angeles, CA, October 31-November 3, 1979.

Hinnebusch, Thomas J. 1992. Interdialectal Borrowing and Contact in Swahili, Paper delivered at the 35th Annual Meeting of the African Studies Association, Seattle, WA, 20-23 November 1992. Atlanta, Georgia: African Studies Association, Emory University.

Hinnebusch, Thomas J & Derek Nurse (ed.). 1993. *Swahili and Sabaki: A Linguistic History.* Berkeley, Los Angeles and London: University of California Press.

Hinnebusch, Thomas J. & Derek Nurse. 1981. Spirantization in Chaga, *Sprache und Geschichte in Afrika* 3:51-78.

Hinnebusch, Thomas J., Derek Nurse & Martin Mould. 1981. Studies in the Classification of Eastern Bantu Languages. (*Sprache und Geschichte in Afrika*, Beiheft 3.) Hamburg: Helmut Buske.

Hoenigswald, Henry M. 1960. *Language Change and Linguistic Reconstruction.* Chicago: The University of Chicago Press.

Hoijer, Harry. 1956. Lexicostatistics: A critique, *Language* 32:49-60.

Holst, F. 1992. Lexicostatistics and history in Africa, Arbeitspapiere 30:63-88. *Schriftenreihe des Kölner Instituts für Afrikanistik*, University of Cologne.

Hymes, Dell H. 1960a. Lexicostatistics so far, *Current Anthropology* 1:3-44.

Hymes, Dell H. 1960b. More on lexicostatistics, *Current Anthropology* 1:338-345.

Kashoki, Mubanga E. & Michael Mann. 1978. The Bantu languages of Zambia, in: Sirapi Ohannessian, Mubanga E. Kashoki, 47-100.

Ladefoged, Peter, Ruth Glick & Clive Criper (eds.). 1972. *Language in Uganda.* London: Oxford University Press.

Lehmann, D. A. 1978. Languages of the Kafue Basin: Introductory Note, in: Sirapi Ohannessian, Mubanga E. Kashoki, 101-120.

Mann, Michael. 1980. Similarity analyses and the classification of the Bantu languages, in: Luc Bouquiaux, pp. 583-591.

Meeussen, A. E. 1956. Lexico-statistiek van het Bantoe: Bobangi en Zulu, Kongo-Overzee 22:86-89.

Meeussen, A. E. 1980 [1969]. *Bantu Lexical Reconstructions.* Tervuren: Musee Royal de l'Afrique Centrale.

Möhlig, Wilhelm J. G. 1977. Zur frühen Siedlungsgeschichte der Savannen-Bantu aus lauthistorischer Sicht, in: Wilhem J. G. Möhlig, Franz Rottland, and Bernd Heine, Zur Sprachgeschichte und Ethnohistorie in Afrika, 166-193. Berlin: Neue Beiträge Afrikanistscher Forschungen.

Möhlig, Wilhelm J. G. 1978. Versuch einer historischen Gliederung der nordöstlichen Bantusprachen auf lautvergleichender Grundlage, *Afrika und Übersee* 61:175-189.

Möhlig, Wilhelm J. G. 1979. The Bantu nucleus: its conditional nature and its historical significance, *Sprache und Geschichte in Afrika* 1:109-141.

Möhlig, Wilhelm J. G. 1980a. Bantu languages, in: Bernd Heine, Wilhelm J. G. Möhlig, 11-58.

Möhlig, Wilhelm J. G. 1980b. Lehnworteforschung und Ethnohistorie, *Paideuma* 26:7-20.

Möhlig, Wilhelm J. G. 1980c. Dialektgrenzen und Dialektkontinua im Bantu-Sprachgebiet von Kenia: zum Problem der Grenzfindung und Grenzgewichtung, in: Joachim Göschel, Pavle Ivic, Kurt Kehr, Dialekt und Dialektologie: Ergebnisse des Internationalen Symposions Zur Theorie d. Dialekts, Marburg/Lahn, 5-10 September 1977, 291-306. Wiesbaden: Steiner.

Möhlig, Wilhelm J. G. 1980d. La dialectométrie: une méthode de classification synchronique en Afrique, in: Guarisma, Gladys & Suzy Platiel, eds., 27-45.

Möhlig, Wilhelm J. G. 1981. Stratification in the history of the Bantu languages, *Sprache und Geschichte in Afrika* 3:251-316.

Möhlig, Wilhelm J. G. 1986a. Introduction à la dialectométrie synchronique, in: Guarisma, Gladys & W. J. G. Möhlig, pp. 15-26.

Möhlig, Wilhelm J. G. 1986b. Les parlers bantous côtiers du nord-est, in Guarisma, Gladys, & W. J. G. Möhlig, 45-92.

Möhlig, Wilhelm J. G., Gérard Philippson, Marie-Françoise Rombi, Jürgen C. Winter. 1980. Classification dialectométrique de quelques parlers swahili (swahili du Nord et swahili comorien), in: Guarisma, Gladys & Suzy Platiel, 267-304.

Möhlig, Wilhem J. G., Franz Rottland & Bernd Heine. 1977. *Zur Sprachgeschichte und Ethnohistorie in Afrika.* Berlin: Dietrich Reimer.

Ngonyani, Deo Gratias S. 1994. A Classification of *Southern Tanzanian Languages.* M. A. Thesis. University of California, Los Angeles.

Nurse, Derek. 1979. *Classification of the Chaga Dialects.* Hamburg: Helmut Buske.

Nurse, Derek. 1982a. A tentative classification of the primary dialects of Swahili, *Sprache und Geschichte in Afrika* 4:165-206.

Nurse, Derek. 1987. Towards a typology of diachronic phonological change in Bantu languages, *Journal of the Atlantic Provinces Linguistics Association* 9:100-122.

Nurse, Derek. 1988. The diachronic background to the language communities in southwestern Tanzania, *Sprache und Geschichte in Afrika* 9:15-115.

Nurse, Derek & Thomas J. Hinnebusch. 1993. *Swahili and Sabaki: A Linguistic History.* Berkeley, Los Angeles and London: University of California Press.

Nurse, Derek & George Park. 1988. Regional anthropology and historical linguistics, *Sprache und Geschichte in Afrika* 9:7-14.

Nurse, Derek & Gérard Philippson. 1975. The north-eastern Bantu languages of Tanzania and Kenya: a classification, *Kiswahili* 45.2:1-28.

Nurse, Derek & Gérard Philippson. 1980a. The Bantu languages of East Africa: a lexicostatistical survey, in: Edgar C. Polomé and Charles P. Hill (eds.), 26-67.

Nurse, Derek & Gérard Philippson. 1980b. Historical implications of the language map of East Africa, in: Luc Bouquiaux, 685-714.

Nurse, Derek & Martin Walsh. 1992. Chifundi and Vumba: language shift, not death, in: Matthias Brenzinger (ed.), 181-212.

Ohannessian, Sirapi, & Mubanga E. Kashoki (eds.). 1978. *Language in Zambia.* London: (International African Institute) Oxford University Press.

Olmsted, D. L. 1957. Three tests of glottochronological theory, *American Anthropologist* 59:839-842.

Pfouts, Anita. 1984. Social structure in precolonial Namibia: a linguistic analysis, *Ufahamu* 13.2/3:283-302.

Polomé, Edgar C. & Charles P. Hill. 1980. *Language in Tanzania.* London: International African Institute, by Oxford University Press.

Rombi, Marie-Françoise (ed.). 1989. Le swahili et ses limites. Ambiguïté des notions reçues. Table ronde internationale du CNRS (Sèrves, 20-22 avril 1983). Paris: Éditions Recherche sur les Civilisations.

Schadeberg, Thilo C. 1986. The lexicostatistic base of Bennett-Sterk's Reclassification of Niger-Congo with particular reference to the cohesion of Bantu, *Studies in African Linguistics* 17.1:69-83.

Teeter, Karl V. 1963. Lexicostatistics and genetic relationships, *Language* 39.4:638-648.

Thomason, Sarah G. & Terrence Kaufman. 1988. *Language Contact, Creolization, and Genetic Linguistics.* Berkeley and Los Angeles: University of California Press.

Tunks, Jane. 1993. *A lexicostatistical study of Southern Bantu languages,* Department of Linguistics, UCLA, Los Angeles, California. (Ms in possession of TJH).

Whiteley, Wilfred H. (ed.). 1974. *Language in Kenya.* Nairobi: Oxford University Press.

Williams, R. M. 1973. A lexico-statistical look at Oluluyia, A paper to be read at the Fourth Annual Conference on African Linguistics, April 5-7, 1973. Ms (in possession of TJH).

Winter, Jürgen C. 1980. International classifications of Kilimanjaro Bantu compared: towards an East African dialectometry, in: Guarisma, Gladys and Suzy Platiel (eds.), 101-132.

Appendix 1: Sabaki lexicostatistical table

	El	UP	LP	Ch	Gi	Du	Di	Ng	Mh	Nz	Ma	Mw	Ti	Si	Pa	Am	Jo	Mv	Chi	Vu	Mt	NPe	SPe	Ung	Tu	Mak
UP	61																									
LP	57	73																								
Ch	57	63	59																							
Gi	58	63	60	81																						
Du	56	61	57	78	77																					
Di	52	60	53	68	66	70																				
Ng	57	61	56	59	60	60	56																			
Mh	55	58	54	60	58	58	54	81																		
Nz	54	59	55	59	59	58	56	77	83																	
Ma	57	59	56	59	60	59	59	80	84	83																
Mw	60	62	61	59	59	58	55	64	65	65	66															
Ti	59	67	67	63	63	62	59	70	70	72	71	79														
Si	59	67	64	62	63	62	59	69	69	71	70	79	86													
Pa	61	69	67	64	64	64	60	70	71	72	72	81	90	91												
Am	60	69	66	64	64	63	60	70	71	72	72	80	87	89	91											
Jo	58	66	64	65	63	64	59	66	66	68	67	71	78	80	81	81										
Mv	56	65	62	66	64	63	58	65	65	67	68	69	79	79	79	79	80									
Chi	56	62	60	64	65	62	55	65	65	67	65	67	77	77	79	79	80	78								
Vu	57	62	60	63	64	62	54	65	66	67	68	66	75	77	77	77	76	75	79							
Mt	56	62	62	62	62	58	54	64	64	66	66	65	74	75	76	77	78	75	77	78						
NPe	53	59	59	61	61	57	53	61	60	61	63	62	68	69	70	70	71	72	71	70	73					
SPe	51	59	60	58	59	56	51	60	60	62	64	60	68	69	70	70	71	72	71	70	73	73				
Ung	51	58	59	58	60	57	50	61	60	61	62	61	70	71	72	72	72	72	72	71	73	72	74			
Tu	51	58	59	58	58	56	51	61	58	59	60	59	66	67	68	68	69	69	69	68	69	70	69	71		
Mak	51	58	58	59	59	57	51	63	62	63	64	60	67	68	69	69	69	69	68	70	71	73	72	68	74	
Mn	55	62	60	60	61	57	52	60	60	61	61	63	71	69	71	71	68	67	64	65	66	65	64	66	62	63

Appendix 2: Abbreviations of language names

El	Elwana	Pa	Pate
UP	Upper Pokomo	Am	Amu
LP	Lower Pokomo	Jo	Jomvu
Ch	Chonyi	Mv	Mvita
Gi	Giriama	Chi	Chifundi
Du	Duruma	Vu	Vumba
Di	Digo	Mt	Mtang'ata
Ng	Ngazija	NPe	Northern Pemba
Mh	Mwali	SPe	Southern Pemba
Nz	Nzuani	Ung	Unguja
Ma	Maore	Tu	Tumbatu
Mw	Mwiini	Mak	Makunduchi
Ti	Tikuu	Mn	Mwani
Si	Siu		

Sabaki subgroups (based on Nurse and Hinnebusch 1993:4-19):

(a) Swahili

Lamu Archipelago (Tikuu, Siu, Pate, Amu)

(Southern Somali coast and Lamu archipelago, Kenya)

Mombasa (Mvita, Chifundi, Vumba, etc.)

(Mombasa area, and southern Kenya and northern Tanzania)

Zanzibar (Pemba, Tumbatu, Makunduchi and Unguja)

(b) Mijikenda (Malindi and Mombasa hinterlands, Kenya)

Northern Mijikenda (Chonyi, Giryama, Duruma, etc.)

Southern Mijikenda (Digo and Segeju)

(c) Comorian (Ngazija, Mwali, Nzwani, Maore)

(Comoro Islands archipelago in the Mozambique Channel off the northwest coast of Madagascar)

(d) Mwani (northern Mozambique coast and Kirimba Islands)

(e) Mwiini (Brava Town on the Somali coast)

(f) Elwana (north of the Pokomo dialect cluster along the Tana River in Kenya)

Nasal Vowel Creation without Nasal Consonant Deletion and the Eventual Loss of Nasal Vowels thus Created: The Pre-Bantu Case

JOHN M. STEWART*
Edinburgh

Introduction

This article, somewhat exceptionally for the present volume, is concerned with proto-Bantu reconstruction primarily in the light of the comparison of Bantu languages with other Niger-Congo languages. One would expect such comparative studies to be specially relevant to the reconstruction of proto-Bantu in areas in which the Bantu languages differ markedly from the languages of neighbouring groups, and the focus of this article is in fact on vowel nasalization, which is one of the most significant of these areas. Although proto-Bantu as traditionally reconstructed has neither nasal vowels proper nor even phonologically nasalized allophones of oral vowels, nasal vowels abound not only in non-Bantu (New) Benue-Congo languages such as Yoruba and Igbo but also in (New) Kwa, Gur and Adamawa-Ubangi languages, and look as if they might be reconstructable at least as far back

* I wish to acknowledge that I have greatly benefited from comments by Larry Hyman and Thilo Schadeberg on earlier versions of this work. I retain, however, sole responsibility.

as proto-Volta-Congo, the latest common ancestor of all these languages by Williamson's (1989:21) classification.

Two non-Bantu languages in particular are considered, both of them members of the Potou-Tano subgroup of the Nyo, or Right Bank, subgroup of (New) Kwa by Stewart's (1989b:221) classification: Akan, the dominant language of Ghana, and Ebrié, the language of the area around Abidjan, the capital of the Ivory Coast. Akan and Ebrié are the best-documented languages in the Tano and Potou subgroups respectively of Potou-Tano.

By Williamson's (1989:21) classification, (New) Kwa is a primary branch of Volta-Congo, and Bantu falls within a different primary branch of Volta-Congo, namely (New) Benue-Congo, so that the latest common ancestor of the Bantu languages, Akan and Ebrié is proto-Volta-Congo. Reconstructions of the nonsonorant consonants and the vowels of the latest common ancestor of the Bantu and the Potou-Tano languages, based exclusively on these languages, are to be found in Stewart (1993 (the consonants) and 1983 (the vowels)); these reconstructions serve as a tentative proto-Volta-Congo, though since they are subject to revision in the light of comparison with other daughters of the same protolanguage, and since the identification of that protolanguage as proto-Volta-Congo is similarly subject to revision in the light of evidence against the currently accepted classification, they are best referred to not as proto-Volta-Congo but as proto-Bantu-Potou-Tano.

Stewart (1993, Appendix B) lists 75 comparative pairs (pairs of apparent cognates) across Guthrie's Common Bantu and Akan; this list would be considerably longer if it was not restricted to pairs displaying stem-initial consonant correspondences which were presumed to be derived from proto-Bantu-Potou-Tano nonsonorants.

The present article begins by examining in greater detail, and with special reference to the derivation of proto-Bantu from proto-Bantu-Potou-Tano (pBPT), an issue which arises in my recent study of implosives in Bantu-Gbe-Potou-Tano (Stewart 1995; Gbe is the continuum which includes Ewe), namely that of how best to account diachronically for the differences in the synchronic rules which are presumed to apply in proto-Potou-Tano and proto-Bantu respectively where a stem-initial implosive is preceded by a homorganic nasal prefix. In proto-Potou-Tano the implosive is assimilated to the preceding nasal in all contexts by a rule of Progressive Implosive Nasalization, while in proto-Bantu it is changed into a plain voiced stop by a rule of Implosive Delenization provided no nasal or prenasalized stop follows in second consonant position, in which case either (i) the Implosive Delenization rule applies as usual and the new voiced stop is thereupon immediately changed into a nasal by a version of Meinhof's law (see Section 4) which I shall call the rule of Progressive Voiced Consonant Nasalization, or (ii)—to derive the same output in another way—the Implosive Delenization rule does not apply as it is bled by a rule of Progressive Implosive Nasalization which differs from the proto-Potou-Tano rule of the same name only in that it is contextually restricted. Both the nasalization and the delenization are entirely natural changes since, as Greenberg (1970:131-2) observes, implosives are highly disfavoured after homorganic nasals; although Greenberg mentions only one of the natural changes that occur, namely the one that I am here calling delenization, the other is clearly attested in present-day Ebrié, as we shall be seeing in Section 3.

The situation in pBPT is presumed to be the same as in proto-Potou-Tano, and the situation in proto-Bantu is presumed to be the result of Stop Epenthesis, a sound change whereby a plain voiced stop is inserted between a nasal consonant and an oral vowel; the new stop is interpreted synchronically as an allophone of its implosive counterpart conditioned by the preceding nasal and, where that preceding nasal constitutes a prefix, as the stem-initial consonant. At the stage of BPT-to-Bantu (i.e. the derivation of proto-Bantu from pBPT) at which Stop Epenthesis applies, a vowel in first vowel position is presumed to be nasalized before a consonant which is ancestral to a proto-Bantu nasal or prenasalized stop; this nasalization blocks the application of Stop Epenthesis between the vowel and a preceding implosive in stem-initial position, and the forms originally generated by Progressive Implosive Nasalization survive unchanged. Now as we have seen, these forms can be derived synchronically in two different ways in proto-Bantu: (i) by allowing Implosive Delenization to apply first and then reversing it in part (i.e. making the consonant lenis again) by applying a rule of Progressive Voiced Consonant Nasalization (Meinhof's law), or (ii) by placing a contextual restriction on the Progressive Implosive Nasalization and applying it first, so that Implosive Delenization never applies in the context in question. Diachronically, of course, by the present reconstruction, the plain voiced stops affected by Meinhof's law never were plain voiced stops in the context in question, and Meinhof's law thus appears to be at variance with the historical facts. The alternative to Meinhof's law is to be preferred even on purely synchronic grounds as it is more explanatory: a single structure condition disallows implosives after homorganic nasals, and two different rules serve that condition in different contexts.

As I note in my earlier (1995) article, the situation reconstructed in proto-Potou-Tano and pBPT is essentially the same as that found in present-day Ebrié and suggests that nasal vowels are created in pre-BPT in a manner not encountered by Ferguson (1966) or Greenberg (1966). Ferguson (1966:59) tentatively assumes that "nasal vowels, apart from borrowing and analogical formations, always result from the loss of a primary nasal consonant." Greenberg (1966:508-9) takes this to imply two successive events: first, the creation of nasalized allophones of oral vowels by nasalization before or after a nasal consonant, and second, the raising of these allophones to the status of phonemically nasal vowels by the deletion of the nasal consonant which has conditioned the nasalization. As we shall see presently, the above reconstruction suggests that Ferguson's assumption should be modified so as to admit that the nasalized vowels are sometimes phonemicized not by the deletion of the nasal consonant but by the creation of new [NV] or [VN] sequences in which the vowels are oral, and thus in contrast with the vowels in the existing [NṼ] or [ṼN] sequences. This proposed modification of Ferguson's assumption is both natural and modest: it simply acknowledges that the deletion of the nasal consonant is not the only means by which the nasalization of the vowel can cease to be conditioned by the context.

I suggest that the synchronic rule of Progressive Implosive Nasalization posited in pBPT in the above reconstruction reflects a diachronic rule of Progressive Implosive Nasalization which applies at some stage of pre-BPT—possibly at a stage at which homorganic nasal prefixes originate by the deletion of the vowels in *NV-* prefixes. I also suggest that this diachronic rule is the second of two: by Vowel Nasalization, the first, vowels preceding or following nasal consonants become redundantly nasalized, so that *mɓa etc. vs. *mma etc. become *mɓa etc. vs. *mmã etc., and by Progressive Implosive Nasalization, the second, a stem-initial implosive preceded by a homorganic nasal prefix is replaced by a simple nasal which tolerates a following oral vowel, so that *mɓa etc. vs. *mmã etc. become *mma etc. vs. *mmã etc.—and new [NV] sequences with oral vowels are created. The synchronic consequences of the second rule are highly remarkable: not only does the nasality of the vowels become phonemic as it is no longer conditioned, but that of the nonsyllabic nasals becomes allophonic as it is now conditioned either by a following nasal vowel or by a preceding homorganic nasal, and the language is left without any nonsyllabic nasal phonemes—a situation which survives today not only in Ebrié, which still retains the original implosives, but also, according to Schachter and Fromkin (1968), in Akan, which dominates the Right Bank, or Nyo, subdivision of (New) Kwa, and, according to Capo (1991), in Ewe, which dominates the Left Bank subdivision. Ewe, it might be mentioned, has gone one step further and dropped its homorganic nasals, with the result that, if certain phenomena of very recent origin are disregarded, it can be said to have no underlyingly nasal consonants whatsoever.

The application of Stop Epenthesis in PBT-to-Bantu, of course, by which *mma etc. vs. *mmã etc. become *mba etc. vs. *mmã etc., has the synchronic result of shifting the underlying oral/nasal contrast back from the vowel to the consonant, where it was before the application of Progressive Implosive Nasalization in pre-BPT; the vowels in question are phonetically unchanged, but their nasality is now once again merely allophonic. Note that since, before the diachronic rule of Progressive Implosive Nasalization applies in pre-BPT, a vowel following an implosive is phonologically oral only if it is not followed by a nasal consonant, the application of Progressive Implosive Nasalization cannot result in the creation of *mmam etc. sequences with oral vowels, and that consequently the subsequent application of Stop Epenthesis in BPT-to-Bantu cannot create *mbam etc. sequences.

Sections 1-4 reproduce, in revised and sometimes expanded form, relevant material from my earlier (1995) study. Sections 1 to 3 respectively show how the comparative method supports my reconstruction of (i) pBPT stem-initial *ɓ, *ɗ, (ii) the pBPT homorganic nasal prefix, and (iii) the proto-Potou-Tano rule of Progressive Implosive Nasalization; the latter proto-Potou-Tano rule supports in turn my reconstruction, already seen, of the pBPT rule of the same name. Section 4 looks at the nature of Meinhof's law in the light of the reconstructions.

In Section 5 I examine, in the light of my claim that pBPT had nasal vowels and that in one particular context at least these were created by a process which did not involve nasal consonant deletion, Hyman's (1972) grounds for claiming that his "proto-Benue-Kwa"—which can be taken as equivalent to my pBPT for the present purpose—had no nasal vowels, and that the nasal vowels of the (Old) Kwa languages were invariably created by nasal consonant deletion.

In Section 6 I go on to break new ground in reconstructing in pBPT a synchronic rule of Syllabic Identical Nasal Deletion, applying after Progressive Implosive Nasalization, whereby a syllabic homorganic nasal representing a prefix is deleted before a stem-initial nasal. I show how the subsequent application of the diachronic rule of Stop Epenthesis in BPT-to-Bantu to words in which both synchronic rules had applied since pBPT could account for the origin in stem-initial position of the characteristic Bantu prenasalized stops in which the initial homorganic nasal is nonsyllabic.

In Section 7 I reconstruct in pre-BPT a diachronic rule of Syllabic Identical Nasal Deletion as the source of the synchronic rule of the same name, and credit it with having the effect of raising nasalized voiced continuants generated by an earlier rule of Nasal Weakening to the phonemic status which they have in pBPT in essentially the same way as the diachronic rule of Progressive Implosive Nasalization has the effect of raising nasalized vowels generated by an earlier rule of Vowel Nasalization to the phonemic status which they have in pBPT.

In Section 8 I present a case for treating the nasalized lateral of Umbundu, one of a number of nasalized voiced continuants reported in that language by Schadeberg (1982), as a direct reflex of the nasalized lateral of pBPT, and thus for reconstructing a nasalized lateral in proto-Bantu. The nasalized lateral of pBPT is of course one of the nasalized voiced continuant phonemes created by the diachronic rule of Syllabic Identical Nasal Deletion.

In Section 9 I reappraise, in the light of this, Greenberg's (1951) diachronic explanation of the nasal harmony found throughout most of the western part of the Bantu area. I note that the *n* which manifests the harmony in all Greenberg's examples corresponds to a nasalized lateral in

Umbundu, and suggest that it goes back not to an oral lateral but to a nasalized lateral in proto-Bantu.

1. The reconstruction of proto-Bantu-Potou-Tano stem-initial *ɓ, *ɗ

Table 1 summarizes the correspondences which support my reconstruction of proto-Bantu-Potou-Tano stem-initial *ɓ, *ɗ (Stewart 1993). It is important to note that except in the case of Guthrie's Common Bantu (CB), the segments are defined not in phonemic terms but in terms of binary phonological features (cf. Stewart 1993:5,24). The relevant binary features here are Lenis, Nasal, Implosive, Continuant, Lateral, Voiced, Labial, Coronal, Dorsal; all [+lenis] segments are redundantly [+voiced], all [+lenis, -nasal, -continuant] segments are redundantly [+implosive], and a [+lenis, -nasal, +continuant, +coronal, -dorsal] segment is redundantly [+lateral].

pBPT	*pBantu*	*CB*	*pPotou-Tano*	*pPotou*	*Ebrié*	*pTano*	*Akan*
*ɓ	*ɓ	/*b/	*ɓ	*ɓ	ɓ	*b	b
*ɗ	*ɗ, *l	/*d/	*ɗ	*ɗ, *l	ɗ, l	*d	d

*Table 1. The correspondences which support the reconstruction of stem-initial *ɓ, *ɗ in proto-Bantu-Potou-Tano.*

Table 2 gives a number of comparative series (CS) across Common Bantu (CB) and present-day Ebrié and Akan illustrating the correspondences in Table 1. The tones are not shown for Ebrié, or for Akan where they are predictable (see Stewart 1993:25-6); they are irrelevant for the present purpose. Note that CB, being phonemic, does not show the allophones *ɓ, *ɗ, *l which I reconstruct in proto-Bantu to the exclusion of *b, *d stem-initially where no homorganic nasal prefix precedes.

	'become cooked'	*'faeces' (CB) 'dirt'*	*'stone'*	*'come'*	*'break'*
CB	*-bìd-	*-bį́dò	*-bùè		
Ebrié	-ɓe	a-ɓi	a-ɓu	-ɓa	-ɓɔ
Akan	-bɪ̃ŋ	e-bĩŋ	ɔ-bʊ	-ba	-bɔ
	'bend'	*'ask'*	*'become black'*	*'soft, slow'*	*'hit'*
CB					*búd-
Ebrié	-ɓu	-ɓi	-ɓie	ɓlɛ-ɓlɛ	
Akan	-bu	-bìsá	-bìrí	bìrɛ̀-bìrɛ̀	bʊrʊ
	'eat'	*'lie down, sleep'*	*'extinguish*	*'tongue'*	*'old'*
CB	*-dí-	*-dáád-	*-dį́m-	*-dímì	
Ebrié	-ɗi	-la	(-nɔ̃)	a-lɛ	lɔ-lɔ
Akan	-di	-da	-dũm		ɗɪ-ꜜdáw

Table 2. Comparative series illustrating the correspondences in Table 1.

Proto-BPT *ɓ, *ɗ survive unchanged in proto-Potou-Tano, and also in proto-Bantu and proto-Potou except that, in BPT-to-Bantu and Potou-Tano-to-Potou independently, *ɗ becomes *l before non-ATR vowels (Stewart 1993:12-13,17-18; ATR = Advanced Tongue Root); this means in effect, in each case, that *ɗ becomes *l before all vowels other than *i, *u. Note that this particular sound change, although not specifically mentioned by Greenberg in his account of "the course of events by which [glottalic] consonants originate and undergo characteristic developments which often result in the loss of the glottalic feature" (1970:134), can none the less be seen as a special case of his "hierarchy of dissolution by which the least favored positions will undergo loss of the glottalic feature first" (1970:135). Since "injectives tend to have front articulation" (1970:127) and in each of the two instances of the change in question the language affected is presumed to have had *ɓ, *ɗ and no other implosives, the alveolar position was in each case the one more likely to undergo the loss of the feature [+implosive]. Since "the point of articulation hierarchies of ejectives and injectives are obviously based on preference for a small and large chamber respectively" (1970:139), *ɗ was more likely to undergo the loss of the feature [+implosive] before non-ATR vowels than before ATR vowels because of the smaller size of the chamber.

The implosives of proto-Bantu survive in several present-day Bantu languages spoken in the northwest; in each of the five languages A.24

Duala, A.34 Benga, B.31 Tsɔgɔ, B.52 Nzɛbi, B.53 Tsaangi, CB /*b/ (pB *ɓ) has the reflex ɓ before all vowels, and CB /*d/ (pB *ɗ) has the reflex ɗ before CB *į *u̧ (i.e. the two ATR vowels) only (Guthrie 1967-71 vol.2:30-6). Clearly the correspondence of *ɓ, ɗ* in Ebrié with *ɓ, ɗ* in a number of present-day Bantu languages strongly supports the reconstruction of *ɓ, *ɗ in the protolanguage, namely pBPT.

The implosives *ɓ, *ɗ of proto-Potou-Tano change into *b, *d in Potou-Tano-to-Tano without merging with any existing *b, *d, and these survive unchanged in Akan and nearly all the other Tano languages. The implosives did not however disappear without trace; in the Asante and Akuapem dialects of Akan as well as in a number of other Tano languages, stem-initial *b, d* are still replaced synchronically by *m, n* after homorganic nasal prefixes just as were their implosive antecedents, even though the rule is no longer natural after the sound change as the sequences *mb, nd,* unlike the sequences *mɓ, nɗ,* are universally highly favoured.

2. The reconstruction of proto-Bantu-Potou-Tano homorganic nasal prefixes

The following two homorganic nasal prefixes found in Bantu languages, and reconstructed as *n by Meeussen in his Bantu Grammatical Reconstructions (1967:97) and *ny by Guthrie in his Common Bantu, correspond to homorganic nasal prefixes in Potou-Tano languages and are presumed to go back to homorganic nasal prefixes in proto-Bantu-Potou-Tano: a first person singular subject verb prefix (C.S.2227f in Guthrie's CB), and a plural noun prefix (Bantu class 10, C.S.2209). I shall look at these in turn.

The 1sg. subject prefix *N-* occurs in Akan and other Tano languages but not in Ebrié. In Akan it occurs in the future affirmative tense only, where it is invariably followed by the future prefix *bɛ́-*, e.g. *Ǹ- +bɛ́bá* → (Fante dialects) *m̀bɛ́ba,* (Asante and Akuapem dialects) *mɛ́bá,* 'I shall come'; in all other tenses the 1sg. subject prefix is *mɪ̀-* e.g., *mɪ̀- + ꜝbà* (Fante and Akuapem dialects) *mɪ́ꜝbà* 'I come'. There are grounds for suspecting that this prefix failed to occur in all tenses even in proto-Bantu-Potou-Tano, as Guthrie notes under C.S.2227f that it occurs in only some tenses in D.61 Ruanda, F.31 Nilamba and P.15 Mbunga. In Anyi, which is closely related to Akan within the Tano group, it occurs in some tenses in which it does not occur in Akan, but still fails to occur in all tenses; the following examples are from Burmeister (1982:169-71): ŋ̀gɔ̀lɪ́ 'je suis parti' (cf. Akan mɪ̀kɔ̀ɔɪ), but mɪkɔ́ 'je veux partir/j'irai'..

The plural noun prefix *N-* occurs in both Akan and Ebrié. In Akan it is one of two plural noun prefixes, and in some languages of the Guang subgroup of Tano it is one of a larger number of such prefixes; Snider (1988) reconstructs four such prefixes in proto-Guang, and all four probably go back to proto-Tano. In proto-Bantu, of course, it is, as the class 10 prefix, one of a still larger number of such prefixes, most if not all of which probably go back to proto-Bantu-Potou-Tano.

In my earlier (1995) study I proceed on the provisional assumption that the homorganic nasal prefixes were syllabic in all contexts in pBPT, and I shall proceed on the same assumption here as far as Section 6, where I shall present evidence that they were reduced to zero before a consonant realized as a nasal.

3. The reconstruction of a synchronic rule of Progressive Implosive Nasalization in proto-Potou-Tano

We have already seen, in the Introduction, the grounds for reconstructing in proto-Bantu-Potou-Tano a synchronic rule of Progressive Implosive Nasalization identical to one that we had assumed at that point to be already validly reconstructed in proto-Potou-Tano. Here we look at the grounds for this latter, lower-level, reconstruction.

In Ebrié, which shares with Akan not only the plural noun prefix *N*- which we take to be cognate with the Bantu class 10 noun prefix but also a noncount noun prefix *N*-, and in which, as we have seen, pBPT *ɓ, *ɗ survive, all voiced lenis consonants including *ɓ*, *ɗ* become nasals after either a homorganic nasal prefix or a nasalized vowel (Stewart 1973, Bole-Richard 1982:327-30, Kutsch Lojenga 1985:8-10), as we see in (1).

(1)	N- PL + ɓie 'woman'	→	mmie	'women'
	N- NONCOUNT + la 'sleep' (v)	→	nna	'sleep' (n)
	N- NONCOUNT + nã	→	nnã	'meat'
	mɛ̃- 'I' + ɓa 'come'	→	mɛ̃ma	'I have come'
	mɛ̃- 'I' + lo 'go'	→	mɛ̃no	'I have gone'

In the Asante and Akuapem dialects of Akan, in which language, as we have seen, pBPT *ɓ, *ɗ do not survive as they have been replaced by *b, *d in Potou-Tano-to-Tano, all voiced consonants including *b, d*, by a rule of Progressive Voiced Consonant Nasalization, become nasals after a homorganic nasal prefix (Christaller 1875:10) though not after a nasalized vowel, as we see in the Asante examples in (2).

(2)	mɪ̃̀- 'I' + bá 'come'	→	mɪ̃̀bá	'I come'
	mɪ̃̄- 'I' + ɴ̀ NEG + bá 'come'	→	mɪ̃̀m̀má	'I do not come'

I accordingly reconstruct in proto-Potou-Tano a synchronic rule of Progressive Implosive Nasalization, identical in essence to the Ebrié rule just seen, whereby *ɓ, *ɗ become *m, *n after a homorganic nasal or a nasalized vowel. In proto-Tano I reconstruct a similar synchronic rule of Progressive Voiced Consonant Nasalization whereby, as in the Asante and Akuapem dialects of Akan, *b, *d become *m, *n after a homorganic nasal but not after a nasalized vowel. This is a version of the proto-Potou-Tano rule which survives despite the fact that it has lost its phonetic *raison d'être* after the change from implosives to plain voiced stops; whereas implosives are highly disfavoured after homorganic nasals, plain voiced stops are of course highly favoured.

A synchronic rule which can be dropped without creating any highly marked or impossible phonetic situation has, of course, a reduced chance of survival, and the proto-Tano rule of Progressive Voiced Consonant Nasalization has in fact been dropped in the Fante dialect of Akan; compare Fante *mĩm̀bá* 'I do not come' with the corresponding Asante form in (2). The original purpose of such a rule is commonly to shore up forms which have been undermined by some phonetic change; Meinhof's law is another such "shore-up" rule, as I show in the next section.

4. Meinhof's law (or any rule substituted for it) as a "shore-up" rule.

Meinhof (1913, as quoted by Meeussen 1962) notes that the following rule, a version of which was reported in Ganda by C.T. Wilson in 1882, is not in fact confined to Ganda but occurs also in Bemba and to a very limited extent in certain other Bantu languages: if a prenasalized voiced stop in first consonant position is followed in second consonant position by another prenasalized voiced stop or by a nasal, the prenasalized stop in first consonant position is reduced [by the assimilation of the oral element to the nasal element] to a simple nasal. The rule is commonly known today as Meinhof's law or Meinhof's rule, though Meinhof himself called it Ganda law. It is now known to apply in very many more Bantu languages; for an updated statement of its distribution see Meeussen (1962).

Schadeberg (1987) distinguishes three main variants of the rule: the Ganda variant seen above, which applies whether there is a prenasalized stop or a nasal in second consonant position, the Lamba variant which applies only where there is a prenasalized stop in that position, and the Umbundu variant which applies only where there is a simple nasal in that position. It is of course the Ganda variant that I reconstruct in proto-Bantu, whose synchronic status in present-day Ganda is most recently examined in considerable detail by Katamba and Hyman (1991).

As we have seen in the Introduction, I suggest that we have to choose, in the reconstruction of proto-Bantu, between (i) a synchronic rule of Progressive Voiced Consonant Nasalization, a version of Meinhof's law, which applies after the Implosive Delenization rule and which does not directly reflect any diachronic rule (the plain voiced stops affected never having been plain voiced stops diachronically in the context in question), and (ii) a contextually restricted synchronic rule of Progressive Implosive Nasalization which applies before the Implosive Delenization rule and bleeds it and which represents a partial retention of the contextually unrestricted Progressive Implosive Nasalization rule of pBPT. Because we have this choice it is particularly important that we should distinguish between what I shall call Meinhof's structure condition, which specifies, whether in

Meinhof's own or in anyone else's terms, a context in which prenasalized voiced stops are inadmissible, and Meinhof's law or rule, which states how, in Meinhof's own view, Meinhof's structure condition is met where it would otherwise be violated; it is of course to Meinhof's law or rule that I am proposing an alternative, not to Meinhof's structure condition.

There are very many Bantu languages (55 according to Meeussen 1962:26) in which Meinhof's structure condition appears to be completely absent. This has a simple diachronic explanation, whether we postulate Progressive Voiced Consonant Nasalization (Meinhof's law) or Progressive Implosive Nasalization (my preferred alternative) in proto-Bantu. To look at the latter option first, these languages have exploited the fact that once the Progressive Implosive Nasalization rule is no longer the only rule whereby the disfavoured nasal-implosive sequences are eliminated, there is no articulatory obstacle in the way of dropping that rule altogether and allowing the Implosive Delenization rule to apply to all nasal-implosive sequences in all contexts. These languages can be said to have completed a two-stage transition from (i) the exclusive use of Progressive Implosive Nasalization (in the pre-Stop Epenthesis period) to (ii) the use of Implosive Delenization to the total exclusion of Progressive Implosive Nasalization.

We now turn to the other option, namely the postulation of Progressive Voiced Consonant Nasalization (Meinhof's law) in proto-Bantu. This rule differs from the Progressive Voiced Consonant Nasalization postulated in proto-Tano (see Section 3) only in that it is contextually restricted: it applies only if the voiced consonant is followed by a nasalized vowel (or, to restate it in Meinhof's own terms, only where a simple nasal or a prenasalized stop follows in second consonant position). In each case the rule changes a plain voiced stop into a nasal after a homorganic nasal, and in each case it represents an articulatorily unwarranted retention, or partial retention, of an earlier natural rule which changed an implosive into a nasal after a homorganic nasal—articulatorily unwarranted since, as we saw in the last section, whereas implosives are highly disfavoured after homorganic nasals, plain voiced stops are highly favoured. In neither case does the rule reflect a diachronic rule whereby plain voiced stops become nasals after homorganic nasals.

In each case the original purpose of the rule is to shore up forms which have been undermined by phonetic change. In neither case does it serve any universal structure condition, and the Progressive Voiced Consonant Nasalization (Meinhof's law) of proto-Bantu has been simply dropped in a large proportion of Bantu languages just as the Progressive Voiced Consonant Nasalization of proto-Tano has been simply dropped in Fante.

Note that although Progressive Implosive Nasalization, my preferred alternative to Progressive Voiced Consonant Nasalization (Meinhof's law) in proto-Bantu, is less directly comparable to the Progressive Voiced Consonant Nasalization of proto-Tano, it is still a "shore-up" rule.

5. Hyman's exclusive reliance on nasal consonant deletion as the source of nasal vowels in (Old) Kwa

Hyman's (1972) case for taking nasal consonant deletion to be the only source of nasal vowels in (Old) Kwa is stated in terms of what I regard as an unwarranted assumption which he makes about his "proto-Benue-Kwa," the latest common ancestor of Benue-Congo, which includes Bantu, and Kwa. His "proto-Benue-Kwa" (pBK) can be regarded as equivalent to my proto-Bantu-Potou-Tano (pBPT) for the present purpose. Whereas I assume that nasal vowels were already present in pBPT (in one particular context at least) and were lost (in that context) in BPT-to-Bantu, Hyman assumes that they were absent in both pBK and proto-Kwa and were created in the course of the development of the various Kwa languages from proto-Kwa; he writes (1972:172-3):

> Considerable evidence for the treatment of nasalized vowels [in Kwa] as the historical product of proto *VN$ (via [*VÑ$]) is ... available. While I know of no extensive well-documented study, occasional correspondences with Bantu cannot be missed. In (7) I have compared three Nupe forms with the corresponding proto roots I have reconstructed for Proto-Bamiléké, which I consider to be Bantu: ...
>
> (7) Nupe gã̀ : PBké *`gàm´ 'to speak'
>
> Nupe kã́(nã́) : PBké *`kán` 'monkey'
>
> Nupe kã́ : PBké *`káŋ´ 'to fry'
>
> Here we see that while Nupe has /ã/ in all three words, Proto-Bamiléké possessed three distinct morpheme-final nasal consonants. It seems then that in the derivation of nasalized vowels in Kwa (with reservations about certain dialects of Akan), the distinction between final /m/, /n/ and /ŋ/ has been neutralized. Other such examples are readily available.
>
> Evidence like that presented in (7) should be enough to convince any skeptic that the proto language that was the ancestor of Nupe (as representative of Kwa) and Bamiléké (as representative of Benue-Congo), for which I shall use the *ad hoc* label Benue-Kwa, did not have nasalized vowels, but instead allowed morpheme-final nasal consonants.

This is invalid as evidence that proto-Benue-Kwa did not have nasal vowels. Consider the comparative pairs across Anyi and Akan in Table 3, which are taken from Stewart (1976:127-8 and 1993: Appendix A); Anyi and Akan are both members of the close-knit Central Tano group:

	'become used up'	*'weep'*	*'fight'*	*'become cooked'*	*'dig'*	*'kill'*
pCTano	*-sã	*-sũ	*-kʊ̃	*-bɪnɪ̃	*-fũnũ	*-kũm
Akan	-sã	-sũ	-kʊ̃	-bɪ̃ŋ	-fũnũ	-kũm
Anyi	-sã	-sũ	-kɔ̃	-bɛ̃	-fũ	-kũ

Table 3. Comparative pairs across Akan and Anyi demonstrating that apparent evidence for the creation of nasal vowels by the loss of a final N(V) is invalid as evidence that the protolanguage, which in this case is proto-Central Tano, did not have nasal vowels.

Hyman would presumably accept pairs such as the three on the right as evidence that the protolanguage did not have nasal vowels, but pairs such as the three on the left show that he would be in error.

Now let us look at how Hyman accounts for the creation of those nasal vowels which I consider to be created not by the loss of any nasal consonant but as a consequence of Progressive Implosive Nasalization. He derives [mṼ] and [nṼ] sequences such as those of Ebrié, in which prevocalic nasals are synchronically variants of implosives, from proto-Kwa *ɓVNV and *ɗVNV respectively, as in (3) (1972:191):

(3) proto-Kwa *ɓVNV > ɓNV > ɓmV > mmV > Ebrié [mṼ]
proto-Kwa *ɗVNV > ɗNV > ɗnV > nnV > Ebrié [nṼ]

The most obvious objection to this is the absence of any evidence that the nasal posited in second consonant position ever existed in the roots in question. One expects a claim that nasal vowels have been created as a result of the loss of a nasal consonant to be supported by Ṽ = VN or Ṽ = NV sound correspondences showing direct evidence of that consonant in related languages which have not undergone the same change, but despite the fact that there is no shortage of related languages, no such correspondences have ever been found.

A second objection is that the comparative evidence that we now have suggests that although the reconstruction of the forms *ɓVNV and *ɗVNV is indeed justified in pre-BPT, these developed in a very different way; an example is pre-BPT *-ɓɪnɪ > *-ɓɪ̃nɪ̃ > pBPT *-ɓɪ͠lɪ > *-ɓɪnɪ̃ > proto-Tano and proto-Central Tano *-bɪnɪ̃ > *-bɪŋ > the Akan form -bɪ̃ŋ 'become cooked,' which we have already seen in Table 3. Compare pBPT *-ɓɪ͠ɪ > *ɓɪlɪ > proto-Bantu *-ɓɪl- (CB *-bíd-) 'become cooked'. All the changes posited here are discussed in Section 7 below; see in particular the last paragraph.

6. The reconstruction of a synchronic rule of Syllabic Identical Nasal Deletion in proto-Bantu-Potou-Tano

Up to this point I have been proceeding on the assumption that the homorganic nasal prefixes of proto-Bantu-Potou-Tano were syllabic in all contexts. In this section I propose the reconstruction in pBPT of a rule of Syllabic Identical Nasal Deletion, applying after Progressive Implosive Nasalization, which reduces them to zero before a consonant realized as a nasal.

The homorganic nasal prefixes are generally nonsyllabic in present-day Bantu languages: where the stem begins with a consonant they are commonly realized as zero or as the nonsyllabic nasal element of a prenasalized obstruent according to whether or not the stem-initial consonant is realized as a nasal. I assume that this situation goes back to proto-Bantu, despite the fact that there are some present-day Bantu languages in which the prefixes are not nonsyllabic in either context. One such language is Ganda, which, as it happens, also has the distinction of figuring prominently in the literature on Meinhof's law; the examples in (4) of the plural noun prefix of class 10, which are taken from Tucker (1962:125-6) and in which Tucker's transcription is retained, illustrate:

4)	lù-muli	pl.	\`m-muli	'reed'
	lù-nakù		\`n-nakù	'day'
	lù-bengo		\`m-mengo	'grindstone'
	lù-limì		\`n-nimì	'tongue'
	lù-bu		\`m-bu	'series'
	lù-lira		\`n-dira	'umbilical cord'

It is not implausible to suggest that here the nasal prefix may have become syllabic and tone-bearing at some stage of Bantu-to-Ganda simply by the dropping of its differences in syllabic and tone-bearing status from the singular prefix with which it is in contrast.

The homorganic nasal prefixes are generally syllabic in Akan, but except in the case of one of them, the negative prefix, which is not presumed to go back to pBPT, they sometimes have a zero variant in the non-Fante dialects where the following consonant is realized as a nasal by virtue of Progressive Voiced Consonant Nasalization. The examples in (5) are from the Asante dialect; (5a-b) illustrate the plural noun prefix *Ǹ*-, (5c-d) the noncount noun prefix *Ǹ*-, and (5f) the first person singular (1sg) subject prefix *Ǹ*-. The material on the first two of these prefixes is from my own field notes. Note that the third prefix, the sg subject prefix *Ǹ*-, survives only before the simple future tense prefix *bɛ́*- and thus never occurs in a context in which a syllabic, or nonzero, variant would be expected; in all other tenses the 1sg subject prefix is *mĩ*-, as we saw in Section 2. L = low tone, H = high tone, and ↓ = downstep.

```
(5)  a.  a- + kʊra        →    akʊra     'old man'
         |     | |              | | |
         L     L H              L L H

         N- + kʊra        →    ŋkʊra     'old men'
         |      | |             | | |
         L      L H             L L H

     b.  a- + yʷʊwa       →    ayʷʊwa    'plate''
         |        |  |          |   | |
         L        H↓H           L   H↓H

         N- + yʷʊwa       →    ɲʷʊwa     'plates''
         |        |  |              | |
         L        H↓H           L   H↓H

     c.  N- + suo         →    nsuo      'water'
         |      | |             | ||
         L      HH              L HH

     d.  N- + gʊ          →    ŋʊ        'oil'
         |     |                |
         L     H               L H

     e.  ɔ- + bɛba        →    ɔbɛba     'he will come'
         |     | |              | | |
         L     H H              L H H

     f.  N- + bɛba        →    mɛba      'I will come'
         |     | |                | |
         L     H H             L  H H
```

I take the zero variant which is found both in Bantu and in Akan as evidence for the reconstruction in pBPT of a rule of Identical Nasal Deletion (note that I have not yet justified reconstructing the nasal as syllabic before deletion) which applies after Progressive Implosive Nasalization and which reduces the homorganic nasal to zero before a consonant realized as a nasal. I assume that, like Progressive Implosive Nasalization, it directly reflects a diachronic change which took place at some stage of pre-BPT; and I also assume that the diachronic Identical Nasal Deletion took place at a later stage than the diachronic Progressive Implosive Nasalization just as the synchronic Identical Nasal Deletion applies after the synchronic Progressive Implosive Nasalization.

I consequently assume that at the stage of BPT-to-Bantu immediately before that at which Stop Epenthesis intervened, both Progressive Implosive Nasalization and Identical Nasal Deletion applied, with the result that the addition of a homorganic nasal prefix had the effect of changing stem-initial *ɓa, *ɓãm etc. to *ma, *mãm etc. Then when Stop Epenthesis intervened, it changed *ma etc. to *mba etc. without changing the syllablic status of the initial nasal, and thereby created the prenasalized voiced stops which I reconstruct in proto-Bantu.

As we saw earlier, the plain voiced stop inserted by Stop Epenthesis is interpreted synchronically as the initial consonant of the stem. Now if we make the reasonable assumption that the homorganic nasals of pBPT—at least when they were word-initial—were, as in Akan, invariably syllabic in those contexts in which they were not deleted by the Identical Nasal Deletion rule, Stop Epenthesis would appear to have created an unstable situation in which word-initial homorganic nasals were syllabic before plain voiceless stops but nonsyllabic before plain voiced stops. It is plausible to suggest that the situation was stabilized by the intervention of a diachronic rule of Homorganic Nasal Desyllabization which merged the syllabic variant with the nonsyllabic variant, and had the synchronic result that the homorganic nasal prefixes became nonsyllabic in their base forms. The nonsyllabic homorganic nasal prefixes of proto-Bantu are thus adequately accounted for in terms of direct or indirect consequences of Stop Epenthesis in BPT-to-Bantu, and I therefore reconstruct the homorganic nasal prefixes of pBPT as invariably syllabic where they do not undergo Syllabic Identical Nasal Deletion.

One might expect that where the stem began with a simple *m or *n, diachronic Syllabic Identical Nasal Deletion would completely eliminate the distinction between the presence and the absence of the prefix, at least on the segmental tier. As we shall see in the next section, however, there is ample evidence that this did not happen: that "before" the double nasals *mm, *nn were reduced to the single nasals *m, *n, the single nasals *m, *n were reduced to the nasalized voiced continuants *β̃, *l̃ by a diachronic rule of Nasal Weakening. I write "before" in quotes as the two diachronic rules could have applied together as a push-chain to substitute the new contrasts *m* vs. *β̃* and *n* vs. *l̃ for the outgoing *mm* vs. *m* and *nn* vs. *n*; however that may be, I assume that Syllabic Identical Nasal Deletion had the effect of raising the nasalized voiced continuants to phonemic status in essentially the same way as Progressive Implosive Nasalization had the effect of raising the nasalized vowels to phonemic status.

7. The creation of the nasalized voiced continuants of proto-Bantu-Potou-Tano

I have elsewhere posited the following nondorsal voiced lenis consonantal segments in proto-Volta-Congo, which can be equated with pBPT for the present purpose: ɓ, ɗ, l, m, n, 'β̃, l̃ (Stewart 1989a:80, Figure 13). In the present article I drop the initial raised comma of the 'β̃, as the lenisness which it indicates is predictable, being a consequence of the nasalization.

Of course the proposals first outlined in Stewart (1995) and further elaborated in the present article demand a radical revision of the derivation of these segments from their antecedents in the pre-BPT of just before

Progressive Implosive Nasalization (PINas), and I now tentatively propose the derivation in (6) for the stem-initial nondorsal voiced lenis consonantal segments (note that the restriction to stem-initial excludes oral l), both alone and in combination with a prefix nasal which has been deleted by the synchronic rule of Syllabic Identical Nasal Deletion:

(6)									
Pre-BPT before PINas	ɓ	ɗ	m	n	mɓ	nɗ	mm	nn
Progressive Implosive Nasalization					mm	nn		
Nasal Weakening			β̃	l̃				
Syllabic Identical Nasal Deletion					m	n	m	n
Proto-Bantu-Potou-Tano	ɓ	ɗ	β̃	l̃	m	n	m	n

Two of the three rules which apply in this derivation, namely Progressive Implosive Nasalization and Syllabic Identical Nasal Deletion, the ones which apply where pre-BPT has *mɓ* or *nɗ*, have already been considered in some detail. While Progressive Implosive Nasalization applies in (6) only where pre-BPT has *mɓ* or *nɗ*, Syllabic Identical Nasal Deletion applies also where pre-BPT has *mm* or *nn* and would merge these with *m* or *n* respectively if the latter were not first dissimilated to *β̃* or *l̃* respectively by Nasal Weakening, which changes a nonsyllabic simple nasal to a nasalized voiced continuant where no syllabic identical nasal precedes. Note that after Syllabic Identical Nasal Deletion, the nasalized voiced continuant consonants are phonemes in their own right and not mere allophones of the simple nasals. Note also that simple nasals no longer occur initially in the underlying forms of stems, and that a stem-initial simple nasal in a surface form now indicates the presence of a prefix whose syllabic nasal has been synchronically deleted.

As Schadeberg observes in his article on 'Nasalization in UMbundu' (1982:109), "Nasalized consonants are universally infrequent." Because of this we would hardly expect them to be created otherwise than as part of a package whereby the cost was offset by some benefit. Under the present proposal, Nasal Weakening and the more widely applicable Syllabic Identical Nasal Deletion together constitute such a package: Syllabic Identical Nasal Deletion eliminates double nasals in a language in which consonant clusters are exceptional, but at the price of the creation, by Nasal Weakening, of nasalized consonants to allow the substitution of the new contrasts *m* vs. *β̃ and n* vs. *l̃* for the outgoing *mm* vs. *m and nn* vs. *n.*

The case for reconstructing pBPT *l̃ is convincingly illustrated by the four comparative pairs across Akan and Common Bantu in Table 4 taken from Stewart (1989a:53); for these, by the present proposals, pBPT*l̃ is reconstructed not only in first consonant position but also in second consonant position:

Akan	-yɛŋ	-yʷɛŋ	-ɲʷ̃ɪnɪ̃	-ɲʷɪ̃nɪ̃
	'bring up (child)'	'watch'	'bitter'	'cool, cold'
Common Bantu	*-dèd-	*-dòd-	*-dùdù	*-dį̀dį̀
	'look after (child)'			
cf. Proto-Bantu	*-lɛl-	*-lɔl-	*-lʊlʊ-	*-lili-

*Table 4. Comparative pairs across Akan and Common Bantu which support the reconstruction of *-CVCV forms with *l̃ in both consonant positions in proto-Bantu-Potou-Tano.*

Table 5 shows the derivation of the Akan forms from the forms posited in pre-BPT at the stage just before Vowel Nasalization, and Table 6 shows the derivation of the proto-Bantu forms from the proto-Bantu-Potou-Tano forms already derived in Table 5.

	'bring up'	*'watch'*	*'bitter'*	*'cool, cold'*
Pre-BPT before V Nasalization	*-nɛnɪ	*-nɔnɪ	*-nʊnʊ	*-nunu
1. V > [+nasal] / N	*-nɛ̃nɪ̃	*-nɔ̃nɪ̃	*-nʊ̃nʊ̃	*-nũnũ
2. N > [+cont] except / N	*-l̃ɛ̃l̃ɪ	*-l̃ɔ̃l̃ɪ	*-l̃ʊ̃l̃ʊ̃	*-l̃ũl̃ũ
Proto-Bantu-Potou-Tano	*-l̃ɛ̃l̃ɪ	*-l̃ɔ̃l̃ɪ	*-l̃ʊ̃l̃ʊ̃	*-l̃ũl̃ũ
1. l̃ > ỹ / C1	*-ỹɛ̃l̃ɪ	*-ỹɔ̃l̃ɪ	*-ỹʊ̃l̃ʊ̃	*-ỹũl̃ũ
2. V > [-round] / ỹ __		*-ỹʷɛ̃l̃ɪ	*-ỹʷɪ̃l̃ɪ	*-ỹʷɪ̃l̃ɪ
3. [-hi, -lo] V > [-nasal]	*-yɛnɪ̃	*-yʷɛnɪ̃		
Proto-Central Tano	*-yɛnɪ̃	*-yʷɛnɪ̃	*-ỹʷ̃ɪl̃ɪ	*-ỹʷ̃il̃i
1. nɪ̃, nĩ > ŋ / C2V2	-yɛŋ	-yʷɛŋ		
2. [+nasal] C > [-cont] /_ [+hi] V			*-ɲʷ̃ɪnɪ̃	*-ɲʷ̃ini
Akan	-yɛŋ	-yʷɛŋ	-ɲʷ̃ɪnɪ̃	-ɲʷ̃inĩ

*Table 5. Derivations of the Akan reflexes of forms reconstructed as *-nVnV in pre-Bantu-Potou-Tano and as *-l̃Ṽl̃Ṽ in proto-Bantu-Potou-Tano.*

	'look after'	*'watch'*	*'bitter'*	*'cool, cold'*
Proto-Bantu-Potou-Tano	*-l̃ɛ̃l̃ɪ	*-l̃ɔ̃l̃ɪ	*-l̃ʊ̃l̃ʊ̃	*-l̃ũl̃ũ
1. [+cont] C > [-nasal]	*-lɛlɪ	*-lɔlɪ	*-lʊlʊ	*-lulu
2. u > i /[+coronal] C__				*-lili
3. V > Ø /__ suffix	*-lɛl-	*-lɔl-		
Proto-Bantu	*-lɛl-	*-lɔl-	*-lʊlʊ	*-lili
cf. Common Bantu	*-dèd-	*-dòd-	*-dùdù	*-dį̀dį̀

*Table 6. Derivations of the proto-Bantu reflexes of forms reconstructed as *-nVnV in pre-Bantu-Potou-Tano and as *-l̃ Ṽl̃ Ṽ in proto-Bantu-Potou-Tano.*

Pre-BPT 1 and 2 in Table 5 are the Vowel Nasalization and Nasal Weakening rules already seen.

The third of the BPT-to-Central Tano rules in Table 5 calls for comment as in effect it does more than merely denasalize mid vowels: in the service of a structure condition of Nasalization Harmony, whereby adjacent sonorant continuant segments agree in their specification for [nasal], a consonant preceding a denasalized mid vowel is denasalized and a consonant following it is replaced by a simple (noncontinuant) nasal. The Nasalization Harmony condition is a surviving synchronic consequence of the diachronic rule of Nasal Weakening in pre-BPT.

The first of the BPT-to-Bantu rules in Table 6, similarly, has an effect beyond merely denasalizing the nasalized continuant consonants: in the service of the Nasalization Harmony condition, the vowels adjacent to the denasalized consonants are also denasalized.

It will be seen that of all the rules posited in Tables 5 and 6, there is only one which applies in only one of the four derivations and which might because of that be more open to suspicion of being *ad hoc*, and that is BPT-to-Bantu.2, which changes *u* to *i* after a coronal consonant. In fact the same rule is presumed to account also for the *u* = *i* (CB *į*) correspondence in Akan *-dũm* = Common Bantu **-dį́m-* 'become extinguished, extinguish'.

The proto-Central Tano nasalized lateral *l̃ shown in C2 position in Table 5 and its oral counterpart *l have both survived in Nzema, which, as a member of the Central Tano group, is one of the languages most closely related to Akan. Both the oral and the nasalized lateral have, however, been lost in Akan, having been replaced by *r* and *n* respectively, e.g. Nzema *fʊfʊlɛ* = Akan *fʊ́!fʊ́rʊ* 'new', Nzema *ɲ-j̃ĩl̃ɪ̃* = Akan *ɲcĩnĩ* 'salt'. For a comparative study of the consonants at C2 in the Central Tano ('Central Volta-Comoé') languages see Stewart (1976:127-141).

The sound correspondence Akan n or ŋ = CB *d which I now derive from pBPT nasalized *l̃ at C2 as in Tables 5 and 6 is illustrated by the further comparative pairs in (7a), most of which are reproduced from Stewart

(1989a:84). The pairs in (7a) may be compared with those in (7b), also from Stewart (1989a:84), which illustrate the correspondence Akan *r* = Common Bantu (CB) *d derived from pBPT oral *l at C2:

(7) a.	Akan	˙ɲ-cĩnĩ	'salt'	CB	*-kédè	
		-h̃ĩnĩ	'itchy'		*-pèdè	
		-mĩnĩ	'swallow'		*-mèd-	
		-mĩnĩ	'throat, gullet'		*-mèdò	
		ɛ̀-cʷɪnĩ	'nose'		*-yúdù	
		-tʊ̃nʊ̃	'forge'		*-tʊ́d-	
		o-kũnu	'husband'		*-kúdù	'older sibling, adult, old person, important person'
		-sɛŋ	'become suspended'		*-déd-	
		-bĩŋ	'become cooked'		*-bíd-	
		e-bĩŋ	'dirt'		*-bɪ́dò	
b.	Akan	-bʊrʊ	'hit'		*-búd-	
		ɔ̀-sʊ́ꜝrʊ̀	'top, sky'		*-jùdú	
		-ciri	'abstain'		*-gɪ̀d-	
		a-huru	'foam'		*-pʊ́dò	

It will be seen that in the last two pairs in (7a), the Akan entry ends in *ŋ* and not in the $n\tilde{V}$ sequence which the rules in Table 5 on their own lead us to expect wherever the preceding vowel is high. The two Akan forms in question, namely those for 'become cooked' and 'dirt', are however entirely regular: Akan has ŋ to the exclusion of $n\tilde{V}$ not only after the mid vowels *ɛ, ɔ, e, o*, but also after any vowel which is preceded by a voiced stop. In the Kwa languages, as Hyman (1972) has noted, nasal vowels are rare after implosives (though not after plain voiced stops) just as the nasal vowels *ɛ̃, ɔ̃, ẽ, õ* are rare in any context. I suggest that the first of the two Akan forms is derived as follows: pBPT *ɓĩl̃ɪ > (by vowel denasalization after implosive, with automatic *l̃* > *n* after oral vowel as in BPT-to-Central Tano.3 in Table 5) *ɓɪnĩ > (by implosive becoming plain voiced stop) proto-Tano and proto-Central Tano *bɪnĩ > (by Central Tano-to-Akan.1 in Table 5) *-bɪŋ > (by high vowel nasalization before nasal) Akan *-bɪ̃ŋ* 'become cooked.' Note that although by the first change the first vowel is denasalized after the implosive, by the second change the implosive becomes a plain voiced stop and thereby facilitates the eventual renasalization of the vowel by the last change.

8. The loss of nasalized voiced continuants in Bantu

If the reconstruction in the preceding section is correct, the nasalized voiced continuants of pBPT which still survived were completely wiped out, together with the phonological nasalization of the adjacent vowels, by the diachronic rule BPT-to-Bantu.1 in Table 6, which I shall call Continuant Denasalization. The C2 sound correspondence Akan *n* or *ŋ* = proto-Bantu oral *l (CB *d), which I derive from pBPT nasalized *-l̃, looks very convincing indeed—it is illustrated above by no fewer than fourteen comparative pairs—and it seems impossible to conceive of a scenario whereby the nasal = oral correspondence is the result not of the loss of the nasality in BPT-to-Bantu by Continuant Denasalization or some other such diachronic change but of the acquisition of the nasality at some stage of BPT-to-Akan.

The pBPT reconstruction does however raise doubts about the traditional proto-Bantu and Common Bantu reconstructions on which it rests. Three of the Common Bantu items with C2 *d corresponding to Akan *n* or *ŋ* listed in (7a) have reflexes with a nasalized lateral in Umbundu, namely *-ɲũl̃ũ* 'nose' (Schadeberg, pers. com.), *-tɛ̃l̃-* 'forge' and *-kũl̃ũ* 'old person' (both Schadeberg 1982:116), and as the most obvious explanation is that the Umbundu reflexes have inherited the nasalized lateral unchanged from pBPT via proto-Bantu, the traditional proto-Bantu may be incorrect and I may be in error in locating Continuant Denasalization in BPT-to-Bantu instead of in the relevant post-Bantu derivations.

Evidence that the pBPT nasalized lateral survives in proto-Bantu not only at C2 but also at C1 is provided by Umbundu *-l̃ã* 'intestines' (Schadeberg 1982:114-5), which appears to have been inherited unchanged from pBPT *-l̃ã (which is of course presumed to be derived from pre-BPT *-na by pre-BPT.1-2 in Table 5). The Akan form is *-ya-* and it appears to be derived as follows: pBPT *-l̃ã > (by BPT-to-Tano.1 in Table 5) *-ỹã > (by a new rule of Continuant Denasalization discussed below) *-ya > (by the item ceasing to occur without the addition after it of *-mũ* inside' or some other item) > *-ya-*. The traditional CB form is of course *-dà.

The new Continuant Denasalization rule posited here appears to apply in Central Tano-to-Akan (CT-to-Akan) at the same stage as rule CT-to-Akan.2 in Table 5, whereby nasalized voiced continuants become simple (noncontinuant) nasals; I shall call this latter rule Nasalized Continuant Strengthening. Both rules appear to serve an innovatory structure condition which disallows nasalized voiced continuants: Nasalized Continuant Strengthening changes these sounds into simple nasals before high vowels, and Continuant Denasalization denasalizes them elsewhere. In effect, however, Continuant Denasalization does more than merely denasalize the consonant: it also triggers the denasalization of the following vowel in the service of the Nasalization Harmony condition which we have already seen in the discussion of rules BPT-to-Central Tano.3 in Table 5 and BPT-to-Bantu.1 in Table 6; it will be recalled that the second of these, which is also a Continuant Denasalization rule, not only denasalizes the nasalized voiced continuants but also, in effect, in the service of the Nasalization Harmony condition, triggers the denasalization of the adjacent nasalized vowels.

There is even a good case for reconstructing a nasalized lateral in proto-Bantu purely on the basis of the internal Bantu evidence provided by regular sound correspondences across (a) Umbundu, which displays the nasalization harmony seen above, whereby any unbroken sequence of voiced sonorant continuants within a specified domain is either oral or nasalized throughout, (b) those Bantu languages which display nasal harmony (as distinct from nasalization harmony), and (c) those Bantu languages which display neither nasalization harmony nor nasal harmony. In languages with nasal harmony, *Vn* occurs to the exclusion of *Vl* after a nasal. Umbundu and the nasal harmony languages together occupy a continuous area in the west which constitutes about half of the total Bantu area; for a map see Greenberg (1951:816). I look at the correspondences in question in the next section.

9. Nasal harmony and nasalization harmony in Bantu languages

Greenberg (1951:816-7) writes as follows:

> Some Bantu languages, among which are Herero, Kongo, Luba, Ila, etc., have not merely two but four variants of some of the verb derivational suffixes under discussion. These additional forms occur when the final consonant of the suffix is *l*, which is then replaced by *n* if the final consonant of the verb root is *m* or *n*. We have thus, in addition to the vowel harmony already discussed, a tendency for a nasal consonant in the verb to be followed by one in the suffix, which has the forms *-in-* and *-en-* in place of *-il-* and *-el-* when a nasal consonant precedes, [e.g.] *kotam-a* 'to bow down', *kotam-in-a* 'to bow down to'...
>
> In general, in those languages of the Bantu family in which nasal harmony occurs in the verb suffixes, [in] words that contained in Proto-Bantu the succession of consonants *m-l*, [that *m-l*] has been replaced by *m-n* as a regular rule of phonetic development. Ila, which, as we have seen, is a language in which the verbal suffixes in *l*, change *l* to *n* after a preceding nasal consonant, shows *man-a* 'to finish' (< Proto-Bantu *mal-a), *men-a* 'to grow' (< Proto-Bantu *mel-a), *min-a* 'to swallow' (< Proto-Bantu *mil-a) ... On the other hand, Nyamwezi, a language of East Africa, which does not have nasal harmony in its verb suffixes, has *mal-a* 'to finish', *mel-a* 'to grow', and *mil-a* 'to swallow'.

Umbundu, however, although it is one of the languages listed by Greenberg as having nasal harmony, turns out not to have true nasal harmony whereby *Vn* occurs to the exclusion of *Vl* after a simple nasal, but rather what I am here calling nasalization harmony, whereby (among other things) a nasalized lateral occurs to the exclusion of an oral lateral after a nasalized vowel, whether that vowel owes its nasality to a preceding simple nasal or to a preceding nasalized voiced continuant. Schadeberg writes as follows (1982:119; note that subject to certain restrictions which can be disregarded for the present purpose, a vowel is nasalized if it is adjacent to a nasalized consonant and Schadeberg leaves its nasality unmarked):

> "There are several verbal extensions in which *-Vl-* varies with *-Vl̃-*. Two of these are semantically transparent, and for these the distribution of allomorphs is predictable:
>
> (27) -Vl̃- / {N,C̃} __
> -Vl- / elsewhere
>
> The same distribution applies to the allomorphs *-ile/-ele/-il̃e/-el̃e* of the "final" suffix marking certain past tenses. The two extensions are the Applicative *-il-/-el-/-il̃-/-el̃* and the Separative *-ul-/-ol-/-ul̃/-ol̃-*. Below I give relevant examples containing the Separative extension ...
>
> (28) N__: óku.pémul̃à 'to cut hair'
> C̃__: óku.sól̃ol̃à 'to take out seam'

The nasalized lateral of Umbundu corresponds to the simple nasal of the true nasal harmony languages not only in verbal extensions and suffixes but also within the verbal root; compare Umbundu *óku.mal̃à* 'to finish' (Schadeberg 1982:119) with Ila *man-a* 'to finish' (Greenberg *op. cit.*). Umbundu *ókw.inà* 'to swallow' (Schadeberg 1982:119), which has *n* at C2, has lost the *m at C1, and is clearly less comparable with Ila *min-a* 'to swallow'.

Greenberg, then, notes a *n* = *l* correspondence within Bantu both at C2 and in verbal extensions, and it is clear from Schadeberg's data on Umbundu that there is in fact an (a) *l̃* = (b) *n* = (c) *l* correspondence in each of these contexts. It is understandable that Greenberg, on the basis of the limited *n* = *l* correspondence, should reconstruct *l in proto-Bantu and posit a change to *n* after *NV*, even though this is a costly hypothesis as the change is not universally frequent and has no obvious articulatory motivation. The establishment of the fuller *l̃* = *n* = *l* correspondence suggests that we should instead reconstruct nasalized *l̃ in proto-Bantu and posit two unconditioned changes: to *n* by a Nasalized Continuant Strengthening rule identical to that posited above in Central-Tano-to-Akan (except that it is unconditioned), and to oral *l* by the Continuant Denasalization rule posited above in BPT-to-Bantu but now relocated in the relevant eastern post-Bantu derivations. Both of these rules have the same obvious articulatory motivation: the replacement of nasalized voiced continuants, which have a highly marked status.

The (a) *l̃* = (b) *n* = (c) *l* correspondence, however, occurs only in the context of a preceding simple nasal, and we still have to account for the correspondence (a) *l̃* = (b) *l* = (c) *l* (i.e. Umbundu *l̃* = non-Umbundu *l*) which occurs elsewhere: we still have to account for the fact that in the languages which display nasal harmony, proto-Bantu *l̃ has the reflex *l* instead of *n* in certain circumstances. I suggest that the Nasalized Continuant Strengthening rule is bled by an earlier rule of Vowel Denasalization which denasalizes any nasalized vowel after an oral consonant in the service of an innovatory structure condition of CV Nasality which requires any CV sequence to be either oral or nasal throughout—and that this Vowel Denasalization triggers the denasalization, in the service of the Nasalization Harmony condition, of any following nasalized voiced continuants, e.g. *-tũl̃- > *-tul̃- > *-tul-* 'to forge'. As a consequence of the earlier application of the diachronic rule of Stop Epenthesis, of course, CV sequences with oral vowels already meet the CV Nasality condition. It would appear that after Vowel Denasalization, no phonemically nasalized vowels or phonemically nasalized continuant consonants survive. A comparable rule of Vowel Denasalization would appear to have reduced the nasal vowels to subphonemic status in Guang-to-Northern Guang (cf. Snider 1989; Guang is a subgroup of Tano).

It will be clear that in the western Bantu languages generally apart from Umbundu, the merger of *l̃ with *n by Nasalized Continuant Strengthening results in the loss of what remains of the nasalization harmony which first emerges in pre-Bantu-Potou-Tano as a synchronic consequence of Nasal Weakening, and in the emergence in its place of Greenberg's nasal harmony.

10. Conclusion

Many questions remain unanswered. It would appear that nasalized continuants reverted to simple nasals not only by the post-Bantu Nasalized Continuant Strengthening rule just seen, but also elsewhere in post-Bantu as well as in pre-BPT and BPT-to-Bantu, at various stages and in various contexts. A pre-BPT reversion to *m, for instance, could account for the correspondences Akan/Ebrié *m* = proto-Bantu stem-initial *m (see 'swallow' and 'throat' in (7a)) and Akan *m* = proto-Bantu stem-final *mb (from *m by the BPT-to-Bantu rule of Stop Epenthesis before a vowel-initial suffix), provided at least that the nasalized continuant *β̃ was allowed to survive in second consonant position in certain—admittedly as yet far from obvious—circumstances to account for the Common Bantu stem-final contrast between *m (my proto-Bantu *β̃) and *mb.

More ample data is available on the nasalized lateral than on any of the other nasalized continuants, and I have not considered any of the others in detail above. Further work in this area, with special reference to Umbundu, should prove rewarding, but note that although Umbundu does have a few instances of *ṽ*, in no instance does this appear to be a reflex of proto-Bantu *β̃; in fact proto-Bantu *β̃ appears not to have occurred stem-initially and to have reverted to *m* stem-finally in Bantu-to-Umbundu.

The main conclusion in the context of the present volume, however, is that the application of the comparative method across Bantu and non-Bantu languages is of much greater significance for the reconstruction of proto-Bantu than is generally appreciated. If non-Bantu languages are disregarded, "Meinhof's law" seems to suggest that the prenasalized voiced stops are older that the simple nasals that replace them, but comparison with the Potou-Tano languages suggests the contrary: once we have posited (i) Vowel Nasalization and Progressive Implosive Nasalization in pre-BPT to account for the origin of the nasal vowels of BPT, and (ii) Stop Epenthesis in BPT-to-Bantu to account for the origin of prenasalized stops (with nonsyllabic nasal element) in proto-Bantu, we do not need to posit any further sound change to account for the origin of "Meinhof's law"—the changes we have already posited predict it. This virtually cost-free account assumes of course that the simple nasals in question are older than the prenasalized stops.

We have similarly seen that if non-Bantu languages are disregarded, western Bantu languages appear to have acquired nasal harmony by a diachronic change from a proto-Bantu voiced oral consonant to a simple nasal where the preceding consonant was a simple nasal, but that comparison with the Potou-Tano languages suggests instead that proto-Bantu had not an oral consonant but a nasalized continuant in the contexts in question and that the most significant diachronic change involved was *denasalization* in the *eastern* Bantu languages.

References

Bole-Richard, Rémy. 1982. L'ébrié, in: Georges Hérault (ed.), *Atlas de Langues Kwa de Côte d'Ivoire*. Abidjan: Institut de Linguistique Appliqueé, Université d'Abidjan, et Agence de Coopération Culturelle et Technique, 307-57.

Burmeister, Jonathan. 1982. L'agni, in: Georges Hérault (ed.), *Atlas de Langues Kwa de Côte d'Ivoire*. Abidjan: Institut de Linguistique Appliqueé, Université d'Abidjan, et Agence de Coopération Culturelle et Technique, 155-172.

Capo, Hounkpati B.C. 1991. *A Comparative Phonology of Gbe*. (Publications in African Languages and Linguistics, 14.) Berlin: Foris and Labo Gbe.

Christaller, Johann Gottlieb. 1875. *A Grammar of the Asante and Fante Language called Tshi (Chwee, Twi)*. Basel: Evangelical Missionary Society. (Republished 1964 by Gregg Press, Farnborough.)

Christaller, Johann Gottlieb. 1881. *A Dictionary of the Asante and Fante Language called Tshi (Chwee, Twi)*. Basel: Evangelical Missionary Society.

Ferguson, Charles A. 1966. Assumptions about nasals: a sample study in phonological universals, in: Joseph H. Greenberg (ed.), *Universals of Language*, 2nd edition. Cambridge, MA: MIT Press, 53-60.

Greenberg, Joseph H. 1951. Vowel and nasal harmony in Bantu languages, *Zaïre* 5: 813-20.

Greenberg, Joseph H. 1966. Synchronic and diachronic universals in phonology, *Language* 42.2: 508-17.

Greenberg, Joseph H. 1970. Some generalizations concerning glottalic consonants, especially implosives, *International Journal of American Linguistics* 36: 123-45.

Guthrie, Malcolm. 1967-71. *Comparative Bantu*. 4 vols. Farnborough: Gregg.

Hyman, Larry M. 1972. Nasals and nasalization in Kwa, *Studies in African Linguistics* 3: 167-205.

Katamba, Francis & Larry M. Hyman. 1991. Nasality and morpheme structure constraints in Luganda, *Afrikanische Arbeitspapiere* 25: 175-211.

Kutsch Lojenga, Constance. 1985. The tones of the Ebrié associative construction, *Journal of African Languages and Linguistics* 7: 1-22.

Meeussen, A.E. 1962. Meinhof's rule in Bantu, *African Language Studies* 3: 25-9.

Meeussen, A.E. 1967. Bantu grammatical reconstructions, *Africana Linguistica* 3: 79-121.

Meinhof, Carl. 1913. Dissimilation der Nasalverbindungen im Bantu, *Zeitschrift für Kolonialsprachen* 3: 272-8.

Schachter, Paul & Victoria Fromkin. 1968. *A Phonology of Akan: Akuapem, Asante and Fante.* (UCLA Working Papers in Phonetics, 9.) Los Angeles: University of California.

Schadeberg, Thilo C. 1987. Nasalization in UMbundu, *Journal of African Languages and Linguistics* 4: 109-132.

Schadeberg, Thilo C. 1982. Silbenanlautgesetze im Bantu, *Afrika und Ubersee* 70.1:1-17.

Snider, Keith L. 1988. The noun class system of proto-Guang and its implications for internal classification, *Journal of African Languages and Linguistics* 10: 137-163.

Snider, Keith L. 1989. The vowels of proto-Guang, *Journal of West African Languages* 19.2: 29-50.

Stewart, John M. 1973. The lenis stops of the Potou Lagoon languages and their significance for pre-Bantu reconstruction, in: M.E. Kropp Dakuku (ed.), *Papers in Ghanaian Linguistics* [2]. (Institute of African Studies Research Review, Supplement 4.) Legon: University of Ghana, 1-49.

Stewart, John M. 1976. The final light syllables of Akan (Twi-Fante) and their significance for Volta-Comoe reconstruction, in: H.M.J. Trutenau (ed.), *Languages of the Akan Area: Papers in Western Kwa Linguistics and on the Linguistic Geography of the Area of Ancient Begho.* (Mitteilungen der BAB, 14.) Basel: Basler Afrika Bibliographien, 93-156.

Stewart, John M. 1983. The high unadvanced vowels of proto-Tano-Congo, *Journal of West African Languages* 13.1: 19-36.

Stewart, John M. 1986. Stop epenthesis and Meinhof's law. [Paper presented at the 16th Colloquium on African Languages and Linguistics, Leiden.]

Stewart, John M. 1989a. Fortis/lenis and vowel length in proto-Bantu, *Journal of African Languages and Linguistics* 11: 45-88.

Stewart, John M. 1989b. Kwa, in: John Bendor-Samuel (ed.), *The Niger-Congo Languages*. Lanham: University Press of America, 217-45.

Stewart, John M. 1993. The second Tano consonant shift and its likeness to Grimm's law, *Journal of West African Languages* 23.1: 3-39.

Stewart, John M. 1995. Implosives, homorganic nasals and nasalized vowels in Volta-Congo, in: E. Nolue Emenanjo & Ozo-mekuri Ndimele (eds.), *Issues in African Languages and Linguistics: Essays in honour of Kay Williamson.* Aba: National Institute for Nigerian Languages, 162-70.

Tucker, Archibald N. 1962. The syllable in Luganda, *Journal of African Languages* 1: 122-66.

Williamson, Kay. 1989. Niger-Congo overview, in: John Bendor-Samuel (ed.), *The Niger-Congo Languages*. Lanham: University Press of America, 3-45.

The Historical Interpretation of Vowel Harmony in Bantu

LARRY M. HYMAN
University of California, Berkeley

1. Introduction

Those of us who have assembled at this Table Ronde on Bantu Historical Linguistics share a number of interrelated historical and comparative concerns. First, we are concerned to define the Bantu group as a genetic unit and to determine the place of Narrow and Wide Bantu, Bantoid, etc. within the Benue-Congo branch of Niger-Congo. Second, as a related goal, we share an interest in refining Proto-Bantu (PB) reconstructions and therefore in establishing what was vs. was not present in the parent language. As part of this enterprise, language-internal and cross-linguistic examinations have been necessitated of the changes that have taken place in the ca. 500 Bantu languages. An oft expressed hope is that the variations characterizing Bantu languages can serve as reliable criteria for the internal sub-grouping of the family.

My paper shares all of this concerns. While those of us present (and others) have approached the above four issues in a number of ways, I would like to exemplify a particular strategy that has only occasionally been applied to Bantu, most notably in the work of Yvonne Bastin. This strategy is to focus on widespread phonological phenomena in Bantu that are conditioned in an unusual way by the morphology. Just as arbitrary features of a morphological system are cited as evidence for genetic relation, the idea here is that phonological properties that have arbitrary—or at least unusual—morphological conditions may also serve this genetic marking function. The material for the kinds of studies I advocate here have been accessible for some time, mostly in dictionaries and lexicons, many of which we have acquired, created, or converted to electronic form as part of the Comparative Bantu On-Line Dictionary (CBOLD) project.[1] My purpose in this paper is twofold. First, I document the well-known process of vowel height harmony (VHH) throughout the (Narrow) Bantu domain. For this purpose I have created a Bantu vowel-harmony database which at the time of this writing contains information on 134 languages. Second, I attempt to show that a peculiarity of VHH, namely an asymmetry in how it operates in front vs. back vowels, is a useful criterion to subdivide Bantu into two groups, roughly approximating the Equitorial vs. Savanna Bantu split postulated by other researchers.[2] My tentative suggestion will be that this asymmetry was introduced into proto-Savanna Bantu after this split was effected.

2. Vowel height harmony

A process of vowel height harmony (VHH) has been documented in a wide range of languages from all parts of the Bantu zone. While widely occurring, VHH is subject to considerable variation. I refer to one pattern which occurs with significant frequency as "asymmetric" VHH in this paper. Assuming for the moment the Proto-Bantu (PB) seven-vowel system **į*, **i*, **e*, **ų*, **u*, **o*, **a* reconstructed by Meinhof and van Warmelo (1932), Guthrie (1967-71), Meeussen (1967) and others, the relevant asymmetry can be expressed diachronically as in (1).[3]

---

[1]Both CBOLD and lexical research on Bantu were supported in part by National Science Foundation grant no. SBR93-19415 and SBR96-16330. An earlier version of this paper was presented under the title "Reconstructing Bantu and its Evolution" at a workshop entitled "Pushing Back the Limits of Linguistic Prehistory: Methods, Tools and Results", which I co-organized with Jean-Marie Hombert at the University of California, Berkeley, June 22-23, 1995 under the sponsorship of the France-Berkeley Fund. I would like to thank John Lowe, the co-Principal Investigator of the CBOLD grant at Berkeley, for his considerable help and input to the present study. I would like also to thank the participants at both the Berkeley and the Lyon conferences for their helpful comments and suggestions—particularly Jean-Noël Mabiala for making his Kongo dialect database available to me.

[2]For discussion see Nurse's overview (this volume) as well as other papers in this volume (especially Ehret's).

[3]As we shall see below, this symbolization of the PB vowel system is equivalent to *i, *ɪ, *ɛ, *u, *ʊ, *ɔ, *a, as we find in Nyamwezi in (2), as well as in most seven vowel systems outside NW Bantu.

(1) Asymmetric vowel height harmony

a. front height harmony : *i > e / { e, o } C __

b. back height harmony : *u > o / o C __

As indicated, the degree 2 vowels **i* and **u* are lowered to **e* and **o* after degree 3 (mid) vowels, but with one difference: Whereas *i is affected after both **e* and **o*, **u* is lowered only after **o*. This front-back asymmetry in VHH is observed directly in many languages which have preserved the original seven-vowel (7V) system of PB. Such is the case in Nyamwezi F.22[4] in (2), where the applicative /-ɪl-/ and reversive transitive suffix /-ʊl-/ are illustrated after each of the seven vowels /i, ɪ, e, u, ʊ, o, a/ of the language:

(2) Nyamwezi F.22 (Maganga & Schadeberg 1992)

a.	-βon-él-a	'see + appl'	-hong-ól-a	'break off'
b.	-zeeng-el-a	'build + appl'	-zeeng-ʊl-a	'build'
c.	-βis-ɪl-a	'hide + appl'	-βis-ʊ́l-a	'find out'
	-pɪɪnd-ɪl-a	'bend + appl'	-pɪɪnd-ʊl-a	'overturn'
	-gub-ɪl-a	'put on lid + appl'	-gub-ʊ́l-a	'take off lid'
	-shʊʊn-ɪl-a	'gnaw + appl'	-shʊʊn-ʊl-a	'show teeth'
	-gaβ-ɪl-a	'divide + appl'	-gaβ-ʊl-a	'divide'

In (2a) we see that both /ɪ/ and /ʊ/ are lowered after /o/. As seen in (2b), however, only /ɪ/ is lowered after /e/. The examples in (2c) show that there is no change after the vowels /i/, /ɪ/, /u/, /ʊ/ and /a/. Eleven 7V languages occur in the vowel harmony database which exhibit the above asymmetry: Lega D.25, Holoholo D.28, Nande DJ.42, Kikuyu E.51, Sukuma F.21, Rimi F.32, Kinga G.65, Nyakyusa M.31 and Matumbi P.13.[5]

In Bantu languages with five-vowel (5V) systems, **i* and **u* merge with **į* and **ų*, respectively. The corresponding suffixes typically continue to show the same asymmetry as in seven vowel systems. Thus consider the examples from Kisa E.32 in (3).

---

[4]Throughout this study I shall provide the Guthrie reference letter+number for each cited language, indicating also changes proposed by Tervuren (e.g. shift of some zone D and E languages into a new zone J) or, in a few cases, Tervuren referential designations given to languages not included in Guthrie (1967-71).

[5]We probably should include in this category one additional language, Holoholo D.28, within which "l'opposition phonologique entre les voyelles du premier degré (į,ų) et celles du second (i,u) est de portée restreinte" (Coupez 1955:12).

(3) Kisa E.32 (Sample 1976)

a.	-tsom-el-a	'pierce + appl'	-tsom-ol-a	'pull out'
b.	-rek-el-a	'set trap + appl'	-rek-ul-a	'spring trap'
c.	-βis-il-a	'hide + appl'	-βis-ul-a	'reveal'
	-fu:ng-il-a	'lock + appl'	-fu:ng-ul-a	'unlock'
	-βa:mb-il-a	'spread out + appl'	-βa:mb-ul-a	'spread apart'

The examples in (3a) show the lowering of /i/ and /u/ after /o/, while in (3b) only /i/ lowers after /e/. Finally, these suffixes are realized with /i/ and /u/ after /i/, /u/ and /a/ in (3c). Within the Bantu vowel harmony database 46 languages attest this pattern. These include, among others: Rwanda (DJ.61), Rundi (DJ.62), Nyankore E.13/J.21, Ganda EJ.15, Haya EJ.22, Jita E.25, Shambaa G.22, Swahili G.42, Shi DJ.53, Cokwe K.11, Lwena K.14, Songye L.23, Luba-Kasai L.31a, Bemba M.42, Tonga M.64, Cewa N.31b, Yao P.21, and Shona S.11.[6] It is safe to say that this asymmetry is quite the rule among 5V Bantu languages.[7]

The languages just cited exemplify what I refer to as the "canonical" VHH system in Bantu. Whether having a 7V or a 5V system, canonical VHH is characterized by the following five properties:

(i) Canonical VHH has the above asymmetry. In other words, within asymmetric VHH there is an independence of front height harmony and back height harmony, as indicated in (1).

(ii) Canonical VHH is not conditioned by the degree 4 vowel /a/. Thus, assuming that VHH is a lowering process, as virtually all scholars do, /a/ fails to pattern with degree 3 vowels in conditioning VHH. Instead, by this criterion, /a/ patterns with degree 1 and 2 vowels.

(iii) Canonical VHH does not apply to /a/. Just as /a/ does not trigger lowering in canonical VHH, it also is not targeted for vowel harmony.

(iv) Canonical VHH does not apply to the final vowel (FV) morpheme. By final vowel I mean to refer both to the inflectional final vowels that occur on verbs, e.g. *-i*, *-e*, *-a*, according to tense/aspect etc., as well as final vowels used in derivational morphology, e.g. verb-to-noun derivation.

(v) Canonical VHH does not apply to prefix vowels. Thus, both noun class prefixes and inflectional prefixes on verbs (marking subject, tense/aspect, object etc.), fail to harmonize in languages with canonical VHH.

Defined this way, canonical VHH characterizes 57 languages in the vowel harmony database. As seen in Map 1, these languages are located in

---

[6]As will be elaborated below, front-back differences in VHH are even more widespread than this list of languages would suggest.

[7]Quite strikingly, the only five-vowel Bantu languages that have *symmetric* VHH, i.e. with lowering of *u to [o] after *e as well as after *o, are to be found in zone H, e.g. certain Kongo H.10 dialects (see below).

the Central and Eastern parts of the Bantu region, extending as far South as the Shona group.

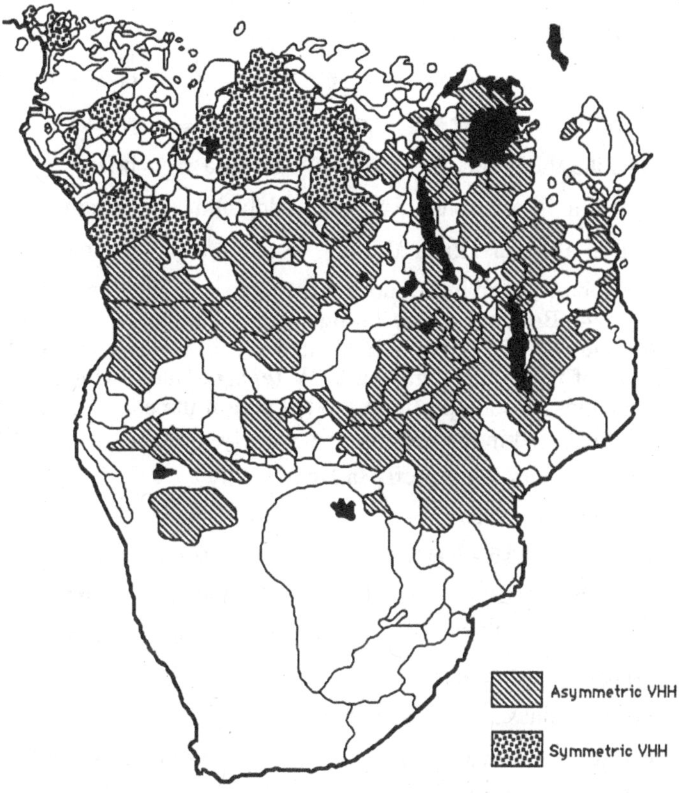

Map 1. Bantu Vowel Height Harmony

Languages, most of which fall outside this contiguous area, differ from the canonical system by providing exceptions to one or more of the five defining characteristics, as summarized below:

(i) Some languages have no VHH, e.g. Punu B.43, Lengola D.12,[8] Suku H.32, Mbala H.41, and Ruund L.53. In these languages, all with 5V, the distribution of mid vowels is severely restricted. Thus in Punu B.43,

[8]Enya D.14 (7V) and N. Binja D.26 (5V) may also belong to this group. In addition, Caga E.62 (5V) is generally believed to not have VHH, since productive suffixes such as applicative -i- do not harmonize. However, Gérard Philippson (personal communication) has pointed out to me that the situation is considerably more complex in polysyllabic forms which are either monomorphemic or which have tightly bound suffixes. Both Caga and similar situations which obtain in zone S (exclusive of Shona S.10) are discussed in §5.

"les phonèmes /e/ et /o/ ne se trouvent qu'en position initiale et radicale" (Kwenzi Mickala 1980:8). As a result, when not /a/, the vowel of a verb extension will always be [i] or [u], as seen in (4), from Blanchon (1995):[9]

(4) No VHH in Punu B.43

a.	-kil-il-a	'repasser'	b.	-kib-ul-a	'découvrir'
	-sub-il-a	'uriner sur'		-fung-ul-a	'révéler'
	-ded-il-a	'obéir à'		-tes-ul-a	'briser'
	-gol-il-a	'se frotter avec'		-dob-ul-a	'extraire, extirper'
	-gab-il-a	'distribuer à'		-gab-ul-a	'séparer'

(ii) Prefixes harmonize in Londo A.11, Bakweri A.22, Nen A.44, Gunu A.62, Koyo C.24, Bobangi C.32, Mongo C.61, Tetela C.71, Kela C.72, Ombo C.76, Budu D.35, Logooli E.41, and Gusii E.42. It is significant perhaps that all of these languages have 7V (except Budu, which has 9V). Harmony of the class 5 noun prefix /e-/ to [ɛ] and of the class 3 noun prefix /o-/ to [ɔ] are illustrated in (5) and (6), respectively, from Koyo C.24:[10]

(5) Harmony of class 5 /e-/ prefix in Koyo C.24

a.	e-símu	'scream'	b.	ɛ-bɛ	'thigh'
	e-túsi	'shoulder'		ɛ-sɛ́gɛ́	'hoe'
	e-bémbo	'debt'		ɛ-bɔ́gɔ́	'arm'
	e-kóró	'skin'		ɛ-sɔ́gɔ́	'hip'
	e-lagá	'promise'			

(6) Harmony of class 3 /o-/ prefix in Koyo C.24

a.	o-lingu	'love'	b.	ɔ-kɛsú	'stream'
	o-kulí	'hill'		ɔ-tɛrɔ	'basket'
	o-yélo	'morning'		ɔ-nɔgɔ	'mouth'
	o-kóro	'clothing'		ɔ-kɔ	'night'
	o-sanga	'rope'			

[9]Note that the only claim made about these languages is that they do not have vowel height harmony. They may in fact have other harmonies. Thus, Fontaney (1980) shows that postradical /a/ and /i/ assimilate to a following /u/, while /a/ also assimilates to a following /i/. She thus analyzes the suffix sequences -imin- and -umun- as /-am-il-/ and /-am-ul-/, respectively. Note in this context that postradical /a/ is actually realized as schwa in Punu, e.g. the FV in all of the examples in (4). Cf. below and Hyman (1998) for discussion of similar assimilations in Yaka.

[10]Based on Gazania (1972) and personal research conducted in Lyon with Mr. Yvon-André Ndzambo.

Besides being found only among certain 7V languages, prefix harmony involves only degree 2 and 3 vowels. That is, /a/ is not involved, as it may be in progressive harmony (see below).

(iii) Among languages that restrict VHH to the stem, the final vowel harmonizes in the B.30 languages (Bobe, Bia, Pinzi etc.), Boma B.82 (B.74b?), Leke C.14, and, in the perfective only, in Kongo H.10 and Yaka H.31. Although we shall return to consider what is "really" going on in Yaka in §4, we illustrate VHH of the perfective final vowel in (7).

(7) Final vowel harmonizing in Yaka H.31 (van den Eynde 1968, Ruttenberg 1971)

a.	tsúb-idi	'vagabonder'	b.	kéb-ele	'faire attention'
	kúd-idi	'chasser qqn'		ték-ele	'vendre'
	kík-idi	'barrer'		sód-ele	'déboiser'
	kás-idi	'lier'		sób-ele	'changer'

In addition, most languages that have extended VHH to prefixes also harmonize the final vowel, e.g. Mongo C.61, Tetela C.71, Gusii E.42.

(iv) The asymmetry is not found in zones A-B-C and Mituku D.13, Gusii E.42, Kuria E.43, Beembe H.11, Vili H.16d, Laadi H.16f, and Mbundu H.21a (see Map 1). Whereas in asymmetric systems VHH fails to obtain in one of the four relevant combinations (**eCu*), it applies in all four environments in these languages (**eCi*, **eCu*, **oCi* and **oCu*). I illustrate symmetric VHH in Mongo-Nkundo C.61 (7V) in (8) and in S. Kongo H.10 (5V) in (9):

(8) Symmetric VHH in Mongo-Nkundo (7V) (Hulstaert 1965)

a.	-kɔt-ɛl-	'couper + appl'	b.	-mɔm-ɔl-	'décoller'
	-kɛnd-ɛl-	'aller + appl'		-mɔ́m-ɔl-	'déshonorer'
	-ét-el-	'appeler + appl'		-bét-ol-	'éveiller'
	-tóm-el-	'envoyer + appl'		-komb-ol-	'ouvrir'
	-íy-el-	'voler [steal] + appl'		-is-ol-	'découvrir'
	-lúk-el-	'pagayer + appl'		-kund-ol-	'déterrer'
	-kamb-el-	'travailler + appl'		-bák-ol-	'détacher'

(9) Symmetric VHH in S. Kongo (5V) (de Gheel 1652)

a.	-somp-el-a	's'attacher à'	b.	-tomb-ol-a	'faire monter'
	-leng-el-a	'dépérir, languir'		-lemb-ol-a	'barrer, effacer'
	-sik-il-a	'soutenir, fortifier'		-vil-ul-a	'mouvoir, remuer'
	-vur-il-a	'surpasser, l'emporter'		-bub-ul-a	'corrompre'
	-land-il-a	'suivre'		-bang-ul-a	'faire violence'

As before, the forms in (8a) and (9a) involve the applicative extension (**-id-*), while those in (8b) and (9b) contain the reversive transitive extension (**-ud-*). It is perhaps worth noting that the data in (9) are taken from de Gheel's (1652) dictionary of a southerly dialect of Kongo H.10 (cf. Laman 1936:lviii). Such dialects of Kongo appear to constitute the only 5V languages with symmetric VHH. This dictionary shows that they have had such harmony for at least three and a half centuries.

(v) Whereas in symmetric languages /a/ does not lower a following vowel, /a/ conditions VHH in Mbundu H.21a, Mbunda K.15, Kwangali K.33, Kwezo K.35, Dciriku K.62, Pende L.11/K.52, Mbundu R.11, Kwanyama R.21, Ndongo R.22, and Herero R.31, all 5V languages.[11] As seen in Map 2, these languages are roughly contiguous, belonging to zones K and R. The illustration in (10) comes from Pende:

(10) Front height harmony (front height harmony) in Pende L.11/K.52 (Niyonkuru 1978)

a.	-lomb-	'demander'	→	gu-lómb-él-a	'demander pour'
	-bemb-	'abandonner'	→	gu-bemb-el-a	'abandonner pour'
	-sas-	'hacher'	→	gu-sas-el-a	'hacher pour'
b.	-díg-	'vendre'	→	gu-díg-íl-a	'vendre pour'
	-túng-	'bâtir'	→	gu-túng-íl-a	'bâtir pour'

While these languages appear to have extended front height harmony, so that the change of /i/ to [e] also occurs after /a/, it should be noted that back height harmony is still restricted to occurring only after /o/:

(11) Back height harmony (back height harmony) of u/o only after /o/ in Pende (Gusimana 1972)

a.	gu-bóg-ól-a	'briser'	b.	gu-seng-ul-a	'absoudre'
	gu-nyóng-ólól-a	'tordre'		gu-shit-ul-a	'défaire (noeud)'
	gu-sómb-ól-óg-a	'sauter'		gu-vumb-ul-a	'déterrer'
				gu-kál-úg-a	'gémir'

[11]Boma B.74b (B.82?), a 7V language, may also fall in this category, though I have not been able to confirm this. Interestingly, Leitch (1996), in fact, shows that the stem sequences [aCɔ] and [aCɛ] are disallowed in favor of [aCe] and [aCo] in a number of zone C languages. Since we independently know that /a/ may become a trigger of retracted tongue root (RTR) harmony outside Bantu, e.g. in Akan (Clements 1985), Yoruba (Archangeli & Pulleyblank 1989) and Gokana (Hyman 1985), we expect that this might also be the case in some of the 7V languages, particularly in zone A. The fact that it is better attested in 5V languages in the Bantu vowel harmony database may only reflect the areal nature of the feature, i.e. characterizing languages in the Southwest part of the Bantu region.

This then provides another argument for the independence of front height harmony and back height harmony.

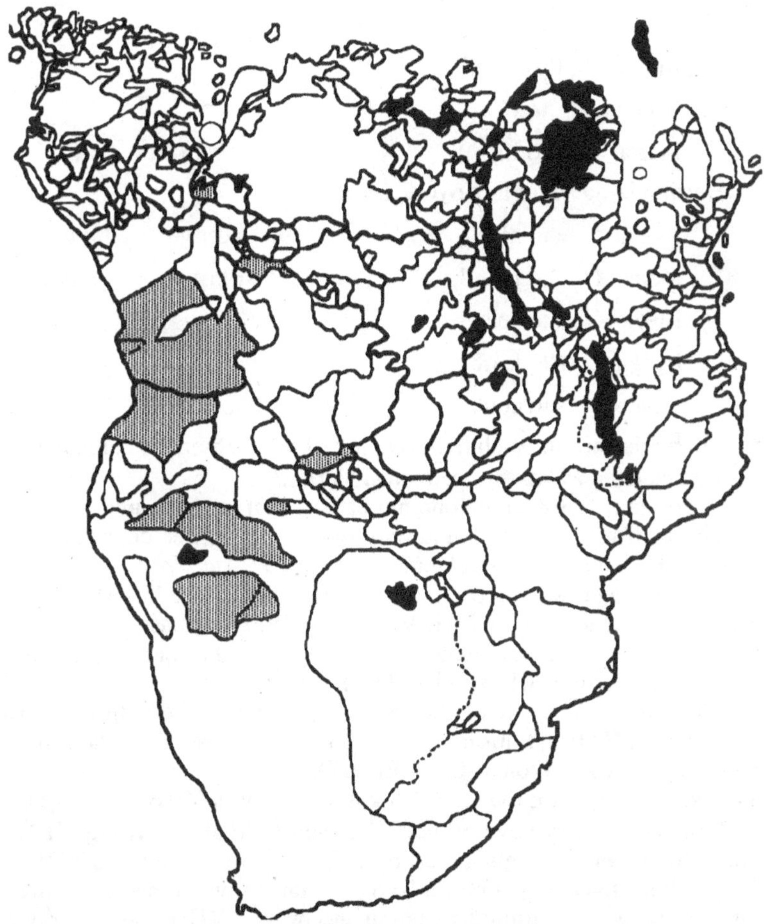

Map 2. Languages Lowering /i/ to [e] after /a/

(vi) /a/ undergoes vowel harmony in Londo A.11, Bakweri A.22, Nen A.44, Gunu A.62, Kota B.25, Nzebi B.52, Tiene B.81, Boma B.74b (B.82), Leke C.14, Koyo C.24, Mboshi C.25, Doko C.31, Lingala C.36d, Ngombe C.41, Leku C.60, Bembe H.11, and Lwalwa L.00. In all of these languages /a/ becomes [ɛ] after /ɛ/ and/or [ɔ] after /ɔ/. This is illustrated with respect to the final vowel /-a/ in Bakweri A.22 and Koyo C.24 in (12) and (13), respectively:

(12) Harmonizing of /a/ in Bakweri A.22 (Hawkinson 1985)

a.	li-sík-a	'to groan/groaning'	b.	i-lɛmb-έ	'to laugh'
	li-tút-a	'to sweep'		i-kɔ́m-ɔ	'to beat'
	i-kot-á	'to light'			
	i-vend-á	'to plait'			
	i-fáf-a	'to hit'			

(13) Harmonizing of /a/ in Koyo C.24 (Gazania 1972)

a.	i-yís-a	'to hide'	b.	i-dzɛg-ɛ	'to laugh'
	i-kund-a	'to plant'		i-lɔg-ɔ	'to bewitch'
	i-wóg-a	'to hear'			
	i-yég-a	'to learn'			
	i-lámb-a	'to cook'			

Of course, by definition, such harmonizing of /a/ is absent in languages that I have characterized as having "canonical" VHH.[12]

With so many parameters, one might ask what is not found? Or, which combinations of features are found only rarely. First, three departures from canonical VHH are restricted to languages with 7V:

(i) All languages having prefixal VHH have 7V. None has 5V.

(ii) All languages having final-VHH have 7V. None has 5V.

(iii) Among the 19 languages in the database that harmonize /a/, all have 7V except Bembe H.11 and Lwalwa L.00.

On the other hand, all of the languages where /a/ conditions vowel lowering have 5V. In addition, of the 18 languages lacking VHH, only 3 have 7V: Duala A.24, Wongo C.85, Enya D.14.

Our focus here is on the front-back asymmetry in VHH. All languages that lack the asymmetry have in fact 7V except for dialectal Kongo H.10.[13] It is interesting that no language has been found with asymmetric VHH and either prefixal harmony or final-vowel harmony. It seems that the asymmetric pattern is limited to languages where VHH affects only the base—i.e. the stem minus the final vowel (Meeussen 1967). As we shall further justify below, the specific asymmetric pattern is a property only of stem-internal VHH. That is, height harmony of the final vowel and prefixes,

[12]It is not clear whether we should view the harmonizing of /a/ as VHH, with which it frequently, though not necessarily, co-occurs. One argument from Koyo for distinguishing the two is that whereas /e, o/ harmonize to [ɔ ,ɛ] in prefixes (as well as in suffixes), as we saw in (5), /a/ harmonizes only in suffixes. Thus we obtain the class 6 plural nouns a-bέɛ 'breasts' (not *ɛ-bέɛ), and a-lɔɔ́ 'thorns' (not *ɔ-lɔɔ́.).

[13]For discussion of Yaka, see Hyman (1998) and below.

when occurring, is strictly symmetric—and, as we have said, typically requires a 7V system.

Before turning to that issue, let us provide further evidence of the independence of front height harmony and back height harmony. First, a group of Southern Bantu languages that includes Lozi K.21/S.34, Luyana K.31, Mbukushu K.33, Makua P.31 and all of zone S except Shona S.10 (e.g. Venda S.21, Tswana S.31, Nguni S.40) lack front height harmony . In these languages the applicative suffix contains an invariant mid vowel /e/, while the causative suffix contains a non-alternating high vowel /i/. In each case, however, *u/o* harmony after [o] is either fully productive, as in asymmetric languages, or is statistically prevalent. For example, in Lozi (5V), "the allodesinence /-ol-/ [and its doubled realization /-olol-/—LMH] occurs with most radicals having radical vowel /o/" (Gowlett 1967:64). Elsewhere one obtains /-ul-/ and /-ulul-/. Hence: *-bóf-a* 'tie' → *-bof-ólol-a* 'untie, release' vs. *-fung-a* 'tie a beast' → *-fung-ulul-a* 'untie a beast'. On the other hand, the applicative is always *-el-*, while the causative is always *-is-*, i.e. neither undergoing VHH. In Mbukushu K.33b (5V), the applicative again has a mid vowel, *-er-* (→ *-en-* after a nasal) and the causative a high vowel -ith- (Fisch 1977:123). However, while these front vowels are exempt from VHH, /u/ is realized [o] after /o/, [u] after /i, e, u, a/. Thus, the reversive suffix and its double alternate between *-or-* (~ *-on-*) and *-ur-* (~ *-un-*): *-ter-a* 'einfüllen', *-ter-ur-a* 'Topf vom Feuer entfernen' vs. *-tong-a* 'stöhnen', *-tong-onon-a* 'beichten'.

It is striking that no Bantu language has front height harmony without back height harmony.[14] We thus see that front height harmony can either be extended to applying after /a/, as in zones K and R, or can be absent, as in Southern Bantu, without any necessary effect on back height harmony. Assuming, following Meeussen (1967), that these harmony systems were once "canonical" in the sense of (1), these examples show that Bantu languages can and do separate front height harmony and back height harmony in their histories.[15] The important observation is that even when a language restructures the inherited situation, a front-back asymmetry typically survives. As another example, consider the possible vowel combinations in Matuumbi P.13 (7V) shown in the table in (14).

---

[14]The one counterexample I once believed to exist is Sukuma F.21 (7V). In this langauge the applicative varies as expected between -el- and -ɛl- (Batibo 1985:167) as does the neuter/stative -ek-/-ɛk- (p.168). The causative also shows VHH but with a slightly more complex pattern: -is-y- after /i, u, a/, -es-y- after /e, o/ and -ɛs-y- after /ɛ, ɔ/. Although the same source appears to report that the reversive /-ol-/ is used as such after all vowels, Batibo (personal communication) has clarified that indeed it lowers to -ɔl- after /ɔ/.

[15]In §5 I shall propose an alternative, namely that PB lacked FHH entirely.

(14) V + XV (postradical vowel) in Matuumbį P.13 (Odden 1996)

V/XV	į	i	e	ų	u	o	a
į	x	—	—	x	—	—	x
ų	x	—	—	x	—	—	x
i	—	x	—	—	x	—	x
u	—	x	—	—	x	—	x
e	—	—	x	x	—	—	x
o	—	—	x	—	—	x	x
a	x	—	—	x	—	—	x

As seen, any of the seven vowels can be followed by postradical /a/, which we can set aside. The restrictions in force are as follows: First, degree 1 high vowels /į, ų/ are followed by another degree 1 high vowel, while the degree 2 high vowels /i, u/ are followed by another degree 2 high vowel. This much is symmetric. On the other hand the degree 3 vowels /e/ and /o/ have asymmetric properties: /e/ can only be followed by /e, ų/, while /o/ can only be followed by /e, o/. Finally, degree 4 /a/ can only be followed by /į, ų/. Whereas in other 7V languages the default high vowels are degree 2 (cf. Nyamwezi in (2) above), in Matuumbi the default high vowels are degree 1, or [+ATR].[16]

This completes the initial survey of VHH. We now turn to questions of reconstruction.

3. Reconstruction of the Proto-Bantu vowel system

The question that arises in the face of the variations outlined in §2 is: What should we reconstruct and for whom? All Bantu? Some subgroup? The problem of whether to reconstruct VHH for PB, and if so, which kind (e.g. symmetric? asymmetric?) is compounded by questions concerning the nature of the vowels themselves in Proto- and pre-Proto-Bantu. We take up these two issues in this and the following section.

While most scholars agree that PB had a system with seven vowels, occasional suggestions of more vowels, either nine or ten, have been heard:

> ...it seems most likely that proto-Bantu had a classic system of CHVH [cross-height vowel harmony—LMH] with nine (or possibly ten) vowels, and that it inherited this system largely unchanged from proto-Volta-Congo. (Stewart and van Leynseele 1979:51)[17]

> La forme à neuf voyelles est notamment attestée dans le groupe Akan de Greenberg, 1963. Stewart 1970, qui désigne ce groupe sous le nom de

[16]For the same reason noun prefixes contain the vowels /į/ and /ų/, not /i/ and /u/. This interpretation differs from that given by Odden (1996), who assumes that the [+ATR] is prespecified.

[17]Stewart (1983) has since come back to his original position (Stewart 1970) that Bantu had 7 vowels, specifically those in (15a,b).

> Volta-Comoe, a émis l'hypothèse que les sept voyelles du protobantou en sont issues. Une hypothèse analogue semble se dégager de faits proprement bantous, à savoir l'alternance, dans les réflexes des langues bantoues contemporaines par rappart au protobantou, de voyelles reflétant le premier degré avec des voyelles reflétant le troisième. (Coupez 1980:67)

Even sticking with the traditional view, as I shall do, which of the 7V systems in (15) should be reconstructed?

(15)	a.			b.			c.		
	į		ų	i		u	i		u
	i		u	ɪ		ʊ	e		o
	e		o	ɛ		ɔ	ɛ		ɔ
		a			a			a	

I assume that the standard Bantu reconstructed system of Meeussen (1967, 1980[1969]) and Guthrie (1967-71) in (15a) is meant to symbolize the phonetically transcribed vowels in (15b). As seen, it is assumed that there was an opposition between tense and lax (or [±ATR]) high vowels. That is, degree 2 vowels are interpreted to be lax high vowels. Mid vowels are also lax, although there is no opposition. In (15c), on the other hand, the proto opposition in tense-laxness (or [ATR]) is assumed to be among the mid vowels: In this system degree 2 vowels are tense mid vowels, while degree 3 vowels are lax mid vowels. The question, then, is which system to reconstruct, (15b) or (15c)?

Part of the difficulty in deciding between these two interpretations can be seen in the inconsistencies that appear in present-day synchronic analysis of different Bantu languages. First, there are studies where the phonological analysis uses (15b), while pointing out that the corresponding phonetic system is (15c). Thus, Kuperus (1985:58) analyzes Londo A.11 with /i, ɪ, e, u, ʊ, o, a/, rather than orthographic /i, e, ɛ, u, o, ɔ, a/, explaining: "The vowels written *e,o* in Londo *sound* like the [+ATR] vowels usually written *e,o*, but they function like the [-ATR] vowels usually written ɪ,*ʊ* or *ɛ,ɔ*. Therefore ATR is used, rather than, say, mid." Similarly, Stappers (1973:3) analyzes Mituku D.13 with /į, i, e, ų, u, o, a/, though pointing out that the vowels are phonetically [i, e, ɛ, u, o, ɔ., a].

In other cases authors are upfront about the difficulty. Thus, Maganga & Schadeberg (1992:26) symbolize the vowel system of Nyamwezi F.22 as /i, ɪ, e, u, ʊ, o, a/, but add: "We have no phonetic evidence for deciding whether the difference between i and u on the one hand and ɪ and ʊ on the other is to be analyzed as an [Advanced Tongue Root] distinction or as one of various degrees of vowel height."

What seems to be part of the difficulty is that the degree 2 vowels are often more close, i.e. more similar to degree 1 vowels, phonetically, than an author's preferred transcription in (15c) would suggest. Thus, concerning the following three languages symbolized with /i, e, ɛ, u, o, ɔ, a/, authors make the following observations:

(i) Bobe B.30: "Les voyelles du second degré d'aperture sont très fermées... et tendent pour cette raison à être confondues avec les voyelles correspondantes du premier degré" (van der Veen 1991:60).

(ii) Doko C.31: "Les voyelles du second degré sont phonétiquement plus proches de celles du premier degré que celles du troisième degré" (Twilingiyimana 1984:3).

(iii) Kela C.75: u/o are "très proches phonétiquement" (Forges 1977:27).

The literature thus shows not only possible disagreement, but also confusion over the phonetics and phonology of the above cited and other Bantu vowel systems. In fact, all three of the systems in (15) have been used to describe individual Bantu languages. A sample of 46 7V systems in the vowel harmony database can be summarized as follows:

(i) 6 languages are symbolized with /į, i, e, ų, u, o, a/: Ombo C.76, Mituku D.13, Holoholo D.28 (6V), Bira D.32, Nande D.42 (7V → 9V phonetically), Matuumbi P.13.

(ii) 6 languages are symbolized with /i, ɪ, e, u, ʊ, o, a/: Londo A.11, Logoli E.41, Kikuyu E.51, Nyamwezi F.22, Rimi F.32, Kinga G.65.

(iii) 33 languages are symbolized with /i, e, ɛ, u, o, ɔ, a/: Bakweri A.22, Duala A.24, Basaa A.43, Gunu A.62, Seki B.22, Kota B.25, Bobe B.30, Pinzi B.30, Himba B.30, Bia B.30, Tsogo B.31, Kande B.32, Nzebi B.52, Tiene B.81, Boma B.82, Leke C.14(6?), Koyo C.24, Mboshi C.25, Doko C.31, Bobangi C.32, Lingala C.36d, Ngombe C.41 (6), Bango C.44, Leku C.60, Mongo C.61, Tetela C.71, Kela C.75, Wongo C.85, Lega D.25, Gusii E.42, Kuria E.43, Sukuma F.21, Nilamba F.31.

(iv) One language, Enya D.14, is transcribed as /į i e ų u o a/ by Koloni (1971) but as /i e ɛ u o ɔ a/ by Spa (1973).

(v) In addition to the above, there are 4 9V languages described with [±ATR] in both high and mid vowels: Budu D.35, Konzo D.41, Tswana S.31, Sotho S.33. In the last two languages, the 8th and 9th vowels /e/ and /o/ can in many cases be interpreted as a tensing of /ɛ/ and /ɔ/ before higher vowels, or before /ʦ/ and /ʤ/ in a fairly transparent way. Konzo D.41, on the other hand, most likely derives these vowels by spreading of [+ATR] from /i, u/, as in mutually intelligible Nande D.42, which I placed in the first group with 7 underlying vowels.

Since the transcriptions in (15a) and (15b) have been said to be equivalent, the first two groups above can be combined to provide 12 7V systems (out of 46) that have been symbolized with a tense-lax opposition in the high vowels (i.e. orthographically, not necessarily "phonologically"). That leaves 34 7V systems for which a tense-lax opposition is instead posited among mid vowels. It would appear that (15c) is more frequently used to transcribe NW Bantu languages (zones A-D), while (15b) is more restricted to Eastern Bantu. However, it is hard to make reliable generalizations from this small sample, particularly as the first group, utilizing (15a), consists largely of a group of Zairian languages (plus Matuumbi P.13).[18]

Of course one question we should consider is whether it matters which of the vowel arrays in (15) represents the proto system, i.e. whether the relevant opposition is one between high vowels or mid vowels. As the above citations indicate, many researchers have found it difficult to decide on the proper analysis of individual languages. In addition, certain recent views on vowel features even attempt a uniform treatment of vowel height and ATR. Clements' (1991), for instance, proposes an aperture theory based on the single feature [open] as a uniform phonological dimension of vowel height [including ATR]. However, his theory is still also capable of distinguishing (15b) and (15c).

While some Bantuists have seen an equivalence in these two transcriptions of seven proto-vowels, others have taken sides on the question. Perhaps the most thoughtful response is seen in Stewart (1970), who argues that (15b) is the more likely reconstruction:

> The situation in Volta-Comoe languages... provides strong evidence for the plausibility of the possible post-Bantu shift (*i, u*) → |ẹ, ọ| but none for the plausibility of the possible post-Bantu shift (ẹ, ọ) → |i, u|. (p.349)
>
> It is worth pointing out that, in the light of this, Professor Guthrie's use of the symbols *į, i, e, a, o, u, ų* rather than *i, e, ɛ, a, ɔ, o, u* in his Common Bantu starred forms is most fortunate. (p.350)

What this would mean is that languages with the system /i, e, ɛ, a, ɔ, o, u/ would have had to have developed it from earlier /i, ɪ, e, u, ʊ, o, a/. In a later article, Stewart (1983:22-23) reaffirms his position:

> I suggest that a sound change *e, o* > ɪ, *ʊ* which is not a merger (and in this case would not have been a merger) is highly implausible phonetically). In the first place the replacing sounds are more highly marked than the replaced sounds, and in the second place I know of no case in which the change can be clearly shown to have occurred.

The idea here is that the widely attested 7V system /i, e, ɛ, u, o, ɔ, a/ would not by itself change to the highly marked one /i, ɪ, e, u, ʊ, o, a/. Stewart's intuition re the relative markedness of /i, ɪ, e, u, ʊ, o, a/, is borne out by Maddieson (1984), who reports only three languages which have an opposition in ATR in the high vowels without a corresponding opposition in the mid vowels.[19]

---

[18]One would also have to make sure that the numbers aren't affected by either the training that the researchers obtained and what was the practice during the time that they studied.

[19]These are Kpelle, Dani and Kunama. Lionel Bender (personal communication), however, has informed me that Kunama does not have this vowel system, but

Besides the examples of the reverse changes in Volta-Comoe discussed by Stewart (1970), Mould (1981:187) suggests the same change to have occurred in Luhya E.40:

> Gusii and Logooli have seven vowel systems by virtue of being Bantu.... Gusii and evidentally all of East Nyanza (e.g. Kuria)... show other adjustments to the system: *į, i, e, ų, u, o, a > i, e, ε, u, o, ɔ, a.*

It is perhaps significant for our purposes that languages that are agreed unambiguously to have the vowel system /i, e, ε, u, o, ɔ, a/ all have symmetric VHH: If their vowel system has been altered since PB, perhaps their vowel harmony system has as well?

Although he uses the transcriptions in (15a) in presenting his comparative series of "Common Bantu" roots, Guthrie (1967) presents two arguments in favor of reconstructing (15c) as the likely pronunciations of these vowels in PB. The first argument is one of frequency:

> ...this series [(15c)—LMH] is the most widespread (series (2) [(15a)] occurring mainly in D.20, 40, 50, F.20, M.10, N.10 and P.10), and in consequence is likely to be closer to the original. (p.61)

However, this may be only the result of the fact that there are so many 7V languages clustered in the Northwest, where (15c) is the normal transcription (see above). In any case, as Stewart (1983) points out, frequency should not be the major guide to reconstruction. My own feeling, in fact, is that if the argument of frequency is relevant at all, it leads to the opposite conclusion: Given that /i, ɪ, e, u, ʊ, o, a/ is an unusual system, it would make more sense to reconstruct it once in PB—or innovate it once—rather than seeing it evolve independently in different Bantu subgroups.[20]

Guthrie's second argument is the following: If *[i, e, ε, u, o, ɔ, a] is reconstructed, then the change of this 7V system to [i, ɪ, e, u, ʊ, o, a] could be seen as an intermediate step on the way to the widely occurring 5V system [i, e, u, o, a]. By Guthrie's reasoning, two sets of sound changes would have occured, as in (16a).

(16)	a.	*e, *o	>	ɪ, ʊ	>	i, u
	b.	*ɪ, *ʊ	>	e, o	>	i, u
	c.	*ɪ, *ʊ	>	e, o		
	d.	*ɪ, *ʊ	>	i, u		

The mid vowels *e, *o are first "closed" to [ɪ, ʊ] and then again to [i, u]. The idea here is that [ɪ, ʊ] are logically mid-way between [e, o] and [i, u],

---

rather a 5V system with a tense/lax opposition. Interestingly Welmers (1962) transcribes Kpelle as /i, e, ε, u, o, ɔ, a/.

[20] The same argument will be made concerning asymmetric VHH: Since it is rare, I propose that it evolved only once, perhaps spreading through contact, rather than arising independently in different Bantu languages.

hence both the change within 7V systems (to [e, o]) and the loss of the distinction between degree 1 and 2 vowels are actually part of the same process. By contrast, a reconstruction as in (16b) would not be coherent: We would not expect the lax high vowels to first become tense mid vowels and then become high. Of course an equally likely explanation of the two changes could be as follows: Let us assume that PB already had the perceptual problem found in many Bantu languages today: Degree 2 vowels were very close perceptually to degree 1 vowels. As a response, languages could have done one of two things. First, they could have reshaped the vowel space as in (16c): *ɪ, *ʊ became [e, o] (and **e*, **o* became [ɛ, ɔ]). Or, second, they could simply have merged *ɪ, *ʊ with *i, *u, thereby yielding a 5V system. The result would be three types of Bantu languages: (i) those with the original system in (15b); (ii) those with the derived 7V system in (15c); and (iii) those with the derived 5V system /i, u, e, o, a/. All three are, of course, attested, although Guthrie claims that (15b) is the most restricted in distribution. Rather than providing an argument against its reconstruction, (15b) could be the original vowel system maintained in somewhat fewer languages because of the natural changes in (16c,d). This is of course related to Stewart's argument in favor of (15b): a sound change of *e, o* > ɪ, ʊ is less natural than the reverse change ɪ, ʊ > *e, o*, which he argues also to be attested in the history of the Volta-Comoé languages.

What other evidence might one bring to bear on the question of choosing the appropriate vowel system for PB, (15b) or (15c)? Perhaps a slight argument in favor of (15b) derives from the fact that the proto degree 2 vowels merge with degree 1 vowels in so many Bantu languages—rarely with the degree 3 vowels **ɛ* and **ɔ*. As seen in Map 3, this has occurred in a wide (largely contiguous) area within the Bantu zone (cf. also Topogram 1 of Guthrie 1967:66). The argument here is that the loss of a tense/lax distinction among high vowels is to be expected, perhaps more than vowel shifts of the sort Mid > High (although these too occur). Perhaps relevant in this context is the fact that the merger of PB degree 1 and 2 vowels is the same for long vowels and short vowels. If the original opposition were one of vowel height, one might expect slight differences in quality (e.g. tense-laxness) and perhaps a merger pattern that is different for long vs. short vowels. A constant ATR specification independent of vowel length is thus consistent with the observed facts.

On the other hand, the same reasoning can be used to argue against (15b) and in favor of (15c). If degree 2 vowels merge with degree 1 because of height similarity, then why do degree 2 and degree 3 harmonize? If we instead assume the proto system /i, e, ɛ, u, o, ɔ, a/, then /e, o/ would be expected to harmonize with /ɛ, ɔ/, from which they differ only in ATR. By this argument, the degree 2 vowels /e, o/ do not harmonize with degree 1 /i, u/, because this is not height harmony, but rather ATR harmony. By contrast, if we assume that the degree 2 vowels were *ɪ and *ʊ, harmonizing with **e* and **o*, phonetically *[ɛ] and *[ɔ], this would have been a height harmony between [-ATR] high and mid vowels. Cross-linguistically, ATR harmony of mid vowels is more expected than height harmony of [-ATR] vowels.

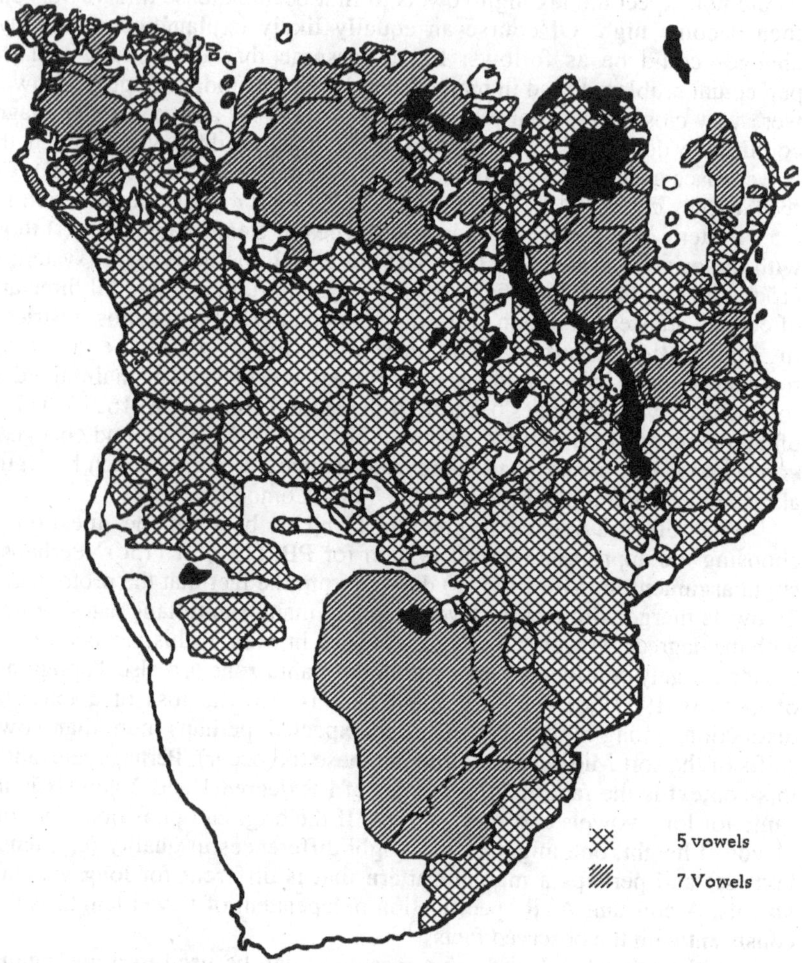

Map 3. 7 vs. 5 Vowels in Bantu Languages

To summarize, (15b) slightly better accounts for the merger of degree 1 and 2 vowels, while (15c) appears to much better account for VHH. So, perhaps the balance is tilted slightly in favor of */i, e, ɛ, u, o, ɔ, a/, which is typically preferred both as a static system as well as a degree 2-3 harmony system. It is important to note, however, that the second part of the conclusion in favor of (15c) depends crucially on there having been VHH in PB, the issue which I address in §4. Another issue: languages with the vowel system /i, e, ɛ, u, o, ɔ, a/ and ATR harmony do not show the front-back asymmetry so prevalent in Eastern Bantu. Could the issue of asymmetric VHH bear on the question of which system to reconstruct? The answer depends on whether asymmetric VHH (or any VHH) can be reconstructed at the PB level. This issue is taken up in the following section.

4. Reconstruction of vowel harmony in Proto-Bantu

The question that we must now address is: What kind of vowel harmony system existed in PB? There are at least three potential answers that must be considered: (i) PB had asymmetric VHH; (ii) PB had symmetric VHH; (iii) PB did not have VHH.[21] Virtually everyone who has commented on the issue agrees that VHH should be reconstructed for PB:

> ...vowel harmony goes back to Proto-Bantu.... vowel harmony... is found widely in Africa outside of the Bantu languages. It is noteworthy that systems similar to that of Proto-Bantu, in that they involve harmonisation of levels, have been described from distant portions of the African continent and from languages which in some cases have no demonstrable genetic relation to each other" (e.g. Twi, Ibo, Moru-Madi group, Lotuko). (Greenberg (1951:818-819).

> Bien que les phénomènes d'harmonie vocalique soient très largement répandus dans le monde et puissent apparaître de manière indépendente par convergence, il semble que le passage de i à e après une voyelle du troisième degré d'aperture puisse être attribué au protobantou ou même à une période antérieure puisque J. Greenberg en a relevé des exemples dans d'autres langues du groupe Niger-Congo." (Bastin 1983a:32).

While Stewart (1970) had once hypothesized that PB or its immediate ancester had had a larger vowel inventory with ATR harmony, he has since modified his position in favor of height harmony in PB:

> We now have good reason, then, to suppose that proto-Bantu lacked advancing harmony in any form, but that it retained advancing as a segmental feature category and that some descendant languages developed advancing harmony in one or the other of two ways: either by reversing the pre-Bantu e, o > ɪ, ʊ shift, therefore introducing single-height harmony as in the case of the Bobangi-type languages [(15c) with symmetric VHH—LMH], or by assimilating all the -Advanced vowels to any +Advanced vowel in the word, thereby introducing cross-height harmony as in the case of Nen". (Stewart 1983:35)

The next question therefore is whether PB VHH was of the symmetric or asymmetric type. Basing himself in part on distributional restrictions of

[21] A fourth possibility not considered here is that PB had a VHH system different from either of those under discussion here. We also will not consider the possibility that PB had other than a 7V system.

vowels in CVCV noun stems, Greenberg (1951) assumes a symmetric system:[22]

> Evidently... the parent Bantu language did not permit vowels of level two and three in successive syllables. The vowel of the third level was lowered to the second level to harmonize with the vowel of the preceding syllable. Thus o was replaced by ɔ and e by ɛ when the preceding syllable had ɔ or ɛ. (Greenberg 1951:814)

However, virtually all other scholars have assumed asymmetrical VHH in PB. Thus, Meeussen (1967:92) states:

> The absence of morphophonemes |e| and |o| in suffixes is worth noticing; this gives free space to the rule stated in 1.7.

The rule in §1.7 to which Meeussen refers is asymmetric VHH:

> |i| appears as /e/ after either |e| or |o|.... Similarly, |u| appears as /o/ after |o| (but not after |e|). (Meeussen 1967:84)

Other representative agreement with Meeussen's position include the following:

> Most Bantu grammars record the paired extensions *-ud-/-uk-. They both appear in two allomorphs conditioned by the preceding vowel but the distribution of the two variants is significantly different from the kind of vowel harmony applying to the front vowel suffixes -iC-:
>
> *-iC; *-uC- / *{į, i, a, u, ų} (C) __
> *-eC-: *-uC- / *e(C) __
> *-eC-; *-oC- / *o(C) __ (Schadeberg 1982:.61)
>
> Le plus souvent la voyelle s'ouvre uniquement lorsqu'elle succède à une autre voyelle postérieure dont le degré d'aperture est plus grande.... Le passage à o après e et o... est relativement rare et apparaît comme une extension du phénomène alors que ce type d'assimilation constituait le trait prédominant pour *-id-.... La distribution très générale de

---

[22]As seen in the quotation a few paragraphs below, Greenberg is of course aware that many Bantu languages have lowering of degree 2 /u/ to [o] only after degree 3 /o/. He is more impressed, however, with both the comparison with non-Bantu harmony systems as well as with his claim that degree 2 and 3 vowels do not cooccur in noun stems in Meinhof and van Warmelo's (1932) PB reconstructions, an issue which I shall address shortly. Let us note, however, that some scholars "misspeak" when characterizing height harmony in Bantu. For example, in presenting their reconstructions of Northeastern Coastal Bantu, Nurse & Hinnebusch (1993:370) state: "The limited vowel harmony...,whereby /-o-/ and /-e-/ occur after stems with mid vowels, and /-u-/ and /-i-/ after nonmid vowels, is an NEC feature, apparently inherited, as it also occurs widely in other eastern Bantu languages." Looking over the discussion, it is clear that they meant to reconstruct an asymmetric system which is remarkably stable in these languages (cf. also Bakari 1985).

> l'assimilation vocalique de la voyelle du suffix *-ud- après une voyelle postérieure (o) indique que ce phénomène peut être attribué au protobantou. (Bastin 1983a:33)

> This rule [VHH] extends to prefixes in a few languages (e.g. Gusii, Llogoori), probably as an innovation. Also [u] lowers to [o] after [e] in some languages (e.g. Kongo), also probably as an innovation. The fact that [u] generally assimilates only after [o] and not [e] may reflect a crosslinguistic tendency according to which one segment, A, is more likely to assimilate to another segment B, to the extent that A and B have more features in common (Kiparsky 1988). (Clements 1991:59)

The earliest recognition of asymmetric VHH I have found comes from Bleek (1862), concerning Herero R.31:

> The rule of vowel harmony is in a very restricted manner carried out in the termination of inversive verbs, -ura or -una, which become -ora or -ona after a preceding o, but retains its sharp vowel after all other vowels, even after the flat a and e." (Bleek 1862:62)

However, in the "first Bantu dictionary" (de Gheel 1652 [van Wing & Penders 1928]), which treats a southerly dialect of Kongo H.10, VHH is clearly symmetric. Recall from earlier discussion that Kongo was cited as the only 5V language (dialect cluster) with symmetric VHH. Relevant forms were cited in (9) in §2. Given the prominence of Kongo in Bantu studies, it is not surprising that it has frequently received special mention:

> However, contrary to the general rule, the u form of suffixes, e.g.-ul-, -uk- occur after e of the verb root instead of the expected -ol-, -ok-. This seems to be generally true of the Bantu languages, though in a few instances, e.g. Kikongo, -ol-, -ok- are the rule." (Greenberg 1951:813).

> In general the presence of a vowel -e- in an extension that is preceded by a radical vowel -e- or -o- corresponds to the presence of a vowel -i- in an extensions preceded by any other radical vowel. When the vowel of an extension is -o- following a radical vowel -o-, this normally corresponds to an extension with a vowel -u- following anly other radical vowel.... In a few languages, such as certain dialects of Kongo, for example, extensions containing a vowel -o- following a radical vowel -o- also have -o- following -e-, as in: S. Kongo -kes-/-kesomon- 'chew/chew up completely', -komb-/-kombomon- 'sweep/sweep up completely', -yal-/-yalumun- 'spread/spread out completely' in other dialects of this language, however, the extended radical of the first two pairs occurs as -kesumun- and -kombumun- respectively. (Guthrie 1962:102)

To summarize, as indicated in the above citations, most Bantuists seem to lean towards reconstructing asymmetric VHH. According to this view, all cases of symmetric VHH would have been innovative. Specifically, as we saw in Map 1, a number of rather disparate languages making up Northwest

Bantu in zones A, B and C, as well as the languages of EJ.40 to the East of Lake Victoria, would have had to innovate harmony of degree 2 *u after degree 3 *e. Since zone ABC languages do not constitute a genetic subgroup of Bantu (Heine 1973), it is unlikely that they would have independently innovated as a one-time change. Instead, one would have to propose that this change spread areally throughout must of the Northwest. The change in EJ.40 would have been an independent development. While this interpretation requires at least two statements, the alternate view that asymmetric VHH was an innovation is a simpler hypothesis to maintain. Asymmetric VHH could be viewed either as the result of areal spread *or* as a one-time innovation affecting the relatively coherent subbranch of Bantu in which it occurs. As Map 1 indicates, these languages are much more homogenous than their complement and corrrespond roughly to the Savanna branch of Bantu, as presented, for example, by Ehret (this volume). It would thus be quite significant if asymmetric VHH were a reliable genetic marker of this subbranch of the family—as I suggested in my presentation at the Table Ronde. In this case symmetric VHH would have existed in PB, with degree 2 and 3 vowels never mixing within stems. We thus would have had phonetic [CɛCɔC] rather than [CɛCʊC], the latter being introduced only later into the Savanna branch.

In support of this proposal was Greenberg's (1951) inquiry concerning the nature of VHH within words with bisyllabic stems:

> The question cannot be investigated further in the verb, since practically all verb roots in Proto-Bantu had only a single syllable and the effects of the addition of a derivational suffix has already been examined. For nouns, adjectives and other parts of speech a review of the forms that have been reconstructed suggests that it is indeed a general rule within Proto-Bantu that sequences of vowels one of which belongs to level three (e or o) and the other of which belongs to level two (ɛ or ɔ) are almost nonexistent. On the other hand, vowels in successive syllables both of which belong to level three or both of which belong to level two are very common" (Greenberg 1951:815).

The claim here is that monomorphemic forms such as noun stems show *symmetric* VHH in PB reconstructions (based on Meinhof and van Warmelo 1932). In fact, even some languages with asymmetric VHH in verbs, show symmetric VHH in bisyllabic noun stems. One such language is Nande DJ.42. As seen in (17a,b), based on Kavutirwaki (1978),

(17) Nande DJ.42 (Kavutirwaki 1978)

a.	-bóh-er-a	'tie + appl'	-boh-ol-a	'untie'
b.	-ses-er-a	'make a bed + appl'	-ses-ul-a	'unmake bed'
c.	-king-ir-a	'close + appl'	-king-ul-a	'open (door)'
	-sun-ir-a	'pinch + appl'	-sun-ul-a	'loosen (from fingers)'

	-land-ir-a	'sew + appl'	-land-ul-a	'unsew'
d.	-hịmb-ịr-a	'build + appl'	-hịmb-ụl-a	'demolish'
	-kụ́mb-ịr-a	'grasp firm + appl'	-kụ́mb-ụl-a	'release grasp'

Nande verb extensions show the classic asymmetric pattern: The applicative suffix is realized -er- after both /e/ and /o/, while the reversive suffix is realized -ol- only after /o/. In other cases the vowel is high.[23] On the other hand, as seen in (18), a quite different pattern emerges in bisyllabic noun stems:

(18) $V_1 + V_2$ in Nande Bisyllabic Noun Stems

V_1/V_2	ị	i	e	ụ	u	o	a
ị	31	—	8	4	—	25	35
i	—	25	—	—	5	29	28
e	14	—	70	4	—	37	28
ụ	29	—	4	7	—	18	32
u	—	15	10	—	43	16	42
o	18	—	16	5	—	46	28
a	21	21	12	17	10	38	113

As seen in the shaded cells, the combinations -CeCi, -CeCu, -CoCi and -CoCu, where a degree 3 vowel is followed by a degree 2 vowel, do not exist in the language.[24] The second of these, -CeCu, contrasts with the pattern found on longer forms, where -CeCuC- is attested to the detriment of -CeCoC-.

Similar observations can be seen in the following plotting of the two vowels of bisyllabic noun stems in Nyamwezi, based on Maganga & Schadeberg (1992).

[23]Rightward spreading of the [+ATR] of the root onto the suffixes in (17d) is a Nande-specific innovation. In fact, (19) shows that [+ATR] [ị, ụ] may not co-occur with [-ATR] [i, u] in either order.

[24]The language is less consistent about sequences where a degree 2 vowel is followed by a degree 3 vowel. Although -CiCe is unattested, -CiCo, -CuCe and -CuCo all are. The only point I wish to make here is that a process by which a degree 2 vowel would have to lower after a degree 3 vowel is symmetric in -CVCV stems but asymmetric in longer stems, specifically, verb stems of the shape -CVCVC- or longer.

(19) $V_1 + V_2$ in Nyamwezi Bisyllabic Noun Stems

V_1/V_2	į	i	e	ų	u	o	a
į	11	5	4	3	6	15	24
i	6	10	---	---	---	7	26
e	11	---	26	4	---	16	14
ų	6	(1)	(1)	6	---	8	25
u	13	10	5	(2)	25	8	24
o	19	---	13	7	---	43	24
a	17	16	13	4	13	32	74

Again, the shaded cells, -CeCi, -CeCu, -CoCi and -CoCu, are completely lacking. Could this be a relic of symmetric VHH in PB?

I think not. First, Greenberg's reliance on Meinhof's limited reconstructions may have affected the overall picture. In (19) I plot out the 7 x 7 matrix of vowels in the bisyllabic stems in Meeussen's (1980[1969]) reconstructions:

(20) $V_1 + V_2$ in Meeussen's Proto-Bantu Bisyllabic Noun Stems

V/FV	į	i	e	ų	u	o	a
į	9	4	4	3	7	14	25
i	6	19	---	2	9	10	36
e	7	5	31	3	6	13	19
ų	2	6	1	3	5	9	12
u	9	25	2	4	58	17	43
o	11	7	16	8	2	60	29
a	16	24	6	9	32	24	113

As seen, although -CeCi, -CeCu, -CoCi and -CoCu reconstructions are not among the most numerous combinations, they do exist and should be examined carefully before concluding that symmetric VHH characterized noun stems in PB.

Nande does, however, underscore an important observation that cuts across the Bantu languages: VHH properties are frequently different within bisyllabic (nominal) -CVCV vs. longer -CVCVC... stems. Using "V_2" to designate vowels in second or later stem syllables, and # to designate word boundary, I refer to this as the independence of V_2C and $V_2\#$ vowel distributions. Harmony of medial vs. final vowels can be quite distinct—even when all vowels belong to the same morpheme.[25] Not only is this the case in Nande, where the opposition is between symmetric vs. asymmetric

---

[25] I thus am not referring to the oft made observation that a FV morpheme does not harmonize in many Bantu languages. See, for example, Leitch's (1996) treatment of this as a parameter within zone C.

VHH, but also in languages where VHH may be lacking in one vs. the other environment.

The ideal languages in which to compare V_2C and $V_2\#$ harmony are of course those like Nande and Nyamwezi, which both have asymmetric VHH and have preserved the 7V system of PB. Unfortunately, the resources in CBOLD are at present accidentally skewed towards 5V languages. In these languages, we have to calculate that /i/ and /u/ represent the merger, respectively, of *į and *i and of *ų and *u. Nevertheless, even 5V languages can be quite revealing of the discrepancies between V_2C and $V_2\#$ harmony.

A case in point is Yaka H.32. The forms in (21), based on Ruttenberg (1971), show that neither the /i/ of the applicative or causative suffixes -il- and -is-, nor the /u/ of the reversive suffixes -uk- and -ul- undergo lowering after /e/ and /o/:

(21)		Applicative -il-			Causative -is-	
	a.	kik-il-a	'barrer pour'	b.	kik-is-a	'faire barrer'
		kud-il-a	'chasser pour'		kud-is-a	'faire chasser'
		kas-il-a	'lier pour'		kas-is-a	'faire lier'
		keb-il-a	'faire attention pour'		keb-is-a	'faire faire attention'
		sol-il-a	'déboiser pour'		sol-is-a	'faire déboiser'
		Reversive intransitive -uk-			Reversive transitive -ul-	
	c.	zib-uk-a	'être ouvert'	d.	zib-ul-a	'ouvrir'
		hul-uk-a	'être sauvé'		hul-ul-a	'sauver'
		bal-uk-a	'être renversé' (camion)		bal-ul-a	'renverser'
		yek-uk-a	'être séparé'		yek-ul-a	'séparer'
		tob-uk-a	'être percé'		tob-ul-a	'percer'

This would seem to suggest that there is no left-to-right VHH in this language. How then to reconcile these data with the fact that the perfective, suffix *-idi* harmonizes to -ele after a mid vowel in (7)? The corresponding perfectives of the forms in (21) show a similar pattern in (22).

(22)		Applicative + Perfective			Causative + Perfective	
	a.	kik-id-idi	'barrer pour'	b.	kik-is-i	'faire barrer'
		kud-id-idi	'chasser pour'		kud-is-i	'faire chasser'
		kas-id-idi	'lier pour'		kas-is-i	'faire lier'
		keb-el-ele	'faire attention pour'		keb-es-e	'faire faire attention'
		sol-el-ele	'déboiser pour'		sol-es-e	'faire déboiser'

Reversive intransitive + Perfective			Reversive transitive + Perfective		
c.	zib-uk-idi	'être ouvert'	d.	zibwel-e	'ouvrir'
	hul-uk-idi	'être sauvé'		hulwel-e	'sauver'
	bal-uk-idi	'être renversé' (camion)		balwel-e	'renverser'
	yek-ok-ele	'être séparé'		yekwel-e	'séparer'
	tob-ok-ele	'être percé'		tobwel-e	'percer'

The realizations in (22a,c) are as in (7): -idi after /i, u, a/ vs. -ele after /e, o/. (22b) shows the same vowel distribution, though in this case the [id] or [el] part of the perfective suffix does not surface. It apparently fuses with the reversive transitive -ul- suffix in (22d) and for some reason requires the vowel [e] even after root /i, u, a/.

As argued in Hyman (1998), the alternation between [i] and [e] found only in the perfective is not a case of the left-to-right VHH we have been considering up to now. Instead, recognizing that the perfective ending reconstructs as *-ɨd-e (Meeussen 1967, Bastin 1983b), what we have in (7) and (22) is a case of where the height feature of the final [e] spreads right-to-left. In order for this process to occur, the root syllable must, however, contain a mid vowel. Hence the process is one of "plateauing": high vowels become mid when wedged between mid vowels. Concerning (22d), the first three forms would be expected to zibwid-i, hulwid-i andbalwid-i, a pattern that is attested in certain Kongo dialects. However, the sequence [wi] cannot occur in Yaka (Hyman 1998). As a second right-to-left harmony process, the height feature of the final [e] thus spreads to convert a [Cwi] syllable to [Cwe], as seen.

With this explanation of the limited (right-to-left) VHH found in Yaka only in the perfective, let us now consider the 5 x 5 matrix of vowels in bisyllabic noun stems in this language:

(23) $V_1 + V_2$ in Yaka Bisyllabic Noun Stems

V_1/V_2	i	e	u	o	a
i	41	—	51	—	66
e	32	(3)	14	56	112
u	61	(1)	124	—	140
o	56	(1)	5	104	94
a	121	—	126	(1)	205

The shaded cells indicate which combinations are not found (or are found only exceptionally, typically in borrowings). As seen, there are two relevant generalizations. First, bisyllabic noun stems do not have the shape CVCe. Second, CVCo noun stems are acceptable only if the first vowel is /e/ or /o/. However, CeCo and CoCo contrast with CeCu and CoCu. What this means is that there has been an on-going change of "peripheralization" finally in bisyllabic noun stems. In the case of the back vowel, the pressure to change *o to [u] has been been successfully countered by the presence of a mid root vowel, which reinforces, as it were, the final *o. In the case of *e, this does not happen: For *e to survive finally, there must also be a preceding *medial* syllable with [e]. Thus, when right-to-left spreading occurs in (22), this has the effect of saving the final [e] of *-i̧d-e. Otherwise we obtain -idi or -is-i, as seen.[26]

The above Yaka discussion establishes two crucial points for our study. First, individual Bantu languages not only potentially inherit, but may also innovate VHH. This is clearly the case in (22d), where VHH is triggered as a response to the unacceptability of [wi] sequences in Yaka. I would conjecture that all VHH is innovative rather than original in Yaka, as in Kongo dialects that also restrict VHH to the prefective.[27] The second important point is that internal vs. final VHH can vary independently from each other. This conclusion is also suggested by Yaka's next door neighbors, the languages/dialects making up Kongo H.10, to which we now turn.

We saw earlier in the data in (9) that some dialects of Kongo have symmetric VHH operating left-to-right within the verb stem. Others, however, lack this harmony and in fact are like Yaka in most respects.[28] This includes the "Mazinga or Central dialect" described by Meinhof & van Warmelo (1932), based on material collected by Laman. The following verb forms, taken from Laman (1936), should be compared to those in (9):

[26]This right-to-left VHH triggered by a final mid vowel also explains the alternation between the final [o] in méésó 'eyes' and méénó 'teeth' vs. the [u] in the corresponding singulars díísú and díínú. The reconstructed roots *-jí̧co and *-jí̧no fuse with the class 6 prefix ma- in the plural, creating the mid vowel in the initial syllable [mee], which in turn protects the final [o] from becoming [u] (as it does in the singular forms). A similar interpretation can be given to the forms in Kongo (Meinhof & van Warmelo 1932:168).

[27]The only reason to "hedge" is that Yaka perfective harmony could be described as a retention in the following way: First, assume that pre-Yaka had standard left-to-right VHH, affecting the derivational suffixes in (21) even in the absence of the perfective. Second, assume that this VHH is subsequently lost as a peripheralization process on medial vowels. The only cases where peripheralization would have failed to apply would be where the whole stem consists of mid vowels: i.e. where peripheralization would have created high vowels surrounded by mid vowels. This analysis would of course not account for the data in (22d), where the penultimate [e] is clearly innovative. It also fails to account for the fact that the perfective ending is -ene (rather than -ini) whenever preceded by a CVCaC- base (Hyman, in press).

[28]A classification of Kongo dialects is found in Laman (1912, 1936) as well as a summary in Meinhof & van Warmelo (1932). See also Mabiala (1996).

(24) No VHH in Central Kongo

a.		b.	
-somp-il-a	's'attacher à'	-tol-ul-a	'casser, briser'
-lèng-il-a	'se flétrir, s'affaisser'	-lẽmb-ul-a	'barrer, effacer'
-sĩik-il-a	'soutenir, fortifier'	-viz-ul-a	'toucher à'
-vud-il-a	'surpasser'	-bũb-ul-a	'corrompre'
-lànd-il-a	'suivre'	-bãng-ul-a	'faire violence'

As seen, in Central Kongo, in contradistinction to Southern Kongo in (9), derivational suffixes do not by themselves undergo VHH. As in Yaka, the perfective ending conditions VHH, with -ili occurring after /i, u, a/ and -ele after /e, o/ (or their nasal variants -ini and -ene).[29]

In his comparative study of six Kongo dialects, Mabiala (1996) considers vowel harmony in Bembe H.11, Vili H.12a, Yombi H.12b, Sundi H.13, Laadi H.16f, and Hangala H.16j. The following tables summarize the distribution of vowels in CVCV stems on the left and CVCVC- stems on the right in three of Mabiala's dialects/languages:[30]

(25) Comparison of 5 x 5 vowel distributions in Kongo dialects/languages

a. Laadi CVCV

V_1/V_2	i	e	u	o	a
i	11	—	21	—	32
e	4	13	—	14	31
u	15	—	31	—	69
o	14	(2)	—	22	53
a	21	—	31	—	80

b. Laadi CVCVC...

V_1/V_2	i	e	u	o	a
i	11	—	7	—	7
e	—	8	—	4	6
u	7	—	22	—	16
o	(3)	2	—	6	1
a	15	—	16	—	23

c. Hangala CVCV

V_1/V_2	i	e	u	o	a
i	19	—	24	—	59
e	(1)	50	—	12	8
u	21	—	51	—	80
o	15	(2)	—	26	45
a	22	—	31	—	94

d. Hangala CVCVC...

V_1/V_2	i	e	u	o	a
i	14	—	7	—	5
e	14	(3)	8	(1)	6
u	8	—	38	—	9
o	7	—	9	(3)	1
a	17	—	26	—	17

[29]The corresponding perfective passive endings are -ulu/-unu and -olo/-ono (Meinhof & van Warmelo 1932:167-8).

[30]In this case, in the addition to CVCVC- verb stems, the survey includes CVCVCV noun stems, which, due to reduplications and borrowings, accounts for some of the exceptions, indicated between parentheses.

e. Yombi CVCV

V_1/V_2	i	e	u	o	a
i	15	—	24	—	46
e	21	—	25	—	33
u	14	—	51	—	64
o	11	—	27	—	40
a	22	—	31	—	85

f. Yombi CVCVC...

V_1/V_2	i	e	u	o	a
i	7	—	5	—	6
e	9	(1)	4	—	5
u	3	—	12	—	4
o	3	—	14	—	1
a	8	—	22	—	5

In (25a) we see that Laadi generally allows CVCe stems only when the preceding vowel is itself /e/. What this means is that CoCi is obtained to the detriment of CoCe, of which there are only two exceptional instances. The four occurrences of CeCi are not shaded in, since it is not clear if they are exceptional. Mabiala's numbers are, of course, somewhat limited and could change as further data are considered. On the other hand, we see that CeCi is disallowed in Hangala in (25c), which in all other respects is identical to Laadi in (25a). The situation in Yombi in (25e) is, however, quite different. Here we see that /e/ and /o/ simply cannot occur as the second vowel in a CVCV stem.

Let us now compare these results with the realization of the internal vowel of CVCVC... stems. While Laadi shows symmetric VHH in (25b), both Hangala and Yombi lack VHH in (25d,f).[31] Yombi is of course consistent in its peripheralization of *e and *o in both final position in CVCV stems and in internal position in CVCVC... stems. However, Hangala is not consistent. While it has only [i] and [u] internally in (25f), it has non-peripheral [e] after /e/ and non-peripheral [o] after both /e/ and /o/. A final mid vowel is peripheralized in all other combinations, including CoCi which occurs to the detriment of *CoCe.

The following summary in (26) shows how Mabiala's six languages/dialects line up with respect to VHH:

(26)

		Stem Shape		VHH	
		CVCV	CVCVC...	CVCV	CVCVC...
a.	Laadi H.16f	CeCe/CeCo	CeCeC/CeCoC	S	S
		CoCi/CoCo	CoCeC/CoCoC	S	S
		(CeCi)			
b.	Hangala H.16j	CeCe/CeCo	CeCiC/CeCuC	S	N
		CoCi/CoCo	CoCiC/CoCuC	A	N

[31]The numbers in (26b) are low and do not clearly show that CoCeC- is preferred over CoCiC-. However, Jacquot's (1962) study makes it clear that VHH is symmetrical in Laadi.

c.	Suundi H.13	CeCe/CeCo	CeCiC/CeCuC	S	N
		CoCi/CoCo	CoCiC/CoCuC	A	N
d.	Yombi H.12b	CeCi/CeCu	CeCiC/CeCuC	N	N
		CoCi/CoCu	CoCiC/CoCuC	N	N
e.	Vili H.12a	CeCi/CeCu	CeCiC/CeCuC	N	N
		CoCi/CoCu	CoCiC/CoCuC	N	N
f.	Bembe H.11	CeCe/CeCu	CeCiC/CeCuC	A	N
		CoCi/CoCo	CoCiC/CoCuC	A	N

In (26) S, A and N stand, respectively, for symmetric, asymmetric and no VHH, respectively. As seen, Laadi is alone among the languages surveyed by Mabiala to have symmetric VHH in both V_2# and V_2C positions. None of the languages in (26b-f) has internal VHH. Hangala and Suundi have the same asymmetric pattern in bisyllabic stems, where CoCi occurs instead of *CoCe.[32] Yombi and Vili, on the other hand, have no VHH in either context. Turning to Bembe in (27f), there appears to be a double asymmetry in bisyllabic stems: CeCe and CoCo instead vs. CeCu and CoCi. On the other hand, Mabiala reports no VHH in CVCVC stems, while Jacquot (1981) indicates that there is symmetric harmony in such cases.[33]

We are now ready to consider what these data may have to say about reconstruction of VHH in PB. Some Kongo dialects are fully harmonizing, while others have no harmony other than in the perfective (which I have claimed to be a right-to-left innovation). If asymmetric VHH is reconstructed, then some Kongo dialects would have generalized it to symmetric (the only such case among 5V Bantu languages), while others would have lost left-to-right VHH altogether (replacing it in some cases with right-to-left perfective harmony). This would seem a rather complex set of developments, as all Kongo dialects would have changed in various directions without any one of them keeping the asymmetric pattern. If we thus instead reconstruct symmetric VHH, then some some dialects could be said to conserve it, while others would have lost it.

Of the two, this second hypothesis thus far seems preferable. In view of the fact that Kongo stands out among 5V Bantu languages (having symmetric VHH), I would further hypothesize that both sets of VHH properties in Kongo dialects were set in motion at a point when these

---

[32]Since the asymmetric pattern in Hangala and Sundi is one of CeCo vs. CoCi, it is the opposite of the Savanna Bantu case, where we obtain CoCeC-, but CeCuC-.

[33]Relevant perhaps to this discrepancy, Laman (1936:lxx) shows VHH variation in Bembe. Thus, kébe 'garder' has the perfective keberi or kebiri. The Bembe material are complicated by the fact that internal vowels also tend to be realized as schwa, an indication of the fact that we are dealing with a form of vowel reduction—which may trigger VHH, peripheralization, "bleaching", or, syncope in extreme cases in Northwest Bantu.

languages had 7V. On the one hand, the dialects with symmetric VHH fit in well in the situation in zone C (Leitch 1996), which have 7V. These also frequently have assimilations of *a to a preceding /ɛ/ or /ɔ/, as we saw in Koyo C.24 in (13). Interestingly, Bembe H.11 is, with Lwalwa L.00 (Ndembe-Nsasi 1972), one of only two 5V languages that also have this property:

> La voyelle de 3ème degré d'aperture [=a] n'apparait jamais précédée d'une voyelle de 2ème degré d'aperture, avec pour conséquence que le morphème /-a/ des noms verbaux présente les variantes [-o] et [-e], respectivement, après 2ème degré postérieur et 2ème degré antérieur" (Jacquot 1962:241).

We thus obtain the following realizations of the final vowel /-a/ on infinitives:[34]

(27)	a.	kù-búl-à	'casser'	b.	ku-ból-ò	'pourrir'
		kù-síís-à	'abandonner'		ku-kéb-è	'garder'
		kùsál-à	'travailler'.			

The hypothesis, therefore, is that both types of Kongo dialects pattern with certain 7V systems in the geographical vicinity. Those which have symmetric suffixal harmony, as in (9), pattern with 7V languages like Mongo C.61, whose symmetric VHH was illustrated in (8). Those which do not have harmony, as in (24), pattern instead with languages like Koyo C.24. Symmetric VHH does occur in this language, as was illustrated in prefixes and CVCV noun stems in (5) and (6). However, as seen in (29), only /i/, /u/ and /a/ occur medially in CVCVC- verb stems:

(28) $V_1 + V_2$ in Koyo CVCVC- Verb Stems

V1/V2	i	e	ɛ	u	o	ɔ	a
i	14	—	—	1	—	—	4
e	14	—	—	2	—	—	—
ɛ	5	—	(2)	1	—	—	(1)
u	19	—	—	3	—	—	2
o	9	—	—	2	—	—	2
ɔ	7	—	—	3	—	(1)	—
a	16	—	—	4	—	—	3

34 Mabiala (1996) has a final schwa on many of his infinitive forms, which suggests, first, that there might be variation, and second that reduction could be a contributing factor, perhaps critical, to the assimilations in question.

In this language, most verbal suffixes have the vowel /i/, as in causative -is- and even reciprocal -in- (from PB *-an-):[35]

(29)	a.	lím-is-a	'extinguish'	b.	yís-in-a	'hide oneself'
		yég-is-a	'teach'		tég-in-a	'meet'
		kɛ́ng-is-a	'make observe'		ɲwɛm-in-a	'have rashes'
		kúr-is-a	'make warm'		kúl-in-a	'separate from each other'
		wóm-is-a	'to dry (tr.)'		wóg-in-a	'agree'
		kɔs-is-a	'soften'		lɔnd-in-a	'follow each other'
		bág-is-a	'make think'		sang-in-a	'amuse oneself'

Internal vowels are clearly peripheralized and exempt from VHH in Koyo. This should be contrasted with the following table of vowel distributions in CVCV stems, which shows that /e, o/ cannot co-occur with /ɛ, ɔ/:

(30) $V_1 + V_2$ in Koyo Bisyllabic Noun Stems

V1/V2	i	e	ɛ	u	o	ɔ	a
i	26	(1)	11	26	—	—	51
e	24	36	—	13	10	—	42
ɛ	17	—	50	10	—	11	(1)
u	27	(1)	(3)	65	—	—	40
o	23	(2)	—	7	66	—	50
ɔ	27	—	—	9	—	72	(2)
a	55	8	—	40	45	—	116

While bisyllabic noun stems show symmetric VHH among mid vowels, internal syllables of verbs have been peripheralized to /i, u, a/. The possibility that stem-internal vowels may undergo a different history than stem-final vowels thus needs to be recognized and factored into the equation.[36] This makes our reconstruction effort that much more difficult.

---

[35]Data are from the Koyo lexicon of 1700+ entries that I developed in Lyon during 1995-1996 with Yvon Dzamba, based loosely on Gazania (1972). All of the verbs that have the shape CVCaC- have a /g/ in C_3 position, e.g. kír-ag-a 'curse', as do the two verbs that have the shape CɛCɛC-, from /CɛCag-/. By comparison, the 84 CVCiC- verb bases divide themselves up among CVCis- (56), CVCin- (16), CVCit- (11) (pronounced [CVCir-]), and CVCing- (1). The 16 CVCuC- verbs have the following C_3 consonants: CVCus- (6), CVCun- (4), CVCum- (3), CVCumw- (2) and CVCul- (1). (Note that Koyo does not have an applicative suffix.)

[36]In Hyman & Inkelas (1997) and Hyman (1998) I have referred to the relevant stem-internal sequence as constituting a "prosodic trough" within which specific phonotactic constraints may hold that do not characterize the "perimeters."

In the next section I attempt to present a different view of what the situation might have been in PB.

5. An alternative hypothesis

In this section I shall depart from the assumptions outlined above and suggest a different view of what might have existed in PB. The position I would like to tentatively advance for consideration is that neither symmetric nor asymmetric VHH existed in PB—at least as concerned suffixes within the verb stem. My proposal will involve both different reconstructions for certain suffixes than usually assumed as well as an historical VHH process that worked quite differently from the way it is normally conceived in synchronic descriptions—whether of PB or of the daughter languages.

Most recent discussions of VHH in PB and present day 7V Bantu languages start from two assumptions. First, VHH involves the assimilation of a degree 2 vowel to a preceding degree 3 vowel.[37] VHH is thus either a lowering process, if one assumes the vowel representations in (15a,b), or a vowel laxing process, if one assumes those in (15c). A second, related assumption, is that insight into this lowering or laxing process is best acquired by examining the alternations that are observed in isolatable verb suffixes such as applicative *-id-, stative *-ik-, reversive *-uk- and *-ud-, etc. In this study I have accordingly followed the general practice of citing such alternations in support of the putative historical processes presented in (1). That is, suffixal *i is realized [e] after a preceding *eC or *oC, while suffixal *u is realized [o] after preceding *oC (and after *eC in "symmetric" VHH systems). I shall now reconsider these assumptions in turn and argue that they should be questioned, if not rejected.

I begin by raising the following question: What is the evidence that degree 2 vowels should be reconstructed with a concomitant lowering or laxing to degree 3—rather than the reverse? It is universally accepted that degree 2 and 3 vowels did not contrast in stem-internal positions, i.e. where these suffixes occur. So why not reconstruct *-ed-, *-ek-, *-ok- and *-od-, etc.? While I am unaware of any explicit argumentation, I imagine the reconstructions with *-iC- and *-uC- to be based, first, on the relatively unmarked status of [i, u] vs. [e, o]. Those taking this view may also see

---

[37]On the other hand, Meinhof (1948) previously reconstructed both *i and *e in specific suffixes, e.g. causative *-ik- vs. intransitive *-ek-. Interesting from my point of view is that Meinhof and van Warmelo (1932:43-46) generally cite suffixes with a front vowel with *e, e.g. -eka and -ela, while suffixes with a rounded vowel are cited either with a high vowel, e.g. -uka and -ula, or with one after the other, e.g. -uka, -oka and -ula, -ola. The intention seems to be to suggest a difference between the front vs. back vowels in verb extensions. This interpretation can also be extracted from Meyer's (1937) historical phonology of Cewa, with its indication of *eka > -eka, -ika vs. *-uka > -uka, -oka (p.186). Meyer thus sees a change of *e > i in the front series vs. *u > o in the back, a view that I will also defend below.

support from the fact that some Bantu languages without VHH disallow [e, o] in stem-internal position, e.g. Punu B.43, Lengola D.12, Suku H.32, Mbala H.41, and Ruund L.53—to which we can also add Yaka H.31 and Easterly Kongo H.10 dialects which allow (right-to-left) VHH only in the perfective—and which otherwise limit internal vowels to [i, u, a]. However, we know that these languages are quite evolved in this and other ways—e.g. in limiting or modifying stem-internal vowels in sequence. As an example, consider the possible internal -VCVC- sequences found in quadrisyllabic (CVC-VCVC-V) verb stems in the Yaka "prosodic trough" (Hyman 1998):

(31) Attested internal -VCVC- sequences in Yaka verbs

a. -ikis- (42), -idil- (10), -ikil- (9), -idik- (5), -inin- (3), -inis- (2)

b. -umun- (56), -ulul- (36), -umuk- (27), -uluk- (9), -unun- (2)

c. -asan- (40), -akan- (34), -alal- (17), -aman- (14), -anan- (6), -amas- (5), -angan- (4), -asal- (3), -angas- (2), -akas- (1)

d. -ukil- (6), -ukis- (1)

The number in parentheses after each sequence indicates how many entries (out of 1781 verbs) appear with this form in the CBOLD version of Ruttenberg (1971). As can be correctly generalized from (31), the only consonants that appear in these two C positions are the four coronals /t, l, n, s/ and the three non-coronals /m, k, ng/ (vs. a much larger inventory in the preceding CVC "perimeter"). In addition, vowels are limited to /i/, /u/ and /a/, which however appear in only four out of nine logical combinations. In (31) I indicate some of the historical innovations which removed non-occurring vowel sequences from the "trough":

(32) Historical innovations yielding trough properties

a.	*-am-uk-, *-am-ud- > -umuk-, -umun-	(positional + reversive)
b.	*-is-an-, *-ik-an- > -asan-, -akan-	(causative/impositive + reciprocal)
c.	*-am-is-, *-am-id- > -amas-/-aman-	(positional + causative/ applicative)

We thus cannot take comfort from such languages, which seem to be moving in the direction of fewer vowel oppositions in stem-internal position in general. While we might take solace from these evolved systems which reveal a tendency to exclude mid vowels from the positions where Bantuists have preferred to reconstruct *i and *u, this only begs the question: Were there never any mid vowels in these positions? It is hard to accept that we would not eventually meet a fuller set of vowels if we could go back far enough in history. So the issue is whether PB is "back far enough" or not. I shall suggest below that it is.

But first let us consider the other intuition that may be involved in the reconstruction of degree 2 vowels. If *-iC- and *-uC- are postulated, then the development of [-eC-] and [-oC-] can be explained as assimilations to the preceding degree 3 vowel. This was seen in the derivation of asymmetric VHH in (1), for instance. If, on the other hand, we were to begin with *-eC- and *-oC-, we would need VHH to be stated as in (33).

(33) Asymmetric VHH reinterpreted

a. front height harmony : *e > i / { i̧, u̧, i, u, a } C __

b. back height harmony : *o > u / { i̧, u̧, i, u, e, a } C __

As seen in (33a), *e would have to raise to [i] after five different vowels, while *o would have to raise to [u] after six different vowels in (33b). Where the mid vowels raise to high vowels after high vowels one could view this as assimilation. However, why should degree 3 *e [ɛ]and *o [ɔ] raise to degree 2 [ɪ] and [ʊ], respectively, when preceded by *a? So, some of the process would seem to be assimilatory, some dissimilatory, clearly a more complicated interpretation of the facts than in (1).

The reasoning in arriving at the interpretation of (1), then, is that VHH is actively conditioned by the preceding vowels. Let us instead consider the possibility that (33) is correct and that the motivation for the changes indicated is "peripheralization," i.e. the tendency for vowels to migrate to the peripheries of the vowel space, becoming /i, u, a/ in "weak" positions (e.g. internally and/or finally). Viewed this way, (33a) could be interpreted as *e becoming [ɪ] except where *e is "reinforced" by a preceding degree 3 vowel. Similarly, (33b) could be interpreted as *o becoming [ʊ] except when reinforced by a preceding *o. Such "passive conditioning" or blocking of a sound change is not unknown in historical linguistics, and can be easily demonstrated with solid Bantu examples.

As shown by Ngunga (1997), for instance, the Yao P.21 suffixes -ik-/-ek- are rounded to -uk-/-ok- in examples such as the following, where they are followed by the reversive suffix -ul-/-ol-:

(34) Rounding of suffixal -ik-ul-/-ek-uk- in Yao P.21

a.	lum-ik-a	'have between the teeth'
	lum-uk-ul-a	'take out of mouth'
	wun-ik-a	'close (book); put together'
	wun-uk-ul-a	'open'
	wuund-ik-a	'store fruit by sealing in pot'
	wuund-uk-ul-a	'take fruit out of sealed pot; unseal'
b.	aan-ik-a	'spread out to dry in the sun'
	aan-uk-ul-a	'gather up sth. spread in sun to dry'

	saj-ik-a	'put on top'
	saj-uk-ul-a	'remove from top of something else'
	taand-ik-a	'spread (bed, mat, table cloth).'
	taand-uk-ul-a	'fold up (table cloth); unmake bed'
c.	kol-ek-w-a	'be hung; be caught by thorns'
	kol-ok-ol-a	'take down sth. that is hung'
	lov-ek-a	'steep in water; soak'
	low-ok-ol-a	'remove from water (from soaking); unsoak'
	tot-a	'sew; rivet; fasten together'
	tot-ok-ol-a	'unpick sewing; unfasten sth fastened'

In (34a,b) /-ik-ul-/ rounds to -uk-ul-, while in (34c), /-ek-ul-/ is realized -ok-ol- by rounding as well as VHH. These examples thus amply demonstrate that there is a rounding harmony affecting the suffixal vowels /i/ and /e/. Now compare the data in (35) with those in (35).

(35) Rounding of -ik-ul- and -ek-ul- fails to occur

a.	sim-ik-a	'fix upright'
	sim-ik-ul-a	'remove what has been fixed upright'
	siind-ik-a	'protect a village or house with medicine'
	siind-ik-ul-a	'unprotect a village or house that was protected with medicine'
	siing-a	'twist strands (of cotton, sisal, etc.) into thread or rope'
	siinj-ik-ul-a	'disentangle, unravel'
b.	eej-ek-a	'place leaning against or on'
	eej-ek-ul-a	'remove what has been placed'
	vel-ek-a	'carry on back (child); bear child'
	vel-ek-ul-a	'swing child from back to hip'
	tej-ek-a	'be easily set (a trap); be cocked.'
	tej-ek-ul-a	'unset (trap), uncock (gun)'

In these examples there is no rounding harmony. A close comparision of these data will reveal that the input -ik-ul- or -ek-ul- sequence is preceded by a back vowel in (34) vs. a front vowel in (35). Note the importance, again, of the form the vowel takes after /a/: Had it not been for the rounding of -ik-ul- to -uk-ul- in (34b), we might have concluded that (34a,c) represented a rounding of -ik- *after* /u/ or /o/, rather than the right-to-left process that it clearly is. Although rounding harmony targets suffix vowels, what is crucial is that the presence of a preceding root vowel /i/ or /e/ blocks the process.[38]

Returning to VHH, Caga E.62 (5V) provides very suggestive evidence that the processes could have been as indicated in (33). This language is generally assumed not to have VHH (cf. note 8), a view reinforced by the fact that the applicative suffix is realized as an invariant -i-. A manual search through Müller (1947), however, tells a different tale, summarized in (36).

(36) Mid V + Mid/High V in Caga CVCVC... Verb Stems

VCVC	All	s	y	k	r	t	d	n	l	š	ny	ng	m	v	w	b
eCeC	83	4	5	9	20	11	2	2	11	7	1	2	7	1	1	—
eCiC	17	6	3	6	2	—	—	—	—	—	—	—	—	—	—	—
oCeC	—	—	—	—	—	—	—	—	—	—	—	—	—	—	—	—
oCiC	29	16	1	8	4	—	—	—	—	—	—	—	—	—	—	—
eCoC	—	—	—	—	—	—	—	—	—	—	—	—	—	—	—	—
eCuC	17	—	1	13	2	1	—	—	—	—	—	—	—	—	—	—
oCoC	53	2	3	11	8	4	1	—	5	2	—	3	5	6	3	2
oCuC	10	—	2	8	—	—	—	—	—	—	—	—	—	—	—	—

The numbers in this table show how many verb stems were found that attest the indicated sequences. Thus, there were 83 stems having the sequence eCeC, 17 having eCiC, and so forth. A count was made only of sequences where a mid vowel is followed by another (non-low) vowel, since an initial survey indicated that there would be extremely few cases where mid vowels follow /i/, /u/ or /a/. The columns headed by s, y, k, r etc. plot the number of examples occurring as a function of the second consonant in the VCVC sequence. Two observations should be made. First, when the mid and following vowel agree in frontness and roundness, VHH applies in about 5/6 of the cases: 83 vs. 17 in the front series and 53 vs. 10 in the back series. Second, when the two vowels different in frontness and roundness,

[38]That only suffixes are affected by this process is seen in examples such as dim-uk-a 'be scared away' and sip-uk-a 'sprout', where the reversive intransitive suffix -uk- does not affect the preceding root /i/. A search of the CBOLD version of Sanderson (1954) reveals only three cases of verbs having the shape CiCuCuCa: -diimbukuka 'tumble; sag; fall over slowly (e.g., a tree or a pole)', -siimbukula 'dig up a plant with roots and soil attached', and -vinukula 'gap (of a wound)'. The first two verbs have a labial consonant preceding the -ukuk- sequence, which I hypothesize to break the blocking effect of the preceding front root vowel. (None of the verbs having the shape CiCiCuCa in the database has a labial second consonant.) The third form is either exceptional or is not derived from vin-ik-ul-a but rather from vin-uk-ul-a—cf. vin-uk-a 'go over (as opposed to go round) an obstacle'.

VHH is impossible. That is, neither oCeC nor eCoC occur in verb stems. In other words, if two vowels in successive syllables are mid, they must be identical.

There are two possible interpretations of these facts: (i) VHH is incipient in Caga and has begun by affecting vowels which agree in frontness and roundness. (ii) VHH is moribund in Caga and has begun by affecting vowels that disagree in frontness and roundness. A major difficulty with the first interpretation is that Caga clearly belongs to the same Eastern Bantu group as other languages in the area which have (canonical) VHH, e.g. Kamba E.55, Shambala G.23, etc. While Caga is somewhat isolated and detached from other Bantu languages, it is hard to conceive of VHH as a recent enough innovation for it to have escaped it. This view is further supported by the facts of contiguous Asu (Pare) G.22 (Kotz 1909). Like Caga, the applicative is non-harmonizing -i- in most cases, e.g. tet-a 'speak', tet-i-a 'speak for someone'. The applicative is however realized as harmonizing -ir-/-er- in frozen forms, e.g. tet-a 'speak', tet-er-a 'cackle'; teka 'get lost', tek-er-a 'get lost on someone'. I therefore adopt the second interpretation: the gradual loss of VHH has been innovated in Caga (and Asu), beginning with applicative -i-.

An additional argument weighs in on the side of gradual loss of VHH in Caga: Note in (36) that the second consonant of disharmonic eCiC and oCuC sequences is more restricted than in the corresponding harmonic sequences eCeC and oCoC. In fact, the only attested disharmonic eCiC and oCuC sequences are: eCis, eCiy, eCik, eCir, oCuy and oCuk, i.e. where the second consonant is [s], [y], [k] or [r]. All of these consonants are involved in suffixal allomorphy in Caga, e.g. causative -is-/-es-, applicative -iy-/-ey-, stative -ik-/-ek-, causative -ir-/-er-. There may therefore be a sporadic differential treatment of stem-internal vowels in cases where a suffix can be identified: Whereas eCeC and oCoC do not become eCiC and oCuC when the second consonant is non-suffixal, these latter may occur, sometimes apparently as variants, when suffixation is involved.

Finally, I should note that 8 of the 17 disharmonic eCiC forms have the sequence emiC vs. only three harmonic emeC forms—two of which are reduplications: *memeluka* 'albern sein, unnützen' and *memes&wa* 'jemdm. mit dem Finger ans Unterkinn fahren' (Müller 1947:199). Similarly, of the 10 disharmonic oCuC forms, 7 have omuk or omuy and one has onuk. By contrast, only one verb, *omoma*, the iterative of *-oma* 'tanzen' (and hence obviously a reduplication), has an omoC sequence. It thus appears that loss of VHH has been further hastened by the presence of a nasal consonant preceding the vowel in question. This presumably correlates with the fact that stem-initial [me], [mo], [ne] and [no] sequences are rare in Caga as in many Bantu languages. A rough count of the number of verb entries in Müller (1947) beginning with /m/ and /n/ is given in (37).

(37) Mid V + Mid/High V in Caga CVCVC... Verb Stems

[NV...]stem	i	e	u	o	a
m	12	3	10	—	26
n	7	1	11	1	11

Thus, rather than having the expected CeNeC and CoNoC sequences, we find CeNiC and CoNuC, respectively. In other words, various factors contribute to the loss of VHH in Caga, as well as to its retention. The important point is that height agreement will generally be maintained when [e] or [o] is preceded by an identical mid vowel.[39] The question now is: if this happened in the history of Caga, why not in the history of Bantu in general?

This, then, is what I believe to be going on in suffixal VHH in Bantu. I propose that the applicative and stative suffixes reconstruct as *-ed- and *-ek-, respectively, which were "peripheralized" to -id- and -ik- in most Bantu languages except where "held back" by a preceding mid root vowel (cf. below for discussion of u/o harmony). Assuming these reconstructions we can now interpret some crucial facts in the following way.

(i) The non-alternating mid vowels of applicative *-ed- and stative *-ek- in Southern Bantu (all of zone S except Shona S.10) and in Makua (P.31) are original. If we assumed the reconstructions *-id- and *-ik-, we would be at a loss to explain why these suffixes employ a degree 3 vowel in these languages—which include the 7V Sotho group, e.g. Tswana S.31.[40]

---

[39]Another example may be Salampasu L.51: "En salampusu, la voyelle i des suffixes s'ouvre en e uniquement après cette voyelle" (Bastin 1986:76). The causative of -end-a 'voyager' is thus -end-esh-a, while the causative of -som-a 'charger un fusil' is -som-ish-a. This could be significant, since Salampasu neighbors Ruund L.53, which has no VHH at all. The interpretation I would propose is that Salampasu i/e VHH has been lost except when an identical /e/ precedes. A slightly different, but case involving comes from Logoli E.41 (7V). Leung (1986:83) shows that the PB final vowel *-e, used in the subjunctive and in the imperative when the verb has an object prefix, is realized [ɪ] after both degree 1 and degree 2 vowels:

kɪ-gʊr-iz-ɪ	'sell it!'	ke-veg-e	'shave it!'
kɪ-dʊy-ɪn̂ɪ	'hit for it!'	ke-n̥oor-e	'obtain it!'
kɪ-guut-ɪ	'defeat it!'	ke-saamb-e	'burn it!'
kɪ-rʊm-ɪ	'bite it!'		

It is clear in this case that *-e > -ɪ unless "held back" by a degree 3 (or 4) vowel, another precedent for what I am proposing here.]

[40]Bastin (1983a) sees this outcome as a possible extension of the -eC- found after *a in languages such as those mentioned in the next paragraph. The argument goes as follows: While *-iC- lowers to -eC- only after mid vowels in most Bantu languages, in several zone K and R languages this process is extended to occurring also after the low vowel *a. Once this happens, this tilts the balance towards the -eC- allomorphs, which occur more frequently—and

(ii) The mid vowel realization of *-ed- and *-ek- following *a in the preceding syllable in Mbundu H.21a, Mbunda K.15, Kwangali K.33, Kwezo K.35, Dciriku K.62, Pende L.11/K.52, Mbundu R.11, Kwanyama R.21, Ndongo R.22, and Herero R.31 is also original. Rather than saying that *-id- and *-ik- lower to -ed- and -ek- by assimilation, in these languages the preceding *a hindered the peripheralization of *-ed- and *-ek- to -id- and -ik- in this account.

(iii) The mid vowel realization of *-ed- and *-ek- following *Ca- roots is also original. Thus, the applicative of *pá- 'give' would have been *pá-ed-a, which in turn would be expected to be realized as [péela], as it is in Bemba M.42, for instance. In a language like Haya.EJ.22, where 'to give for/at' is realized as [héera], an input such as *pá-id-a would have been expected to come out as *[híira] by the normal vowel coalescence rules.

(iv) By setting up these suffixes as *-ed- and *-ek-, we can now resolve a dilemma faced by Bastin (1986) concerning the long causative suffix "-is-" which co-occurs with the short causative *-į-. In many languages, there is a morph -is- which harmonizes to -es- in exactly the same contexts as the applicative, e.g. Bemba M.42, Cewa N.31b, Shona S.11. If the applicative is reconstructed as *-id-, this would suggest that the causative sequence should be reconstructed as *-ic-į-. The problem is that individual languages from all parts of the Bantu zone also show evidence that the vowel of the causative is higher than that of the applicative. Thus, the causative suffix is -is- in Bobangi C.32 in the Northwest vs. applicative -el- (which harmonizes to -ɛl-). Similarly, in the South, the causative suffix is -is- in Lozi K.21/S.34, Luyana K.31, Mbukushu K.33, Makua P.31, Venda S.21, Sotho-Tswana S.30 and Nguni S.40 vs. applicative -el- (neither of which harmonizes). Finally, note that there are traces of this difference even in the East. Thus we have said that the applicative form /há-ir-a/ 'give for/at' is realized [héera] in Haya. However, the causative of /há-/ is [háisa]—even though both suffixes harmonize identically (-ir-/-er- and -is-į-/-es-į-) when following a consonant. We might follow Guthrie's suggestion (reported in Bastin 1986:89) and say that the morph -į- which directly follows the longer morph raised or tensed the vowel of *-ic-į- to -įc-į- so that we sometimes

---

hence are extended to occuring after the rounded vowel as well. While this might seem plausible in 5V systems, where 2 harmony triggers vs. 3 non-triggers changes to 3 vs. 2, in the 7V Sotho group the change would have been from 2 harmony triggers vs. 5 non-triggers to 3 vs. 4, hardly making -eC- the dominant allomorph! If the putative extension of VHH to occurring after *a took place before the 7V > 5V merger, this would thereby weaken this interpretation even further. Finally, as I discuss below, the preponderance of stem-internal [e] (over degree 1 or 2 front vowels) in Tswana S.31 extends beyond recognizable suffixes to characterize so-called "expansions" and unanalyzeable non-initial root syllables. While one could see Tswana analogizing applicative -el- and stative -ek- to all environments, it would seem unlikely to have done the same with corresponding tautomorphemic post-root vowels.

these discrepancies between the vowel of the applicative and the vowel of the causative. Bastin goes as far as to reconstruct *-į̧c-į̧-, with harmony as a secondary development (much as in the case of perfective *-į̧d-e, which historically did not undergo VHH, but which has been "regularized" to undergo VHH in such languages as Bukusu EJ.31c and Bemba M.42. Unlike the perfective, however, there is precious little evidence that her *-į̧c-į̧- conditions frication on preceding consonants, as *į̧ should—and as Bastin herself notes.[41]

My proposal handles both of these problems (higher vowel height than applicative which cannot however be *į̧ because of lack of frication) by recognizing the applicative as *-ed- and the causative as *-ic-į̧-. The applicative harmonizes as above, i.e. except where held back by mid vowels in most harmonizing languages. The causative, on the other hand, has a degree 2 vowel which may lower (lax) as a result of VHH coming to be more general in Bantu languages, or it may tense (peripheralize) instead. Or, as in Haya, it may do a bit of both, depending on whether it follows a consonant or a vowel. Two bits of data further support this view. First, Batibo (1985:168) indicates that Sukuma F.21 (7V) has the interesting realization of causative *-is-į̧-: -į̧s-į̧- after /į̧, ų, a/, -is-į̧- after degree 2 /i, u/, and -es-į̧- after degree 3 /e, o/. This situation contrasts with the "canonical" VHH pattern that characterizes the applicative and stative suffixes which are realized -el- and -ek- after mid vowels, otherwise degree 2 -il- and -ik-.[42]

Why should this be? My hypothesis would be to attribute the difference between these suffixes to a difference in the vowel that is reconstructed in causative *-is-į̧- vs. applicative *-ed- and stative *-ek-. When VHH was introduced into this language, *-ed- and *-ek- harmonized to a preceding degree 2 *i or *u, while *-is- harmonized to a preceding degree 3 vowel. In addition, the degree 1 vowel -į̧- further exerted an influence, causing the degree 2 vowel of (non-harmonized) -is- to become -į̧s- as a secondary development—which was blocked, however, by a preceding degree 2 *i or *u. Again it is the vowel /a/ that tells us what is going on. Had we obtained -is-į̧- after /a/, we might have interpreted the process as left-to-right agreement in [ATR]. However, /a/ is followed by -į̧s-į̧-. Thus, as in the Yao rounding harmony in (34) and (35), the innovation is for -is-į̧- to become

---

[41]Languages which do show such frication often do so by analogy. Thus, Ashton et al (1954) claim that the long causative of Ganda EJ.15 ku-túuk-a 'to arrive, reach' should be ku-túus-is-a, but I have been able to elicit only ku-túuk-is-a. If such forms exist, even marginally, it may be by analogy with the short causative form ku-túus-a whose applicative is ku-túus-iz-a.

[42]Batibo mentions that Swahili might be exerting an influence on these realizations. In addition, causative *-ic- was almost certainly followed by *-į̧- in PB (Bastin 1986), as it is in many Eastern Bantu languages today, e.g. Haya (Trithart 1977). Thus, the possibility is always there that the correct reconstruction could be with the same vowel as the applicative and stative suffixes—and that languages later and independently raised the vowel.

-įs-į- by a right-to-left process, which is secondary to VHH. This process is however blocked when the preceding *i or *u shares the degree 2 vowel height with the suffix -is-.

Corroboration of such a vowel height distinction in verb extensions comes from as far away from Eastern Bantu as Duala A.24 (Ittmann 1939[1978]). In this language both the applicative and stative are realized -e-, e.g. *lóng-a* 'build', *lóng-e-a* 'build for'; *túm-a* 'tear (tr.)', *túm-e-a* 'tear (intr.)'. However, the causative is realized -is- (followed by the final vowel -ɛ): *wút-a* 'become short', *wút-is-ɛ* 'shorten'; *lónd-a* 'to fill (intr.)', *lónd-is-ɛ* 'to fill (tr.). Reconstructing a different vowel in causative *-ic- vs. applicative *-ed- would thus go a long way towards accounting for vowel height differences sporadically noted throughout the Bantu zone.

Now it is conceivable still that the vowel height differences are due to the following degree 1 causative morph *-į- which obligatorily accompanied *-ic- in PB (as in many daughter languages).[43] A close examination of stem-internal vowels, whether suffixal or not, is of course required and has been only partially effected at the time of this writing. Other citations of differential vowel height in Bantu languages include harmonizing impositive -ik-/-ek- vs. non-harmonizing stative -ik- in Ndonga R.22 (Viljoen & Amakali 1978) and Herero R.31 (Meinhof & van Warmelo 1932:44). Since invariant applicative -i- is presumably an innovation in Caga E.62, and since leveling of VHH is likely to hit the most productive suffixes first (e.g. the applicative and stative), it is conceivable that this distinction is a secondary development.[44]

If the causative and applicative suffixes are reconstructed with different vowels, they could have been subject to VHH with slightly different results, as we have seen. However, I wish to consider the alternative hypothesis that PB did not have had stem-internal VHH at all. One area that may shed some light on these questions is the realization of suffixes (and expansions) after CV- roots. I have already alluded to the fact that differences in vowel height between the applicative and causative is sometimes attested only after a vowel, e.g. Haya EJ.22 *hé-er-a* 'give for/at' vs. *hé-is-a* 'cause to give' (from -*há*-). Besides freely combining roots such as *-*pá*- 'give', *-*lí*- 'eat', *-*nó*- 'drink' etc., there are a number of frozen -CV-VC- combinations where the

---

[43]Evidence that would support the tensing of a vowel immediately followed by *-į- would consist of a language in which -įs-į- is non-harmonizing when these two morphs occur in sequence, but harmonizing when another morph, e.g. the applicative, intervenes, i.e. -is-il-į- vs. -es-el-į- (with possible frication of the [l] of the applicative). I know of no such language. However, I am struck by the fact that *-į- tenses mid vowels that precede it in Sotho-Tswana S.30 (cf. discussion of Tswana S.31 below). The question is why *-į- does not affect the vowel of suffixes other than *-ic- to e.g. the applicative. In my account this is because the two sequences were *-ic-į- and *-ed-į-, respectively.

[44]Ndonga apparently uses -ik-/-ek- as its general causative, perhaps productively, whereas Herero utilizes invariant -is- for this purpose.

-CV- "root" does not occur independently. The following list of -CyVVC- and -CwVVC- verbs from Bemba M.42 was presented in Hyman (1995), arranged by the vowel of the hypothetical suffix:

(38)	a.	fu-ik-	(fwíik-)	'dress (tr.), clothe'	*-dṷ́ik-	'clothe'
		fu-is-	(fwiis-)	'spit'	*-tṷ́id-	'spit'
		fu-it-	(fwiit-)	'refuse a gift'		
		ku-ik-	(kwíik-)	'set handle on tool'	*-kúik-	'put into handle'
		ku-il-	(kwíil-)	'earn'		
		pu-il-	(pwiil-)	'sip'		
	b.	fí-uk-	(fyúuk-)	'run away'		
		fí-ul-	(fyúul-)	'dislocate'		
		si-uk-	(šuuk-)	'be lucky'		
		si-ul-	(šuul-)	'dig up, de-stump'	*-dị̯ud-	'disinter'
	c.	fo-el-	(fweel-)	'bend, droop'		
		fo-en-	(fween-)	'scratch'		
		kó-el-	(kwéel-)	'climb'	*-koid-	'climb'
		kó-es-	(kwees-)	'rub'		
		po-ek-	(pweek-)	'have diarrhea'	*-puak-	'have diarrhea'
		pe-et-	(pyeet-)	'wimper'		
		se-el-	(šeel-)	'drag on buttocks'		
		se-et-	(šeet-)	'chew'		
	d.	be-ol-	(byool-)	'belch'		
		se-ob-	(šoob-)	'reproach'		
		se-ok-	(šook-)	'take a detour'		
		se-ol-	(šool-)	'crave meat'		
		se-on-	(šoon-)	'run over, crush'		
	e.	bi-al-	(byaal-)	'sow'	*-bé(j)ad-	'sow'
		fu-al-	(fwáal-)	'get dressed, wear'	*-dṷ́ad-	'wear'
		fí-al-	(fyáal-)	'give birth'	*-bị̯́ad-	'give birth'
		fi-am-	(fyaam-)	'be wedged'		
		kú-at-	(kwáat-)	'have'	*-kúat-	'seize'
		lú-al-	(lwáal-)	'be sick'	*-dúad-	'be ill'
		sí-al-	(šaal-)	'remain'	*-tị̯gad-	'remain'
		si-am-	(šaam-)	'be unlucky'		
		tu-al-	(twaal-)	'take sth. to'	*-túad-	'carry'

Since /s/ becomes [š] only before [i] or the glide [y] in Bemba, I have included forms such as šeet- 'chew' as having the intermediate structure -CyVVC-. Further evidence that this and certain other verbs from (38) have a bimorphemic structure is seen from the verb pairs in (39).

(39)	a.	fu-ik-	(fwiik-)	'dress (tr.), clothe'	*-dų́ik-	'clothe'
		fu-al-	(fwaal-)	'get dressed, wear'	*-dų́ad-	'wear'
	b.	si-uk-	(šuuk-)	'be lucky'		
		si-am-	(šaam-)	'be unlucky'		
	c.	se-et-	(šeet-)	'chew'		
		se-ol-	(šool-)	'crave meat'		
	d.	si-ul-	(šuul-)	'dig up, destump'	*-dįud-	'disinter'
		si-ik-	(šiik-)	'bury'	*-dįik-	'bury'

In both (38) and (39) I have given corresponding reconstructions from Meeussen (1980[1969]). The interesting cases are (38c,d) and (39c), where mid root vowels are involved. Three important observations should be made about these forms:

(i) A mid vowel must glide before another mid vowel, e.g. /pe-et-/ → *pyeet-* 'whimper', rather than simply fusing into a long vowel as elsewhere in the language, e.g. in imbrication (Hyman 1995).[45]

(ii) The vowel /o/ appears directly after the the root vowel /e/, e.g. /be-ol-/ → *byool-* 'belch', even though Bemba is has asymmetric VHH. Bemba thus has words such as *-beluk-* 'knock off (work)' *-lépul-* 'tear', not **-belok-*, **-lépok-* etc.

(iii) Although the consonant [f] appears in Bemba as the reflex of *p and *b before *į and of any obstruent before *ų, the first two forms in (38c), *fweel-* 'bend, droop' and *fween-* 'scratch', appear to require the representations given: fo-el-, fo-en-. Otherwise we have no explanation as to why the vowel is mid.

Of course all of the above falls into place if we abandon the requirement that vowel sequences need to show the same VHH requirements as vowels separated from each other by a consonant. In this case we can have representations such as /si-et-/, /pi-et-/, /bi-ol-/, /fu-el-/ and /fu-en-/. Already Meeussen (1967:87) recognized the problem:

> The presence of vowel /o/ without preceding /o/ in *-pįong-* ['press (out)'] and *-pįom-* ['stammer'] as also of /e/ in *-tįed-* ['slip'] is

[45]Hyman & Katamba (to appear) make a similar observation for Ganda EJ.15. What is also interesting about the Bemba form -pyeet- is that the hypothetical extension is -Vt- and the form hence analyzed as -pe-Vt-, where V = a copy of the preceding vowel (cf. §6). Needless to say, the mid feature can only come from the first vowel.

remarkable; it would seem to suggest an earlier stage of the language which had not yet the Proto-Bantu rules given in 1.7.

By 1.7 Meeusssen is of course referring to VHH. In the following table I have plotted out all of the stem-internal VV sequences in Meeussen's (1980[1969]) reconstructions:

(40) Internal V_1V_2 in Meeussen's Proto-Bantu Verb Stems

V_1/V_2	į	i	e	ų	u	o	a
į	1	1	2	—	5	2	4
i	—	8	—	—	3	—	7
e	—	1	12	—	—	—	1
ų	—	4	—	1	2	—	3
u	—	6	4	—	15	—	9
o	—	2	—	—	—	6	—
a	2	1	—	—	1	—	9

Note first that although internal long vowels occur in the reconstructions, there is only one example each involving the two degree 1 vowels: *-pįįt-* 'be black', *-pų̀ųk-* 'mature'.[46] The effective absence of *ea and *oa can perhaps be attributed to the difficulty of distinguish these from *ia and *ua. While it is not clear what to say about the absence of *eo or *eu, the absence of *oe should be contrasted with Meeussen's reconstruction of both *ue and *oi:

(41) a. *-jued- 'speak' b. *-coid- 'spy'
*-kued- 'whistle' *-koid- 'climb'
*-puen- 'smoke'
*-tuet- 'breathe, wheeze'

It is unclear how *-kued- and *-koid- might have contrasted in PB, or how their reflexes differ in the daughter languages. As seen in (38c), I have identified 'climb' as /ko-el-/ in Bemba. While the number of reconstructed roots with *VV is not large, the table in (40) nonetheless suggests that disharmonic VV sequences were likely to have occurred in PB. Since VHH is definitely more general in CVC-VC- sequences than it is in CV-VC- forms, it would be particularly striking if we could find differences in recognizable -VC- suffixes in one vs. the other structure.The two roots mentioned by Meeussen with *įo in (42b) are contrasted with his five reconstructions with *ųi in (42a).

(42) a. *-dį-ud- 'pull out of grond' b. *-pįom- 'stutter'
*-dįunguk- 'turn round' *-pįonj- 'squeeze out'

[46]Guthrie (1967-1971) has more, but many of these are suspect, either in terms of the proposed shapes of his common forms, or in terms of whether these forms characterized PB.

*-kįud- 'break wind'
*-tįugud- 'wipe off, rub'
*-tįuk- 'shake'

As seen, the forms in (42a) all involve verbs that end in either *-ud- or *-uk-, i.e. the shapes of the transitive and intransitive reversive suffixes, respectively. On the other hand, the two forms in (42b) end in -om- and -onj-, respectively, which do not resemble suffixes. Could this be the difference, then, between the two sets of forms? The question is whether *-ud- and *-uk- behave any differently from other proto round vowels in post-radical position.

A possible answer comes from Southern Bantu. The languages of Guthrie's zone S fall into two distinct groups from the point of view of VHH. The Shona S.10 group has asymmetric VHH exactly as other most other Savannah Bantu languages to its North, e.g. Tonga M.64, Cewa N.31b, Yao P.21. The rest of zone S lacks VHH in the front series, exhibiting, for instance, invariant applicative -el- and stative -ek-, but causative -is-. In the back series, these languages fall into two groups: Certain have VHH in the back series, where -uk- and -ul- are realized -ok- and -ol- after /o/, e.g. Venda S.21 (Murphy 1997[van Warmelo 1937]) and Lozi K.21/S.34 (Gowlett 1967). To this group one can also add Makua P.31 which has invariant applicative -el- and causative -ih-, but alternating u/o in the back series.[47] The other group shows the same facts in the front series, but exhibits a more complex situation concerning internal [u] and [o]. Among these latter languages are Tswana S.31 and Ndebele S.44.

Tswana is typical of the Sotho group in having a recently developed 9V system from the tensing of /ɛ/ and /ɔ/ to [e] and [o]. In many cases the tense variants are predictable, occurring before a following higher vowel or a consonant such as /ts/, itself derived from a following lost historical causative *-į- suffix. However, there are also instances of unpredictable tensing. The following table, based on Creissels (1996) and using his transcription, shows the plotting of the nine potention V1 and V2 vowels in CVCVC-a verb stems:

[47]This is another sense in which Makua, despite its northerly location, belongs with the languages of zone S (cf. Janson 1991/1992 for further discussion).

(43) CVCVC-a verb stems in Tswana (based on Creissels 1996)

V1V2	i	ι	e	ε	u	ɷ	o	ɔ	a
i	12	—	(2)	11	—	17	—	—	8
ι	5	6	3	9	—	—	—	—	10
e	8	—	9	—	—	24	—	—	(1)
ε	—	—	—	22	—	—	—	—	4
u	8	—	—	24	19	3	—	—	10
ɷ	7	(1)	5	14	—	34	—	—	22
o	3	—	10	—	3	23	6	—	—
ɔ	—	—	—	24	—	—	—	16	16
a	25	6	10	52	3	64	—	—	51

Note, first along the top left/bottom right diagonal, that any vowel can be followed by itself, a property that is typical of Southern Bantu, despite other constraints. In addition, of the 68 verbs having the shape CVCiC-a, 52 are causatives, i.e. CVCis-a. Degree 2 /ι/ mostly occurs after itself, but also after /a/. Since /e/ and /ε/ differ only in secondary tensing, if we combine their numbers we see that 195 V_2 vowels are mid vs. only 58 /i/ and 13 /ι/.

The back series shows something quite different. Although /a/ has a very general distribution, tense /u/ occurs only after back vowels. /ɷ/ also occurs generally, though not after /ι/. One possibility is that CιCιC- derives from *CιCɷC-, since internal /ι/ otherwise occurs only after /a/. Finally, note that /o/ and /ɔ/ occur only after an identical mid vowel. This last fact suggests vowel harmony in the back series. However, we also see that contrasting with the 6 cases of CoCoC- and 16 cases of CɔCɔC- are 23 entries with CoCɷC-. In other words, back VHH appears to occur in about 50% of the relevant verb forms. We, thus, obtain verbs such as tɬhɔ́bɔ́χá 'désespérer (intr.)' as well as *tɬòbɷ̀χà* 'peler (intr.)'. If we plot out these 45 verbs as a function of the consonant that follows the /ɷ/, /o/ or /ɔ/, we obtain the following results:

(44) ɔ/o + ɔ/o/ɷ in Tswana CVCVC-a Verb Stems

CVCVC	All	l	χ	t	tl	b	k	m	s	ts	ntsh	tɬh
CɔCɔC	16	2	2	2	5	3	1	1	—	—	—	—
CoCoC	6	—	—	—	—	—	—	—	2	2	1	1
CoCɷC	23	13	6	—	—	—	—	—	2	2	—	—

We are concerned with CVCVC-a verb stems whose last C is /l/ or /χ/: Only 4 out of 22 CɔCɔC-a or CoCoC-a verbs end in one of these two consonants vs. 19 out of 23 CoCɷC-a verbs. In addition, a combined search of CVCVC-a and longer verbs turned up 60 CɔCɔC or CoCoC sequences of which only 3 were CɔCɔl (and none CoCol) vs. 46 cases of CoCɷC, of which 31 had the sequence CoCɷl. In other words, the sequence CoCɷl outnumbers CɔCɔl ten to one! This cannot be accidental.

The picture is even clearer in the 5V Nguni S.40 languages, where similar distributions are found. Within this group I shall briefly consider only Ndebele S.44, based on the CBOLD version of Pelling (1971). The first two vowels of CVCVC... verb stems are plotted in (45).

(45) $V_1 + V_2$ in Ndebele CVCVC... verb stems

V_1/V_2	i	e	u	o	a
i	92	42	8	(2)	36
e	28	99	67	(1)	26
u	29	45	141	—	35
o	19	27	36	75	21
a	52	80	107	—	127

As seen, both /i/ and /e/ occur frequently after all root vowels. This isn't surprising, given that the causative suffix is invariant -is- and the applicative and stative suffixes invariant -el- and -ek-, respectively. Of 220 verbs that begin CVCiC-, only 21 have neither the root vowel /i/, nor have /s/ following the V_2 /i/. The back series, on the other hand, clearly shows, first, that /o/ occurs only after root /o/. However, /u/ may also occur after root /o/. Upon closer inspection of the data in (46), however, we note that the C_3 consonant plays an important role in predicting whether the form will be CoCuC... or CoCoC...:

(46) CoCuC.../CoCoC... in Ndebele Verb Stems

CVCVC	All	l	k	b	d	m	n	ng	nq	s	th	tsh	z
CoCoC	75	10	5	9	3	3	1	2	2	2	7	1	28
CoCuC	36	27	9	—	—	—	—	—	—	—	—	—	—

As seen, all 36 CoCuC... verb stems have either the shape CoCul... or CoCuk.... By contrast, the final consonant of CoCoC... stems can be quite varied. Particularly noteworthy is the fact that 28 verbs have the shape CoCoz. Why should this be?

In order to address this question, let us take a closer look at the distribution of vowels in verb stems that begin with the sequence CVCVz.... The results are displayed in (47).

(47) $V_1 + V_2$ in Ndebele CVCVz... verb stems

V_1/V_2	i	e	u	o	a
i	23	7	—	1	6
e	—	34	8	—	—
u	—	5	28	—	10
o	—	1	—	28	—
a	5	10	13	—	45

A number of important observations can be made from this table. First, as elsewhere, a postradical vowel seems always able to immediately follow an identical preceding root vowel. Hence, the sequences iCiz, eCez, uCuz, oCoz and aCaz are all found in relative abundance. Second, we see that postradical *ez* appears after all root vowels, though less frequently after /u/ and /o/. In fact, there is only one example, *sondez-a* 'bring near', where root /o/ is followed by *ez*. This verb is clearly a causative of the corresponding verb *sondel-a* 'go near', where the *el* sequence may itself be a frozen applicative. If this is so, why aren't there more examples of CoCez? The answer, I believe, derives from the tendancy of S.30 and S.40 languages to modify stem-vowel sequences that disagree in roundness. We already noted with respect to the table in (43) that Tswana lacks CiCuC-, CιCuC- and CιCωC-. We also hypothesized that the latter has been replaced by CιCιC-, noting especially that postradical [ι] occurs mostly after root /ι/. I would, thus, like to suggest a similar scenario here: What would have been pronounced CoCez- is instead realized CoCoz-, i.e. with agreement in rounding. Note that this latter form ends in [z], which is elsewhere associated with causative *-į-. What this means is that one might expect some confusion with CoCul- forms, which normally do not undergo harmony. It was noted in (46) that 10 verbs occur in the database with the shape CoCol... (vs. 27 verbs of the shape CoCul...). As seen now in (48a), six of these 10 verbs are further "extended" by [oz]!

(48)	a.	dondolozel-a	'go along with a staff'
		gombolozel-a	'encircle, surround'
		londoloz-a	'take care of, look after'
		mpompoloz-a	'talk boisterously'
		nyonkoloz-a	'scowl, glower at'
		zongolozel-a	'wind round, wind up'
	b.	godol-a	'cold, feel the cold'
		kopol-a	'peck at'
		lobol-a	'give lobolo [bride price]'
		qobol-a	'cuff gently on the head'

Further, of the four verbs in (48b), one is clearly denominal (lobol-a), while others may be de-ideophonic (see below) or borrowings. It is, therefore, clear that the reversive transitive should be invariant -ul- in Ndebele, even in CoC-ul- forms. The forms in (48a) should therefore not have the extension shape *-oloz-*, but rather *-uluz-*, as in the three examples occurring in the database: *phephuluz-a* 'blow away', *huquluz-a* 'take, appropriate' and *hlukuluz-a* 'annoy, intimidate'. Thus, the development of *oz* from *ez* by assimilation to a preceding /o/ has caused a realignment—and perhaps introduced VHH in the back series in Ndebele.[48,49]

Assimilation may not be the only source of the discrepancy between CoCuC- and CoCoC-. Recall from (46) that there are 9 CoCuk... verbs in Ndebele vs. 5 CoCok.... Since our contention is that the former set is "regular", showing a direct reflex of reversive intransitive *-uk-, it is significant to note in (49) that all but one of these verbs has a corresponding reversive transitive in -ul-:

(49)	hotsh-uk-a	'get pulled out'	hotsh-ul-a	'pull out'
	mony-uk-a	'slip out'	mony-ul-a	'pull out'
	ngcom-uk-a	'come out, slip out'	ngcom-ul-a	'pull out'
	ngcoth-uk-a	'get plucked/pulled out'	ngcoth-ul-a	'pluck/pull out'
	nyom-uk-a	'slip (knot), get pulled'	nyom-ul-a	'slip out knot'
	photh-uk-a	'get round'	photh-ul-a	'grind mealies'
	qoth-uk-a	'get rubbed off'	qoth-ul-a	'rub smooth'
	yoc-uk-a	'get taken off (skin)'	yoc-ul-a	'tear skin off'

---

[48]Of perhaps potential significance to this problem is the fact that semantically related verbs exist with similar forms that cannot exactly be derived from each other. We have cited the verb *zongolozel-a* 'wind round, wind up' in (48). Seven other verbs occur in Pelling (1971) that begin with a zVng... sequence: *zeng-a* 'loiter', *zengel-a* 'hunt, persecute', *zingelez-a* 'go round', *zingelezel-a* 'encircle, surround', *zungelez-a* 'encircle', *zunguz-a* 'sway, wave (tr.)', *zunguzek-a* 'sway (intr.)'. As seen, there appears to be a relatedness, even though the root vowel varies between [e], [o] and [u]. Given the restrictions on vowel sequencing in Ndebele, it would not be without interest to investigate how the suffix might have affected the root vowel, rather than the reverse.

[49]One other issue not mentioned is the potential interaction of reduplication with VHH. In a language with canonical VHH such as Ganda EJ.15, the full reduplication of a verb such as kól-à 'do' as kólàà-kola will mean that an [o] follows an [a], which is disharmonic. We can easily ignore such cases (also in languages where verb stem reduplication is limited to two syllables). However, most Bantu languages have roots that begin with what appears to be the reduplication of the first root syllable, e.g. Ndebele *xoxomela* 'stand on tiptoe'. To test whether this factor might contribute to the occurrence of CoCoC... verbs, I did the following count of $C_iV_iC_iV_iC$... verbs for the 5 vowels in Ndebele. The results are as follows:

C_iiC_iiC...	:	7/92	(8%)	C_iuC_iuC...	:	16/141	(11%)
C_ieC_ieC...	:	12/99	(12%)	C_ioC_ioC...	:	25/75	(33%)
C_iiC_iiC...	:	22/271	(8%)				

Whereas reduplicated first syllables with the vowels /i, e, u, a/ hover around 8-12% of the number of verbs with identical first and second syllable vowels, as seen, a full 33% of CoCoC... verbs appear to be reduplicative. The exact significance of this is not clear, but definitely merits further attention.

god-uk-a	'depart, die of old age'	—	

By contrast, none of the CoCok- verbs has a corresponding CoCol-. Instead, four have a corresponding transitive of the form CoCoz-:

(50)	bhobok-a	'get pierced'	bhoboz-a	'break
	phoqok-a	'snap in two (intr.)'	phoqoz-a	'snap in two (tr.)'
	wohlok-a	'fall/shower down'	wohloz-a	'shake down (tr.)'
	phohlok-a	'get broken, smashed'	bohloz-a[50]	'break, smash'
	tshopok-a	'spring (intr.)'		—

My hypothesis is thast these verbs derive historically from bisyllabic ideophones of the shape CoCo. These ideophones would have been verbalized with intransitive -k- and transitive -z-, hence *wohlo-k-a* 'shower down (intr.)' and *wohlo-z-a* 'shower down (tr.)', etc. Although Pelling (1971) does not have an extensive list of such ideophones, one relevant form does appear in the dictionary: *wohlololo* 'ideophone expressing idea of collapsing', which is clearly related to the two verbs just cited. In other words, there is a potential difference in morphological segmentation between CoC-uk-a vs. CoCo-k-a.[51]

Ideophones are widespread in Bantu, particularly Southern Bantu, and can be assumed to have existed quite early in Bantu linguistic history. They are also known to produce disharmonic verb forms. Thus, in Cewa N.31b, which has canonical (asymmetric) VHH, the following are the complete set of CeCiC- disharmonic verbs in the CBOLD database for that language:

(51)	a.	cheni-m-a	'to shine'	b.	cheni	'shining' (ideo.)
		chezi-m-a	'to shine'		chezi	'shining' (ideo.)
		nyeti-m-a	'to shine'		nyeti	'shining' (ideo.)
		nyezi-m-a	'to shine'		nyezi	'shining' (ideo.)
		pheni-m-a	'to shine'		pheni	'glittering; truly'
		yeti-m-a	'to glitter'		yeti	'shining; glistening'
	c.	tsenjil-á	'to disappear, be out of sight'			

As seen, the six verbs in (51a) all derive from bisyllabic ideophones in (51b), which have the shape CeCi. (The one disharmonic verb in (51c) remains an unaccounted for exception.) Although CeCi is an acceptable bisyllabic stem shape, CeCiC-V is disharmonic.

The verbs in (51) suggest that disharmonic (de-ideophonic) verbs constitute a well-defined semantic glass 'shining' in Cewa. This need not be the case. One of the most extensive documentations of ideophones is

---

[50]As seen, there is an irregular correspondence in the voicing of the initial consonant of the root.

[51]This result should cause one to reponder the conclusion drawn from Caga E.62, whose limited VHH resembles the S.30-S.40 situation in obvious ways.

available from Shona S.11, just to the south of Cewa N.31b. Fortune (1962) indicates that almost every verb has a corresponding ideophone in Shona. Shona, like Cewa, has canonical VHH. While there is significant dialect variation, (52) provides a representative sampling of disharmonic verb stems of the shapes CoCiC- and CoCuC- and their corresponding ideophones (Hannan 1987):

(52) De-ideophonic verbs in Shona and their source ideophones

a. CoCiC- verbs

bóidza	blink, flicker	bói bói ideo. of blinking
chómwira	swallow w/difficulty	chomwí ideo. of swallowing without chewing'
dórika	hop (esp. insects that do not fly)	dóri dóri ideo. of hopping (esp. non-flying insects)
dórinha	run, trot	dóri dóri ideo. of running, trotting
kóira	copulate	kói kói ideo. of copulating
kórofika	be lazy when hoeing	kórófi kórófi ideo. of hoeing lazily
kótsidza	make nod; drowsy; put to sleep	kotsí ideo of nodding with sleep
kotsira	nod with sleep, be asleep	kotsí ideo of nodding with sleep
ngóndika	bend right over (tall person)	ngóndi ideo of bending forwards (tall object)
nyobidza	cause to sink, pulling from below	nyobí nyobí ideo of bobbing (float on fishing line)
nyobika	bob (as fishing-float, when fish are nibbling)	nyobí nyobí ideo of bobbing (of float on fishing line)
pfóridza	make sleepy, cause to fall asleep	pforí ideo of falling fast asleep, going astray
pfórika	become sleepy (not in one's bed), fall asleep	pforí ideo of falling fast asleep, going astray
tóira	shine distantly	tói tói ideo of flickering (esp. in distance)
tórika	hop (insect)	tóri tóri ideo of hopping (insects)
tsómwidza	cause to swallow sth difficult	tsómwi ideo of swalling sth difficult to swallow
tsomwira	swallow something difficult	tsómwi ideo of swalling sth difficult to swallow

b. CoCuC- verbs

hómura	bark (baboon)	hómu ideo. of barking (baboon)
hómuka	turn (inspanned oxen)	hómu inter. turn (to inspanned oxen)
hópuka	be liftable, movable (heavy obj.)	hópu inter: pull (to oxen)
hóura	bark (dog)	hóu ideo. of barking (dog)
kóbvudza	make thick	kobvú adj. thick
kóbvuka	grow thick	kobvú adj. thick
kómuka	turn right round (oxen)	kómu inter: turn! (to oxen); cf. homu

As seen, the ideophones in question have the shapes Co(C)i and Co(C)u. Derived intransitive verbs generally have the shapes Co(C)i-k- and Co(C)u-k-, while the corresponding transitives may have use -r-, -dz- or -s- as their verbalizing consonant. What's important is that VHH may be inhibited, either generally or dialectally, by virtue of a verb's relationship to a corresponding Co(C)i or Co(C)u ideophone in Shona.[52]

In fact, disharmonic verbs can be not only de-ideophonic, but also denominal (usually de-adjectival), as in Ganda EJ.15 (Hyman 1994):

(53)	a.	-gézì-w-al-	'grow wise'	cf.	-gézì	'wise'
		-genyi-w-(al)-	'visit'	cf.	-genyi	'visiting'
	b.	-ógì-w-	'grow sharp'	cf.	-ógì	'sharp'
		-kópì-w-al-	'become common'	cf.	-kópi	'common'
	c.	-zito-w-	'be heavy'	cf.	-zito	'heavy'

In these examples, verb bases are derived from adjectives by suffixing -w-(al)-, a direct reflex of PB *-p-(ad)-. The data in (53a)show forms that begin CeCi-w..., while those in (53b) begin CoCi-w-. In (53c) the verb *-zito-w-*, also disharmonic, is derived from the adjective *-zito* 'heavy' (PB *-dịto). It is frequently disharmonic in Bantu languages with canonical VHH (cf. Shi DJ.53 *zido-h-*; Yao P.21 *-sito-p-*).

In studies on VHH such derivational relationships are often overlooked, as such scholars typically privilege the alternations found in the applicative, stative, causative and other "alternating" suffixes. While these forms are easily isolable, morphologically, they show in language after language that disharmonic verb bases can and do co-exist along side canonical VHH. The examples just considered involve "exceptional" non-harmonizing forms. In

[52]On the other hand, Hannan (1987) includes a smaller number of Co(C)iC- and Co(C)uC- verbs whose corresponding ideophone is not provided. Some of these are indicated as borrowings, e.g. kórisa 'enjoy' (<Nguni), pórisha 'apply polish to surface' (<English], komburena 'complain' (<English).

the discussion of CoCoz... verbs in Ndebele, where we instead have "exceptional" harmony, it was suggested that the existence of ideophones of the shape CoCo might be sought as a partial explanation for some of the observed facts. In other words, de-ideophonic, de-nominal and, ultimately, borrowed verbs, should be carefully considered for their potential relevance in determining the rise and fall of VHH in Bantu.

6. Conclusion

In the preceding sections we have taken a close look at VHH as it is realized throughout the Bantu family. We have considered a number of issues on which VHH depends, including the distribution of the features that define both canonical and non-canonical VHH throughout the Bantu zone. We have also considered the nature of the PB vowel system, specifically, how different interpretations of it might intersect with the job of reconstructing the historical devleopment (and loss) of VHH in the various branches and individual languages. While virtually everything said here must be taken as tentative, I hope to have at least mapped out some of the broad issues with which we must still contend. As seen particularly in §5, this study has led us to take a close look at the distribution of vowels not only within the derived Bantu stem, where most attention on VHH has focused, but in non-derived verb and noun stems as well.

While this study has confirmed many of the prior observations made about VHH in different Bantu languages, I have, however, speculatively, parted company with majority views in certain of my conclusions. First, I have suggested that VHH did not exist in PB—at least not as usually cited with derivational suffixes such as the applicative, stative, causative, reversive etc. Second, in order to account for their differential realization across languages, I have proposed to reconstruct some of these latter suffixes with degree 3 vowels, e.g. applicative *-ed- and stative *-ek- vs. causative *-ic-į-, reversive intr. *-uk-, and reversive tr. *-ud-. In my view, VHH is so often asymmetric in the front vs. back series because of a different in starting point: *-ed- and *-ek- begin as degree 3 vowels, while *-uk- and *-ud- begin as degree 2 vowels. Front height harmony thus involves a raising of *e to degree 2 [ɪ] by a process of "peripheralization", inhibited by the presence of a preceding mid vowel (as well as by /a/ in parts of zones K and R. Back height harmony, on the other hand, involves the lowering of *u to degree 3 [ç] by assimilation to a preceding [ɔ]. The fact that causative *-ic-į- sometimes joins *-ed- and *-ek- in its harmony properties, and sometimes doesn't, is accounted for by reconstructing *-ic- with a degree 2 vowel.

Looked at more specifically, I would claim that these derivational suffixes did not harmonize in PB. That is, they had the same behavior as we suppose both for the inflectional final vowel morphemes *-i, *-e, and *-įd-e and their derivational counterparts, e.g. *-ų, *-o etc. This prior resemblance must certainly have something to do with the tremendous temptation

Bantuists have had to view certain or all of the derivational suffixes as bimorphemic: Intransitive *-k- combines with both *-e- and *-u- (my reconstructed vowels) to form statives and intransitive reversives, while transitive *-d- combines with these same vowels to form applicatives and transitive reversives, and so forth. If front height harmony is largely a peripheralization process (*e > i), as I have suggested, then the process might not have gotten seriously under way until after the ubiquitous final vowel *-a was added to all verb forms lacking an otherwise clearly demarcated inflectional ending (cf. Grégoire 1979 for discussion of this possible interpretation of PB). We Bantuists are struck not only by the possible factoring out of *-d-, *-k- etc., but also by the striking resemblance of the vowel of the deverbal (e.g. agentive) nominalizer -į with the vowel of causative *-į-. Could this latter have been a "final vowel" morpheme? Consider also the resemblance between passive *-u- and the deverbal (e.g. adjectival) nominalizer *-ų. Maybe the longer causative *-ic-į- and the longer passive *-ib-u- were once derivatives of a verb such as 'do', with meaning of 'make do' and 'being done'?[53] Could their earlier status as final vowel's also account for Meeussen's (1967, 1973) contention that causative *-į- and passive *-u- may have had high tone in PB?[54]

Whatever the answer, what is important for the purpose of this study is that there is no apriori reason to reconstruct the same vowel height on all derivational suffixes, which, with the exception of the Meinhof school, has usually been done. Since I have reconstructed *-ed- and *-ek- vs. *-ud- and *-uk-, one might reasonably ask why these vowel heights might have been different in this way in PB? If non-accidental, I would seek an answer in the fact that *-uC- suffixes are more tightly bound with their radical than are *-eC- and *-iC- suffixes. Although Meeussen (1967) and others distinguish between two types of "extension" (suffix vs. expansion), there seems in fact to be good reason to make at least a three-way distinction: (i) relatively productive suffixes such as applicative *-ed-, causative causative *-is-į-, and reciprocal *-an-; (ii) relatively unproductive suffixes such as the reversives *-uk- and *-ud-; and (iii) unanalyzable expansions (see next paragraph). By this typology *-uk- and *-ud- fall in the second category, i.e. somewhere between expansions and productive suffixes. Although there is some variation, they often are restricted to occurring immediately after the verb root, which in most cases cannot occur without a suffix. Coming "early" in the verb stem, *-uk- and *-ud- may also be followed by other suffixes, if valence requirements are met, e.g. the applicative, reciprocal, passive, etc. Thus, in this medial position, they might have been subject earlier to the restriction of having to be [+high].

---

[53]I know that the consonant of the causative suffix cannot be regularly derived from PB *t in all languages, but once proposed that *-ic- could be related to *-kit- 'do'.

[54]See Hyman & Katamba (1990) for further discussion and exemplification.

My view, then, is that stem-internal VHH was not fully formed in PB, and that the verbal derivational suffixes should be reconstructed with more than the three vowels *i, *u and *a. As I have pointed out, most work on VHH has focused on these derivational suffixes, which have often been synchronically represented as degree 2 vowels or as the archiphonemes /ɪ/ and /U/. Constrast this with the frozen "expansions" reconstructed by Meeussen (1967) in (54).

(54) a. *-ų-, *-įm-, *-ųn-, *-įng-
b. *-ang-, *-ab-, *-ag-, *-ak-
c. *-im-, *-om-, *-ong- (these occur only after CV-)
d. *-ut-

What is most striking about the above array is, first, how many degree 1 vowels there are in the expansions in (54a), and second, how utterly lacking degree 1 vowels are in derivational suffixes (except causative -į-). (54b) shows that *a also appears to be prevalent in expansions, just as it is in derivational suffixes, e.g. in the productive reciprocal suffix *-an- 'reciprocal' and the usually non-productive positional *-am- (which, however, does occur as a productive passive suffix in certain areas, e.g. in Mongo C.60).

My contention is that the only overlap between expansion vowels and derivational extension vowels is *a. I must therefore address the expansions in (54c,d), which are purported to contain a degree 2 or 3 vowel. First, as indicated, *-im-, *-om- and *-ong- occur only after a CV- "radical". It is therefore not clear that they should be compared with derivational suffixes, which of course appear after all verb bases. In any case, note that the expansions *-om- and *-ong- are reconstructed with a degree 3 vowel—vs. the degree 2 Meeussen proposes for *-uk- and *-ud-. This leaves the expansion *-ut- in (54d). In order to determine the synchronic status of this proposed expansion, I have searched for CVCut- verb stems in several languages for which CBOLD has on-line dictionaries: Nande DJ.42, Kiga EJ.14, Pende L.11/K.52, Bemba M.42, Cewa N.31b, Yao P.21, Makua P.31, Kalanga S.16, Venda S.21, Ndebele S.44. What I have found is that except for *-íkut-* 'be satisfied (with food)', which may contain an historical reflexive -i-, almost all such verbs exhibit an initial CuCut- sequence (1 exception each in Pende, Makua, Kalanga and Venda; 3 exceptions in the large Kiga corpus). This is consistent with the overall distribution of CVCVt-, which is for the second vowel to agree with the first. (There also are verbs that have the shape CVCat-.) I therefore do not know on what basis Meeussen arrived at the reconstruction of an *-ut- expansion.

Instead, expansion vowels, where they are determinable, do not general reconstruct with either degree 2 or degree 3 vowels, rather with *į, *ų and *a. In other words, they are subject even more to the peripheralization process that clearly affects stem-internal vowels (i.e. what I have called the "prosodic trough"). Expansion vowels are also more subject to assimilation to the preceding (root) vowel than are suffixal vowels. Thus, many of these, including those reconstructed with *a, show a tendency for the vowel to completely assimilate to the preceding vowel. In many languages the process appears to be incomplete. This is what I suspect for the expansion *-at-: Some verbs are realized as CVCat-, while others appear as CV_iCV_it-. If I am correct that expansion vowels were different from suffixal vowels in PB, then this obviously raises the question of why? I have suggested that the vowels of verb suffixes may have been final vowel morphemes, which were perhaps restricted, but this goes only part way towards an explanation. Why couldn't these same FV vowels appear as expansions? Or if they did, why did they become *į and *ų at the PB stage? Unfortunately we don't have good examples of recognizable morphemes appearing with one vowel as an expansion, but with another vowel as a derivational suffix. Or could it be that the expansions *-ų-, *-įm-, *-ųn-, *-įng- are related to passive *-u-, positional *-am-, reversive transitive *-ud- and (?) *-ang-. With Tervuren's recent completion of Bantu Lexical Reconstructions II, it may be possible to study these and related questions with greater certitude.

References

Archangeli, Diana & Douglas Pulleyblank. 1989. Yoruba vowel harmony. *Linguistic Inquiry* 20.173-217.

Archangeli, Diana & Douglas Pulleyblank. 1994. *Grounded Phonology.* Cambridge, Ma.: M.I.T. Press.

Ashton, Ethel O., E. M. K. Mulira, E. G. M. Ndawula & Archibold N. Tucker. 1954. *A Luganda grammar.* London: Longmans, Green & Co.

Bakari, Mohamed. 1985. *The Morphophonology of the Kenyan Swahili Dialects.* Berlin: Dietrich Reimer Verlag.

Bastin, Yvonne. 1983a. Essai de classification de quatre-vingts langues bantoues par la statistique grammaticale. *Africana Linguistica* IX, 9-108.

Bastin, Yvonne. 1983b. *La finale -IDE et l'imbrication en bantou* (Annales, Série IN-8, Sciences Humaines, no. 114.) Tervuren: Musée Royal de l'Afrique Centrale.

Bastin, Yvonne. 1986. Les suffixes causatifs dans les langues bantoues, *Africana Linguistic* X, 55-145.

Batibo, Herman. 1985. *Le Kekusuma (langue bantou de Tanzanie): Phonologie, morphologie.* Paris: Editions Recherche sur les civilisations.

Bleek, Wilhelm H. I. 1862. *A comparative grammar of South African languages.* Part I. Phonology. London: Trübner & Co. [Reprinted Westmead, England: Gregg International, 1971]

Bourquin, Walther. 1955. Notes on the 'close vowels' in Bantu. *African Studies* 14:49-62.

Clements, George N. 1985. Akan vowel harmony: a nonlinear analysis. In Didier Goyvaerts (ed.), *African linguistics: Essays in memory of M. W. K. Semikenke.* Amsterdam: Benjamins, 55-98.

Clements, George N. 1991. Vowel height assimilation in Bantu languages. *Proceedings of the Seventeenth Annual Meeting of the Berkeley Linguistics Society*, Special Session on African Language Structures, 25-64.

Coupez, André. 1955. Esquisse de la langue holoholo. Tervuren: Musée Royal de l'Afrique Centrale.

Coupez, André. 1975. La variabilité lexical en bantou. *African Languages/Langues Africaines* 1.164-203.

Coupez, André. 1980. Traces de dix voyelles en protobantou. *Africana Linguistica* VIII, 65-73.

Creissels, Denis. 1996. Tswana electronic dictionary provided to CBOLD.

de Gheel, Georges. 1652. *Le plus ancien dictionnaire bantu: het oudste Bantu-woordenboek.* Translated into French and Dutch by J. van Wing and C. Penders. [1928]. Leuven.

Ehret, Christopher. 1999. Subclassifying Bantu: The evidence of stem morpheme innovations. In this volume.

Fisch, Maria. 1977. *Einführung in die Sprache der Mbukushu, Ost Kavango, Namibia* (Wissenschaftliche Forschung in Südwestafrika 15. Folge.) Windhoek: S.W.A. Scientific Society.

Fontaney, Louise. 1980. Le verbe. In François Nsukka (ed.), *Éléments de description du punu.* Lyon: Université Lyon2, 51-114.

Forges, Germaine. 1977. *Le kela; langue bantoue du Zaïre (Zone C): Esquisse Phonologique et Morphologique.* Paris: Société d'Etudes Linguistiques et Anthropologiques de France.

Fortune, George. 1962. *Ideophones in Shona.* Cape Town: Oxford University Press.

Ganzania, Rollande. 1972. *Aspects phonologiques et morphologiques du koyo.* Thèse de Troisième Cycle, Grenoble.

Gowlett, Derek F. 1967. Morphology of the Verb in Lozi M.A. thesis. Johannesburg: University of Witwatersrand.

Greenberg, Joseph Harold. 1951. Vowel and nasal harmony in Bantu languages. *Revue Congolaise* 8:813-820.

Grégoire, Claire. 1979. Les voyelles finales alternantes dans la conjugaison affirmative des langues bantoues centrales, *Journal of African Languages and Linguistics* 2:141-172.

Gusimana, Barthelemy. 1972. *Dictionnaire pende-français* (Editions du CEEBA. Série 3, vol. 1.) Bandundu: CEEBA.

Guthrie, Malcolm. 1962. The status of radical extensions in Bantu languages. *Journal of African Languages* 1:202-220.

Guthrie, Malcolm. 1967-71. *Comparative Bantu: An Introduction to the Comparative Linguistics and Prehistory of the Bantu Languages*, Vols. I-IV. London: Greggs.

Hannan, M. 1987. *Standard Shona Dictionary.* Salisbury: College Press.

Hawkinson, Annie K. 1985. Bakweri verb morphology. PhD dissertation, University of California, Berkeley.

Heine, Bernd. 1973. Zur genetischen Gliederung der Bantu-Sprachen, *Afrika und Übersee* 56:164-185.

Hulstaert, G. 1965. *Grammaire du Lɔmɔngɔ*. Deuxième Partie: Morphologie. Tervuren: Musée Royal de l'Afrique Centrale.

Hyman, Larry M. 1985. *A theory of phonological weight*. Dordrecht: Foris.

Hyman, Larry M. 1994. Conceptual issues in the comparative study of the Bantu verb stem, In Salikoko S. Mufwene & Lioba Moshi (eds), *Topics in African Linguistics*. Amsterdam: Benjamins, 3-34.

Hyman, Larry M. 1995. Minimality and the prosodic morphology of Cibemba imbrication. *Journal of African Languages and Linguistics* 16, 3-39.

Hyman, Larry M. 1998. Positional prominence and the 'prosodic trough' in Yaka. *Phonology* 15.1.

Hyman, Larry M. & Sharon Inkelas. 1997. Emergent templates: the unusual case of Tiene. In Viola Miglio & Bruce Morén (eds), *Selected phonology papers from H-OT-97* (University of Maryland Working Papers in Linguistics 5), 92-116.

Hyman, Larry M.—Francis X. Katamba. 1990. Spurious high-tone extensions in Luganda. *Journal of South African Languages* 10.142-158.

Hyman, Larry M.—Francis X. Katamba. In press. The syllable in Luganda phonology and morphology. In Harry van der Hulst & Nancy Ritter (eds), *The syllable: views and facts*. Berlin: Mouton deGruyter.

Ittmann, Johannes. 1939. Grammatik des Duala, Supplement to *Zeitschrift fur Kolonialsprachen* 20. Translated into French [1978] by L.A. Boumard, *Grammaire du Duala*. Douala, Cameroon: Collège Libermann.

Jacquot, André. 1962. Notes sur la phonologie du Beembe (Congo). *Journal of African Languages* 1:232-242.

Jacquot, André. 1981. *Etudes Beembe (Congo)*. Paris: ORSTOM.

Janson, Tore. 1991/92. Southern Bantu and Makua. *Sprache und Geschichte in Afrika* 12/13:1-44.

Kavutirwaki, K. 1978. *Lexique nande-français, français-nande*. Kinshasa-Gombe: Editions du Sec. Gén. de l'Episcopat du Zaïre.

Koloni, Jean. 1971. Eléments de morphologie et de vocabulaire de la langue enya. Mémoire. Kinshasa: Université Lovanium).

Kotz, Ernst. 1909. *Grammatik des Chasu*. Archiv für das Studium deutscher Kolonialsprachen, X. Berlin: George Reimer.

Kuperus, Juliana. 1985. *The Londo word*. Tervuren: Musée royal de l'Afrique centrale.

Kwenzi Mikala, Jérome. 1980. Esquisse phonologique du punu. In François Nsukka (ed.), *Éléments de description du punu*. Lyon: Université Lyon2, 7-18.

Laman, Karl E. 1912/ *Grammar of the Kongo language*. New York.

Laman, Karl E. 1936. *Dictionnaire kikongo-français, avec une étude phonétique décrivant les dialectes les plus importants de la langue dite kikongo.*

Bruxelles. Reprinted [1964]: Ridgewood, N.J.: The Gregg Press International.

Leitch, Myles. 1996. Vowel Harmony of the Congo Basin: An Optimality-Theoretic Analysis of Variation in the Bantu C. Zone, Ph.D. Dissertation, University of British Columbia.

Leung, Elizabeth Woon-Yee. 1986. The Tonal Phonology of Llogori: a study of Llogoori verbs. M.A. Thesis, Cornell University.

Mabiala, Nguimbi. 1996. Vowel harmony in Kongo CVCV and CVCVC... stems, Laboratoire Dynamique du Langage, Lyon. [Unpublished MS.]

Maddieson, Ian. 1984. *Patterns of Sounds*. Cambridge [Cambridgeshire] ; New York : Cambridge University Press.

Maganga, Clement & ThiloC. Schadeberg. 1992. *Kinyamwezi: grammar, texts, vocabulary*. Köln: Koppe.

Meeussen, A.E. 1967. Bantu grammatical reconstructions, Annalen van het Koninklijk Museum voor Midden-Afrika 61:79-121.

Meeussen, A.E. 1980 [1969]. Bantu Lexical Reconstructions. Tervuren: Koninklijk Museum voor Midden-Afrika.

Meeussen, A.E. 1973. Comparative Bantu test cases for method. African Language Studies 14:79-121.

Meinhof, Carl. 1948. Grundzüge einer vergleichenden Grammatik der Bantusprachen. Second edition. Hamburg: Echardt & Messtorff.

Meinhof, Carl & Nicolaas J. van Warmelo. 1932. *Introduction to the phonology of the Bantu languages*. Translated, revised and enlarged in collaboration with the author and Dr. Alice Werner by Nicolaas J. van Warmelo. Berlin: Dietrich Reimer Verlag.

Meyer, Emmi. 1937. Etymologische Lautlehre des Nyanja. Zeitschrift für Eingeborenen-Sprachen 27.1-34, 129-155, 184-211.

Mould, Martin. 1981. Greater Luyia. In Thomas H. Hinnebusch, Derek Nurse & Martin Mould (eds), *Studies in the Classification of Eastern Bantu Languages.* (Sprache und Geschichte in Afrika, Beiheft 3.) Hamburg: Helmut Buske Verlag, 181-236.

Müller, Emil. 1947. *Wörterbuch der Djaga-Sprache (Madjame-Mundart) gesprochen am Kilimandjaro in Ostafrika.* (Supplement no. 25 to *Zeitschrift für Eingeborenen-Sprachen*.) Berlin: Dietrich Reimer.

Murphy, Lynne. 1997. Venda electronic dictionary provided to CBOLD. (Based on Van Warmelo, N. J. 1937.)

Ndembe-Nsasi, D. 1972. Esquisse phonologique et morphologique de la langue lwalwa. Lumbumbashi: Université Nationale du Zaïre.

Ngunga, Armindo. 1997. Lexical phonology and morphology of Ciyao. Ph.D. dissertation, University of California, Berkeley. (To appear, Stanford: C.S.L.I.).

Niyonkuru, Lothaire. 1978. Phonologie et morphologie du giphende. Mémoire, Université Libre de Bruxelles.

Nurse, Derek & Thomas Hinnebusch. 1993. *Swahili and Sabaki: A linguistic history*. Berkeley and Los Angeles: University of California Press.

Odden, David. 1996. *The Phonology and Morphology of Kimatuumbi.* (The Phonology of the World's Languages series.) Oxford: Clarendon Press.

Pelling, Rev. James N. 1971. *A Practical Ndebele Dictionary.* Harare: Longman Zimbabwe (Pvt.) Limited.

Ruttenberg, P. 1971. *Lexique yaka-francais, français-yaka.* Kinshasa.

Sample, Ward A. 1976. The application of rules in the phonology of Olukisa. Ph.D. Dissertation, Indiana University.

Sanderson, George M. 1954. *A dictionary of the Yao language.* Zomba, Nyasaland: Government Printer.

Schadeberg, Thilo C. 1982. Derivation. University of Leiden. [Unpublished MS.]

Spa, Jaap J. 1973. *Traits et tons en enya: phonologie générative d'une langue bantoue.* Tervuren: Musée Royal de l'Afrique Centrale.

Stappers, Leo. 1973. *Esquisse de la langue mituku,* Annales No. 80. Tervuren: Musée Royal de l'Afrique Centrale.

Stewart, John & Helene van Leynseele. 1979. Underlying cross-height vowel harmony in Nen (Bantu A.44). *Journal of African Languages and Linguistics* 1:31-54.

Stewart, John M. 1970. Tongue root position in the Volta-Comoe languages and its significance for the reconstruction of the original Bantu vowel sounds. *African Language Studies* 11.340-350.

Steward, John M. 1983. The high unadvanced vowels of Proto-Tano-Congo. *Journal of West African Languages* 13:19-36.

Trithart, Lee. 1977. Causatives and instruments, in: Ernest Rugwa Byarushengo, Alessandro Duranti, & Larry M. Hyman (eds), *Haya grammatical structure.* (Southern California Occasional Papers in Linguistics 6.) Los Angeles: University of Southern California, 89-98.

Twilingiyimana, Chrysogone. 1984. *Elements de description du doko.* (Annales, Linguistique 116.) Tervuren: Musée Royal de l'Afrique Centrale.

van den Eynde, Karel. 1968. *Eléments de grammaire yaka.* Kinshasa: Université Lovanium.

van der Veen, Lolke J. 1991. Etude Comparée des parlers du groupe Okani B 30 (Gabon). Thèse; Université Lumière Lyon2.

Viljoen, Johannes Jurgens & Amakali. 1978. *A handbook of Oshiwambo.* Pretoria: University of South Africa.

Van Warmelo, Nicolaas J. 1937. *Tshivenda-English Dictionary.* (Ethnological Publications VI.) Pretoria: Union of South Africa Department of Native Affairs.

Welmers, William E. 1962. The phonology of Kpelle. *Journal of African Languages* 1:69-93.

Remarks on the Sound Correspondences between Proto-Bantu and Tswana (S.31), with Particular Attention to Problems Involving *j (or *y), *į and Sequences *NC

DENIS CREISSELS
Laboratoire Dynamique du Language (CNRS/Université Lumière Lyon2)

1. Introduction

The subgroup of Bantu languages labeled S.30 in Guthrie's classification (often termed Sotho subgroup or Sotho-Tswana subgroup) is certainly a genetically valid grouping within the Bantu family. Its homogeneity is obvious, and it shows very clear-cut contrasts with all the other groups of Bantu languages located in the same geographical area. The Sotho-Tswana subgroup is the only group of southern Bantu languages in which the seven Proto-Bantu vowels are maintained as distinct phonemes, and the way it treats the prenasalized consonants of Proto-Bantu is rarely found elsewhere in the Bantu family.

A number of studies have already been devoted to the comparative study of the Sotho-Tswana languages and dialects: Tucker (1929), Ponelis (1973), Dickens (1977), De Wolf (1981), Dickens (1984). The historical phonology of the Sotho-Tswana languages occupies an important place in Dickens (1986), and, as regards specifically Tswana, some indications can be found in Cole (1955) and Malepe (1968) too. Among recent works, Dickens (1986) must be pointed out as particularly interesting. These studies, as well as Guthrie (1967-71), propose what seems to be fairly reasonable hypotheses on the evolutions leading from the sound system of Proto-Bantu to the Sotho-Tswana sound systems. The aim of this paper is, on the one hand, to make these hypotheses more precise by discussing some apparently irregular correspondences that might well reflect regular sound changes with a relatively restricted conditioning, and on the other hand, to show how a careful study of the conditioning of the Tswana reflexes of Proto-Bantu and of the cases when the regular correspondences are not satisfied can contribute to the discussion of certain problems of reconstruction.

In this connection, in order to avoid any misunderstanding, it is very important to keep in mind the precise value given here to the symbol ° in notations such as (1).

(1) *-jį́b- 'steal' -útsw-á < °-ų́bų-

The precise meaning of such a notation is that:

- *-jį́b- 'steal' is generally considered by Bantuists as a valid reconstruction;
- the same meaning is expressed in Tswana by *-útsw-á*, and, in spite of the fact that the phonetic similarity is at first sight not obvious, it is possible to put forward the hypothesis of a historical relationship with this reconstruction: the vowels are different, but they belong to the same degree, and the presence of a labial consonant in the Bantu reconstruction may explain the presence of a labial vowel in the Tswana form; on the other hand, it is easy to establish that /ts/ is the regular reflex of *b in certains contexts;
- however, given the regularities in the correspondences between Bantu reconstructions and Tswana words, *-útsw-á* cannot be analyzed as the result of the evolution of a protoform *-jį́b-* undergoing only the historical processes reflected in regular correspondences as they can be established by comparing the current Bantu reconstructions with Tswana;
- on the other hand, this Tswana form could be the result of the evolution of a protoform *-ų́bų-* undergoing only the historical processes reflected in regular correspondences.

In other words, a notation such as °-ų́bų- has in this paper a strictly heuristic value. I don't claim that the notations introduced by the symbol ° represent forms that really existed as dialectal variants of the Bantu protoform, or as more or less irregular developments of the Bantu protoform in Proto-S.30. I don't exclude that perhaps further studies will lead to the conclusion that some of these forms are in some way or another historically valid, but this question need not be raised here. The point is that, once the regularities in sound correspondences between Bantu reconstructions and the lexicon of an individual Bantu language are assumed to be established on a relatively firm basis, it seems to me necessary to investigate carefully the portion of the lexicon of this language which seems to be related to Proto-Bantu, yet cannot be predicted by applying mechanically rules of correspondence to Bantu reconstructions, and the use of the symbol ° is nothing more than a practical way of making apparent the problems raised by Tswana words that do not fit the main regularities of correspondence with the current Bantu reconstructions.

The Tswana forms quoted in this study are transcribed in a broad phonetic transcription whose symbols must be taken with their value in the IPA alphabet. This means in particular that, in this transcription of Tswana, vowels of degree 1 are represented by /i/ and /u/, vowels of degree 2 are represented by /ɩ/ and /ɷ/, /j/ represents the palatal approximant (or semi-vowel), and /qh/ represents an aspirate uvular stop (or affricate). The reason why this transcription of Tswana ignores the distinction between /f/ and /h/ will be explained in section 5.1.

The quotation form of verbs is the stem of the disjunctive form of the present positive, characterized by a final *-a* and by the absence of a grammatical H tone.

Nouns and verbs are quoted with their basic tonal melody, defined as the tonal melody realized in contexts that do not require the application of any particular rule, i.e. the tonal melody realized when the only tone rules put into action are those operating within the limits of the unit itself[1]. This means in particular that the basic tonal melody disregards the H tone retraction process operating automatically in Tswana before every pause.
Bantu reconstructions are generally quoted in accordance with Meussen (1980). Many details have been specified and some corrections have been introduced with the help of Yvonne Bastin, Claire Grégoire and Baudouin Janssens; they also gave me indications about the reliability of the individual reconstructions, which was crucial in order to avoid making wrong hypotheses on the basis of insufficiently reliable reconstructions. I am deeply grateful to them for their help.

2. The main regularities concerning syllabic structures

2.1. General remarks

Bantu reconstructions depart from the canonical syllabic structure CV on the following points: they may include sequences NC, they may include double

---

[1] As a result of this process, the tonal melody actually uttered by Tswana speakers when they pronounce words in isolation is often different from their basic tonal melody; for example, the citation form *mɷ̀sàdí* 'woman' corresponds to a phonetic realization [mɷ̀sádì] when this word is uttered in isolation (note the lengthening of the penultimate vowel, which is also automatic before a pause).

vowels, and they may include vowel sequences. The aim of section 2 is to make clear the main regularities concerning (a) the treatment of these non-canonical syllabic structures in Tswana, and (b) the creation of new cases of non-canonical syllabic structures in Tswana.

2.2. The treatment of Proto-Bantu sequences NC

2.2.1. Sequences *NC not interrupted by a morpheme boundary and the notion of «strong reflex»

Given a sequence *NC not interrupted by a morpheme boundary, the first element N always disappears in the languages of the Sotho-Tswana subgroup, but the consonant representing the second element C is generally different from the consonant representing the same Proto-Bantu consonant in other contexts (see examples in section 5.2). It is convenient to term «strong reflexes» the consonants that regularly correspond to Proto-Bantu consonants immediately preceded by nasals, and to term «weak reflexes» the Tswana consonants corresponding regularly to Proto-Bantu consonants not immediately preceded by nasals:

(2) *C > C_{strong} / N ___
*C > C_{weak} / V ___ or # ___
*N > Ø / ___ C

From the point of view of historical processes, this means that, at an early stage in the history of the languages of the Sotho-Tswana group, there was an allophonic variation: most oral consonants had different allophones depending on whether they were immediately preceded by a nasal or not; later in the history of this subgroup of Bantu languages, the first element of sequences NC not interrupted by a morpheme boundary disappeared. One can imagine that perhaps in a first stage it was not properly speaking deleted, but rather assimilated to the following consonant, but there seems to be no evidence in support of such a hypothesis.

2.2.2. Sequences *NC interrupted by a morpheme boundary

Given a sequence *NC in which C is the initial consonant of a noun stem and N represents the prefix of class 9 or 10, the consonant *C has in Tswana exactly the same reflexes as in sequences *NC not interrupted by a morpheme boundary (see examples in section 5.2), but the nasal receives a different treatment. The nasal representing the prefix of class 9 or 10 has been deleted only in combination with stems comprising at least two syllables. In combination with monosyllabic stems, its reflex is a L-toned syllabic nasal, as in the following examples[2]:

[2]The presence of this L-toned syllabic nasal in ǹtɬɛ́, ɲ̀-tʃ(w)á and ŋ̀-kwɛ̀ implies that historically, whatever the original syllabic status of the vowel sequence in lexemes reconstructed as $*CV_1V_2$ may have been, these lexemes were already

(3) *-dá 9 'louse' ǹ-tá / dìǹ-tá
*-jâɩ̨ 9 'outside' ǹtɬɛ́
*-gòɩ̨̀ 9 'leopard' ŋ̀-kwɛ̀ / dìŋ̀-kwɛ̀
*-búà 9 'dog' ɲ̀-tʃ(w)á / dìɲ̀-tʃ(w)á
*-jù 9 'house' ǹ-tɬʊ̀ / mà-tɬʊ̀

2.3. Other cases of creation of syllabic nasals in Tswana

Syllabic nasals may be present within Tswana lexemes; when the lexemes in question correspond to a Bantu reconstruction, the syllabic nasal can be predicted by the following rule:

(4) *NV > syllabic nasal, iff V is a vowel of degree 1
*-gènɩ̨̀ 1 ›stranger' mʊ̀-èŋ̀ / bà-èŋ̀
*-jànɩ̨́ 14 'grass' bʊ̀-dʒàŋ́
*-nų̀nk- 'smell' -ŋ̀qh-à
*-mɩ̨́mba 9 'abdomen' ḿpá

The following correspondence can be explained with the same rule applying to an ancient form of class 9 reinterpreted as the stem:

(5) *-jɩ̨́ngí 'many' -ńtsí < °-n-ɩ̨́ngɩ̨

Another case of creation of syllabic nasals concerns the noun prefix of class 1, the noun prefix of class 3 and the object marker of class 1, i.e. reflexes of *mù- (with a vowel of degree 2, i.e. a vowel which is generally maintained, even when following a nasal). In Tswana, these three morphemes are generally realized as *mʊ̀-*, but they are obligatorily represented by a syllabic nasal when they are prefixed to a stem beginning with /b/, and /b/ in contact with this syllabic nasal changes into /m/. For example:

(6) *-bòmbó 3 'bridge of the nose' m̀-mɔ̀pɔ́ / mɩ̀-bɔ̀pɔ́

The replacement of *mʊ̀-* representing the same morphemes by a syllabic nasal is also possible (but not obligatory) in contact with stems beginning with /h/.

The last case of creation of syllabic nasals in Tswana concerns the prefix of class 1 *mʊ̀-*; irrespective of the nature of the following consonant, in ancient forms of class 1 whose prefix has been reinterpreted as the first syllable of the stem (which means that the old plural formed by substituting *bà-* for *mʊ̀-* is replaced by a new plural formed by adding to the singular form the prefix *bó-* of class 2a), the prefix *mʊ̀-* tends to be replaced by a syllabic nasal. For example:

monosyllabic at the stage when the rule deleting the prefix of class 9/10 before non-monosyllabic stems operated.

(7) *-bį ada 1 'cross-cousin' ǹtsálá / bó-ǹtsálá < °-mù-bį ada

2.4. The Tswana reflexes of the vowel sequences of Proto-Bantu, and the origin of the vowel sequences of Tswana

2.4.1. General remarks

The precise meaning of the sequences VV and V_1V_2 in Bantu reconstructions is not clear: did the vowels belong to the same syllable, or did they constitute two successive syllable nuclei separated by an empty onset? But what is important to point out here is that in Tswana, sequences *VV or *V_1V_2 always correspond to a single syllable nucleus and are treated differently from sequences *VCV or *V_1CV_2 in which the ancient consonant in intervocalic position has dropped.

Among the Proto-Bantu consonants commonly found in intervocalic position, *g has generally no segmental reflex in Tswana (see section 2.4.5), but the regular reflex of *VgV or *V_1gV_2 in Tswana is a sequence of two vowels constituting two successive syllable nuclei separated by an empty onset. In other words, whatever the ancient status of *VV or *V_1V_2 may have been, we must assume that, at the stage when the deletion of *g created new vowel sequences, the ancient sequences *VV or *V_1V_2 had already the status of single nuclei and not of sequences of nuclei separated by an empty onset, since if it were not the case, Tswana would have lost every trace of the distinction between Proto-Bantu sequences *VV or *V_1V_2 and sequences VV or V_1V_2 resulting from the deletion of *g.

2.4.2. The treatment of double vowels

The double vowels of Proto-Bantu always correspond to a single syllable nucleus in Tswana, and the Tswana reflexes of double vowels are identical to the reflexes of the corresponding single vowels. More generally, there is nothing in Tswana that could be analyzed as an indirect trace of ancient double vowels. By contrast with many other Bantu languages, Tswana has no trace of an ancient distinction between long and short vowels in its tonal morphology. The Tswana reflexes of Bantu reconstructions with double vowels could be predicted as well from protoforms with single vowels.

2.4.3. Vowel sequences in which the second vowel is more open than the first one

In Tswana forms corresponding to Bantu reconstructions with a vowel sequence whose second element is more open than the first one, as a rule the second vowel of the reconstructed sequence is maintained with the status of syllable nucleus. Depending on its nature and on the nature of the preceding consonant, the first vowel may leave traces of its presence in two different ways: it may be maintained as a semi-vowel, and it may condition a particular reflex of the preceding consonant: the reflexes of several Proto-Bantu consonants immediately followed by certain vowel sequences are different from the reflexes of the same consonants followed by a single vowel or by a double vowel (this question will be treated in detail in section 5.5). For example:

(8) *-pɩ́à 'new' -ʃá

*-búà 9 'dog' ɲ̀-tʃ(w)á / dìɲ̀-tʃ(w)á

*-dúad- 'be ill' -lwál-á

2.4.4. Vowel sequences whose second element is *i̯

A difference between Guthrie's reconstructions and the reconstructions listed in Meeussen (1980) is that vowel sequences whose second element is *i̯ are almost totally absent from Guthrie's reconstructions. In this connection, it is worth noting that Tswana provides evidence in support of the reconstruction of such vowel sequences:

- sequences *ai̯ account for the fact that the corresponding Tswana forms may have any of the front vowels /ɩ/, /e/, /ɛ/ (with in several cases a dialectal variation between /ɩ/ and /ɛ/) and not the /a/ expected from the *a posited by Guthrie:

(9) *-dàì̯ 'long' -léèlé (cl. 9 [télèlé])[3]

*-jâi̯ 9 'outside' ǹtɬɛ́

*-tâi̯ 6 'saliva' mà-thɩ́ < °mà-ntái̯

- sequences *oi̯ account for the fact that the corresponding Tswana forms, in the same way as those corresponding to reconstructions with a sequence *ai̯, may have any of the front vowels /ɩ/, /e/, /ɛ/ (with in several cases a dialectal variation between /ɩ/ and /ɛ/), but have in addition a semi-vowel /w/ and a reflex of the preceding consonant identical to that occurring more generally under the influence of vowel sequences beginning with a non-close back vowel, which cannot be explained from reconstructions with a single *o as those posited by Guthrie:

(10) *-mòì̯ 'one' -ŋwɩ̀

*-gòì̯nà 9 'crocodile' kwènà / dɩ̀-kwènà

*-kó-ì̯ 1 'son-in-law' mɷ̀-χwɛ́ / bà-χwɛ́

2.4.5. The deletion of *g

With very few exceptions, Proto-Bantu vowels separated from each other by *g are reflected in Tswana by two distinct syllable nuclei separated by a syllable onset which, depending on the precise nature of the vowels in question, may remain empty or associate with a semi-vowel. Noun stems

[3] The form of cl. 9 suggests that *-léèlé* originates from a triplicated form of the Proto-Bantu root.

reconstructed with an initial *g are almost always reflected in Tswana by noun stems whose initial vowel never fuses with the vowel of the prefix, which means that their initial vowel is preceded by an empty onset reflecting the ancient presence of *g, since in other cases (see section 2.5.2) initial vowels of noun stems are involved in interactions with the vowel of the prefix (the particular problem raised by Tswana verb stems with an initial vowel will be discussed in section 2.5.4). In other words, the regular non-conditioned (or minimally conditioned) reflex of *g not immediately preceded by a nasal is an empty syllable onset:

(11) *-bògó 9 'buffalo' pɔ̀ɔ́ / dì-pɔ̀ɔ́ 'bull'
*-jògṵ̀ 9 'elephant' tɬòù / dì-tɬòù
*-gànjà 7 'palm of the hand' sɩ̀-àtɬà / dì-àtɬà
*-gṵ̀bà 3 'bellows' mɷ̀-ùbà / mɩ̀-ùbà

2.5. Tswana reflexes of reconstructions including *j

2.5.1. General remarks

The reconstruction of Proto-Bantu *j is a difficult and controversial question. Non-initial *j is not frequent in Bantu reconstructions, and almost always non-initial *j occurs as the second element of a sequence *nj, whose regular reflex in Tswana is /tɬ/ or /ts/, depending on the following vowel (see section 5). A detailed examination of the comparative series for which Meeussen (1980) gives a reconstruction with an initial *j reveals that, apart from a few noun stems belonging exclusively to class 9/10, most of the time only a very limited number of languages provide evidence supporting the reconstruction of an initial consonant. In such cases Guthrie's reconstructions have an initial *y instead of the initial *j found in Meeussen (1980).

Tswana data clearly supports the reconstruction of two different types of initials corresponding roughly to Guthrie's *y and *j. However, the evidence provided by Tswana (and more generally by the languages of the Sotho-Tswana subgroup) does not support the hypothesis of an ancient distinction between two different consonants (as suggested by Guthrie's notation), but rather of a distinction between reconstructions with an initial *j and reconstructions whose initial should perhaps be posited as *(j) in order to account for the fact that in many languages (including Tswana and its closest relatives) the observed reflexes are incompatible with the hypothesis of the (relatively) recent deletion of an initial consonant and support rather the hypothesis of the (relatively) ancient absence of any initial consonant.

As already explained in section 2.4.5, *g not preceded by a nasal has generally no segmental reflex in Tswana, but the fact that two vowels separated from each other by *g are maintained as distinct syllable nuclei proves that a consonant was still present at the stage when the rules reducing the vowel sequences posited in Bantu reconstructions were phonetically active. Nothing similar can be observed in the case of *j: among the Tswana forms corresponding to reconstructions with *j not immediately preceded by a nasal, the prevailing regularity is clearly that everything happens as if no consonant were present at the stage when the rules reducing the vowel sequences of Proto-Bantu were phonetically active.

However, there are some complications with the analysis of the verb stems of Tswana beginning with a vowel; this is the reason why nouns are examined first. On the other hand, the reflexes of Bantu reconstructions beginning with a syllable *jį (*yį by Guthrie) raise particular problems which cannot be conveniently discussed now; we will return to them in section 6; in sections 2.5.2 to 2.5.4, the reconstructions beginning with *jį (or *yį) are not taken into account.

2.5.2. Initial *j in noun stems combining with prefixes reconstructed as *CV

As a rule, in the Tswana reflexes of noun stems reconstructed with an initial *j and combining with a prefix reconstructed as *CV (i.e., with a prefix other than those of class 5, 9 or 10), the vowel of the prefix and the first vowel of the stem are treated in the same way as immediate sequences of vowels within stems. The only difference is that in some cases, in an apparently unpredictable way, either the vowel of the prefix is simply deleted (instead of changing into a semi-vowel and/or inducing a modification of the preceding consonant), or the first vowel of the stem is deleted (and in that case, the Tswana form keeps no trace of the first syllable of the reconstructed stem).

In other words, whatever the validity of reconstructions with an initial consonant may be for the other subgroups of the Bantu family, the languages of subgroup S.30 (and in particular Tswana) demand to accept at least the possibility of variants of these reconstructions with no initial consonant:

(12)	*-jédį 3 'moonlight'	ŋwèdí	< °mù-édį
	*-jànį́ 14 'leaf, grass'	bὼ-ʤàŋ́	< °bù-bù-ànį́
	*-jánà 1 'child'	ŋw-àná / b-àná	< °mù-ána
	*-jàdí 1 'girl'	ŋw-àlί / b-àlί	< °mù-àdí
	*-jápà 15 'armpit'	lὶ-χwáhá / mà-χwáhá	< °dì-kù-ápa
	*-jákà 3 'year'	ŋwàχá / dì-ŋwàχá	< °mù-áka
	*-jòngó 14 'brain'	bὼ-bɔ̀kɔ́ / mà-bɔ̀kɔ́ 'brain'	< °bù-bù-òngó
		mὼ-kɔ́ / mὶ-kɔ́ 'marrow'	< °mù-òngó
	*-jòjá 'body hair, fur'	bὼ-bὼá	< °bù-bù-ògá[4]

[4]The reconstruction *-jòjá 'body hair, fur' includes both an initial *j and a non-initial *j, but the Tswana form points to a protoform °-ògá, because the reflex of

*-jògà	14 'mushroom'	lɩ̀-bɷ̀à / mà-bɷ̀à	< °dì-bù-ògà
*-júkì	14 'honey'	bɷ̀-tshɩ́ 'sweetness'	< °bù-únki [5]
*-júkɨ̀	3 'smoke'	mɷ̀-sí / mɩ̀-sí	< °mù-úkɨ

We observe that in several cases, the fusion of the ancient prefix with the first syllable of the stem has been followed by the adjunction of an additional prefix (sometimes identical with the original prefix, sometimes different).

2.5.3. Initial *j in noun stems combining with prefixes reconstructed as *N

As a rule, initial consonants in contact with the prefix of class 9/10 are treated in the same way as consonants immediately preceded by a nasal belonging to the same morpheme, which confirms the reconstruction of the prefix of class 9/10 as a nasal consonant. In this context, *g, whose reflex in other contexts is an empty onset, is represented in Tswana by /k/ or /ts/, depending on the following vowel. But in the case of noun stems corresponding to a reconstruction with an initial *j and combining with the prefix of class 9/10, a distinction must be made between cases of initial *j treated in this context in the same way as non-initial *j preceded by a nasal and cases of initial *j treated in a different way; the fact that the Tswana reflexes of *-jàdà 9 'hunger' and *-jádà 11 'nail' have different initials excludes the possibility of a conditioning:

- in the case of certain noun stems of class 9/10 reconstructed with an initial *j, we must assume that an initial sequence NC was still present at the time when the rule deleting N followed by an oral consonant operated, since the Tswana reflexes of these stems begin with /tɬ/ or /ts/, i.e. with the consonants recognized as the regular reflexes (depending on the following vowel) of an internal sequence *nj:

(13)	*-jìdà	9 'path'	tsɩ̀là / dì-tsɩ̀là
	*-jàdɨ́	9 'lightning'	tɬàdí / dì-tɬàdí
	*-jàdà	9 'hunger'	tɬàlà
	*-jâɨ	9 'outside'	ǹtɬɛ́

the second vowel of the stem (*a) is immediately preceded by an empty syllable onset, which constitutes in Tswana the regular reflex of *g.

[5] *bɷ̀-tshɩ́* points to a protoform °-únki slightly different from the reconstruction *-júkì, because /tsh/ is the regular reflex of *nk followed by a front vowel, whereas the regular reflex of *k followed by a front vowel and not preceded by a nasal is /s/.

*-jògù̧ 9 'elephant' tɬòù / dì-tɬòù
*-jù 9 'house' ǹ-tɬɷ̀ / mà-tɬɷ̀
*-jùgú 9 'ground-nut' tɬɷ̀ɷ́ / dì-tɬɷ̀ɷ́ *'voandzeia subterranea'*

- by contrast, some other noun stems belonging to class 9/10 equally found with an initial *j in Meeussen (1980) have a Tswana reflex beginning with a syllable NV; this means that, at the time when the rule deleting N followed by an oral consonant operated, the nasal representing the prefix of class 9/10 was not the first element of a sequence NC (in that case, it would have been deleted), but rather the onset of a syllable NV; in other words, we must assume that such noun stems were already devoid of initial consonant at this stage of the history of the Sotho-Tswana languages; it is interesting to observe that the following list includes *-júkì 9 'bee' / 14 'honey', already encountered in (12) (section 2.5.2) in combination with the prefix of class 14:

(14) *-jàmà 9 'meat' nàmà / dì-nàmà < °n-àmà
*-jàmbɪ́ 9 'God' nàpɪ́ 'the god of wisdom' < °n-àmbɪ́
*-jádà 11 'nail' lɷ̀-nálá / dì-nálá[6] < °dù-n-áda
*-játì 9 'buffalo' nárɪ́ / dì-nárɪ́ < °n-áti
*-jóngà 9 'hip' nɔ́ká / dì-nɔ́ká < °n-ónga
*-jókà 9 'snake' nɔ́χá / dì-nɔ́χá < °n-óka
*-jùnɪ̧ 9 'bird' nɔ̀ɲánɪ́ / dì-nɔ̀ɲánɪ́ < °n-ùnɪ̧-ani
*-jùndò 9 'hammer' nɔ̀tɔ̀ / dì-nɔ̀tɔ̀ < °n-ùndò
*-júkì 9 'bee' nótshɪ́ / dì-nótshɪ́ < °n-únki

In such cases, protoforms with an initial *j cannot account for the way the prefix of class 9/10 is treated in Tswana, and the simplest explanation of such reflexes of noun stems combined with prefixes of class 9/10 would be provided by protoforms with an initial vowel constituting the nucleus of a syllable whose onset was the nasal consonant representing the prefix.

2.5.4. *j at the beginning of verb stems

Things are different in the case of verb stems, but they do not contradict the conclusions drawn from the observation of nouns, because nouns show particularities whose historical implications are fairly clear, whereas verbs by themselves would not permit to draw any conclusion concerning the problem discussed here.

---

[6]In this case, the stem of the singular form must probably be explained as remade by analogy with the plural form of class 10.

The verb stems of Tswana corresponding to a reconstruction with an initial *j are not different from those corresponding to reconstructions with initial *g: in both cases the initial vowel of the verb stem constitutes in Tswana the nucleus of a syllable which, in spite of the fact that its onset is empty, never fuses with any prefix. For example:

(15)				
	*-jím- 'stand'	-ɛ́m-á		< °-ím-
	*-jèp- 'avoid'	-ɛ̀h-à	'keep out of harm's way'	< °-èp-
	*-jánik- 'dry in the sun'	-ánɛ́χ-á		< °-ánik-
	*-jàd- 'spread'	-àl-à		< °-àd-
	*-jádịm- 'borrow'	-ádím-á <		< °-ádịm-
	*-ját- 'split'	-ár-á	'lance an abcess, operate'	< °-át-
	*-jác-am- 'gape, yawn'	-átɬhám-á		< °-ác-am-
	*-jànk- 'swing'	-àqh-à		< °-ànk-
	*-jón- 'damage, spoil'	-ɔ́nál-á	'become worn out'	< °-ón-
	*-júm- 'become dry'	-ɔ́m-á<		< °-úm-

The absence of interaction with prefixes seems at first sight to contradict the hypothesis of protoforms devoid of initial consonant. But a careful examination of the data shows that, in the case of verb stems, an initial empty onset does not necessarily constitute the trace of an ancient consonant. The point is that some aspects of the behavior of these stems in Tswana cannot be explained as the mere result of historical processes affecting stems whose initial consonant would have been deleted in a relatively recent past (as in the case of noun stems corresponding to reconstructions with an initial *g).

The crucial observation is that, in contexts where initial consonants constituting the weak reflexes of Proto-Bantu consonants are replaced by the corresponding strong reflexes (for example, when a deverbative noun stem combines with the prefix of class 9), all verb stems beginning with a vowel take without exception an initial /k/, irrespective of the following vowel and of the consonant posited in the corresponding reconstruction. If the empty onset at the beginning of these verb stems were the regular reflex of *g or *j, the strong form of the initial should be /tɬ/ or /ts/ at least in certain cases; for example:

- *ɔ́mɛ́lɛ́l-à* 'become dry' originates from a root reconstructed as *-júm-; the derived noun of class 9 is *kɔ́mɛ́lɛ́lɔ̀*, which contradicts the rule according to which the regular reflex of *j preceded by a nasal and followed by a back vowel is /tɬ/;
- the plural of *lɷ̀-ɛ̀tɔ̀* 'travel', derived from *-ɛ̀t-à*, is *dì-kɛ̀tɔ̀* (class 10); according to the reconstruction *-gènd- an initial /ts/ would be expected,

since /ts/ is the regular reflex of *g preceded by a nasal and followed by a front vowel.

This leads to the conclusion that the behaviour expected in the case of stems originating in protoforms beginning with *g followed by a non-front vowel has been extended by analogy to all verb stems beginning with a vowel, whatever their initial may have been in a more distant past and irrespective of the nature of their first vowel. Thus, there is nothing, in the Tswana reflexes of Bantu verb roots currently reconstructed with an initial *j, that could be analyzed as the unambiguous trace of an initial consonant, and the conclusions drawn from the observation of noun stems can be accepted as valid for Tswana as a whole: all the evidence provided by this language points to a variant of Proto-Bantu in which *j occurred only as the second element of internal sequences *nj or at the beginning of a few noun stems of class 9 /10.

3. The main regularities concerning tone

3.1. Tonal correspondences in verb stems

Irrespective of their morphological complexity and of their length, the verbal lexemes of Tswana divide into two tone classes, and derived verbs always belong to the same tone class as the root from which they originate. Tswana verbs traceable to a Bantu root have generally the same tone as the corresponding reconstruction; for example:

(16) *-dìm- 'cultivate' -ɪ̀m-à
*-gènd- 'walk, travel' -ɛ̀t-à
*-bɨ́n- 'dance' -bín-á
*-dí- 'eat' -ʤ-á

3.2. Tonal correspondences in noun stems

Tswana monosyllabic noun stems corresponding to a reconstructed noun stem have generally the same tone as the corresponding reconstruction; for example:

(17) *-dɨ̀ 3 'root' mʊ̀-dì / mɪ̀-dì
*-gɨ̀ 9 'fly' ǹ-tsì / dìǹ-tsì
*-dá 9 'louse' ǹ-tá / dìǹ-tá
*-tá 14 'bow' bʊ̀-rá / mà-rá

Tswana dissyllabic noun stems divide into three tone classes: leaving aside a very small number of exceptions that are not relevant in a historical perpective[7], one can say that in the case of dissyllabic noun stems, HH and

[7]The only dissyllabic noun stem with a HL contour in all contexts I have found in the speech of my main informant is *tíì* 'tea'.

HL are not lexically distinct contours, but rather contextual variants of the same lexical contour; noun stems belonging to this tone class have a tonal melody HL when they immediately precede a pause or when they constitute the head of a NP and immediately precede certain modifiers, and a tonal melody HH in all the other contexts.

The following examples show that, as a rule, reconstructed dissyllabic noun stems with tonal sequences *LL and *LH are realized unchanged in Tswana, whereas Tswana has merged *HH and *HL into the tone class «HH with a contextual variant HL»:

(18) *-jògų̀ 9 'elephant' tɬòù / dì-tɬòù
*-pòkù 4 'blind person' sì-hòhù / dì-hòhù
*-bògó 9 'buffalo' pɔ̀ɔ́ / dì-pɔ̀ɔ́ 'bull'
*-dùngú 9 'porcupine' nʊ̀kʊ́ / dì-nʊ̀kʊ́
*-cį́mbá 9 'wildcat' tshípá / dì-tshípá 'genet(*genetta genetta*)'
*-kádį́ 1 'woman' bʊ̀-χádí 'cattle given to the girl's family to conclude marriage negotiations'
*-dį́mù 3 'god, spirit' mʊ̀-dímʊ́ / mì-dímʊ́
*-tį́kù 14 'night' bʊ̀-síχʊ́ / mà-síχʊ́ < °bù-cį́ku

In cases when the first syllable of a noun stem reconstructed with a tonal contour *HH or *HL has fused with a prefix, it may happen that the syllable resulting from the fusion retains in Tswana the L tone of the prefix, and that the H tone of the first syllable of the stem associates with the following syllable; the result is a regular correspondence between Proto-Bantu *HH or * HL and Tswana LH:

(19) *-jánà 1 'child' ŋw-àná / b-àná < °mù-ána
*-jákà 3 'year' ŋwàχá / dì-ŋwàχá < °mù-áka

There are however exceptions:

(20) *-jápà 15 'armpit' lì-χwáhá / mà-χwáhá < °dì-kù-ápa
*-jį́bà 3 'thorn' mútɬwá / mítɬwá < ° mù-į́njua

4. The main regularities concerning vowels

4.1. The vowel system of Proto-Bantu and the vowel system of Tswana

The seven vowels of Proto-Bantu distinguish four degrees of aperture, numbered from 1 (close) to 4 (open):

(21)

	front (unrounded)		*back (rounded)*
ap. 1	į		ų
ap. 2	i		u
ap. 3	e		o
ap. 4		a	

Tswana has 9 phonologically distinct vowels:

(22)

	front (unrounded)		*back (rounded)*
ap. 1	i		u
ap. 2	ɩ		ɷ
ap. 3a	e		o
ap. 3b	ɛ		ɔ
ap. 4		a	

The numbering of two different degrees as respectively 3a and 3b is motivated by synchronic as well as diachronic considerations. From the historical point of view, the Tswana vowels of degree 3a and of degree 3b are regular reflexes (depending on the context) of Proto-Bantu vowels of degree 3. From the synchronic point of view, in spite of the fact that the vowels of degree 3a and the vowels of degree 3b must be analyzed as distincts phonemes (since the choice is unpredictable in certain contexts at least), there is still in Tswana a particular relation between these two couples of vowels: they can contrast only in certain contexts, and in contexts in which they cannot contrast, vowels of degree 3b are automatically replaced by the corresponding vowels of degree 3a.

4.2. The regular Tswana reflexes of Proto-Bantu vowels in the absence of a particular conditioning

As a rule, Proto-Bantu vowels have Tswana reflexes of the same degree and with the same value of the feature front / back; if no vowel of degree 1 or 2 exerts an influence on them (see 4.3), Proto-Bantu vowels of degree 3 regularly correspond to Tswana vowels of degree 3b:

(23) *-gį̀d- 'abstain from, avoid' -ìl-à
*-kį̀d- 'grind' -sìl-à

*-dìm- 'cultivate' -lɩ̀m-à
*-dɩ̀d- 'cry' -lɩ̀l-à

*-gènd- 'walk, travel'	-ὲt-à
*-gèd- 'flow'	-ὲl-à
*-dà 6 'intestines'	lì-là / mà-là
*-dá 9 'louse'	ǹ-tá / dìǹ-tá
*-bón- 'see'	-bɔ́n-á
*-bòd- 'rot'	-bɔ̀l-à
*-dúm- 'bite'	-lʊ́m-á
*-túm- 'send'	-rʊ́m-á
*-kų́m- 'become rich'	-húm-á
*-bų́ 5 'earth'	m̀-mú / mì-bú

4.3. Contexts in which Tswana vowels of degree 3a are regular reflexes of Proto-Bantu vowels of degree 3

Proto-Bantu vowels of degree 3 occurring in non-final syllables regularly correspond to Tswana vowels of degree 3a if the nucleus of the following syllable is a vowel of degree 1 or 2:

(24)	*-gènị 1 'stranger'	mʊ̀-èŋ̀ / bà-èŋ̀
	*-déet- 'bring'	-lérí[8]
	*-cónị 9 'shame'	dì-tɬhɔ́ŋ́
	*-jògụ̀ 9 'elephant'	tɬòù / dì-tɬòù

4.4. Contexts in which Tswana vowels of degree 3 are regular reflexes of Proto-Bantu vowels of degree 2

In the first syllable of roots reconstructed with an initial *j, Proto-Bantu vowels of degree 2 regularly correspond to Tswana vowels of degree 3. When the roots in question are verb roots, we know that Tswana gives no hint of the exact nature of their ancient initial, but we observe that none of the nominal roots concerned by this correspondence presents traces of an ancient initial consonant. It is therefore possible to propose the following rules:

(25) *i > ɛ or e / ≠ ___N (≠ represents the left boundary of a stem)

*u > ɔ or o / ≠ ___N

[8] *-lérí* 'bring' and *-ítsí* 'know' have (except in the perfect positive) an invariable final vowel instead of the regular flexional endings of verbs.

*-jím- 'stand'	-ɛ́m-á	< °-ím-
*-jìmb- 'dig'	-ɛ̀p-à	< °-ìmb-
*-júm- 'become dry'	-ɔ́m-á	< °-úm-
*-júkì 9 'bee'	nótshí / dì-nótshí	< °n-únki[9]

A regular correspondence between Proto-Bantu vowels of degree 2 and Tswana vowels of degree 3 concerns also the vowel *i of the extensions *-ik-, *-id-, as well as post-radical *i's likely to belong to frozen extensions. For example:

(26) *-dį́mid- 'get lost' -tímɛ́l-á

*-jánik- 'dry in the sun' -ánɛ́χ-á

An important difference whith the case of vowels belonging to roots is that there is nothing similar with extensions having a back vowel of degree 2. Moreover, nasals seem to play no role here. Consequently, it seems reasonable to assume that the lowering of vowels of degree 2 belonging to roots and the lowering of vowels of degree 2 belonging to extensions result from two independent historical processes.

4.5. Tswana reflexes of Proto-Bantu vowels in contact with other vowels

As already explained in section 2.4:

- in vowel sequences whose second element is more open than the first one, the regular reflex of the second vowel is generally maintained in Tswana as a syllable nucleus, whereas the first vowel may be maintained as a semi-vowel and/or condition the occurrence of a particular reflex of the preceding consonant, but vowel sequences interrupted by a morpheme boundary do not always conform to this regularity;
- the Tswana reflex of the vowel sequence *aį may be any of the three non-close front vowels of Tswana (i.e. any vowel combining the feature «front» originating from *į and the feature «open» originating from *a);
- the vowel sequence *oį has the same reflexes as *aį, with the addition of the semi-vowel /w/, and the consonant preceding such a vowel sequence is treated in the same way as before any other vowel sequence beginning with a non-close back vowel.

[9] This is the only case in which the vowel of degree 2 involved in this correspondence is not followed by a nasal in the current reconstruction, but the following consonant is represented in Tswana by its strong reflex, which points to the presence of an ancient nasal.

4.6. Deletion of vowels following a nasal

The regular cases of deletion of vowels following a nasal (resulting in the creation of syllabic nasals) have already been described in section 2.3.

5. The main regularities concerning consonants

5.1. The consonant system of Proto-Bantu and the consonant system of Tswana

Leaving aside the controversial question of the precise phonetic nature of certain Proto-Bantu consonants, most Bantuists would agree on the following presentation of the consonant system of Proto-Bantu (O = order, S = series – the numbering of orders and series in this chart is arbitrary):

(27)

	O1	*O2*	*O3*	*O4*
S1	p	t	c	k
S2	b	d	j	g
S3	m	n	ɲ	

The classification of the consonant phonemes of Tswana according to their phonetic nature can be presented in the following way[10]:

(28)

ph	th	tɬh	tsh	tʃh	kh	qh	
p	t	tɬ	ts	tʃ	k		
b	d[/l]			ʤ			
[f]			s	ʃ		χ	h
m	n			ɲ	ŋ		
	r						
		l[/d]					

The following chart presents a different classification, in which phonemes characterized by similar combinatory properties and/or morphological behaviour are systematically grouped (even in cases when such a grouping leads to contradictions with a classification based on the phonetic nature of phonemes); not unexpectedly, such a classification permits a simpler account of the relation between the consonants of Proto-Bantu and their Tswana reflexes:

---

[10]The so-called «semi-vowels» are not included in this inventory. Generally speaking, one can argue that semi-vowels are not true consonants, but rather vocalic segments functioning as syllable onset, and the properties of the semi-vowels of Tswana are in total accordance with this analysis of semi-vowels.

(29)	O_1	O_2	O_3	O_5	O_6	O_{4a}	O_{4b}	O_7
S_{1a}	(f)	r		s	ʃ		χ	h
S_{1b}	ph	th	tɬh	tsh	tʃh	kh	qh	
S_{2a}	b	d/l			ʤ			
S_{2b}	p	t	tɬ	ts	tʃ	k		
S_3	m	n		ɲ	ŋ			

The numbering of the orders in this chart is motivated by the wish of making apparent the relation between the consonant orders of Tswana and the consonant orders of Proto-Bantu: in principle, the consonants grouped in the orders numbered O_1, O_2, O_3, O_{4a} and O_{4b} are unambiguously the unconditioned (or minimally conditioned) reflexes of the Proto-Bantu consonants belonging to orders with the same numbering in chart (27), whereas most consonants belonging to orders O_5, O_6 and O_7 result from processes which took place in specific contexts and led to the neutralization of certain ancient distinctions between consonants, as will be explained in detail below:

- the consonants of order O_5 are the regular reflexes of the Proto-Bantu consonants of orders O_3 or O_4 followed by front vowels, but they are also the reflexes of Proto-Bantu consonants of any order followed by vowel sequences beginning with a vowel of degree 1 (see section 5.5.2 and 5.5.4);
- the consonants of order O_6 are mainly the reflexes of the Proto-Bantu consonants of order O_1 followed by vowel sequences beginning with a vowel of degree 2 or 3, but /ʤ/ is also the regular reflex of *d followed by a vowel sequence beginning with a front vowel of degree 2 or 3 (see sections 5.5.3 and 5.5.5);
- /h/ is the non-conditioned reflex of *p not preceded by a nasal, but it is also the reflex of *k followed by *ų (see section 5.4.1).

As regards series, the consonants belonging to S_{1a} et S_{2a} are those which undergo a modification in contexts requiring «strengthening» (with a problem concerning /ʤ/: in some Tswana dialects this consonant is not affected by strengthening, in other dialects it alternates with /tʃ/).

The notation *d/l* means that in Tswana, [d] and [l] must be analyzed as representing the same phoneme: the allophone [d] occurs as the onset of syllables whose nucleus is a vowel of degree 1, whereas [l] occurs as the onset of syllables whose nucleus is a vowel of degree 2, 3 or 4.

The notation (f) means that certain Tswana dialects have no labial fricative in their phonetic inventory; in the dialects having a labial fricative, it must be analyzed as a distinct phoneme, but the dialects without labial fricative substitute /h/ for it.

This status of the labial fricative raises a problem. In the kind of study carried out here, it is desirable to have access to data of dialects with a maximum of phonological contrasts, because this can help to make precise hypotheses about the protoforms from which the observed forms are likely to originate. Unfortunately, the available Tswana data (including the data I collected with my informants) either concern dialects without labial fricative or have been collected with informants having in their individual speech a more or less free variation between /f/ and /h/, which seems to be a very common situation among Tswana speakers[11]. In such conditions, it seemed to me preferable to limit this study to the case of Tswana dialects without labial fricative.

5.2. The Tswana reflexes of Proto-Bantu consonants in the absence of any particular conditioning

The following sections will describe various factors conditioning the occurrence of particular reflexes of Proto-Bantu consonants. When none of these factors is present, the correspondences between Proto-Bantu consonants and Tswana consonants listed in the following chart are regular (in this chart, ø indicates the absence of segmental reflex[12]):

(30)

	O_1	O_2	O_3	O_4
S_1	*p > h	*t > r	*c > tɬh	*k > χ
S_2	*b > b	*d > d/l	*j > Ø	*g > Ø
S_3	*m > m	*n > n	*ɲ > n	

*-jápà 15 'armpit' — ɩ̀-χwáhá / mà-χwáhá < °dì-kù-ápa
*-pá- 'give' — -h-á

*-játì 9 'buffalo' — nárɩ́ / dì-nárɩ́ < °n-áti
*-tá 14 'bow' — bὼ-rá / mà-rá

*-pácà 5 'twin' — ɩ̀-hátɬhá / mà-hátɬhá
*-cúá 3 'termite' — mὼ-tɬhwá / mɩ̀-tɬhwá

---

[11] It is often said that the distinction is maintained, at least for initial consonants, at a morphological level: /h/ alternating with /kh/ is allegedly a «true» /h/, whereas /h/ alternating with /ph/ represents an underlying /f/, but in fact, when questioned about these alternations, Tswana speakers often hesitate and/or contradict themselves.

[12] As already explained in section 2, *g and *j share the property of having segmental reflexes in certain contexts only, but their case is nevertheless very different: even when it has no segmental reflex, *g regularly corresponds to an empty syllable onset analyzable as the trace of the presence of a consonant in a relatively recent past; by contrast, in the Tswana forms corresponding to reconstructions with *j not preceded by a nasal, there remains no trace of the ancient presence of a consonant.

*-bókò 5 'arm'	ĺì-tsɔ́χɔ́ / mà-bɔ́χɔ́
*-kúnì 11 'firewood'	lɷ̀-χɷ́ŋ́ / dì-qhɷ́ŋ́
*-dì̧bà 7 'pool'	sì-dìbà / dì-dìbà well
*-bí̧n- 'dance'	-bín-á
*-bìd- 'boil'	-bìl-à
*-dí̧mù 3 'god, spirit'	mɷ̀-dímɷ́ / mì-dímɷ́
*-dìm- 'cultivate'	-ĺìm-à
*-mì̧n- 'press, squeeze (esp. the nose)'	-mìn-à
*-bón- 'see'	-bɔ́n-á
*-nàì̧ 'four'	-nɛ̀
*-kóɲ- 'fold'	-χɔ̀n-à 'bend a limb'

5.3. The Tswana reflexes of Proto-Bantu consonants preceded by a nasal and not followed by a vowel or a vowel sequence exerting a particular influence

As already explained in section 2.2, in sequences *NC not interrupted by a morpheme boundary, N disappears in Tswana, but (except in the case of *c, which has no distinction between a weak reflex an a strong reflex) a trace of the presence of N remains through the choice of the strong reflex of C. If in such a sequence N represents the prefix of class 9/10, the only difference is that, in the case of monosyllabic stems, the reflex of the nasal is a L-toned syllabic nasal.

The strong reflexes of Proto-Bantu consonants in contexts where no vowel or vowel sequence exerts a particular influence are summarized in the following chart:

(31)

	O_1	O_2	O_3	O_4
S_1	*p > ph	*t > th	*c > tɬh	*k > qh
S_2	*b > p	*d > t	*j > tɬ[13]	*g > k

[13]As already explained in section 2.5, this correspondence confirms the necessity of distinguishing two types of initials equally represented by *j in Meeussen (1980); the reason is that the combination of an initial *j with prefixes of class 9/10 is not always treated in the same way as sequences *nj within stems. In some cases (see section 2.5.3), the result of the combination of a noun stem reconstructed with an initial *j with prefixes of class 9/10 is a Tswana form with an initial /n/, which points rather to protoforms devoid of initial consonants.

*-pépò 9 'wind'	phíhɔ́ / dì-phíhɔ́	< °n-pípo
*-pàdá 9 'impala antelope'	phàlá / dì-phàlá	
*-ntù 1 'human being'	mɷ̀-thɷ̀ / bà-thɷ̀	
*-càká 9 'thicket'	tɬhàχá	
*-cónį 9 'shame'	dì-tɬhóŋ́	
*-jànk- 'swing'	-àqh-à	< °-ànk-
*-kúpá 9 'tick'	qhɷ́há / dì-qhɷ́há	
*-cį́mbá 9 'wildcat'	tshípá / dì-tshípá 'genet *(genetta genetta)*'	
*-bògó 9 'buffalo'	pɔ̀ɔ́ / dì-pɔ̀ɔ́ 'bull'	
*-gènd- 'walk, travel'	-ɛt-à	
*-dá 9 'louse'	ǹ-tá / dìǹ-ta	
*-gìnjá 15 'late summer'	lì-χwètɬá	< °dì-kù-ìnjá
*-jàdà 9 'hunger'	tɬàlà	
*-bùngú 7 'worm'	sì-bɷ̀kɷ́ / dì-bɷ̀kɷ́	
*-gòįnà 9 'crocodile'	kwènà / dì-kwènà	

There is however a problem with the fact that, in a relatively great number of cases, a Proto-Bantu consonant not preceded by a nasal is represented in Tswana by its strong reflex, and not by the reflex expected according to the regularities established in section 5.2.

When strong reflexes appear at the beginning of noun stems combined with prefixes other than those of class 9/10, a possible explanation is that perhaps the noun in question belonged originally to class 9 in the singular and to class 10 in the plural, so that the strong reflex could be the trace of a frozen prefix of class 9/10, but such an explanation is excluded in the cases of verb stems. Given the relatively great number of Proto-Bantu verb stems corresponding to Tswana forms with an apparently irregular strong initial, the question of an explanation of this (apparent?) irregularity must be raised, but before trying to propose a solution, it would be necessary to make a systematic study of the verb stems of Tswana beginning with consonants of series S_{1b} or S_{2b}[14].

There are only a few cases in which a consonant in intervocalic position in a non-problematic Bantu reconstruction corresponds to the Tswana

[14]Similar facts are encountered in Bantu languages belonging to other subgroups; Janssens (1993) observes in Ewondo a correlation between prenalization and intransitivity which leads him to the hypothesis of an ancient mid-voice marker *n*-.

consonant which is in principle the strong reflex of the consonant in question. They must certainly be considered as isolated exceptions.

But strong reflexes not predicted by the regularities posited above are particularly frequent in the case of Tswana consonants corresponding to the onset of the second syllable of reconstructions beginning with *jį; this issue will be discussed in detail in section 6[15].

5.4. Reflexes of Proto-Bantu consonants conditioned by the nature of the following vowels

5.4.1. The non-problematic cases

The reflexes described in section 5.2 and 5.3 can be considered as the regular reflexes of Proto-Bantu consonants when the following vowel does not exert any particular influence, but certain consonants have particular reflexes when followed by certain vowels. The regularity of the influence of the vowel on the consonant can be considered as certain in the case of *c, *k, *j, *g followed by a front vowel, and in the case of *k followed by *ų:

(32)	*c or *k not preceded by a nasal	>	s /— *į, *i, *e
	*c or *k preceded by a nasal	>	tsh /— *į, *i, *e
	*-bícì 'raw, fresh, unripe'		lɷ-bísí 'fresh milk'
	*-cį́mbá 9 'wildcat'		tshípá / dì-tshípá 'genet (*genetta genetta*)'
	*-kímbà 5 'dung'		lì-sípá / mà-sípá
	*-kį́į̀ 9 'eyebrow'		ǹtshí 'eyelash'
(33)	*j or *g preceded by a nasal	>	ts /— *į, *i, *e
	*-genje 3 'mane'		mɷ-ɛ̀tsɛ̀ / mì-ɛ̀tsɛ̀
	*-jìdà 9 'path'		tsìlà / dì-tsìlà
	*-jį́ngí 'many'		-ńtsí < °-n-į́ngį
	*-gį̀gè 9 'locust'		tsìè
	*-gį̀ 9 'fly'		ǹtsì / dì-ǹtsì

15 The following two cases should perhaps be also explained in relation with the presence of *į (see section 6):

*-bàįj-	'carve'	-bètɬ-à	< °-bàįnj-
*-dèk-	'allow'	-lètɬ-à	< °-dàįnj-

(34) *k not preceded by a nasal > h / — *ų
*k preceded by a nasal > kh / — *ų

*-kų́tà 6 'fat' mà-húrá
*-kų́dų̀ 9 'tortoise' khúdú / dì-khúdú

Note that the influence of vowels on consonants results in neutralizations:

- *k and *c followed by a front vowel have the same reflexes;
- preceded by a nasal and followed by a front vowel, *g and *j have the same reflexes;
- when not preceded by a nasal, *p and *k followed by *ų have the same reflexes.

5.4.2. The problem of *t followed by *į

At first sight, certain correspondences suggest that the regular reflex of *t not preceded by a nasal is /s/ before *į. However, these correspondences are not very numerous, and they are not very reliable either, since they concern comparative series for which alternative reconstructions with *c have been proposed. Moreover, there is approximately the same number of relatively reliable reconstructions with *t followed by *į corresponding to Tswana forms with /r/ (and not with /s/); for example:

(35) *-tįtį- 3 'hair' mʊ̀-rírí / mì-rírí
*-pį́tį 9 'hyena' phírí / dì-phírí

We must also take into account the fact that there are, in contact with non-front vowels, unquestionable cases of *t corresponding to /tɬh/, which is in principle the unambiguous reflex of a palatal:

(36) *-táànó` 'five' -tɬhánʊ́ < °-cánu
*-tákųn- 'chew' -tɬháhún-á < °-cákųn-

Therefore, it seems preferable to reject the analysis of /s/ as the regular reflex of *t followed by *į, and to consider that in the following correspondences, the Tswana form is not directly related to the Proto-Bantu form beginning with *t, but rather to a variant with an initial *c[16]:

(37) *-tįngà 11 'sinew' lʊ̀-síká 'vein' < °dù-cį́nga
*-tį́g- 'leave behind' -sí-á < °-cį́g-
*-tįkù 14 'night' bʊ̀-síχʊ́ / mà-síχʊ́ < °bù-cį́ku

[16]The most plausible explanation from a historical point of view is that this partial merger of *t and *c observed in Tswana in the context ___*į reflects a variation in Proto-Bantu rather than a conditioned change taking place at some stage of the history of subgroup S.30.

5.5. Reflexes of Proto-Bantu consonants immediately followed by a vowel sequence

5.5.1. General remarks

In this section, a problem is that, given the scarcity of most combinations V_1V_2 in Bantu reconstructions, it is impossible to find satisfying illustrations for certain regularities of correspondence which are however very plausible, by analogy with other well-established correspondences.

The discussion is based on the assumption that vowel sequences whose first element is a vowel of degree 1 must be distinguished from those whose first element is a vowel of degree 2 or 3[17]. In at least some cases, the necessity of this distinction is obvious, and in such cases, the reflexes of consonants followed by a vowel sequence whose first element is a vowel of degree 2 or 3 have a more natural and more straightforward phonetic explanation than those conditioned by a vowel sequence whose first element is a vowel of degree 1. This suggests that historically, the change induced by vowel sequences whose first element is a vowel of degree 1 took place in a relatively distant past, so that the immediate result of this change may have been modified by subsequent evolutions.

5.5.2. Reflexes of Proto-Bantu consonants before a vowel sequence beginning with *į

On the basis of the available correspondences and of the existence of morphophonological alternations traceable to the influence of ancient vowel sequences on consonants, in spite of some problematic cases, it is reasonable to assume that before vowel sequences beginning with *į, the distinctions of place of articulation are neutralized, and that the only possible regular reflexes of Proto-Bantu consonants in such a context are /s/ (for consonants of series S_1 not preceded by a nasal), /tsh/ (for consonants of series S_1 preceded by a nasal), /ts/ (for consonants of series S_2, preceded by a nasal or not), and /ɲ/ (for consonants of series S_3). As already explained in section 5.4, identical reflexes are observed before a single vowel *į, but only for consonants belonging to orders O_3 and O_4. Note that, in Tswana forms corresponding to reconstructions with a vowel sequence begining with *į, the modification of the consonant is the only trace of the ancient presence of *į.

(38)	*-díkį- 'lead to pasture'	-dís-á	< °-dį́kį-
	*-bį́ad- 'give birth'	-tsál-á	
	*-bį́ada 1 'cross-cousin'	ǹtsálá / bó-ǹtsálá	< °mù-bį́ada
	*-bį́-uk- 'wake up and rise'	-tsώχ-á	

---

[17]Vowel sequences whose first element is /a/ never exert an influence on the preceding consonant.

*-gèd-į- 'try' -èts-à 'imitate'
*-búud-į- 'ask' -bɷ́ts-á
*-gį̀i 3 'village' mɷ̀-tsì / mì-tsì

5.5.3. Reflexes of Proto-Bantu consonants before a vowel sequence beginning with a front vowel of degree 2 or 3

In this section, *I* represents a front vowel of degree 2 or 3. It has been established in section 5.4 that the only consonants having special reflexes when followed by a front vowel of degree 2 or 3 are the consonants belonging to orders O3 and O4 (and among them, the consonants belonging to series S2 are concerned only when preceded by a nasal). These consonants can be expected to have the same reflexes when followed by a vowel sequence beginning with the same vowels, and the available illustrations confirm this hypothesis.

(39) *kI or *cI not preceded by a nasal > s / — V
*kI or *cI preceded by a nasal > tsh / — V
*gI or *jI preceded by a nasal > ts / — V

*-kígam-o 3 'head-rest' mɷ̀-sámɔ́ / mì-sámɔ́
< °mù-kíam-o
*-kíá 7 'stump of a tree' sì-sáná / dì-sáná
*-kí- 'dawn' s-á

Among the consonants having no special reflex when immediately followed by a single front vowel of degree 2 or 3, several correspondences provide evidence supporting the hypothesis of special reflexes before vowel sequences beginning with a front vowel of degree 2 or 3 in the case of *p ,*b and *d:

(40) *pI not preceded by a nasal > ʃ(w) / — V
*pI preceded by a nasal > tʃh(w) / — V
*-pí- 'become burnt' -ʃ(w)-á
*-píà 'new' -ʃ(w)á

(41) *bI not preceded by a nasal > ʤ(w) / — V
*bɨ preceded by a nasal > tʃ(w) / — V

*-béad- 'sow' -ʤ(w)ál-á

(42) *dI not preceded by a nasal > ʤ /___V [18]

*-dí- 'eat' -ʤ-á

*-dìàngò 3 'doorway' mʊ̀-ʤàkɔ̀ / mì-ʤàkɔ̀

Things are less clear in the case of the other consonants. Rules (43) are relatively productive in the morphology of Tswana, in particular in the formation of diminutives, but nothing ensures that these rules reflect in a straightforward way the historical evolution of the consonants in question. On the contrary, certain observations suggest that they involve at least a certain degree of confusion between weak and strong reflexes and between the modifications historically induced by semi-vowels originating from vowels of degree 1 and those induced by semi-vowels originating from vowels of degree 2 or 3; such confusions are not surprising if one takes into account that these rules concern mainly the formation of diminutives by suffixation, and that historically, this mechanism seems to be relatively recent.

(43) mI > ŋw /___V

rI > tsh /___V (/r/ is the regular reflex of *t)

lI > ʤ /___V (/l/ is the regular reflex of *d before a non-close vowel)

nI > ɲ /___V

5.5.4. Reflexes of Proto-Bantu consonants before a vowel sequence beginning with *ų

On the basis of the available correspondences and of the existence of morphophonological alternations traceable to the influence of ancient vowel sequences on consonants, in spite of some problematic cases, it is not unreasonable to assume that before vowel sequences beginning with *ų, in the same way as before vowel sequences beginning with *į, the distinctions of place of articulation are neutralized, and that the only possible regular reflexes of consonants in such a context are /s/ (for consonants of series S_{1a}), /tsh/ (for consonants of series S_{1b}), /ts/ (for consonants of series S_{2a} and S_{2b}) and /ɲ/ (for consonants of series S_3). A difference with the case of the vowel sequences beginning with *į is that *ų followed by another vowel is represented in the corresponding Tswana forms by the semi-vowel /w/.

---

[18]In the absence of correspondences illustrating this configuration, it is difficult to propose a hypothesis for the case of *dI in the context *N — V*, since in most Tswana dialects, /ʤ/ constitutes an exception to the rules of alternation between the consonants of series S_{2a} and S_{2b}.

(44)	*-kṵ́- 'die'	-sw-á	
	*-kṵ́á 14 'heritage'	bὼ-swá	
	*-kṵ́ù 11 'death'	lὼ-sώ	
	*-bṵ́ang- 'mix'	-tswák-á	
	*-dṵ̀- 'come out, come from'	-tsw-à	
	*-gṵ́ɪ̀ 3 'arrow'	mὼ-tswɪ́ / mɪ̀-tswɪ́	< °mù-gṵ́ḭ
	*-jámṵ- 'suck the breast'	-áɲ(w)-a	< °-ámṵ

5.5.5. Reflexes of Proto-Bantu consonants before a vowel sequence beginning with a back vowel of degree 2 or 3

In this section, *U* represents a back vowel of degree 2 or 3. By contrast with the case of vowel sequences beginning with a front vowel of degree 2 or 3, it is relatively easy to establish the regularities concerning the reflexes of consonants followed by vowel sequences beginning with a back vowel of degree 2 or 3, because the rules of formation of passives by adjunction of -w- (reflex of *-u-) can be considered as reflecting the historical changes involving such vowel sequences. Special reflexes conditioned by a vowel sequence beginning with a back vowel of degree 2 or 3 are observed only for the consonants belonging to order O_1:

(45)	*pU not preceded by a nasal	> ʃ(w) / — V	
	*pU preceded by a nasal	> ʃh(w) / — V	
	*-pòḭ́ 'ostrich'	ɲ̀tʃh(w)é / bó-ɲ̀tʃh(w)é	
(46)	*bU not preceded by a nasal	> ʤ(w) / — V	
	*bU preceded by a nasal	> ʧ(w) / — V	
	*-jànḭ́ 14 'leaf, grass'	bὼ-ʤàŋ́ grass	< °bù-bù-ànḭ
	*-búà 9 'dog'	ɲ̀-ʧ(w)á / dìɲ̀-ʧ(w)á	
(47)	*mU > ŋw / — V		
	*-jédḭ 3/15 'moonshine'	ŋwèdí	< °mù-édḭ
	*-jánà 1 'child'	ŋw-àná / b-àná	< °mù-ána
	*-jàdí 1 'girl'	ŋw-àlí / b-àlɪ́	< °mù-àdí
	*-mòḭ̀ 'one'	-ŋwɪ̀	

6. The Tswana forms corresponding to protoforms beginning with *jį (or *yį) and related questions

6.1. Problems raised by the Tswana forms corresponding to reconstructions beginning with *jį (or *yį)

6.1.1. General remarks

The following chart gives the entire list of the Tswana forms for which a plausible correspondence can be proposed with Bantu reconstructions with a first syllable *jį (or *yį) representing comparative series with a relatively wide geographical distribution:

(48)			
	*-jį́n- 'dip'	-ín-á	< °-į́n-
	*-jį̀n-am- 'bend down'	-ìnàm-à	< °-į̀n-am-
	*-jį́nà 5 'name'	lì-íná / mà-íná	< °dì-gína
	*-jį́nò 5 'tooth'	lì-ínɔ / mɛ̀nɔ́	< °dì-gíno/°mà-íno
	*-jį́ngí 'many'	-ńtsí	< °-n-į́ngį
	*-jį́ngid- 'enter'	-tsɛ́n-	< °-ngén-
	*-jį́b- 'steal'	-ʊtsw-á	< °-ɲbų-
	*-jį̀j- 'come'	-tł-à	< °-nj̀- ~ °-į̀nj-[19]
	*-jį́j-ad- 'become full'	-tłál-á	< °-njád-
	*-jį́ji(b)- 'know'	-ítsí[20]	< °-į́nji
	*-jį́jì 6 'water'	mètsí ~ mètsí	< °mà-į́nji ~ °mà-į́njį
	*-jį́jùkùdù 1 'grand-child'	mʊ̀-tłʊ́χʊ́lʊ́ / bà-tłʊ́χʊ́lʊ́	< °mù-njúkúdú
	*-jį́gų- 'hear'	-útłw-á	< °-ɲnjų-
	*-jį́gų̀à 3 'thorn'	mútłwá / mítłwá	< °-mù-į́njųa
	*-jį̀p-ud- 'serve food'	-tshʊ̀l-a	< °-mpį̀-ud-
	*-jį̀t-id- 'pour'	-tshɛ̀l-à	< °-ntį̀-id-
	*-jį́cò 5 'eye'	lì-ítłhɔ́ / mà-tłhɔ́	< °dì-gíco / °mà-có
	*-jį́kut- 'become satisfied'	-qhʊ́r-á	< °-nkút-
	*-jį̀kò 11 'ladle'	lʊ̀-sɔ̀ / dìǹ-tshɔ̀	< °dù-kį̀ò

[19]The variant °-į̀nj- accounts for the fact that, in contact with this root, the morpheme *-a-* marking the disjunctive form of the present positive may change into *-e-*.

[20]See note 8.

*-jį̀kò 5 'hearth'	lì-ísɔ́ / mà-ísɔ́	< °dì-gį́kį̀o
*-jį́ncí 3 'daytime' 'middle of the day'	mʊ̀-tshíχàrí	< °mù-ncí-kàtí
*-jį̀ncì 3 'pestle'	mʊ̀-tshì / mì-tshì	< °mù-ncì

It is interesting to add the following three correspondences, in spite of the fact that they rely on comparative series with a relatively limited geographical distribution, because they show the same particularities and therefore confirm the existence of a specific problem:

(49)	*-jįp- 'clear away'	-ǹtsh-à 'take out'	< °-nį̀mpį-
	*-jįkab- 'perforate'	-tɬhàb-à	< °-càb-
	*-jįtuk- 'become startled'	-tshʊ̀χ-à	< °-ntį̀uk-

It is striking that, out of the 25 correspondences listed above, only 2 (the first two in the list) conform with the regularities established in the preceding chapters. In most cases, the protoform from which the Tswana form could be predicted by applying in a mechanical way the rules accounting for these regularities is more or less different from the current reconstruction of the root in question.

Some of the irregularities observed here concern only a small number of cases, and therefore can hardly be considered as typical of the reconstructions beginning with *jį (ou *yį); however, their accumulation is somewhat surprising; let us have a quick look at them:

- in four cases, Tswana has an unambiguous trace of an ancient initial consonant, which suggests rather a protoform with an initial *g (*-jį́nà 5 'name', *-jį́kò 5 'hearth'), sometimes in variation with a protoform devoid of initial consonant (*-jį́nò 5 'tooth'), and sometimes in variation with a protoform in which the first syllable is absent (*-jį́cò 5 'eye');
- in three cases (*-jį́gų 'hear', *-jį́gų̀à 'thorn' et *-jįkab- 'perforate') the Tswana form has the unambiguous reflex of a palatal, whereas the corresponding consonant in the reconstructed form is a velar;
- in three cases, the Tswana form has a vowel different from the regular reflex of the vowel of the reconstructed form; this difference may be the result of assimilation processes, but it cannot be considered as regular: *-jį́ngí 'many', *-jį́jì 6 'water,' *-jį́gų 'hear'; in the case of *-jį́ngid- 'enter', the presence of /ɛ/ in the Tswana form is regular if we assume that this vowel belongs to a frozen extension (see section 4.4.2); the same can be said about *-jį̀t-id- 'pour';
- in the case of *-jį́b- 'steal' and *-jįp- 'clear away', the Tswana form points to a protoform with an additional vowel;
- in the case of *-jį́ngid- 'enter' and *-jįp- 'clear away', the Tswana form points to a protoform with a nasal consonant instead of *d (in the case of *-jį́ngid- 'enter') or of *j (in the case of *-jįp- 'clear away').

But what is particularly interesting is that certain of the irregularities observed in the correspondences listed above, either have an obvious phonetic relation with the structure of the reconstructions in question, or occur with such a frequency that the question of their relation with the reconstruction of an initial syllable *ji̧ (ou *yi̧) must be raised, even if at first sight the nature of this relation is not obvious.

6.1.2. The absence of reflex of the first syllable in many Tswana forms corresponding to reconstructions beginning with *ji̧ (ou *yi̧)

As a rule, the number of syllables of a Tswana form is equal to the number of vowels in the corresponding Bantu reconstruction, except in cases when the Bantu reconstruction includes a vowel sequence (see section 2.4). Given this regularity, the absence of a syllabic reflex of the first syllable in a relatively great number of Tswana forms corresponding to Bantu reconstructions with a first syllable *ji̧ (or *yi̧) calls for an explanation. This phenomenon occurs in 12 cases (out of 25):

(50)	*-jí̧ngid- ‘enter’	-tsɛ́n-	< °-ngén-
	*-jì̧j- ‘come’	-tɬ-à	< °-nj̀- ~ °-ì̧nj-
	*-jí̧j-ad- ‘become full’	-tɬál-á	< °-njád-
	*-jí̧jùkùdù 1 ‘grand-child’	mὼ-tɬώχώlώ / bà-tɬώχώlώ	< °mù-njúkúdú
	*-jì̧p-ud- ‘serve food’	-tshὼl-à	< °-mpì̧-ud-
	*-jì̧t-id- ‘pour’	-tshɛ̀l-à	< °-ntì̧-id-
	*-ji̧tuk- ‘become startled’	-tshὼχ-à	< °-ntì̧uk-
	*-ji̧kab- ‘perforate’	-tɬhàb-à	< °-càb-
	*-jí̧kut- ‘become satisfied’	-qhώr-á	< °-nkút-
	*-jì̧kò 11 ‘ladle’	lὼ-sɔ̀ / dìǹ-tshɔ̀	< °dù-kì̧ò
	*-jí̧ncí 3 ‘daytime’	mὼ-tshíχàrí ‘middle of the day’	< °mù-ncí-kàtí
	*-jì̧ncì 3 ‘pestle’	mὼ-tshì / mì-tshì	< °mù-ncì

This phenomenon can certainly be considered as a confirmation of the hypothesis according to which, at least in the variety of Proto-Bantu which was the direct ancestor of the languages of subgroup S.30, the stems for which Guthrie proposes a reconstruction with an initial *y were in fact devoid of initial consonant (see section 2.5). But it points also to an ancient process of initial *i̧ deletion, whereas nothing similar seems to have affected the other initial vowels.

However, a certain number of Bantu roots reconstructed by Guthrie with a first syllable *yi̧ (which consequently had presumably an initial *i̧ in the direct ancestor of the languages of subgroup S.30) were not affected by this process of initial *į deletion, and it does not seem possible to propose a rule according to which this deletion could be considered as regular iff certain conditions were met.

6.1.3. The irregular presence of strong reflexes in many Tswana forms corresponding to reconstructions beginning with *jį (or *yį)

Out of the 25 correspondences listed in 6.1.1, in 4 cases the first syllable *jį (or *yį) of the reconstructed form is immediately followed by a sequence NC, and the Tswana form has the strong reflex of the consonant in question, which is perfectly regular. But a strong reflex is present in 12 other cases in which no sequence NC is present in the reconstructed form:

(51)	*-jı̀j- 'come'	-tł-à	< °-nj̀- ~ °-ı̀nj-
	*-jíj-ad- 'become full'	-tłál-á	< °-njád-
	*-jíji(b)- 'know'	-ítsí	< °-ínji-
	*-jíjì 6 'water'	mètsí ~ mètsí	< °mà-ínji ~ °mà-ínjį
	*-jíjùkùdù 1 'grand-child'	mò-tłóχólò / bà-tłóχólò	< °mù-njúkúdú
	*-jígų- 'hear'	-útłw-á	< °-ųnjų-
	*-jígų̀à 3 'thorn'	mútłwá / mítłwá	< °-mù-ínjųa
	*-jįp- 'clear away'	-ǹtsh-à 'take out'	< °-nı̀mpį-
	*-jı̀p-ud- 'serve food'	-tshò l-à	< °-mpı̀-ud-
	*-jįtuk- 'become startled'	-tshòχ-à	< °-ntı̀uk-
	*-jı̀t-id- 'pour'	-tshèl-à	< °-ntı̀-id-
	*-jíkut- 'become satisfied'	-qhór-á	< °-nkút-

Moreover, compared to the 12 cases of unambiguous strong reflexes contradicting the absence of a sequence NC in the reconstructed form, the list of 25 correspondences given in section 6.1.1 includes only 2 cases of unambiguous weak reflexes, and one of them concerns a correspondence in which the Tswana form points rather to a protoform with an initial *g:

(52)	*-jı̀kò 11 'ladle'	lò-sò / dı̀n-tshò	< °dù-kı̀ò
	*-jíkò 5 'hearth'	lì-ísó / mà-ísó	< °dì-gíkio

Therefore, there is a very strong statistical correlation between the presence of what was presumably an initial *į and the occurrence of the strong reflex of the following consonant in the corresponding Tswana form. From a strictly formal point of view, this could be accounted for by enlarging the definition of the contexts conditioning the choice of strong reflexes: a rule according to which the context *≠ i̧ — (or perhaps *yi̧ — , or *i̧ — with the condition that no consonant precedes immediately i̧) requires the choice of strong reflexes would account for a relatively great number of correspondences and would leave only very few exceptions. It remains however the problem of the historical and phonetic interpretation of such a rule. At least two scenarios can be imagined, if we accept the current hypothesis that no nasal was present at the onset of the second syllable of most Proto-Bantu forms currently reconstructed with a first syllable *ji̧ (or *yi̧):

- A first hypothesis, already suggested by Eiselen (1924), is that *i̧ exerted on the following consonant the same influence as a nasal; the fact that some languages (outside of subgroup S.30) have nasals in the reflexes of the roots in question does not contradict this hypothesis, since these nasals might have been introduced later by analogy with the more common situation in which strong reflexes co-occur with nasals.
- Another hypothesis, already proposed by Bourquin (1932-3) is that at a first stage *i̧ induced the insertion of a nasal which consequently exerted its influence on the following consonant.

However, neither of these two solutions is entirely satisfactory, since both rely on the hypothesis of phonetic changes whose naturalness is at least questionable. The possibility of Proto-Bantu forms including both *i̧ and a nasal should perhaps be seriously considered. But such a question cannot be solved on the basis of a single language (or of a single group of languages). Tswana data unquestionably shows that there is a problem with a certain type of reconstructions whose relation with the corresponding Tswana forms cannot by described in a simple and satisfactory way, but it would not make sense to propose a solution before testing its compatibility with the data of a variety of languages belonging to different subgroups of the Bantu family.

6.1.4. Cases in which a consonant following *ji̧ (ou *yi̧) is treated by Tswana as if it were followed by a vowel sequence beginning with *i̧

Among the irregularities observed in the list of correspondences given in section 6.1.1, the one we are going to examine now is from a statistical point of view less important than those examined in sections 6.1.2 and 6.1.3, but it is not less interesting, because it suggests a fairly natural explanation of the alternations affecting the initial consonant of certain noun stems when they combine with the prefix of class 5 (see section 6.2). In the following 6 correspondences, the consonant constituting the onset of the second syllable in the reconstructed form is represented in Tswana by a consonant which could be its regular reflex before a vowel sequence beginning with *i̧:

(53) *-jịp- 'clear away' -ǹtsh-à 'take out' < °-nịmpị-
*-jị̀p-ud- 'serve food' -tshʊ̀l-à < °-mpị̀-ud-
*-jịtuk- 'become startled' -tshʊ̀χ-à < °-ntị̀uk-
*-jị̀t-id- 'pour' -tshɛ̀l-à < °-ntị̀-id-
*-jị̀kò 11 'ladle' lʊ̀-sɔ̀ / dìǹ-tshɔ̀ < °dù-kị̀ò
*-jị́kò 5 'hearth' lì-ísɔ́ / mà-ísɔ́ < °dì-gị́kịo

First, it is important to observe that in 5 cases out of 6, the Tswana consonant unambiguously points to the presence of a vowel sequence beginning with *ị, and that this problem could not be solved by proposing a variant of the reconstructed form with a palatal consonant, since the Tswana reflexes of palatals not followed by front vowels are lateral plosives.

The second important observation is that, by contrast with the question discussed in section 6.1.3., a plausible phonetic explanation of this irregularity can be proposed, according to which a copy of *ị was inserted immediately after the following consonant:

(54) ị C V > ị C ị V

It must however be emphasized that this cannot be considered as a general property of *ị, since there is no trace of such a phenomenon in the Tswana reflexes of reconstructed forms where *ị constitutes the nucleus of a syllable whose onset is a non-problematic consonant. Therefore, it seems reasonable to assume that this process was limited to occurrences of *ị not immediately preceded by a consonant (which once again supports the hypothesis that, at least in the direct ancestor of the languages of the Sotho-Tswana subgroup, the stems currently reconstructed with an initial *y were in fact devoid of initial consonant).

6.2. Consonant reflexes in contact with the prefix of class 5

When Tswana noun stems originating from a Proto-Bantu root combine with the prefix of class 5, in most cases the initial consonant of the root in question is represented by its regular reflex as described in section 5. However, in a certain number of cases, we observe in combination with the prefix of class 5 an initial consonant different from the regular reflex of the initial consonant of the reconstructed root. Leaving aside a few problematic cases the following list can be established:

(55) *-bókò 5 'arm' lì-tsɔ́χɔ́ / mà-bɔ́χɔ́
*-búmb- 'mould pottery' -bʊ́p-á > lì-tsʊ́pá 'clay'

*-támà 5 'cheek' lì-sámá / mà-rámá
*-tambo 5 'bone' lì-sápɔ́ / mà-rápɔ́
*-tàngá 5 'cattle-post' lì-sàká / mà-ràká
*-tákò 5 'buttock' lì-sáχɔ́ / mà-ráχɔ́

*-dìm-	'cultivate'	-lɩ̀m-à > lɩ̀-tsɩ̀mà	'communal work in the fields'
*-dàmb-	be hungry	-làp-à 'be tired' > lɩ̀-tsàpà	'tiredness'
*-kúmį	5 'ten'	lɩ̀-sɷ́mɛ́	

It is important to observe that this irregularity disappears when the same stems combine with other prefixes[21], and that in the case of deverbative stems, the initial consonant of the verb is the regular reflex of the initial consonant of the reconstructed root.

But the crucial observation is that, in all the correspondences listed above, the form of class 5 would be perfectly regular (with the only exception of the final vowel of *lɩ̀-sɷ́mɛ́*) if an additional *į were present immediately after the initial consonant of the stem:

(56)
lɩ̀-tsɔ́χɔ́ < °lì-bį́oko
lɩ̀-tsɷ́pá < °lì-bį́umba

lɩ̀-sámá < °lì-tį́ama
lɩ̀-sápɔ́ < °lì-tį́ambo
lɩ̀-sàká < °lì-tį̀àngá
lɩ̀-sáχɔ́ < °lì-tį́ako

lɩ̀-tsɩ̀mà < °lì-dį̀ìmà
lɩ̀-tsàpà < °lì-dį̀àmbà

lɩ̀-sɷ́mɛ́ < °lì-kį́ume

This is reminiscent of the observations made in section 6.1.4, and the same phonetic explanation can be considered.

In section 6.1.4 we have observed that it is not infrequent that a consonant immediately preceded by *į is treated in Tswana as if it were immediately followed by a vowel sequence beginning with *į, provided the *į in question does not form a syllable in combination with a non-problematic consonant, and that in addition to that, such a *į tends to be deleted and to leave the modification of the following consonant as the only trace of its ancient presence.

In this connexion, it must be kept in mind that the current grammatical reconstructions (see Meeussen (1967)) suggest that the present prefix of class 5 of Tswana (lɩ̀-) originates in a reanalysis of the ancient augment of class 5, and that the prefix of class 5 was originally *į̀-. Consequently, the prefix of class 5 of Tswana can be considered as the reflex of *di-į-. Starting from that, a possible explanation of the alternations affecting certain noun stems in combination with the prefix of class 5 is that *į representing the

[21] Note however that the situation is becoming confused, and that Tswana speakers tend to use indiscriminately both forms of such stems with the prefix of class 5 and with the prefix of class 6.

ancient prefix of class 5 was involved in the same processes as the presumably initial *ị of the stems whose Tswana reflexes have been analyzed in section 6.1, with which it shared the property of not constituting the nucleus of a syllable CV: it has never been maintained as a distinct syllable nucleus, which is perfectly regular since it was always immediately preceded by another vowel (see 2.5.2), but the following consonant may be treated by Tswana as if it were followed by a vowel sequence beginning with *ị, a possible explanation being the insertion of a copy of *ị immediately after the consonant in question, as proposed in section 6.1.4.

Moreover, in some cases, Tswana consonants which are in principle strong reflexes of Proto-Bantu consonants occur as the result of the alternation induced by the prefix of class 5, and a nasal is even present in the singular form of the Tswana reflex of the following Bantu root:

(57) *-bùè 5 'stone' lɪ̀-ǹtswɛ̀ / mà-ʤɛ̀

Note that the plural stem is the regular reflex of *-bùè (see section 5.5.5) whereas the singular stem implies the influence both of a nasal and of a vowel sequence beginning with *ị, since in the context *N* ___ *ue*, /tʃ/ would be expected instead of /ts/ (see sections 5.5.2 and 5.5.5)

This confirms the similarity between the phenomena occurring at the junction between prefix and stem in class 5 and those characterizing the reflexes of roots currently reconstructed with a first syllable *yị. However, in the case of the prefix of class 5 an additional complication follows from the fact that a morphological (rather than phonological) explanation of strong reflexes occuring at the initial of noun stems is always possible.

6.3. The reflexive prefix

It is interesting to examine the properties of the reflexive prefix (or mid-voice prefix) of Tswana in the light of the observations presented in sections 6.1 and 6.2; the point is that this prefix, although invariably represented by *-i-* , exerts on the initial of the stem exactly the same influence as a nasal: when the stem begins with a consonant constituting from the historical point of view the weak reflex of a Proto-Bantu consonant, in contact with the reflexive prefix the strong reflex of the same Proto-Bantu consonant is substituted for it. For example, the reflexive form of *-bɔ́n-á* 'see' < *-bón-is *-í-pɔ́n-á*.

An important observation is that, by contrast with the noun prefixes of class 9 and 10 (which modify the initial of noun stems exactly in the same way as the reflexive prefix modifies the initial of verb stems), even in the case of monosyllabic stems, no nasal occurs at the junction of the reflexive morpheme and of the verb stem to which it is prefixed (for example, the reflexive form of *-f-á* give is *-í-ph-á* appropriate—compare with *m̀-ph-ɔ́* / *dìm̀-phɔ́* gift). Therefore, the hypothesis of a protoform like °-ịn- would be in contradiction with the rule according to which, given a sequence *NC where N belongs to a prefix whereas C constitutes the initial of a monosyllabic stem, N changes into a L-toned nasal (see 2.2.3). On the other hand, the hypothesis of a protoform °-į- is not satisfactory either, since it implies the generalization of a phonetic process (the insertion of a nasal immediately after *į) whose motivation remains somewhat mysterious.

6.4. The Tswana reflexes of *-kádį́ 1 woman

A regular reflex of *-kádį́ 1 woman is attested in Tswana:

(58) *-kádį́ 1 'woman' bʊ̀-χádí 'cattle given to the girl's family to conclude marriage negotiations'

However, the Tswana word for «woman» is *mʊ̀-sádí / bà-sádí*, and it is at first sight not obvious wether it must be considered as related to this root or as having an entirely different origin.

A popular etymology, motivated by the traditional distribution of roles in Tswana society, relates *mʊ̀-sádí* to the verb *-sál-á* 'remain, stay': *Mosadi ke mosala-gae* 'A woman is a person staying at home'. This etymology is perfectly possible from a strictly morphological point of view, but it is nevertheless dubious, since the possibility of the semantic shift 'person staying (at home)' > 'woman' does not seem to be confirmed by other languages. The facts observed in this chapter suggest rather considering the possibility of a relationship with the Bantu root reconstructed as *-kádį́.

The Tswana stem *-sádí* cannot be the regular reflex of *-kádį́, but it could be a regular reflex of °-kį́adį. On the other hand, in ràqhádí paternal aunt it is possible to isolate *-qhádí*, which could be a regular reflex of °-nkádį. In other words, the possible Tswana reflexes of the Bantu root for 'woman' point to an ancient variation °-kádį ~ *-nkádį ~ -kį́adį*.

Given the observations about the Tswana reflexes of Bantu reconstructions with a first syllable *jį (or *yį) and the alternations affecting the initial of noun stems combining with the prefix of class 5, a plausible hypothesis is that °-kį́adį comes from a more ancient form °-į́kadį whose initial was involved in the variation *į ~ įn ~ n ~ Ø* described in section 6.1[22]; this does not provide an explanation, but it is not uninteresting to observe that the list of the Bantu roots whose reflexes point to such a variation could probably be extended by the addition of roots whose current reconstruction does not include a first syllable *jį or *yį.

7. Conclusion

Problems of Bantu reconstruction cannot be solved on the basis of data limited to a single language or to a single subgroup of languages. But a careful examination of the correspondences between the current reconstructions and the lexicon of a particular Bantu language is nevertheless

[22]Bourquin (1932-3) puts forward a similar hypothesis for the Bantu root currently reconstructed as *-ntʊ̀ 'human being', arguing that the reflexes of this root in some Bantu languages point to protoforms like *-ì(n)tʊ̀.

useful, since specific difficulties in establishing regular correspondences in the particular case of reconstructed forms presenting certain configurations are an indication that perhaps certain current hypotheses should be revised. In the particular case of Tswana, the contrast between the obvious regularity of most correspondences and the extreme difficulty in establishing regularities in the case of reconstructions of the type examined in section 6 is absolutely striking. It would not be wise to propose a revision of these reconstructions (and possibly of other reconstructions whose reflexes raise similar problems—see section 6.4) on the sole basis of the difficulties encountered in trying to find rules accounting for their relation with the corresponding forms in this particular language, but I would not be surprised if a detailed study of their reflexes in other languages confirmed the necessity of a revision.

References

Bourquin, W. 1932-3. Entstehung von Nasalen durch den Einfluss von i in Bantu, *Zeitschrift für Eingeborenen Sprachen* XXIII: 195-202.

Cole, D. T. 1955. *An Introduction to Tswana Grammar*, Longman, Cape Town.

De Wolf, P. P. 1981. Consonant Change from Proto-Bantu to Northern Sotho and Multivalued Feature Expression, *Africana Marburgensia* 14.2: 11-42.

Dickens, P. 1977. Grammar Simplification via Rule Inversion: The Effect of Historical Deletion of Nasals on Modern Sotho, *African Studies* 36: 161-70.

Dickens, P. 1984. The History of So-called Strengthening in Tswana, *Journal of African Languages and Linguistics* 6.2: 97-125.

Dickens, P. 1986. *Qhalaxarzi Phonology*, University of the Witwatersrand, Johannesburg.

Eiselen, W. 1924. Die Veränderungen des Konsonanten durch ein vohergehendes i in den Bantusprachen, *Zeitschrift für Eingeborenen Sprachen* XIV: 81-153.

Guthrie, M. 1967-71. *Comparative Bantu*, 4 vols, Gregg International, Farnborough.

Janssens, B. 1993. *Doubles réflexes consonantiques: quatre études sur le bantou de zone A*, PhD thesis, Université libre de Bruxelles, Brussels.

Malepe, A. T. 1968. Classification of Tswana Dialects, *Limi* 5: 61-68.

Meeussen, A. E. 1967. Bantu Grammatical Reconstructions, *Africana Linguistica* III: 79-121.

Meeussen, A. E. 1980. *Bantu Lexical Reconstructions*, Musée Royal de l'Afrique Centrale, Tervuren, Belgium, Archives d'anthropologie n° 27.

Ponelis, F. 1973. *Studies in Northern Sotho Phonological Dynamics*, University of South Africa, Pretoria.

Tucker, A. N. 1929. *The Comparative Phonetics of the Suto-Chuana Group of Bantu Languages*, Longmans, Green & Co., Londres.

Vowel Systems and Spirantization in Southwest Tanzania

CATHERINE LABROUSSI
Institut National des Langues et Civilisations Orientales, Paris

The aim of the present paper is to examine the nature of the relationship between two well known historical evolutions in Bantu, spirantization and vowel reduction. Supportive data, first- as well as second-hand, come from the Lake Corridor Area in Southwestern Tanzania and small adjoining territories of Zambia and Malawi; they cover Guthrie's M.10, 20 and 30 groups, plus Wungu (F.25), Kinga (G.65), Ngonde (unclassified but clearly belonging to M.30). Other languages like Bemba (M.42) or Holoholo have also been taken into consideration, although to a lesser extent. In the following sections, I will briefly refer to current views on the topic (§1), establish a methodological distinction (§2) on the basis of which all data will be examined and categorized (§3); I will then proceed to the interpretation of the data, by proposing a historical scenario of a 2-stages structural evolution for spirantization and its incidence on the vowel system (§4), completed and counterbalanced by a consideration of the role that non-genetic (i.e., areal and sociolinguistic) factors have played in the formation of the current situation (§5). Some general conclusions on the main topic of this paper will be formulated in section §6.

1. Background

Previous treatments of this issue have not failed to stress the apparent interdependence of occurrence between these two major phonological changes in Bantu: "...for reduction to occur when spirantization does is so widely attested, giving the impression that it is a necessary adjunct of the change, *that for it not to happen, is quite surprising*" (Hinnebusch 1981:72, my own italics).

At the same time it has been acknowledged that as general as this co-occurrence can be, it doesn't seem to involve any direct causal relationship between the two changes, in the form of either a drag-chain or a push-chain: "I consider both changes as being independently well motivated, and while admitting *the possibility that the phonological system as such may favour or disfavour certain changes*, I argue that areal norm and areal spread are the major reasons for the widespread combined occurrence of spirantization and 7>5, in that (apparent) order" (Schadeberg 1995:73, my own italics). In more specific structural terms, the interdependence that characterizes the two changes lies, not in direct push- or drag-chain relations, but in the dynamics of the overall phonological system: "I suggest that t*he vowel system is protected precisely by the poverty of the consonantal feature system*" (Schadeberg 1995:81, my own italics).

While fully agreeing with Schadeberg on the independence, the structural conditions (see italicized quotations above) and the influence of an areal norm in the spread of such phonetic changes as vowel reduction, I will try to elucidate, based on more extensive regional data:

(1) The reason for the seemingly atypical behaviour of spirantizing/7-vowel (7V) languages, most of which are situated in and around the Lake Corridor.

(2) Any further structural implications that underlie this 'chain-reaction' evolution of spirantization followed by—but not preceded by (see Schadeberg 1995)—the 7V>5V merger.

(3) The extent to which areal diffusion has played a role in each one of these changes.

2. Method of approach

Before we examine the linguistic facts in the Corridor, we should explicitly distinguish two aspects of the same phenomenon, called in a general way 'Spirantization':

(1) Historically speaking, the phonetically-motivated (C+high vowel) process, through incremental steps, ended up in the fricativization of stops (*pį > ... > fi). As a result, a new correlation ([±continuant]) and new phonemes (/f/ + increased occurrence of /s/ or /f, v/ + increased occurrence of /s, z/) were finally introduced in the phonological system of the evolving languages (cf. also §3.1.1.).

(2) Synchronically speaking, an active morphophonemic process of spirant/stop alternations (for example p/f, t/s, k/s), where the spirant is phonologically determined by a following (surfacing or underlying) High vowel. These alternations occur in certain predefined morphological

contexts. Four such contexts have been isolated, in reference to Proto-Bantu (PB) (reconstructions from Meeussen 1967):

(a) *-ụ (adjectival derivation suffix)

(b) *-į- (causative extension)

(c) *-į (nominal—and especially agentive—derivation suffix)

(d) *-įde (perfective and/or past tense ending)

Where this morphophonemic (MP) mechanism occurs, the feature of |MP Alternation| is added to the definition of the morphemes, associated to the above-mentioned morphs—see for instance Nyakyusa {causative}:

Morph 1: |-i-| (phonetically realized as a Glide) + |MP alternation in stem-final consonant|, {direct}: 'do/cause sth. on s.o. or sth.'[1]

Morph 2: |-Isi-| (phonetically realized as either [-isy-] or [-esy-]),[2] {indirect}: 'make s.o. do/cause sth.'

3. The data

When the data are examined in the light of the distinction outlined above—and especially with regard to the second synchronic aspect of spirantization—a pattern emerges.[3] More specifically, some morphological contexts are more or less universally affected by spirantization, others are less frequently affected. An hierarchy of these contexts according to universal presence of spirantization gives (from more frequent to less frequent):

(1) *The interior of morphemes*, both affixes and verbal/nominal stems, that is where no morphological border separates the consonant from the following (surfacing or underlying) High vowel. Spirantization is attested morpheme-internally in all languages of the corpus, although for the same context, it is only partially present in Holoholo (cf.§3.1.4).

---

[1]I have not attempted a detailed study of the modalities of the causative yet, so this analysis may be overgeneralized. As it becomes clear from diachronic and comparative data though, this functional and semantic differentiation of the two Causative morphs, if it ever existed, is becoming fuzzed today.

[2]This compound causative morph reflects either Common Bantu item *-ic-, CS 2187 or *-ikį- CS 2191a (Guthrie 1967-70, 4:215, 216). The first underspecified vowel is harmonizing with the vowel of the verb stem.

[3]The data are presented in broad phonetic transcription (sometimes indicated as [ ]), except when specified otherwise: namely, slashes / / have been used to indicate a phonemic transcription with no reference to the morphophonemic situation—somewhat in the classical structuralist way—or the output of morphophonemic rules. Vertical bars indicate a morphophonemic transcription, i.e. the underlying representation of a lexeme. Note that the International Phonetic Alphabet has been used throughout. Vowel length has been noted in all contexts (i.e. both contrastive and phonetically-determined) only in the case of languages where it is phonemic. Tones, being irrelevant to this discussion, are omitted even in the proto-Bantu items.

(2) *Adjectival *-ų and causative *-į-*. These two MP contexts are the most frequently spirantizing, since they are associated with spirantization in every language in which they appear. However, the first is not present in all corpus languages and the second is, in some languages, competing with another non-spirantizing causative morph (cf. §3.1. and §4.1.2.)

(3) Agentive **-į*. Inter-linguistic and intra-systemic variation is observed, as in some languages, this context is systematically spirantizing, while in others it is only partially or sporadically so.

(4) *Past/Perfect tense *-įde*. It is the least affected MP context across languages. Bastin 1983 arrives at the same conclusion while examining the frequency of consonant modifications before *-įde (see for instance her remarks on page 27) compared to that of other spirantizing contexts and especially of causative *-į-.

Presence/Absence of MP alternation before the last spirantizing context *-įde is here considered as the decisive criterion for the categorization of some linguistic systems as "fully spirantizing" as well as for the historical interpretation that will follow, due to the fact that *-įde is the most general and most productive of all four spirantizing contexts. For, while not all verbal stems can yield a—semantically and pragmatically acceptable—nominal or adjectival derivative, nor, similarly, do all verbal bases permit causativization, every verb has a past or perfect tense in its inflectional paradigm. As will be further argued in §4.1.2, adopting and promoting spirantization as a morphophonemic feature of this past tense, spreads this change all through the verbal system, thus rendering it irreversible. In that sense, and since all other environments in my corpus languages have been more extensively affected by this historical innovation, spirantization before *-įde cannot but be the last, and most decisive, step of the whole process.

The synchronic situation can also be viewed as a continuum. At the same time, the data analysis attempted in the following section suggests that 7V languages tend to cluster around one of its poles, namely the least affected by spirantization (cf. also Table 10 in §4). A simplified version of this continuum is presented here, as this evolution is undoubtedly more gradual than the discrete categories distinguished below would lead us to believe:

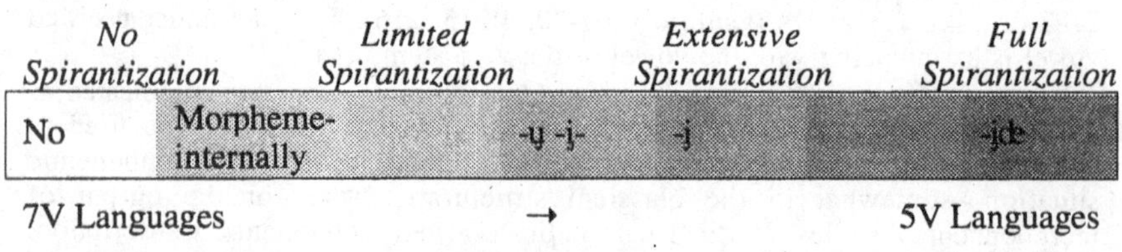

Figure 1. Continuum of evolution for spirantization and vowel reduction

In the next section, I will present the data following this pattern. Thus, the two polar situations (i.e., no or limited spirantization + 7V vs. full spirantization + 5V) will be examined first, followed by other cases found, called Intermediate by virtue of the intermediate positions they occupy in the continuum when the combination of their spirantizating pattern and their vowel system is taken into account. The relation between this spirantization pattern and the evolution of 7V- to 5V systems will be fully discussed in sections §4 and §5. Note that most PB items figuring in the examples are taken from Meeussen [1980], while some come from Guthrie's Common Bantu Comparative Series (1967-70).

3.1. Limited spirantization in 7V Languages

3.1.1. Nyakyusa

As an example of this situation, Nyakyusa (M.30) has 7 phonemic vowels, which are rather clearcut in terms of audibility and seem to be stable as far as the possibility of an oncoming merger is concerned. Furthermore, vowel length is clearly phonemic. The spirantizing process, where it applies, gives the following results:

*(N)b, p	/__į	>	fi	(N = Homorganic Nasal)
*(N)d, g, t, k	/__į	>	si	
*(N)b, d, g, p, t, k	/__ų	>	fu	

Table 1. Spirantization rules in Nyakyusa

In Table 1 we see (i) the merger of voiced and voiceless PB consonants in the Nyakyusa reflexes, (ii) the merger of all orders in front of the Back High vowel to only one labial reflex, and (iii) the phonetic rule which further eliminates non-syllabic nasals in front of spirants, keep the inventory of the newly introduced syllabic segments to two: [fi, fu].[4] For [s], due to its merging with the reflex of *c (> s), was not new in the system although spirantization increased its occurrence before High vowels. As a result, /s/ is now a fully settled phoneme, contrary to [f].[5] Regarding the phonetic impact of spirantization, Nyakyusa contrasts sharply with

---

[4]One could argue that, since linguistic change is not teleological (cf. Ohala 1993:262), the late and independently-motivated phonetic rule of nasal deletion should not be taken into account here and that the new syllabic segments introduced by spirantization are really four. The point I wish to make here is that, nasal deletion, whether it was a chained or an independent innovation, contributed to the maintainance of the 7 pre-spirantization vowels by further limiting the phonetic products of spirantization. These remarks fully concord with the position taken by Schadeberg (1995) cited in §1.

[5]Nevertheless, in spite of its still defective distribution, in this paper I consider /f/ in Nyakyusa and Ndali as a partially-integrated phoneme by virtue of its participation in the [±continuant] correlation together with his Alveolar counterpart /s/ and with his velar [+back] counterpart /h/.

Inamwanga, a language placed in the opposite pole of the continuum (cf. §3.2.1).

The same contrast exists in the morphophonemic domain, as in Nyakyusa not all possible morphophonemic environments have been affected by these diachronic changes, and even in affected environments exceptions are frequently found (first-hand data and Schuman 1899, Konter-Katani n.d. and Voorhoeve & Mwangoka n.d.):

Morpheme-internally

Non-transparent[6] spirantization occurs widely in the lexicon, i.e., morpheme-internally:

(1) a. ɪŋgafi 'paddle' < *-kapį 'paddle'
b. ɪkɪsiɣe 'eye, eyelid' < *-kįge 'eyebrow, eyelash'
c. -fuunda 'instruct' < *-tų́nd- 'teach, instruct'
d. ʊmfiimba 'corpse' < *-bįmba 'corpse'
e. ɪndefu 'beard' < *-dèdų 'beard, chin'
(cf. ʊrʊteefu/iindeefu 'big mat', probably a derivative from a lost verb *-teNC-)
f. -fwiima 'hunt' < *-gų́ím- 'hunt'
g. iilaasi 'bambou' < *-dangį́ 'bambou'

Nonetheless, there still exists an opposition of high/non-high vowels in the same consonantal contexts which normally should have been eliminated by spirantization irrespectively of the PB or innovative origin of the lexical items. This gives the impression of an unaccomplished change:

(2) a. ʊbʊriɾi 'worm' ≠ ʊβʊriɾi 'kind of big mat'
b. -kuɾa 'blow (wind)' ≠ -kʊra 'grow (animates)'
c. -βina 'be sick' ≠ -βɪfwa 'get ripe'
d. -ipuuta 'pray' ≠ -pʊʊɾa 'thresh'

It is still not clear whether these frequently encountered lexemes that contain high vowels following stops were introduced in the language after the historical process was extinct, or whether they represent remnants of an earlier stage that spirantization, being "aborted" before completion, failed to affect. In both cases, the fact remains that spirantization in Nyakyusa hasn't had a thorough effect either in the lexicon or in the morphophonemic

[6]By non-transparent I mean irretrievable through synchronic analysis, as opposed to transparent (= input and change retrievable) by virtue of the alternation between actual reflexes.

system, which further suggests that the phonetic processes implicated in the change have not been active for a long period of time.

Across MP borders

In Nyakyusa, transparent spirantization, functionning as a morphophonemic mechanism occurs as follows:[7]

Adjectival derivation through *-ų, although not the unique adjective-producing mechanism in Nyakyusa, is general and productive:

(3) a. -erees-j-a 'widen up' → -ereef-u 'wide'

b. -ɣor-ok-a 'be straight' → -ɣorof-u 'straight, innocent'

Still, many instances of frozen derivatives, without association to a source verbal item, are found, a fact which might contribute to the weakening of spirantization as an active MP mechanism:

(4) a. -kaf-u 'dry; hard; healthy' < *-kád- 'become dry'

b. -toof-u 'soft' no *-toNC- 'be soft'- cf. Nyiha ex.(42b)

Even before causative *-į-, the same tendency towards deactivation of the MP process is nowadays manifested in the preference of speakers for non-spirantizing *-ikį- (> -Isy-) forms. Thus, although in my data and in other actual sources causative forms using spirantizing morph *-į- are found, they seem to be infrequent compared to non-spirantizing *-ikį- causatives:

(5) a. -sook-a 'come out' →-soos-j-a 'take sth. out'

b. -dʒoŋg-a 'escape' →-dʒoos-j-a /dʒonsja/ 'make sth.disappear'

but

(6) a. -βudʒ-a 'return' → -βudʒ-ɪsj-a ~ -βus-j-a 'cause to return'

b. -pon-a 'be healed' → -pon-esj-a 'heal s.o.'

c. -and-a 'start' → -and-ɪsj-a 'make s.o. begin'

Moreover, previously spirantizing forms reported by Schumann 1899, e.g. in (7), have actually been replaced by the non-spirantizing *-ikį-forms—cf. (8) from my own data—without consideration of semantic conditioning (cf. end of §2):

(7) a. -sɪm-a 'be put out' → -sɪm-j-a 'put out fire'

b. -end-a 'walk' → -ees-j-a 'cause to walk'

---

[7]For all examples of spirantization in these four morphophonemic contexts no corresponding PB item will be given, since what is of interest here is the synchronic process of alternations—irrespectively of the origin of the verbal stem—and not the evolution of proto-consonants, which is represented in the Tables accompanying each language.

	c.	-soβ-a 'get lost'	→	-sof-j-a	'lose sth.'
(8)	a.	-sɪm-a idem	→	-sɪm-ɪsj-a	
	b.	-end-a "	→	-end-esj-a	(Swahili influence?)
	c.	-soβ-a "	→	-soβ-esj-a	

Finally, the lexicalization of spirantizing causative verbs attained either through semantic differenciation of the derivative or loss of the non-extended verbal base contributes to the weakening of spirantization after *-i̧- as an active MP process:

(9) a. no *-naŋg- or *-laŋg- -naŋgɪsj-a 'to show'
(cf. Ndali -ɾangiʃ-a 'to show')

b. no *-idʒ-? -idʒɪsj-a 'obey,respect'

c. no *-ɾaaɾ-uk- -ɾaaɾʊsj-a 'ask'

d. -ʊʊɾ-a 'buy' → -ʊʊɾ-ɪsj-a 'sell'

e. -maɲ-a 'know' → -maɲ-ɪsj-a 'teach'

Spirantization in the environment of the agentive *-i̧ is rare. Its presence, rather than being determined by any structural criteria, seems to have been the result of a stylistic or sociolinguistic tendency, favouring adoption of some spirantizing lexemes while disfavouring that of others.[8] In active synchronic derivation, only non-spirantizing agentive nouns are obtained. Seen from a diachronic perspective, spirantization in the agentive noun context seems to have regressed in favour of the corresponding non-spirantizing form. Thus, where variation between spirantizing and non-spirantizing forms was noted by Carl Schumann in the 1890's, as in (10),

(10) ʊmbomb-i ~ ʊmboof-i 'worker' ← -βomb-a 'work'

only non-spirantizing forms survive today. Synchronic data for Nyakyusa show predominance of this non-spirantizing tendency:

(11)	a.	-βomb-a	'work'	→	ʊm̩bomb-i	'worker'
	b.	-paap-a	'bear child'	→	ʊm̩paap-i	'parent'
	c.	-keet-a	'see'	→	ʊn̩keet-i	'eye witness'
	d.	-pok-a	'save'	→	ʊm̩pok-i	'saviour'
	e.	-ɾoŋg-a	'settle cases'	→	ʊn̩doŋg-i	'judge'
	f.	-ɾoβ-a	'to fish'	→	ʊn̩doβ-i	'fisherman'

[8] In this respect, it is suggestive that two Agentive nouns are found always spirantizing in all Corridor languages: these are *-pond-i̧ '-ironsmith' and *-dog-i̧ '-sorcerer'.

	g.	-hɪɪdʒ-a	'steal'	→	ʊŋhɪɪdʒ-i	'thief'
	h.	-ɣoɣ-a	'kill'	→	ʊŋgoɣ-i	'killer'
	i.	-toɾ-a	'win'	→	ʊn̩toɾ-i	'winner'
	j.	-swɪɪɾ-a	'feed'	→	ʊn̩swɪɪɾ-i	'feeder, caretaker'

But:

(12)	a.	-tendeeɾ-a	'to spy'	→	ʊntendees-i	'spy'
	b.	-kʊɾ-a	'grow up'	→	ʊŋkʊs-i	'adult'
	c.	-loɣ-a	'bewitch'	→	ʊndos-i	'sorcerer'
	d.	-pond-a	'forge, beat'	→	ʊmpoos-i	'ironsmith'

Finally, and most importantly, there is no trace of spirantization in the stem-final consonant of a verb in the past or perfect tense, i.e., before the morph *-ɨde (only perfect tense forms are given):

(13)	a.	-peet-a	'winnow'	→	mbeet-iɾe	'I have winnowed grain'
	b.	-sek-a	'laugh'	→	sek-iɾe /nsekiɾe/	'I have laughed'
	c.	-dʒoβ-a	'speak'	→	ndʒoβ-iɾe	'I have spoken'
	d.	-βʊʊɾ-a	'say'	→	mbʊʊɾ-iɾe	'I have said'
	e.	-and-a	'start'	→	naand-iɾe	'I have started'

3.1.2. Kinga

The same behaviour as regards MP spirantization is also found in neighbouring Kinga (G65) also a 7V language, with phonemic vowel length, although spirantizing rules differ (data come from Wolff 1905 and Schadeberg 1973):

*(N)b, p, t, k	/__ɨ	>	si / __ {C, #}	(>s / __V)
*d, g	/__ɨ	>	tsi/ __ {C, #}	(>ts / __V)
*Nd, Ng	/__ɨ	>	nzi / __ {C, #}	(>nz / __V)
*(N)b, d, g, p, t, k	/__ʉ	>	su	

= end of lexeme

Table 2. Spirantization rules in Kinga

It is remarkable that spirantization in this language is exclusively assibilating: whatever the nature of the proto-consonant, no labial Fricative has been created. Spirantization seems general morpheme-internally as well as in the contexts of adjectival *-ʉ, cf. (14), and causative *-ɨ-, cf. (15), although the limited available data didn't permit me to locate any existing disfunctioning, as in the case of Nyakyusa:[9]

(14) a. -ɣolok-a 'be straight' → -ɣolos-u 'straight'
b. -valaal-a 'be white' → -valaas-u 'white, light'

(15) a. -tsov-a 'speak' → -tsos-a 'make s.o. speak'
b. -kʋl-a 'grow' → -kʋts-a 'make s.o. or sth. grow'
c. -homb-a 'pay' → -hos-a 'make s.o. pay'

As for agentive derivational suffix *-i̯, Wolff considered spirantization in Kinga agentive nouns as only occurring "in älteren Wort-formen" while "in jüngeren Formen bleiben die Konsonanten unverändert" (1905:4), although no synchronic variation pairs are given:

(16) a. -pond-a 'forge' → ʋm̩poonz-i 'ironsmith'
b. -tekel-a 'sacrifice' → ʋn̩tekets-i 'priest'
c. -dwad-a 'to fear' → ʋn̩dwats-i 'fearful person'
d. -ɣend-a 'go' → ʋn̩genz-i 'companion'

But:

(17) a. -pok-a 'save' → ʋm̩pok-i 'saviour'
b. -loβ-a 'to fish' → ʋn̩doβ-i 'fisherman'
c. -βʋmb-a 'mould' → ʋm̩bʋmb-i 'potter'
d. -tseŋg-a 'build' → ʋn̩tseŋg-i 'builder'

Finally, no trace of spirantization is found in front of *-i̯de:

(18) a. -koŋg-a 'follow' → aŋkoŋg-ile 'he has followed him (Pfct)'
b. -cov-a 'talk' → ndaacov-ile 'I talked (Remote past)'
c. -lol-a 'see' → twaavʋlol-ile 'we saw it (Rm past cl.14)'

3.1.3. Safwa

Spirantization rules in Safwa, the northern neighbour of Nyakyusa, are as follows (first-hand data and Voorhoeve n.d.):

[9] Transcription of Kinga data has been somewhat modified to suit current practice, but is closely following the phonetic description of segments included in Wolff (1905), checked against data from Schadeberg 1973.

*(N)b	/__į	>	(N)vi	*(N)b, g	/__ų	>	(N)vu
*(N)d, g	/__į	>	(N)zi	*(N)d	/__ų	>	(N)vu~zu
*(N)p	/__į	>	(N)fi	*(N)p, k	/__ų	>	(N)fu
*(N)t, k	/__į	>	(N)si	*(N)t	/__ų	>	(N)fu~su

Table 3. spirantization rules in Safwa

Furthermore, a somewhat different situation obtains compared to that in Nyakyusa: Safwa maintains the vowel length opposition, but the situation concerning vowel quality is far from clearcut: according to Voorhoeve (n.d.), the phonetic distance between high and mid-high vowels is sometimes audible, most other times difficult to hear, so that he prefers describing it as a 5V system. My personal experience from interviews with two Safwa informants confirms this impression of an inconsistent, not sharply differenciated use of seven phonetic vowels. But unlike Voorhoeve, I prefer treating Safwa as a 7V language actually undergoing reduction of its vowel system, and thus follow a 7V phonetic notation.

Although the data are incomplete (no detailed study has been done on formal variation, or the functioning of the compound causative |-Isi-| and its interaction with spirantizing |-i-|), spirantization seems to be regular in the first three cases, that is before *-ų, *-į-, and *-į:

(19) a. -lʊl-a 'coagulate, curdle' → -lʊz-u 'curdled (milk)'
b. ʊŋgolos-u 'saint' cf. Nyakyusa ex. (3b) and Kinga ex. (14a)
c. -sjev-u 'shrewd' (-sjeβ-?)

(20) a. -buuh-a (< *k) 'rise' → -buus-j-a 'lift'
b. -gul-a 'buy' → -guz-j-a 'sell'
c. -teeg-a 'get lost' → -teez-j-a 'lose'
d. -tuumb-a 'run' → -tumv-j-a 'drive away'

(21) a. -paap-a 'bear a child' → ʊm̩paaf-i 'parent'
b. -log-a 'bewitch' → ʊn̩noz-i /ʊndozi/ 'sorcerer'
c. -dʒend-a 'walk' → ʊn̩dʒenz-i 'wanderer'

But even if data on the previous contexts are not conclusive, absence of spirantizing before *-įde places Safwa in this category:

(22) a. -dʒaat-a 'stroll' → tʊdʒaat-ile 'we have strolled'
b. -lol-a 'see' → aandol-ile 'he saw me'
c. -dʒeend-a 'walk' → adʒeend-ile 'he has walked'

3.1.4. Holoholo

Holoholo is here considered as an external reference supporting the general argument of this paper. The data, adapted to the general set-up of the paper, are taken from Coupez 1955. Being a 7V language, Holoholo has undergone spirantization to a very limited extent. More specifically, the change has apparently been active only in the phonetic context of Alveolar consonants:

*d, t /__ į,ų > s

Table 4. Spirantization rules in Holoholo

This very limited lexical spirantization can be seen in the following examples:

(23)	a.	simo	'spear'	<	*-tų́mo	'spear'
	b.	ndesi	'beard'	<	*-dedų	'beard'
	c.	mbusi	'goat'	<	*-búdį	'goat'

But:

(24)	a.	mbila	'rain'	<	*-bų́dá	'rain'
	b.	ndʒogi	'elephant'	<	*-dʒogų	'elephant'

Moreover, across morphological borders no MP alternations are found, except in the case of causative *-į- and even then only the Voiced Alveolar segment /l/ is spirantizing:

(25)	-lɩl-a	'cry'	→	-lɩs-j-a	'make s.o. cry'

But:

(26)	-ning-a	'tighten up'	→	-ning-j-a	'hurry up'

On the contrary, agentive nouns with *-į, and past/perfect forms with *-įde do not show any trace of spirantization:

(27)	a.	-ib-a	'steal'	→	ngib-i	'thief'
	b.	-bjal-a	'bear (child)'	→	-bjal-i	'parent'
	c.	-tong-a	'be ill'	→	-tong-i	'ill'
(28)	a.	-lol-a	'look'	→	ʊlol-ile	'you have looked'
	b.	-bʊk-a	'cross'	→	ndʒabʊk-ile	'I have crossed'
	c.	-lond-a	'follow'	→	nsimʊlond-ile	'I haven't followed him'

3.2. Full spirantization in 5V Languages

3.2.1. Inamwanga

Typical of this category, Inamwanga has a 5V system whereas long vowels are only phonetic, being determined by syllable position: in fact, in most words and especially in careful articulation, the penultimate contains a very long vowel, somewhat in the Zulu manner. Thus, Inamwanga has undergone a general reduction of its vowel system in both vowel quality and vowel length. On the contrary, spirantization as seen from the following rules, has introduced eight new sequences in the language: [fi, mfi, vi, mvi, fu, mfu, vu, mvu]. This proliferation is all the more visible in the MP domain where the stop/spirant alternation mechanism is fully exploited. (first-hand data and Busse 1940-41):

*(N)b	/__į	>	(N)vi	*(N)b, g	/__ų	>	(N)vu
*(N)d, g	/__į	>	(N)zi	*(N)d	/__ų	>	(N)zu
*(N)p	/__į	>	(N)fi	*(N)p, k	/__ų	>	(N)fu
*(N)t, k	/__į	>	(N)si	*(N)t	/__ų	>	(N)su

Table 5. Spirantization rules in Inamwanga

The following examples illustrate spirantization rules of Table 5:

(29)	a.	imvwi	'grey hair'	< *-bųi	'grey hair'
	b.	-vumbika	'bake in ashes'	< *-gųmb-ik-	'bake in ashes, cover'
	c.	-fukama	'kneel down'	< *-kųkam-	'kneel down'
	d.	-sunda	'instruct'	< *-tųnd-	'teach, instruct'
	e.	uluwazu	'rib'	< *-badų	'rib'
but:	f	-vukuta	'work bellows'	< *-dųkut-[10]	'work the bellows'
	g.	-vimba	'swell'	< *-bįmb-	'swell'
	h.	ulufjo <-fiØo	'kidney'	< *-pįgo	'kidney'
	i.	ulusje <-siØe	'eyelash'	< *-kįge	'eyelash, eyebrow'

As a morphophonemic process, spirantizing alternations are regular in all morphological contexts, including the most productive *-įde. However,

---

[10]It is very interesting that throughout the Corridor, even in languages like the Southern Mwika Group or Nyiha where the reflexes *d, t /__ų are uniformly sibilants (i.e. / z, s /), this verbal stem is exclusively found with a labial reflex.

in Inamwanga adjectival derivatives are generally obtained through other derivational mechanisms than the *-ụ suffix. Among these, the most frequent is the form |Augment-Adjectival Prefix-Radical-e| of denominative -p- qualification verbs, like *-zi-p-a* 'be nice' and *-wi-p-a* 'be bad':

(30) umuntu u-mu-[wi-p]-e
man Cl.1 A-AdjPfx-[be bad]-AdjSfx
'a bad man'

As a result, adjectives in |-u| are very rare. More specifically, the only one found in Inamwanga is frozen:

(31) -wenz-u/-benz-u 'red' ← *CB -bèng- 'become red'

Causative *-į- and agentive *-į are regularly associated with spirantization:

(32)	a.	-ik-a	'come down'	→	-is-j-a	'take sth. down'
	b.	-kal-a	'buy'	→	-kaz-j-a	'sell'
	c.	-onk-a	'suckle (child)'	→	-ons-j-a	'breast feed'
(33)	a.	-kwat-a	'bear a child'	→	umukwas-i	'parent'
	b.	-longol-a	'lead, guide'	→	ecilongoz-i	'leader'
	c.	*-dog -	'bewitch'	→	umuloz-i	'sorcerer'
	d.	-womb-a	'work'[w ~ Ø]	→	umuwomv-i	'worker'

But most importantly, the past/perfect tense in *-įde shows a well developed paradigm of MP alternations:

(34)	a.	-pap-a	'carry on back'	→	apaf-ile	'she has carried... (perfect)'
	b.	-vukut-a	'blow bellows'	→	wavukus-ile	'he blew...(past)'
	c.	-talik-a	'start'	→	mwatalis-ile	'you pl. started (past)'
	d.	-iw-a < *b	'steal'	→	twiv-ile	'we have stolen (perfect)'
	e.	-wol-a	'rot'	→	zjawoz-ile	'they rotted (cl.10-past)'
	f.	-samb-a	'bathe,wash'	→	nasamv-ile	'I washed myself (past)'
	g.	-send-a	'take'	→	insenz-ile	'I have taken (perfect)'
	h.	-ɲuŋg-a	'sift grain'	→	waɲunz-ile	'she sifted grain

				(past)'
i. -tont-a	'get tired'	→	natons-ile	'I got tired '
j. -koŋk-a	'follow'	→	wakons-ile	'he followed'

The same maximal use of synchronic spirantizing mechanisms, in combination with a 5V system, is encountered in the all the other languages which, together with Inamwanga, constitute the Southern Mwika group[11] i.e., Lungu, Mambwe and the variety of Fipa spoken in the southern part of Ufipa (e.g. in the town of Mwazye where my informant came from), which I call, in order to distinguish it from its central/northern counterpart, Southern Fipa.

3.2.2. Lungu

Kagaya (1987) treats Lungu as a 5V language with a vowel-length opposition. Its spirantization rules are identical to those in Inamwanga—cf. Table 5. The only difference is found among synchronic alternations where, due to further evolution of *b to [j] (replacing [w] where no rounded vowel either precedes or follows) one more alternation, namely j/v is added to the existing w/v labials alternation—see example (36a) below. Adjectival *-ų is limited to example (35):

(35) -jenz-u 'red' cf. Inamwanga ex.(31)

On the other hand, MP spirantization is regular in causative *-į- forms:

(36)	a. -kaj-a	'become hot'	→	-kav-j-a	'heat sth.'
	b. -oŋk-a	'suckle (child)'	→	-ons-j-a	'feed at the breast'
	c. -omb-a	'be wet'	→	-omv-j-a	'wet sth.'
	d. -poŋg-a	'get lost'	→	-ponz-j-a	'lose'

As only the following agentive noun in *-į is found in Kagaya (1987), generalizations are not possible:

(37) -luŋg-a 'hunt' → umulunz-i 'hunter'

On the contrary the same regularity as in Inamwanga is encountered in the past/perfect tense *-įde:

(38)	a. -pit-a	'walk'	→	-pis-ile
	b. -lol-a	'see'	→	-loz-ile
	c. -tamb-a	'watch'	→	-tamv-ile

[11] See Nurse (1988) for the lexicostatistic classification of the Mwika group in general. The distinction of a Southern Mwika group—thus isolating the variety of Fipa called "Sukuma"—is entirely my own, based on lexicostatistic, phonemic and morphophonemic considerations, thoroughly analysed in Labroussi (1998).

d. -vwint-a 'throw' → -vwins-ile

3.2.3. Southern Fipa

Southern Fipa is a 5V language, and, insofar as my limited first-hand data permit me to judge, vowel length is not phonemic. Nurse (1988:105) seems to confirm my analysis, since the structural features described in his Table 5 about what he calls "Fipa", coincide more or less with the structural profile of the variety called here "Southern Fipa". Spirantization rules in this variety are identical to those of Inamwanga and Lungu, as resumed in Table 5. In order to illustrate these, some morpheme-internal reflexes are given below:

(39) a. uwazi 'blood' < *-gadį 'blood'

b. izija 'lake' < *-dįba 'pool, depth'

c. isumo 'spear' < *-tųmo 'spear'

d. icifuwa 'chest' < *-kųba 'chest'

e. ulufjo 'kidney' < *-pįgo 'kidney' cf. (29h)

My first-hand data are very limited to permit any definitive conclusions as to its MP spirantizing pattern. Therefore, I have tentatively included Southern Fipa in the same category as Inamwanga and Lungu based on the most general structural (i.e.,lexical and phonological) ressemblances between these languages. The only adjective in *-ų found is the same as in Inamwanga and Lungu:

(40) -jenz-u 'red'

No data have been obtained on causative verbs or agentive nouns, but spirantization seems regular in the past/perfect tense using *-įde:

(41) a. ukuzip-a 'be good' → kutazif-ile 'it's not good (cl.15)'

b. ukupit-a 'leave,go' → japis-ile 'they left'

c. ukuvwang-a 'say,speak' → wavwanz-ile 'he said'

3.2.4. Nyiha

Full spirantization in all possible morphological contexts occurs also in Nyiha, a language adjoining the Southern Mwika Group in the central part of the Corridor. Nyiha has 5 phonemic vowels and my first-hand data suggest that phonemic vowel-length is either lost or currently dying out. Nurse (1988:104) seems to share the same opinion concerning the phonemic status of vowel-length in Nyiha. Moreover, the spirantizing rules valid for the Southern Mwika Group (cf.Table 5) also apply in its case (first-hand data and Busse 1960).

Contrary to the Southern Mwika Group, adjectival derivation through *-ų is frequent and productive, and spirantizing always appears:

(42) a. -βol-a 'rot' → -βoz-u 'rotten'

b. -tont-a 'be mild,calm' → uβutons-u 'mildness'

The same regularity is observed in causative derivatives using *-į-, as well as in agentive derivatives using *-į:

(43) a. βaβ-a 'hurt intr.' → -βav-w-a /βavja/ 'hurt (trans.)'

b. -izul-a 'be full' → -izuz-j-a 'fill up'

c. -bomb-a 'work' → -βomv-w-a /βomvja/ 'cause to work'

d. -and-a 'start' → -anz-j-a 'cause to start'

e. -oŋk-a 'suckle(child)' → -ons-j-a 'feed at the breast'

(44) a. no * -βiNC- → umuβinz-i 'hunter'

b. -kal-a 'buy' → umukaz-i 'merchant'

c. -teleh-a < *k 'to cook' → umuteles-i 'cook'

Once more, a systematic use of MP alternations in found in the past/perfect tense *-įde:

(45) a. -paap-a 'carry on the back' → ampaaf-ile 'she carried him'

b. -seh-a 'laugh' → nases-ile 'I laughed'

c. -mel-a 'grow (plants)' → βumez-ile 'it grew cl.14'

d. -zeŋg-a 'build' → twazenz-ile 'we built'

According to Busse 1960, spirantization is also activated by the /-*ite*/ past tense morph:

(46) a. -ot-a 'warm oneself' → nos-ite 'I warmed myself'

b. -and-a 'start' → nanz-ite 'I started'

This MP behaviour before *-ite* is in fact unique. As comparative data from Bastin 1983 show, in most languages where this morph appears, it is not associated with spirantization of preceding stem consonant. This fact must be due to the quality of its initial vowel, which as Bastin concludes was probably a non-tense vowel (still Mituku and Matuumbi (P.13), both 7V languages, have an initial tense vowel). Only in Nyiha (also in a single verbal item in Shambala) does this spirantizing before *-ite* appear, and it could be interpreted as a maximal exploitation of this alternating mechanism, spread by analogy even in contexts where it is not normally expected.

3.2.5. Lambya—"Nyiha-like" variety

The same pattern of regular spirantization in all possible contexts is found in the variety of Lambya,[12] reported by Busse (1939-40), which I call "Nyiha-like" Lambya, in opposition with the variety I studied which is "Ndali-like". (In Table 10, the former variety figures as Lambya 2, while the latter as Lambya 1.)

3.3. Intermediate Situations

Between the two polar situations analysed above—i.e., 5V + maximal spirantization and 7V + minimal spirantization—a continuum of intermediate situations can be broken into two subgroupings:

3.3.1. Limited spirantization in 5V Languages

Among the Corridor languages, Ndali of Tanzania and Ngonde of northern Malawi are placed in this category. They both clearly belong to the Nyakyusa group and their spirantization pattern is similar to that of Nyakyusa. As to their vowel systems, the Tanzanian variety of Ndali spoken in Ileje District as well as the Malawian variety described by Vail 1972, both have undergone reduction and share a 5V system, while they both maintain a clear vowel length opposition. On the contrary, no conclusions can be formulated on Ngonde's vowel system, as my limited data come from two young Malawian informants on a trip to Tanzania. Their vowel system was clearly reduced to 5 vowels with no long/short opposition, but it is quite possible that a 7V Ngonde variety is spoken in the rural areas of Ngondeland and by elder members of the community. In this second case, Ngonde would be even more close to Nyakyusa and should be placed in the polar category of 7V languages having undergone limited spirantization (i.e., §.3.1). Lambya 1, or the "Ndali-like" variety, shows the same morphophonemic behaviour as Ndali, and is thus placed in this subgroup. Furthermore, at the western extreme of the Corridor, Bemba is another 5V language making a restricted use of MP spirantizing mechanisms.

---

[12]In fact Lambya is an interesting—maybe typical—case of a dispersed linguistic community, living in others' linguistic territories and adopting many of the standards of the dominant host society. It is yet too early to determine the extent to which each aspect of their linguistic system has been affected by cohabitation and convergence with neighbouring dominant languages but it seems at first glance that no domain (phonology, morphology and especially vocabulary) has been spared. Nevertheless, its ultimate linguistic affiliations must be sought in the Nyika group (or maybe the superordinate Nyika/Mwika grouping).

3.3.2. Ndali

The data come both from a personal research in Tanzania and from the malawian variety of Ndali studied by Vail (1972). Spirantization rules are shared by both varieties:

*(N) b, p	/__ į	>	fi
*(N)d, g, t, k	/__ į	>	si > ʃi
*b, d, g, p, t, k	/__ ų	>	fu

Table 6. Spirantization rules in Ndali

The presence of spirantization in the four MP contexts is restricted to adjectival -ų and causative -į-:

(47)	a.	-keseef-u	'red'	(no alternating examples found)
	b.	-kaf-u	'hard; healthy'	

(48)	a.	-pjat-a	'be sharp'	→	-pjaʃ-a /sja/	'sharpen'
	b.	-βuuɾ-a	'say'	→	-βuuʃ-a	'ask'
	c.	-it-ik-a	'answer back call'	→	-it-iʃ-a	'call s.o.'
	d.	-oɣo-p-a	'fear'	→	-oɣo-f-j-a	'frighten'
	e.	-soβ-a	'be lost'	→	-sof-j-a	'lose sth.'

As in Nyakyusa, the non-spirantizing |-Isi-| morph seems to compete with |-i-| since the distribution of these two causative morphs doesn't seem to be ruled by any semantic considerations:

(49)	a.	-pon-a	'be healed'	→	-pon-eʃ-a	'heal s.o.'
	b.	-swiɣ-a	'be startled'	→	-swiɣ-iʃ-a	'startle'
	c.	-ɾit-a	'be tired'	→	-ɾit-iʃ-a	'tire s.o.'
	d.	-sumb-a	'be calm'	→	-sumb-iʃ-a	'calm s.o.'
	e.	-kind-a	'run'	→	-kind-iʃ-a	'chase'

Spirantization is fossilized in agentive nouns:

(50)	a.	-ɾoɣ-a	'bewitch'	→	umuɾoʃ-i	'sorcerer'
	b.	-pond-a	'forge'	→	umupooʃ-i	'ironsmith'

But:

(51)	a.	-paap-a	'bear child'	→	umupaap-i	'parent'
	b.	-keet-a	'witness,observe'	→	umukeet-i	'eye-witness'
	c.	-swiiɾ-a	'feed'	→	umuswiiɾ-i	'herdboy'

d. -oc-a /oki/ 'roast' → umwoc-i /k/ 'roaster'

e. -piidʒ-a 'to cook' → umupiidʒ-i 'cook'

The same MP context in Malawian Ndali seems to be even less spirantizing:

(52) a. -tendeer-a 'watch' → umutendeer-i 'watchman'

b. -tuur-a 'help' → umutuur-i 'helper'

c. -pond-a 'forge' → umupond-i 'ironsmith'

Note that this last item is always found in its spirantizing form across the Corridor languages. The possibility of a loan from a non-spirantizing language seems rather weak as Ndali is entirely surrounded by spirantizing languages and, moreover, diffusion of smithing techniques and iron objects into the Ndali community can, in historical times, be traced to communities speaking spirantizing languages (mainly Kinga—cf. Kalinga 1979).

Finally, the *-ite* past/perfect tense morph, used exclusively in the case of non-extended -CVC- verbal stems, behaves as a non-spirantizing context, its most frequent behaviour according to Bastin 1983's analysis. But, in spite of the fact the *-įde context is absent—which is here considered as the crucial context for deciding whether spirantization is complete or not—Ndali's behaviour in the other three morphological contexts is conservative enough for it to be considered as a language with a "limited spirantizing pattern".

3.3.3. Ngonde

My personal data on Ngonde have been completed by a word list collected by Owen Kalinga and kindly made available to me by Michael Mann of SOAS. I'm grateful to both for this material. Spirantization rules being identical to those of Nyakyusa, as shown in Table 1, only the data will be shown here. Some reflexes of spirantization morpheme-internally are given here for reference:

(53) a. ilifumbi 'egg' < *-tųmbi 'egg'

b. ulufumbi 'dust' < *-gųmbi 'dust'

c. ikilefu 'chin' < *-dedų 'beard, chin'

d. ikisiɣe 'eye' < *-kįge 'eyelash, eyebrow'

e. iiŋgafi 'paddle' < *-kapį 'paddle, oar'

The spirantizing morph *-ų is used regularly, although as source verbs are not available, it cannot be judged whether it is active as a derivation mechanism:

(54) a. -kaf-u 'hard' < *-kad- 'become dry'

b. uβutalalif-u 'cold' ← -talal-ik-a? < *-tadad-a 'cold'

As in its northern neighbour, Nyakyusa, past/perfect tense morph *-i̧de has not caused spirantization in stem-final position:

(55)	a.	-sek-a	'laugh'	→	nasek-ile	'I laughed'
	b.	-ɣul-a[13]	'buy'	→	naɣul-ile	'I bought'
	c.	-timb-a	'beat'	→	am̩timb-ile	'he beat her'

3.3.4. Lambya—'Ndali-like' variety

As has already been mentioned, the variety of Lambya spoken in parts of Ileje District where the Lambya intermingle with the Ndali, presents more cases of disfunctioning in its alternational pattern than the variety reported by Busse 1939-40. It is a 5V language with a phonemic length opposition which spirantizes as follows (first-hand data):

*(N)b	/_ i̧	>	(N)vi	*(N)b, g	/_ u̧	>	(N)vu
*(N)d, g	/_ i̧	>	(N)zi	*(N)d	/_ u̧	>	(N)zu ~ vu
*(N)p	/_ i̧	>	(N)fi	*(N)p, k	/_ u̧	>	(N)fu
*(N)t, k	/_ i̧	>	(N)si	*(N)t	/_ u̧	>	(N)su ~ vu

Table 7. spirantization rules in Lambya

The morph *-u̧ is associated with spirantization, whereas the same frozen adjectives as in the Nyakyusa group appear in Lambya:

(56)	a.	-toof-u	'soft'			
	b.	-kaf-u	'hard; healthy'			
	c.	-βor-a	'rot'	→	-βoz-u	'rotten'

But:

(57)	a.	-swep-u	'bright, white'			
	b.	-fiit-a	'be black'	→	-fiit-u	'black, dark'

Is the vowel /u/ in these last two examples etymologically *-u̧ or *-u? (cf. Meeussen 1967:95). Due to vowel reduction, but also to the ambiguous behaviour of this variety in regard to spirantization, the answer is not self-evident.

Spirantizing causative *-i̧- seems regular. Still, some verbs appear with a non-spirantizing compound morph with no apparent reason:

---

[13]The corresponding stem in Nyakyusa is l-ʊl-l. In both languages considerable mixing must have taken place regarding lexemes that contain *g in stem-initial position, as both reflexes (i.e. *g > ɣ and *g > Ø) are attested. Proportions have not been established yet, but it seems indicated that lexemes containing the /ɣ/ reflex are of more recent introduction.

(58) a. -pjat-a 'be sharp' → -pjas-j-a 'sharpen'
b. -ik-a 'come down' → -is-j-a 'take sth. down'
c. -ɣur-a 'buj' → -ɣuz-j-a 'sell'
d. (*-ruβ-?) → -ruv-j-a 'forget'

But:

(59) a. -oŋk-a 'suckle (child)' → -oŋk-ezj-a 'feed at the breast'
b. -soŋk-a 'be well lit (fire)' → -soŋk-ezj-a 'poke up fire'

The origin of this harmonizing, non-spirantizing -Izy- in the last two examples is not clear. It could represent {causative + applicative} *-id-į-, a possibility which however is not supported by the non-applicative semantism of the two extended verbs. We could also imagine that Lambya has copied the use of non-spirantizing -Isy- in these verbs from Ndali and Nyakyusa. In this second case, voicing of the Lambya consonant is irregular, since the compound -Isy- causative contains an etymological voiceless consonant.

Spirantizing agentive nouns with the *-į suffix are not infrequent, although some do not spirantize. Prefixation of deverbatives ending in *-į with class 14 ubu- or class 3 umu- produces abstract nouns:

(60) a. -iβ-a 'steal' → umwiv-i 'thief'
b. -totomer-a 'to desire' → uβutotomez-i 'desire cl.14'
c. -roɣ-a 'bewitch' → umuroz-i 'sorcerer'
d. -cind-ik-a 'to respect' → umucinz-i 'respect cl.3'

But:

(61) a. -mat-a 'mould' → umumat-i 'potter' (cf. Ndali)
b. -paap-a 'bear child' → umupaap-i 'parent' (cf Ndali)

Besides, Ndali-like Lambya, in contrast to Nyiha-like Lambya, makes an exclusive use of non-spirantizing *-ite* in its past/perfect paradigm. Still, a detailed dialectological and sociolinguistic study must be undertaken before either of the two tendencies can be ascribed to Proto-Lambya, i.e. do the conservative Lambya imitate the innovative Nyiha or do the innovative Lambya imitate the conservative Ndali? It is interesting to note that acceptance of the conservative tendency as a Proto-Lambya feature isolates Nyiha as the only innovative language of the Nyika group (M20 in Guthrie's classification) and justifies the (identical) conservatism of Safwa as a feature commonly shared from Proto-Nyika.

3.3.5. Bemba

Bemba is also put in this category as a 5V language attesting limited MP spirantization. Briefly, regular spirantizing alternations occur before the *-į-causative extension, affecting the stem consonant even cyclically in case of {causative + applicative} (cf. Hyman 1994). The *-į agentive nouns do appear with a spirant stem-final consonant, but they seem to be losing ground to |-ka- -a| forms (Larry Hyman, personal communication). This tendency has the effect of limiting the contexts where MP spirantization applies. I have no data on *-ų adjectives, although if they occur, they should normally be accompanied by spirantization. But, the decisive criterion is, once again, total absence of spirantization in the stem-final consonant preceding *-įde. Not only is this past/perfect tense ending non-spirantizing, it is also harmonizing with the stem vowel, exactly as the *-id- Applicative extension. This fact might lead us to consider that in Bemba, this morph |-Ile| is not comparable to its cognate in Ndali or in any other language that doesn't spirantize in its context.

However, seen in a historical perspective this differentiation is not justified. For in fact, the identification—or confusion—between a tense (i.e., *į of *-įde) and a non-Tense (i.e., *i of *-id-) vowel is very unlikely to happen in a 7V language and indeed to my knowledge there is no 7V language where it occurs (see also comparison of *-id- and *-įde initial vowels in Bastin 1983). This further means that in Bemba it can't have occurred but *after* reduction of the vowel system had taken place. Meanwhile, for spirantization to be inexistant in past/perfect context, we must suppose that by the time vowel reduction (and subsequent identification of *-id- and *-įde initial vowels) took place, phonetic spirantizing processes were already extinct, otherwise they would have affected stem consonants in this context. In other words, it is partly because spirantization in front of *-įde was already blocked and partly because vowel reduction had already occurred, that identification of the initial vowels in *-įde and *-id- was made possible.

Thus, as it can be seen from the historical scenario proposed here, Times 1 and 2 of Bemba's evolution fit well into Stage A of spirantization (cf.regional scenario in §4):

T1: Loss of spirantization before affecting *-įde context →

T2: Vowel reduction →

T3: Identification of initial vowels in *-įde and *-id- and consequent harmonizing of |-Ile|.

Time 3 on the contrary, being a late individual innovation, is irrelevant to the present issue. For the purposes of this typology, the fact remains that *-įde in Bemba is not a spirantizing morphophonemic context.

3.3.6. Apparently Full spirantization in 7V Languages

This category stands for the fourth member of possible combinations of spirantization with the vowel system (i.e., Full spirantization + 7V). Two languages have been placed in this category as being 7V languages which seem both to use the spirantizing alternation mechanism in all four MP contexts examined here. But, as the adverb "apparently" suggests, the regularity of the MP spirantizing pattern is doubtful and a more adequate explanation must be sought for the irregularities in these two languages.

3.3.7. Fipa-Sukuma

I call Fipa-Sukuma the linguistic variety spoken in the central and northern part of Ufipa. In the literature, all linguistic varieties spoken across the Ufipa Plateau are covered by the relatively new and—linguistically speaking—vague term "Fipa". Reference has already been made to the southern variety called here Southern Fipa (§3.2.4). In fact, a survey of different studies and classifications where "Fipa" is included, reveals that they can not all possibly refer to the same linguistic system. As I further argue in Labroussi (1998), based on phonological considerations, Fipa-Sukuma and Southern Fipa are not even dialectal varieties sharing the same common ancestor, as only a much deeper separation time can account for their phonological divergence.

Speakers of the central part of Ufipa were traditionally called—and are still locally known as—"Sukuma", an ethnonym which has apparently nothing to do with the Sukuma of northwestern Tanzania. More interestingly, Sukuma groups are mentioned in Bemba traditions all across Bembaland as well as in the first Europeans' reports as the original inhabitants of these territories (see Willis 1981 and Roberts 1973).

Fipa-Sukuma possesses the neatest 7V system of the Corridor, with a maximal audible distance between high and mid-high vowels. Furthermore, a neat distinction between long/short phonemic vowels is observed. Like in all other 7V languages(cf. §3.1.1 for the same point in Nyakyusa), the presence of tense vowels after stops as well as the contrastive distribution of tense and non-tense vowels in the same consonantal environments—i.e., both after stops and the Alveolar spirant—gives the impression that historical spirantization has had a limited impact in the lexicon, which in itself suggests a premature loss of the phonetic processes involved (first-hand data and Willis 1978):

(62) a. ɪcɑitɪɪndɪ 'cow dung' ≠ ɪntiindi 'back'

(compare the second lexeme with spirantizing Nyiha *insinzi* 'back')

b. ɪɪntilya 'elephant' ≠ ʊn̩silya 'salt'

c. -cɪn-a < ki 'to danse' ≠ -ciind-a < ki 'to play'

Spirantization rules in this language are different from the southern Fipa variety, in that Fipa-Sukuma has devoiced all the reflexes of PB voiced consonants before High vowel:

*(N)b, p	/__ i̧	>	fi	*(N)b, g, p, k	/__ ų	>	fu
*(N)d, g, t, k	/__ i̧	>	si	*(N)d, t,	/__ ų	>	su

Table 7. Spirantization rules in Fipa-Sukuma

As for its MP alternations pattern, the general picture points to spirantization being present in all four MP contexts. However, on closer examination this pattern doesn't seem as clearcut as the commonly shared Maximally-spirantizing pattern of the Southern Mwika languages or their eastern neighbour, Nyiha.

Contrary to the other Mwika languages to its south, including Southern Fipa, Fipa-Sukuma makes a general use of the *-ų adjectival suffix in parallel with the verbal qualification mechanism that these languages almost exclusively use. In this case, MP alternation is active and regular:

(63)	a.	-talıı-mp-a	'be short'	→	-talıf-u	'short'
	b.	-ful-a	'be plenty, abound'	→	-fus-u	'many, abundant'
	c.	-jii-p-a	'be bad'	→	-jiif-u	'bad'
	d.	-sıı-p-a	'be good'	→	-siif-u	'good'
	e.	-cee-p-a	'be small'	→	-ceef-u	'small'

Spirantization is regular in the context of the causative morph *-į-. Due to insufficience of data it is not clear whether compound non-spirantizing |-Isi-| occurs in semantically determined contexts (i.e., as {indirect causative}) or if it is competing with spirantizing *-į-, as in Nyakyusa or Ndali:

(64)	a.	-fik-a	'arrive'	→	-fiʃ-a /sja/	'cause to arrive'
	b.	-kal-a	'buy'	→	-kaʃ-a	'sell'

but

(65) -sak-a 'marry (man)' → -sak-ıʃ-a 'find a bride for one's son'

The most frequent agentive derivation in Fipa-Sukuma is the |ka-Rad-a| form. Nevertheless, some Agents ending in spirantizing *-į are found:

(66)	a.	-fjaal-a	'bear a child'	→	ʊn̩fjaas-i	'parent'
	b.	-ij-a	'steal' < *-dʒįb-	→	ʊmwif-i	'thief'

In this last example, is the derivational mechanism transparent? As no other examples, nominal or verbal, where [j] (from *b in a non-rounded vocalic environment) alternates with [f] are found, this derivational transparency seems uncertain. Compare with Lungu example (36a).

With the past ending *-įde, while Whiteley (1964) reports regular spirantization,[14] I have noted inconsistencies quite untypical of the Mwika group: in some cases both spirantizing and non-spirantizing variants were

14But the formulation of a rule of morphophonemic alternations, doesn't imply lack of sociolinguistically determined variation.

independently obtained from my two informants and later on judged as acceptable, in some others only the non-spirantizing form was produced and, upon questioning, considered as "the correct one". Non-spirantizing -ile forms are also found in the Sukuma oral literature published in Willis (1978):

(67) a. -ʊmool-a 'kill' → waŋgʊmoos-ile 'he killed me'
b. -kal-a 'dry' → twaakas-ile 'we dried (sth.)'

But:

(68) a. -paap-a 'bear child' → wapaap-ile 'she bore a child'
b. -loot-a 'dream' → náloot-íle ~ náloos-íle 'I dreamt (yesterday)'
c. " " → náàlót-íĺé 'I dreamt (remote past)'
d. -sak-a 'marry(man)' → waasak-ile 'he married (remote past)'
e. -it-a 'call' → nkwit-ile 'I have called you (perfect)'
f. -sumb-a 'throw' → wásumb-ile 'you threw'
g. -lond-a 'be after sth.' → walond-ile 'he went after..'
h. -sap-a 'be dirty' → apasap-ile 'it has become dirty cl.16'

3.3.8. Wungu

Wungu is an intriguing language as attempts to its classification can show (cf. Nurse 1983). It shares enough with every language group in and around the Corridor to represent a peripheral member, but not enough to be indiscutably classified in any one of them. I therefore prefer to place it alongside a macro Mwika-Nyika group in my own lexicostatistic grouping. It is also a 7V language but quite different from Fipa-Sukuma: the audible difference between the two highest orders is at most times minimal and rather difficult to grasp, and even my old and very sharp informant was confused with the vowel quality of some words. In the case of my younger informant, it was impossible to keep a consistent 7 vowel notation. The same indeterminacy obtains with vowel length, which seems to be mostly dependent on emphasis and a careful vs. fast articulation, in the Inamwanga or Nyiha̧ manner. In this respect, the contrast with the neat Long/Short vowels opposition in Fipa-Sukuma is very marked. Spirantization is governed by the following rules (first-hand data):

*(N)b	/__į	>	vi	*(N)b, d, g	/__ų	>	-vu
*(N)d, g	/__į	>	zi				
*(N)p	/__į	>	fi	*(N)p, t, k	/__ų	>	-fu
*(N)t, k	/__į	>	si				

Table 8. Spirantization rules in Wungu

The same kind of inconsistency has been found with Wungu's spirantization pattern, although it has not been satisfactorily enquired into. The morphs *-ų and *-į- always occur with the inevitable spirantizing of the preceding consonant:

(69) a. -dʒegeʒ-a /zja/ 'tie loosely' → -dʒegev-u 'weak, feable'

b. -tjelef-u 'soft' cf. Inamwanga -telep-e
'soft' from -tele-p-a 'be soft'

(70) a. -ik-a 'go down' → -iʃ-a /sja/ 'take sth. down'

b. -sʊβ-a 'return' → -sʊv-j-a 'return sth.'

c. -kal-a 'dry (intr.)' → -kaʒ-a /zja/ 'dry sth.'

d. -sʊnd-a 'come close' → -sʊʒ-a 'bring sth. close'

The same is not always the case with the agentive *-į where a certain number of stems don't alternate. Still, sample derivatives in all three MP enviroments are not enough to be conclusive:

(71) a. -zond-a 'lead the song' → ʊn̩zond-i 'lead singer'

b. -sʊŋg-a 'guard, watch' → ʊn̩sʊŋng-i 'watchman'

c. -saβ-a isao 'make a fortune' → ʊn̩saβ-i 'rich man'

But:

(72) a. -lel-a 'bear a child' → ʊn̩dez-i 'parent'

b. -iβ-a 'steal' → ʊmwiv-i 'thief'

c. *-dog- 'bewitch' → ʊn̩doz-i 'sorcerer'

d. -βaβ-a 'hurt' → ʊwʊβav-i [w~Ø] 'pain cl.14'

As for the past tense *-įde paradigm (the perfective aspect is rendered by the |-a-Rad-a | form), parallel to a majority of spirantizing *-įde forms, a variation of spirantizing/non spirantizing forms has been noted in some cases, only non-spirantizing forms obtained in others. The idiolect of a third informant, characterized by the other two as more "Safwa-like" was even less spirantizing. The following verbal forms have been obtained from Informant 1, an old man, from the village of Maleza:

(73)	a.	-βal-a	'go'	→ waβaz-ile	'he went'
	b.	-teel-a	'speak'	→ twateez-ile	'we spoke'
	c.	-loot-a	'dream'	→ naloos-ile	'I dreamt'

But:

(74)	a.	-lel-w-a	'be born'	→ walel-il-w-e	~
				walez-il-w-e	'you were born'
	b.	-and-a	'begin'	→ twand-ile	'we begun'
	c.	-zeŋg-a	'build'	→ twazeŋg-ile	'we built'
	d.	-βaβ-a	'hurt'	→ kwambaβ-ile	'it hurt me cl.15'
	e.	-paap-a	'carry on back'	→ apaap-ile	'she carried on the back'

More non-spirantizing past tenses were obtained by Informant 3, a younger man from the town of Galula:

(75)		-teel-a	'speak'	→	nateez-ile 'I spoke'

But:

(76)	a.	-lamb-a	'cross river'	→	βalamb-ile	'they crossed'
	b.	-βal-a	'go'	→	naβal-ile	'I went' (cf. ex.71a)
	c.	-sek-a	'laugh'	→	nasek-ile	'I laughed'

4. Historical scenario

The typological facts outlined above, can be further grouped in the following general table of spirantizing situations in conjunction to vowel systems:

	-Rad-	**-ụ*	**-į-*	**-į*	**-įde*	*Vowel-Systems*
Holoholo	~+	?	~+	_	_	7V, L/S
Kinga	+	+	+	~+	_	7V, L/S
Nyakyusa	+	+	+	~+	_	7V, L/S
Ndali	+	+	+	~+	Ø	5V, L/S
Ngonde	+	+	+	?	_	5V?
Safwa	+	+	+	+	_	7V→5V, L/S
Lambya 1	+	+	+	~+	Ø	5V, L/S
Bemba	+	?	+	+	_	5V, L/S
Fipa-Sukuma	+	+	+	~+	~+	7V, L/S
Wungu	+	+	+	~+	~+	7V→5V, L/S?

Lambya 2	+	+	+	+	+	5V, L/S
Nyiha	+	+	+	+	+	5V, L/S
Southern Fipa	+	+	+	+	+	5V, L/S?
Inamwanga	+	+	+	+	+	5V
Lungu	+	+	+	+	+	5V, L/S

-Rad-: Morpheme-internal spirantization
~: Variation (or restriction in certain consonantal contexts) in the application of spirantizing rule
?: Situation unknown or doubtful
Ø: Not in use
L/S: Phonemic contrast between Long and Short vowels

Table 10. Spirantization patterns and vowel systems in the corpus languages

These facts, also represented in the continuum of §3, suggest the following diachronic scenario:

4.1. Structural evolution of spirantization

Whether genetically or areally determined, spirantization is too important and complexe a change to have undergone completion within a unique evolutional sequence, common to every linguistic group. This fact can be seen in the variety of reflexes and their distribution in the present day languages. In phonological terms, spirantization has led, as Schadeberg 1995 stressed, from the rather simple PB consonantal system—in terms of series, orders and correlations—to the more developed systems of present day spirantizing languages. This statement has been proved particularly true concerning some of the languages presented in this paper, of which Inamwanga ans Nyiha are typical examples.

On the other hand, the chronology of this complexe change is not yet easy to establish. A first impression of a "two-gear spirantization" has already been mentioned. It is also tempting to make a guess as to which of the phonetic environments could have triggered off the whole series of evolutions. These environments combine phonetic naturalness with generality of attestation through the Bantu domain even in the case of very conservative—but nevertheless affected by spirantization—languages like Holoholo and Tswana:[15]

(1) First of all, syllables containing a front high glide /CjV/ (j = non-syllabic i)—cf. both Tswana and Holoholo. The spirantizing force of this environment has been stressed by Bastin 1983. In Holoholo for instance, although most consonants have remained untouched by spirantization morpheme-internally, *d has uniformly turned into [s] in this phonetic

[15]For Holoholo see Coupez 1955; for Tswana see Creissels (in this volume).

environment, even when it is crossed by a morphological border as in causative verbs.

(2) From consonants, first Alveolar and then Velar (and Palatal) consonants merging to Post-alveolars in front of *į and among these, especially voiced segments. Möhlig (1977) has argued for a later involvement of velars based on *g /__HV conservative languages. But Tswana spirantizes regularly the voiceless Velar consonant (*kį > si),[16] while only occasionally its alveolar counterpart (*tį > si ~ ri). For the alveolar voiced phoneme see Holoholo (*dį >si).

(3) Probably *ų combined with labialization of preceding consonants—cf. Nyakyusa. Möhlig (1977) argues that the relative ancientness of consonantal modifications before *-ų is to be seen in the uniformity and development of the phonetic evolutions. This point however needs further consideration, as examination of data from Eastern Bantu languages show non-negligible variation (i.e., both labials and sibilants, affricates and fricatives are attested) in the reflexes of PB consonants before *-ų.

With respect to the dichotomy that formed the basis of the present discussion (lexical vs. morphophonemic spirantization), all relevant phonetic evolutions can be integrated into a framework involving two main structural/functional stages, somewhat arbitrarily delimited, since the whole process was surely continuous.

4.1.1. Stage A

The various phonetic processes that constitute the phonological change globally refered to as "spirantization" are first triggered off morpheme-internally, that is, where no morphological boundary is blocking the influence of the tense high vowels on preceding consonants. Affixes, and more precisely prefixes (i.e., pre-stem or -theme elements), being peripheral to languages where everything centers around the stem, were probably affected the first. This type of progress, first morpheme-internally and then across morphological boundaries, has already been noted by Bastin (1983:25) in regard to spirantization.

In fact the detailed sequence should be (a) morpheme-internally in affixes, (b) stem-internally and (c) across MP borders as it can also be observed in other (morpho-)phonological changes actually in progress or by synchronic comparison and typological analysis in these and other Bantu languages. See for instance the evolutional pattern of palatalization in the Corridor, where the first three cases distinguished in the table can be grouped as morpheme-internal situations as opposed to the fourth (only Palatalization before /i/ is considered):

---

[16]The fact that it extends spirantization to all Front, non-Low Vowels doesn't affect the argument, since the structural tendency towards spirantization is judged to be initiated by High Vowels.

		Nyakyusa	*Ndali*	*Lambya*	*Nyiha*	*Inamwanga*
(1)	cl.7 prefix (ki-C, -V)	-	+	+	+	+
(2)	other /ki-V/ (as in *-joki-a 'to burn')	-	+	+	+	+
(3)	Stem-internally	-	-	+	+	+
(4)	/k-iC/ (+MP border) (*-biik-id-a 'to put Appl.')	-	-	-	+	+

Table 9. Palatalization of /ki/ in Corridor languages

As this table shows, Inamwanga and Nyiha are still the most innovative languages of my corpus in spreading phonetic changes across morphophonemic borders.

Back to the topic of this paper, spirantization begins, roughly at the same time that it affects stems, to spread across morphemes under the influence of the most (phonetically) favourable MP borders and affect the most responsive consonants. Based on comparison of the corpus languages, and especially conservative languages, the first MP environment to undergo spirantization has been the stem-final position preceding causative *-į-. Shortly after that, phonetic spirantizing processes must have extended to stem-final position before the adjectival *-ų, since among the languages of the corpus that use this morph, those who attest no more than causative *-į- MP spirantizing, also spirantize *-ų.

4.1.2. Stage B

Spirantization extends to the agentive *-į context, and finally to the past/perfect paradigm with *-įde. This very context constitutes the threshold of morphologization of the whole change, for once the feature |+ MP Alternation| is introduced into the production of the perfect/Past tense, spirantization becomes a central element of the inflectional morphology, thereby consolidating its regularity in the derivational part of the morphology as well.

Up to that moment—that is before adopting spirantization in the context of *-įde—there was always a possibility of minimizing this morphologization, by using the conservative "auto-defensive" mechanisms of fixing and lexicalization of derivatives, or the substitution of the original non-derived lexeme by a new irrelevant one. We can observe these conservative mechanisms in action since the 19th century until today in Nyakyusa. The same mechanisms seem to function in Ndali and according to Wolff (1905) in Kinga. What we have in these cases is *regression* of spirantization, seen as the normal behaviour of a conservative MP system. On the contrary, at the end of this second stage, spirantization changes its aspect: from a mainly phonological change, it becomes morphologically oriented by maximally exploiting its applicability in all possible MP contexts. We could in this second case talk about *expansion* of spirantization. As we have seen in §3.2.4. for Nyiha, this expanding tendency has been observed even in contexts where no etymological High vowel can be reconstructed with certainty.

4.2. Phonemic systems in the Corridor

4.2.1. Languages with limited MP spirantization and their vowel systems

Thus languages attesting minimal/restricted MP spirantization have undergone Stage A and the first steps of Stage B which constitute a transitional phase to morphologization. But the whole process was for the first time blocked when spirantization before *-ịde was imminent, that is before attaining the critical point of morphologization. Whereby, the various phonetic processes were deactivated before the global change reached completion. Languages like Bemba seem to have accomodated their MP system to fully integrate the newly created alternations although lexicalization of derivatives is not unknown. In more conservative languages like Nyakyusa and Kinga, and even Ndali, the post-deactivation reaction with respect to existing MP alternations is, as it has already been mentioned, to rehabilitate the ancient non-alternating pattern (regression of spirantization). As our most ancient sources testify,[17] this final rehabilitation stage for these languages took place quite recently, as late as the nineteenth century, which in its turn means that historical spirantization was active in the MP domain until relatively late in parts (or the whole?) of the Corridor.

Whether this conservative morphophonemic behaviour constitutes a shared historical feature (i.e., motivated by a common "stylistic" choice among two structural alternatives, conservatism or innovation) or separate individual evolutions (i.e., structurally well motivated in each case) it is too early to say. I can't help feeling though, that such a central element in the structural profile of all these languages can't be *le fruit du hasard*; maybe we should face the possibility of an inherited ancestral tendency, with the classificational consequences that it entails. All the same, we cannot rule out the possibility that this tendency, either towards blocking MP spirantization or towards promoting it, has been horizontally transmitted (i.e. diffused) to other languages in contact (see §5.2.). On one condition: that this transmission took place when spirantization in the recipient language was still evolving and its outcome was yet unsettled. Only then could we talk about a "diffused change". As I will try to demonstrate in §5.2.2., this cannot be the case in either Fipa-Sukuma or Wungu, which

---

[17] Schumann's data were collected in 1890 and published in 1899, Wolff's in the first years of the 20th century.

show the signs of "structural interference"—as analysed by Weinreich (1953)—between two already settled systems.

Now to link this evolution with the other major theme of this paper, what is happening all this time in the vowel systems of these languages? I think the correct answer is: "Nothing was necessarily happening in them".. Spirantization was then still a phonetic change centered on the consonants under modification, and even though a new correlation was finally added in the phonological system, new phones are still not fully phonologized yet. The only difference with the situation prior to spirantization has been that a certain instability in the balance between vowels and consonants was created, thus opening new possibilities for restructuring.

At the point where conservative languages blocked spirantization in the MP domain, two options were open for their vowel systems:

(1) Preserve 7V system—this is still the situation in Nyakyusa, Kinga, Holoholo and other spirantizing 7V languages as well as in Safwa until very recently

(2) Follow natural tendency for innovation and merge to 5V—this happened in Ndali, Bemba and, if my data are correct, in Ngonde.

4.2.2. Languages with Full MP spirantization and their vowel Systems

In the languages of this group (i.e., Southern Mwika Group and Nyiha; Wungu and Fipa-Sukuma will be examined in §5.1.2) spirantization was deactivated only after Stage B had reached completion. From this point of view, these languages were too innovative for their vowel system to be left untouched. Therefore, following the continuously decreasing phonetic distance between the two higher orders and the resulting confusion (actually taking place in Safwa or, as I believe, in Wungu), merger of the old 7V system to a 5V system was inevitable.

As it has already been established, the evolution towards the 5V systems can be linked to the overall structure of the phonological system, more precisely the enrichment of the consonantal system. The present paper further argues that in spirantizing Bantu languages it is the enrichment of the underlying morphophonemic structure as a whole that necessarily involves restructuring (i.e. reduction) of the vowel system.

Seen in a time perspective, the whole process can be represented as a sequence of four evolutionary steps:

T1: Stage A of spirantization (all spirantizing languages)
T2: [Vowel reduction—optional]
T3: Stage B of spirantization (only the most innovative languages)
T4: Vowel reduction—necessary

5. The Areal Factor

Let us now consider the role of non-structural factors in the progression of these two changes. Since vowel reduction has more or less been established by Schadeberg 1995 as a well-motivated change regardless of spirantization, we should rather adopt the view that each of the two changes can be—and possibly has been—incited or accelerated independently by the sociolinguistic environment, rather than consider both changes as necessarily diffused *en bloc*. This approach is also justified by the data, as it will become clear from the following discussion. Under the term "sociolinguistic environment" are considered, not only the commonly discussed phenomena of contact and diffusion, but also intimate-contact-situations like convergence of different linguistic strata.

5.1. The Spread of vowel reduction

The influence of regular contacts with linguistic communities where no opposition between high and mid-high vowels was maintained must have been very important for the more conservative languages of this region, for there clearly exists an areal patterning of 5V vs. 7V languages, which cuts across groups that show undoubted genetic bonds, of which the most salient example is the Nyakyusa group.

The Nyakyusa-speaking communities (i.e., Nyakyusa proper, Kukwe, Selya...), being relatively isolated from the rest of the Corridor by physical barriers, maintained close relations only with their eastern neighbours, the Kinga, as isolated as themselves. Regular contacts were also kept with their northern neighbours, the Poroto fraction of the Safwa, a group even more isolated than the other two (cf. Wilson 1958). Furthermore, the nineteenth century saw the overwhelming spread and influence of the Sangu, a military and linguistically conservative group, into their territories.

On the other hand, the Ndali community was geographically and socially dissociated from the Nyakyusa and more open to the innovative savanna groups to their west. Being actively implicated in the regional commerce (cf. Kalinga 1979) they participated in the introduction and spread of the new pronunciation habits, of which vowel reduction and /ki/ or /si/ Palatalization are two examples. As for Ngonde, if the 5V system observed in my young informants' speech is a widespread feature, it can certainly be supported by the social and political expansionism of the Ngonde kingdom, which incorporated many innovative linguistic groups (among them Lungu/Mambwe and Lambya).

Another areal split of this type separates Nyiha and Lambya from their more conservative affiliated languages, Safwa and Malila, although more research is needed to clear up this picture. Nowadays, with the establishment of contacts between the isolated Safwa and the more innovative groups, the former's 7V system seems about to collapse. Nothing more is known about the situation in Malila.

These networks of contacts, reflecting the distribution of vowel systems, divide the Corridor into:

(1) *An Eastern conservative enclave*, inwardly turned and mutually-supportive, open only to the North, where another conservative bloc survives (Kimbu, Sangu, Konongo etc.)

(2) *A Western innovative zone*, spreading far into Central and Southern Africa.

5.2. The Spread of spirantization

Several important questions are related to this issue:

(a) Is there a more or less uniform chronological schedule for the emergence, spread and completion of spirantization throughout Eastern Bantu? For instance, are there cases where spirantization is still an active phonetic process?

(b) Is spirantization diffusable? Has it in effect been diffused? Under what conditions?

I will not attempt here to give direct answers to these questions. I will only deal in a general way with what bears directly on a point that hasn't been treated so far, namely the situation in Fipa-Sukuma and Wungu. But before this discussion, let's ask a general but inevitable question: What should spirantization look like while being an active change?

5.2.1. Model of change

The study of linguistic evolution has shown that the main caracteristics of a phonological change in progress are:

(1) It is *regular* and *general*, that is, applying wherever its structural conditions are met without reference to semantic factors, although some lexemes and fields precede, for sociolinguistic or stylistic reasons, in the creation or adoption of a new pronunciation "fashion". The change is said to be extinct either when all relevant contexts have been affected by the phonetic rules into operation, or when rule application is blocked prematurely, after what, remaining relevant contexts appear unaffected.

(2) Sound change is, in acoustic and articulatory terms, abrupt (cf. Ohala 1993:266). But, where complex phonological changes like spirantization are concerned, the process refered to as "sound change" is *gradual* in the sense that it modifies the speech habits of the speakers by one phonetic step at the time. The attempt to determine "how large a 'quantum jump' is permitted between two segments" (Lass 1978:251),—i.e., the size of this phonetic step, which in its turn determines the "abruptness" of the phonetic change, is not yet definitely resolved: for what we know, it could be either language-specific or universally-determined (cf. Lass 1978:251-259). Focusing on the phonetic dimension of spirantization, Hyman (1978) has analysed the intermediate phonetic steps, usually overlooked when spirantization is 'telescoped', i.e., seen as a finite phonological change where only the input and output are of interest. These intermediate steps include some stage of aspiration and/or affrication, followed by deaffrication (for example *pi > p^{hi} ~ p^{fi} > pfi > fi). I should further like to stress the fact that, irrespectively of their phonetic content and their number,

intermediate stages are not only possible or optional, but necessary for the transformation of a stop to a fricative.[18] The importance of this point will be evident in the analysis of the Fipa-Sukuma and Wungu material.

(3) In sociolinguistic terms, the most prominent—and observable—feature of a change in progress is synchronic *variation between two competing forms*, representing two consequent steps of the change separated only by one "quantum leap" as specified in the language . The fate of the potential change can be statistically estimated by measuring the proportion of occurrence of each form in the speech of one individual and of the community as a whole.[19]

Therefore, spirantization should be said to be actively occurring in a present day language if the above conditions are met.

5.2.2. Two sociolinguistic (and structural) accidents

Lambya is not considered here, although it certainly represents a very interesting case of "socioliguistic accident". The difference with the other two exceptional varieties, Wungu and Fipa-Sukuma, is that, Lambya being a 5V language, the irregularity is not so much intra-systemic as cross-dialectological. Lambya behaves either as a minimally-spirantizing or as a maximally-spirantizing language, following the environment it's in. Still, the data are insufficient and it is more than possible that structural irregularities emerge with a more detailed research, in which case a similar interpretation like the following one would be proposed.

According to the scenario of evolution outlined above, the profile of Wungu and Fipa-Sukuma is considered abnormal. Normally, an innovative language shouldn't maintain a conservative vowel-system. And, normally, an innovative language should behave so without hesitation and inconsistency. Could it be that these two languages are actually still undergoing the final Stage of spirantization (whether inherently motivated or by diffusion) whereby, in accordance with the scenario, vowel reduction is imminent? In other words, do we have here two quite normal innovative MP systems, of the Inamwanga type, even though the whole process has, for some unknown reason, been retarded?

I have three good reasons why this isn't so:

(1) The timing of this so-called active change is wrong.

In every other language of the Corridor spirantization either has already been extinct for about a century or more now or it hasn't occurred at all (cf. Kimbu). To what extent this statement about chronology is applicable to the rest of Eastern Bantu is not of the present study to decide. Hinnebusch, Nurse, and Mould (1981:17) remark on Sukuma/Nyamwezi: "in Sukuma/Nyamwezi there is considerable evidence that spirantization is now

---

18This statement concerns more speicifically [f, v, s, z], not [β, ð, ɣ], for which no intermediate step is necessary, as the situation in Spanish can show.

19These are very general principles, resumed in Lass 1984.

beginning there". At first sight however, spirantization in these languages, seen in the light of the principles outlined in §5.2.1., seems more random and frozen than active (data from Maganga and Schadeberg 1992 for Nyamwezi, Batibo 1985 for Sukuma). Regardless of facts in West Tanzania, the ambiguous behaviour of Fipa-Sukuma and Wungu, seen under the chronological perspective in the Corridor, is hard to explain.

(2) The nature of the signs of this so-called active change is wrong.

We have previously determined in theory what spirantization should look like while still being an active change (§5.2.1). In the lexicon of both Fipa-Sukuma and Wungu, wherever spirantization has occurred, it has by now already produced its final output, i.e., spirant consonants and a new stops/spirants correlation, which is the most common outcome across spirantizing Bantu. Consider now in practice the historical derivation of a past/perfect tense form both in Wungu and Fipa-Sukuma. The lexical item chosen is the PB *-kád- 'become dry'. Remember that Fipa-Sukuma is a devoicing language, while Wungu has kept the correlation of voice in its spirant reflexes:

	a. Wungu	*b. Fipa-Sukuma*
Input	*-kad-i̧le	*-kad-i̧le
(1) Affricate stops/__HV	-kadile~kad^{z}ile~kadzile	-kadile~kad^{z}ile~kadzile
{Devoice Affricates}	-	{- kadzile~ka^{t}sile
(2) Deaffricate/Spirantize	-kadzile~ka^{d}zile~kazile	-katsile~ka^{t}sile~kasile}
		{-kadzile~ka^{d}zile~kazile
{Devoice spirants}	-	-kazile~kasile}
Output	-kazile	-kasile

{...}: either—or[20]
NUMBERING: necessary rule ordering

Table 11. Model of observable synchronic variation within a diachronic linguistic change

Irrespectively of the accuracy of the phonetic modifications suggested, what should be synchronically observable in the speech of one speaker, if spirantization was indeed active, is minimally-distanced variation [1~2] or [2~3] or [3~4] in a series of phonetic changes ordered 1-2-3-4. And, since in Wungu and Fipa-Sukuma we are apparently dealing with the closing stages of spirantization, something like [Affricated~Deaffricated] forms should be

[20] I include here two possibilities of ordering for devoicing, that is, early devoicing of affricates, or late devoicing of spirants, though only detailed comparative study will establish which type of evolution, among these cited here or others, is the most plausible.

regularly found in the contact of agentive *-į or past/Perfect *-įle. However, as all the available data show, no such systematic variation is found.

Instead, both languages attest selective, more-than-one-step-apart formal variation. We actually find juxtaposed the input and the output of a complex change that certainly took centuries and more than one phonetic step to be completed. For instance, Fipa-Sukuma varies between [ti] < *tį as in *náloot-íle* and [si] < *tį as in *náloos-íle*—example (68b). In other forms only [pi, ti, ki] of a non-spirantizing variety appear, while still in others only the regular final [fi, si] of a spirantizing variety are obtained. Within a single linguistic system, this variation is normally synchronically impossible.

One more point should be stressed: for spirantization to produce a well-formed output, the only phonetically correct input is a stop consonant and not any corresponding lenited form. This statement bears more particularly on the voiced input segments, often represented in Eastern Bantu as *B, *L, *G (see for instance Hinnebusch 1981) due to the usually lenited variants found today in non-prenasalized environnements and which should be a phonetic feature of early Eastern Bantu. However, only *b, *d and *g can result to spirants through affrication. Thus, even if we accept that spirantization is attained through one phonetic step and that its input and output can coexist in synchronic variation, this variation would have to be between [b, d, g] on one hand and [v, z] or [f, s] on the other. In practice, variants like **waled-ilwe* ~ *walez-ilwe* should alternate in Wungu example (74a). But this is once more not the case. The non-spirantizing, lenited forms like *walel-ilwe* or *kwaambaβ-ile*, ex. (74d), which coexist with spirantizing forms both in Wungu and in Fipa-Sukuma, are in reality the normal output of a language that hasn't undergone spirantization in this context. Such a variety has subsequently undergone lenition rule affecting PB voiced stops not only in the context of the non-tense vowels (for example *d > l /__a,o,e,ʊ,i) but also before the tense high vowels (*d > l /__i,u); evidently, this change occurs only where spirantization hasn't eliminated these stops. Therefore, according to the derivation which follows, *walel-ilwe* and *walez-ilwe* cannot but constitute two different outputs produced in two different linguistic varieties by two different phonetic evolutions:

	a. spirantizing variety	*b. Non-spirantizing variety*
Input	*-ded-įd-u-e	*-ded-įd-u-e
1. Affricate stops/__HV	-dedz-id-u-e	-
2. Deaffricate/Spirantize	-de^{d}z-id-u-e~dez-id-u-e	-
3. Lenit Voiced stops	-lez-il-u-e	-lel-il-u-e
Output	-lezilwe	-lelilwe

Table 12. Historical derivation of a spirantizing and a non-spirantizing variant

The evolution of column b has occurred for instance in Nyakyusa example (13d) from PB *-buud- and Kinga example (18c) from PB *-dod-. Let's sum up the facts: In Fipa-Sukuma and Wungu, the existence of both spirantizing and non-spirantizing past/perfect tense or agentive forms cannot be the sign of active spirantization affecting the last morphophonemic environments. Actually, the type of variation observed is not intra-systemic but trans-systemic.

(3) The vowel quality in the so-called active change is wrong.

To consider vowel reduction as imminent for Wungu is not a far-fetched prediction, given the phonetic instability and frequent confusion of the two highest orders in this language. But as I am arguing here, spirantization in Wungu is already extinct and therefore, this imminent vowel reduction is not directly linked to it. However, things are very different in Fipa-Sukuma, where the phonetic clarity of the 7V system makes vowel reduction a improbable outcome in the near future, therefore contradicting once more the hypothesis of an active closing stage of spirantization.

Since the possibility of an active change is ruled out, there remains one plausible interpretation for the situation in Wungu and Fipa-Sukuma. According to it, inconsistencies in the pattern aren't but the manifestation of structural interference between the two polar MP systems in contact. What must have, for instance, been introduced in the linguistic system called Fipa-Sukuma—an essentially conservative language—is not so much active morphophonemic spirantization as spirantization's result, the *produit fini* in the form of a set of synchronic rules. Only by the non-phonetic nature of the diffused object, can the immunity of the vowel system be explained.

We could think that diffusion through contact is enough for the adoption of the innovative MP mechanism in replacement to a more conservative system; but this replacement seems too radical to have been diffused by simple contact. Bemba has been in contact with the Southern Mwika Group for centuries (cf. Roberts 1973) and it hasn't been tempted to introduce spirantization in the production of the past/perfect tense. In a similar manner, Safwa has been more and more exposed to Nyiha influence since the 19th century. The impact of this contact can already be seen in the ongoing reduction of Safwa's 7V system. Still, no sign that Safwa is adopting spirantization in front of *-i̯de is found. More intimate contact is, I believe, necessary for such situations to emerge and 'diffusion' should be replaced by 'structural mixing'. In fact, this structural mixing is part of an overall social and linguistic convergence between populations coming from two different horizons in each case:

(1) For the Fipa-Sukuma—populations of the Southern Mwika group (i.e., Southern Fipa, Lungu, Mambwe, Wanda, Inamwanga) in intimate cohabitation with the Sukuma, a group of ultimately different origins, difficult to establish as yet. The cosmopolitan character of the "Fipa" society has already been stressed out by Willis (1981); it is also visible in

the linguistic structure, of which the spirantizing MP system is but one aspect. The unity of the Mwika lexicostatistic group is another.

(2) For the Wungu—populations of the Southern Mwika type, intermingling with populations of the Kimbu (or Safwa?) type. Although little is known about the history of this group, I believe that detailed ethnographic and historical research will confirm this population mixing' hypothesis.

6. Conclusions

In this paper, I have attempted to detect any other parameter that might determine the historical links between spirantization and vowel reduction, described by Schadeberg (1995) as a structural balance between the consonantal and the vocalic sub-systems. After examining and categorizing the Corridor data, the impression remains that vowel reduction, once a certain threshold of structural complexity in the consonantal system is crossed, is potentially an independent innovation, liable to areal diffusion without regard to the spirantizing pattern of the languages in contact. In fact, the evolution of certain 5V languages in the Corridor (Ndali, Bemba, Wungu, Safwa) can be best explained if vowel reduction is considered an innovation in its own right.

By distinguishing between (a) spirantization as a phonological change having affected the lexicon in an opaque manner and (b) spirantization as a morphophonemic change having introduced a new mechanism of alternations in today's languages, the structural relation between vowel reduction and spirantization is further elucidated. Thus, the degree of interdependence between these two changes and the necessity of occurrence of vowel reduction after spirantization is not simply a function of the structural balance in a language's phonemic system. It is, more precisely, a function of how profoundly spirantization has affected the synchronic morphophonemic system, by creating a general and systematic alternation mechanism between stops and spirants. The deeper this spirantizing action has been in the morphophonemic domain,—'deeper' refering to the most productive spirantizing context *-i̹de—the more it entails the reduction of the vowel system.

Under this new parameter, 7V languages having undergone spirantization (Nyakyusa, Kinga...) appear quite normal, since, as data analysis shows, spirantization in their case is limited to the lexicon and to the less compromizing morphological contexts (derivation). Similarly, 5V languages having undergone only the same limited pattern of spirantization (Ndali, Bemba...) also behave in a normal expected way, since, vowel reduction can become active through inherent or areal motivation. It must be stressed though, that once vowel reduction is activated as a phonetic process, it necessarily blocks any further progression of spirantization by eliminating its determining phonetic environment: in these 5V languages as well as in the case of spirantizing 7V languages, spirantization's phonetic mechanisms seem to have been short-lived.

The most direct interdependence between the two changes is apparent in the most structurally innovative languages, i.e., those that have undergone spirantization in all possible morphophonemic environments thus modifying significantly their morphophonemic systems (both derivation and inflection). In these languages (Inamwanga, Lungu, Nyiha etc.) vowel reduction is indeed considered as a necessary adjunct of spirantization. Furthermore, a difference of timing must be supposed in their case, for, in order to attain all possible environements, spirantizing processes must have been active for a longer period of time.

This pattern of behaviour being established, the possible combination of a fully innovative (i.e., spirantizing) morphophonemic system with a conservative 7V system is considered abnormal. Unless material from different parts of the Bantu territory proves this combination to be regular and frequent, thereby invalidating the reasoning in this paper, an explanation of a different order must be sought for the few apparently contradictory cases. I suggest that this explanation must involve a more detailed knowledge of sociolinguistic and historical networks in the area where the abnormal pattern occurs. There is a strong possibility that the present day situation reflects the "structural mixing" of two (or more?) languages in contact. If this is indeed so, the impact of such a contact should also be detectable in other parts of the language structures (cf. Thomason & Kaufman 1988). Such an explanation is offered here for the two Corridor languages which combine extensive (but inconsistent) MP spirantization with a 7V system, i.e., Wungu and Fipa-Sukuma.

Finally, as the historical scenario proposed in this paper suggests, it is the overall spirantizing profile (not only phonological but also morphophonemic) of each language that should be taken as a global genetic criterion for classification.

It should be borne in mind that this paper is only an introductory discussion to a huge and very promising subject that embraces the whole domain of Eastern Bantu. Only the Corridor languages are here explicitly treated and the conclusions cannot but be partial and provisional. Furthermore, limitations are imposed by the relatively insufficient volume of data, since for this type of analysis an extensive dialectological survey is necessary. Thus, in spite of the categorical tone sometimes adopted, what I have tried to do, much more than provide easy solutions, is to attract the interest of other comparatists to this direction of research. Only with collective comparative work will more mysteries of the Bantu expansion be resolved.

References

Bastin, Y. 1983. *La finale verbale -IDE et l'imbrication en Bantu.* Tervuren: Musée Royal, no 114.

Batibo, H. 1985. *Le kesukuma (langue bantu de Tanzanie): phonologie, morphologie*. Paris: Editions Recherche sur les Civilisations.

Busse, J. 1939-40. Lambya Texte, in *Zeitschrift für Eingeborenen Sprachen* , 30(3): 250-72.

Busse, J. 1940-41. «Lautlehre des Inamwanga» in *Zeitschrift für Eingeborenen Sprachen* 31(1): 21-50.

Busse, J. 1960. *Die Sprache der Nyiha in Ostafrika*. Berlin: Akademie Verlag

Coupez, A. 1955. *Esquisse de la langue Holoholo*. Annales du Musée Royal du Congo Belge, Vol. 12.

Creissels, D. 1999. "Remarks on the sound correspondences between Proto-Bantu and Tswana (S.31) (with particular attention to problems involving *j (or *y), *į and *NC sequences). In this volume.

Dominicy, M. & D. Demolin (eds.) 1995. *Sound Change*. Amsterdam: John Benjamins.

Fisiak, J. (ed). 1978. *Recent developments in Historical Phonology*. The Hague-Mouton.

Guthrie, M. 1967-70. *Comparative Bantu*. 4Vols. London: Cregg.

Hinnebusch, T. 1981. Northeast Coastal Bantu, in T.Hinnebusch, D.Nurse, & M. Mould (eds). 21-125

Hinnebusch, T., D. Nurse & M. Mould, (eds). 1981. *Studies in the Classification of Eastern Bantu Languages. S.U.G.I.A.* 3.

Hyman, L. M. 1977. Phonologization, in A.Juilland (ed), 407-418.

Hyman, L. M. 1994. Cyclic phonology and morphology in Cibemba. In J. Cole and Charles Kisseberth (eds.), *Perspectives in Phonology,* 81-112. Stanford: C.S.L.I.

Jones, C. (ed). 1993. *Historical Linguistics: Problems and Perspectives*. London: Longman.

Juilland, A. (ed). 1977. *Linguistic studies presented to Joseph H.Greenberg*. Saratoga: Anma Libri.

Kagaya, R. 1987. *A classified vocabulary of the Lungu language*. Tokyo: Institute for the Study of Languages & Cultures of Asia and Africa.

Kalinga, O. 1979. Trade, the Kyungus and the emergence of the Ngonde Kingdom of Malawi, *International Journal of African Historical Studies* 12(1): 17-39.

Konter-Katani, M. No date. *A Nyakyusa-English Wordlist*. Leiden (polycopied).

Labroussi, Catherine. 1998. *Le Couloir de Lacs — Contribution linguistique à l'histoire des populations du sud-ouest de la Tanzanie*. [PhD dissertation, INALCO].

Lass, R. 1978. Mapping constraints in phonological reconstruction: on climbing down trees without falling out of them, in: J.Fisiak (ed), 245-284.

Lass, R. 1984. *Phonology*. Cambridge University Press.

Maganga, C. & T. Schadeberg. 1992. *Kinyamwezi-Grammar, Texts, Vocabulary*. Köln: R.Köppe Verlag.

Meeussen, A. E. 1967. Bantu grammatical reconstructions, *Africana Linguistica*. Tervuren: Musée Royal de l'Afrique Centrale, 61(3): 81-121.

Meeussen, A. E. [1980]. *Bantu Lexical Reconstructions*. Tervuren: Musée Royal de l'Afrique Centrale, n°27. Reprint 1956(27).

Möhlig, W. 1977. Zur frühen Siedlungsgeschichte der Savannen-Bantu aus lauthistorischer Sicht, in W. Möhlig, F. Rottland & B. Heine (eds), 166-193.

Möhlig, W., F. Rottland & B. Heine (eds). 1977. *Zur Sprachgeschichte und Ethnohistorie in Afrika*. Berlin: Dietrich Reimer.

Nurse, D. 1988. The diachronic background to the language communities of Southwestern Tanzania, *S.U.G.I.A.* 9: 15-115.

Ohala, J. 1993. The phonetics of sound change, in: C. Jones (ed), 237-278.

Roberts, A. 1973. *A History of the Bemba*. London: Longman.

Schadeberg, T. 1973. Kinga: A restricted tone system, *Studies in African Linguistics* 4(1): 23-47.

Schadeberg, T. 1995. Spirantization and the 7-to-5 vowel Merger in Bantu, in: M. Dominicy & D. Demolin (eds), 73-84.

Schumann, C. 1899. Grundriss einer Grammatik der Kondesprache, *Mitteilungen des Seminars für Orientalische Sprachen* 2: 1-86.

Thomason, S.G. & T. Kaufman, 1988. Language contact, creolization, and genetic linguistics. Berkeley: University of California Press.

Vail, L. 1972 . The noun classes of Ndali, *Journal of African Languages* 11(3): 21-47.

Voorhoeve, J. 1973. Safwa as a restricted tone system, *Studies in African Linguistics* 4(1): 1-21.

Voorhoeve, J. No date. *A Grammar of Safwa*. Leiden (polycopied).

Voorhoeve, J. & Ng. Mwangoka. No date. *Cursus ki-Nyakyusa*. Leiden (polycopied)

Weinreich, U. 1953. *Languages in contact*. New York: Linguistic Cercle of N.Y.

Whiteley, W. 1964. Suggestions for recording a Bantu language in the field, *Tanzania Notes & Records* 62: 1-19.

Willis, R. 1978. *There was a certain man—spoken art of the Fipa*. Oxford: Clarendon Press.

Willis, R. 1981. *A State in the Making—Myth, History and Social Transformation in Pre-colonial Ufipa*. Bloomington: Indiana University Press.

Wilson, M. 1958. *Peoples of the Nyassa-Tanganyika Corridor*. Cape Town: School of African Studies.

Wolff, R. 1905. *Grammatik der Kingasprache*. Berlin: D.Reimer.

Katupha's Law in Makhuwa

THILO C. SCHADEBERG*
University of Leiden

Introduction

J. M. M. Katupha, in his M.Phil. thesis on the Makhuwa dialect E-Saaka, makes the following observation about co-occurrence restrictions of aspirated consonants (1983:27):

> There are certain constraints on the choice of consonants in successive syllables at least within the lexeme. Thus, while there are found sequences such as: –asp...–asp. (-tek-), –asp...+asp. (-tath-), +asp...–asp. (-that-), the sequence +asp…+asp. is not found, although it may occur across morpheme boundaries.
>
> e.g., Kha-ƫhunale "he did not want"
>
> In some circumstances this leads to the de-aspiration of plosives,

* Several colleagues have critically commented on earlier versions of this paper, and I would like to thank them for their suggestions: Yvonne Bastin, Derek Nurse, John M. Stewart, and the editors of this volume, Larry M. Hyman and Jean-Marie Hombert. I am particularly grateful to Charles W. Kisseberth, who has worked on various Makhuwa dialects for a number of years and was kind enough to share with me his views on the topic discussed in this paper. I have incorporated most of his comments, but we should note that, unfortunately, he did not have access to the bulk of his Makhuwa materials when he wrote to me.

e.g.,	-phwe-	'to get broken'	but	-pwes-	'break'.
	-khum-	'come out'	but	-kumih-	'take out'.

This is probably a regular morpho-phonological process but the rules have not been investigated yet.

In this article, I attempt a slightly more detailed investigation of the synchronic and diachronic processes involving aspiration in Makhuwa, and I suggest the name "Katupha's Law" for th'e specific process of Deaspiration. I also compare Deaspiration in Makhuwa to that in Swahili, and in a final section I look at a possible relationship between Katupha's Law and Dahl's Law.

1. Restriction on aspiration in Makhuwa

Makhuwa, spoken in Mozambique and in neighbouring Tanzania and bearing the code P.31 in Guthrie's referential classification, has aspirated and non-aspirated voiceless plosives (and affricates) at four or five points of articulation, depending on the particular dialect and/or the description. (In this article, I follow the orthographic conventions which are customary in Mozambique and have been accepted by NELIMO, 1989.)

(1)	*bilabial*	*dental*	*retroflex*	*palatal*	*velar*
	p	t	tt	c	k
	ph	th	tth	ch	kh

The distinction bears a high functional load in the lexicon which is not surprising given the absence of distinctive voicing in the phonological system.

(2)	o-pak-a	'to do, to make'	o-phak-a	'to befriend'
	o-tek-a	'to build'	o-thek-a	'to peel'
	o-ttap-a	'to overcook'	o-tthap-a	'to dance for joy'
	o-kom-a	'to hit with hammer'	o-khom-a	'to blow'

The above minimal pairs are from Katupha (1983:23). His ESaaka does not have an aspirated palatal affricate, but some other dialects do. The following two examples are from Prata (1990).

(3)	ocapa	'to wash (clothing)'	ochanana	'to fear'

There are no restrictions as to the position of the aspirated consonant within the stem, even in the presence of other voiceless plosives capable of being aspirated (examples from Prata 1990).

(4)	ottipha	'to extinguish'	otthukula	'to untie'
	ottokottha	'to ripen'	ottikhela	'to throw (appl.)'
	okulakuttha	'to move about'	ottikitthela	'to rub (appl.)'

Katupha says that the restriction holds "at least within the lexeme", and he gives an example with the negative formative *kha-* which may freely precede a verb stem containing an aspirated consonant *(vide supra).* More precisely, we may say that the restriction holds within the stem; the stem being that part of a word which contains the root as well as derivational and—in the case of verbs—inflectional suffixes. The restriction applies to the whole stem, not just to adjacent syllables.

Counterexamples, i.e. words with two aspirated consonants, are rare in Makhuwa dictionaries. In Prata's Makhuwa-Portuguese dictionary (1990; ca. 500 pages), I have searched the section on infinitives (conveniently put together by being cited with the nominal prefix *o-* or *w-)* as well as the nouns of class 9 starting with the prefix *e-* where for historical reasons stem-initial aspirated consonants may be expected to be particularly frequent (see below); I have only cursorily looked at other sections of the dictionary. In this way, I have collected the following apparent counterexamples:

(5)	ethalapha	'tax receipt; work done instead of tax, receipt for such work'
		cf. ethalapa 'small gift of meat' [for the chief?]
		cf. Prata 1973 etalapha 'tax receipt'
	ethethemere	'trembling; greed'
		cf. otetemera, ottettemera 'to tremble';
		cf. Prata 1973 etetere 'earthquake'
	ekhaikhai	'truth' cf. Prata 1973 ekaikhai idem; this is also the form supported by Kisseberth (pers. comm.)
	epharaphara	'peritoneum; insect sp.' cf. ephara 'an animal whose skin is used for drums'
	ephitophito	'hammer made from ebony, mace' cf. ephito idem
	nikhovokhovo	'drop, drizzle of rain'
	nikuphe-kuphe	'fan'
	otupha-tupha	'to jump many times'
		cf. otupha 'to jump'

otthuwa-tthuwa 'to come and go, to be very busy'
cf. otthuwa 'to emit smoke'

The first item is the only one which does not involve reduplication, and its value as a counter-example is rather dubious because the expected form with only one aspirated consonant is given in Prata's earlier dictionary. The second example involves partial reduplication, and again the transcription appears to be uncertain. The other examples all have fully reduplicated stems. We cannot exclude the possibility that the restriction on aspirated consonants is less strict for reduplicated stems, but we return to the issue in the following section.

2. Deaspiration in Makhuwa

Bound morphemes with aspirated consonants are rare in Makhuwa. No nominal class prefix or concord prefix has an aspirated consonant, and more importantly, there is no verbal extension with such a consonant which would give us a chance to observe what happens when two aspirates come together within one stem. However, Prata (1990) contains a significant number of examples where the addition of the causative extension *-ih-* or one of its shorter allomorphs involving *x* [ʃ] coincides with loss of aspiration in the stem, both at C_1 and C_2.

(6)	ottipha	'to extinguish (itr.)'	ottipiha	'to extinguish (tr.)'
	okhuma	'to leave'	okumiha	'to extract, to make leave'
	othuma	'to buy'	otumiha	'to sell'
	otuthuwa	'to be frightened'	otutuxa	'to frighten'
	ophattuwa	'to occur, to evolve'	opattuxa	'to make appear, to produce'
	ophiya	'to arrive'	opixa	'to make arrive'
	ophweya	'to break (itr.)'	opwexa	'to break (tr.)'

I believe that these examples are too systematic to be discarded as transcription errors. In addition, all the examples selected here are confirmed by Centis 1985. True, in most derived causative verb stems the dictionary does not indicate loss of aspiration, and some of the words cited here appear in two shapes, i.e., *ottiphiha* and *ophattuxa*. Some such variability may be real[1], but it is also possible that Prata has "regularized" the spelling in an

---

[1] Kisseberth (pers. comm.) writes: "I did a very systematic study of this [deaspiration in causatives, TCS] for Ikorovere and Imitthupi... and there are many examples of the phenomenon. On the other hand, it is clear that deaspiration is not enforced to the same extent in all contexts and all dialects... It seems to me that the variation is most prevalent when the consonants are not in adjacent syllables." This would agree well with our observation that

attempt to keep the stem constant. This would be understandable given his being unaware of a productive phonological process.

Additional support for the process of Deaspiration comes from reduplication. We have already seen in (5) that Prata (1990) contains several examples of fully reduplicated stems where Deaspiration does not seem to apply. However, there are also examples where it does:

(7)	epwittipwitthi	'sheep, ram'
	nipattapattha	'horn (for blowing)'; also nipattapatta, nipalapatta

The item 'sheep' is confirmed in this shape by all my sources on Makhuwa (and I have checked it personally with several speakers). It is also interesting to look at verb stems with partial reduplication, i.e., verbs which in all probability are historically derived by doubling the initial syllable of the stem: -cvCVC-. Such verbs usually carry an iterative meaning, often describing movements which consist of many oscillating repetitions. The identification of such verbs often relies on semantic intuition since the underived verb is generally not attested.

(8)	okakhara	'to rain, with big drops'; cf. okakarexa (caus.) idem
	okukhusula	'to gnaw'
	opephera	'to have sexual intercourse'
	otuthunya	'to limp'
	otuthuwa	'to be frightened, to be startled'
	ottitthima	'to flash (of lightning) and thunder'
	ottutthumera	'to sprinkle (salt, dust, incense etc.) on sth.'
	ottyatthya	'to jump from one branch to another (iter.)'

Examples as these are abundant in Prata (1990). They have a plain plosive as C_1 and an aspirated plosive as C_2. The inverse, such as *otthottonka* 'to stress', is rare, but in one case both forms are given with the same meaning: *okhukusula.* (Of course, sequences of two syllables with identical non-aspirated consonants are also frequent.)

The examples involving reduplication suggest that Deaspiration applies in Makhuwa to all but the last aspirated C in a stem. We shall see in the next section that the same process underlies Deaspiration in the causative derivation, and I shall refer to this process as "Katupha's Law".

3. On the origin of aspirated consonants in Makhuwa

According to Meinhof (1908) and Guthrie (1967-71), aspirated (voiceless) consonants in Makhuwa have basically two sources: prenasalized voiceless

---

Deaspiration is less regular in full than in partial reduplication, compare (5) with (8).

stops and voiceless stops before a high closed vowel. In the absence of any detailed historical study of the Makhuwa sound system we provisionally accept these statements even if it is clear that much more is needed to account for a more respectable portion of aspirated consonants in present Makhuwa.

Guthrie's statement about the development of Bantu obstruents in Makhuwa (vol. 3, p. 60) can be summarized as follows:

(9)	*PB*	*elsewhere*	*/_ į*	*/_ ų*	*PB*	*elsewhere*
	*p	v	ph	?	*mp	ph
	*t	r	tth	tth	*nt	tth
	*c	th	h	?	*nc	th
	*k	Ø	x	kh	*nk	kh
	*b	Ø	h	?	*mb	p
	*d	l	r	r	*nd	tt
	*j	?	?	?	*nj	t
	*g	Ø	c	?	*ng	k

I have adapted Guthrie's spelling of Makhuwa to the standard NELIMO orthography. I have also corrected his elsewhere reflex of *c from unaspirated to aspirated dental, on the strength of *-cek- > *-they-* 'laugh' and *-cum- > *-thum-* 'buy'. Guthrie himself does not give a single Makhuwa reflex for *c, at least not in position C_1. Also, I have put a question mark where Guthrie gives *c* as the elsewhere reflex of *j; Guthrie's only examples for initial *j are *mcana* 'yesterday' (< *janá) and *-teka* 'build' (< *-jeng-). Guthrie considers the second item to attest an irregular "nasal increment", i.e., the reflex does not attest the reconstructed item but would be regular if the reconstruction were *-njeng-*, which it isn't.

The changes conditioned by prenasalization survive in some alternations involving the nominal prefix of classes 9/10 *N-.

(10) *-tatu > -raru 'three' araru 2, miraru 4, mararu 6, ttharu 10

*-pít- > ovira 'to pass' ephirọ 9 'path'

We can now explain why the causative verb extensions behave like aspirated consonants. The most common, "long" allomorph in Makhuwa *-ih-* derives from the sequence *-įcį- (Bastin 1986); other consonantal changes representing the causative extension derive from the short allomorph *-į-. We assume the following derivations; cf. the examples given in (6):

(11) *-cum-įcį-a > -thumithya > -tumithya > -tumiha 'to sell'

*-pį́k-į-a > -phikhya > -pikhya > -pixa 'to make arrive'

*-uk-į-a	> -ukhya	> -uxa	(intr. sep. + caus.)
cf. *-uk-a	> -u(w)a		
*-ik-į-a	> -ikhya	> -ixa	(stative + caus.)
cf. *-ik-a	> -i(y)a		

I would like to propose that the strengthening influences exercised by high closed vowels and by prenasalization are not unrelated. There are indications in Makhuwa pointing to the evolution of nasality in the context of high closed vowels, especially *į.

Firstly, the class 5 nominal prefix is *ni-* or *n-* in Makhuwa where almost all other Bantu languages have i- or li-, the latter derived from *di-į- (the original Bantu nominal prefix preceded by the augment). The following examples are from Frizzi (1982); note that the nominal prefix is *n-* before coronal consonants and *ni-* before all other consonants

(12) nivaka 'spear' nikhumi 'ten'

ntata 'hand' nikhuva 'bone'

Secondly, the perfective stem is formed by inserting n before the stem-final consonant (and adding the final vocalic suffix *-e*). This process is known in Bantu studies as "imbrication" and goes back to the incorporation of a high closed vowel *į into the stem:

(13) -tenke[2] < *-teįke < *-tek-įle perfective stem of o-teka 'to build'

-linve perfective stem of o-liva 'to pay'

-vinre perfective stem of o-vira 'to pass'

Thirdly, some remarkable changes occur in verbs derived from stems with initial *(j)į.

(14) a. *-(j)įkada 'to sit' > w-ikhala

*-(j)įpaga 'to kill' > w-ipha

b. *-(j)įpaga 'to kill' > w-ivva (other dialectal
variants:

winva and wiiva)

*-(j)ı́ba 'to steal' > w-iyya (other dialects: wiiya)

*-bı́na 'to dance' > w-inna (other dialects: wiina)

c. *-(j)ímba 'to sing' > w-ippa (other dialects: w-ipa)

*-dida 'to cry' > w-inla ~ w-unla

---

2 Note the absence of aspiration in *-tenke*. The sequence *nk* is not a prenasalized consonant but contains the moraic nasal *n*.

In (14a), the strong reflexes *kh* and *ph* are obviously conditioned by a preceding rather than following *į. They are equal to the reflexes of the prenasalized consonants *nk and *mp.

The examples in (14b) are from the Ikorovere dialect (Kisseberth, pers. comm.). Here, the reflexes are geminated consonants, a kind of strengthening, too, but different from the regular "strong" reflexes of prenasalized consonants.

The examples in (14c) are remarkable in that they attest similar changes in the environment of the historical degree 2 vowel *i. The item 'to sing' is again from Ikorovere (Kisseberth, pers. comm.), the item 'to cry' from unspecified dialects (Prata 1990). I shall not attempt to offer any explanation for these cases.

Finally, another case of strengthening in the shape of consonant gemination due to the influence of a preceding (historically) high closed front vowel *į occurs with nouns of class 10. In some Makhuwa dialects (cf. Prata 1960:7ff.), nouns have identical shapes in classes 9 and 10, the nominal prefix being e- plus whatever traces are left of the original Bantu prefix *N (prenasalization). In other dialects, the synchronic nominal prefix is *e-* in class 9 and *i-* in class 10. This difference is a reflex of the different augments: class 9 *ji-, class 10 *jį. Now, in the Eeratti dialect as observed by Kisseberth (pers. comm.), all stem initial consonants are geminated in class 10. For example, the word for 'drum' in Eeratti is *ekoma* 9/*ekkoma* 10 (< *ji-ngoma / jį-ngoma), where other dialects have *ekoma*/*ekoma* or *ekoma*/*ikoma*.

A difficult but interesting problem is posed by the pair *o-vitha* 'to hide (tr.)' and *w-i-pitha* 'to hide oneself'. It brings us to the question of the relative chronology of Makhuwa sound changes. We have seen in (9) that Makhuwa has undergone two major sound shifts:

(15)	Voicing-and-Weakening (VW):	*p t k > v r Ø
		*b d g > Ø l Ø
	(Post-)Nasal Strengthening (NS):	*Np Nt Nk > ph tth kh
		*Nb Nd Ng > p tt k

VW affects single obstruents (as in the left elsewhere column in (9)); NS affects prenasalized obstruents (as in the right elsewhere column in (9)); it somehow also extends to other environments involving high vowels although the details have not been worked out. If these two processes are ordered at all they must have occurred in the sequence here given because NS did not feed VW. In other words, the [p] derived from [mb] by NS did not change further to [v] by VW.

Katupha's Law, on the other hand, clearly applies to the output of NS. This chronological order agrees with the derivation of the reflexive verb 'to hide oneself' where the strong reflex of *p is conditioned twice: by the preceding and by the following *į; the reflex is p rather than ph because of

Katupha's Law. Note that dental aspirated th is the unconditioned reflex of *c; stem-internal *į has no strengthening influence on a following consonant: cf. *o-phiya* 'to arrive' < *-pįk-. However, the derivation of the underived verb *o-vitha* seems to force us to order VW after Katupha's Law:

(16)	NS	KL	VW?	
*-jį́-pį́c-a	> -i-phitha	> -i-pitha		'to hide oneself'
*-pį́c-a	> -phitha	> -pitha	> -vitha	'to hide (tr.)'

I would like to propose the following solution for this problem: At some stage, the reflexive morpheme -i- is assumed to have conditioned verb stem-initial alternations such as *v/p r/tth Ø/kh*. The verb 'to hide' was special in having a strong reflex in both the reflexive and the non-reflexive forms. The non-reflexive form with the weak reflex *v* was created by analogy. Later, paradigm levelling occurred on a larger scale and the reflexive prefix generally lost its strengthening influence on stem-initial consonants. The proposed changes are schematized in (17) with the semi-fictitious verb stem -pata given as the model serving for the analogical change.

(17)	*the model*		*'to hide (oneself)'*	
	simple	*reflexive*	*simple*	*reflexive*
stage 0	-pata	-į-pata	-pįca	-į-pįca
VW + NS >	-vara	-i-phara	-phitha	-i-phitha
Analogy			-vitha	
KL >				-i-pitha
Par. Lev. >	-vara	-i-vara		

I assume that two factors may be involved protecting the verb 'to hide (oneself)' from partaking in the final, general paradigm levelling: this verb is presumably frequent in both its simple and in its reflexive form, and the stem-initial consonants are not one of the typical alternating pairs.

Note that Prata 1990 gives both *ovitha* and *opitha* (in addition to *wipitha*), but Matos 1974 as well as Frizzi 1982 give only *ovitha/wipitha*. (Prata frequently lists what clearly are variant forms of the same lexical item without indicating whether these are notational uncertainties or dialectal variants, and if the latter, to which kind of Makhuwa each form belongs. This is rather unfortunate if one wants to use his publications for comparative purposes.) In any case, this is another example showing the strengthening influence of *į on a following consonant.

Makhuwa has a significant number of loan words from Swahili that are probably older than the recent (twentieth century) influence of Swahili on all languages of interior East Africa. (Note that only a small part of the speakers of Makhuwa lives in Tanzania; the vast majority lives in

Mozambique and does not speak Swahili.) In such words we encounter many aspirated consonants which have no regular Bantu correspondences. Consider the following words:

(18)	epakha	'cat' < *i-N-paka ??	cf. Sw. paka (or p^haka)
	opatthana	'to be friends'	cf. Sw. kupatana 'to reach agreement'
	opatikhana	'to be able, to get'	cf. Sw. kupatikana 'to be obtainable'

The regular derivation of the first word would be *mpaka > *phaka > *phaa, which would probably be reflected as something like **mwala-pha, cf. similar derivations involving the addition of the element *mwala-* in *mwalakhu* 'chicken' < *N-kúkú and *mwalapwa* 'dog' < *N-búa. Only if we could assume "Aspiration SHIFT" and order it prior to the loss of k, then this word would be a regular cognate. Since Makhuwa shows no sign of Aspiration Shift, epakha must be a loan, most likely from Swahili.

In the two verb forms which I regard to be related to Swahili kupata 'to get', there is a possible historical source for aspiration at C_1 but not at C_2. If the Proto-Sabaki reconstruction *-įpata (Nurse and Hinnebusch 1993:590) is correct we may expect Makhuwa *o-phara*, if however we start from the Meinhof-Guthrie reconstruction *-pát- then we would expect Makhuwa *o-vara*. In fact, both exist with the senses 'to hold, to seize, to attach'; in addition, Prata 1990 gives *o-phatta* with a similar meaning. There is no internal explanation for the strong reflexes of C_2 and the specific semantic changes of the extended verbs are additional clues that these items were borrowed from Swahili.

We conclude that in loans from Swahili all voiceless stops were interpreted as aspirates, and that only the last aspirated consonant was retained, in agreement with Katupha's Law.

4. Aspiration in Swahili

Since Swahili is another East African Bantu language where aspiration is distinctive (though only in some dialects), it may be worthwhile to look for a comparable process of Deaspiration.

In KiUnguja and KiMvita, the aspirated consonants p^h t^h k^h derive from Bantu *mp *nt *nk. This is the only direct source for aspirated consonants in Swahili, hence the functional load of aspiration is much lower than in Makhuwa. Aspiration is not marked in standard orthography but is noted in Sacleux 1939 and in Slavíková and Bryan 1973 (and also in several editions of poetic texts), but many younger speakers of the relevant dialects do not make or even recognize the distinction. Slavíková and Bryan 1973 report the speech of Sheikh Yahya Ali Omar of Mombasa (KiMvita) and of Sheikh Kassim Hafidh of Zanzibar (KiUnguja).

(19) *N-puda > p^{h}ua 'nose'

*N-tope > t^{h}ope 'mud'

*N-kóndo > k^{h}ondo 'war'

*mu-ntu > mt^{h}u 'person'

*-nụnk-a > -nuk^{h}a '(to) smell'

Voiceless prenasalized consonants are extremely rare in roots. The two examples cited above ('person', 'to smell') are probably the best attested such roots in Bantu. However, examples are plentiful in word-initial position with nouns of classes 9/10 where the homorganic nasal is provided by the nominal prefix. Adjectival stems with initial voiceless plosives show the expected alternation. Aspirated consonants are also the regular phonotactic result (in KiMvita and other northern dialects) whenever the morpheme °ni- (1sg) precedes a voiceless consonant in a verbal form:

(20) cl. 10 °N-kuu > k^{h}uu 'big' °N-tatu > t^{h}atu 'three'

cl. 2 °wa-kuu > wakuu °wa-tatu > watatu

°ni-ta-ku-pa > t^{h}akupa 'I shall give (to) you' (Sacleux 1909:12)

Slavíková—Bryan 1973 note three examples of Aspiration Shift:

(21) *-kant-a > -k^{h}ata Y.A.O./Mv; -k^{h}ata ~ -kat^{h}a K.H./Ung 'cut'

*-tunt-a > -t^{h}uta Y.A.O./Mv 'pant'; -tut^{h}a K.H./Ung. 'throb'

*ki-ntu > k^{h}itu ~ kit^{h}u 'thing' Y.A.O./Mv, K.H./Ung

To these we may add *-k^{h}eti* or *-k^{h}e̞ti* 'to sit' (depending on the dialect), a compound stem derived from the perfective stem of the verb *-kaa*, followed by the noun *nt̪^{h}i* 'ground' in its northern Swahili shape (cf. Nurse and Hinnebusch 1993:161, 552).

In the case of Aspiration Shift, the aspiration is transferred to the preceding consonant which must be capable of aspiration, i.e., a voiceless plosive. It seems that the process is more regular for the speaker of KiMvita than for the speaker of KiUnguja. In all known examples, the shift is from the ultimate to the penultimate syllable, in other words, the target of Aspiration Shift is the stressed syllable. No further retraction of aspiration occurs, as can be seen in the word for 'bed', *kit^{h}anda* (Mv), where the aspiration is not shifted to the initial consonant of the prefix *ki-*.[3] It should

[3] The position of the aspiration is faithfully reflected in the cognate (or borrowed) items *kinanda* in Mwani and *cinanda* in Makonde; in both languages the reflex of *nt is *n*. However, the same word has also been borrowed into Makhuwa as *ekhittantta* where its prefix has been reinterpreted as part of the stem. According to what we observed at the end of the previous secion, we would have expected that both voiceless consonants of Swahili *kit^{h}anda* were

also be noted that the stressed penultimate syllable does not attract aspiration from a preceding syllable, as can be seen in *tʰakupa* (see (20) above).

The following example is significant because it indicates that these dialects of Swahili do not only have Aspiration Shift but also Deaspiration.

(22) *-kont-a 'knock' >> °N-kont-o > kʰoto 'children's game with hitting of fingers

Here, both consonants are expected to be aspirated since they are derived from prenasalized voiceless plosives, but only the first one preserves this property. If this were a general process, then we might expect one of the consonants in the output of (23) to lose its aspiration.

(23) °ni-ta-kʰata > tʰakʰata > ?

°ni-ta-kʰeti > tʰakʰeti > ?

In fact, Alamin Mazrui (pers. comm.) has confirmed the KiMvita form *tʰakʰeti* with two aspirated consonants. Sheikh Yahya (the same who was the source for Slavíková—Bryan 1973), however, prefers the form *ntakʰata* for KiMvita, but knows the form given in (23) from more northern dialects such as KiAmu; interestingly, he adds that it would be difficult to maintain two aspirated consonants in one word.[4]

In this context it is interesting to note the word for 'shark'. Sacleux 1939 gives *pʰapa* for all northern dialects ("DN", which include Mvita but not Unguja). He also cites *mbamba* for rural ShiNgazidja ("Ngaz. 2"). Kisseberth (pers. comm.) cites *mphaampha* for ChiMwiini. Bleek 1856 gives *mama* for KiMwani ("Cap[e] Delgado"), though this word is not recognized by modern speakers. In these varieties of Swahili, *mp is reflected as *mph* (Mwiini), *mb* (Ngazidja), and *m* (Mwani). This would indicate an internal reconstruction for 'shark' as *mpampa, with Deaspiration in KiMvita. (There is no indication that either rural ShiNgazidja or KiMwani have applied a rule of "aspiration harmony" by which aspiration spreads from one consonant to another.)

In Swahili, therefore, the processes of Aspiration Shift and Deaspiration both work in the same direction, at least in the domain consisting of the last two syllables of the word: aspirated consonants will occur only on the first suitable consonant. This is different from the situation in Makhuwa in two respects: Firstly, Makhuwa has no Aspiration Shift and therefore allows aspirated consonants anywhere in the word. Secondly, Deaspiration takes the inverse direction from Swahili and preserves only the last aspiration in the

---

interpreted as aspirated, but we fail to understand why it is the second one that lost its aspiration contrary to the general workings of Katupha's Law.

[4]I would like to thank Dr. A. Mazrui and Sh. Yahya for their long-distance help. I am also grateful to Ridder Samsom, SOAS, for consulting Sheikh Yahya on my behalf.

word. Swahili and Makhuwa are, however, alike in that they both allow but one aspirated consonant in the relevant domain.

5. Deaspiration and Dahl's Law

Meinhof (1904:299) formulated Dahl's Law as follows:

> Wenn in einem Wortstamm zwei aufeinanderfolgende Silben mit einer stimmlosen Explosiva beginnen, so wird die erstere stimmhaft.
>
> [When two successive syllables in a stem each begin with a voiceless plosive, then the first of these becomes voiced.]

Meinhof named the law after the missionary Edmund Dahl who had discovered it in Nyamwezi. The law, or traces of it, occur, in one form or another, in a wide range of East African Bantu languages. After describing Dahl's Law for Nyamwezi, Meinhof adds (p.300):

> Ob *k, t, p* echte Tenues oder Aspiraten sind, kann für unseren gegenwärtigen Zweck gleichgültig sein.
>
> [For our present purpose it is irrelevant whether *k, t, p* are pure voiceless or aspirated consonants.]

Three decades later, in Meinhof and Van Warmelo's *Introduction to the phonology of the Bantu languages* (1932:181) we find a new formulation of the same sound shift where aspiration has shifted from irrelevance to central importance:

> When two successive syllables each begin with an aspirate, the first of these loses its aspiration and becomes voiced.

The authors' inspiration for their change of mind becomes clear from an added footnote: "We draw particular attention to the similarity to the Greek law of dissimilation mentioned on p. 19." Although I can't find anything but Grimm's Law mentioned on that page or the adjacent ones it is clear that Meinhof and Van Warmelo refer to Grassmann's Law, or more precisely, to its second clause (here quoted from Collinge 1985:47):

> Given two consonant-groups in a word, separated by a vowel and themselves aspirated, and provided that they are within the same root, then one (and normally the first) is deprived of its breath feature.

Collinge (1985), in his book on *The laws of Indo-European,* devotes a whole appendix to "Dahl's law in Bantu" (pp. 279–281) because, as he says, "this law is often paraded, usually by name only, by Indo-Europeanists who are eager to justify their canonic shifts by demonstrating parallels elsewhere". Meinhof and Van Warmelo's description of Dahl's Law leaves room for many misunderstandings as is evidenced by Collinge's summary. Since Meinhof and Van Warmelo 1932 is probably the main source on Dahl's Law for non-Bantuists, it may be worthwhile to clarify a few points.

- In Nyamwezi, the domain of Dahl's Law is the root; prefixes are not affected by it and suffixes do not trigger it. There are only a handful of cases such as *-dw-ɩ́k-a* 'put a load on one's head' where the root is derived from (and also appears synchronically) as /-tʊ́-/. But in other languages Dahl's Law has a much wider domain. (For Dahl's Law in Nyamwezi, cf. Maganga—Schadeberg 1992:23–25).

- As for the historical ordering of Dahl's law in Nyamwezi, consider *lʊ-gohé* 'eyelash' < *lu-kópe. I am not aware of any arguments that would justify the conclusion that Dahl's Law post-dates the (inconsistent) Nyamwezi shift *p > *h*. However, in languages where Dahl's Law produces synchronic alternations, it is true that it may or may not be triggered by reflexes of voiceless stops of quite different phonetic substance, and it may even be triggered by voiceless consonants originating from voiced ones. Such cases offer excellent grounds for dating the lifespan of Dahl's Law in particular languages. (A much more extensive description may be found in Davy—Nurse 1982.)
- The Nyamwezi word for 'fat, oil' is *magutá* < *ma-kų́ta. The form *mavutha* is either a misprint in Meinhof—Van Warmelo 1932 or else a form from the neighbouring Sumbwa language. The Sumbwa fricative *v* is not an intrusion from Swahili but the regular result of spirantization of *g (<*k) before *ų (pace Collinge 1985:280).

As to the role of aspiration in the workings of Dahl's Law, there can be no doubt that it applies to voiceless stops irrespective of their reflexes being aspirated or not. It is true that in some languages, such as Nyamwezi and, even more so, in closely related Sukuma, all voiceless stops are aspirated, but this feature is not distinctive. No language is known where Dahl's Law applies to aspirated voiceless stops but not to non-aspirated ones. This makes Dahl's Law look much less similar to Grassmann's Law; the real parallel to which is Katupha's Law.

Meinhof—Van Warmelo (1932) have nothing to say on how they conceive the link between Dahl's Law and Grassmann's Law. What I would like to propose here is that Dahl's Law builds on the output of Katupha's Law in the following way.

(a) At some stage, all voiceless stops became aspirated: [p^h, t^h, k^h].

(b) Katupha's Law reduced the first in a sequence of two aspirates to a plain stop.

(c) Dahl's Law changed unaspirated voiceless stops into voiced ones.

Here are some considerations which, I believe, lend some plausibility to these hypotheses.

(i) The reconstructable Bantu consonant system contains just eight simple obstruents which are generally represented as *p t c k, b d j g. There can be little doubt about the correctness of this reconstructed system in a phonemic sense, but the phonetic values of some of these obstruents is open to questioning. The voicing distinction between the two series is not controversial. The "palatal" members *c and *j often behave differently from the other obstruents and may have been fricatives (*s, *z; cf. Meeussen 1967). The voiced obstruents *b d g may have been continuants rather than stops. Meinhof reconstructed *β l ɣ; his case appears to be the strongest for *l and the weakest for *ɣ. Stewart (1993) considers *b and *d to have been [ɓ] and [ɗ/l]. Whatever the precise phonetic nature of these consonants was at certain stages of Bantu prehistory, there certainly was room for making the two series maximally distinct. For voiceless stops, aspiration would have been a natural enhancement of their voiceless nature. This is what I postulate for stage A.

(ii) Dahl's Law, when taken by itself, is phonetically rather puzzling: Why would any language object to a sequence of two totally unmarked consonants? (Cf. Collinge 1985:261 who speaks of Indo-European *tek* as "a sequence which only a very strange tongue would ostracize".) On the other hand, each of the two processes here proposed under stages B and C appears to be better motivated and more natural. Deaspiration (Katupha's Law) simplifies a sequence of two marked consonants by un-marking one of its members, and the new Dahl's Law then maximizes the phonetic difference between aspirated and non-aspirated voiceless stops by adding voice to the latter class of consonants.

(iii) The historical depth of Dahl's Law is a problem because its reflexes occur in a wide area in East Africa but rarely in a consistent, regular way. The present hypothesis treats apparent parallel occurrences of Dahl's Law as "drift" based on the earlier, widespread Katupha's Law. (This argument would loose some of its strength if D. Nurse, this volume, has indeed fixed the historical depth of Dahl's Law.)

Of course, Makhuwa itself has no obvious traces of Dahl's Law which is not surprising given the general voicing of voiceless plosives. It is unlikely (though logically not impossible if we assume that the voiced series of Bantu obstruents originally was *β l ɣ) that Dahl's Law applied to pre-Makhuwa (without producing a partial merger between the voiced and the voiceless series) and that its effects became later obliterated by "Voicing-and-Weakening".

References

Bastin, Yvonne. 1986. Les suffixes causatifs dans les langues bantoues, in: *Africana Linguistica* 10:55–145. Tervuren: Musée royal de l'Afrique Centrale.

Bleek, Wm. H. J. 1856. *The languages of Mosambique: vocabularies of the dialects of Lourenzo Marques, Inhambane, Sofala, Tette, Sena, Quellimane, Mosambique, Cape Delgado, Anjoane, the Maravi, Mudzau, &c. drawn from the manuscripts of Dr. Wm. Peters, M. Berl. Acad.* London: Harrison and Sons.

Centis, Gino. 1985. *Método macua.* Anchilo: Centro Catequético Paulo VI.

Collinge, N. E. 1985. *The laws of Indo-European.* Amsterdam: John Benjamins.

Davy, J. I. M. & Derek Nurse. 1982. Synchronic versions of Dahl's Law: the multiple applications of a phonological dissimilation rule, *Journal of African Languages and Linguistics* 4:157–195.

Frizzi, Giuseppe. 1982. *Dicionário de emakhuwa-português e portugués-emakhuwa.* Lichinga.

Guthrie, Malcolm. 1967–71. *Comparative Bantu.* 4 vols. Farnborough: Gregg International.

Katupha, José Mateus Muária. 1983. *A preliminary description of sentence structure in the e-Sáaka dialect of e-Mákhuwa.* M.Phil. thesis, School of Oriental and African Studies, London.

Katupha, José Mateus Muária. 1991. *The grammar of Emakhuwa verbal extensions.* PhD diss., School of Oriental and African Studies, London.

Maganga, Clement & Thilo C. Schadeberg. 1992. *Kinyamwezi: grammar, texts, vocabulary.* Cologne: Rüdiger Köppe.

Matos, Alexandre Valente de. 1974. *Dicionário português–macua.* Lisbon: Junta de Investigações Científicas do Ultramar.

Meeussen, A. E.. 1967. Bantu grammatical reconstructions, in: *Africana Linguistica* III, pp. 79–121. (Annales, 61.) Tervuren: Musée royal de l'Afrique Centrale.

Meinhof, Carl. 1904. Das Dahlsche Gesetz, *Zeitschrift der Deutschen Morgenländischen Gesellschaft* 57:299–304.

Meinhof, Carl. 1908. Linguistische Studien in Ostafrika: XIV. Makua, *Mitteilungen des Seminars für Orientalische Sprachen* 11:85–131.

Meinhof, Carl & N. J. van Warmelo. 1932. *Introduction to the phonology of the Bantu languages.* Berlin: Dietrich Reimer / Ernst Vohsen.

NELIMO. 1989. *Relatório do I seminário sobrae a padronização da ortografia de línguas moçambicanas.* Maputo: INDE & UEM.

Nurse, Derek & Thomas J. Hinnebusch. 1993. *Swahili and Sabaki: a linguistic history.* Berkeley and Los Angeles: University of California Press.

Prata, António Pires. 1960. *Gramática da língua macua e seus dialectos.* Cucujães: Sociedade Portuguesa das Missões Católicas.

Prata, António Pires. 1973. *Dicionário português-macua.* Cucujães: Sociedade Missionária Portuguesa.

Prata, António Pires. 1990. *Dicionário macua–português.* Lisbon: Instituto de Investigação Científica Tropical.

Sacleux, Charles. 1909. *Grammaire des dialectes swahilis.* Paris: Procure des PP. du Saint-Esprit.

Sacleux, Charles. 1939. *Dictionnaire swahili-français.* Paris: Institut d'Ethnologie, Musée de l'Homme.

Slavíková, Magdalena & Margaret M. Bryan. 1973. Comparative Bantu: the case of two Swahili dialects, *African Language Studies* 14:53–81.

Stewart, John M. 1993. The Second Tano consonant shift and its likeness to Grimm's Law, *Journal of West African Languages* 23,1:3–39.

*HH and *HL Tone Patterns in Bemba and the Bemba Tone System

GERARD PHILIPPSON
Institut National des Langues et Civilisations Orientales, Paris & Laboratoire Dynamique du Language (CNRS/Université Lumière Lyon2)

Introduction

This paper discusses the origin of the tone patterns exhibited by nominal and verbal stems in Bemba, a Bantu language of Zambia, and concludes that two diachronic processes, Tone Doubling (still active in the language) and Tone Lowering, supply the background for the present-day patterns, whereas learning mistakes at the time the two processes were in operation probably account for irregularities in tonal correspondences with reconstructed Common Bantu forms.

A notable aspect of tone correspondences among present-day Bantu languages is that, however exotic any one system might appear, it does not generally prove very difficult to relate to a simple two-tone system, leading for instance to four disyllabic tone patterns *HH[1], *HL, *LH, *LL, such as that reconstructed by Guthrie himself for Common Bantu (henceforth CB)[2].

---

1 The following conventions are used : H means High tone, L means Low tone; a star indicates a reconstructed form.

2 For readers who might not be clear about what is meant by CB, Guthrie defined it as the inventory of lexical and grammatical items found to exhibit regular sound correspondences among contemporary Bantu languages (the procedure for

Although Guthrie's tonal typology is not too explicit (the best account is by Carter, 1973), he established a distinction between "clear" tone systems - i.e. systems in which the tone patterns exhibited by an actual language are identical to CB (*HL = HL, *HH = HH, etc., a good example being Asu, G 22 in Guthrie's referential classification, although Guthrie 1967-71 erroneously describes it as exhibiting reduced tonal distinctiveness[3]) - and "fully distinctive" tone systems. In the latter, one finds four disyllabic tone patterns, like in CB, but there is no one to one correspondence: thus, to take a seemingly extreme case, Luba (L.33) has the correspondences *HH = LL, *HL = LH, *LH = HL and *LL = HH.

If we now turn to the case of Bemba (M.42) a language which Guthrie thoroughly studied, to the extent of writing his Ph.D. dissertation on its tone system (Guthrie 1945), we find that he considered it as belonging to his "fully distinctive" category, without specifying which were the patterns deviating from their CB counterparts. Although dedicated to the tone system of Bemba, his dissertation sheds no light on this point since it is exclusively synchronic.

1. Bemba

In a remarkable paper (Meeussen, 1976), A.E. Meeussen established convincingly that several of Guthrie's reconstructed CB items had been given erroneous tone patterns and he endeavoured (successfully) to correct them. Of interest to us, however, is that in the same article he claimed, basing himself on J.C. Sharman's data as well as his own, that Bemba did not in fact exhibit four reconstructible tone patterns in disyllabic stems but only three, CB *HH and *HL stems having fallen together to give Bemba HH (with an insignificant number of exceptions, some of which perhaps being loans). In my own study of Eastern Bantu tone systems (Philippson 1992) I followed Meeussen, out of trust for his exceptional competence in the subject of Bantu tonology, and because the rather meagre Bemba data in my possession[4] seemed to confirm, for about half a dozen usually crucial items (see 3.2.1. below) that his was indeed the correct analysis.

With the publication by M. Mann of Guthrie's Bemba vocabulary (Guthrie and Mann, 1995) a host of new data has become available which compels one to look at the situation with an unprejudiced eye and to

establishing the inventory is to be found in Guthrie 1967-71). It is not meant to be the reconstruction of a proto-language (although Guthrie did also propose Proto-Bantu correspondences, these are no more than a glorified CB; cf. Möhlig 1976 and 1980 for a sound criticism)

[3] It is worth emphasising, in the hope of preventing potential users of Guthrie's otherwise valuable work from going astray, that there are very many errors in his tonal references.

[4] Collected from Mr. Makasa Kasonde in the mid-eighties, during the course of the late Pierre Alexandre's Bantu seminar.

conclude that, in this one case, Guthrie was right against Meeussen (and, in a modest way, Philippson...)[5].

To start with, it is clear that CB *HL stems correspond to HH in Bemba. There is a wealth of examples, e.g. *-mbúʃí* 'goat' (CB **-búdį̀)*, *-límí* 'tongue' (CB **-dímį̀)*, *-nsókś* 'snake' (CB **-jókà)*, *-kúní* 'piece of firewood' (CB **-kúnį̀)*, and many others.

This being established, we turn to CB *HH stems. First of all, it is worth remembering that Guthrie had posited as being *HL a number of stems that Meeussen reconstructed as *HH in his 1976 article. In each case for which the evidence is sufficient, I found Meeussen to be right. Nevertheless, in some cases it can be hypothesised that Guthrie's misallocation of a *HH stem was caused by his overreliance on Bemba.

We can start by distinguishing two groups:

(i) Those that were reconstructed as *HL by Guthrie but as *HH by Meeussen; I identified 8 of these in Bemba, namely

-ŋgókó	'chicken'	-mfúmú	'chief'
-kúlú	'big'	-mpúŋgú	'eagle'
-mbúlú	'monitor lizard'	-káʃí	'wife'
-pémbe	'horn'	-fína	'pus'

As can be seen, 6 out of 8 appear in Bemba with the HH tone pattern that we otherwise know to be the reflex of CB *HL. In other words, this set of items explains, so to speak, the dual error of Guthrie and Meeussen: the former "knew" that *HH and *HL have different reflexes in Bemba and so reconstructed all Bemba HH stems as CB *HL[6]. As for Meeussen, he "knew" that the reconstructed pattern of those items must be *HH and so judged that Bemba did not distinguish reflexes of *HL from *HH[7].

(ii)Those reconstructed as *HH by Guthrie and either accepted or at least not challenged by Meeussen[8]. There are 14 occurrences in Guthrie and Mann's Bemba vocabulary, of which:

- 3 are HH:

-séké	'seed'	-ŋkáfí	'paddle'
-mbéú	'vegetable garden'		

5 One might argue that the two writers refer to different dialects with different tonal realisations, but the "feel" of the evidence leads me to think that it is not so and that Meeussen was genuinely mistaken (so was Sharman, apparently).

6 He either overlooked "horn" and "pus" whose Bemba HL tone pattern should have led him to reconstruct CB *HH, or else decided that more compelling evidence from other languages pointed to CB *HL.

7 He then must have decided that "horn" and "pus" were exceptions too...

8 In one lone example they both must be wrong: the item seen in Bemba *ícilémá* 'illness' has reflexes in many languages all of which point to a reconstruction *-démà not *-démá as maintained by both Guthrie and Meeussen.

- 11 are HL:

-sánsu	'twig'	-ténde	'heel'
-ʃínde	'clod'	-líba	'trap'
-ála	'fingernail'	-ʃíma	'well'
-kúɲu	'fig-tree'	-kópyo	'eyelash'
-kúpa	'tick'	-ŋkúnda	'pigeon'
-púta	'boil'		

If we add the two *HH stems erroneously considered as *HL by Guthrie (*-pémbe* and *-fína*, see 3.2.1.1. above), we find that 14 CB *HH stems give HL in Bemba as against 9 that give *HH. Out of the latter, one (*-káʃí* 'wife') is well attested as *HH throughout the Bantu field, but Luba-Shaba (L 33) has *-kaʒí*, also a *HL reflex; so perhaps the HH pattern of Bemba does reflect a regional CB *HL pattern for this one item. The same seems to apply to *-séké* 'seed' (Luba-Shaba *-seké*), whereas the word *-mbéú* 'vegetable garden' might not be directly related to the CB stem **-béyú* 'seed' (it might conceivably be a loan). In other words, there are only 5 Bemba HH stems which seem incontrovertibly to reflect CB *HH.

On the other hand, the evidence for *HH = Bemba HL is not that very much stronger. Only 6 HL stems are straightforwardly *HH, namely *-fína* 'pus', *-pémbe* 'horn', *-sánsu* 'twig', *-ténde* 'heel', *-ʃínde* 'clod', *-líba* 'trap'. The others vary from mixed evidence (for instance *-kúpa* 'tick' would reflect *HH, along with Duala A.24 *-wówá* and Asu G.22 *-ŋgúhá*, but Kikuyu E. 51 *-ŋgohá* and Rwanda J.61 *-gúha* are both *HL) to chaos (*-kópyo* 'eyelash' is skewed segmentally since the CB stems reconstructs **-kópé*; the segmental skewing is shared by Luba-Shaba *-kópyô* whose tones would however correspond to *LH; other languages have variously *HL as Rwanda *-ŋgóhe* or Asu *-γóhe*, or else *LL as Zulu S.42 *-k^{h}op^{h}e* or LH as Tsonga S.53 *-ŋkohé* or again *HH as Shi J.53 *-góhe*).

Nevertheless, since there are a very large number of Bemba HH stems reflecting CB *HL (cf. 3.1. above), I will assume that Bemba HL does reflect, by and large CB *HH. The question will nevertheless remain: whence the confusion in the reflexes? The rest of the paper will try to address this issue.

The correspondence Bemba HH = CB *HL is buttressed by the following fact: verbo-nominal stems in Bemba as in most Bantu languages are made up of a radical followed by a final vowel /-a/. If we look at -CVC- radicals, the resulting disyllabic stems can be of only two shapes in Bemba: either LL as in *-lima* 'cultivate' or *-kumba* 'gather grass', or else HH, as in *-pítá* 'pass' or *-bómbá* 'work'.

Now the first series of examples shows that the final vowel must itself be L otherwise we would expect forms such as **-limá* or **-kumbá* which are non-existent; if this is so how is it that this very same final /-a/ appears as H in the second series of examples? The obvious answer seems to be that the H lexically associated to the radicals *-pít-* or *-bómb-* doubles onto the final vowel. We will call this process Tonal Doubling (TD) and will formulate it thus:

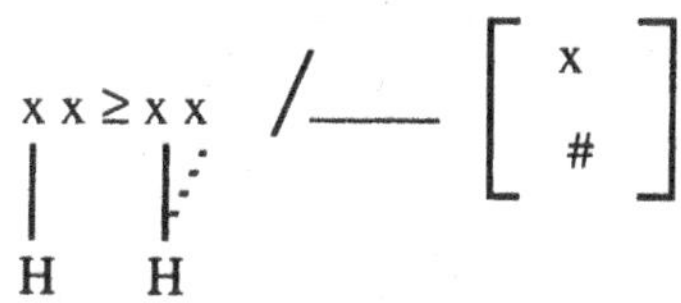

The rule says in essence that a H linked to a mora will spread to the next toneless mora provided either a word boundary or another toneless mora follows[9].

TD is operating with longer stems as well, for instance -CVCVCV verb stems will fall into just two groups as for instance *-kulula* 'clean up' vs. *-céléka* 'filter', and likewise -CVCVCVCV subdivides into two groups as exemplified by *-tuntukila* 'appear unexpectedly' vs. *-kólóŋgana* 'assemble'. In other words infinitive verb stems in Bemba appear either as all L or else with H on their first two moras, other moras, if any, being L. Note that one never sees a single H surfacing in this context.

TD thus suggests a plausible explanation for the correspondence Bemba HH = CB *HL. If H tones in Bemba always double onto a following L syllable, then it is easy to see that all original *HL stems must eventually surface as HH by TD.

This process of TD is well attested in other Bantu languages such as Gweno (G.65 in Guthrie's referential classification) or Nyamwezi (F.22), two Bantu languages of Tanzania. In both these languages however the effect of TD is to neutralise, either in some contexts only (as in Gweno) or in all contexts (as in Nyamwezi), the contrast between *HH and *HL stems.

2. Other languages

And yet, the data adduced above showed us that some at least of the CB *HH stems have remained distinct from *HL (the contrast being realised in an 'inverted" way, as HL and HH respectively). How is it then that original *HH stems have turned into HL?

Since this change appears as an example of dissimilation it is most tempting to resort to a dissimilatory process well attested in Eastern Bantu languages, and known under the name of Meeussen's Rule, in short MR (cf. Goldsmith 1984 and Philippson 1998). MR has the effect of turning the

---

9 Note that the rule seems to take as its target *moras* in verb stems, including infinitives, but *syllables* in noun stems, including deverbatives. The conditioning of this distinction is not entirely clear to me, although I assume it to have to do with the stage where verb vs. noun stems receive their final tones: this stage must be earlier for noun than for verb stems, which are subject to derivational processes practically throughout the lexical level. A similar situation has been reported for Sukuma.

second of two successive underlying H syllables into L, as in the following Rundi (D.62) example:

(1) narázibáriira 'I was sewing them' (cl. 10)[10]

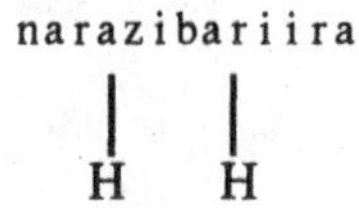

(2) narábariira 'I was sewing'

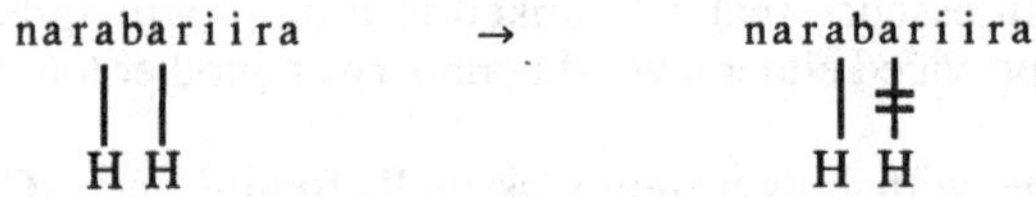

In the first example (1) there is no contiguity between the H located on the Tense Aspect Marker (TAM) prefix */-ara-/* and the first stem H so no application of Meeussen's rule takes place; contrariwise, in the last example (2) these two H tones are in immediate succession and the second one (the radical H) is disassociated.

Now MR is a very widespread synchronic process in the Bantu languages of the Lacustrine region and has definitely played an important role in the evolution of tone systems there. In Bemba however, there is absolutely no synchronic occurrence of MR whatsoever, as the following verbal examples show:

- between S(ubject) C(oncord) and TAM:

(3) báléeséka 'they're laughing'[11]

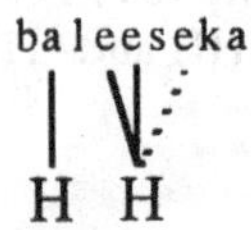

The H of the prefix */bá-/* does not dissimilate the following TAM */-léé/*; cf. *tuléeséka* 'we're laughing' with a Low tone SC.

- between SC and stem:

[10] Note that in this tense the H tone on the radical is morphologically determined; /-bar-/ is underlyingly a L radical.

[11] It will be recalled that a H spreads onto a following L syllable (mora in verbs)

(4) bábútúka... 'they run...'[12]

babutuka

H H

cf. tubútúka... 'we run...'

- between SC and O(bject) C(oncord):

(5) bákálíma... 'they cultivate it' (cl. 12)...

bakalima

H H

cf. *tukálíma*... 'we cultivate it...'

- between OC and stem:

(6) tukáfísá... 'we hide it' (cl. 12)...

tukafisa

H H

cf. tumufísá... 'we hide you (pl.)...'

- within stems, see below.

We are thus apparently justified in denying the presence of MR in contemporary Bemba. How can we then explain the diachronic change *HH > HL? A first answer might be that MR did operate at some point in the past, long enough to dissimilate *HH stems into HL, then disappeared. Although not entirely impossible, this solution seems as unlikely as it is unenlightening. Another line of reasoning presents itself however. In a number of Bantu languages, a process known as "downstepping" slightly lowers the second of two successive H tones. In a language such as Asu (or Pare, G.22; cf. Odden 1985), this process operates in several contexts, of which one is of interest to us: before pause, the last of two successive H tones lowers, thus (I indicate downstepping by a raised "!" in front of the downstepped syllable):

(7) ŋkúkú θáno 'five chickens' versus

(8) ŋkú$^!$kú # 'chickens'

In Shambaa (G 23; cf. Kähler-Meyer 1962, Odden 1982, Philippson, 1992), two successive H syllables are normally separated by a downstep, so that the language distinguishes:

---

12 This form cannot be used without a complement.

```
(9)   mbúzí 'goat'      and     (10)   ŋgó!tó 'sheep'
      mbuzi                             ŋgoto
      |.·                               | |
      H                                 H H
```

The representations make it clear that in the case of *mbúzí*, we are faced with a single H which has spread (very much like the rule TD in Bemba, although at the post-lexical, not the lexical, level[13]) whereas with *ŋgó!tó*, there are two Hs. Downstep in Shambaa always intervenes between two H syllables, whether they are both lexical, like in *ŋgó!tó*, or in contact following TD, like in

```
(11)  mbúzí !ntátú 'three goats' (lexically mbúzi, ntátu)
      mbuzi ntatu
      |.·   |.·
      H     H
```

What is of interest to us here is the case of two stem Hs since we seek to explain the fate of *HH in Bemba. First of all, it should be noted that Shambaa cannot be of direct use to solve our problem, since it has entirely collapsed CB *HH and *HL to HH (i.e. a single H plus TD), thus apparently going all the way in the direction that Bemba only embarked upon. All present-day H!H stems in Shambaa seem to be due to loans[14], apart from a few deverbative stems ending in /-wa/ and thus probably underlyingly trisyllabic. Nevertheless, the fact that Shambaa incontrovertibly *does* lower the second of every two successive H tones offers a tempting model for Bemba diachrony.

Let us suppose that this process of downstepping successive Hs (paralleling as it does TD, attested in both Shambaa and Bemba), did in fact operate in Bemba at the time TD was developing; its function then could be very naturally explained, namely maximising phonological contrasts between stems which would otherwise neutralise if *HL > HH while *HH remains as it is. Now, it is clear that all Bantu languages having undergone TD, did not in fact in the long run escape this particular neutralisation: we only have to look at Sukuma (F.21) or Nyamwezi (F.22) to realise this fact

---

13 Moreover the rule operates not only on two syllables but over much longer stretches, if available.

14 I might be oversimplifying a complex situation. Suffice it to say that for all the Bemba HL stems < CB *HH which have a Shambaa equivalent, the latter is HH (without downstep). A number of vexing problems remain, like Shambaa *-mpá!ʃá* 'twins' and Bemba *-mpása* 'id.', both pointing to *HH, whereas Guthrie reconstructs *-pácà —not disputed by Meeussen, and confirmed in my database by Duala (A.24), Kikuyu (E.51), Luba (L.33) and Rwanda (D.61)!

(cf. Philippson, 1992 and 1998). Indeed, even Bemba did not entirely escape it, since we saw above that a number of indisputably CB *HH stems turn out as Bemba HH. But that a *tendency* towards maintaining distinctiveness operated seems plausible. What we must admit of course is that this distinctiveness-inducing process was maximised in Bemba, by not only downstepping the second stem syllable, but by lowering it entirely - a not unreasonable assumption[15].

3. Verb stem tonal melodies

But an interesting observation arises: we saw earlier that MR does not operate in Bemba and we adduced many examples from outside the verb stem to confirm this fact. Now lowering, either by downstepping or otherwise, does not operate there either[16]. In other words, the process of downstepping followed by lowering that we postulated seems to have applied within stems only. But what of verb stems then? If we seek a better insight into the diachrony of Bemba tone rules, we should also try to analyse the synchronic typology of tonal patterns to be found there.

The first fact worthy of notice is that, rather than a succession of single tones, stem tones must be analysed as "melodies" (cf. Philippson, 1992). The major melodies found in verb stems are the following:

(i) Lexical tone on radical syllable (doubling by TD if H) and L on all other stem syllables; this melody is found in the infinitive, in numerous tenses with an /-a/ suffix, probably formed on the infinitive, in a few other tenses such as the /-ile/ Yesterday Past and in numerous deverbatives in /-o/ and /-i/:

(12)	tukatutuma	'we'll tremble';	tukabútúka	'we'll run'
(13)	twaaʃítile[17]	'we brought';	twaacítíle	'we did'
(14)	umúsambilo	'wash-basin'	<	/-sambil-/;
	úmuʃílíko	'type of medicine'	<	/-ʃílik-/

---

[15] In contrast, absolute lowering could not take place in Shambaa since: (1) downstepping is a post-lexical process and operates iteratively (how low can you get ?!) and (2) more crucially, there exists in Shambaa a HL tonal category whose origin is to be found in stems having a long radical syllable historically (length contrasts were diachronically neutralised in Shambaa but their tonal effects persist).

[16] There is in fact downstepping in the Bemba verbal system, but this is a very late process operating exclusively on the basis of resyllabification (cf. Sharman and Meeussen, 1955).

[17] The H appearing on the radical comes from the doubling of the H on the /-á-/ TAM; this H is itself disassociated from the TAM after resyllabification, since rising tones are disallowed in Bemba: *tuáʃitile* → *tuáʃítile* (TD) → *twaáʃítile* (resyllabification) → *twaaʃítile* (rising tone simplification) (cf. Philippson, 1992 for a detailed discussion).

(ii) Lexical tone on radical syllable followed by a complex melody LH. It appears to be found exclusively with object relative forms where the subject prefix is equally associated with a H. Notice that the H of the LH melody associates with the final vowel, the L part associating with all the intervening vowels between the radical and the final vowel; ex.:

(15) éko túkásokolokelá 'that is where we'll jump to'

(16) éko túkapítílilá 'that is where we'll pass by'

The H from a H radical obeys TD, as seen above; but a difference occurs when only one mora separates the radical from the final: in this case a radical H either[18] doubles onto the following syllable in which case the final vowel will associate to the L of the LH melody and the final H will remain floating, as in

(17) éko túkabútúka 'that is where we'll run'

Otherwise, TD is blocked and the H of the LH melody associates to the final vowel, as in

(18) éko túléesápiká 'that's where we're searching'

Example (17) has the underlying representation in (10) and undergoes TD in (20):

(19)

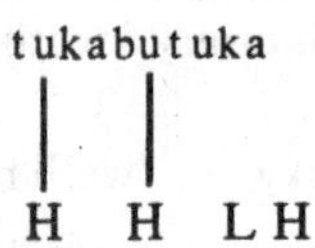

(20)

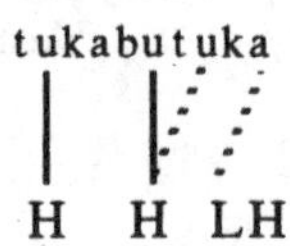

The most natural explanation (if one accepts, as I do, rule ordering) is to consider that in this case TD precedes the anchoring of the LH melody. Since this melody is determined by morphological factors (the presence of a H toned relative prefix) its anchoring must take place at the lexical level and thus TD must be a lexical rule as well. This is confirmed by the fact that TD is strictly confined within word boundaries as we saw above.

As regards example (18), it would seem that here anchoring to the final vowel precedes TD and bleeds it normally by removing its context:

(21)

---

18 The literature is not entirely clear on this point. Sharman and Meeussen claim the optionality exists for some forms and not for others, but they leave many forms unmentioned. Guthrie's data indicate variation, sometimes on the basis of context, but most of the time without justification.

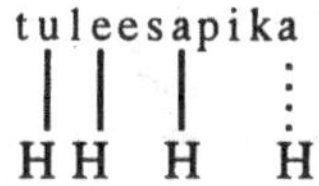

with TD not applicable. Either way, TD remains a lexical rule.

This melody is found (always, it seems, in its second variant) with deverbative agentive noun stems, formed with an /-a/ F(inal) V(owel) and a /ka-/ prefix. The FV is always associated to the H of the LH melody, except when a H radical syllable immediately precedes the FV, that is in -CV(V)CV stems, where the L associates to the FV and the H disappears:

(22) kasúmiká 'chief's cup-bearer' < -súmik-

(23) kafúndiʃá 'teacher' < -fúndiʃ-

(24) kafúla 'smith' < -fúl-

(25) kabúúʃa 'questioner' < -búúʃ-

The proposed analyses are given in (26) and (27):

(26)

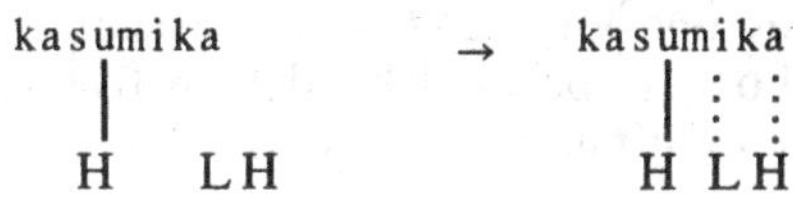

(27)

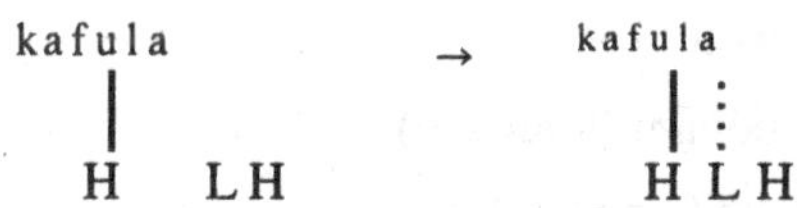

Let us reflect on this LH final melody; it is strange to see Low tones as part of a rule since they obviously play no role at the underlying level; indeed the fact that TD does not take the presence of L tones in consideration *except* in the variant we are now discussing where a L does have a blocking effect shows *a contrario* that Ls are absent elsewhere in the derivations. In the case of the relative tenses where the H tone is introduced at the very end of the derivation, after all other tones have been associated, and on the basis of the prefixal tone which it echoes, it might be possible to claim that default Ls *have* been introduced already and that the association of the final H takes this presence into consideration. But it does not seem possible to me to treat deverbative agentive nouns in the same fashion. It was mentioned above that noun stem tone patterns must be established at an earlier stage in the derivation, when default L tones should not reasonably be present, and I do not find any contrary evidence in the language[19]. I thus consider the LH melody in deverbative agentives as being the remnant of the diachronic process postulated above, which absolutely lowered the second of two successive Hs. To be sure, we might have expected the final H to be lowered as well, but the process might have operated iteratively from left to right, or alternatively the final H might have escaped lowering to enhance the deverbative pattern which otherwise would just emerge as the one described immediately above, i.e. lexical tone on the radical syllable and no other H. I wish to emphasise here that while the justification of the process as sketched here is very tentative, we are still a long way from fully understanding diachronic tonal processes at work in Bantu stems. In principle, in verb stems the tone of the FV associates to all syllables (or moras as the case may be) separating it from the radical syllable /mora, but there are exceptions which appear difficult to convincingly account for at present (cf. Philippson, 1992, Chapter 4, for a brief discussion of these).

A final point: another tone melody can be evidenced which appears thus: lexical tone on radical syllable followed by H on all other stem syllables; this melody is typical of negative tenses, and is also found in some positive tenses, e.g. the Far Past; this pattern, which is obviously indistinguishable from the basic one[20] in -CVCV stems bearing a lexical radical H, is found in a handful only of polysyllabic deverbative stems; it is on the other hand evidenced in a fair number of underived noun stems (cf. Appendix Z):

(28) tatwaakatutúmé 'we won't tremble';

tatwaakabútúké 'we won't run'

(29) twaaʃitílé 'we bought (long ago)';

twaacítílé 'we did (long ago)'

Now, we are faced with an apparent contradiction: how do we reconcile the process of lowering described above with this pattern which not only *does not* lower successive Hs, but even brings together a radical H and a derived H melody with no tonal effect at all?

The only way we can account for this melody is to assume that we are here faced with a single H severally associated and not two (or more) successive Hs. This would satisfactorily explain the absence of lowering, since a single H could obviously not be affected. Now, whereas it is not difficult to posit a single H associating to both the FV and the extensions (i.e. the syllables between the radical and the FV), since this is a very widespread process in Bantu, accounting for the lack of lowering between

---

19 Admittedly, the evidence is not as complete as we might wish—a good, thorough, theoretically-grounded descriptive monograph on the Bemba tone system is sorely needed—but sketchy as it is, it seems sufficient to support the claims I am making.

20 That is, the one involving just TD .

the *radical* H and this post-radical H melody appears more problematic. The only way for the lowering not to occur is for the radical H to fuse with the post-radical melody (by an OCP-like stipulation) at a very early stage in the derivation, say at stem-level, assuming this to be a valid lexical stage[21]. We would thus get something like this:

(30) underlying

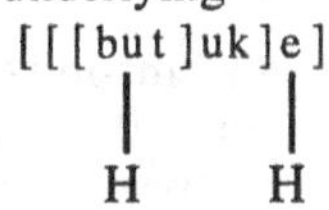

(31) extension association

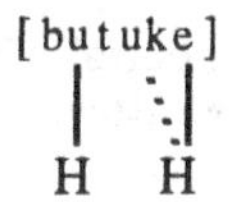

(31) H-fusion (by OCP?)

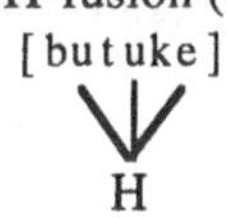

If one accepts this line of reasoning, it must be recognised that this melody associates in a fashion totally different from the LH melody, which seems rather to have as its aim the prevention of any contiguity between different Hs. It must also be acknowledged that if this synchronic process correctly explains the non-lowering of originally successive Hs, it did not apply to CB *HH stems, where the two Hs were not subjected to this OCP-like fusion, but on the contrary underwent the lowering process. This is not particularly surprising since these nominal stems were not derived, in contradistinction to verb stems, and thus did not meet the structural description of the fusion rule[22].

---

21. Doubts have been expressed about the validity of the Bantu stem as a stage in derivation within the framework of lexical phonology, but by and large such a stem-level for rule application seems to me fairly well motivated (cf. Philippson, 1992).

22 It is noteworthy that something very similar occurs in Shambaa, which we have already seen as a possible model for tone-lowering in Bemba: in Shambaa also, where two successive H's are normally separated by a downstep (cf. 6), there is no such downstep between a radical H and the H associating to the extensions from the FV. Here too the same OCP-like fusion must be at work at stem-level.

3. Conclusions

In conclusion, we can envision the following diachronic developments:

(a) a process of Tone Doubling associates a H tone to the following mora, thus turning *HL stems into HH

(b) to enhance distinctiveness, a downstep appears between two successive H tones, thus turning *HH into H!H. Later on the downstepped H becomes absolutely lowered

(c) in the course of the learning process, some *HH stems mistakenly get re-allocated to the *HL > HH category - this makes sense, if we assume the doubling process to somewhat antedate downstepping, however slightly. We could in fact, as suggested above, consider TD as leading towards a neutralisation of the *HH/*HL contrast (as in Shambaa) and downstepping as being a later reaction against such a neutralisation.

(d) in longer stems, mostly verbal, the tendency to neutralisation is resisted by either fusing all stem Hs together, or alternatively, systematically demarcating two successive Hs by a L.

Whether this analysis offers a valid model for understanding Bemba tonal diachrony remains to be put to the test of: (1) a more in-depth multi-dialectal study of the Bemba tone system and (2) better comparative data on neighbouring languages.[23]

References

Carter, H. 1973. Tonal data in Comparative Bantu, *African Language Studies* 14: 36-52.

Goldsmith, J. 1984. Meeussen's Rule, in M. Aronoff & R. Oehrle (eds.), *Language sound structure: Studies in phonology presented to Morris Halle by his teacher and students*. Cambridge: MIT Press.

Guthrie, M. 1945. The tonal structure of Bemba. [Unpublished Ph.D. thesis, University of London.]

Guthrie, M. 1967-71. *Comparative Bantu*. 4 vols. Westmead: Gregg

Guthrie, M. (comp.) & M. Mann (ed.). 1995. *A vocabulary of Icibemba*. (African Languages and Cultures. Supplement 2.) SOAS

Kaehler-Meyer, E. 1962. Studien zur Tonalen Struktur der Bantusprachen: Shambala, *Afrika und Uebersee*. 46: 1-43.

Meeussen, A. E. 1976. Notes on tone in Bantu nominal stems, *African Languages/ Langues africaines*. 2: 60-70

Moehlig, W. J. G. 1976. Guthries Beitrag zur Bantuistik aus heutiger Sicht, *Anthropos*. 71: 673-715

23Since writing this paper, it has come to my notice that several South-Eastern Bantu languages, such as Shona (S 10) and Nguni (S 40) have a similar apparent inconsistency in the reflexes of *HH/*HL, applying in virtually the same set of items as in Bemba.I intend to investigate the wider situation in a forthcoming article.

Moehlig, W. J. G. 1980. Bantu languages in B. Heine & W.J.G. Moehlig (eds.) *Language and dialect atlas of Kenya.* 1: 13-53

Odden, D. 1982. Tonal phenomena in Kishambaa, *Studies in African Linguistics.* 13, 2: 177-208.

Odden, D. 1985. Three dialects of Kipare, in G. Dimmendaal (ed.) *Current approaches to African linguistics* 3. Dordrecht: Foris, 257-80.

Philippson, G. 1992. Tons et accent dans les langues bantu d'Afrique Orientale: étude comparative typologique et diachronique, [Unpublished Doctorat d'Etat dissertation, Université Paris V.]

Philippson, G. 1998. Tone reduction vs. metrical attraction in the evolution of Eastern Bantu tone systems, in L. Hyman & C. Kisseberth (eds.), *Theoretical aspects of Bantu tone.* Stanford.

Sharman, J.C. & A.E. Meeussen. 1955. The representation of structural tones, with special reference to the tonal behaviour of the verb in Bemba, Northern Rhodesia, *Africa.* 25: 393-404.

Appendix

1) Trisyllabic underived HHH stems in Bemba:

-mmámbálá	'hoop iron'	-búúkílá	'snag in path, pointed'
-ɲcéénéné	'large queen termite'	-fwámbák(w)á	'sheath of knife'
-ŋkákáʃí	'bitterness of unripe fruit'	-ŋkálámó	'lion'
-ŋkáŋgálá	'warty cucumber'	-kólóbwé	'snare for animals'
-kólócí	'very old person'	-kóŋgóló	'stalk of fruit'
-ŋkúbílí	'barrel-shaped drum'	-ŋkúŋgúlú	'bull elephant'
-ŋkwíŋgílí	'metal bracelet'	-láálílá	'shrub sp.'
-lékésé	'long bundle tied in grass'	-lúndúʃí	'tall person'
-lúŋgúlé	'hot spring'	-néŋéné	'very small ant'
-ɲɲéɲjélé	'bell'	-ŋgólólí	'laughter'
-pámbátá	'edible caterpillars'	-páŋgálá	'bull waterbuck'
-mpásásé	'uproar'	-pélélé	'termite sp.'
-pémbélé	'rhino'	-sákátá	'handful'
-sáŋgátí	'tree sp.'	-sélémbá	'tree sp.'
-nséŋgélé	'genet sp.'	-nsóŋkóló	'bull eland'
-ʃémbélé	'tsetse'	-ʃúndápwá	'incurable illness'
-táláwé	'hail'	-ntándálá	'kudu'
-tééléélwé	'peace after fighting'		

2) Quadrisyllabic underived HHHH stems in Bemba:

-mbúlúmíná	'axe handle not yet bored'	-kúúkúútílá	'white root cassava'
-cóólóbóndó	'trickle (of water)'	-tútúlúmé	'contempt of taboo'
-nsélébéndé	'village green'	-nsábáwílé	'flood of water'
-sépélélá	'rain driven in under verandah'	-túntúmíná	'unbroken, undamaged thing'
-ʃímíníʃí	'last echoes'	-sónsóŋkélá	'cape'
-célécésé	'undercooked "cikanda" (an edible tuber)'		

3) Anomalous deverbative HHH stems (2 out of 3,500 items):

-bútúkô	'running'	-céɲjéló	'cunning'

4) Anomalous deverbative HHHH stems (5 out of 3,500 items):

-fíʃílíʃá	'hiding place'	<	-fís-
-bílíkíʃá	'alarm'	<	-bíl-
-ŋkáláűʃí	'jumbler of words'	<	-kálaw-
-kőkőtőlő	'crust'	<	-kőkotol-
-ʃíndíkílá	'parting words of ill-omen'	<	-ʃíndik-

L’augment en bantou du Nord-Ouest

CLAIRE GRÉGOIRE & BAUDOUIN JANSSENS
Musée Royal de l'Afrique Centrale, Tervuren &
Université Libre de Bruxelles

1. Introduction

Depuis le colloque de Viviers, la majorité des bantouistes s’accordent pour considérer que le Wide Bantu constitue un continuum linguistique. Les principaux arguments avancés en faveur de l’existence de ce continuum sont issus de l’examen du système des classes nominales. Pourtant il est encore difficile aujourd’hui d’élaborer un modèle satisfaisant pour rendre compte de l’évolution historique qui a dû être celle des morphèmes préfixés aux thèmes nominaux dans cet ensemble linguistique.

Les reconstructions proposées à cet égard pour le Narrow Bantu se caractérisent notamment par le fait qu’elles incluent l’existence de l’augment ou prépréfixe. Segmentalement identique au préfixe pronominal, ce morphème s’antépose au substantif dans certaines conditions grammaticales ou syntaxiques qui sont, de manière générale, liées à l’expression de la détermination.

Différents chercheurs[1] ont évoqué l’existence possible d’anciennes séquences de type Augment + Préfixe nominal en dehors du Narrow Bantu. Cette hypothèse a notamment été avancée en vue d’expliquer le fait qu’en Western Grassfields, les préfixes nominaux sont majoritairement de type

---

1 Hyman (1980b), Voorhoeve et Leroy (n.d.), Boum (1981), Grégoire (1983), Janssens (1985, 1992) et d'autres.

vocalique et qu'ils sont dotés d'un ton haut, sauf aux classes 1 et 9 où le ton est bas, ce qui est également le cas des préfixes pronominaux reconstruits par Meeussen (1967) pour le Narrow Bantu. Stallcup rejetait toutefois cette argumentation en estimant que: "There is no direct evidence that Grassfields Bantu ever had a pre-prefix. The only evidence for it at all is the high tone prefixes themselves and this is a circular argument. Furthermore, evidence for a pre-prefix in Northwest Narrow Bantu (zones A, B, C) is scanty and its extent and influence are not well known in this area." (1978: 236).

S'il est vrai que, depuis cette date, les acquis documentaires relatifs aux langues bantoues des zones A, B et C ont considérablement augmenté, l'augment n'a jamais été étudié de manière systématique dans cette partie du domaine. De Blois (1970), dont l'article est la seule étude comparative générale de ce morphème en bantou, n'a pu envisager que des données encore lacunaires. On a donc pensé que, pour sortir progressivement du cercle vicieux dénoncé par Stallcup, une voie s'offrait à la recherche: il fallait, dans un premier temps, réfléchir aux problèmes posés par l'augment dans les zones bantoues du Nord-Ouest, voir si ce morphème y était ou non attesté de manière claire, étudier les traces éventuelles qu'il y avait laissées et, le cas échéant, décrire l'évolution propre aux séquences préfixales complexes dans cette partie de l'aire linguistique. Cette démarche pouvait être particulièrement fructueuse puisqu'en zones A, B et C, les préfixes nominaux de type vocalique et/ou les préfixes nominaux à ton haut sont très fréquents notamment aux classes 1, 3, 4 ou 6 et que quelques langues de zone A distinguent une classe 6 et une classe 6a, problématique que l'on retrouve intégralement en dehors du bantou étroit. En 1973 déjà, Meeussen écrivait que: "A correct view of the augment as a correspondance in Bantu may enable us to bridge a gap between Bantu and the other Benue-Congo languages." (1973: 13). Or il est clair que, sans envisager la problématique de l'augment telle qu'elle se pose dans les langues du Nord-Ouest, on ne peut avoir une vue comparative correcte de ce morphème dans l'ensemble bantou.

Cette étude est loin d'être achevée. On se limitera donc ici à rassembler un certain nombre de données et à montrer qu'elles constituent un ensemble cohérent dont il y a moyen de dégager un schème d'évolution pour les séquences Augment + Préfixe nominal. Dans une étape ultérieure, ce schème d'évolution devra être confronté avec ce que l'on peut observer dans d'autres systèmes linguistiques relevant ou non du Narrow Bantu.

2. Langues à augments fonctionnels

De Blois (1970) ne consacre qu'un seul paragraphe aux langues bantoues du Nord-Ouest. Il y suggère que le myene (B.10) et le yambasa (A.60) attestent très probablement des traces d'augment, mais il ne tire aucune conclusion ferme des données parcellaires dont il disposait. Même à l'heure actuelle, la documentation n'est pas toujours suffisamment explicite. On peut noter cependant que Motingea (1996) a reconstruit l'augment en proto-Ngiri

(C.30) et que, selon Bokamba (1971) et Kamanda Kola (1991), le zamba atteste un augment dont la représentation varie selon les classes, mais qui s'oppose à son absence de la même façon que dans certaines langues bantoues centrales. C'est ce que montrent les exemples suivants, empruntés à Kamanda Kola:

(1)	a.	bábâ:ná bànd òdâ:nà	'les enfants jouent'
	b.	bâ:ná bànd òdâ:nà	'des enfants jouent'
(2)	a.	ímúntɔ̀dù ímwà mwâ:sì	'le nombril de la femme ...'
	b.	ímúntɔ̀dù ímwà ómwâ:sì	'le nombril de la femme en question...'
	c.	ímúntɔ̀dù mwà mwâ:sì	'le nombril d'une femme'
(3)	a.	ímídɛ́kɛ̀	'les nasses'
	b.	ò mídɛ́kɛ̀	'dans les nasses'
(4)	a.	bábâ:ná	'les enfants'
	b.	bâ:ná díbòà	'neuf enfants'
	c.	ínswě:	'les poissons'
	d.	ńswě: nsámbó	'sept poissons'
(5)	a.	ízíkèì	'l'oeuf'
	b.	zíkèì zídò	'quel oeuf?'

Les exemples cités sous (1) attestent un augment articulé qui est présent ou absent selon que le substantif est déterminé vs indéterminé (ou, selon Bokamba, spécifié vs non spécifié). En (2) on voit que le même conditionnement explique la présence ou l'absence de l'augment à l'initiale du connectif. Quant aux exemples (3), (4) et (5), ils montrent qu'en zamba, l'augment est absent lorsque le substantif est soit précédé d'un locatif, soit accompagné d'un déterminant numéral ou interrogatif, ce qui est très souvent le cas dans les langues bantoues centrales. Les problèmes soulevés par l'absence fréquente de l'augment après un morphème locatif ont été discutés dans Meeussen (1973: 13) et dans Grégoire (1975: 159-163). On se limitera donc à noter que le substantif accompagné d'un déterminant interrogatif est, par essence, non spécifié et qu'il en va souvent de même du substantif accompagné d'un numéral. Dans ce dernier cas cependant, la spécification du substantif est possible si l'on se réfère à la totalité des entités dénombrées comme c'est le cas dans des énoncés tels que: 'les neuf enfants...' ou 'les sept poissons...'. Mais ce type de syntagme est très rarement recueilli par les descripteurs et nous ignorons comment il s'exprime en zamba. On en trouve toutefois des exemples en ngubi et en bubi, comme on le verra ci-dessous en (8) et (10).

En ngubi (B.40), Puèch (1988) a décrit, à partir des exemples repris en (6), un augment *í*- ou ´- qui disparaît lorsque le substantif est accompagné d'un déterminant numéral:

(6) a. ímwà:tsì, ímyà:tsì 'veine(s)'

b. myà:tsì mìbáyì 'deux veines'

c. íŋâ:ŋgà 'le guérisseur'

d. ŋà:ŋgà mô:sí 'un (numéral) guérisseur'

On notera toutefois que le texte publié par Aleko et Puèch (1988) paraît attester de réelles oppositions entre la présence et l'absence de l'augment tonal, même dans le cas où le substantif est accompagné d'un déterminant numéral, oppositions qui sont exactement celles que permet un augment fonctionnel:

(7) a. ...rá ɓàɣísí ɣò

'ce ne sont pas des génies'

b. ...rá múɣisí wà:fúmá ɣú mà:mbà

'c'est un (= le?) génie qui est sorti de l'eau'

(8) a. ...rá àɣwétsá (...) nà ɓàɣétù ɓàbáyì

'il est venu avec deux femmes'

b. βàmbé báɣètù ɓàɓáyì ɓànàɓá ná ɗì:mì...

'Comme les deux femmes étaient enceintes ...'

Enfin, l'examen des notes bubi (A.30) recueillies par Guarisma (1977-78) paraît montrer que, dans cette langue aussi, l'augment vocalique est absent ou présent à l'initiale du substantif accompagné d'un numéral selon que le sens est indéterminé ou déterminé (exemples 9 et 10) et qu'il est généralement absent après le morphème locatif *hɛ́* 'il y a' (exemple 11).

(9) a. òwàysóò, àβàysóò 'la femme, les femmes'

b. òβòyɛ́:ḿ ɔ́kí βàysóò bébàttá 'mon père a trois femmes'

(10) a. èpwáà, ìpwáà 'le chien, les chiens'

b. nɔ̀á yérà?á là pwá yéǹcɔ́ 'six serpents et cinq chiens'

c. ìpwáà cátɔ́báà yɔ́ βóyɛ:ḿ 'les trois chiens de mon père'

(11) a. àβàtɛ 'les pierres'

b. ètɛ́llɛ wèlàá hɛ́ βàtɛ 'sur le chemin, il y a des pierres'

D'autres langues pourraient être citées, mais le zamba, le ngubi et le bubi suffisent à montrer que, dans chacune des zones du Nord-Ouest, il existe des langues qui possèdent, non des traces d'augments, mais bien des augments articulés et fonctionnels dont l'utilisation est comparable à ce que l'on décrit dans certaines langues bantoues centrales.

3. Langues à augments partiellement fonctionnels

3.1.

On s'intéressera plus particulièrement ici à deux langues, le doko (C.30) et le myene (B.10), dans lesquelles une voyelle initiale—qui se comporte généralement comme l'un des constituants segmentaux du préfixe nominal ou comme le préfixe nominal lui-même—peut encore être identifiée comme un augment au travers de fonctionnements particuliers qui sont toutefois extrêmement figés.

3.2.

Les exemples présentés en (12) montrent que le doko, décrit par Twilingiyimana (1984), utilise des morphèmes préfixaux de type V̌- lorsque le thème substantival commence par une consonne et qu'il utilise des morphèmes préfixaux de type V̌C(V)- lorsque le thème commence par une voyelle:

(12)	a.	cl 1, 2	ókônzì, ákônzì	'chef(s)'
			ómáná, ábáná	'enfant(s)'
	b.	cl 3, 4	ópúté, ípúté	'rat(s)'
			ómêŋgà, ímêŋgà	'huile(s)'
	c.	cl 5, 6	íhú, áhú	'jour(s)'
			ídínó, ámínó	'dent(s)'
	d.	cl 14, 6	ópîpò, ápîpò	'force(s)'
			óbôhò, ámâhò	'visage(s)'
			ógbálé, ámálé	'maladie(s)' [2]
	e.	cl 9, 10	énzóí, ínzóí	'abeille(s)'
			ékôpì, íkôpì	'langue(s)'
			ékútú, íkútú	'calebasse(s)'

La voyelle initiale n'est toutefois pas représentée en présence de l'interrogatif 'combien' ou dans certains syntagmes exprimant les rapports de parenté, ce qui représente des conditions typiques d'absence d'augment

2 Devant certaines voyelles situées à l'initiale du thème, la séquence préfixale de classe 14 ó-bú- → óbw- est représentée par ógb-.

dans les langues centrales. On a ainsi, par exemple, *mínó máŋgá* 'combien de dents' (et non: *ámínó màngá), *mán á mbí* 'mon enfant' (et non: *ómán á mbí) etc...

En classes 9 et 10, les séquences préfixales sont de type V́N- ou V́-selon que la consonne initiale du thème est sonore ou sourde. L'exemple *kút íbà* 'deux calebasses' montre toutefois que la voyelle initiale n'est pas représentée lorsque le substantif est accompagné d'un déterminant numéral. Or, dans ce même type de syntagme, les morphèmes préfixaux de type V́- à ton haut qu'utilisent les substantifs de classes 4, 5 et 6 dont le thème commence par une consonne, peuvent facultativement être remplacés par des morphèmes de type CV̀-, à ton bas. C'est ce que montrent les exemples cités en (13):

(13) a. íbúlù 'la nuit'

b. áhú 'les jours'

c. ípúté 'les rats'

mais:

d. dìbùlú dímósì 'une nuit'

e. màhú máhátó 'trois jours'

f. mìpúté mibá 'deux rats'

Il est clair que les emplois où figurent des morphèmes préfixaux alternants de type C-, -CV̀-, ou Ø sont des emplois où il est fréquent que les langues bantoues centrales n'utilisent pas l'augment. Même si l'emploi du préfixe CV̀- est facultatif lorsque le nom est déterminé par un numéral, il est incontestable qu'il s'agit là d'un archaïsme, non d'une innovation. On peut donc en conclure que la voyelle à ton haut qui disparaît ou est remplacée par une séquence CV̀-, est bien un ancien augment, partiellement articulé encore. Ainsi l'alternance entre les morphèmes préfixaux de type V́- et de type CV̀-, que l'on observe dans les divers emplois des substantifs de classes 4, 5 et 6 dont le thème est à initiale consonantique, ne peut s'expliquer qu'en admettant qu'un préfixe nominal CV̀- est représenté lorsque l'augment est exclu, et que la présence de l'augment entraîne, par contre, la disparition de ce préfixe.

On notera enfin qu'établir des séquences de type V́- CV̀-, permet de rendre compte de la tonalité des substantifs dont le thème a une première voyelle à ton bas. Tout se passe en effet comme si le ton haut de l'augment était redoublé sur le PN et modifiait ensuite la tonalité du thème lorsque la représentation du PN ou de sa voyelle est nulle. On peut en effet poser:

dì+bùlú → dìbùlú

mais:

í-dì+bùlú → í-dí+bùlú → í-´+bùlú → í+búlǔ → íbúlù

On a ainsi schématiquement :

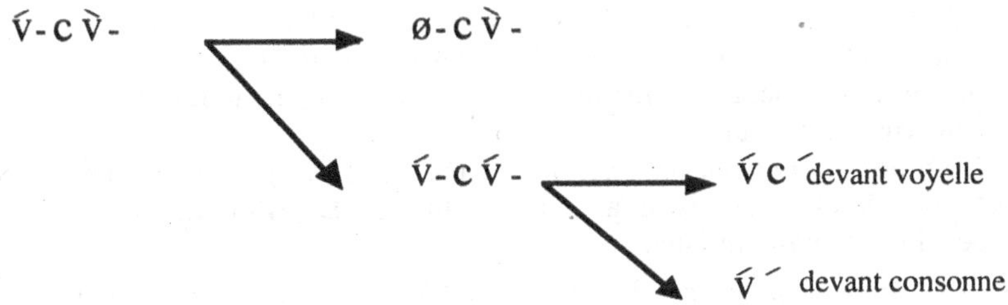

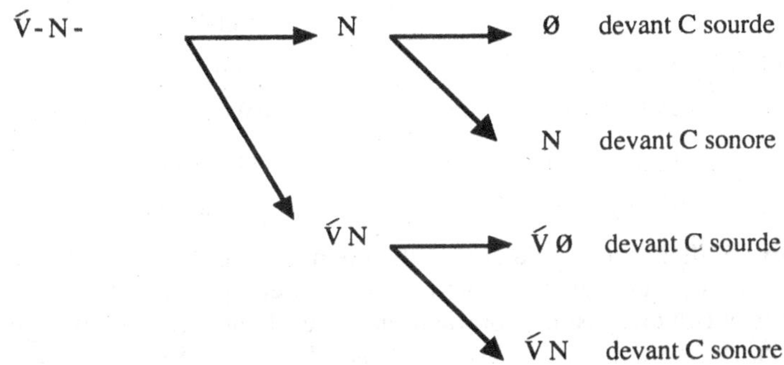

3.3.

Les phénomènes observables en myene (B.10) sont analogues à ceux qui viennent d'être décrits en doko. On les résumera brièvement car ils sont partiellement variables d'après la classe dont il s'agit et présentent donc une certaine complexité. Nous nous limiterons de plus au myene-nkomi dont la situation nous est plus familière que celle des autres parlers myene.

A la classe 10, les substantifs et les adjectifs du myene-nkomi attestent canoniquement une séquence préfixale de type iN- comme le montrent les exemples qui suivent:

(14) cl 9, 10 ḿbwà, ímbwà 'chien(s)'

ìmbw ímpólò 'de gros chiens'

ìmbw ínáyì ou m̀bwá náyì 'quatre chiens'

Le dernier de ces exemples montre également que la voyelle [i] de cette séquence disparaît facultativement dans le substantif et le déterminant, à condition que celui-ci soit un numéral. Dans ce cas, la consonne nasale est clairement tonale, au même titre que celle de la classe 9. Ce fait, de même que les commutations observables dans les formes adjectivales: cl 2 *àlá* vs cl 10 *ìndá* vs cl 9 *ǹdá* 'long(s)' oblige synchroniquement à considérer la nasale comme faisant partie du préfixe. La voyelle [i] est donc certainement un augment historique, même s'il n'est pas sûr qu'il faille l'analyser comme telle en synchronie, puisque la classe 10 serait alors la seule classe à manifester un augment fonctionnel et que, de surcroît, elle le ferait au travers d'une alternance facultative.

Comme le montrent les exemples cités en (15), le comportement des substantifs de cl 9 et 8 est exactement celui que De Blois décrit dans les langues dites à augment latent:

(15) a. cl 9 àré n' ìmbwá mpólò 'il a un gros chien'
ákė m' ínyɔ̀nì 'les oeufs de l'oiseau'
ìndʒɛ́ɣɔ̀ sétɔ́ndè nyámà 'les léopards aiment la viande'
b. cl 7, 8 èrérè, rérè 'arbre(s)'
èzɔ́mbɔ̀lɔ̀, yɔ́mbɔ̀lɔ̀ 'balai(s)'
ìɣómí ny' írérè 'une dizaine d'arbres'
n' ìyɔ́mbɔ̀lɔ̀ 'avec les balais'

Ces substantifs n'ont pas d'augment directement identifiable, sauf après le connectif et l'associatif où apparaît un augment [i] auquel on peut certainement attribuer aussi la modification en [e] de la finale *-a* du verbe précédent dans: *ìndʒɛ́ɣɔ̀ sétɔ́ndè nyámà*. En effet, lorsque ce même verbe est suivi d'un pronom substitutif, sa finale est *-a*: *ìndʒɛ́ɣɔ̀ sétɔ́ndà nyɔ́* 'les léopards l'aiment (le mouton, cl. 5)'. La même chose peut être dite de l'associatif et du connectif dont la voyelle est [a] comme le montrent les exemples (16):

(16) a. àbyá nà yɛ 'il est venu avec lui (cl. 1)'
b. èbándá zá ɣélò 'une peau claire (litt.: de rougeur)'

Aux classes autres que 8, 9 et 10, les substantifs ont une voyelle initiale dans tous leurs emplois, le degré de détermination étant marqué par le schème tonal. Les exemples de classes 3/4 cités en (17) sont représentatifs de la situation générale:

(17) a. òlóndà, ìlóndà 'le(s) fruit(s)'
b. ìɣómí ny' ílóndà 'une dizaine de fruits'
c. àré n' ìlòndà ɣ^{ɥ} ótòndó wɛ̀ 'il a des fruits dans son panier'

d.	àbyá n' ì lóndà	'il est venu avec les fruits'
e.	èdʒíβ' òlóndà	'il cueille le fruit'
f.	èdʒíβ' ìlóndà	'il cueille les fruits'

A eux seuls, ces exemples ne permettent pas d'affirmer que la voyelle initiale du substantif *òlóndà, ìlóndà* est un ancien augment, mais cette hypothèse devient plausible lorsqu'on les envisage simultanément avec ceux cités en (14) et (15). On notera aussi qu'en myene-nkomi la plupart des séquences préfixales sont de type VC- ou VCS- lorsque le thème commence par une voyelle:

(18)	a.	cl 1, 2	òŋwánà, àwánà	'enfant(s)'
	b.	cl 3, 4	òŋwáŋgà, ìmyángà	'morceau(x) de fer'
	c.	cl 5, 6	ìnyàŋgò, àmàŋgò	'petit(s)' (adjectif)
	d.	cl 14, 6	òwárɔ̀, àmárɔ̀	'pirogue(s)'

En outre, les exemples cités en (19) montrent que, si le thème substantival ou adjectival commence par une consonne labiale *p, v,* ou *w*, parfois identifiable par la commutation, la séquence préfixale est de type Vm- aux classes 1, 3, 4 et 6 ainsi d'ailleurs qu'à la classe 10, quoiqu'elle provienne alors de V N - :

(19)	a.	cl 3, 4	òmpéndè, ìmpéndè	'jambe(s)'
	b.	cl 5, 6	ìwúmù, àmbúmù	'ventre(s)'
	c.	cl 10	ìmbónì	'chèvre(s)'
	d.	-wé 'mauvais'	cl 2 àwé ; cl 1 et 3 òmbé; cl 6 àmbé; cl 4 et 10 ìmbé	
	e.	-vóló 'gros'	cl 2 àvóló ; cl 1 et 3 òmpóló; cl 6 àmpóló; cl 4 et 10 ìmpóló	

En résumé, on peut donc dire que le myene-nkomi a conservé la trace d'un augment fonctionnel en classe 10, qu'il a un augment latent aux classes 8 et 9 et un augment figé à toutes les autres classes. Aux classes où existe un augment figé, on peut postuler qu'à partir des anciennes séquences préfixales de type V-CV-, la langue a:

- effacé ou semi-vocalisé la voyelle du préfixe nominal devant une voyelle
  Ex: *òŋwáŋgà, ìmyángà* 3, 4 'morceau(x) de fer'
- effacé la voyelle du préfixe nominal de type mV- devant une consonne labiale
  Ex: *òmpéndè, ìmpéndè* 3, 4 'jambe(s)'

- effacé la totalité du préfixe nominal devant une consonne quelconque
  Ex: *òtɔ́ndò, ìtɔ́ndò* 3, 4 'panier(s)'

4. Langues à augments résiduels

Dans des langues comme le tuki ou le gunu (A.60), la situation est particulièrement intéressante parce que, tout en présentant à certaines classes des séquences préfixales analogues à celles que l'on a décrites jusqu'ici, ces langues ne paraissent attester aucun fonctionnement qui permette d'identifier des augments de manière directe. De plus, elles ont une classe 6 et une classe 6a entièrement distinctes. Les exemples tuki qui suivent sont repris à Hyman (1980a) et à Musada (1996)[3].

(20)	a.	cl 1, 2	mòtò, bàtò	'personne(s)'
			mwànā, bànā	'enfant(s)'
			òkōtó, bàkōtó	'femme(s)'
			òŋgìnī, bɔ̀ŋgìnī (Hyman)	'étranger(s)'
			ùŋgìnī, bìnī (Musada)	'étranger(s)'
	b.	cl 3, 4	òhòmbā, ìhòmbā	'nez'
			òtēmā, ìtēmā	'coeur(s)'
			ɔ̀mbɔ̀ɔ̄, ìmbɔ̀ɔ̄	'bras'
			ɔ̀ŋgòlō, ìŋgòlɔ̄	'pied(s)'
			ùŋgūté, ìŋgūté	'bouche(s)'
	c.	cl 5, 6	ììgìī, àŋgìī	'oeuf(s)'
			ìjɔ̀ŋgɔ̄, àŋjɔ̀ŋgɔ̄	'lance(s)'
			ìtānē, àtānē	'pierre(s)'
			ìbùmù, àmbùmù	'ventre(s)'
			ìbāné, àmbāné (ou àŋbāné)	'sein(s)'
			nìó, àŋgīó	'dent(s)'
			nìsō, àŋgīsó	'oeil, yeux'

On voit, qu'à part dans quelques substantifs de classe 1 où le préfixe est mò-, les préfixes des classes 1, 3, 4 et 6 pluriel de 5, sont de type VN- si la consonne initiale du thème est une consonne sonore *b, d, j, g*, mais de type V- si la consonne initiale du thème est une consonne sourde. Un exemple comme *ùŋgìnī,* pluriel: *bìnī* 'étranger(s)', et quelques substantifs de classes 5, 6 comme *nìó,* pluriel: *àŋgīó* montrent de plus

3 Les sources sont relatives à deux variantes dialectales distinctes qui diffèrent, notamment, par leurs systèmes vocaliques.

que la séquence préfixale comporte une nasale devant les thèmes à initiale vocalique, quelle que soit l'origine de la vélarisation de cette nasale.

On peut donc observer non seulement que le préfixe de classe 6, pluriel de 5, se comporte exactement comme ceux des classes 1, 3 et 4 (ce que Hyman avait déjà constaté), mais encore que le traitement des séquences préfixales propres à toutes ces classes, est analogue à celui qui a été décrit en myene-nkomi.

Les classes 6a et 18 ont, quant à elles, un préfixe de type mV- dont la représentation est stable. La classe 18, dont le PN est *mù-/mò-*, forme le pluriel de la classe 19. La classe 6a, dont le préfixe est de type *mà-*, sert à former les substantifs qui désignent des liquides ou des masses; elle sert aussi de pluriel à la classe 14 et à des substantifs inclus dans des appariements non canoniques; elle est enfin utilisée dans la dérivation nominale déverbative.

(21)	a.	cl 19, 18	ìtɔ̄ŋgɔ́, mùtɔ̄ŋgɔ́	'corne(s)'
	b.	cl 6a	màtīá	'eau'
			mɔ̀wɔ́	'vin'
			màwūtē	'graisse'
			màbāné	'lait'
	c.	cl 14, 6a	wùsī, màsī	'jour(s)'
			wùsyō, màsyō	'visage(s)'
	d.	-bùw- 'récolter'	mèbùwè	'(saison des) récoltes'
		-wùt- 'cultiver'	mèwùtè	'saison des cultures'
		-mān- 'finir'	màmānā	'fin'

On notera que, s'il n'est pas synchroniquement additif en tuki, le préfixe nominal de classe 18 pourrait l'avoir été à l'origine s'il avait un lien avec le préfixe locatif de classe 18 attesté en bantou central. Ce lien ne peut être démontré, mais on remarquera cependant que divers parlers kongo peuvent, pour les substantifs locatifs signifiant 'endroit', utiliser la classe 18 pour exprimer le pluriel des classes 16 et 17 (Laman, 1912: 84, Ndonga Mfuwa, 1995: 141). En ce qui concerne la classe 6a, la situation est plus complexe. Pour ce qui est des substantifs désignant des noms de masses et de liquides, on peut admettre, comme Voorhoeve et Leroy (n.d.) l'avaient suggéré, qu'ils représentent un champ sémantique peu sensible à l'opposition déterminé/indéterminé et que l'absence d'augment y est donc explicable. Quant à la classe 6a incluse dans un appariement, son préfixe est additif dans un certain nombre de cas au moins. Ainsi dans *hɔ̀mà/màhɔ̀mà* 16/6a 'endroit(s)', le préfixe de classe 6a est, historiquement au moins, additif par rapport à un préfixe locatif de classe 16, tandis que dans *ìhɔ́ɔ̄/màpɔ́ɔ̄* 4/6a 'marmite(s)', l'alternance consonantique montre qu'il précède un préfixe de type N-.

La même observation peut être faite en gunu où l'on trouve non seulement des appariements 14/6a, mais aussi des appariements 14+N/6a+N:

(22)	a.	cl 5, 6	ìbènú, àmbènú	'noix de cola'
	b.	cl 14, 6a	bùbènú, màbènú	'colatier(s)'
	c.	cl 14+N/6a+N	bòmpòndó, màmpòndó	'cocotier(s)'
			bómpɛ̀lɛ̀, mámpɛ̀lɛ̀	'papayer(s)'

Or en nomande, langue très proche du gunu, Scruggs (1983) fait observer que les substantifs de classe 9 font non seulement leur pluriel en 10, mais aussi en 6+10 avec le sens plus spécifique de 'beaucoup de... ', 'un grand nombre de... '. Un sens analogue paraît aussi être lié au pluriel 6+N du mankon où Leroy (1977) signale que *fɨngwáŋə* signifie 'du sel', alors qu'en classe 6+N *mɨngwáŋə* signifie 'des tas de sel'. On notera que l'emploi additif du PN6 pour exprimer un sens collectif, totalisateur ou quantitatif a été signalé par de très nombreux auteurs, tant dans le bantou du Nord-Ouest que dans le bantou central. Cet emploi a d'ailleurs été relevé par Kadima (1969: 164). Ce sens collectif pourrait aussi être celui des substantifs déverbatifs de la classe 6a du gunu (*-gìd-* 'battre' → *mègìdé* 'bastonnade') ou du tuki (*-bùw-* 'récolter' → *mèbùwè* 'récoltes').

A propos des substantifs déverbatifs, il est curieux de constater qu'en tuki et en gunu, leur préfixe est dépourvu d'augment, qu'en nomande, selon Scruggs, le préfixe de cl.1 est *o-* mais qu'il est *mu-* dans les déverbatifs qui désignent l'agent et enfin qu'en tiv, selon Hyman, le préfixe de cl 3 est *o-* (ou Ø) mais qu'il est *m-* dans les déverbatifs. Une telle convergence appelle sans doute la réflexion et devrait être expliquée.

Il serait également utile de vérifier si, de façon générale, l'augment n'a pas tendance à être absent lorsque le préfixe nominal est additif ou l'a été historiquement. Tel est en effet souvent le cas en bantou central, notamment pour les préfixes additifs des classes locatives. S'il paraît hors de doute que l'on doit reconstruire des augments en classes 16, 17 et 18, d'assez nombreuses langues n'attestent plus d'augment à ces classes ou les attestent uniquement sous une forme latente, alors qu'elles ont encore un augment segmental aux classes non locatives. Le lecteur se reportera à Grégoire (1975: 156-159) où cette question se trouve discutée.

Si des études ultérieures (portant, par exemple, sur les préfixes diminutifs ou augmentatifs) aboutissaient à confirmer la fragilité de l'augment des préfixes additifs, on tiendrait peut-être une piste permettant d'expliquer l'existence simultanée de deux classes 6 en bantou du Nord-Ouest. La séquence préfixale de cette classe aurait en effet connu deux types d'emplois distincts. L'augment y aurait été utilisé de manière régulière lorsque la séquence intervenait dans la formation du pluriel de la classe 5.

Par contre, il n'aurait pas été utilisé dans les substantifs collectifs désignant des liquides ou des masses ainsi que dans les pluriels collectifs formés par addition de préfixe. L'ancienne séquence préfixale de classe 6 aurait alors produit deux allomorphes distincts dans leurs emplois. Ces allomorphes seraient devenus autonomes et les systèmes auraient alors engendré deux classes différentes en créant de nouveaux préfixes d'accord.

Tout cela reste, bien entendu, à démontrer. Pourtant il est intéressant de noter que, selon Hyman (1980b), les langues Western-Grassfields ont une classe 6a dont les accords sont de type *mə̀*– et dotés d'un ton bas, alors que ceux de la classe 6, pluriel de 5, ont un ton haut. Cette situation pourrait éventuellement s'expliquer si l'on admettait que les accords de la classe 6a sont issus d'un calque qui s'est opéré directement à partir de l'allomorphe *mà*– de la séquence préfixale sans augment.

5. Observations finales

Hyman (1980b) avait déjà attribué la coexistence des classes 6 et 6a du tuki à l'évolution différenciée d'une séquence *a-ma-*. Notre contribution consiste donc à montrer que ce processus s'intègre dans un ensemble cohérent d'évolutions diachroniques qui sont, de plus, observables dans des zones où l'existence ancienne de l'augment ne fait aucun doute.

La littérature, même récente, attribue souvent l'apparition des préfixes nominaux de type vocalique à l'effacement de la consonne dans des structures de type CV-. S'il est clair que tel peut être effectivement le cas dans certaines langues et/ou à certaines classes (comme la classe 7 par exemple), nous pensons avoir montré que l'occurrence des préfixes de type V- doit parfois être attribuée à l'effacement complet du préfixe nominal qui ne laisse subsister que le seul augment vocalique. Cette procédure est en effet la seule qui puisse justifier le fait que le doko fasse alterner un préfixe de type V́- à ton haut et un préfixe de type CV̀- à ton bas aux mêmes classes et dans les mêmes substantifs, uniquement en fonction de la nature du déterminant qui figure dans le syntagme nominal. Elle est aussi la seule qui puisse expliquer de manière satisfaisante l'occurrence des préfixes vocaliques du myene-nkomi. Elle vaut aussi pour le tuki et le gunu aux classes dont le préfixe ne comporte pas de consonne nasale. Il semble bien que ce processus soit dû à des contraintes de type prosodique relatives aux schémas syllabiques des substantifs, contraintes qui semblent avoir joué aussi dans certaines langues bantoues centrales. Plusieurs de ces langues, en effet, ne conservent l'augment que dans les substantifs dont le thème est monosyllabique ou dans ceux dont le thème commence par une voyelle. Ceci a pour effet d'aligner la majorité des substantifs sur un modèle canonique comportant trois syllabes dont la première peut être issue soit de l'augment, soit du préfixe nominal. De Blois (1970: 94) cite des exemples intéressants à cet égard en gisu (J30) où l'on a:

(23) a. ba–ba–ndu 'les gens'

b. ga–ma–gi 'les oeufs'

mais:

c. b a – k a n a 'les filles'

En ce qui concerne, plus particulièrement, les séquences préfixales de type V_1-mV_2- des classes 1, 3, 4 ou 6, les problèmes posés sont plus complexes. Ces séquences peuvent avoir subi le traitement général qui efface le préfixe nominal, mais elles peuvent aussi avoir été réduites à V_1N- par perte de la voyelle préfixale et le myene-nkomi atteste simultanément ces deux traitements ainsi que nous l'avons montré plus haut au paragraphe 3.3. Comme, par ailleurs, la nasale d'une séquence VN- peut, dans certaines langues, être effacée devant une consonne sourde, il peut être difficile de reconstituer l'évolution exacte qui a mené aux préfixes vocaliques de ces classes et la question doit être envisagée dans chaque langue en particulier. On notera que, quel que soit le traitement qu'ont subi les séquences V_1-mV_2-, leur aboutissement répond aux mêmes contraintes prosodiques que celles que nous avons évoquées plus haut. L'apparition des préfixes de type VN- a souvent été expliquée comme le résultat d'une métathèse: mV_2- > V_2N-. Nous pensons que l'hypothèse que nous proposons ici est préférable puisqu'elle s'intègre dans un processus général. L'effacement de la voyelle V_2 du préfixe nominal situé dans une séquence V_1-mV_2- aboutit en effet à la perte d'une syllabe, ce qui est aussi le cas lorsque le préfixe tout entier est effacé dans une structure de ce type ou dans une structure V_1-CV_2-.

En résumé—et en nous limitant aux séquences dans lesquelles figure un augment ainsi qu'aux thèmes à initiale consonantique—on peut schématiser les divers processus que nous avons relevés de la manière suivante:

(1) V_1-CV_2 + C ... > V_1 + C ...

(2) V_1-mV_2 + C ... > V_1 + C ... ou V_1 (N) + C ...

Un travail comparatif considérable est encore nécessaire pour montrer que ces schémas valent également pour d'autres langues bantoues du Nord-Ouest que nous n'avons pas pu envisager ici. Ce travail est indispensable car il est clair que le même résultat peut s'expliquer différemment selon les langues et même selon les classes dans une même langue.

Si un tel travail aboutissait à des résultats concluants, il serait sans doute fructueux de réenvisager, dans une perspective semblable, les préfixes vocaliques qui apparaissent dans les langues bantoïdes non bantoues puisque certaines d'entre elles attestent des faits qui ne sont pas sans rappeler ceux que nous avons relevés en Narrow Bantu. Ainsi, par exemple, le préfixe nominal de classe 6 du kenyang est *bà-* ou *mà-*, mais *àm-* lorsque le thème commence par une consonne labiale; en ejagham, le préfixe nominal de classe 6 est *à-* devant une consonne, mais *àm-* devant une voyelle:

(24)	a.	kenyang		
		cl.6	bàfɔ́	'graisse'
			mànɔ̀ŋ	'sang'
		cl 5, 6	àwɔ́, àmɔ́	'bras'
			nɛ́bɨ́, ámɨ́	'sein(s)'
	b.	ejagham		
		cl 5, 6	èβê, àβê	'sein(s)'
			èyə̂d, àmə̂d	'oeil, yeux'
			èyə̂ŋ, àmə̂ŋ	'dent(s)'

De même en menchum, Boum (1981) admet que, sur le plan historique, l'hypothèse la plus vraisemblable pour expliquer les préfixes nominaux de certaines classes, consiste à leur attribuer une structure de type VC- qui se réduit à V- devant consonne, mais à C- devant voyelle.

Quant à savoir si une investigation menée dans cette perspective aboutirait à des résultats probants, on ne le saura pas avant de l'avoir terminée. Considérer que le Narrow Bantu est plus conservateur qu'innovateur en ce qui concerne le système des classes nominales nous paraît être une hypothèse tout à fait plausible. Peut-être serait-il temps de développer de façon systématique et cohérente ce que certains auteurs ont déjà exprimé à ce sujet. Miehe (1991) a montré que les préfixes à nasale, loin d'être une innovation propre au bantou comme l'avait soutenu Greenberg (1963), ont probablement une origine beaucoup plus ancienne. Williamson (1993) a, pour sa part, montré qu'on trouve des traces claires de séquences 'augment + préfixe' dans divers groupes New Benue-Congo non bantous. Si d'autres études confirmaient ces acquis, elles remettraient en question la théorie communément admise selon laquelle le bantou serait un rejeton tardif du Benue-Congo.

Références

Aleko, Hilaire & Gilbert Puèch. 1988. Notes sur la lagune Ngove et les Ngubi, *Pholia* 3: 257-269.

Bokamba, Georges D. 1971. Specificity and definiteness in Dzamba, *Studies in African Linguistics* 2: 217-237.

Boum, Marie Anne. 1981. Le syntagme nominal en modele. [Thèse de doctorat non publiée, Rijksuniversiteit te Leiden.]

De Blois, Kees F. 1970. The Augment in the Bantu Languages, *Africana Linguistica* IV: 85-165.

Essono, Jean Jacques M. 1974. Description phonologique du tuki (ati), langue Sanaga. [Mémoire non publié, Université de Yaoundé.]

Essono, Jean Jacques M. 1980. Morphologie nominale du tuki (langue Sanaga). [Ms non publié, Université de Yaoundé.]

Greenberg, Joseph H. 1963. *The Languages of Africa.* The Hague: Mouton.

Grégoire, Claire. 1975. *Les locatifs en bantou.* Tervuren: Musée royal de l'Afrique Centrale, Annales en sciences humaines 15.

Grégoire, Claire. 1983. Quelques hypothèses comparatives sur les locatifs dans les langues bantoues du Cameroun, *Journal of West African Languages* 13, 2: 139-164.

Guarisma, Gladys. 1977-1978 Enquête sur la langue bubi. Questionnaire QIL. [Ms non publié.]

Hyman, Larry M. 1980a. Esquisse des classes nominales en tuki, in: Larry M. Hyman (ed), *Noun classes in the Grassfields Bantu Borderland.* Los-Angeles: University of Southern California —SCOPIL 8: 1-26.

Hyman, Larry M. 1980b. Reflections on the nasal classes in Bantu, in: Larry M. Hyman (ed), *Noun classes in the Grassfields Bantu Borderland.* Los-Angeles: University of Southern California —SCOPIL 8: 179-207.

Hyman, Larry M. & Francis X. Katamba. 1993. The Augment in Luganda: Syntax or Pragmatics?, in S.M. Mchombo (ed), *Theoretical Aspects of Bantu grammar* 1. Stanford: CSLI Publications, 209-256.

Janssens, Baudouin. 1985. Quelques objectifs de recherche comparative en zone A, communication au *Colloque international du CICIBA sur l'identité et les migrations bantoues,* Libreville 1-6 avril 1985. [Ms non publié.]

Janssens, Baudouin. 1992. Review of Gudrun Miehe (1991) *Die Präfixnasale im Benue-Congo und im Kwa - Versuch einer Wiederlegung der Hypothese von der Nasalinnovation des Bantu* , *Afrikanistische Arbeitspapiere* 30: 175-181.

Kadima, Marcel. 1969. *Le système des classes en bantou.* Leuven: Vander.

Kamanda Kola. 1991. Eléments de description du zamba, langue bantoue (C.31e) du Zaïre. [Mémoire de licence spéciale non publié, Université libre de Bruxelles.]

Laman, K. E. 1912. *Grammar of the Kongo Language.* New-York [No indication of publisher.]

Leroy, Jacqueline. 1977. Morphologie et classes nominales en mankon. [Thèse de Doctorat de 3ème cycle, non publiée, Université de la Sorbonne Nouvelle, Paris.]

Meeussen, A. E. 1967. Bantu Grammatical Reconstructions. *Africana Linguistica* III:80-121.

Meeussen, A. E. 1973. Test cases for method, *African Language Studies* 14: 6-18.

Miehe, Gudrun. 1991. *Die Präfixnasale im Benue-Congo und im Kwa - Versuch einer Wiederlegung der Hypothese von der Nasalinnovation des Bantu.* Sprache und Oralität in Afrika, Frankfurter Studien zur Afrikanistik, Band 5, Berlin: Dietrich Reimer.

Motingea Mangulu. 1995. *Etude comparative des langues Ngiri de l'entre Ubangi-Zaïre.* Leiden: University, Research School CNWS.

Musada, Augustin. 1996. Eléments de description du tuki (langue bantoue du Cameroun, A62). [Mémoire de DEA non publié, Université libre de Bruxelles.]

Ndonga, Mfuwa. 1995. *Systématique grammaticale du kisikongo (Angola)*. Lille: Atelier national de reproduction des thèses.

Puèch, Gilbert. 1988. Augment et préfixe nominal en ngubi, *Pholia* 3: 247-256.

Stallcup, Kenneth L. 1978. *A comparative perspective on the Phonology and Noun Classification of three Cameroon Grassfields Bantu Languages: Moghamo, Ngie and Oshie*. Ph.D. Thesis, Stanford University, Ann Arbor: University Microfilms International.

Rekanga, Jean-Paul. 1989. Essai de grammaire gunu (langue bantoue du Cameroun, A62). [Mémoire de licence spéciale non publié, Université libre de Bruxelles.]

Scruggs, Terri R. 1983. *Le système des classes en nomande*. Yaoundé: Société Internationale de Linguistique.

Twilingiyimana, Chrysogone. 1984. *Eléments de description du doko*. Tervuren: Musée royal de l'Afrique Centrale, Annales en Sciences humaines 116.

Voorhoeve, Jan & Jacqueline Leroy. n.d.. Le bantou périphérique. [Ms non publié.]

Williamson, Kay. 1993. The Noun Prefixes of New Benue-Congo, *Journal of African Languages and Linguistics* 14, 1: 29-45.

Les formes nomino-verbales de classes 5 et 15 dans les langues bantoues du Nord-Ouest

PASCALE HADERMANN
Musée Royal de l'Afrique Centrale, Tervuren

1. Introduction

Ce travail a pour objet d'analyser principalement les formes nomino-verbales de classe 5 et 15 telles qu'elles peuvent apparaître dans les langues bantoues des zones A, B, C et D[1]. Nous estimons qu'une meilleure compréhension des phénomènes morpho-syntaxiques, qui peuvent caractériser les formes nomino-verbales dans cette région, peut apporter des éléments décisifs au niveau de la reconstruction de ces formes en proto-bantou. L'infinitif de classe 15, bien attesté dans les langues actuelles a été reconstruit pour le proto-bantou par Meinhof, Meeussen et Guthrie et même pour le proto-benue-congo par De Wolf (1971). Pour ce qui est de la forme de la classe 5, il faut noter qu'il existe actuellement, à travers tout le domaine bantou, une forme nominale déverbative qui désigne l'action exprimée par le verbe et qui accepte souvent l'appariement 5/6. On peut donc supposer qu'en proto-bantou on a eu simultanément une forme de type

[1] Il faut noter que certaines langues de notre corpus construisent leur infinitif dans une classe autre que la classe 5 ou 15 et que dans un nombre relativement important de langues l'infinitif peut être amené par un morphème locatif ou comporter des traces d'un morphème locatif.

*kò-RV-à et une autre de type *ì-RV-à. La question qui se pose est de savoir quelle était la nature grammaticale originelle de ces deux formes. Si l'on pousse l'hypothèse jusqu'au bout, on pourrait imaginer quatre possibilités: (1) il y a eu en proto-bantou deux infinitifs, (2) la forme en *kò- était infinitif et celle en *ì- substantif déverbatif, (3) la forme en *kò- était substantif déverbatif et celle en *ì- était infinitif, (4) les deux formes étaient substantifs déverbatifs. A partir de l'étude de formes nomino-verbales dans les langues du Nord-Ouest, nous essaierons de trouver des arguments plaidant en faveur de l'une de ces quatre possibilités.

Rappelons que selon Forges, *La classe de l'infinitif en bantou* (1983), la forme de classe 15 serait une forme nomino-verbale alors que la forme de classe 5 serait un substantif déverbatif qui aurait désigné à l'origine le procès et qui aurait acquis des traits verbaux suite à la disparition progressive de la classe 15. Or, ce n'est pas parce que la classe 15 nominale tend à disparaître (cf. Doneux, 1967), que la classe 15 nomino-verbale est nécessairement soumise à la même tendance. Forges (1983: 262) note d'ailleurs elle-même que la classe 15 nominale et la classe 15 de l'infinitif ne disparaissent pas dans les mêmes langues. Ainsi, le raisonnement de Forges ne nous paraît pas apporter d'arguments convaincants, d'autant plus qu'elle n'a tenu compte que de l'infinitif en isolation. Nous sommes d'avis que, pour déterminer le statut grammatical ancien d'une forme donnée, il faudrait également étudier ses emplois en contexte.

Le plan de notre travail se présente comme suit: nous analyserons d'abord les attestations des formes nomino-verbales à PN5 et à PN15 pour étudier ensuite le phénomène de la métatonie, qui est posée par Meeussen (1967: 111) comme une caractéristique de l'infinitif de classe 15 mais qui peut également caractériser certaines formes verbales conjuguées. Elle consiste à attribuer à la finale d'une forme nomino-verbale ou d'une forme verbale un ton haut si celle-ci est suivie d'un complément[2]. Nous terminerons notre travail par un bref aperçu de l'emploi des morphèmes aspecto-temporels dans la conjugaison. Pour cette étude nous partons de l'idée que certains formatifs peuvent être issus d'anciens auxiliants (cf. Nsuka Nkutsi, 1986). Lorsque l'auxiliant est suivi d'une forme nomino-verbale et que la construction “Auxiliant + Forme nomino-verbale” est soumise à des procédures de grammaticalisation aboutissant à la création d'un nouveau morphème aspecto-temporel, le préfixe de la forme nomino-verbale peut laisser des traces au sein de ce morphème. On aurait encore pu envisager d'autres paramètres, tels que la présence au sein des formes examinées de morphèmes typiquement verbaux comme le négateur, l'infixe objet ou la postfinale ou on aurait pu étudier les fonctions syntaxiques que

---

2 A dessein, nous n'utilisons pas le terme d'objet parce que la fonction syntaxique du syntagme qui suit le verbe ne nous paraît pas toujours facile à identifier. Il serait certes intéressant d'étudier le rapport syntaxique entre le verbe à ton haut métatonique et le syntagme suivant, étude que nous n'avons pas envisagée ici.

les différentes formes peuvent assumer au sein d'un énoncé. Dans le cadre d'une recherche qui a l'ambition de proposer des conclusions historiques valables, il faudra certainement tenir compte de ces autres critères. Toutefois, notre but ici n'est pas de tirer des conclusions comparatives mais de faire quelques constatations concernant le fonctionnement de l'infinitif tel qu'il se présente dans les langues bantoues du Nord-Ouest. Plusieurs de nos observations nécessiteraient d'ailleurs de plus amples vérifications et ne sont mentionnées ici que comme indications de pistes à creuser.

Pour ce qui est du corpus, nous avons fait un choix assez arbitraire dans la documentation que nous avions à notre disposition pour les zones A, B, C et D, mais nous avons tout de même veillé à avoir au moins une langue représentant chaque sous-groupe à l'intérieur d'une zone. La liste des langues dépouillées et les références se trouvent à la fin de l'article.

2. Le préfixe de l'infinitif

2.1. Préfixe nominal de classe 15

Alors que Forges (1983) affirme que l'infinitif de classe 15 est moins bien repésenté dans les langues du Nord-Ouest, nos données montrent que cet infinitif a une belle répartition à travers le domaine que nous avons envisagé. Il est plus particulièrement attesté en: A.31 bubi[3] (ɔ-), A.34 benga (o-), A.43 basaa (Ø-, 15 d'après les accords), A.44 nen (o-), A.46 nomaande (o-), A.60 tuki (o-), A.62a gunu (gu-), A.83 makaa (Ø-[4]), B.40 ngubi (ɣú-), B.41 eshira (gu-, gú), B.42 sango (u-), B.44 lumbu (u-) B.52 nzebi (u-), B.61 mbete (hɔ-)[5], B.82 boma (ko-), B.86 dzing (ku-), B.87 mbuun (ku-), C.36d lingala (ko-), C.44 boa [pakabete] (ko-), C.53 sogo, C.55 kele (o-), C.63 ngando (o-), D.10 mokpa (ko-), D.13 mituku (ko-), D.14 enya (ko-), D.25 lega (ko-), D.26 binja-Sud (ko-), D.28 holoholo (ko-), D.30 bodo (ko-)[6], D.55 buyi ('o-, ho-).

Quelques remarques s'imposent à propros de la forme que prend le PN15. Nous avons trois réalisations différentes: $C_{vélaire}$V-, V- et $C_{glottale}$V-. Il est clair que la première forme est un réflexe direct de la proto-forme *ko-. Afin de justifier l'identification du préfixe vocalique comme un ancien morphème de classe 15, nous avons, dans la mesure du

3 D'après Rwakazina (1971: III/84), le bubi connaîtrait une forme infinitivale à préfixe *ala-/ale-*. Dans les sources que nous avons consultées, nous n'avons pas pu identifier un morphème pareil et il est donc difficile de déterminer à quelle classe cette forme aurait pu appartenir. Notons qu'en bubi le préfixe de classe 5 est *ri-*, précédé éventuellement de l'augment *e-*.

4 D. et T. Heath (1982, p. 4) attribuent à l'infinitif un PN ø de classe 3, ceci sur base des accords. Le makaa qui n'a plus que 10 classes nominales a probablement fusionné les classes 3, 11, 14 et 15.

5 Il est difficile d'identifier le degré d'aperture dans la notation d'Adam (1954). Dans son introduction, il pose le système suivant: i, è, é, a, o, ô, u, ü.

6 L'infinitif en ko- est donné par Bokula (1966), alors qu'il a un PN9 chez Asangama (1983).

possible, vérifié les accords et contrôlé si *k peut s'amuïr dans les langues en question, ceci en nous basant essentiellement sur le réflexe du PN7 *ke-. La consonne *k étant une consonne extrêmement fragile, en tous cas à l'initiale d'un préfixe, la réalisation vocalique du préfixe de l'infinitif pourrait être attribuée à une classe 15 ancienne, même si synchroniquement ce préfixe est posé comme appartenant à une autre classe[7].

La réalisation $C_{glottale}V$- du PN est attestée en mbete (B.61) et en buyi (D.55). En buyi, où il existe également un infinitif en ϱ–, la forme en ho– est utilisée dans des formes verbales complexes:

(1) buyi D.55

kobɛ́lɛ holɔ̃ba 'He was fishing'

Etant donné le sens progressif de la forme ('il était en train de pêcher = il est dans le fait de pêcher'), il nous paraît possible d'analyser ho- comme le résultat d'une contraction entre un préfixe locatif (ha- < *pa-) et un préfixe infinitival o-. Cette hypothèse est confirmée par le fait que *p donne régulièrement h en buyi et que *k s'amuït:

*p > h:	*-pé-	> -he-	'cuire'	*-pét-	> -heth-	'passer'
*k > Ø:	*-(j)áka	> -áa	'année'	*-kóme	> -óme	'dix'

Le PN ho- du mbete (B.61) pourra probablement être analysé de la même manière, mais les données sont moins claires et il est difficile de trouver des réflexes *h* issus de *p. Le seul exemple que nous ayons trouvé est *pá- > *-ha-* 'donner'. De plus, *k peut donner *h* en mbete:

*k > h:	*ko-$_{PL}$17	> ho ndjo	'dans la case'
	*-tóko 'jour'	> -tcuhu	'jour'

ho- pourrait donc aussi bien être le réflexe direct du préfixe de classe 15.

2.2. Préfixe nominal de classe 5

Dans toutes les zones que nous avons examinées, nous avons relevé des langues où l'infinitif se caractérise par la présence d'un préfixe nominal de classe 5. L'infinitif de classe 5 ne doit pas être confondu avec le substantif déverbatif de classe 5; contrairement à ce dernier, l'infinitif est en principe monoclasse et peut être employé comme forme de citation du verbe. Les langues qui attestent un infinitif de classe 5 sont: A.11 londo (dì–), A.15 akoose (a-), A.24 duala (j- ou Ø-), A.32 noho (i-), A.42 bankon (i-), A.53

---

7 Une autre analyse possible serait d'interpréter *u-/o-/ɔ–* comme une trace de l'augment. Dans le cadre d'une telle hypothèse (voir dans ce volume le travail de Cl. Grégoire et B. Janssens) l'identification de la classe à laquelle appartiendrait l'infinitif deviendrait plus difficile, parce que ce morphème vocalique peut représenter l'augment de classes 1, 3, 11, 13, 14 et 15 (voire 17 et 18).

bafia (r ɨ –), A.70 groupe pahouin (a-), A.80 bajele[8] (e-), A.84 koozime (e-), A.86c mpyemo (a-), B.30 pove (Ø-), B.30 geviya (e-), B.31 tsogo (e-), C.35b bolia (i-), C.37 buja (i-), C.60/65 ntomba-Inongo[9] (i-), C.75 kela (di- ou i-), D.12 lengola (i-).

Le préfixe nominal de classe 5 a donc les représentations suivantes: Ci-/Ce-, i-/ e-, a-, Ø-. Pour ce qui est de la réalisation Ci-/Ce-, elle est issue de la séquence Augment5-PN5 du proto-bantou: *de-i-. Les préfixes de type *i-* ou *e-* pourraient en principe être rattachés historiquement à des classificateurs de plusieurs classes. Afin de les identifier comme des formes de classe 5, nous nous sommes basée sur les accords.

(2) koozime A.84

eto lâm 'my departure' (= aller de moi; lâm < li-a-m, li-: préfixe pronominal de classe 5)

Quant à la réalisation Ø, elle est une caractéristique très répandue du PN5 devant les thèmes nominaux, du moins à initiale consonantique, et l'absence de PN à l'infinitif reflète donc une situation devenue normale pour cette classe qu'on ne peut identifier qu'en tenant compte des accords:

(3) pove B.30

sembák'ɛ éndendé gyó gyá paká góndé wáɲ'ɛ

'Chanter est une chose difficile pour les enfants'

(ɛ: démonstratif faible de classe 5, é–: préfixe verbal de classe 5)

En bobangi (C.32), où l'infinitif n'a pas de préfixe représenté, il nous semble difficile de lui attribuer la classe 5 parce que les thèmes nominaux de cette classe prennent un PN *li-* devant consonne et un PN *z-* devant voyelle. Nous n'avons pas relevé d'occurrences d'accord exercé par l'infinitif. La même situation se produit en kumu (D.23) où l'infinitif est constitué du thème verbal et de la finale *-a* et où Harries (1958) ne fournit aucun renseignement quant aux accords. Le kako (A.93) constitue un autre cas problématique. Le système de classes y a été considérablement réduit: il n'existe plus que deux marques qui désignent toutes les deux le pluriel: *ɓè-* pour les "êtres animés et corps célestes", *mɛ̀–* pour les "objets non animés" (cf. Ernst, 1989: 4). On pourrait voir dans *ɓè–* un vestige du PN2 et dans *mɛ̀–* un résidu du PN4 ou du PN6. Etant donné ce système classificatoire lacunaire, il nous est impossible de déterminer à quelle classe nominale l'infinitif du kako a pu appartenir.

Quant à la réalisation *a-*, elle est attestée en mpyemo:

[8] Le bajele, qui n'est pas repris dans la classification de Guthrie, est un parler proche du mvumbo (A.81).

[9] Ce parler est différent du ntomba C.35a.

(4) mpyemo A.86c

à-gwō mórì

'tuer quelqu'un'

à- est synchroniquement un préfixe nominal de classe 5, qui fait son pluriel en *mɛ̀-* et qui a des accords en *r-*, mais la question se pose de savoir si, d'un point de vue comparatif, il existe vraiment un rapport entre ce *a-* et la classe 5 *dé-ì- telle qu'elle a été reconstruite en proto-bantou. Rappelons que dans les langues du Nord-Ouest, le système des classes nominales se caractérise souvent par des rapprochements et des fusions par rapport à la situation du proto-bantou. En moghamo par exemple[10], le PN de classe 7 est *a-*. Selon Stallcup (1980: 222), les classes 7 et 8 auraient d'abord eu toutes les deux un préfixe *i-*. Comme il n'y avait pas de distinction singulier-pluriel, la classe 7 aurait emprunté le PN de classe 6, emprunt qui était facilité par le fait que la classe 6 et la classe 7 avaient les mêmes accords en *j-*.

Mais il existe peut-être une autre explication pour la forme *a-* du préfixe nominal de classe 7 en moghamo. Rappelons que la forme proto-bantoue du PN7 est *ke- et celle du PN12 *ka-. On pourrait envisager que la forme *a-* du PN7 en moghamo représente l'aboutissement d'une fusion des classes 7 et 12. Ce type de fusion peut encore être observé synchroniquement dans certains parlers du groupe B.20 (le kele, le ngom et le mbangwe; cf. Jacquot, 1983) qui ont pour la classe 7 une forme *gy-* devant un thème à initiale vocalique et une forme *a-* devant un thème à initiale consonantique:

(5) ngom B.22b

a. gyíà 'danse' gyédì 'barbe'

b. àkíŋù 'cadavre' àlésà 'os (sing.)'

La variante *gy-* du préfixe représente sans doute le préfixe nominal *ke-; la variante *a-* est probablement le réflexe du préfixe *ka-.

D'autre part, le préfixe de classe 7 peut avoir été confondu avec le préfixe de la classe 5 dans les langues qui n'ont pas maintenu la consonne *k en position initiale. Ainsi, on pourrait imaginer que dans des langues où le système des classes nominales a été profondément perturbé, il y ait eu des rapprochements entre les classes 5 et 7, entre les classes 7 et 12 et indirectement entre les classes 5 et 12. Ces fusions pourraient expliquer l'apparition d'un préfixe de type *a-* à la classe 5.

En mpyemo, le préfixe *a-* de l'infinitif semble toujours porter un ton structurel bas alors que dans des langues du groupe A.70, comme l'ewondo, il est tantôt bas, tantôt haut. En ewondo, l'attribution de la classe 5 à la forme en *à-* est entre autres motivée par les accords (cf. 6.b). La forme à préfixe *á-* à ton haut est à mettre en rapport avec la présence d'un prépréfixe locatif, comme le montrent l'analyse structurelle de *ǎdi* en (6.c) et l'accord

10 Le moghamo est une langue du groupe momo.

en (6.d)[11]. En (6.d) *-nə* est précédé du préfixe verbal de classe 16 ó– qui, d'un point de vue historique, remonte plutôt à une préfixe de classe 17.

(6) ewondo A.72a

a. adí = àPN5-dí

'manger' (dans les fonctions nominales et dans la conjugaison)

b. adí dŏe ánə abé

'Ta façon de manger est mauvaise' (= Manger de toi est mauvais)

c. ádi = áPN16–àPN5–dí > âdí > ádǐ > ádi

'manger' (en emploi absolu)

d. ábàl ŏnə...

'Sarcler est...'

L'infinitif à PN5 est donc bien représenté dans les langues de notre corpus, surtout à l'extrême Nord-Ouest (zone A). De plus, si l'on tient compte des langues qui attestent simultanément des formes nomino-verbales de classes 5 et 15, l'aire de répartition pour les deux infinitifs s'étend considérablement.

2.3. Préfixes nominaux de classes 5 et 15

Nous avons relevé une série de langues qui se caractérisent par la présence simultanée de deux formes nomino-verbales monoclasses. C'est le cas des langues B.25 kota, B.85 yans, C.25 mboshi, C.30 doko, C.30 lifonga, C.30 likata, C.61 parlers mongo, C.83 bushong, D.32 bira, D.43 nyanga, D.54 bembe.

Nous espérions trouver dans ces langues à deux formes nomino-verbales des indications relatives au statut ancien de ces formes. Toutefois, dans des langues comme le kota, le lifonga, le likata, le bira, les formes de classes 5 et 15 semblent coexister arbitrairement. Dans d'autres parlers, tels que le yans et le mongo[12] l'utilisation de l'une ou l'autre forme nomino-verbale est attribuée à des variations dialectales. Ce n'est qu'en mboshi, en nyanga et en bembe que nous avons relevé des différences, subtiles parfois, entre la forme de classe 5 et celle de classe 15.

---

[11] Le réflexe de *pa- est *va-* dans les langues A7.0. Cependant le préfixe *và-* n'est attesté que devant le substantif locatif *-óm* "endroit" et le démonstratif *-ɛ́ɛ̀* "là". Partout ailleurs dans l'expression de la localisation le prépréfixe locatif de classe 16 est *á-*. Ce *á-* représenterait d'un point de vue historique plutôt l'augment de classe 16.

En ewondo le préfixe pronominal de classe 5 est *dí-* et le préfixe verbal de classe 5 est *á-*.

[12] Ce qui semble caractéristique des parlers C61, c'est la présence d'une forme nomino-verbale à préfixe nasal et sa coexistence avec une autre forme nomino-verbale qui appartient, selon le parler en question, à la classe 5 ou à la classe 15.

En mboshi (C.25), où il n'existe plus de classe 15 nominale, la forme de classe 5 est, selon Fontaney (1989: 94), employée comme forme de citation du verbe, après le verbe *ìkànzà* 'interdire' (cf. 7.a) et après des formes prépositionnelles (cf. 7.b). Après les auxiliaires et dans les formes verbales périphrastiques, c'est la forme en *o-* qui est attestée (cf. 7.c et 7.d):

(7) mboshi C.25

a. bâ ákànzì bísí *ìdzwà* lá mbyèngì

'They forbade us to go hunting'

b. bísí lékyè àswéngé ásárè *míìtóngà* láyâ

míìtóngà < mi itonga < ma itonga

'We took three months building it'

c. wà ásí *òɸyémbá* òyíí

'He has already walked a lot'

d. ngá îdzwà *òsìngá* ìkándé

'I'm going to wash the clothes'

On peut observer, en (c) et (d), que la forme nomino-verbale en *o-* construit son objet directement tandis qu'en (b) le substitutif semble être introduit par un connectif: *láyâ* = *lá*Connectif + *yâ*. En outre, l'infinitif en *o-* a une finale à ton haut métatonique, alors que la finale de la forme en *i-* n'est pas soumise à la métatonie. Ces quelques éléments paraissent indiquer que les deux formes n'ont pas tout à fait le même statut grammatical en mboshi.

En nyanga (D.43), l'infinitif est de classe 5, mais lorsqu'il comporte un infixe réfléchi, il prend le préfixe de classe 15:

(8) nyanga D.43

a. etéma rasómá

'creuser est dur'

b. kwinama kwasómá

'se pencher est dur'

Si l'on considère que la présence d'un infixe réfléchi est caractéristique d'une forme verbale, on interprétera la forme de classe 15 comme étant plus verbale que celle de classe 5[13].

---

[13] Nous retrouvons la même situation en mbuun (B.87) où, d'après Polak (1983), le préfixe de l'infinitif est *ka-* avec une variante Ø devant infixe objet et une variante *ku-* devant infixe réfléchi.

En bembe (D.54), Meeussen (1953: 390)[14] mentionne l'existence de deux infinitifs qui se caractérisent respectivement par un préfixe *'e-* et *'o-*. La différence entre ces deux infinitifs est que la forme en *'o-* prend un ton haut métatonique, alors que celle en *'e-* est insensible à la métatonie et a toujours une finale à ton bas.

(9) bembe D.54

a. 'ohóláná 'mnombá

'sortir de la maison' (-hólana 'sortir')

b. 'ehólana 'mnombá

'sortir de la maison'

Les différences observées en mboshi, en nyanga et en bembe paraissent indiquer un fonctionnement différent (plus "verbal"?) pour les formes de classe 15. Toutefois, on ne peut pas se baser sur trois langues pour tirer des conclusions à prétention historique.

2.4. Conclusion

De ce rapide survol, il ressort que les infinitifs de classe 5 et de classe 15 sont bien représentés dans les langues bantoues du Nord-Ouest, comme on peut l'observer sur la carte suivante où sont situées la plupart des langues de notre corpus[15]:

De plus, toute une série de langues se caractérise par la présence simultanée de formes nomino-verbales de classe 5 et de classe 15. Dans la majorité de ces langues, ces formes semblent pouvoir assumer les mêmes emplois et leur coexistence est souvent attribuée à des variations dialectales au sein d'une même langue. Ce n'est qu'en mboshi, en nyanga et en bembe que nous avons pu observer un fonctionnement différent pour les formes de classe 15. Mais on ne peut pas se baser sur trois langues pour tirer des conclusions quant au statut grammatical qu'auraient eu ces formes à un stade plus ancien du bantou.

Toujours à la recherche de critères distinctifs, nous examinerons maintenant l'application du phénomène de la métatonie aux différentes formes nomino-verbales.

---

14 Dans la description du bembe telle qu'elle a été réalisée par Mutombo (1973), l'infinitif de classe 15 a été relevé dans le parler de Madinde, alors que l'infinitif de classe 5 est récolté dans le parler d'Abada. Mutombo a noté l'existence du ton haut métatonique à certains tiroirs verbaux mais ne le fait pas intervenir dans le cadre des formes infinitivales.

15 La carte a été réalisée avec le logiciel Bantu Mapmaker 3, créé par le Prof. Thilo C. Schadeberg. Nous le remercions d'avoir mis ce logiciel à notre disposition.

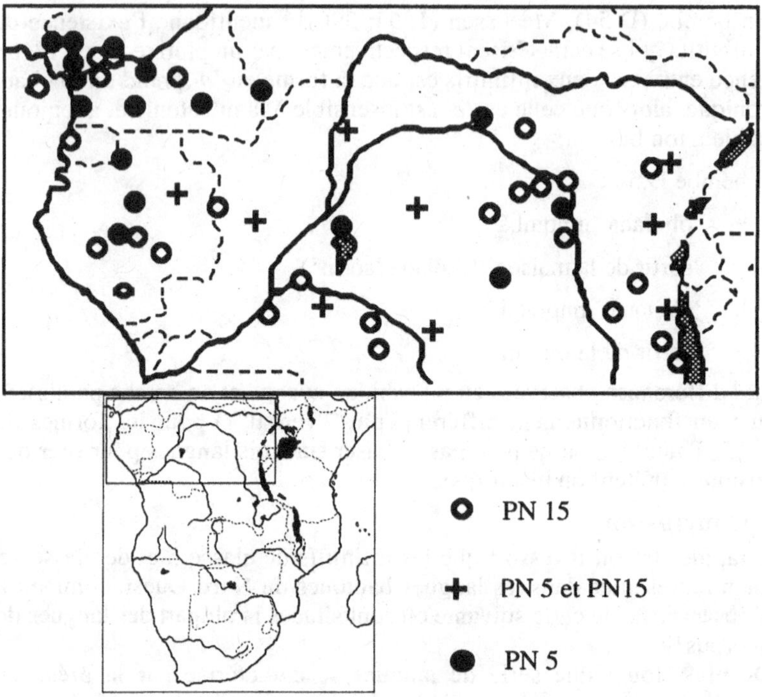

Figure 1. Distribution des infinitifs de classe 5 et 15

3. La métatonie

3.1. Définition et réalisation de la métatonie

La métatonie consiste à attribuer à la voyelle finale de l'infinitif, ou d'une forme verbale, un ton haut si celui-ci est suivi d'un complément. Ailleurs la finale de l'infinitif a un ton bas. La nature syntaxique exacte du complément semble assez variable: dans certaines langues le complément ne peut être qu'un objet direct, dans d'autres langues, dont fait partie le lega, le complément peut aussi être un locatif:

(10) lega D.25

a. kwĕngela
'entrer'

b. kwĕngélá ko busyô
'entrer dans la chambre'

En lega le ton haut de la voyelle finale se redouble sur la voyelle des extensions.

Beaucoup d'auteurs réduisent le contexte d'application de la métatonie à une opposition "ton haut à l'intérieur de l'énoncé (absence de pause)/ ton bas en fin d'énoncé (pause)". Toutefois, si l'on examine les exemples cités, ils se laissent en général ramener à un conditionnement ±complément:

(11) buyi D.55

a. okáboa

'to build'

b. okábőá sɛsɛ

'to build a house'

c. okáboa wákế

'his (way) of building'

En (11.b), *okáboa* 'bâtir', accompagné de son objet *sɛsɛ* 'maison', est soumis à la métatonie. En (11.c), où *okáboa* est suivi d'un possessif ('de lui') qui renvoie à l'agent du procès 'bâtir', la finale *-a* ne prend pas de ton haut métatonique.

Ajoutons aussi que, même si l'on pose la métatonie comme un processus qui consiste à attribuer à une forme verbale un ton haut si elle est au milieu de l'énoncé et un ton bas si elle se trouve en fin d'énoncé, ce n'est pas la position qui conditionne l'alternance tonale: d'autres mots peuvent en effet avoir un ton haut ou bas peu importe s'ils sont au milieu ou à la fin de l'énoncé.

(12) lega D.25

twăsǒké ǹdí nakwěká

'nous passerons si je te porte'

D'autre part, il n'est pas toujours aussi facile de repérer des illustrations de la métatonie. Dans les exemples (10) et (11), nous avons des attestations directes de la règle, alors que dans les cas suivants il faut tenir compte d'autres règles tonales qui agissent simultanément, telles que le redoublement ou le déplacement tonal.

(13) fang A.75

ábàgəlě bôt

'garder des gens' (ábàgəlè 'garder')

Dans cet exemple le ton haut métatonique se joint au ton bas de la voyelle finale pour engendrer un ton montant et en même temps il se redouble pour s'associer au ton du préfixe: bà-òt > bá-òt > bôt.

(14) songye L.23

a. kusepa mûntu (< kù-sèp-á mù-ntù)

'rire avec quelqu'un'

b. kusepá mfumú (< kù-sèp-á m-fùmú)

'rire avec le chef'

c. kusepa kwǎmbwá ǹkubúlúka

'le rire d'un chien c'est aboyer'

En (14.a) le ton haut se déplace à droite pour se combiner au ton bas du préfixe nominal tandis qu'en (14.b), où le préfixe du nom suivant est une nasale, le ton haut reste sur la finale. En (14.c) *kusepa* est suivi d'un syntagme connectival qui réfère à l'agent du procès exprimé par l'infinitif et dans ce contexte la métatonie ne s'applique pas.

(15) eshira B.41

a. ɣutsîbiɣə diɣuyi

'fermer la porte' (ɣutsibiɣə 'fermer')

b. níkásúmbísí mípálə

'je vais vendre des bananes plantains' (ɣusúmbisə 'vendre')

c. níkásúmbisi matotu

'je vais vendre des bananes douces'

Dans l'exemple (15.a) le verbe 'fermer' est un verbe à radical bas mais, lorsqu'il est suivi de complément, il a la tonalité des nominaux °BH: *mufûdu* 'jeune homme' (cf. Blanchon, 1988: 76). Avec des verbes à radical haut, c'est un pont tonal qui se déclenchera à condition qu'il y ait un ton haut dans le mot suivant (cf. 15.b et c).

Ces quelques illustrations montrent qu'il n'est pas toujours simple de reconnaître l'éventuelle intervention d'un ton haut métatonique. Pour faciliter la tâche et limiter au maximum la confusion avec d'autres règles telles que celle du pont tonal haut, on devrait de préférence chercher des radicaux verbaux à ton bas. En outre, il ne faut pas prendre toutes les alternances tonales qui peuvent se manifester aux formes verbales, et plus particulièrement à l'infinitif, comme relevant de la métatonie. La métatonie est une règle tonale dont le conditionnement est syntaxique, son application est liée à la présence d'un complément après la forme verbale.

Meeussen, dans ses reconstructions grammaticales du bantou (1967: 111), semblait mettre en rapport la métatonie avec les formes nomino-verbales de classe 15. Cependant, des formes verbales autres que l'infinitif se caractérisent par une alternance tonale conditionnée par le contexte syntaxique.

(16) lega D.25

a. tokobolota tɔngɔ

'nous tirons également'

b. tokobolɔ́tá mòzígi

'nous tirons la corde'

Ces alternances ne relèveraient-elles pas de la métatonie? Nous verrons dans les paragraphes qui suivront que l'opposition "*–á* devant complément/ *-à* ailleurs" dans une forme verbale peut relever de la métatonie si la forme verbale en question est issue d'une structure complexe comportant un infinitif.

Mais que faire des alternances tonales apparaissant dans des formes verbales qui n'ont aucun rapport avec l'infinitif?

(17) sotho S.33

a. kɩ̀tsùbìlè lɩ́-ǹnà

'J'ai fumé (djt) moi aussi'

b. kɩ̀tsùbílè lɩ́-jɛ̀nà

'J'ai fumé (cjt) avec lui/elle'

c. hàkɩ́bínɩ̀ lɩ́-ǹnà

'Je ne chante pas (djt) moi non plus'

d. hàkɩ́bínɩ́ lɩ́-jɛ̀nà

'Je ne chante pas (cjt) avec lui/elle'

e. kɩ̀tɬàbíná lɩ́-ǹnà

'Je chanterai (djt) moi aussi'

f. kɩ̀tɬàbínà lɩ́-jɛ̀nà

'Je chanterai (cjt) avec lui/elle'

En a. le verbe 'fumer' est suivi de *lɩ́-ǹnà* qui est coréférentiel avec l'actant-sujet du verbe, alors qu'en (b) 'fumer' est accompagné d'un argument qui, du point de vue pragmatique, apporte une nouvelle information (cf. Creissels, 1996: 111). Cette différence syntaxique se manifeste par une opposition tonale entre (a) et (b): en (a) la forme verbale est entièrement basse alors qu'en (b) il y a un ton haut sur l'avant-dernière syllabe. On retrouve ces mêmes alternances à d'autres tiroirs (cf. c/d, e/f) où l'opposition tonale se manifeste sur la voyelle finale. Notons que la distinction tonale n'est pas identique partout puisqu'en c/d on a une alternance conjoint-ton haut final/disjoint-ton bas final alors qu'en e/f c'est exactement l'inverse. De plus, l'alternance disjoint-conjoint est dans certaines formes verbales marquée par un élément segmental (cf. 18) tandis qu'à d'autres formes verbales la différence disjoint-conjoint semble ne pas exister (cf. 19).

(18) sotho S.33

a. kɩ̀jàbínà lɩ́-ǹnà

'Je chante (djt) moi aussi'

b. kɩ̀bínà lɩ́-jɛ̀nà

'Je chante (cjt) avec lui/elle'

(19) sotho S.33

a. kɩ̀kábínà lɩ́-ǹnà

'Je peux chanter (djt) moi aussi'

b. kɩ̀kábínà lɩ́-jɛ̀nà

'Je peux chanter (cjt) avec lui/elle'

Creissels (1996) a relevé la même distinction conjoint-disjoint en swati, entre autres au parfait où il existe une opposition à la fois segmentale et tonale entre les formes du conjoint et du disjoint:

(20) swati S43

a. bántfwànà básébéntìlè nàbó

'The children too have worked (djt)'

b. bántfwànà bàsèbènté nàbó

'The children have worked (cjt) with them'

Toutes ces alternances segmentales et supra-segmentales, disjoint-conjoint et métatonie, résultent probablement d'une même stratégie qui consiste à marquer le rapport existant entre la forme verbale et la suite de l'énoncé. Pourtant, il est difficile de déterminer si les différentes réalisations de cette stratégie pragmatique sont reliées historiquement, ou si elles se sont développées indépendamment à partir de structures différentes. Pour ce qui est de la métatonie proprement dite, nous essaierons de formuler quelques hypothèses après avoir étudié sa distribution dans notre corpus de langues bantoues du Nord-Ouest.

3.2. La distribution de la métatonie

Selon Meeussen (1967) la métatonie peut être attribuée au proto-bantou. Elle est bien attestée dans les langues de notre corpus[16]: duala (A.24), le

---

16 Pour cet aspect de notre étude, nous nous sommes exclusivement basée sur les langues pour lesquelles l'existence de la métatonie est déjà mentionnée dans les sources. Dans le cadre d'une étude exhaustive de la métatonie, il serait cependant indispensable de contrôler dans les autres systèmes la tonalité des formes nomino-verbales et verbales.

groupe pahouin (A.70), eshira (B.41), sango (B.42), nzebi (B.52), teke (B.70), mboshi (C.25), libinza (C.31), mbudza (C.36c), ebango (C.40), mituku (D.13), enya (D.14), lega (D.25), binja-Sud (D.26), bodo (D.30), nyanga (D.43), bembe (D.54) et buyi (D.55). Comme elle a aussi été relevée dans des langues bantoues plus centrales et plus méridionales, la métatonie a certes une belle distribution.

(21) bangubangu L.27

a. 'uvundagaɲiʃa

'faire mélanger'

'vundagáɲíʃá byőső

'tout faire mélanger'

b. tulusáhula

'Nous parlons'

tulusáhulá kíbangubángu

'Nous parlons kibangubangu'

3.2.1. La métatonie, l'infinitif de classe 15 et les formes verbales dérivées de cette forme

La première observation que nous avons faite, c'est que les langues qui possèdent un ton haut métatonique et qui construisent leur infinitif en classe 15, appliquent ce ton haut métatonique systématiquement à cet infinitif (cf. aussi les exemples 10, 11 et 15).

(22) sango B.42

ùbâ:tə̀ bàtsîbì

'manger des excréments'

versus: ùbà:tə̀

'manger'

De plus, la métatonie se manifeste à certains tiroirs verbaux qui se caractérisent souvent par une marque aspecto-temporelle en *o-*, par exemple une forme du futur proche en enya (cf. 23), du présent en lega (cf. 24) et en binja-Sud, du passé en binja-Sud (cf. 25), du passé et du consécutif en bodo (cf. 26), du passé en nyanga (cf. 27):

(23) enya D.14

bő:miná sénɔ í ñ̃ñama (< bá–ó–ko–min–á)

'ils vont avaler la viande' (komina 'avaler')

versus: ḿmbɛ ká:ómina

'sinon il (cl. 12) risque d'avaler'

(24) lega D.25

bekobolótá mózígi

'ils tirent la corde' (=ba-eko-...)

versus: bekobolota tɔngɔ

'ils tirent également'

(25) binja-Sud D.26

tosósombéécá nyumú

'nous venons de rassembler les arachides'

versus: tosósombeeca

'nous venons de rassembler'

(26) bodo D.30[17]

ndí tátápɔa ɗisǐni, tótogboká ɓácwá ámuyí

(< tà-ó-tò-gbòk-á....)

'lorsque nous traversâmes la rivière, nous rencontrâmes les Pygmées de l'autre rive'

versus: átɔgboka ɓáná amuduu wóɗísǐni

'il alla trouver les enfants au bord de la rivière'

(< á-tɔ̀-gbǒk-à ɓà-àná: la métatonie ne caractérise pas le passé à marque -tɔ̌-)

(27) nyanga D.43[18]

twákotémá boʃa

'nous avons creusé une fosse (ce matin)'

versus: twákotéma

'nous avons creusé (ce matin)'

Nous verrons dans le point (4) que ces marques en *o-* sont issues d'anciennes constructions complexes constituées d'un auxiliant et du préfixe de l'infinitif *ko-*. L'intervention de la métatonie dans ces formes s'explique donc par la présence sous-jacente d'un infinitif, autrement dit, d'un point de vue historique, ces formes verbales seraient des structures complexes.

---

[17] En bodo (D30) l'infinitif, que Bokula (1966) pose en classe 15 avec des accords en *i-* et que Asangama (1983) pose en classe 9, n'est pas soumis à la métatonie. Notons qu'en bodo l'objet est toujours marqué par la présence d'un ton haut sur le préfixe.

[18] En nyanga (D.43) où l'infinitif a le préfixe *ko-* devant l'infixe réfléchi et le préfixe *e-* partout ailleurs, la métatonie ne se manifeste pas aux formes nomino-verbales.

Le mbudza (C.36c) possède un infinitif de classe 14 *wo- -i*, dont la finale est toujours basse, mais cette langue atteste le phénomène de la métatonie au futur (*-kó- -a*) et au présent habituel (*-kó- -ak-a*).

(28) mbudza C.36c

tokómotómá moto

'nous enverrons quelqu'un'

versus: tótotóma tɛ́

'nous n'enverrons pas'

La marque aspecto-temporelle des tiroirs à ton haut métatonique n'est pas nécessairement en *o-*, mais il importe alors de noter que ces tiroirs réfèrent le plus souvent au futur: par exemple en mbudza le conditionnel à marque – ´ –, en binja-Sud le tiroir à marque *-nga-* (cf. 29) et en nyanga le tiroir à marque – ˣ*a*- (cf. 30).

(29) binja-Sud D.26

ningasombéécá bilaala

'je vais rassembler les feuilles mortes'

versus: ningasombeeca

'je vais rassembler'

(30) nyanga D.43

twătémá boʃa

'nous creuserons une fosse (aujourd'hui)'

versus: twătéma

'nous creuserons (aujourd'hui)'

Comme le futur est souvent issu d'une construction analytique, on pourrait se demander si l'application du ton haut métatonique à la finale de certains tiroirs du futur n'est pas un indice de la présence sous-jacente d'un infinitif. Mais pourquoi le préfixe de l'infinitif n'aurait-il pas laissé des traces dans ces formes alors qu'il en laisse tant à d'autres tiroirs? D'une part, il faut signaler que, dans certaines langues, on retrouve tout de même aux tiroirs du futur des résidus du PN de l'infinitif, comme nous le verrons dans le paragraphe 4. D'autre part, il se pourrait que les marques *-nga-*, – ˣ*a*-, et autres, relevées en mbudza, en binja-Sud et en nyanga ne doivent pas être mises en rapport avec un ancien auxiliant: ces morphèmes auraient été de vrais "formatifs" en proto-bantou et auraient été originellement suivis du thème verbal (cf. Meeussen, 1967: 113). C'est alors par analogie avec les tiroirs analytiques que la métatonie se serait appliquée à ces tiroirs simples.

3.2.2. La métatonie et la forme nomino-verbale de classe 5

Dans des langues qui attestent simultanément deux infinitifs, telles que le bembe et le mboshi, la métatonie ne semble pas intervenir à la forme de classe 5. Ainsi, en bembe la métatonie caractérise la forme de classe 15, le futur (*-ò- -a*) et le présent (*-dè-mò -a*, cf. 31). En mboshi elle apparaît seulement à la forme à PN *o-* et au présent (–`–   –*a*, cf. 32).

(31) bembe D.54

a. todemosádángá m̀'andá

'nous sommes en train d'écrire une lettre'

versus: todemosádanga

'nous écrivons'

b. byodá bídemomíná m̀ măki

'Les crapauds jouent dans l'eau'

versus: 'ádemomína

'il est en train de jouer'

(32) mboshi C.25

a. ngá îdzwà òsìngá ìkándé

'I'm going to wash the clothes'

b. wà âdzá àswé àyíí

'He eats a lot of fish'

c. bísí wáá lèsí òdzâ, lêbínà

'After we've eaten, we'll dance'

d. ópèrá ɔ̀pɛ́ ngá àbɔ̀ɔ̀?

'Can you give me a hand?'

e. ádzwè là dâ mbóà, míìdzwà ɔ̀pɛ̂ là mwásì

'They went with it to the village, to go and give it to the whife'

En (32.a) l'infinitif a une finale *-a* à ton haut. Dans les autres exemples on observe que les radicaux -CV qui ont une tonalité descendante lorsqu'ils ne sont pas suivis d'un objet, se caractérisent par un ton haut devant un objet. Les exemples (d) et (e) sont intéressants du point de vue syntaxique: en (d) ngá 'moi' est objet de la forme verbale ɔ̀pɛ́ qui subit la métatonie; par contre, en (e) *mwáasì* 'femme' est introduit par *là* et ne fonctionne donc pas comme objet de ɔ̀pɛ̂, ce qui explique pourquoi la forme verbale ne se caractérise pas par une finale à ton haut.

En duala, où l'infinitif est de classe 5, la métatonie existe à l'impératif, au présent en *-ma-* et au parfait sans marque aspecto-temporelle mais elle ne touche pas l'infinitif:

(33) duala A.24

na mabolá mó

'ich gebe es'

versus: na mabola ndé

'ich gebe ja'

3.2.3. La métatonie et les autres formes nomino-verbales

Certaines langues, qui construisent leur infinitif dans une classe autre que la classe 5 ou 15, appliquent le phénomène de la métatonie tant à leur forme infinitivale, qu'au sein de la conjugaison. C'est, entre autres, le cas du teke (infinitif probablement de classe 7) et du libinza (infinitif de classe 11).

(34) teke B.70

gáɲwá lákàyà

'to smoke tobacco'

versus: gáɲwà

'to drink'

(35) libinza C.31b

áyâ lokózá ó ndáku yandé

'he should come to eat at his house'

versus: yambo ya lozâ, bato...

'before eating, people...'

Les langues du groupe A.70 qui, rappelons-le, ont des formes nomino-verbales à préfixe *á–* (classe 16+5) et à préfixe *à-* (classe 5) présentent un cas intéressant pour l'analyse. En fang-ntumu, Ondo-Mebiame (1991-1992: 707) cite des exemples d'alternance tonale de type métatonique pour les formes à préfixe *á–* (cf. 36.a). La question qui se pose est de savoir si cette alternance se manifeste également aux formes à préfixe *à-*. Malheureusement, les quelques illustrations de formes nomino-verbales en *à-* suivi d'un objet que nous avons trouvées (cf. 36.b) ne permettent pas vraiment de trancher si oui ou non la métatonie y est attestée. En (36.b) *à:tùk* 'laver' est suivi de *ŋɔ̄* 'lui' et a un préfixe *à-* à ton bas[19]. Comme la finale *-e* n'est pas réalisée, on aurait pu s'attendre à une modification de la tonalité du radical dans le cas de la métatonie. Or, il ne se produit aucune alternance tonale, ce qui pourrait montrer que la forme à PN5 ne serait pas soumise à l'action de la métatonie.

---

19 Nous n'avons pas d'explication pour la longueur de la voyelle *à*.

(36) fang A.75

a. ábàgəlě minə́ná

'garder une femme'

versus: ábàgəlè

'garder'

b. àmànə́ kə̀ à:tùk ŋə́ ŋó:

'il finit d'aller laver son le corps' (=... lui le corps)

3.3. Conclusion

D'après les données du duala, du mboshi, du bembe (et aussi du nyanga, cf. note 18) la forme nomino-verbale de classe 5 se distinguerait donc des autres formes nomino-verbales. Mais comment interpréter cette différence? L'absence de la métatonie aux formes de classe 5 indiquerait-elle que celles-ci sont plus verbales ou plus nominales que les formes de classe 15? Pour répondre à cette question, il est avant tout indispensable d'arriver à une meilleure compréhension de la métatonie elle-même et de son origine. Avec les données que nous fournit notre corpus, il nous est impossible de trancher cette problématique de manière définitive. Une étude générale de la métatonie présuppose en effet une connaissance globale du système tonal de chaque langue, connaissance dont nous ne disposons pas pour le moment. Ainsi, nous nous limiterons à formuler quelques hypothèses et à en discuter la portée.

Rappelons que certains auteurs, tels qu'Angenot pour l'ewondo (1971), expliquent l'existence du ton haut métatonique à l'infinitif par un connectif sous-jacent. Le connectif sert généralement à introduire le déterminant d'un syntagme nominal. L'infinitif, en tant que forme *nomino*-verbale, devrait aussi construire ses déterminants (compléments) indirectement. Quoiqu'en ewondo, l'objet de l'infinitif ne soit pas introduit par un morphème connectival, Angenot pose l'existence d'un connectif en structure profonde qui, en surface, est représenté par un ton flottant haut. Ce ton flottant se placerait sur la voyelle finale de l'infinitif et rendrait ainsi compte de l'alternance tonale manifestée sur cette voyelle. La présence du ton haut métatonique au sein de la conjugaison verbale devrait s'expliquer par des mécanismes analogiques s'appliquant à partir de l'infinitif.

Toutefois, d'un point de vue diachronique, l'hypothèse d'un ton haut métatonique issu d'un connectif sous-jacent ne nous convainc pas. Premièrement, si l'on accepte cette hypothèse, la tonalité des séquences "infinitif+complément" devrait être analogue à celle d'autres structures où l'on pourrait imaginer l'existence d'un connectif sous-jacent, telles que les noms composés. Or, en sango par exemple, langue où l'on peut poser l'existence d'un connectif "invisible" dans le cadre des noms composés (cf. Blanchon, 1990: 40-41), la tonalité des séquences "infinitif+complément" (cf. 37.c) est différente de celle qu'on retrouve dans les composés (cf. 37.b).

(37) sango B.42 (Blanchon, 1990, pp.40-1)

a. ùbà:tə̀

'manger'

b. ìbǎ:tə́–tsîbì

'bousier': le ton haut du connectif "invisible" rend la finale haute et le radical montant

c. ùbâ:tə̀ bàtsîbì

'manger des excréments': cf. supra, profil tonal des nominaux Bas-Haut

Deuxièmement, la construction indirecte du complément d'objet d'un infinitif[20] n'est généralement attestée que dans des emplois obligeant l'infinitif à s'aligner sur le système des nominaux, tels que la fonction sujet (cf. 38). D'ailleurs, dans certaines langues, l'infinitif reste dans un rapport direct avec son objet, même en fonction sujet (cf. 39).

(38) nkomi B.11e[21]

ìpákìlyà s'óyèmbò wáwɔ̀ sádúɔ̀ m̀byámbyɛ̀

'Le fait de commencer leur chanson était bien' (= Commencer de la chanson d'eux...)

(39) libinza C.31b

lopá mosɔlɔ lólo loláu

'To give wealth is good'

Contrairement à ce que nous venons d'observer pour les formes nomino-verbales de classe 15 (et autre), il semble que pour les formes nomino-verbales de classe 5 la construction indirecte du complément est plus fréquente. Ainsi, nous avons vu qu'en mboshi la forme nomino-verbale en *o-*, à ton haut métatonique, est dans un rapport direct avec son complément, tandis que celle en *i-*, sans ton haut métatonique, construit son complément indirectement (cf. supra, exemple 7). Le mboshi présente donc la distribution complémentaire suivante:

---

20 Notons que pour le syntagme qui désigne l'agent du procès exprimé par l'infinitif, la construction indirecte est généralement la construction canonique (cf. entre autres l'exemple 14.c).

21 La fonction de *oyembo wawɔ* est pourtant ambigüe: *-pakìlya* 'commencer' peut avoir en nkomi un sujet ±animé; *oyembo wawɔ* pourrait donc aussi bien être objet de *-pakilya* (cf. 'on commence la chanson') que sujet (cf. 'la chanson commence').

	Nomino-verbal de classe 15 + complément	*Nomino-verbal de classe 5 + complément*
métatonie	+	–
connectif	–	+

Tableau 1. Distribution de l'emploi du connectif et de la métatonie en mboshi.

Cette distribution pourrait constituer un argument en faveur du rapport "connectif-métatonie". Pourtant, nous sommes d'avis qu'il faut interpréter l'emploi du connectif et la métatonie comme des processus de hiérarchisation semblables mais en même temps profondément différents. Le connectif est utilisé lorsque la forme nomino-verbale s'intègre au paradigme des nominaux pour lesquels la structure canonique est "Déterminé-Connectif-Déterminant". En revanche, la métatonie est plutôt une caractéristique de l'emploi verbal de l'infinitif, emploi dont le schème de base est "Verbe-Objet".

La deuxième hypothèse qu'on pourrait envisager consiste à établir un lien entre la métatonie et l'augment. L'augment est un morphème pré-préfixal, reconstruit à ton haut. Dans un certain nombre de langues bantoues où il n'est plus attesté segmentalement, l'augment peut avoir laissé son ton haut. Ce ton, flottant, peut alors s'associer au nom qu'il précède. On peut imaginer que, dans un contexte "Verbe–Ton flottant haut$_{(\text{<Augm})}$–Nom$_{\text{compl}}$", le ton haut, au lieu de s'associer au nom, aille se mettre sur la finale de la forme verbale et soit ainsi responsable de l'alternance "ton haut s'il y a un complément qui suit/ton bas s'il n'y a pas de complément". Cette hypothèse qui consiste donc à expliquer la métatonie par la présence d'un ton flottant haut provenant d'un ancien augment a entre autres été formulée par Schadeberg (1995: 179): "Metatony, then, could very well be the incorporation of the same floating high tone into the preceding verb form. Much will depend on the geographical spread of metatony, which, ideally, should be adjacent but not overlapping with the area where complements are marked tonally."

Comme nous l'avons signalé au début de ce passage consacré à la métatonie, nous ne nous sommes pas livrée à une étude générale des règles tonales des différents systèmes linguistiques que nous avons envisagés et nous ne pouvons pas trancher la problématique du lien augment-métatonie. Notons tout de même que la métatonie, si elle se manifeste dans la conjugaison verbale, semble plutôt caractériser les formes affirmatives que les formes négatives, ce qui n'est pas sans rappeler le fonctionnement de l'augment: dans certaines langues, les noms précédés d'une forme verbale négative ne prennent pas d'augment. Quelques langues de notre corpus attestent cependant la métatonie à des formes verbales négatives.

(40) mbudza C.36c

tőtomotómá moto tɛ́

'nous n'enverrons personne'

versus: tőtotóma tɛ́

'nous n'enverrons pas'

(41) nyanga D.43

ntétwákotémá boʃa

'nous n'avons pas creusé une fosse (ce matin)'

versus: ntétwákotéma

'nous n'avons pas creusé (ce matin)'

De plus, si le ton haut métatonique est à mettre en rapport avec un ton flottant haut issu d'un augment, il est difficile d'expliquer pourquoi la métatonie ne se manifeste qu'à certains tiroirs de la conjugaison (en principe ceux pour lesquels on peut poser la présence sous-jacente d'une forme nomino-verbale). A cela s'ajoute que le complément d'un verbe à ton haut métatonique n'est pas nécessairement nominal; il peut être pronominal (cf. exemples 30.d et 31). Or, l'emploi de l'augment avec des formes pronominales est exceptionnel. Donc, l'hypothèse qui consiste à relier le ton haut métatonique à la présence ancienne d'un augment se heurte également à des contre-arguments[22].

Ainsi sommes-nous, à ce stade de notre recherche, plutôt tentée d'interpréter la métatonie comme un phénomène propre à l'infinitif de classe 15. La métatonie serait un processus de marquage du lien que l'infinitif entretient avec son complément et consisterait en un ton haut qui s'associe à la finale. Ce serait le caractère ambigu, à la fois nominal et verbal, de l'infinitif qui nécessiterait un marquage spécifique lorsqu'il entre dans une construction avec complément. L'infinitif de classe 15, s'il est suivi immédiatement de son complément, s'aligne sur les formes verbales et la métatonie sert probablement à souligner ce type de rapport particulier entre une forme nomino-verbale et un complément. Pour expliquer l'absence de la métatonie dans les infinitifs de classe 5, nous pensons qu'il faudrait se tourner vers cet autre substantif déverbatif à appariement 5, 6 qui, par contagion, aurait bloqué une plus grande intégration de la forme nomino-verbale de classe 5 au paradigme verbal.

---

22 Nous n'avons pas fait de recherche sur la tonalité des formes nomino-verbales suivies de compléments appartenant à la classe 1a. Si les formes nomino-verbales (ou verbales) se caractérisaient dans ce contexte également par un ton haut final, on aurait un autre argument contre l'hypothèse "rapport métatonie-augment", puisque les substantifs de classe 1a ne prennent pas d'augment.

4. Les marques aspecto-temporelles

L'infinitif apparaît régulièrement comme constituant de formes verbales périphrastiques, issues de constructions de type "verbe + objet nomino-verbal". Ces structures, lorsqu'elles ont été soumises à des procédures de grammaticalisation, aboutissent à la création de morphèmes aspecto-temporels issus de mécanismes de contraction entre l'auxiliant et par exemple le PN d'une forme nomino-verbale. Dans ce qui suit, nous citerons d'abord les morphèmes aspecto-temporels qui pourraient contenir un résidu du PN15 **ko-*, c'est-à-dire par des morphèmes qui se caractérisent par la présence d'une voyelle postérieure fermée[23]. Ensuite, nous essaierons de trouver des traces de préfixes d'autres formes nomino-verbales dans les différents paradigmes de marques aspecto-temporelles que nous avons étudiés.

4.1. Les marques en o-

Les marques en *o-* existent dans presque toutes les langues pour lesquelles nous avons pu dépouiller le système verbal[24], peu importe que leur infinitif soit de classe 15 ou d'une autre classe: A.11 londo (PN5), A.24 duala (PN5), A.44 nen (PN15), A.60 tuki (PN15), A.70 pahouin (PN5 ou 16+5), A.83 makaa (PNØ), A.84 koozime (PN5), A.86c mpyemo (PN5), B.11a mpongwe (PN10bis), B.11e nkomi (PN17+10bis), B.25 kota (PN5 ou15), B.30 pove (PN5), B.30 geviya (PN5), B.41 eshira (PN15), B.42 sango (PN15), B.82 boma (PN15), B.85 yans (PN5 ou 15), C.25 mboshi (PN5 ou 15), C.32 bobangi (PNØ), C.35a ntomba (PN9), C.35b bolia (PN5), C.36c mbudza (PN14), C.40 motembo (PN14), C.40 ebango (PN14), C.55 kele (PN15), C.61 les parlers mongo (PN5 ou 15), C.71 tetela (PN9), C.75 kela (PN5), C.83 bushong (PN16?), D.10 mokpa (PN15), D.12 lengola (PN5), D.14 enya (PN15), D.23 kumu (PNØ), D.25 lega (PN15), D.26 binja-Sud (PN15), D.28 holoholo (PN15), D.30 bodo (PN9 ou 15), D.43 nyanga (PN5 ou 15), D.54 bembe (PN5 ou 15) et D.55 buyi (PN15).

Cependant, il n'est pas toujours facile de montrer que ces morphèmes aspecto-temporels en *o-* sont issus de séquences où il y a eu contraction entre un Auxiliant et un $PN_{Infinitif}$. Seules les langues qui attestent des marques temporelles de type *-Coo-* et *-(C)VCo-* permettent de démontrer de manière plus ou moins définitive cette origine (respectivement "Aux_{CV} + ko-" et "$Aux_{(c)V}$ + ko-").

Pour ce qui est des marques de type *-Coo-*, nous avons relevé en mpyemo (A.86c), au passé récent ("venir de"), une marque *–lɔɔ–* pour laquelle on pourrait envisager une origine *-li-ko-*, *-li* représentant une forme du verbe "être". En nkengo (C.61), une des formes du futur comporte la marque *-too-*, qui pourrait refléter une séquence ancienne *-ta-ko-* où *-ta-*

---

23 Les marques aspecto-temporelles, reconstruites pour le proto-bantou, se sont bien conservées dans les langues de notre corpus: *-a-*, *-á-*, *-ma-*-, *-ka-* (et *-nga-*?).

24 Nous n'avons analysé le système verbal que pour la moitié des langues de notre corpus (56 langues).

remonterait à un verbe "aller". En mboshi (C.25) et en binja-Sud (D.26), le passé s'exprime à l'aide d'une marque *-soo-* qui provient sans doute de *-sa-ko-*, *-sa-* étant assez fréquemment utilisé comme marque du passé. En binja-Sud (D.26), le tiroir du passé à marque *-soo-* se caractérise par un ton haut métatonique, ce qui est une preuve supplémentaire pour l'analyse du morphème *-soo-* en *-sa-ko-*.

(42) binja-Sud D.26

tosőosombéécá bilaala

'nous avions rassemblé des feuilles mortes'

En ce qui concerne les marques *-(C)VCo-*, elles proviennent probablement de séquences de type "$Aux_{(c)v}$ + ko-". La liste des formes relevées est reproduite dans le tableau (2).

marque[25]	*passé*	*présent*	*futur*
-aho-	buyi (PN15)		
-ako-	nyanga (PN5 ou 15)	mokpa (PN15), bodo (PN9)	kumu (PNø-)
-eko-		lega (PN15)	
-oko-		enya (PN15)	
-ndoko-			kela (PN5)

Tableau 2. Les marques -(C)VCo-.

Notons que la métatonie s'applique souvent à la finale des tiroirs formés des marques *-(C)V-ko-*, ce qui est un argument supplémentaire en faveur de notre hypothèse *-(C)V-ko-* < "Auxiliant + $PN_{Infinitif}$". La métatonie caractérise les tiroirs à marque *-aho-* relevée en buyi, à marque *-ako-* en nyanga (mais non pas en bodo où la métatonie apparaît cependant à d'autres tiroirs), à marque *-eko-* en lega et à marque *-oko-* en enya. Pour ce qui est de cette dernière forme, relevée par Spa (1973), la première voyelle *o* peut s'expliquer par assimilation. En outre, il est intéressant de noter que dans la variante décrite par Koloni (1971), cette marque semble s'être réduite à *–o-*:

25 Nous ne nous intéresserons pas au comportement tonal des ces marques parce que nous n'avons pas encore d'idée précise des paramètres qui pourraient expliquer la tonalité. L'irrégularité au niveau tonal est peut-être un indice d'intégration relativement récente de ces formations au paradigme des marques aspecto-temporelles, comme nous l'a suggéré le Prof. D. Nurse (comm. pers.).

(43) enya D.14
a. Spa: mőkőṃmbola
'ils sont en train de jeter' (< má-ő-ko-ninb-od-a)
b. Koloni: tôbúka
'nous sommes en train de couper' (< tő-ˣo-bűk-a)

Donc, l'évolution qui s'est produite en enya peut être schématisée de la manière suivante: *-V-ko-* > *-o-ko-* > *-o-o-* > *-o-*

Le kela (C.75) et le kumu (D.23), qui par ailleurs font leur infinitif en classe 5, n'attestent pas de métatonie. La forme *-ndoko-* du kela (C.75) montre une généralisation de la voyelle *o* au sein du paradigme des marques aspecto-temporelles. Selon nous, contrairement à ce qui s'est passé en enya, la première voyelle *o* de *-ndoko-* ne s'explique pas par assimilation en kela, mais par une réanalyse des différentes marques. Ainsi, le kela possède un morphème *-ndo-* pour traduire le présent progressif. Ce morphème peut être issu de la séquence *-nda-ko-* > *-nda-o-*, dans laquelle *-nda-* serait à mettre en rapport avec le morphème locatif *nda* signifiant 'à, dans'. La marque *-ndo-* subit une usure telle que le locuteur kela ne se rend plus compte de la présence sous-jacente d'un préfixe de l'infinitif. Pour indiquer le futur, il va recourir à cette marque du présent *-ndo-* et lui juxtaposer la forme-nomino-verbale en *ko-*.

L'utilisation de marques en *-ko-* dans des langues comme le kela et le kumu est un indice en faveur de la présence ancienne d'une forme nomino-verbale de classe 15, à moins qu'on n'explique leur emploi dans ces langues par le phénomène de l'emprunt. Pourtant, selon nous, l'emprunt ne saurait rendre compte du grand nombre de marques en *o-* et de la diversification de leurs emplois dans les langues du Nord-Ouest.

Dans les autres langues, où le morphème aspecto-temporel se présente sous une forme *-(C)o-*, nous ne disposons pas de ces indices pour démontrer que la marque en question provient de la contraction d'un ancien auxiliant avec le PN de l'infinitif *ko-*. Cependant, l'alternance avec des morphèmes en *a-* au sein de la langue même ou dans des parlers voisins paraît corroborer notre hypothèse. Dans le tableau (3) qui ne se veut pas complet, nous énumérerons la majorité des marques aspecto-temporelles relevées en ne distinguant que trois grandes catégories temporelles: le passé, le présent et le futur[26].

---

26 Nous n'avons pas tenu compte de la voyelle finale des différents tiroirs, qui n'est pas nécessairement *-a*. En effet, nous estimons que les marques en *-o*, après l'achèvement des procédures de grammaticalisation, ont pu s'étendre à différents tiroirs pour lesquels il n'est pas nécessaire de poser une origine "Auxiliant + Infinitif" et pour lesquels la finale ne doit donc pas nécessairement être *-a*. Pourtant, une étude systématique des finales pourrait peut-être révéler l'existence d'autres formes nomino-verbales sous-jacentes telles que la forme de classe 14 qui se termine souvent en *-i/-e*.

marque	*langue*	*temps*
-no-	nen nkomi tuki	passé (// -na-) passé futur
-mo-	londo	passé (// -ma-)
-mbo-[27]	pove ntomba kela	passé passé passé
-to-	yans bushong kumu binja-Sud bolia nkengo nkomi kele tetela nkutsu bodo	passé passé passé présent passé, présent, futur présent, futur futur futur futur futur futur
-so-	kele kumu	passé passé
-ndo-	nen ntomba kele kela	présent présent présent présent
-nko-/-ngo-	motembo nen koozime kota ntomba motembo	présent futur (// -na-) futur futur (-ango-) futur futur
-yo-	bolia parlers mongo nkengo tetela kela	passé, présent, futur passé, présent présent, futur futur futur (infinitif)

Tableau 3. Les marques -Co-.

27 *-mbo-* peut-il être analysé en *-mba-o-* et si oui comment analyser l'élément *-mba-*? Est-il à mettre en rapport avec *-ba*, forme du verbe 'être', qui aurait été renforcée par une nasale?

Les marques de type *-Co-* sont également attestées en tetela (C.71) où elles ont comme particularité de pouvoir être suivies de la nasale *n*, préfixe de l'infinitif en tetela.

(44) tetela C.71

léék ló nkàmbá

'je suis en train de travailler'

Si l'on analyse le morphème du progressif *lo* comme issu d'une ancienne séquence *-la-ko-*, où *ko-* serait le PN de l'infinitif, la présence de la nasale s'explique difficilement. En revanche, si l'on prend *ko-* pour un morphème de classe 17, la séquence devient plus plausible: on aurait une succession de la marque *-la-*, suivie du prépréfixe locatif et du préfixe nominal de l'infinitif. Si on accepte cette hypothèse, on pourrait remettre en question l'analyse proposée précédemment pour les autres marques, ou du moins pour les marques qu'on pose comme issues d'un auxiliant qui désignait à l'origine un mouvement, telles que par exemple *-yo-* et *-to-* provenant respectivement de *-ya-ko-* et de *-ta-ko-*, puisqu'un verbe de mouvement est en principe accompagné d'un syntagme locatif. Cependant, comme dans les langues où les morphèmes *-yo-* et *-to-* sont attestés, il n'y a généralement plus de trace segmentale d'un préfixe de l'infinitif[28], il est très difficile de vérifier cette supposition. Des données supra-segmentales pourraient fournir des indications mais nous n'avons pas encore abordé cet aspect de l'analyse. De toute manière, même si *ko-* avait été un prépréfixe locatif, il aurait probablement été suivi du préfixe de classe 15 et on aurait eu une structure *-Ca-ko-ko-*. En effet, un préfixe nominal d'une autre classe aurait sans doute donné lieu à une évolution vocalique différente.

Avant de passer à l'étude de marques formées d'une voyelle antérieure fermée, il nous reste à signaler l'existence de nombreux tiroirs, essentiellement du présent et du futur, en *-ko-/-go-/-gu-* dans lesquels l'ancien auxiliant s'est probablement amuï en laissant parfois une trace tonale. Egalement très fréquentes sont les marques aspecto-temporelles *-o-* qui apparaissent au temps du passé, du présent et du futur. Nous ignorons pour le moment si ces marques s'expliquent par la chute de la consonne *k*, par une contraction de séquences de type *-V-ko-* (comme cela semblait être le

---

28 Des langues telles que le mpongwe et le nkomi, où il y a alternance consonantique à l'initiale du radical, fournissent des indices en faveur de l'analyse de *-ko-*, trace du prépréfixe locatif.

mpongwe B.11a

mitodyena "je verrais", mais myayeni "j'ai vu"

Pour expliquer l'alternance consonantique *dy/y*, on pose pour *mitodyena* la structure sous-jacente *mi-to-di-yen-a* < *mi-ta-yo-di-yen-a*. Dans cette forme structurelle *di* serait un morphème de classe 10bis et *yo* un prépréfixe locatif.

cas en enya) ou par un simple alignement sur les autres morphèmes aspecto-temporels.

En guise de conclusion, les marques aspecto-temporelles en *o-* sont bien réparties à travers le domaine envisagé et apparaissent dans des langues qui n'attestent plus nécessairement une forme nomino-verbale en *ko-*. Le rapport entre ces marques en *o-* et un infinitif de classe 15 ne fait cependant pas de doute et leur existence dans des langues qui construisent actuellement leur infinitif dans une classe autre que la classe 15 est, selon nous, un indice en faveur de la présence ancienne d'une forme nomino-verbale de classe 15 dans ces langues. Ainsi, l'infinitif de classe 15 aurait eu anciennement une distribution plus importante encore.

5.2. Les marques en i-/e-

L'analyse de ces marques, que nous venons seulement d'entamer, nous a posé beaucoup de problèmes. On pourrait en effet partir d'une hypothèse analogue à celle défendue pour les marques aspecto-temporelles en *o-* et soutenir que des séquences constituées d'un auxiliant en *-a* suivi d'une forme nomino-verbale à PN5 vocalique (*i-*) auraient pu être à l'origine de marques aspecto-temporelles à voyelle antérieure *e-* ou *ɛ* – d'après le système phonologique de la langue. Malheureusement, les données ne sont pas aussi simples à interpréter.

Premièrement, si l'on attribue aux formes en *-a* une origine verbale, elles pourront prendre les affixes verbaux. Ainsi, elles pourront être suivies d'une finale verbale qui n'est pas nécessairement *-a* mais qui peut se présenter aussi sous forme de *-i* (à rattacher en général pour les temps du passé à la finale *– i d ɛ). Des morphèmes de type *-me-* pourraient alors dériver de structures de type "*-ma-i* + auxilié", où *-ma-* serait à mettre en rapport avec la reconstruction *-màd- 'finir'[29]. D'un point de vue sémantique, le sens de *-màd- 'finir' explique pourquoi les marques qui en dérivent s'emploient le plus souvent au passé:

(45) teke B.70

mé mì búlá mbììnà

'I have broken the pot'

Deuxièmement, étant donné qu'une des formes reconstruites pour le verbe 'être' est *-de, il est difficile de déterminer dans certaines formes verbales la nature des marques de type -de/di-, -le/li-, -e/i-.

(46) makaa A.83

mə̀ è wíínŋg ómpyê

'I will chase away the dogs (later today)'

---

29 La marque *-me-* peut donc être issue de *-mà (d)-i ou de *-mà (d)- i d ɛ avec imbrication:

*-mad– i dɛ > -ma i dɛ > -medɛ > -mee > -me.

Dans cet exemple, *è* est-il une forme du verbe 'être' ou la trace d'un préfixe nominal? Rappelons que le makaa construit son infinitif à l'aide d'un PN Ø- qui, d'après les accords, se rattacherait historiquement à un PN15; donc on tendrait plutôt à interpréter *è* comme une forme de verbe 'être'. Toutefois, le koozime (A.84), parler proche du makaa, atteste un infinitif en *e*- qui est utilisé après une forme *lɨ* signifiant, d'après Beavon (1991: 62) 'in, at':

(47) koozime A.84

bé lɨ́ èfùmò mímbĕr

'they are building houses'

Par analogie avec les données du koozime, on pourrait supposer que la forme *è wííŋg* du makaa est une forme nomino-verbale mais, pour le moment, aucun argument ne nous permet de justifier cette supposition.

Donc, il est extrêmement difficile d'identifier les traces d'un éventuel PN5 dans les différents paradigmes des marques aspecto-temporelles de type -*CV*-. Néanmoins, certaines langues présentent des marques à voyelle longue où la longueur semble s'expliquer par la présence sous-jacente d'un PN de l'infinitif.

(48) yans B.85

m'asiikiɛ

'je dois partir'

La marque -*sii*- pourrait être analysée en -*sa*-*i*-.

En guise de conclusion, il est très difficile de retrouver des traces de formations issues de "Auxiliant + PN5" dans les langues de notre coprus, parce que la présence d'une voyelle antérieure dans une marque aspecto-temporelle peut s'interpréter de différentes manières. L'identification est moins douteuse pour les morphèmes à voyelle longue et leur existence montre qu'anciennement les formes nomino-verbales de classe 5 ont pu faire partie de constructions verbales complexes qui, par la suite, se sont grammaticalisées pour donner lieu à des marques aspecto-temporelles devenues inanalysables.

6. Conclusion

De l'analyse du préfixe des formes infinitivales dans plusieurs langues des zones A, B, C et D, il ressort que la classe 15 est bien représentée dans les formes nomino-verbales et que, là où elle n'est plus attestée à l'infinitif actuel, elle a dû exister à un stade plus ancien de l'histoire de la langue comme le montrent les marques aspecto-temporelles en -*o*. Les langues du Nord-Ouest n'infirment donc pas l'hypothèse de l'existence d'une forme infinitivale de classe 15 en proto-bantou.

Quant à la forme de classe 5, elle est tout aussi bien représentée dans les langues de notre corpus, avec peut-être une plus grande concentration d'attestations à l'extrême Nord-Ouest. Cette forme nomino-verbale de classe 5 semble dans beaucoup de cas être équivalente à celle de classe 15 et assumer les mêmes emplois. Probablement, elle a pu faire partie d'anciennes constructions verbales complexes, qui après avoir subi des procédures de grammaticalisation, ont donné lieu à la création de marques aspecto-temporelles. Malheureusement, il nous est, jusqu'à présent, très difficile de retracer ce genre d'évolutions pour les formes de classe 5.

Dans notre étude, nous avons relevé un critère distinctif important pour la détermination du fonctionnement des formes nomino-verbales: la métatonie. La métatonie ne semble pas s'appliquer aux formes de classe 5 tandis qu'elle touche fréquemment les infinitifs de classe 15 et les formes verbales qui peuvent être ramenées à des structures complexes constituées de cet infinitif. Pour interpéter cette différence nous serions tentée de partir de l'hypothèse que les formes des classes 5 et 15, d'un point de vue sémantique, n'étaient probablement pas synonymes. La forme de classe 15 aurait plutôt référé au procès en acccomplissement, supposant éventuellement un actant-objet non spécifique, alors que la forme de classe 5 aurait désigné le procès accompli. Il faudrait bien sûr chercher des arguments qui mettent en évidence cette différence sémantique, recherche que nous n'avons pas entamée ici[30]. C'est la différence sémantique qui explique, selon nous, pourquoi la forme de classe 15 s'intègre plus fréquemment dans des constructions verbales complexes.

Si notre hypothèse initiale n'était pas infirmée par des phénomènes qu'on observera dans d'autres langues bantoues, nous pourrions être amenée à supposer qu'il y a eu, à un stade plus ancien du bantou, des formes nominales déverbatives presque équivalentes de classes 5 et 15, ce qui explique aussi leur coexistence dans quelques langues de notre corpus. Dans d'autres langues une des deux formes a été spécialisée dans un emploi qu'on pourrait qualifier d'infinitif et la deuxième forme a été perdue ou réservée à d'autres emplois.

Références

1. Ouvrages généraux

Bastin, Y. 1989. El prefijo locativo de la clase 18 y la expresión del progresivo presente en Bantu, *Estudias Africanos, Revista de la Asociación Espanola de Africanistas* IV/6: 35-55; IV/7: 61-86.

Creissels, D. 1995. La structure tonale des bases verbales aux différents tiroirs de la conjugaison en sotho sud, Communication présentée au 25° Colloque de Linguistique Africaine de l'Université de Leiden, 28-30/8/1995.

30 Un critère intéressant dans ce genre d'étude pourrait être selon nous l'analyse du prédicat verbal lorsque ces deux formes nomino-verbales ont la fonction-sujet. Ainsi lorsque, nous faisions des recherches quant au fonctionnement de l'infinitif de classe 15 en fonction sujet, nous avons constaté que les prédicats étaient le plus souvent de type généralisant.

Creissels, D. 1996. Conjunctive and disjunctive verb forms in Setswana, *South African Journal of African Languages* 16/4: 109-115.

Doneux, J. 1967. Données sur la classe 15 nominale en bantou, *Africana Linguistica* III: 1-22.

Forges, G. 1983. La classe de l'infinitif en bantou, *Africana Linguistica* IX: 257-263.

Guthrie, M. 1967-1971. *Comparative Bantu: an introduction to the comparative linguistics and prehistory of the Bantu languages*. Vols 1-4. Farnborough: Gregg International Publishers.

Jacquot, A. 1983. *Les classes nominales dans les langues bantoues des groupes B.10, B.20, B.30 (Gabon-Congo)*. Paris: ORSTOM.

Meeussen, A.E. 1954. *Linguïstische schets van het Bangubangu*. Tervuren: Musée Royal du Congo belge.

Meeussen, A.E. 1967. Bantu grammatical reconstructions, *Africana Linguistica* III: 79-121.

Meinhof, C. 1948. *Grundzüge einer vergleichenden Grammatik der Bantusprachen*. (2° éd.) Hamburg: Verlag Von Eckardt & Messtorff.

Nsuka Nkutsi, F. 1986. Formatifs et auxiliaires dans les langues bantoues: quelques critères de détermination, *Africana Linguistica* X: 337-364.

Polak, L. 1983. L'infixe réfléchi en bantou, *Africana Linguistica* IX: 271-304.

Rwakazina, A.M. 1971. Formes verbales en bantou. [Thèse de doctorat non publiée, ULB-Bruxelles.]

Schadeberg, T.C. 1995. Object diagnostics in Bantu, in: E. Nolue Emenanjo & Ozo-mekuri Ndimele (éds), *Issues in African languages and linguistics. Essays in honour of Kay Williamson*. Aba: National Institute for Nigerian Languages, 173-180.

Schadeberg, T.C. 1996. Bantu Mapmaker 3. Leiden: Rijksuniversiteit te Leiden.

Stallcup, K. 1980. The Momo languages, in: L. Bouquiaux (éd.), *L'expansion bantoue*. Paris: SELAF, I: 193-224

Stappers, L. 1964. *Morfologie van het Songye*. Tervuren: MRAC.

2. Le corpus: sources

Londo A.11

Kuperus, J. 1985. *The londo word*. Tervuren: MRAC.

Akoose A.15

Hedinger, R. 1982. The verb in akoose. [Ms. non publié.]

Duala A.24

Ittman, J. 1939. *Grammatik des Duala (Kamerun)*. Berlin-Hamburg: Reiner-Friederichen-De Gruyter.

Bubi A.31

Meeussen, A.E. s.d.. Notes sur le bubi (liste de verbes). [Ms. non publié.]

Rurangwa, I.M. 1985. Enquête linguistique sur le bubi, langue bantu insulaire de Guinée Equatoriale (Phonologie et système de classes), in: T. Obenga (éd.), *Les peuples bantu. Migrations, expansion et identité culturelle.* Paris—Libreville: Editions L'Harmattan—CICIBA, 1: 77-100.

Noho A.32

Schadeberg, T.C. 1980. La morphologie verbale du bantou commun et les langues bantoues du Cameroun, in: L. Bouquiaux (éd.), *L'expansion bantoue.* Paris: SELAF, II: 503-509.

Benga A.34

Nassau, R.H. 1892. *Mackey's grammar of the Benga-Bantu language.* New York: American Tract Society.

Bankon A.42

Spellenberg, F. 1922. *Die Sprache der Bo oder Bankon in Kamerun.* (3° Beiheft zur Zeitschrift für Eingeborenen Sprachen.) Berlin-Hamburg: D. Reimer & C. Boysen.

Basaa A.43

Dimmendaal, G. 1976. Aspekten van het basaa. [Mémoire non publié, Rijksuniversiteit te Leiden-Leiden.]

Nen A.44

Dugast, I. 1971. *Grammaire du tunen.* Paris: Editions Klincksieck.

Nomaande A.46

Wilkendorf, P. 1986. The marking of tense in nomaande, *Journal of West African languages* XVI/1: 63-74.

Wilkendorf, P. 1991. Floating high tones in Nomaande locatives, in: S. Anderson (éd.), *Tone in five languages of Cameroon.* Arlington: University of Texas—SIL, 61-72.

Wilkendorf, P. 1991. Le système temporel et aspectuel de la langue nomaande, in: S. Anderson & B. Comrie (éds), *Tense and aspect in eight languages of Cameroon.* Arlington: University of Texas—SIL, 105-146.

Bafia A.53

Bessong, A.D.P. & I.A. Mel'cuk. 1983. Un modèle formel de la conjugaison bafia (à l'indicatif), *BSOAS* XLVI/3: 477-528.

Guarisma, G. 1982. Le syntagme verbal à modalité de temps et à modalité d'aspect en bafia, in: G. Guarisma, G. Nissim & J. Voorhoeve (éds), *Le verbe bantou.* Paris: SELAF, 57-77.

Guarisma, G. 1990. La négation en bafia: langue bantoue A.53 du Cameroun, *Linguistique Africaine* 4: 65-78.

Gunu / nugunu A.60 / A.62

Gerhardt, P. 1989. Les temps en nugunu, in: D. Barreteau & R. Hedinger (éds), *Descriptions de langues camerounaises.* Paris: ACCT—ORSTOM, 283-314.

Orwig, C. 1991. Relative time reference in Nugunu, in: S. Anderson & B. Comrie (éds), *Tense and aspect in eight languages of Cameroon*. Arlington: University of Texas—SIL, 147-162.

Tuki A.61 ou 64

Biloa, E. 1995. *Functional categories and the syntax of focus in Tuki*. München—Newcastle: Lincom Europa.

Pahouin A.70

Piper, K. 1989. *Aspektstruktur im Pahouin. Zur verbalen Morphologie nordwestlicher Bantusprachen*. Hamburg: H. Buske.

Ewondo A.72a

Angenot, J.P. 1971. *Aspects de la phonétique et de la morphologie de l'éwondo*. (Ph.D. diss.) Leiden: Rijksuniversiteit te Leiden.

Essono, J.-J. M. 1993. Description synchronique de l'ewondo, bantu (A.72a) du Cameroun. Phonologie—Morphologie—Syntaxe. [Thèse de doctorat non publiée, 2 vols., Université de la Sorbonne Nouvelle-Paris III.]

Fang A.75

Ondo-Mebiame, P. 1991-1992. De la phonologie à la morphologie du fang-ntumu parlé à Aboumezok (Bantu A.75). [Thèse de doctorat non publiée, 2 vols., Université libre de Bruxelles-Bruxelles.]

Bajele A.80

Renaud, P. 1976. *Description phonologique et éléments de morphologie nominale d'une langue de Pygmées du Sud-Cameroun: les Bajele (Bipindi)*. Yaounde: ONAREST—ALCAM.

Makaa A.83

Heath, D. & T. Heath. 1982. *Notes on the mekaa noun class system*. Cameroun: SIL.

Heath, D. & T. Heath. 1982. *Relative clauses in mekaa*. Cameroun: SIL.

Heath, D. 1991. Tense and aspect in Makaa, in: S. Anderson & B. Comrie (éds), *Tense and aspect in eight languages of Cameroon*. Arlington: University of Texas—SIL, 3-15.

Heath, D. 1991. Tone in the Makaa associative construction, in: S. Anderson (éd.), *Tone in five languages of Cameroon*. Arlington: University of Texas—SIL, 3-28.

Koozime A.84

Beavon, K. 1979. Studies in the discourse grammar of konzime. A bantu language of Cameroun. [Unpublished Ph.D. dissertation, University of Texas-Arlington.]

Beavon, K. 1991. Koozime verbal system, in: S. Anderson & B. Comrie (éds), *Tense and aspect in eight languages of Cameroon*. Arlington: University of Texas—SIL, 47-103.

Bangando A.86

Boursier, D., J. Mokoto & U. Wiesemann. 1984. Les verbes en bangando, *Journal of West African Languages* XIV/2: 103-123.

Mpyemo A.86

Biandji, D. 1990-1991. Le verbe en mpyemo, langue bantu. [Mémoire de maîtrise non publié, Université de Bangui-Bangui.]

Kako A.93

Ernst, U. 1989. *Lexique kako–français, français-kako avec tableaux de conjugaisons.* Yaounde: SIL.

Ernst, U. 1991. Temps et aspect en kako, in: S. Anderson & B. Comrie (éds), *Tense and aspect in eight languages of Cameroon.* Arlington: University of Texas—SIL, 17-45.

Mpongwe B.11a

Gauthier, J.M. 1912. *Grammaire de la langue mpongwée.* Paris: s.éd.

Ogouamba, P.A. 1990. Etude morpho-syntaxique du verbe en mpongwé, parler B11 du Gabon. [Mémoire de licence non publié, Université Omar Bongo-Libreville.]

Nkomi B.11e

Grégoire, Cl. 1996. Nkomi: communication personnelle.

Kota B.25

Piron, P. 1990. Eléments de description du kota, langue bantoue du Gabon, B25. [Mémoire de licence non publié, Université libre de Bruxelles-Bruxelles.]

Pove B.30

Mickala-Manfoumbi, R. 1993-1994. Essai de grammaire pove: langue bantoue du groupe B.30. [Thèse de doctorat non publiée, Université libre de Bruxelles-Bruxelles.]

Geviya B.30

Blanchon, J. 1988. Une langue mixte en voie de disparition: le geviya, *PHOLIA* 3: 53-69.

Van der Veen, L. 1988. Caractéristiques principales du groupe B30, *PHOLIA* 3: 271-290.

Van der Veen, L. 1991. Etude comparée des parlers du groupe Okani B 30 (Gabon). [Thèse de doctorat non publiée, Université Lumière-Lyon 2.]

Tsogo B.31

Marchal-Nasse, C. 1979. Esquisse de la langue tsogo: phonologie, morphologie. [Mémoire non publié, Université libre de Bruxelles-Bruxelles.]

Ngubi B.40

Puech, G. 1988. Augment et préfixe nominal en ngubi, *PHOLIA* 3: 247-256.

Gisira/eshira B.41

Dodo-Bounguendza, E. 1992-1993. Esquisse phonologique et morphologique du gisira, langue bantoue (B41) du Gabon. [Thèse de doctorat non publiée, Université libre de Bruxelles-Bruxelles.]

Blanchon, J. 1988. Relèvements tonals en eshira et en massango: première approche d'une tonologie comparée du groupe bantou B 40, *PHOLIA* 3: 71-85.

Sango B.42

Blanchon, J. 1988. Relèvements tonals en eshira et en massango: première approche d'une tonologie comparée du groupe bantou B 40, *PHOLIA* 3: 71-85.

Blanchon, J. 1990. Noms composés en massango et en nzebi de Mbigou (Gabon), *PHOLIA* 5: 31-48.

Lumbu B.44

Blanchon, J. 1984. Présentation du yi-lumbu dans ses rapport avec le yi-punu et le ci-vili à travers un conte traditionnel, *PHOLIA* 1: 7-35.

Duma B.51

Adam, J. 1954. *Grammaire composée mbede—ndumu—duma*. Montpellier—Brazzaville: Mémoires de l'Institut d'Etudes Centrafricanes 6.

Nzebi B.52

Blanchon, J. 1990. Noms composés en massango et en nzebi de Mbigou (Gabon), *PHOLIA* 5: 31-48.

Marchal-Nasse, C. 1989. De la phonologie à la morphologie du nzebi, langue bantoue (B52) du Gabon. [Thèse de doctorat non publiée, Université libre de Bruxelles-Bruxelles.]

Mbede B.61

Adam, J. 1954. *Grammaire composée mbede—ndumu—duma*. Montpellier—Brazzaville: Mémoires de l'Institut d'Etudes Centrafricanes 6.

Ndumu B.63

Adam, J. 1954. *Grammaire composée mbede—ndumu—duma*. Montpellier—Brazzaville: Mémoires de l'Institut d'Etudes Centrafricanes 6.

Teke B.70

Fontaney, L. 1970. Notes towards a description of Teke (Gabon), *PHOLIA* 1: 47-70.

Kukuya B.78

Paulian, C. 1975. *Le kukuya: langue teke du Congo: phonologie—classes nominales*. Paris: SELAF.

Boma B.82

Stappers, L. 1989. *Boma. Eine Sprachskizze*. Hamburg: H. Buske Verlag.

Yans B.85

Rottland, F. 1970. *Die Verbformen des Yanzi*. Leiden: Rijksuniversiteit te Leiden.

Dzing B.86

Ruzicka, K.F. 1956. Infinitive in Swahili, *Archiv Orientalni* 24: 57-116 + 294-333.

Mboon B.87

Bwantsa-Kafungu, S.-P. & A.E. Meeussen. 1970-1971. Notes mbuun. [Ms. non publié.]

Leke C.00

Vanhoudt, B. 1987. *Eléments de description du leke. Langue bantoue de zone C*. Tervuren: MRAC.

Mboshi/bunji C.25

Fontaney, L. 1988. Mboshi: Steps towards a grammar. Part 1, *PHOLIA* 3: 87-167.

Fontaney, L. 1989. Mboshi: Steps towards a grammar. Part 2, *PHOLIA* 4: 71-131.

Doko C.30

Twiligiyimana, C. 1984. *Eléments de description du doko*. Tervuren: MRAC.

Lifonga C.30

Motingea, Mangulu. s.d. [1990]. *Parlers riverains de l'entre Ubangi-Zaire. Eléments de structure grammaticale*. (Etudes Aequatoria, 8.) Mbandaka: Centre Aequatoria.

Likata C.30

Motingea, Mangulu. s.d. [1990]. *Parlers riverains de l'entre Ubangi-Zaire. Eléments de structure grammaticale*. (Etudes Aequatoria, 8.) Mbandaka: Centre Aequatoria.

Zamba C.30

Motingea, Mangulu. s.d. [1990]. *Parlers riverains de l'entre Ubangi-Zaire. Eléments de structure grammaticale*. (Etudes Aequatoria, 8.) Mbandaka: Centre Aequatoria.

Libinza C.31b

Van Leynseele, H. 1976-1977. An outline of Libinza grammar. [Mémoire non publié, Rijksuniversiteit te Leiden-Leiden.]

Bobangi C.32

Whitehead, J. 1899. *Grammar and dictionary of the Bobangi language as spoken over a part of the upper Congo, West Central Africa*. London: Kegan Paul, Trench, Trübner.

Ntomba C.35a

Bastin, Y. 1989. El prefijo locativo de la clase 18 y la expresión del progresivo presente en Bantu, *Estudias Africanos, Revista de la Asociación Espanola de Africanistas* IV/6: 35-55; IV/7: 61-86.

Bolia C.35b

Bastin, Y. 1989. El prefijo locativo de la clase 18 y la expresión del progresivo presente en Bantu, *Estudias Africanos, Revista de la Asociación Espanola de Africanistas* IV/6: 35-55; IV/7: 61-86.

Lingala C.36

Heine, B. 1991. Auxiliaries in African languages: the Lingala case, *Proceedings of the 17th Annual Meeting of the Berkeley Linguistic Society*, 106-119.

Mbudza C.36c

Bemon-Musubao, B. 1971. Eléments de grammaire mbudza. [Mémoire non publié, Université Lovanium-Kinshasa.]

Buja C.37

Rwakazina, A.M. 1971. Formes verbales en bantou. [Thèse de doctorat non publiée, Université libre de Bruxelles-Bruxelles.]

Motembo C.40

Molembo Masimo. 1987. Formes verbales comparées des langues motembo et lingombe, *Annales Aequatoria* 8: 307-316.

Ebango C.40

Motingea, Mangulu. 1995. Esquisse de l'ebango: langue bantoue du groupe C40, *Afrikanistische Arbeitspapiere* 41: 5-50.

Ngombe C.41

Molembo Masimo. 1987. Formes verbales comparées des langues motembo et lingombe, *Annales Aequatoria* 8: 307-316.

Pakabete C.44

Motingea, Mangulu. 1995. Aspects du pakabete: langue zaïroise de la frontière bantoue-oubanguienne, *Afrika und Übersee* 78: 199-230.

Lebeo C.45

Kähler-Meyer, E. 1955. Zur Genealogie des Adjektive im Bantu, in: J. Lukas (éd.), *Afrikanistische Studien*. Berlin: Akademie Verlag, 64-75.

Sogo C.53

Stoop, H. 1989. Les préfixes du sogo (C 53), *Annales Aequatoria* 10: 127-140.

Lokele C.55

Carrington, J. s.d.. *Esquisse d'une grammaire lokele*. Stanleyville.

Ngando C.60

Hulstaert, G. 1987. Les parlers des Bangando méridionaux, *Annales Aequatoria* 8: 205-288.

Loleku C.60

Hulstaert, G. 1982. *Esquisse de la langue des Eleku.* Bandundu: CEEBA.

Lokalo C.61

Hulstaert, G. 1988. Le parler des Lokalo orientaux, *Annales Aequatoria* 9: 133-171.

Lokonda C.61

Hulstaert, G. & Ilonga Mpongo. 1989. Les verbes en lokonda, *Annales Aequatoria* 10: 201-221.

Lonkundo C.61

Hulstaert, G. 1938. Praktische grammatica van het Lonkundo (Lomongo). Antwerpen: De Sikkel.

Lonkengo C.61

Hulstaert, G. 1970. *Esquisse du parler des Nkengo.* Tervuren: MRAC.

Ntomba Inongo C.65

Gilliard, L. 1928. *Grammaire pratique lontomba.* Bruxelles: Editions de l'Essorial.

Ombo C.69

Meeussen, A.E. 1952. *Esquisse de la langue ombo.* Tervuren: MRAC.

Tetela C.71

Omatete, Alonge-Dikonda. 1982. Description du verbe dans la morphologie de la langue tetela. [Mémoire non publié, Université libre de Bruxelles-Bruxelles.]

Lonkutsu C.73

Motingea, Mangulu. 1989. Esquisse grammaticale du lonkutsu, *Annales Aequatoria* 10: 91-116.

Kela C.75

Forges, G. 1977. *Le kela: langue bantoue du Zaïre (zone C): esquisse phonologique et morphologique.* Paris: SELAF.

Bushong C.83

Vansina, J. 1959. *Esquisse de grammaire bushong.* Tervuren: Musée Royal du Congo Belge.

Mokpa D.10

Motingea, Mangulu. 1990. Esquisse de la langue des Mokpá (Haut-Zaïre), *Afrika und Übersee* 73: 67-100.

Lengola D.12

Stappers, L. 1971. Esquisse de la langue lengola, *Africana Linguistica* V: 255-307.

Mituku D.13

Stappers, L. 1973. *Esquisse de la langue mituku.* Tervuren: MRAC.

Enya D.14

Koloni, J. 1971. Eléments de morphologie et de vocabulaire de la langue enya. [Mémoire non publié, Université Lovanium-Kinshasa.]

Spa, J.J. 1973. *Traits et tons en enya: phonologie générative d'une langue bantoue.* Tervuren: MRAC.

Lega D.25

Meeussen, A.E. 1971. *Eléments de grammaire lega.* Tervuren: MRAC.

Binja-sud D.26

Meeussen, A.E. & F. Sebassoni. s.d.. Notes binja-Sud. [Ms. non publié.]

Holoholo D.28

Coupez, A. 1955. *Esquisse de la langue holoholo.* Tervuren: MRAC.

Kamba Muzenga, J.G. 1987. Phonologie historique du holoholo, *Annales Aequatoria* 8: 317-348.

Schmitz, R. 1912. *Les Baholoholo.* Bruxelles: Collection des monographies ethnographiques.

Bodo D.30

Asangama, N. 1983. Le budu, langue bantu du nord-est du Zaïre: esquisse phonologique et grammaticale. [Thèse de 3ème cycle non publiée, INALCO—Université de la Sorbonne Nouvelle, Paris III.]

Bokula, F.X. 1966. Eléments de grammaire et de vocabulaire de la langue bodo. [Mémoire non publié, Université Lovanium-Kinshasa.]

Bira D.32

Dz'ba, Dheli Susa. 1972. Esquisse grammaticale du bira. [Mémoire non publié, Université Nationale du Zaïre-Lubumbashi.]

Meinhof, C. 1939. Die Sprache der Bira, *Zeitschrift für Eingeborenen Sprachen* 24/4: 241-286.

Kumu D.37

Harries, L. 1958. Kumu: a sub-Bantu language, *Kongo-Overzee* 24/4-5: 265-296.

Nyanga D.43

Kadima, M. 1965. Esquisse phonologique et morphologique de la langue nyanga, *Africana Linguistica* II: 55-111.

Bembe D.54

Mutombo, H.D. 1973. Ebauches de grammaire de la langue bembe et du dialecte kalamba:yi de la langue luba kasayi. [Mémoire non publié, Université libre de Bruxelles-Bruxelles.]

Meeussen, A.E. 1953. De talen van Maniema (Belgisch-Congo), *Kongo-Overzee* 19: 385-391.

Buyi D.55

Meeussen, A.E. 1951. Notes buyu. [Ms. non publié.]

Future and Distal *-ka-*'s: Proto-Bantu or Nascent Form(s)?*

ROBERT BOTNE
Indiana University

1. Introduction

In Bantu verbal morphology, one of the most common morphological forms is *-ka-*. Although one finds numerous functions and meanings of this form across the Bantu domain, the focus of this paper will be on just two of these: its temporal use as a (post-hodiernal) future formative and its spatial use as a distal marker indicating location of an event/action away from the deictic center. The presentation and discussion of each type will comprise three parts: its geographical distribution, its grammatical distribution, and its potential sources of origin. The complexity of the issue of whether either or both of these morphemes can be reconstructed for Proto-Bantu or should

* Portions of this article were first presented at the Round Table on Bantu Historical Linguistics, Lyon, France (June 1, 1996). It has benefitted from discussions with and comments from many participants at the conference. In particular, I would like to thank Pascale Hadermann and Tom Gueldeman for their extensive comments, as well as Larry Hyman and Jean-Marie Hombert for raising issues about the analysis and presentation. I also wish to thank Beatrice Wamey, Bertrade Mbom, Ellen Kalua, Deo Ngonyani, and Loveness Schafer for providing data on Oku, Basaa, Ngonde, Ndendeule, and Ndali, respectively. The views presented here, for which I am entirely responsible, do not necessarily represent those of the editors or of the participants at the round table.

be considered nascent in Bantu precludes definitive answers here. Rather, the discussion is intended to provide a general overview of the body of data available and some of the issues involved.

The discussion is organized in the following manner. First, a brief overview of previous work in this area is presented (§2). Second, a synchronic map of the distribution and use of distal -KA- is laid out (§3). This is followed by a consideration of potential soure(s) of -KA-, particularly as a locative clitic (§4). Next, the distribution of (post-hodiernal) future -KA- is outlined (§5) and subsequently compared with that of distal -KA- (§6). The concluding section (§7) presents a summary of the discussion and indications of future directions of research.

2. The working hypotheses of Meeussen and Guthrie

The historical status of the two -KA- forms in question has been the subject of tentative hypotheses at best. Meeussen (1967) rather tentatively lists *-ka-* as a future tense formative, but warns that the "list of tense formulae, ... [is] intended as illustrating guesses rather than as real reconstructions" (p. 116). He further tempers the listing of -KA- among tense formatives by suggesting that it is "probably rather a limitative" (p. 109), the term "limitative" referring to "[a] special position between formative and infix... attested in a limited number of languages; the result [being] that little can be said about proto-forms occurring in that position..." (p. 109). Meeussen also notes the relevance to this discussion of infinitival forms in *ka-*, noting that it suggests rather "a connection with the 'motional' limitative *-ka-* ['go to do'] than with cl. 12. The whole question is very involved." (p. 111).

Guthrie (1967-71), like Meeussen, proposes a tentative reconstruction of -KA- as a future marker, his comparative series C.S. 2248: "C.S. 2248 could well reflect some Proto-Bantu tense sign in view of its geographical distribution and the uniformity of tonal distinctiveness in the infix in all entries." (vol. 4: 242) Unlike Meeussen, he makes no mention of a motional -KA-. Meinhof (1910), however, reconstructs a verb root *-ka-* 'go' based on Ngonde and Herero motional *-ka-*'s and Swahili consecutive *-ka-*. Bourquin (1923) and Meeussen (1967) follow Meinhof in reconstructing a verb *-ka-* 'go'.

Given the very tentative and limited nature of this previous body of work, several questions need to be addressed concerning the historical status of -KA- forms. First, what is the geographical distribution in the Bantu domain of distal -KA-? How does its grammatical distribution in various languages relate to this geographical distribution? What was (or were) its source(s), if it is not reconstructable for Proto-Bantu? A locative affix? A verb of motion? Is there a connection with infinitival *ka-*? Second, what is the geographical distribution of future -KA-? Its grammatical distribution?

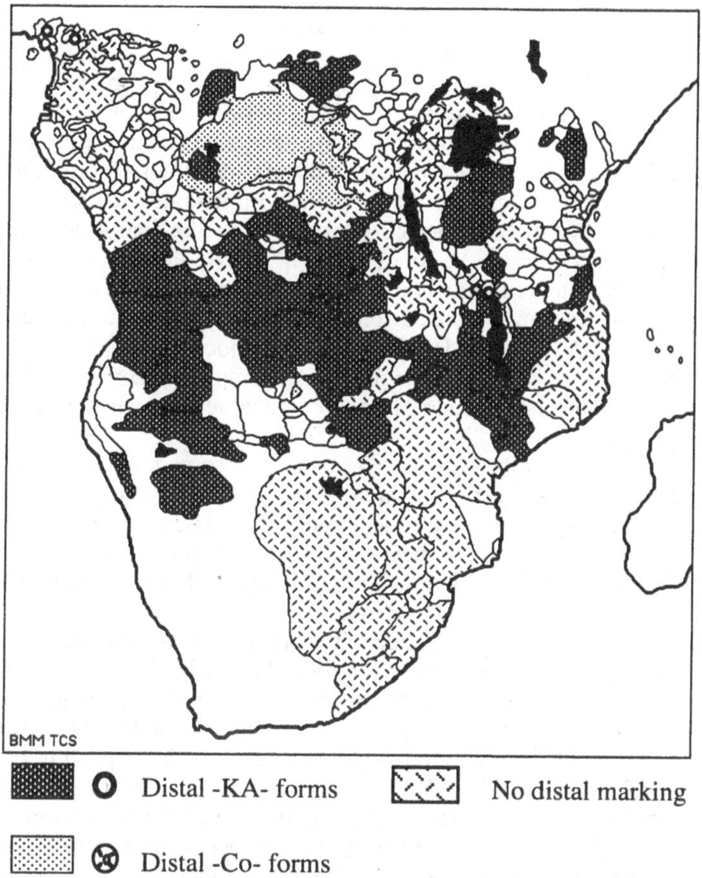

Map 1. Distribution of distal -KA- across Bantu[1]

How do these compare with distal -KA-? Can a historical connection be posited between future -KA- and distal -KA-? Although it is not possible, at this time, to provide conclusive answers to all of these questions, the data are, nevertheless, suggestive of potential paths of evolution.

3. Distal *-ka-*

Of approximately 150 languages spread across the Bantu domain that I have been able to consider, 51 employ distal -KA- in at least one construction. (See Appendix for list of languages.) However, -KA- is only one form of

[1]Maps were produced using Bantu Mapmaker 3 (1996), created by Thilo Schadeberg and John B. Lowe, whom I thank for making it available.

distal marker found among Bantu languages. Several others are *-yo-*, *-to-*, and *-ko-*. Map 1 illustrates not only the distribution of -KA- languages, but also that of the -Co- languages. Languages that appear not to have any kind of distal marker are indicated by cross-hatching. One caveat, however: it is not possible to completely discount these languages at this time because authors have not always included data on distal use in their descriptions.

Two aspects of the distributional pattern immediately stand out. First, although distal -KA- occurs across a large part of the Bantu domain, it is most heavily concentrated in zones K, L, M, N, P, and R, i.e., across the south-central Bantu area. Second, distal markers of any type apparently do not occur at all in zones B, D, J, and S, and only in a few languages in zones A, C, E, F, G, and H. That is, areal pockets in the northwest, comprising zones A, B, and H; the northeast, comprising zones D, G, J; and the southeast, comprising much of zone P and zone S; generally lack distal marking.

Although the data show distal -KA- to be widespread, the general lack of this formative in the northwest area—with the exception of Londo and Tunen—and the high frequency of occurrence in the south-central area require explanation. In particular, are these various -KA- forms cognate, or do they have different historical sources? In either case, do the data reflect a Proto-Bantu formative or a later development?

Before turning to these questions, it is appropriate to consider the grammatical distribution of distal -KA-. The focus here is the intensity of use in a language as gauged by its use in the imperative, subjunctive, indicative, and infinitive. Map 2 provides a general overview of such a distribution. However, note that authors do not always provide full descrip-tions of such phenomena; a language listed as only using -KA- in the imperative, for example, might also use it in the subjunctive, a fact which may not have been noted in the grammar(s) consulted. Of particular note in this distribution is that the use of -KA- is, to some extent, predictable.

The simplest use of -KA- is either in an imperative (1) or a subjunctive (2) construct.

(1) Use of distal -KA- in imperative only: "go and V" or "V elsewhere"

C.30	Mabembe	*ka*-ROOT-a	(Motingea 1991)
C.31	Ngiri	*ka*-ROOT-e	(Motingea 1996)
C.44	Ebango (Bua)	*ka*-ROOT-a	(Motingea 1995)
L.32	Kanyok	*ka*-ROOT	(Stappers 1986)
M.54	Lamba	*ka*-ROOT-e	(Doke 1938)
N.44	Sena	*ka*-ROOT-e	(Anderson 1897)
P.22	Mwera	*ka*-ROOT-e	(Harries 1950)

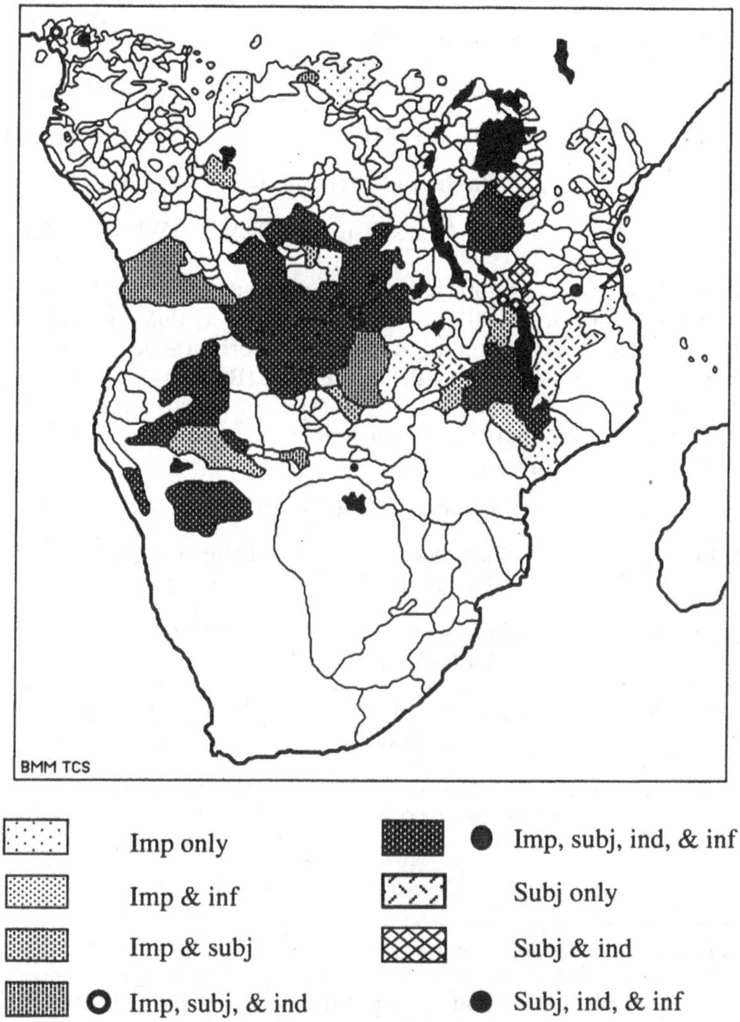

Map 2. Map of the grammatical distribution of distal -KA-

(2) Use of distal -KA- in subjunctive only

E.51	Gikuyu	SP-*ka*-ROOT-e	(Fut)[2]	(Barlow 1960)
E.55	Kamba	SP-*ka*-ROOT-e	(Fut)	(Farnsworth 1957)
G.64	Pangwa	SP-*xa*-ROOT-e	(Fut)	(Stirnimann 1983)
M.52	Lala	ka-SP-*ka*-ROOT-e	(Hort)	(Madan 1908a)
P.21	Yao	SP-*ka*-ROOT-e	(Fut)	(Whiteley 1966)

Yao P.21 also has a future indicative construction incorporating distal -*ka*- which has the form ti-SP-ka-ROOT-e. However, this construction is clearly a grammaticalization of a one-time periphrastic form having auxiliary -*ti* 'say, do' followed by the subjunctive (Botne 1998).

If a language uses distal -KA- in two types of constructions, these are predominantly the imperative and subjunctive (3), with a few using it only in the subjunctive and indicative (4).

(3) Use of distal -KA- in imperative and subjunctive

A.11	Londo	ká-ROOT-e SP-kà-ROOT-e	(Kuperus 1985, 1982)
C.34	Sakata	ká(á)-ROOT SP-ká-ROOT-í	(de Witte 1955)
L.21	Kete	ka-ROOT(-a) SP(-a)-ka-ROOT(-a)	(Kamba Muzenga 1980)
L.62	Nkoya	ka-ROOT-e SP-ka-ROOT-e	(Yukawa 1987)

[2]The following abbreviations are used:

Acc	Accompli	Imp	Imperative	PoHo	Post-hodiernal
Dir	Directional	ImF	Immediate Fut	Pr	Present
Dis	Distal	Ind	Indicative	Prf	Perfective
Dur	Durative	Indef	Indefinite	Prog	Progressive
F	Future	Inf	Infinitive	Pst	Past
FV	Final vowel	Loc	Locative	RmF	Remote fut
Foc	Focus	MedF	Medial Fut	S	Singular
Fut	Future	NrF	Near Fut	TomF	Tomorrow fut
HoF	Hodiernal Fut	P	Person	VRmF	Very remote fut
Hort	Hortative	Pl	Plural		

M.21	Ndali	kà-ROOT-e SP-ká-ROOT-e	(Field notes—RB)
N.21	Tumbuka	ka-ROOT-a-ni SP-ka-ROOT-e	(Diocese of Mzuzu 1970)
N.31	Ngonde	ka-ROOT-e SP-ka-ROOT-e	(Field notes—RB)
N.41	Nsenga	ka-ROOT-e SP-ka-ROOT-e	(Ranger 1928)
R.22	Ndonga	ka-ROOT-e sp-ka-root-e	(Viljoen and Amakali 1978)

(4) Use of distal -KA- in subjunctive and indicative only

F.21	Sukuma	SP-ká-ROOT-e SP-ko-ka-ROOT-a	 (Fut)	(Batibo 1985)
G.61	Sango	SP-ká-ROOT-age [Form not provided]		(Heese 1920)
P.13	Kimatuumbi	SP-ka-ROOT-é SP-ka-ROOT-a	 (Fut)	(Odden 1996)

One language, Nyungwe N.43, differs from this pattern in that it uses distal -KA- in the imperative and the infinitive (5), but apparently not in the subjunctive.

(5) Use of distal -KA- in imperative and infinitive

N.43	Nyungwe	k^{h}a-ROOT-e ku-kÓa-ROOT-a	(Courtois 1888)

The next group of languages uses distal -KA- in three construction types: imperative, subjunctive, and indicative (6).

(6) Use of distal -KA- in imperative, subjunctive, and indicative

C.37	Ebuja	ka-ROOT-e sp-ka-root-e SP-ko-ka-ROOT-a	 (Fut)	(Toulmond 1937)
H.21	Kimbundu	ka-ROOT-e sp-a-ka-root-e SP-a-ka-ROOT-a	 (Fut)	(Chatelain 1888-89)
K.38	Mbukushu	ka-ROOT-e sp-ka-root-e		(Fisch 1977)

		mbo-SP-na-ka-ROOT-a	(Pst)	
L.41	Kaonde	ka-ROOT-i		(Broughall Woods 1924)
		SP-ka-ROOT-e		
		SP-a-ka-ROOT-a	(Pst)	
P.10	Ndendeule	ka-ROOT-a		(D. Ngonyani, p.c.)
		sp-ka-root-é		
		cha-SP-ka-ROOT-a	(Fut)	

Tunen A.44 differs from these languages, using a directional *-ka* in subjunctive (hortative), indicative, and infinitive constructions (7), but apparently not in the imperative.

(7) Use of distal -KA- in subjunctive, indicative, and infinitive

A.44	Tunen	SP-T-kā ROOT		(Dugast 1971)
		sp-ka-root		
		o-ka-ROOT	(Hort)	

Finally, there is a large set of languages spread across the central portion of the Bantu area that use distal -KA- in all four types of constructions (8).

(8) Use of distal -KA- in imperative, subjunctive, indicative, and infinitive

F.22	Nyamwezi	ka-ROOT-é		(Maganga and Schadeberg 1992)
		SP-ka-ROOT-é ??		
		SP-laa-ka-ROOT-ée		
		ku-ka-ROOT-a	(Fut)	
K.11	Chokwe	ka-ROOT-e		(Martins 1990; White 1947)
		SP-ka-ROOT-e		
		mu-SP-ka-ROOT-a		
		ku-ka-ROOT-a	(MedF)	
K.13	Luchazi	ka-ROOT-e		(White 1947)
		SP-ka-ROOT-e		
		SP-ka-ROOT-a		
		ku-ka-ROOT-a	(MedF)	
K.14	Lwena	ka-ROOT-e		(Horton 1949; White 1947)
		SP-ka-ROOT-e		
		na-SP-ka-ROOT-a		
		ku-ka-ROOT-a	(MedF)	

K.19	Nganguela	ka-ROOT-e		(Lecomte 1938)
		SP-ka-ROOT-e		
		SP-ka-ROOT-a		
		ku-ka-ROOT-a	(Fut)	
K.22	Lunda	ka-ROOT-e		(White 1947;
		SP-a-ka-ROOT-e		Fisher [1963])
		SP-a-ka-ROOT-a		
		ku-ka-ROOT-a	(MedF)	
K.33	Kwangari	ka-ROOT-e		(Dammann 1957)
		SP-ka-ROOT-e		
		na-SP-ka-ROOT-a ??		
		ku-ka-ROOT-a	(Fut)	
L.31a	Luba-Kasayi	ka-SP-ROOT-e		(Willems 1988)
		SP-ka-ROOT-e		
		SP-ká-ROOT-i		
		ka-ka-ROOT-a	(Pst)	
L.33	Luba-Shaba	ka-SP-ROOT-e		(Munyarugero 1975;
		???		Gillis 1973)
		SP-a-ká-ROOT-íde		
		ku-ka-ROOT-a	(Pst)	
L.35	Sanga	ka-ROOT-e		(Roland 1937)
		SP-ka-ROOT-e		
		SP-ka-ROOT-a		
		ku-ka-ROOT-a	(ImF)	
N.31	Chewa	ka-ROOT-e		(Watkins 1937;
		SP-ka-ROOT-e		Hetherwick 1914)
		SP-ka-ROOT-a		
		ku-ka-ROOT-a	(Fut)	
R.21	Kwanyama	ka-ROOT-e		(Turvey et al. 1977;
		SP-ka-ROOT-e		Brincker 1891)
		SP-ka-ROOT-a		
		ku-ka-ROOT-a	(Fut)	
R.31	Herero	ka-ROOT-e		(Hendrikse 1981)
		SP-ka-ROOT-e		
		SP-ka-ROOT-a		
		ku-ka-ROOT-a	(Fut)	

These data reflect an implicational relationship among the types of constructions in which distal -KA- can be found. Use in the infinitive always implies use in the imperative and, with the sole exception of Nyungwe N.43, in the indicative, while use in the indicative always implies use in the subjunctive. Except for a few languages in the northern and central eastern areas (sole exception: Lala M.52, but this may be a lack of descriptive completeness in Madan 1908a) and for Tunen A.44 in the northwest, use in the subjunctive implies use in the imperative. Schematically, the implicational relationships can be displayed as follows:

Imperative ← ← ← Infinitive
⇑ ⇓
Subjunctive ← Indicative

As important as the apparent implicational relationship is the fact that the overwhelming majority of the languages use distal -KA- in the imperative, suggesting that this may have been the primary point of origin of this marker for most languages. However, six of eight languages not permitting use of distal -KA- in the imperative occur in the east, indicating a different possible origin in the subjunctive.

4. Source(s) of distal -KA-

Distal -KA- constructions are often given a reading "go and V". Given this motional quality, a likely source would appear to be a verb of movement. Tunen A.44 provides an example of a language which appears to derive an "itive" (direction away)[3] -KA- from the verb "go". According to Dugast (1971), Tunen has two directional constructions, one indicating movement away (9a), the other movement towards (9b), the speaker.

(9) Tunen A.44 (Dugast 1971)
a. SP T-*ka* (OBJ) ROOT — movement away — [< -ákan 'go']
b. SP T-nda (OBJ) ROOT — movement towards

Dugast (1971:253) proposes that the -ka of (9a) "est sans doute une contraction du verbe 'aller', -ákan." This origin-in-a-verb-of-motion hypothesis finds support in two areas. First, directional marking through the use of "go" verbs can be found in other Southern Bantoid languages of northern Cameroon. For example, in Tikar (10), we can see the origins of a comparable construction in which the auxiliary verb still maintains the sense "leave". And Hyman (1981:69) indicates for Noni (11) that "ègɛ̄ǹ '& went' is a directional verb which is required to indicate motion towards [a place]." A similar construction is found in Oku (12) and Ghomala?-Bamileke (13), both Grassfields Bantu languages.

[3] The term "itive" (< Lat. *ire* 'go') was apparently coined and first used by Schadeberg (1990).

(10) Tikar (Stanley 1991)

à	kèn-ϕ	kɔ'	nswi'	pyì	nywi
il	partir-Prf	botte	paille	tomber	corps

'Il est partie se jeter sur la botte de paille.'

(11) Noni [Beboid] (Hyman 1981)

bɔ́	cí	nɔ́ɔ̀	lewtɛ̀	ɛ̀gɛ̄ǹ	fɔ̀wǎy	[gɛn 'go']
3P	P2	FOC	run	& went	market	

'They ran to the market.'

(12) Oku [Grassfields, Ring] (B. Wamey, p.c.)

ɣene	ɲínɔ́	ndúu	əʊwěy	[ndú 'go']
3P	run.PROG	go.PROG	market	

'They are running to the market.'

(13) Ghomala?-Bamileke [Grassfields, Mbam-Nkam] (Nissim et al. 1977)

wáp	dʌ	tá	ǎ	yə	gɥə́	gɔ́	m	lɔ́ktà
ils	prendre-ACC	père	moi	celui	grand	aller	vers	hópital

'Ils ont emmené mon grand-père á l'hopital.' [gɔ́ 'go']

Second, a variety of narrow Bantu languages lend further support to a possible verbal source for distal -KA-. The verb *-kɛ́* 'go' is used in an itive role, similar to that noted in the southern Bantoid languages, in a past indicative in Basaa A.43 (14), in the present and imperative in Ewondo A.72 (15), and in the imperative in Ngombe C.41 (16). Note in both Basaa and Ngombe the obligatory presence of a locative following the motion verb.

(14) Basaa A.43 (B. Mbom, p. c.)

ŋ-kɛ̂	+	ì	+	Verb Root	'went to V'
PST-go		LOC			

(15) Ewondo A.72 (Redden 1979)

a.	mɑ-kə	tsá(b)	ndzaag		'I'm going to gather firewood'
	1S-go	gather	firewood		
b.	kə-lə̀	wa-wulu	á	ndzɔ́ŋ	'I'm going to gather firewood'
	go-?	2S-walk	LOC	road	

(16) Ngombe C.41 (Motingea 1996)
kɛ́ á loké maɗíbá 'va puiser l'eau' [-kɛ́ 'go']
go LOC puiser eau

Other "go" verbs also occur with itive uses. Mokpa D.10?? (17) uses the verb *-kɔ́ya* 'partir', Ntomba C.66 (18) the verb *-ta* 'aller, partir'; Lozi S.34 (19) the verb *-ya* 'go'.

(17) Mokpa D.10? (Motingea 1990)
a. ta ntsɔkɔ mbéyá 'appelle ta mère'
appelle ta mère ?

b. kô-tá-é ntsɔkɔ mbéyá 'va appeller ta mère'
va-appeller-FV ta mère ? [< -kɔ́ya 'partir']

(18) Ntomba C.66 (Gilliard 1928)
a. to-kos-e 'va prendre' [< -ta 'partir, aller']

b. yo-lamb-e biomba 'viens préparer la nourriture' [< -ya 'venir']

(19) Lozi S.34 (Gorman 1950)
a. mu-yo-bon-a 'go (Pl) and see' [< -ya 'go' + ku-INF]

b. mu-to-ng-a 'come (Pl) and get (it)' [< -ta 'come' + ku-INF]

As apparent from the examples in (18b) and (19b), the verb 'come' may also be used with a directional "ventive" sense. A further example is found in Eleku C.36g (20), in which the source verb *-ya* 'venir' develops a directional use, either itive or ventive.

(20) Eleku C.36g (Hulstaert 1982)
yǒ-koá mai 'viens/va chercher l'eau'
[yá + ǒ + koa]
come-LOC of place-get

Finally, in Luguru G.35 (21), the verb *-ká* 'go' is used to form a periphrastic itive indicative, while in Sakata C.34 (22) it occurs in an itive imperative.

(21) Luguru G.35 (Scheerder—Tastevin 1950)
na ye k-o-ka uku-gula kwa waHindi
et lui 3S-PR-aller INF-acheter chez Hindous
'et lui, il va (le) vendre chez les Hindous'

(22) Sakata C.34 (de Witte 1955)
káá pə 'ga geef' ['go give'] [-ká 'go']

These data suggest that use of a verb of motion, such as 'go' or 'come', in a periphrastic construction in order to indicate direction is and was a productive process in Bantu not limited to a particular motional verb. The data also reveal that certain languages required a locative particle or clitic following a verb of motion. In Eleku (20), this clitic is /ǒ/, a locative of place; in Basaa (14) it is /ǐ/. In Mabiha P.25 and Tumbuka N.21, locative clitics are also used following verbs of motion, as in (23) and (24), respectively.

(23) Mabiha P.25 (Harries 1940)

ŋ-gw-ena ku-ku-lihinga 'I am going to bathe.' [<-hena 'go']
1S-PR-go LOC-INF-bathe

(24) Tumbuka N.21 (Diocese of Mzuzu n.d.)

a. n-iza m(u)-ku-mu-phalira-ni 'I will come and tell you.'
1S-come LOC-INF-2P-tell-2P

b. wa-k(a)-iza ka-tola vingoma 'S/he came to get maize.'
3S-PST-come DIS-fetch maize

c. wa-ka-ya ka-tola vingoma 'S/he went to get maize.'

Notice in Tumbuka that verbs of motion may be followed either by the locativized infinitive with *mu-ku-* or by the distal infinitive in *ka-*. A similar case in Songye L.23 (25) is discussed by Stappers as follows: "Morfologisch is dit weer een T.4 van het werkwoord *kuya (gaan) dat in de infinitief niet voorkomt. Gevolgd door een infinitief met °ka- als prefix in plaats van °ku- duidt het de beweging aan." (Stappers 1964: 179) ["Morphologically, this is again a T.4 of the verb *kuya (to go) that does not occur in the infinitive. Followed by an infinitive with °ka- as prefix instead of °ku-, it indicates motion to." Translation—RB]

(25) Songye L.23 (Stappers 1964:179)

tufunínê tuyaa ka-kuná 'we gingen planten'
3P-be 3P-go KA-plant ['we were going to plant']

Willems (1988: 109) makes the same point about Luba-Kasayi L.31: "...après les verbes *kuya* ['go'] and *kuenda* ['go'] le prefixe de l'infinitif [i.e., *ku*] est souvent remplacé par *ka*." The imperative form may also occur without the verb of motion, but in this case it requires a final *-e* rather than *-a*, as a comparison of (26a) and (27) shows.

(26) Luba-Kasayi L.31 (Willems 1988: 109)

a. yâ ka-kuata nzò:lo 'va prendre une poule'
go LOC-catch chicken

b. nda ka-mòna, tung' 'va voir, dis'

(27) Luba-Kasayi L.31 (Willems 1988: 107)
ka-kuàt-e 'va prendre'

Willems also points out that "...parfois on entend la particule *ka* avec le sens de venir," as illustrated in (28).

(28) Luba-Kasayi L.31 (Willems 1988: 109)
ku:àngatè tshimuma etshi 'viens prendre ce fruit'
[ka-u-angat-e]
LOC-2S-take-FV fruit this

However, as the example in (28) clearly shows, this construction is not the same as that in (27), which has the sense of "go". The *ka-* in (28) appears in a construction which apparently cannot be preceded by a verb of motion and, more importantly, one which is followed by a subjunctive form in *-e*, a typical pattern in Bantu when verbs occur in sequence in the imperative. This indicates that the *ka-* of (28) had a verbal origin. Given the ventive use, the verb was most likely 'come'. The most probable form would have been *yaka* 'come (imp)', with eventual loss of the initial syllable. Compare, for example, Kela C.75 which, according to Forges (1977: 86), has *di-yà* 'to come' in normal use, but *-yaka* when used as an auxiliary. This latter is of particular relevance because it suggests that auxiliary constructions included a particle *ka* following the verb of motion 'come' and preceding the main verb root. Consequently, the evidence points towards not only a potential verbal origin for distal -KA-, but also a locative one in clitic *ka*.

Locative *ka-* in Bantu, unlike the common Bantu locative clitics PA, KU, and MU, is not widespread. Nevertheless, there are a small number of languages across the Bantu domain that have this clitic. Significant for the aims of this paper, this clitic appears as a directional locative—in some cases in opposition to locative *ku-* —and as an infinitive prefix. Gérard (1924:45), for example, describing Lebeo C.45, states that *ka* is a "préposition indiquant une relation de lieu" and is a "signe de l'infinitif" (29).

(29) Lebeo C.45 (Gérard 1924)
SP-ba ka-ROOT-a 'aller V'
want INF-Stem

Similarly, Harries (1959: 189) indicates that in Nyali D.33 "[t]he [verb] stem may take prefix *ka-* or *i-* in... verbal constructions corresponding to the uses of the infinitive."

(30) Nyali D.33 (Harries 1959)
asá ka-murá 'He has gone to the field.'
3S-go LOC-field

In Bushong C.83, according to Vansina (1959: 37) "[l]e locatif est un préfixe *á-* ou *ká-*." It is also an infinitival prefix (31).

(31) Bushong C.83 (Edmiston n.d.; Vansina 1959)
ba-wela ka-shahala mboka 'they are about to dig the road'
3P-be about to INF-hoe road

-KA- may also come to denote the purpose of the action, as in Sena N.44 (32).

(32) Sena N.44 (Anderson 1897)
w-a-enda ka-saka nkuni 's/he has gone to get firewood'
3S-PST-go LOC-look for firewood

Further evidence of locative *ka* in Bantu can be seen in Fang A.75 (33) and Lozi S.34 (34), Ombo C.69 (35), Gusii E.42 (36), and Luyana K.31 (37).

(33) Fang A.75 (Galley 1964)
ká 'á gauche; derriere'
kô 'á droite; devant'

(34) Lozi S.34 (Gorman 1950)
ka "used to express 'at, in, on' in phrases of time;
ku "used to express 'in the time of'"

(35) Ombo C.69 (Meeussen 1952)
a. bákindí kámị [< ká-amị 'LOC-mon']
'ils sont chez moi (ici)'

b. bákindí kamị [< ka-amị 'LOC-mon']
'ils sont chez moi (au loin)'

(36) Gusii E.42 (Whiteley 1960)
ká-i 'where' [< *-pí 'where']

(37) Luyana K.31 (Givón 1970)
a. i-ná-ká-kél-a 'I came, way over there.'
1S-PST-DIS-come-FV

b. i-ná-kú-kél-a 'I came, here.'

That an archaic locative *ka-* is found in Bantu should not be entirely unexpected. De Wolf (1971: 59) proposes reconstructing *ka locative-temporal for Proto-Benue-Congo, finding evidence of it in a variety of languages. Among Bantoid languages, one finds *ká/ka* indicating place or direction away/to in Mambila (Northern Bantoid; Meyer 1939-40), kə-r [kə́r] 'towards' in Tiv (Southern Bantoid; Abraham 1940), and káyər 'into' in Jarawa (Southern Bantoid; Lukas and Willms 1961).

Another aspect of the use of *ka*-, illustrated in Mabembe C.30 (38), provides further support for a locative analysis. In (38a), we see that in the imperative the *ka*- form may be preceded by a verb 'go', here *kɛndɛ́*. In (38b), on the other hand, we find what Motingea calls an "infinitif sans marque". He indicates that there cannot be two consecutive *ka*'s, and opts to gloss the one present as 'va', speculating "qu'il s'agit du phénomène d'haplologie" (p. 31). However, in a list of common verbs, including that for 'go', he does not list or discuss a verb stem *-ka*. The lack of consecutive *ka*-'s can be explained if we assume that the source of *ka*- here is not a verb, but rather a locative clitic that appeared only following verbs of motion, which could be deleted, leaving the *ka*- as the surface source of the sense "go and".

(38) Mabembe C.30 (Motingea 1991)

a. kɛndɛ́ ká-tóká `mái ó dzidziba
   va LOC-puiser eau á source
   'va puiser de l'eau á la source'

b. ká kɔlɔ́ na bangó
   va dire á eux
   'va leurs direm'

Other languages provide additional evidence of a verb of motion plus locative infinitive construction. Among them are Londo A.11 (39), Kimbundu H.21 (40), Sena N.44 (41), and Tumbuka N.21 (42).

With respect to the origins of distal -KA-, these data suggest that there were at least three different paths: 1) via a directional verb such as *-ka* or *-ta* 'go (away)' found in a periphrastic indicative construction, as, for example,

(39) Londo A.11 (Kuperus 1985) (Bruens 1948)

	(Kuperus 1985)	(Bruens 1948)
a. ka-lang-e	'go read'	'read'
b. nde ka-lang-e	'come on, read'	'go and read'

[nde 'go (imp)']

(40) Kimbundu H.21 (Chatelain [1888-89] [1964])
   ndé ka-sumb-e 'go and buy' [compare with the verb *-ia* 'go']

(41) Sena N. 44 (Anderson 1897)
   ndoko ka-m-pang-e 'Go and tell him.'
   go (IMP) LOC-3S-tell-FV [compare with the verb *-pita* 'go']

(42) Tumbuka N.21 (Diocese of Mzuzu n.d.)
luta-ni ku-ya ka-wona 'Go (pl.) and see.'
go-PL to-go LOC-see

in Tunen A.44; 2) via an imperative form of a verb 'go (away)' followed by a bare root in the subjunctive, as in Sakata C.34; or 3) via a locative clitic affixed to the main verb when preceded by a verb of motion, found in many languages. These possible paths are schematically represented in (43).

(43) Possible paths of evolution of distal -KA-
a. SP + *ka* STEM < Directional verb *-ka* 'go (away)'
b. *ka* ROOT-e < Imperative 'go' followed by subjunctive
IMP SUBJ
c. Vb_{dir} *ka*-ROOT-e < Locative affix following directional verb

The data also appear to suggest that distal -KA- was not fully established as such in Proto-Bantu. Rather, there appears to have been a creative potential for motional constructions, as evidenced by the wide variety in forms of 'go' and 'come' motion verbs that have been employed for this purpose and by the erratic areal use of this pattern in the northwest Bantoid/Bantu area. But such constructions must have still been transparent, both in composition and meaning. That is, *-ka* must have been one of several viable motion verbs and *ka-* a quasi-viable locative clitic. Furthermore, of the two languages in the northwestern area that have distal -KA- constructions, Londo A.11 and Tunen A.44, it is clear that distal -KA- in Tunen has a verbal origin, as in (43a), Londo either the imperative/ subjunctive (43b) or the locative one (43c), or both. Both of these cases can be accounted for as nascent forms in Proto-Bantu, culminating at a later time in relatively fixed forms.

Nevertheless, the issue of the origins of distal -KA- merits much additional investigation. Important evidence could be gleaned from a comparison of tonal behavior of -KA- forms, which has not been included here for two reasons. First, many data sources do not indicate tone. Second, there are often differences between surface tone and proposed underlying tone that is significant. Kuperus (1985), for example, suggests that Londo *ka-* has an underlying low tone, though it surfaces with a high tone. Which of these to use in a comparison is not readily apparent. Close comparison of -KA- usage in very similar areal groups should also lead to further insights.

5. Future -KA-

Like distal -KA-, the distribution of the future formative -KA- is widespread over the Bantu domain, as indicated by the mapping of its distribution in Map 3. In addition to future markers having the simple form *-ka-*, two other formatives, both having the general form *-Vka-*, are indicated on the map. In the central northern area of the Bantu domain, several languages occur with a future form -EKA-, as illustrated by the examples in (44).

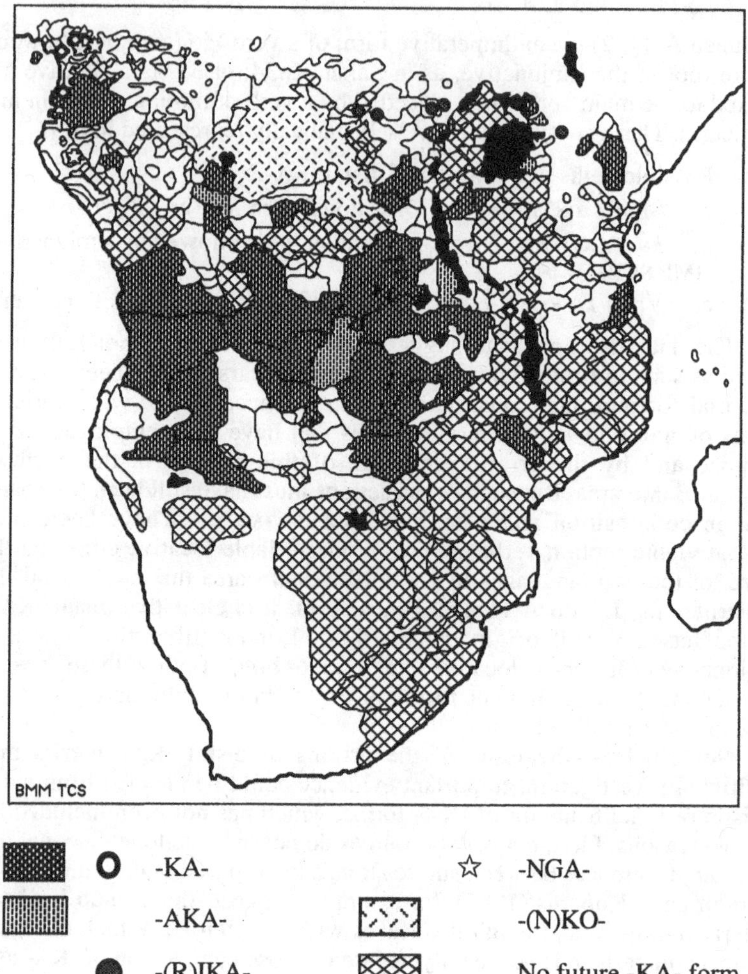

Map 3. Geographical distribution of future -KA-

(44) Future formatives in -EKA-

a.	C.50 Likile	SP- *éká-* ROOT- a	Fut	(Carrington 1977)
b.	D.14 Enya	SP- *eka-* ROOT- ea	Fut	(Spa 1973)
c.	D.33 Nyali	SP- *ɪká-* ROOT- a	Fut (Nr)	(Tucker and Bryan 1957)

That these *-Vka-* forms are not simple morphological units, at least historically, is suggested by the fact that other languages in the area have e- as the future formative (45) and by the fact that Likile, for example, constructs the negative future with *-ka-* and not *-eka-* (46).

(45) Future formatives in -E-

a.	C.53 Gesogo	SP- *e-* ROOT- a	Fut	(Harries 1955)
b.	J.51 Hunde	SP- *e-* ROOT- a	Fut (Hod)	(Mateene 1992)

(46) Likile C.50 future negative (Carrington 1977)
SP-*tí-ká*-ROOT -a

The remote future formative *-rika-* in Llogoori E.41 (47) is similar to the future formatives listed in (44) above. However, the difference in the vowel quality of the formative (1st degree of aperture vs. 2nd degree) and in the suffixal vowel— *-e* rather than *-a* —suggests a different origin. Since the the near future formative is *-ri-*, one can reasonably analyze *-rika-* as *-ri+ka-* (cf. Mould 1981 for a different analysis), which quite possibly could have been suppletive "be" plus a locative *ka-* complement. Compare this, for example, with Luchazi K.13 which has a remote future derived from suppletive "be" plus a *ka*-infinitive, SP-li ka-ROOT-a.

(47) Llogoori E.41 (Leung 1991)

SP-*rika*-ROOT -e   Fut (Rm)

A second subset of *-Vka-* formatives is comprised of those languages having a future formative -AKA-, as listed in (48).

(48) Future formatives in -AKA-

a.	D.28 Holoholo	SP- *àkà-* ROOT- a	Fut	(Coupez 1955)
	K.22 Lunda	SP- *aka-* ROOT- a	Fut (Rm/Dis)	(White 1947)
	M.41 Taabwa	SP- *aka-* ROOT- a	Fut	(De Beerst 1898)
b.	D.33 Nyali	SP- *aká-* ROOT- ɪ	Fut (Rm)	(Tucker and Bryan 1957)

c.	E.41	Llogoori	SP- *raka*-ROOT- e	Fut (Rm)	(Leung 1991)
	J.25	Kwaya	SP- *aka*-ROOT- e	Fut (Rm)	(Sillery 1920)
	J.32	Luhya	SP- *axá*-ROOT- e	Fut (Rm)	(Mould 1981)
	J.34	Saamia	SP- *axá*-ROOT- e	Fut (Rm)	(Mould 1981)

As with the -EKA- forms, the -AKA- forms appear to be analyzable into two parts. In Holoholo (48a), for example, the future negative occurs without the *-a-* (49a), while in Taabwa (49b) it is optional. Moreover, in Taabwa the present/near future is formed with the morpheme *-a-* alone (50a), while the future subjunctive has only *-ka-* (50b).

(49) Future negatives

a.	*a*-SP-*kà*-ROOT -*í*	Holoholo D.28	(Coupez 1955)
b.	*ta*-SP-(*a*)*ka*-ROOT-*a*	Taabwa M.41	(De Beerst 1898/1902)

(50) Taabwa M.41 (De Beerst 1898/1902)

a.	SP-*a*-ROOT-*a*	Pr/nr fut
b.	SP-*ka*-ROOT-*e*	Fut subj

The cluster of northeastern languages (48c) appear to have derived from the same original construction. Although Mould (1981) analyzes *-raka-* as a single formative, other evidence suggests separable parts. Llogoori, itself, has an indefinite future formative *-ra-*, which suggests that *-ka-* was a separate element combined with it to create a new tense formative. Second, Sumbwa F.23 has a pair of futures which make the same distinction (51).

(51) Sumbwa F.23 (Capus 1900)

a.	SP-*la*-*ka*-ROOT-*a*	Rm Fut
b.	SP-*la*- -ROOT-*e*	Mid Fut

Although there is no evidence in Lunda or Nyali, I suggest that they are also cases of two morphemes combining to form one formative. Hence, the *-Vka-* cases can be considered in conjunction with simple -KA- future forms.

The mapping of the areal distribution of future -KA- provides an important perspective on its wide range of occurrence in Bantu. However, equally as important for understanding its history and development is its distribution and use in the grammars of particular languages, as was the case with distal -KA-.

Close observation of the occurrence of future -KA-'s shows that -KA- occurs in four kinds of constructions with a future reading, usually some kind of post-hodiernal future; these include the indicative, subjunctive, infinitive, and imperative. The most pervasive use of this future -KA- is found in the indicative. In 30 of the 55 languages having a future -KA-, the -KA- is found only in the indicative (52). (For languages marked with an asterisk, the sources do not discuss other areas of the grammar. Hence, they may use *-ka-* elsewhere as well.)

(52) Languages having only indicative future -KA-

A.31	Bube	SP-(k)a-ROOT-a	RmF	(Justo 1991; Juanola 1890)
A.42	Bankon	SP-ɣá-ROOT-a	F	(Spellenberg 1922)
A.46	Nomaande*	SP-ká-SP ROOT SP-kà-SP ROOT	PoHoF IndefF	(Wilkendorf 1991)
A.62a	Nugunu*	SP-gaá-ROOT	HoF	(Gerhardt 1989)
B.52	Nzebi	SP-ká-ROOT	RmF	(Marchal-Nasse 1989)
B.85	Yansi	SP-N°-ka-ROOT	MedF	(Mayanga 1985)
C.31b	Libinza	SP-kV-ROOT-ì SP-kV-ROOT-á	MedF RmF	(van Leynseele 1976/77)
C.34	Sakata	SP-kə́-ROOT-a	RmF	(Ikamba 1987)
D.25	Lega	SP-ka-ROOT-a	RmF	(Waseka 1988)
D.26	Binja-Sud	SP-ká-ROOT-a	IndefF	(Hennin n.d.)
E.41	Llogoori*	SP-ra-ka-ROOT-e	RmF	(Leung 1991)
F.23	Sumbwa	SP-la-ka-ROOT-a	RmF	(Capus 1900)
J.25	Kwaya	SP-a-ka-ROOT-e	MedF	(Sillery 1920)
J.31	Masaba	SP-ka-ROOT-e	TomF	(Purvis 1907)
J.32	Luhya*	SP-a-xá-ROOT-e	RmF	(Mould 1981)
J.34	Saamia*	SP-a-xá-ROOT-e	RmF	(Mould 1981)
J.51	Hunde*	SP-ka-ROOT-a	HoF	(Mateene 1992)
J.61	Ha	SP-ro-ka-ROOT-a	VRmF	(van Sambeek n.d.)
K.19	Nganguela	SP-ka-ROOT-a	F	(Lecomte 1938)
K.31	Luyana	SP-ká-ROOT-a	NrF	(Givón 1970)
K.51	Mbala	SP-ga-ROOT-a	PoHoF	(Ndolo 1972)

L.41	Kaonde	SP-ká-ROOT-a	PoHoF	(Wright 1977)
L.62	Nkoya	SP-kà-ROOT-a	PoHoF	(Yukawa 1987)
M.42	Bemba	SP-kà-ROOT-a SP-ká-ROOT-a	TomF RmF	(Givón 1969)
M.52	Lala	SP-ka-ROOT-a	RmF	(Madan 1908a)
N.43	Nyungwe	SP-k^{h}a-ROOT-a	NrF	(Courtois 1888)
P.22	Mwera	ci-ka-SP-ROOT-e	MedF	(Harries 1950)
R.11	Umbundu	SP-ka-ROOT-a	F	(Schadeberg 1990; Valente 1964)
R.22	Ndonga	ota-SP-ka-ROOT-a	F	(Viljoen and Amakali 1978)
S.34	Lozi	SP-ka-ROOT-a	F	(Gorman 1950)

Several languages in the northwest have futures marked by -NGA- forms (53). In Ewondo A.72, however, there is also a future of the form SP-n-ROOT, suggesting that -NGA- forms may have been historically, at least, complex forms comprised of *-n-* and *-ka-*.

(53) Languages having indicative future -NGA-

A.62a	Nugunu	SP-ngà-ROOT	RmF	(Gerhardt 1989)
A.72	Ewondo	SP-ŋ-gâ-ROOT	RmF	(Redden 1979; Abega 1976)
B.31	Tsogho	SP-nga-ROOT	F	(Walker n.d.)

Several languages use future -KA- in two areas of the grammar. Benga A.34 and Kwanyama R.21 use it in both the indicative and infinitive (54), while six other languages use it in the indicative and the subjunctive (55).

(54) Languages having indicative and infinitve futures with -KA-

A.34	Benga	SP-ka-ROOT-a-ndi ka-ROOT-a	F–Ind F–Inf	(Pérez e Sorinas 1928)
R.21	Kwanyama	oha-SP-ka-ROOT-a oku-ka-ROOT-a	F–Ind F–Inf	(Turvey et al. 1977; Brincker 1891)

(55) Languages having future indicative and subjunctive with -KA-

E.55	Kamba	SP-ka-ROOT-a nĩ-SP-ka-ROOT-a SP-ka-ROOT-e	NrF–Ind RmF–Ind F–Subj	(Farnsworth 1957)
L.33	Luba-Shaba	SP-a-ka-ROOT-a SP-ka-ROOT-e	RmF–Ind F–Subj	(Munyarugero 1975; Gillis 1973)
M.41	Taabwa	SP-a-ka-ROOT-a SP-ka-ROOT-e	F–Ind F–Subj	(De Beerst 1898)
M.54	Lamba	SP-a-ka-ROOT-a SP-ka-ROOT-e	F–Ind F–Subj	(Doke 1938)
M.61	Lenje	SP-ka-no-ROOT-a SP-ka-ROOT-e	RmF–Ind F–Subj	(Madan 1908b)
M.63	Ila	SP-ka-ROOT-a SP-ka-ROOT-e	RmF–Ind F–Subj	(Smith [1964])

Seven languages extend use of the future formative -KA- to the infinitive (56) or to the imperative (57).

(56) Languages having future indicative, subjunctive, and infinitive

E.51	Gikuyu	SP-kā-ROOT-a SP-ka-ROOT-e gũ-ka-ROOT-a	RmF–Ind F–Subj F–Inf	(Barlow 1960; Gecaga 1960)
K.11	Chokwe	mu-SP-ka-ROOT-a SP-ka-ROOT-e ku-ka-ROOT-a	RmF–Ind F–Subj F–Inf	(Martins 1990; White 1947)
K.13	Luchazi	SP-ka-ROOT-a SP-ka-ROOT-e ku-ka-ROOT-a	RmF–Ind F–Subj F–Inf	(White 1947)
K.22	Lunda	SP-a-ka-ROOT-a SP-ka-ROOT-i ku-ka-ROOT-a	RmF–Ind F–Subj F–Inf	(Fisher 1963; White 1947)
L.34	Hemba	SP-ka-ROOT-a SP-ka-ROOT-anga SP-ka-ROOT-e ku-ka-ROOT-a	NrF–Ind RmF–Ind F–Subj F–Inf	(van der Meiren 1912)

L.35	Sanga	SP-ka-ROOT-a	F–Ind	Roland 1937)
		SP-ka-ROOT-e	F–Subj	
		ku-ka-ROOT-a	F–Inf	

(57) Languages having future indicative, subjunctive, and imperative

D.28	Holoholo	SP-a-ka-ROOT-a	F–Ind	(Coupez 1955)
		SP-ka-ROOT-e	F–Subj	
		ka-ROOT-é	F–Imp	

One language, Lwena K.14, exhibits use of future -KA- in all of the constructions (58).

(58) Languages having future indicative, subjunctive, imperative, and infinitive

K.14	Lwena	na-SP-ka-ROOT-a	RmF–Ind	(Horton 1949;
		SP-ka-ROOT-e	F–Subj	White 1947)
		ka-ROOT-e	F–Imp	
		ku-ka-ROOT-a	F–Inf	

This distribution of future -KA- across grammatical constructions, when plotted on a map (Map 4), shows the densest use to come in the south-central area of the Bantu domain.

These data, like those in the case of distal -KA- noted previously, again suggest an implicational relationship among future -KA- constructions across languages. In particular, the data indicate that use of -KA- in the infinitive or subjunctive always implies use in the indicative. Use of -KA- in the imperative implies use in the subjunctive. The drawing below summarizes these relationships schematically:

Indicative ← Subjunctive ← Imperative
↑
Infinitive

If correct, such an implicational relationship provides strong evidence that future -KA- originated in indicative constructions and only later spread to other constructions.

There are apparent exceptions to this claim. For example, in Tonga M.64, we find use of future -KA- only in the subjunctive (59).

(59) Tonga M.64 (Collins 1962)

watwaambila kuti tu-ka-bool-e

'the told us that we come the day after tomorrow'

However, if we look at formation of simple indicative futures, we find that both are relatively recent periphrastic constructions based on auxiliary *-ya* 'go' (near future) or *-zi* stem of 'come' [<-*zya*] (remote future) plus the infinitive. Quite likely, a simple indicative construction with formative -KA- was replaced by these periphrastic innovations.

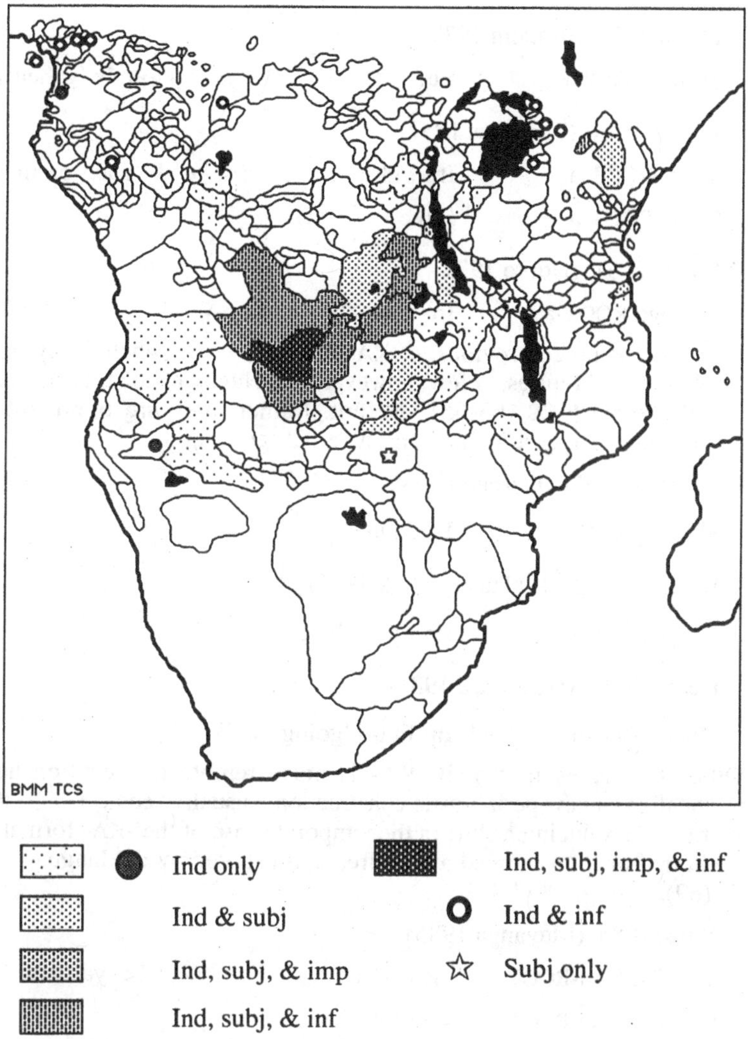

Map 4. Grammatical distribution of future -KA-

Determining the origins of future -KA-'s is even less certain than it was for distal -KA-. Nevertheless, there are several observations which may help in guiding us towards a solution. First, it can be seen from the examples in (60) to (62) that grammaticalized "go + V" constructions in Bantu tend to become imminent or near futures, though occasionally there are exceptions, as in Hunde J.51 (67).

(60) Duala A.24 (Ittmann 1939)

SP-m-ɛndɛ́ INF	Fut	[< -ɛndɛ 'gehen']

(61) Myene B.11 (Teisseres 1957)

SP-kɛ-ROOT-a	Im Fut	[< -kɛnd- 'aller, partir']
SP-be-ROOT-a	Fut	

(62) Mbala K.51 (Ndolo 1972)

SP-anga ROOT-a	Im Fut—'be going to V'	[< -ang- 'aller']

However, as noted previously, -KA- futures are overwhelmingly post-hodiernal "remote" futures. A few, however, like Nugunu A.62a, Kwanyama R.21, and Herero R.22 (63-65), are not. Rather, they are imminent or hodiernal futures, suggesting, perhaps, a verbal 'go' origin.

(63) Nugunu A.62a (Gerhardt 1989)

SP-gaá-ROOT	Hod Fut

(64) Kwanyama R.21 (Turvey et al. 1977)

SP-ka-ROOT-a	Im Fut—'be going to V'

(65) Herero R.31 (Hendrikse 1981)

SP-ka-ROOT-a	Im Fut—'going to V'

Other languages in which -KA- is not a remote future often have grammaticalized a new periphrastic construction—usually "come + V"—as a remote future, producing a shift in the temporal sense of the -KA- formative to a hodiernal or more immediate future, as illustrated by the languages in (66) to (69).

(66) Yansi B.85 (Mayanga 1985)

a.	SP-N°-ya-ROOT	Rm Fut	[< -ya 'venir']
b.	SP-N°-ka-ROOT	Im Fut	

(67) Hunde J.51 (Mateene 1992)

a.	SP-génde-ROOT-a	Post-Hod Fut	[< -gɛnd- 'aller']
b.	SP-ka-ROOT-a	Hod Fut	

(68) Nyungwe N.43 (Courtois 1888)

a.	SP-dza-ROOT-a	Rm Fut	[< -dza 'vir']
b.	SP-k^ha-ROOT-a	Nr Fut	

(69) Mwera P.22 (Harries 1950)

a.	ci-SP-jie-ROOT-a	Rm Fut	[< -ji- 'come']
b.	ci-ka-SP-ROOT-e	Med Fut	

Other evidence indicates that some future -KA-'s derived from *ka-* infinitive prefixes. In Bushong, for example, futures are constructed from the a *ka-* infinitive (70). In the remote future, the verb itself is repeated in its infinitival form. Subsequent loss of the first root would produce the kind of future construction evident elsewhere.

(70) Bushong C.83 (Edmiston n.d.; Vansina 1959)

a.	SP-ROOT-ká-ROOT	Rm Fut	
b.	SP-wela ká-ROOT	Im Fut	[< -wela 'want']

And in Tumbuka N.21 a ventive future is formed from auxiliary 'come' plus a *ka-* infinitive (71). The potential loss of *-iza-* in further grammaticalization would again lead to the common -KA- future form found elsewhere.

(71) Tumbuka N.21 (Diocese of Mzuzu 1970)

SP-iza-ka-ROOT-a Ventive Fut [< -iza 'come' + ka- infinitive]

The discussion so far has pointed to possible origins of -KA- futures in auxiliary verbs or *ka-* infinitives, scenarios similar to those discussed for distal -KA-. However, other observations suggest that a future -KA- is, unlike distal -KA-, reconstructable for Proto-Bantu. First, whereas distal -KA- is almost entirely absent from the northwest Bantu area, future -KA- is found in a number of languages in this area: Bubi A.31, Benga A.34, Bankon A.42, Ewondo A.72, Fang A.75; Nzebi B.52, Yansi B.85; Libinza C.31b, Sakata C.34. Second, unlike the case with distal -KA-, some non-Bantu Southern Bantoid languages also posess a -KA- future. Tikar (72) is one such case. Nomaande and Nugunu (Yambasa), (73) and (74), respectively, are two others. They are of potential interest because of their location and classification. Although classified as Bantu A.46 and A.62, respectively, by Guthrie, they have been reclassified as part of the Mbam group (Southern Bantoid) in Watters and Leroy (1989).

(72) Tikar (Stanley 1991)

à kà	yɛn-kà	ɓyin	'Il vous aura vu.'
il FUT	voir-PRF F	vous	

(73) Nomaande A.46 or Mbam (Wilkendorf 1991)

u-ká-a	námb-áka	'Elle (le) préparera (demain).'
3S-RmF-3S	préparer-DUR	

(74) Nugunu A.62a or Mbam (Gerhardt 1989)

SP gaá Root	Fut (Tod or Tom)
SP nga Root	Fut (remote)

The fact that two of the languages in this classificatory border area have -KA- futures adds further support to the hypothesis that the form can be reconstructed for Proto-Bantu. However, this does not imply that all languages currently possessing a future -KA- inherited it from Proto-Bantu.

6. Distal vs future -KA-

In separating distal from future uses of -KA-, it seems highly likely that distal -KA- originated in imperative constructions, post-hodiernal future -KA- in simple indicative constructions. This hypothesis finds support not only in the survey and discussion developed previously, but also in the facts associated with individual languages. In a number of languages that have both distal and future -KA-'s, there is a clearcut distinction between them. In Nyungwe N.43 (75), for example, distal -KA- occurs only in the imperative, future -KA- only in the indicative. Neither occurs in the subjunctive.

Sanga L.35 and Nkoya L.62, (76) and (77), respectively, permit distal -KA- in both the imperative and the subjunctive, but only future -KA- in the simple indicative.

(75) Nyungwe N.43 (Courtois 1888)

a. k^ha-gon-e 'vá dormir' ['go sleep']

b. *a-ka-Root-e

c. a-k^ha-sung-a 'guardarei' ['he will stand guard']

(76) Sanga L.35 (Roland 1937)

a. ka-dy-e 'va manger (ailleurs)'

b. a-ka-dy-e 'qu'il aille manger (ailleurs)'

c. u-ka-pot-a 'il achètera'

(77) Nkoya L.62 (Yukawa 1987)

a. ka-mu-mónesh-é 'Show him' (somewhere else)

b. u-ka-mu-mônesh-e 'That you show him' (somewhere else)

c. ba-ka-môn-a 'They will see' (post-hodiernal future)

Lala M.52, which apparently does not allow distal -KA- in the imperative, does use it in the subjunctive, but only future -KA- in the indicative (78).

(78) Lala M.52 (Madan 1908a)

a. ??ka-Root-e

b. n-ka-tem-e 'I should go and cut'

c. tu-ka-tem-a 'We will cut (some time)'

(79) Nganguela (Lecomte 1938)

	Distal -KA-	*Future -KA-*	
a.	ka-lek-e 'vai dizer'		Imperative
b.	tu-ka-nw-e 'vamos beber cerveja'		Subjunctive
c.	a-ka-handek-a 'êle irá falar'	va-ka-ts-a 'hão-de morrer'	Indicative
d.	ku-ka-land-a 'ir comprar'		Infinitive

Overlap of the two uses in particular languages also supports different points of origin. In Nganguela K.19 (79 above), the use of distal -KA- has spread through the grammar, so that it occurs in the imperative, subjunctive, indicative, and infinitive, whereas future -KA- (79c) is restricted to the indicative.

In Gikuyu E.51 and Kamba E.55, on the other hand, the reverse has occurred. Future -KA- has spread to the subjunctive and infinitive, while distal -KA- has been retained only in the subjunctive (80).

(80) Gikuyu E.51 (Barlow 1960)

	Distal -KA-	*Future -KA-*	
a.		gũ-ka-negeni-a 'to upbraid (at a later time)'	Infinitive
b.	ũ-ga-tem-e '(that) you cut the tree (dist)'	ũ-ga-tem-e '(that) you cut the tree (later)'	Subjunctive
c.		nĩ-n-ga-gwat-a 'I will take hold (post-hoF)'	Indicative

In Ndonga R.22, the two uses overlap in the subjunctive, but are distinct in the imperative and indicative (81).

(81) Ndonga (Viljoen and Amakali 1978)

	Distal -KA-	*Future -KA-*	
a.	ka-long-e 'go work'		Imperative
b.	u-ka-land-e '(that) you should go and buy'	a-ka-dhim-e '(that) he extinguish the fire'	Subjunctive
c.		ota-ndi-ka-dhan-a 'I will play'	Indicative

Extensive spread of the use of both distal and future -KA-'s through the grammar is found in the southwest area of Bantu. In Luba-Shaba L.33, Sanga L.35, Chokwe K.11, Luchazi K.13, and Lunda K.22, the overlap is complete except for the imperative, where no future use is found. Examples from Sanga (82) illustrate this discrete (i.e., non-overlapping) use of the two.

(82) Sanga (Roland 1937)

	Distal -KA-	*Future -KA-*	
a.	ka-dy-e 'va manger (ailleurs)'		Imperative
b.	a-ka-dy-e 'qu'il aille manger'	a-ka-pot-e 'qu'il achète [plus tard]'	Subjunctive

c.	n-ka-dy-a 'je vais manger (ailleurs)'	u-ka-pot-a 'il achètera'	Indicative
d.	ku-ka-dy-a 'aller manger (ailleurs)'	ku-ka-sak-a 'vouloir [futur]'	Infinitive

In Lwena K.14 (83), the overlap of distal and future is complete.

(83) Lwena K.14 (Horton 1949; White 1947)

	Distal -KA-	*Future -KA-*	
a.	ka-mu-lwez-e 'show him (elsewhere)'	ka-mu-lwez-e 'show him (later)'	Imperative
b.	ngu-ka-ci-ling-e 'that I do it (elsewhere)'	ngu-ka-ci-ling-e 'that I do it (later)'	Subjunctive
c.	na-va-ka-lim-a 'they will hoe (later at some other place)'	na-va-ka-ci-ling-a 'they will do it (post-hoF)'	Indicative
d.	ku-ka-has-a 'to be able (elsewhere)'	ku-ka-has-a 'to be able (later)'	Infinitive

Significantly, use of the two -KA-'s appears to be, in all of the languages mentioned, mutually exclusive; they cannot be used together in the same expression, nor have the two meanings merged into one morpheme expressing, simultaneously, both meanings. However, there are two languages—Kimbundu H.21 and Kimatuumbi P.13—in which the two senses are combined in just one *-ka-* morpheme. Chatelain ([1964]: 47), for example, states that the indicative future with *-ka-* "indica um tempo futuro com mudança de logar mais distante que o futuro II" (84). A similar statement could be made for Kimatuumbi (85).

(84) Kimbundu H.21 (Chatelain [1964])

	Distal and future -KA-	
a.	tu-a-ka-bang-e 'that we will [go] make'	Subjunctive
b.	tu-a-ka-bang-a 'we will [go] make'	Indicative
c.	ndé ka-sumb-e 'go and buy'	Imperative

(85) Kimatuumbi P.13 (Odden 1996)

Distal and future -KA-

a. nį-ka-tuúmbuk-e — Subjunctive
'I should go fall'

b. nį-ka-túumbuk-a — Indicative
'I will go fall'

In sum, comparison of distal and future -KA- has pointed towards different initial uses in the grammars of Bantu languages. Subsequently, either distal or future use, or both, has spread to other constructions, eventually leading in some languages to complete overlap of the two forms.

7. Summary and directions for future work

It has been my intent in this paper to provide a general overview of the distribution and use of the form -KA- in two of its various functions, as distal marker and as future formative. While the histories of both are complex, the discussion has illuminated several general patterns. First, the grammatical distribution of distal -KA- suggests an origin in an imperative construction. Nevertheless, the somewhat different results in eastern Africa suggest the possibility of a subjunctive origin there. In either case, although there appear to be several potential sources of distal -KA-, -KA 'go (away)' as the first verb of a complex imperative-subjunctive serial construction or KA- as a locative clitic following a directional verb must be considered the most likely sources. The near lack of distal use in the northwest and its widespread occurrence in the south-central Bantu area suggest that it was nascent in Proto-Bantu, not yet a true verbal affix. Further insight into the origins of distal -KA- may come from a consideration and comparison of the range of distribution of languages having a set of aspectual-like markers in a distinct "limitative" category and those having distal -KA-.[4]

Second, both the geographical and grammatical distributions suggest that a future -KA- can be reconstructed for Proto-Bantu. Not only is it widespread in Bantu, but it occurs in many languages of the northwest area. The data also lead us to conlcude that it originated in a simple indicative construction. Nevertheless, some -KA- futures clearly arose from other sources at a later time. For individual languages many details not considered in this general survey remain to be examined. Some languages have two future morphemes of the form -KA-, differing usually in tone or prenasalization. How are these related? Does near versus remote fıture use indicate two original sources, or simply language internal differentiation of

[4] I thank Larry Hyman and Jean-Marie Hombert for pointing out the potential significance of such a comparison.

one? Which is cognate with -KA- in languages that have only one future -KA- morpheme?

This overview provides a first step in mapping out the historical evolution of distal and future -KA-'s. What is needed to clarify and verify this rather coarse initial picture of -KA- is more complete and accurate data, including tonal information, from individual languages. Evidence needs to be adduced as well to determine the nature and role of borrowing in promulgating spread of these morphemes. In addition, distal -KA- needs to be compared with the distribution and use of the so-called "subsecutive" -KA-, which seems to be quite common in those areas where distal -KA- is less-commonly found.

References

Abega, P. 1976. *L'Organisation du Verbe Ewondo*. Yaounde: Université de Yaounde.

Abraham, R. C. 1940. *The Principles of Tiv*. London: Crown Agents for the Colonies.

Anderson, W. G. 1897. *An Introductory Grammar of the Sena Language*. London: Society for Promoting Christian Knowledge.

Barlow, A. Ruffell. 1960. *Studies in Kikuyu Grammar and Idiom*. Edinburgh: William Blackwood & Sons, Ltd.

Batibo, Herman. 1985. *Le kesukuma: phonologie, morphologie*. Paris: Editions Recherche sur les Civilizations.

Botne, Robert. 1998. The evolution of future tenses from serial 'say' constructions in Central Eastern Bantu. *Diachronica* XV, 2.

Bourquin, Walther. 1923. *Neue Ur-Bantu-Worstämme*. Berlin: Dietrich Reimer. (Reprinted 1969, Nendeln, Liechtenstein: Kraus Reprint.)

Brincker, P. H. 1891. *Lehrbuch des Oshikuanjama*. Stuttgart and Berlin: W.P. Spemann.

Broughall Woods, R. E. 1924. *A short Introductory Dictionary of the Kaonde Language*. London: The Religious Tract Society.

Bruens, A. 1948. Het Londo. *Kongo-Overzee* 14:87-106.

Capus, A. 1900. Grammaire de shisumbwa. *Zeitschrift für afrikanische und oceanische Sprachen* 3: 1-123.

Carrington, J. F. 1977. Esquisse morphologique de la langue likile (Haut-Zaire). *Africana Linguistica VII*, 65-88. Annales — Sciences Humaine N° 90. Tervuren: Musée Royal de l'Afrique Centrale.

Chatelain, Heli. 1888-89. *Grammatica Elementar do Kimbundu*. Geneva. Reprinted Gregg Press International, 1964.

Collins, B. 1962. *Tonga Grammar*. London and Salisbury, Zambia: Longmans.

Coupez, André. 1955. *Esquisse de la langue Holoholo*. Sciences de l'Homme N° 12. Tervuren: Musée Royal du Congo Belge.

Courtois, Victor José. 1888. *Elementos de Grammatica Tetense*. Moçambique: Imprensa Nacional.

Dammann, Ernst. 1957. *Studien zum Kwangali*. Hamburg: Cram, De Gruyter & Co.

De Beerst, Gust. 1898/1902. Essai de grammaire tabwa. *Zeitschrift für afrikanische und oceanische Sprachen* 2: 271-383.

De Wolf, Paul. 1971. *The Noun Class System of Proto-Benue-Congo*. The Hague and Paris: Mouton.

de Witte, P. 1955. *Taalstudie Bij de Sakata*. (Annales, Sciences de l'Homme N° 10). Tervuren: Musée Royal du Congo Belge.

Diocese of Mzuzu. 1970. *Tumbuka Grammar*.

Doke, Clement M. 1938. *Textbook of Lamba Grammar*. Johannesburg: Witwatersrand University Press.

Dugast, Idelette. 1971. *Grammaire du tunen*. Paris: Editions Klincksieck.

Edmiston, Althea Brown. n.d. *Grammar and Dictionary of the Bushonga or Bukuba Language*. Congo Mission: Congo-Belge.

Farnsworth, E. M. 1957. *A Kamba Grammar*. n.p.

Fisch, Maria. 1977. *Einführung in die Sprach der Mbukushu*. Windhoek: S.W.A. Wissenschaftlichen Gesellschaft.

Fisher, M. K. 1963. *Lunda-Ndembu Handbook*. Lusaka: Northern Rhodesia Publications Bureau.

Forges, Germaine. 1977. *Le kela: langue bantoue du Zaire*. Paris: SELAF.

Galley, Samuel. 1964. *Dictionnaire Fang-Français et Français-Fang suivi d'une grammaire fang*. Neuchatel: Éditions Henri Messeiller.

Gecaga, B. Mareka. *A Short Kikuyu Grammar*. Nairobi: Macmillan Kenya.

Gerhardt, Phyllis. 1989. Le temps en Nugunu. In *Descriptions de langues camerounaises*, Daniel Barreteau and Robert Hedinger (eds), 315-361. Paris: Orstrom.

Gérard, P. 1924. *La langue lebeo: Grammaire et vocabulaire*. Bruxelles: Vromant & Co.

Gilliard, L. 1928. Grammaire synthétique de lontomba. Bruxelles: Éditions de l'Essorial.

Gillis, A. 1973. *Mwendela Kiluba: Grammaire pour debutants*. Gent: Henri Dunantloan.

Givón, Talmy. 1969. Studies in Chibemba and Bantu linguistics. *Studies in African Linguistics*, supplement 3.

Givón, Talmy. 1970. *The Si-Luyana Language: A preliminary linguistic description*. Lusaka: Institute for Social Research, University of Zambia.

Gorman, W. A. R. 1950. *Simple Silozi: A guide for beginners*. London: Longmans Green and Co.

Guthrie, Malcolm. 1967-1971. *Comparative Bantu* (4 volumes). Farnborough: Gregg International Publishers, Ltd.

Hadermann, Pascale. 1996. Formes verbales complexes et grammaticalisation de la structure Infinitif + $\text{Verbe}_{\text{conjugués}}$ dans quelques languages bantoues de zones B et H. *Studies in African Linguistics* 25, 2: 155-170.

Harries, Lyndon. 1940. An Outline of Mawiha Grammar. *African Studies* 14: 91-146, 410-433.

Harries, Lyndon. 1950. *A Grammar of Mwera*. Johannesburg: Witwatersrand University Press.

Harries, Lyndon. 1955. Grammar of Gesogo. *Kongo-Overzee* 21: 420-440.

Harries, Lyndon. 1959. Nyali, a Bantoid language. *Kongo-Overzee* 25: 174-205.

Heese, Paul. 1920. Die Sango-Sprache. *Zeitschrift für Eingeborenen-Sprachen* 10: 87-106.

Hendrikse, H. 1981. *The Concepts Mood and Sentence Type in a Herero Grammar with Theoretical Aims*. Grahamstown: Dept. of African Languages, Rhodes University.

Hennin, R. n.d. *Kizimba—Binja-Sud*. n.p.

Hetherwick, Alexander. 1914 *A Practical Manual of the Nyanja Language*. Nyasaland and Northern Rhodesia: The African Lakes Corp., Ltd.

Horton, A. E. 1949. *A Grammar of Luvale*. Johannesburg: Witwatersrand University Press.

Hulstaert, G. 1982. *Esquisse de la langue des eleku*. Bandundu: CEEBA Publications.

Hyman, Larry M. 1981. *Noni Grammatical Structure*. SCOPIL N° 9. Los Angeles: Department of Linguistics, UCLA.

Ikamba, Monse. 1987. *Elements de grammaire sakata*. Bandundu: CEEBA Publications.

Ittmann, Johannes. 1939. *Grammatik des Duala*. Berlin. Reprint, Kraus, Nendeln, Liechtenstein, 1969.

Juanola, Joaquín. 1890. Grammatica de la Lengua Bubi—Fernando Poo. Madrid: Imprenta de A. Pérez Dubrill.

Justo, Bolekia Boleká. 1991. *Curso de lengua Bubi*. Malabo: Centro Cultural Hispano-Guineano.

Kamba Muzenga, J. G. 1980. *Esquisse de grammaire kete*. Annales, Sciences Humaines N° 104. Tervuren: Musée Royal de l'Afrique Centrale.

Kuperus, Juliana. 1982. The morphology of (Ba-)Londo verb tenses. In *Le verbe bantou*, G. Guarisma, G. Nissim, and J. Voorhoeve (eds), 19-56. Paris: SELAF.

Kuperus, Juliana. 1985. *The Londo Word*. Annales, Sciences Humaines N° 119. Tervuren: Musée Royal de l'Afrique Centrale.

Lecomte, L. 1938. *Elementos de Gramática Ganguela*. Collocated by Domingos Vieira Baião. Lisboa: Centro dos Estudos Fililógicos.

Leung, Elizabeth Woon-Yee. 1991. The tonal phonology of Llogoori: A study of Llogoori verbs. *Working Papers of the Cornell Phonetics laboratory* N° 6.

Lukas, J. & A. Willms. 1961. Outline of the Language of the Jarawa in Northern Nigeria (Plateau Province). *Afrika und Übersee* 45,2: 1-66.

Madan, A. C. 1908a. *Lala-Lamba Handbook*. Oxford: The Clarendon Press.

Madan, A. C. 1908b. *Lenje Handbook*. Oxford: The Clarendon Press.

Maganga, Clement and Thilo C. Schadeberg. 1992. *Kinyamwezi: Grammar, Texts, Vocabualary*. Köln: Rüdiger Köppe Verlag.

Mangulu, Motingea. 1990. Esquisse de la langue des Mokpa (Haut-Zaire). *Afrika und Übersee* 73: 67-100.

Mangulu, Motingea. 1991. Notes Mabembe. *Frankfurter Afrikanistische Blätter* 3: 14-34.

Mangulu, Motingea. 1995. Esquisse de l'ebango: langue bantoue du groupe C.40. *Afrikanische Arbeitspapiere* 41: 5-49.

Mangulu, Motingea. 1996. *Étude comparative des langues ngiri de l'entre Ubangi-Zaire*. Leiden: Research School CNWS.

Marchal-Nasse, Colette. 1989. De la phonologie à la morphologie de nzebi, language bantoue du Gabon. Thése de doctorat, Université Libre de Bruxelles.

Martins, João Vicente. 1990. Elementos de Gramática de Utchokwe. Lisboa: Instituto de Investigação Científica Tropical.

Mateene, Kahombo. 1992. *Essai de grammaire du kihunde: syntaxe, morphologie, et phonologie melangés*. Munster:

Mayanga, Tayeye. 1985. *Grammaire Yansi*. Bandundu: CEEBA Publications.

Meeussen, A. E. 1952. *Esquisse de la langue ombo*. Annales — Sciences de l'Homme, Linguistique N° 4. Tervuren: Musée Royal du Congo Belge.

Meeussen, A. E. 1954. *Linguistische Schets van het Bangubangu*. Sciences de l'Homme N° 5. Tervuren: Musée Royal du Congo Belge.

Meeussen, A. E. 1967. Bantu Grammatical Reconstructions. *Africana Linguistica III*, pp. 79-121.

Meeussen, A. E. 1969. *Bantu Lexical Reconstructions*. Tervuren: Musée Royal de l'Afrique Centrale.

Meeussen, A. E. 1971. *Elements de grammaire lega*. Archives d'Ethnographie N° 15. Tervuren: Musée Royal de l'Afrique Centrale.

Meinhof, Carl. 1910. *Introduction to the Phonology of the Bantu Languages*. Berlin. Trans. and rev. by N. J. v. Warmelo. Berlin: Dietrich Reimer, 1932.

Meyer, Emmi. 1939-40. Mambila-Studie. *Zeitschrift für Eingeborenen-Sprachen* 30: 1-52, 117-48, 210-32.

Mould, Martin. 1981. Greater Luyia. In *Studies in the Classification of Eastern Bantu Languages*, T. H. Hinnebusch, D. Nurse, and M. Mould, 181-261. Hamburg: Helmut Buske Verlag.

Munyarugero, Nkiko. 1975. *Esquisse grammaticale de la langue luba-shaba*. Lubumbashi: Université Nationale du Zaire.

Ndolo, Pius. 1972. *Essai sur la tonalite et la flexion verbale du gimbala.* (Archives d'Anthropologie N° 19). Tervuren: Musé Royal de l'Afrique Centrale.

Odden, David. 1996. *The Phonology and Morphology of Kimatuumbi.* Oxford: The Clarendon Press.

Pérez Gaspar & Lorenzo Sorinas. 1928. Gramatica de la Lengua Benga. Madrid: Editorial del Corazón de María.

Purvis, John B. 1907. *A Manual of Lumasaba Grammar.* London: Society for Promoting Christian Knowledge.

Ranger, A. Sidney B. 1928. *Chinsenga Handbook.* London: Sheldon Press.

Redden, James E. 1979. *A Descriptive Grammar of Ewondo.* Occasional Papers in Linguistics #4. Carbondale: Dept. of Linguistics, SIU.

Roland, Hadelin. 1937. Grammaire de la langue kisanga. Missions Benedictines: Abbaye de Saint-André les Bruges.

Schadeberg, Thilo C. 1990. *A Sketch of Umbundu.* Köln: Rüdiger Köppe Verlag.

Scheerder & Tastevin. 1950. Les waluguru. *Anthropos* 45: 241-286.

Sillery, Anthony. 1932. A sketch of the Kikwaya language. *Bantu Studies* 6: 273-308.

Smith, Edwin. 1907. *A Handbook of the Ila Language.* Oxford. Reprinted Gregg Press Inc., 1964.

Spa, Jaap J. 1973. *Phonologie generative d'une langue bantoue.* Archives d'Anthropologie N° 20. Tervuren: Musée Royal de l'Afrique Centrale.

Spellenberg, Friedrich. 1922. *Die Sprache der Bo oder Bankon in Kamerun.* Berlin. Reprinted Kraus , 1969.

Stanley, Carol. 1991. Description morpho-syntaxique de la langue tikar. Epinay sur Seine and Yaoundé: Société Internationale de Linguistique.

Stappers, Leo. 1964. *Morfologie van het Songye.* Annales — Linguistique N° 51. Tervuren: Musés Royal de l'Afrique Centrale.

Stappers, Leo. 1986. Kanyok: Eine Sprachskizze. *Afrikanistische Arbeitspapiere* (sondernummer).

Stirnimann, Hans. 1983. Praktische Grammatik der Pangwa-Sprache. Freiburg: Universitätsverlag Freiburg Schweiz.

Teisseres, U. 1957. *Methode pratique pour apprendre l'Omyenez* (2nd. ed., rev. by V. Dubois). Paris: Société des Missions Evangelique de Paris.

Toulmond, Léon. 1937. Essai de grammaire d'ebudja. *Congo* 18,2: 361-376, 481-525.

Tucker, A. N. & M. A. Bryan. 1957. *Linguistic Survey of the Northern Bantu Borderland,* Vol. 4 (Languages of the eastern section Great Lakes to Indian Ocean). London, New York, Toronto: Oxford University Press.

Turvey, B. H. C., W. Zimmermann & G. B. Toapopi. 1977. *Kwanyama-English Dictionary.* Johannesburg: Witwatersrand Press.

Valente, José Francisco. 1964. *Grammática Umbundu*. Lisboa: Junta de Investigações do Ultramar.

van der Meiren, J. 1912. *Grammaire de la langue kiluba-hemba*. Bruxelles: Ministère des Colonies.

van Leynseele, Hélène. 1976/77. An Outline of Libinza Grammar. Leiden.

[van Sambeek, J.] n.d. *Petite Grammaire Kiha*. n.p.

Vansina, J. 1959. *Esquisse de grammaire bushong*. (Sciences de l'Homme N° 23). Tervuren: Musés Royal du Congo Belge.

Viljoen, J. T. & P. Amakali. 1978. *A Handbook of Oshiwambo*. Pretoria: University of South Africa.

Walker, André. n.d. Essai de grammaire tsogho. Brazzaville: Institut d'Études Centrafricains.

Waseka, Lungumbu Bweni. 1988. La conjugaison en lega. *Journal of Asian and African Studies* 35: 85-111.

Watkins, Mark. H. 1937. *A Grammar of Chichewa*. Suppl. to *Language*, N° 24.

Watters, John R. & Jacqueline Leroy. 1989. Southern Bantoid. In *The Niger-Congo Languages*, John Bendor-Samuel (ed.), 431-449. Lanham, New York, London: University Press of America.

White, C. M. N. 1947. A comparative survey of the verb forms in four languages of the west central Bantu group. *African Studies* 6,1: 1-20.

Whiteley, W. H. 1960. *The Tense System of Gusii*. Kampala: East African Institute of Social Research.

Whiteley, W. H. 1966. *A Study of Yao Sentences*. Oxford: The Clarendon Press.

Wilkendorf, Patricia. 1991. Le système temporel et aspectuel de la langue nomaándé. In *Tense and Aspect in Eight Languages of Cameroon*, Stephen C. Anderson and Bernard Comrie (eds), 105-146. Dallas: SIL and the University of Texas, Arlington.

Willems, Em. 1988. Le tshiluba du Kasayi. (5th ed.) Kananga: Éditions de l'Archdiocèse.

Wright, J. L. 19. Kaonde: A brief description of the language. In *Language in Zambia: Grammatical Sketches* (vol. 1), Michael Mann, Mubanga E. Kashoki, and J. L. Wright (eds). Harare: Institute for African Studies, University of Zambia.

Yukawa, Yasutoshi. 1987. A tonological study of Nkoya verbs. In *Studies in Zambian Languages*, Y. Yukawa (ed.), 129-184. Tokyo: Institute for the Study of Languages and Cultures of Asia and Africa (ILCAA).

Appendix

Future -KA-

Zone A

A.31	Bubi	[-(k)a-]
A.34	Benga	[-ka-]
A.42	Bankon	[-ɣá-]
A.46	Nomaande	[-ká-]
A.62a	Nugunu	[-gaá-]
A.75	Fang	[-kə́-, -kœ́-]

Zone B

B.52	Nzebi	[-ká-]
B.85	Yansi	[-aka-]

Zone C

C.31b	Libinza	[-kV-]
C.34	Sakata	[-kə́-]
C.50	Likile	[-eka-]
C.83	Bushoong	[ká-]

Zone D

D.14	Enya	[-eka-]
D.25	Lega	[-ká-]
D.26	Binja-sud	[-ká-]
D.28	Holoholo	[-aka-]
D.32	Bira	[-ɽiká-]
D.33	Nyali	[-ɪka-]

Zone E

E.51	Gikuyu	[-ka-]
E.55	Kamba	[-ka-]

Zone F

F.23	Sumbwa	[-ka-]

Zone H

H.21	Kimbundu	[-ka-]

Zone J

J.25	Kwaya, Ruri	[-aka-...-e]
J.31	Masaba	[-ka-...-e]
J.32	Luhya	[-axá-...-e]
J.41	Konzo	[-ka-]
J.42	Nande	[-ka-]
J.61	Ha	[-ka-]

Zone K

K.11	Chokwe	[-ka-]
K.13	Luchazi	[-ka-]
K.14	Lwena	[-ka-]
K.19	Nganguela	[-ka-]
K.22	Lunda	[-aka-]
K.31	Luyana	[-ká-]
K.51	Mbala	[-ga-]

Zone L

L.33	Luba-Shaba	[-ká-]
L.34	Hemba	[-ka-]
L.35	Sanga	[-ka-]
L.41	Kaonde	[-ka-]
L.62	Nkoya	[-ka-]

Zone M

M.21	Ndali	[-ka-]
M.41	Taabwa	[-ka-]
M.42	Bemba	[-ká-, -kà-]
M.52	Lala	[-ka-]
M.54	Lamba	[-ka-]
M.61	Lenje	[-ka-]
M.63	Ila	[-ka-]
M.64	Tonga	[-ka-]

Zone N

N.43	Nyungwe	[-k^{h}a-]

Zone P

P.13	Kimatuumbi	[-ka-]
P.22	Mwera	[-ka-]

Zone R

R.11	Umbundu	[-ka-]
R.21	Kwanyama	[-ka-]
R.22	Ndonga	[-ka-]

Zone S

S.34	Lozi	[-ka-]

Future -NGA-

Zone A

A.62a	Nugunu	[-ngà-]
A.72	Ewondo	[-ngá-]

Zone B

B.31	Tsogho	[-nga-]

Distal or directional -KA-

Zone A

A.11 Londo
A.44 Nen

Zone C

C.30? Ebudza-Molua
C.30? Likata
C.30 Mabembe
C.31a Loi
C.31s Balobo
C.34 Sakata
C.37 Buja
C.44 Ebango (Bua)

Zone E

E.42 Gusii
E.51 Gikuyu
E.55 Kamba

Zone F

F.21 Sukuma
F.22 Nyamwezi

Zone G

G.61 Sango
G.64 Pangwa

Zone H

H.21 Kimbundu

Zone K

K.11 Chokwe
K.13 Luchazi
K.14 Lwena
K.19 Nganguela
K.22 Lunda
K.31 Luyana

Future -(N)KO-

Zone C

C.35	Bolia	[-ngó-]
C.75	Kela	[-kó-]
C.61	Mongo	[-ngó-]
C.65	Ntomba	[-ngó-]
C.66	Ntomba	[-ngóó-]
C.71	Tetela	[-kó-]

Zone K (cont'd)

K.33 Kwangari
K.38 Mbukusha

Zone L

L.21 Kete
L.27 Bangubangu
L.31a Luba-Kasayi
L.32 Kanyok
L.33 Luba-Shaba
L.35 Sanga
L.41 Kaonde
L.62 Nkoya

Zone M

M.21 Ndali
M.31 Ngonde
M.52 Lala
M.54 Lamba
M.64 Tonga

Zone N

N.21 Tumbuka
N.31 Chewa-Nyanja
N.41 Nsenga
N.43 Nyungwe
N.44 Sena

Zone P

P.10 Ndendeule
P.13 Kimatuumbi
P.22 Mwera
P.21 Yao

Zone R

R.11 Umbundu
R.21 Kwanyama
R.22 Ndonga
R.31 Herero

Distal -Co-

Zone C

C. 35	Bolia	[-tó-]
C.36g	Eleku	[-kó-]
C.61	Losikongo	[-yó-]
C.65	Ntomba	[-yǒ-]
C.66	Ntomba	[-to-]
C.68	Yenge (Mbole)	[-só-]
C.71	Tetela	[-to-]
C.81	Ndengese	[-ko-]

Zone D

D.12	Lengola	[-ko-]
D.14	Enya	[-kó-]

Zone S

S.34	Lozi	[-yo-]

Languages apparently w/o future -KA-

Zone A

A.11	Londo
A.24	Duala
A.44	Tunen
A.53	Kpa (Bafia)
A.74	Bulu
A.81a	Bujeba
A.83	Makaa
A.84	Koozime
A.93	Kako

Zone B

B.11	Myene
B.43	Punu
B.51	Duma
B.61	Mbede
B.63	Ndumu
B.77b	Fumu
B.88	Lwel

Zone C

C.35	Bolia
C.36g	Eleku
C.37	Ebudja
C.45	Lebeo
C.65	Ntomba-Inongo
C.66	Ntomba-Bikoro
C.71	Tetela
C.75	Kela

Zone D

D.12	Lengola
D.13	Mituku
D.43	Nyanga

Zone E

E.42	Gusii

Zone F

F.21	Sukuma
F.22	Nyamwezi
F.32	Rimi

Zone G

G.11	Gogo
G.23	Shambala
G.24	Bondei
G.42	Swahili
G.61	Sango

Zone H

H.16k	Zoombo

Zone J

J.11	Nyoro-Nkore-Kiga
J.15	Luganda
J.22	Haya
J.24	Kerebe
J.53	Shi
J.61	Kinyarwanda-Rundi

Zone K

K.33	Kwangari
K.38	Mbukushu
K.52	Pende
K.53	Kwezo

Zone L
L.21 Kete
L.22 Mbagani

Languages apparently w/o future -KA- (cont'd)

Zone L (cont'd)
L.23 Songye
L.31a Luba-Kasayi

Zone M
M.14 Lungu
M.31 Ngonde

Zone N
N.21 Tumbuka
N.31 Chewa-Nyanja
N.41 Nsenga
N.44 Sena

Zone P
P.10 Ndendeule
P.21 Yao
P.23 Makonde
P.25 Mawiha

Zone P (cont'd)
P.31 Makua
P.32 Lomwe

Zone R
R.31 Herero

Zone S
S.10 Shona
S.21 Venda
S.31 Tswana
S.32 N. Sotho
S.33 S. Sotho
S.34 Lozi
S.41 Xhosa
S.42 Zulu
S.43 Swati
S.44 Ndebele
S.53 Tsonga

Languages apparently w/o distal -KA-

Zone A
A.24 Duala
A.31 Bubi
A.34 Benga
A.42 Bankon
A.46 Nomaande
A.53 Kpa (Bafia)
A.62a Nugunu
A.72 Ewondo
A.74 Bulu
A.75 Fang
A.81a Bujeba
A.83 Makaa
A.84 Koozime
A.93 Kako

Zone B
B.11 Myene
B.31 Tsogho
B.43 Punu
B.51 Duma
B.52 Nzebi

Zone B (cont'd)
B.61 Mbede
B.63 Ndumu
B.74 Boma
B.77b Fumu
B.85 Yansi
B.86 Idzing
B.88 Lwel

Zone C
C.31r Libinza
C.32 Bobangi
C.69 Ombo
C.83 Bushoong

Zone D
D.12 Lengola
D.13 Mituku
D.25 Lega
D.26 Binja-Sud

D.28 Holoholo
D.33 Nyali

Languages apparently w/o distal -KA- (cont'd)

Zone D (cont'd)
D.43 Nyanga

Zone E
E.43 Kuria

Zone F
F.23 Sumbwa
F.32 Rimi

Zone G
G.11 Gogo
G.23 Shambala
G.24 Bondei
G.36 Kami
G.42 Swahili

Zone H
H.16 Kongo
H.31 Yaka

Zone J
J.11 Nyoro-Nkore-Kiga
J.15 Luganda
J.22 Haya
J.24 Kerebe
J.25 Kwaya
J.31 Masaba
J.32 Luyia
J.42 Nande
J.53 Shi
J.61 Kinyarwanda-Rundi-Ha

Zone K
K.33 Kwangari
K.51 Mbala*
K.52 Pende
K.53 Kwezo

Zone L
L.22 Mbagani
L.25 Budya
L.34 Hemba

Zone M
M.14 Lungu
M.41 Taabwa
M.42 Bemba
M.61 Lenje
M.63 Ila

Zone P
P.23 Makonde
P.25 Mawiha
P.31 Makua
P.32 Lomwe

Zone S
S.10 Shona
S.21 Venda
S.31 Tswana
S.32 N. Sotho
S.33 S. Sotho
S.34 Lozi
S.41 Xhosa
S.42 Zulu
S.43 Swati
S.44 Ndebele
S.53 Tsonga

Tense and Aspect in Great Lakes Bantu Languages

DEREK NURSE & HENRY R. T. MUZALE
Memorial University, Newfoundland

1. Introduction.

1.1. Scope and aims

Over the first few months of 1996 we examined tense and aspect (henceforth TA) systems in the Great Lakes Bantu languages of East Africa.[1] We had

We would like to thank John Hewson, Bob Botne, and the editors for their comments on this text. The usual disclaimers apply.

[1]We looked in most detail at TA in *Haya* and also examined data from some 30 other varieties (our most reliable source languages are *italicized*): Zinza, Nyambo, *Kerewe*, *Nkore/Kiga*, Nyoro/Tooro, *Ganda*, *Soga*, Gwere, six dialects of Luhya (Masaaba, *Saamia*, Wanga, Bukusu, Isukha, *Logooli*), *Gusii*, *Suba*, Kuria, *Ngurimi*, Shashi/Sizaki, *Ikizu*, Zanaki, *Ruri*, Regi, Jita, Kwaya, *Rwanda*, Rundi, Hangaza, Shubi, Ha. Also in some detail at a Sukuma dialect (*Nkiiya*).

For some we had better data because it came from some or all of: good published sources, reliable field notes made by Muzale (1994, 1996) and/or Nurse (1970s), good papers written in the 1970s at the UDSM by student first language speakers: Zinza, Nyambo, Kerewe, Nkore/Kiga, Nyoro/Tooro, Ganda, Soga, Gwere, some Luhya and Mara languages, Ruri, Regi, Jita, Rwanda, Hangaza, Shubi, Ha. For the others the data was of lesser quality and quantity. Our primary source in nearly all cases was our own data.

two primary and one secondary goal. The first was to analyze how TA works in these languages, with a view to a possible later extension to a larger set of Bantu languages. The second was to see how far this analysis might lead to reconstructions of earlier TA systems, both for Great Lakes and for Bantu in general.[2] The third was to see whether or how TA systems might be used as a tool for historical classification. Classification in Bantu has languished for two decades in the shadow of lexicostatistics. We thought it was time for an experiment with new approaches. This applies to Great Lakes and to Bantu in general. Although in the main text we do not deal in any depth with this third goal, we do come back to it briefly in the Conclusion.

This paper was originally intended to set out our results from the first two goals and we hoped to be able to present a more or less complete analysis and reconstruction. As will be seen, there were problems we did not anticipate. So this paper reports on progress and on the difficulties, and indicates future directions.

1.2. Target languages: The Great Lakes languages

We use the term *Great Lakes* as a descriptive label and do not assume that it necessarily has genetic or historical validity. While the assumption of such a set of languages with historical validity has clearly been fruitful as a working hypothesis for historians[3], such hypotheses need to be proven linguistically first, and, once accepted, then combined with non-linguistic facts. Great Lakes has not really been proved linguistically yet, although it seems likely that large parts of it will ultimately cohere genetically.

Despite this, for working purposes we accept the following as subsets of Great Lakes:

(i) Rutara (Kerewe, Zinza, Nyambo-Haya, Nkore-Kiga, Nyoro-Tooro: Guthrie's E.11-4, 21-4).
(ii) N(orth) Nyanza (Ganda, Soga, Gwere, Syan, etc: E.15-17).
(iii) Luhya, including Logooli (E.30 plus E.41).

We refer to the whole set of Bantu languages around Lake Victoria as Great Lakes, recognize a number of subgroups within it (cf section 1.2), and use Schoenbrun's referential system of geographically-based names. For more on Great Lakes, see Nurse (this volume).

[2]Mould 1981 is the first and only attempt at a reconstruction of part of the TA systems for part of Great Lakes. He reconstructs on the basis of data from Luhya, North Nyanza, and Nyoro-Tooro. Guthrie's Common Bantu lists reconstructed individual morphemes with glosses, based on his test languages, but is not a reconstruction of any system formed by the individual morphemes.

[3]Schoenbrun 1990 is a fine example of what can be achieved historically by assuming the linguistic notion of Great Lakes and combining it with certain archaeological correlates. This thesis is a very coherent presentation of Great Lakes history from 3000BP to 1000BP.

(iv) Mara (Gusii, Suba, Kuria, Ngoreme, Simbiti, Zanaki, Shashi, Nata: E.40+, less E.41).
(v) Suguti (Ruri, Regi, Kwaya, Jita: E.25+).
(vi) W(est) Highlands (Rwanda, Rundi, Shubi, Hangaza, Ha, Vinza: D.60).

We accept additional small subsets within Great Lakes (Bastin 1978, Schoenbrun 1990). Further, there are other minor languages only mentioned in the literature (see the article by Nurse in this volume). Since we have no data at all or no adequate data on these, we have to ignore them.

The quality and quantity of data available for the thirty or so target languages varied. Our data was best for Haya, because it is Muzale's native language and because it is otherwise well analyzed (Hyman and Byarushengo 1984). We wanted to be sure that for each of the six subsets above we had at least one principal language for which reasonable data was available. For subsets for which we had access to more than one language with reasonable data we used them all: these are the languages italicized in footnote 1. It is our impression that TA systems change quite readily and that TA categories and morphemes are subject to influence from systems in adjacent languages[4], so when selecting our sample languages we tried where possible to be careful with data from languages on the geographical edge of their group because these might have been modified by contact in recent centuries: thus northern Luhya has interacted historically with Syan/Gwere/Soga, Nyoro/Tooro with Ganda, and almost all Kerewe are today bilingual in Jita. We represent the intersection of tense and aspect as a matrix (see Table). As most of our sources did not present their data in this framework we had to adapt their data. We thought we had reasonable data for each subset but as it turned out for reasons explained below, this was not always so. For practical purposes, we cannot present the data from all 30 languages, so we illustrate our approach in the Table using one language (Haya) alone.

When making generalizations we have had to be careful about evidence from Gusii and West Highlands. Some linguists (Whiteley 1960, Nurse and Rottland 1991-2) have wondered whether Gusii really belongs with Great Lakes at all, or at the very least, whether it might have started as an E.50 language and become more Great Lakes-like as its community interacted with its Mara neighbors.[5] For W. Highlands, while nonverbal features support or do not contradict its membership of Great Lakes, its TA system differs so much from that of other Great Lakes languages as to cast doubts on whether the two can be derived from a single original ancestral system.

[4]Even across the boundaries of language families. See Dimmendaal, forthcoming.

[5]Some of Gusii's aberrant features also appear in the northern Mara languages, specifically Suba and Kuria, but at present it is hard to say whether they were also once outsiders, or because some of Gusii's aberrant features have rubbed off on them.

We have therefore attached less importance to Gusii and W. Highlands data in the reconstructions.

1.3. Achievements and problems

We started out with Haya forms used in what have been called main clause affirmatives (MCAs). We started with this kind of data because it shows the largest set of semantic contrasts and categories (e.g., number of discrete pasts and futures) and because it was the kind of data most readily available for our other languages, too. That is, there are some languages where such contrasts in main clause negatives (MCN), relative clause affirmatives (RCA) or negatives (RCN) might be as numerous as those in MCAs, and there are others which have less contrasts in MCNs, RCAs, or RCNs than in MCAs, but, as far as we know, there are no languages which had more contrasts outside the MCAs. So if we wanted to see the fullest range of TA contrasts and categories in contemporary systems and see how they work, MCAs were the place to start. Section 2 (aspect) and section 3 (tense), below, have a typological overview of these systems, while section 4 deals with some unclear categories. We have ignored some categories, such as conditionals, completely.

Problems arose with the section on reconstruction. In phonological reconstruction, one is regularly faced with two or more competing possible alternative forms. The choice between them depends on a number of principles. One is what might be called the majority rule: all other things being equal, one chooses as the reconstructed form something identical or similar to what the majority of languages have today, because it is easier to assume that only a minority of languages will have changed. But things are not always equal, in which case one has recourse to a second guiding principle: which of the alternative reconstructions of components of a proto-system makes most sense within the system. This is already trickier because, whereas most phonologists have ideas about plausible consonant or vowel systems, ideas about plausible TA systems are less advanced, and thus also the place and nature of components within any system. Even trickier is the third principle: the choice of one reconstruction over another is directly linked to the possible processes linking a proto-form to contemporary forms (e.g., is *x > y more or less plausible than *y > x?). Again, we have reasonable knowledge of the set of plausible phonological changes but, despite recent progress (e.g., Bybee et al 1994), our ability to judge between alternative forms of change between TA systems is less advanced in general. We found ourselves faced with alternative reconstructions and possible changes which were hard to evaluate. One component of this proved particularly difficult. MCA forms are only one dimension of a system with several dimensions, and when we find that the category of, for example, "present" or "near past" is realised by different morphology in MCAs and MCNs and relatives, how do we judge what the older situation might have been? In which category does change typically occur first and where are remnant or older forms most likely to be retained?

There is a suggestion that change tends to occur in MCAs rather than in the other structures so, if the forms of MCAs differed from those in MCNs, RCAs, and RCNs, the latter may represent retention. By omitting such data, we are eliminating vital information that might help us distinguish innovation from retention. At this point it became obvious that our ability to talk about change and thus reconstruction was limited by our focus on the forms in MCAs. We also felt that our restricted knowledge of the tonal features of some morphemes hampered us.

At the end of each subsection in 2, 3, and 4, below, we discuss what we think are likely reconstructions. We do not attempt a complete set of reconstructions in all cases. Where we are reasonably sure, we offer concrete suggestions. Where we are not sure (e.g., as in Pasts), we merely list forms and categories.

2. Aspect in Great Lakes

We assume that a discrete verbal TA form has a meaning or range of meanings different from that of other verbal TA forms in the same language, and that all such forms fit into a coherent system. We concentrate here on positive, non-relative, non-conditional forms, the forms of MCAs. All Great Lakes languages show both tense and aspect. Aspect is represented in the Table in vertical columns, tense by horizontal rows. This implies an analysis where tense and aspect are and have been strictly distinct. This is not so. It is our general impression that forms can extend their semantic range, and even eventually lose their original meaning, and that aspects can become tenses, though we see little evidence for movement in the opposite direction. We also have the impression that new tense markers have arisen from auxiliaries, but have no obvious evidence whether there was necessarily an intermediate aspect stage.

Great Lakes languages distinguish formally at least four aspects and most have five. It will be seen that we include under aspect both one- and two-word forms. In the latter, the first word is an tense-marked auxiliary and the second (lexical) word carries the aspect.

In what follows, unless stated otherwise, examples are from Haya. Haya examples are tone-marked, in most cases the others are not, for want of the facts. The Haya tones are not surface tones but those at a stage before the application of phrase-final rules. Some are part of imposed grammatical patterns (cf. Hyman and Byarushengo 1984).

2.1. Simple

Column two in the Table presents the Simple form. Morphologically, Simple is the unmarked, or little marked, form (e.g., English *walked* vs *has walked* or *was walking*), on which other forms in the paradigm are often based. Other models would imply that the lack of marking in these forms means a lack of aspect, but no verbal form is without aspect, regardless of its marking. Semantically, Simple forms often represent the event as a complete whole. That is, if asked what they do for a living, people might answer "We buy", where the emphasis is on the action in general, not on whether it is happening now (Present Progressive), or whether it happens regularly (Habitual). The lines between the three can obviously be so narrow that Simple, Progressive, and Habitual forms often coalesce.

Simplest of all in Great Lakes are Simple Presents, as exemplified by:

(1) tu-ø-gur-á 'we buy' (/-gura/)

a form shared by nearly all Great Lakes languages. The Suguti form, *e-cí-ø-gur-a* [6] 'we are buying', is slightly different in that it has the augment affixed to what is otherwise just the person marker affixed to the bare stem. In most of Mara, Simple, Progressive, and even Near Future are indicated by an apparent innovation *-ra-*.

The data here strongly supports a reconstructed Simple Present, marked by a zero postsubject marker and suffixal *-a*, e.g., *sp-ø-ROOT-a.[7]

2.2. Progressive

Column three shows the Progressive, where the event is represented as ongoing at the time of reference. Where time is not indicated formally, it is usually the time of speaking, usually the present. For all aspects, the Present form is typically a single word form, and tenses build time reference on to this, either by additional morphology in the single word form, or by adding a tense marked auxiliary. We take the present form as basic and in most cases it is a single word form.[8] Where present Progressive is clearly different from Simple and Habitual, it takes one of two main shapes. One is initial *ni-*, occurring in most of Rutara in single and compound forms but in Kerewe (and Regi) only in compounds (see also 4.1, below):

(2) Haya, Nyambo, Zinza,
Nkore, Tooro *ni*-tu-ø-gur-á 'we are buying'
Kerewe tw-á-ri-ga *ni*-tu-ø-gúra 'we were buying'
Regi c-a-ri-ka *ni*-ci-ø-kura 'we were buying'

The other is a form containing an aspect marker which rather obviously derives from an older or underlying two-word construction 'be (locative) plus verbal noun=infinitive/*-li* + *ku-*. Constructions like this, with be plus

---

[6]This Suguti *ci-* (/ki-/) 'we' is not cognate with the reflexes of *tu-* found in most but not all Great Lakes languages. It occurs only in forms referring to present/near future and augment-less forms are also possible. While we are not entirely sure of its meaning, it seems to be linked to focus or certainty.

[7]Our own data does not contain enough comparative information to enable us to say anything about the tone pattern of this, or any of the other patterns set out here.

[8]The main exception is West Highlands, where Progressive is formed by adding an auxiliary to the Simple. So Rwanda *tu-ra-gura* 'we buy' and *tu-ri-ho tu-(ra)-gur-a* 'we are buying'.

locative, are common across Bantu and in many other languages worldwide. In some of our languages, they occur in positive and negative forms, thus:

(3) Soga tu-*li+ku*-gula/ti-tu-*li+ku*-gula 'we are buying/are not buying'

while in others, e.g., Haya, it is restricted to negatives and relatives:

(4) ti-tú-*rí+ku*-gura 'we are not buying'

and in a few, it is reduced to *-ku-*:

(5)	Kerewe	tu-*ku*-gura	'we are buying, we buy, we will buy'
	Suba	*ni*-to-*ko*-gora	'we are buying, we buy'

Allowing for the possibility that our data may be incomplete, this *(-li+) ku-* construction occurs in one form or meaning in two nonadjacent sets of languages: Rutara, Soga, Gwere, Masaaba, and Gusii, Kuria, and Suba. (Suba combines #ni- with *-(le)ko-* and Simple with Progressive).

The impression given by the forms in (1) and (2) above is that Simple tends to be unmarked whereas Progressive is marked. While that is true for a majority of Great Lakes languages, it is not true for all. Some (like Ganda) do not distinguish the two meanings, having merged the contrastive forms (in either direction), and in some others, especially along the eastern side of the lake, the morphologically simpler form is the Progressive. Others merge Progressive and Habitual and indicate the merged form by a single word form, usually marked by *-anga/-aga*.

Reference to past or future time is then achieved by adding a tense sign to these forms. In Suguti, and in West Highlands in some tenses, this means a one word version of the present, modified by prefix and/or suffix (italicized below), thus:

(6)	Ruri	e-ci-ø-gur-a-*ga*	'we buy'
		ci-*a*-gur-a-ga	'we used to buy, were buying'
		ci-*aka*-gur-*e*-ga	'we will buy regularly'

In the other languages the auxiliary 'be' showing tense (italicized below) is placed before the lexical verb showing aspect (often the forms in (2)), so

(7)	tw-*áa*-bá ni-tu-ø-gurá	'we were buying (Near Past)'
	tu-*raa*-bá ni-tu-ø-gurá	'we will be buying (Near Future)'

Two forms of 'be' occur as the auxiliary, *-li* and *-ba*. We see no obvious geographical or functional pattern to the distribution of these two.[9]

[9]For Luhya, Mara, and much of N.Nyanza, our data is too sketchy to allow meaningful generalization. In all Rutara except Kerewe *-ba* "be" is the main or only form used in MCAs. In Suguti, Kerewe, W. Highlands, and Ganda (= all N. Nyanza?), *-ba* appears in MCAs in futures and *-li* in some or all pasts. In W. Highlands *-ri* is used in the present whereas in Ganda it is *-ba*. For more detailed discussion of the roles of *-ba* and *-li*, see Botne 1986.

It is noteworthy that although Kerewe today has no independent present progressive such as *ni-tu-ø-gul-a,* it does use such a form as the second member of two-word compounds, suggesting its recent replacement in the present.

Some Great Lakes languages have a contrast between forms such as (future):

(8)	Nkore	tu-rya-ba ni-tu-ø-gura	'we'll be buying (we-fut-be + progressive-we-buy)'
		tu-rya-ba tu-ø-gura	'we'll be buying habitually (we-fut-be + we-buy)'

There is reasonably strong evidence here for reconstructing a proto-Great Lakes Progressive category, distinct from Simple and Habitual, at least in the Present. How this Present Progressive was marked is less clear. Two patterns predominate: one with the grammaticalized *-li+ku-* ('be + locative'), the other with initial #ni-. Our guess is that #ni 'progressive' is an expansion of some other function such as #ni "focus" (see section 4.1): note that it is the only aspect or tense marker that is verb initial. In that case the *-li+ku-* pattern may originally have indicated progressive. But even with reconstructing *-liku-* we have to be wary: how far back can it be projected? As a marker of Progressive it is fairly widespread inside and outside Great Lakes, and its grammaticalization path is transparent. This suggests that *-li+ku-* > *-liku-* happens often so while the evidence from outside Great Lakes suggests it happened early in Bantu, at a pre-Great Lakes stage, it might also have happened again at a post-Great Lakes point.

Non-present Progressives are also not easy to project backwards. What could we assume for nonpresent Progressives for a proto-Great Lakes: oneword forms or compounds? In general we assume a cycle. Compound forms get grammaticalized over time into single word forms but also there is an going tendency for analytic compounds to arise spontaneously alongside synthetic forms. We assume this is a continuous process and at present we see no obvious reason not to assume the possible existence of both analytic and synthetic forms for proto-Great Lakes.

2.3. Habitual

Column four presents the Habitual: event occuring regularly or repeatedly. In some of our languages, for some time periods, Progressive and Habitual are, or can be, expressed, identically, whereas in others Habitual is a distinct category. For semantic reasons, Habitual does not cooccur with all tenses: not with Near or Mid Past or Near Future.

Habitual is most often expressed by a one word form with a suffix, of the shape *-anga* (N. Nyanza, Luhya, Mara) or *-aga* (the rest). Although our data is incomplete, it suggests most Great Lakes languages can use the suffix in combination with past, "present", and future reference. In some languages it only cooccurs with certain tenses (mostly past) and in a few it has disappeared: Habitual is then replaced by a two word form (cf Nkore in (8)). Rwanda *-aga* is restricted to past progressive ("doing something all day/month long") as Rwanda does not seem to distinguish progressive and habitual.

Incidentally, the marker *-a(n)ga* appears in Haya, Kerewe, Nkore, and Ganda in some imperatives and negative perfects but not in the equivalent positives (in Nkore that is the only place it appears). This suggests the possibility that it occurred earlier in a wider set of (MCA) contexts.

The data are thus almost unanimous in supporting a Habitual marked by **-anga/-aga*. The evidence suggests it could be combined with the zero Present and with at least one past and one future: by their nature, habituals would not be expected to co-occur with any or all pasts and futures but would be most likely to refer to far pasts and futures. The most commonly attested Past Habitual has the shape *sp-a-ROOT-a-(n)ga*: although we have less evidence for Future Habitual, the most common form is *sp-raa-ROOT-a(n)ga*. We would tentatively suggest these two, and the *sp-ø-ROOT-a-(n)ga* Present, as reconstructible.

2.4. Perfect

The next column shows Perfect, whereby the speaker looks back at an event completed and either the results of that event live on into the time of reference or that event is of present relevance. Thus English *he has lived here for 20 years*, with the implication that he is still living here (vs *he lived here for twenty years*, where he is no longer living here) or Swahili *a-me-lala* 'she went to sleep, she is therefore now asleep (and so cannot talk to you)'.

All languages express Present Perfect by a single word form and all (most?) use the suffix *-ile*.[10] Perfect is most widely expressed by prestem zero and poststem *-ile*. Haya, Nyambo, Zinza, Kerewe have *a...ire*for regular verbs but *ø...ire* in statives (and in the Middle Past), so

(9) ba-*áa*-guz-ire 'they have already bought', but

ba-ø-nagí-iré 'they are asleep = they have fallen asleep'

Rwanda has a mixed situation, with *ø...ire* in the present, but *a...ire*in compound pasts and futures, so:

---

[10]We use the shape [ile] for general reference. In some languages, this is its shape, in other languages [r] or some intermediate sound appears, and in other languages the suffix is reduced to a vowel. In all 5-vowel languages the suffix causes modifications of the verb stem.

Most languages here do not distinguish /l/ from /r/. We write <l> and <r> as we find them.

(10) Rwanda tu-ø-guz-e 'we have bought'

but

tw-á-ri tw-*á*-guz-e 'we had bought '

and

tu-zaa-ba tw-*á̲*-guz-e 'we will have bought'

As in the Progressive, nonpresents often consist of a two word compound, a tensed form of 'be' in the first word followed by a perfect form of the lexical verb.The distribution of *-ba* 'be' and its suppletive form *-li* in the Perfect is much as in the Progressive (cf fn. 9). In both progressive and perfect, the major exception to compound forms for non-presents is in Suguti, which favors single word forms, with aspect at suffix and tense at prefix.

There is thus strong evidence for a reconstructed single word present Perfect, expressed by *ø...ile. For non-present Perfects for proto-Great Lakes we make the same assumption as for progressives: there is a cycle in which compound forms get grammaticalized over time into single word forms but also there is an going tendency for analytic compounds to arise spontaneously alongside synthetic forms. As for nonpresent progressives, we see no obvious reason not to assume the possible existence of both analytic and synthetic forms for proto-Great Lakes.

At the same time, the *-ile* suffix is also used as a tense marker in Great Lakes, in two predominant forms, *ø...ile* and *a...ile*.[11] Where these cooccur, the first always refers to a more recent event than the latter, so Gwere:

(11) tw-a-gul-ile 'we bought (Middle Past)'

tu-ø-gul-ile 'we bought (Near Past)'

As both are widespread, we assume the shift from aspect to tense marker happened early (cf 3.2).

2.5. Persistive

The final column presents the Persistive, a term for what is often traditionally labelled 'Be still...ing'. Here an event is depicted as having started at some prior point and as being still ongoing. In other languages this is represented by the progressive plus adverb (French *toujours*, English *still*, Swahili *bado*, German *noch*). In Great Lakes languages, this is expressed by derivatives of prestem *-kiaa-.[12] As with other aspects, the

[11]This apparent extension from marker of perfect aspect to marker of past tense also occurs outside Great Lakes, for example in Sukuma. The other markers that co-occur less often with *-ile* are *-aka-*, *-ka-*, *-ra-*, *-ara-*, and conditional markers such as *-andi-*, and persistives *-kiaa-*, *-ki-*.

[12]This prefix might have consisted of two morphemes, since, while most Great Lakes languages show reflexes of *-kyaa-*, a few have just [ki], and some, like Haya, have [kya:] or [ki] in partly but not completely complementary

present form is a single word (*tu-kiáa-gur-a*) and past and future forms are compounds with this as the second word.

So for the present we reconstruct prestem *-kiaa- (*sp-kiaa-ROOT-a). Past and future forms were likely compounds with this as the second word and a tense marked auxiliary as the first.

Other aspects are also possible in these languages.[13] Finally, although we have not shown this, in many Great Lakes languages a verb form can (by definition) show only one tense, but more than one of the aspects mentioned (see Table, comment #1).

3. Tense in Great Lakes

Some Great Lakes languages, as Haya, have a tense system with six members:

(a) Far Past represents an event which occurred before yesterday, assuming the event or action lends itself to that kind of temporal categorization.

(b) Middle Past represents an event which occurred yesterday.

(c) Near Past represents an event which occurred very recently, so recently that it forms an extension of the present. 'Very recently' depends on how a language sets its parameters. For Haya and Rutara, it refers to today, for Sukuma *-il* refers to an event of the last few minutes.

For events which occur infrequently but regularly and predictably, say, once a year (such as certain farming activities), Near Past represents the most recent (i.e.this year's) occurrence of the event, Middle Past last year's, and Far Past would represent any occurrence of the event before that. In neighbouring languages such as Sukuma, if the point of reference is other than today, then the Near Past immediately precedes that, and so on. Futures have similarly flexible reference.

Some Great Lakes languages (e.g., N. Nyanza) have a fourth category, a Very Near Past.

(d) Present represents an event between past and future. Forms representing Simple Present are unmarked or little marked. How long the present lasts varies from language to language: thus a form such as Suguti *eki-ø-gura* translates as 'we buy, we are buying, we will buy from now for several days into the future' and it even appears to refer backwards some distance in some Suguti languages whereas in most Great Lakes languages it covers only a short time period.

---

distribution: *-kya(a)-/-ca(a)-* all Rutara, W.Highlands, Ganda, south Mara, Suguti; *-ki-/-ke-* scattered W.Highlands, Haya, Kerewe, Logooli, north Mara; *-si-/-shi-* Luhya; *-kaa-* Soga.

If this started as two morphemes, the second would have been *-a(a)-* 'Past', consonant with its current meaning of an event that started in the past, and the second would have been -ki-, indicating 'ongoing'.

[13]Thus Mara and Suguti languages can distinguish varying degrees of certainty in the same (usually future) tenses (= mood ?).

(e) Near Future represents an event which is going to occur today or tomorrow.

(f) Far Future represents an event which will occur after tomorrow.

Other Great Lakes languages have fewer or more than these six temporal distinctions.

Thus West Highlands has a Far Past (before today), a Near Past (starting earlier today), a Present (now to end of the day), and a Future (after today).

Soga has an extra past (so Far Past, Middle Past, Near Past, and Very Near Past) and an extra future (so Near, Indefinite, and Far Future). These extra categories need confirming. Ruri has a third future category (Near, Middle, Far) and a further future distinction certain vs noncertain. These again need confirming.

To use Haya as a norm and to compare the others to it by saying that they have more or less categories is at this point just a descriptive device and implies no special categorial or historical status for Haya or its system.

3.1. Futures

We start with future tenses because they are most transparent. Great Lakes languages vary in how they categorize future time and the geographical patterns of categorization tend to mirror those for past time. So West Highlands languages (all?) typically have only one future and, morphologically though not tonally, only one past.[14] The majority have two (Near Future (today, tomorrow, next 24 hours?) versus Far Future). A few have three futures: as we will see for past time, the languages with most distinctions are in North Nyanza and Luhya. Mara and Suguti may also be involved but Mara data are not good and Suguti has categories referring to future time whose reference is unclear to us: multiple futures or is it degree of certainty (mood)?

Given this categorial variation, we started by working from common morphological patterns. Apart from very local patterns specific to one or two dialects or languages, five morphological patterns for future are found widely in Great Lakes:

- a shape *-laa-* referring to Near Future occurs through Great Lakes.[15]

[14]Botne (p.c.) does not agree with this formulation. For instance, for future reference, he agrees that there is a Far Future *-zaa-* in Rwanda and that the Present *-ra-* refers to present and to future within today, but he points out that events within today can also be referred to by two other forms: a two word form with *-ri* 'be'+ bu-ROOT-e (e.g. *tu-ri bu-gur-e*), and the periphrastic form with 'come' and infinitive. Thus there is one Far Future and three forms referring to today. The semantic difference between the three is unclear, and, as far as we know, has not been carefully examined.

[15]Rwanda *-zaa-* refers to all futures and other W.Highlands languages have this, *-zoo-*, or *-roo*. Apparently alone in W. Highlands, Ha has *-laa-*. Botne (1990) discusses the etymology of *-zaa-*. Most W. Highlands has *-ra-* with different

- a shape *-li-* referring to Far Future occurs throughout Great Lakes except W. Highlands.
- a form of 'come + infinitive'. It refers predominantly to some kind of near future.[16] In some it is fully grammaticalized, in others it is still an auxiliary. In some it is an alternative to *-laa-*, in others it is semantically similar but distinct. We feel that it is a relatively recent innovation.
- Luhya, Suba, and parts of Suguti have a form referring predominantly to far future in *-(a)ka-* plus suffixal *-e*.[17] Where it cooccurs with *-li-* with reference to far future, the difference is not clear but at least in some cases it refers to indefinite future, a semantic feature which appears to be an innovation along the eastern side of the lake. This, plus the limited geographical distribution, suggests this is also a relatively recent innovation.
- the subjunctive marker *-e* is associated with some near future reference in all but West Highlands. In Rutara and North Nyanza this association only occurs in the negative (Near Future):

(12) ti-tuu-gur-é[18] 'we will not buy (negative of tu-raa-gur-á)'

but in Luhya, Mara, and Suguti it occurs in affirmatives:

---

reference (see 4.2), and if this was originally the same morpheme (?) we do not know why it should be short-vowelled, as W. Highlands otherwise keeps inherited length.

Our data for Luhya, Mara, and Suguti are not clear about vowel length for this morpheme. The liquid has become a nasal in N. Nyanza and parts of adjacent N. Luhya. In the so-called Elgon group of Kalenjin older *l went unconditionally to n: in at least parts of the Bukusu area no longer Kalenjin speaking, some place names have twin names, one with /l/, the other with /n/. Could this otherwise unexplained shift of [laa] to [naa] be connected to a Kalenjin substratum?

[16]In one or two dialects of Luhya it may refer to far future but our data were not good.

[17]E.g. Suba *tw-aka-gor-ɛ*. Some dialects have *-ka-*, others *-aka-*, and in Logooli *-rika-/-raka-* appears. Due to the operation of the Luhya Law, the [k] appears regularly as [x] or [h] in Luhya. In Suba *-aka-* appears to represent the Near Future, in Ruri it appears to represent the Middle Future, and throughout Luhya it refers to Far Future.

[18]As can be seen, associated with the suffix is a zero prestem marker and the vowel of the subject is lengthened. See section 4.4 for discussion.

(13) Ruri ci-la-gur-e 'we will buy (near future, not certain)'
ci-aka-gur-e 'we will buy, (middle future, certain), if we buy'
ci-aka-gur-e-ga 'we will buy regularly'

It cooccurs with several prestem markers of future, mostly, but not exclusively, Near Future. Where these languages distinguish certain and noncertain futures, *-e* is most often associated with the noncertains. Our interpretation of this is that subjunctive marks nonfactuals, that the future is nonfactual, and especially negative and noncertain future. So it is not surprising that subjunctive comes to refer to future(s).[19] It also does in other Bantu languages.

This analysis leads to fairly clear conclusions. Both *-laa-* 'Near Future' and *-li-* 'Far Future' are widely enough spread and cognate in Great Lakes languages to be assumable for Proto-Great Lakes. At least within east and southern African Bantu these morphemes do not appear widely with these meanings so they might here be tentatively assumed to be innovations. Both are absent from W.Highlands, from which it can be concluded that: either W.Highlands is not part of Great Lakes: or, if it is, then these innovated after W.Highlands and the other languages had parted: or W.Highlands lost them since proto-Great Lakes.

The association of *-e* with future reference, either negative, or positive, or uncertain, or all, also appears widely enough spread to be assumable for proto-Great Lakes also, with the same caveat about W.Highlands. What meaning would be assigned to it? It is clear enough that it is linked to Near, not Far, Future; it is linked with uncertain, contrasted with certain, Near Future, in the relevant (Suguti) languages; and the likely bridge from subjunctive via nonfactualness. Whether it was associated with positive or negative Near Future is not clear.

The other two patterns, the *-aka-....-e* and 'come + infinitive' have a different status. They have a limited geographical distribution. The second at least is not fully grammaticalized in all languages. These, plus the likelihood that these are not inherited from PB, suggest these as post-proto-Great Lakes innovations.

So we assume: *-laa- Near Future; *-li- Far Future, and *-e "(1) subjunctive (2) associated in some as yet undefined way with Near Future reference".

3.2. Pasts

Generalizing about past is harder than about future tenses in these languages. A few languages, such as West Highlands, have only two time

[19] An objection to this is that the *-e* might be expected to be associated with far future as far future is less 'factual' than near future.

divisions;[20] 'earlier today' versus 'before today'. Others, apparently the majority, have a three way division, usually 'earlier today: Near Past' versus 'yesterday: Middle Past' versus 'before yesterday: Far Past'. Still others, all in North Nyanza, Luhya, and Mara, distinguish four pasts, adding a 'just past' to the foregoing. Finally, all these languages have a Perfect aspect, which, of course, also contains a component of past reference. Within any subgroup, the past tenses of most member languages work similarly[21], but they show startling permutations of the morphology representing these four or five categories.

As for future, we proceed from considering common morphological patterns to asking what categories they represent or might have represented. Two patterns have an areal distribution wider than one language but not as wide as Great Lakes.

One is *-aka-*, a marker of the nearest past, so

(14) Logooli kw-aka-gor-a 'we just bought'

This spreads throughout N.Nyanza and Luhya and laps over into adjacent parts of Nyoro/Tooro and northern Mara (?), that is, the languages to the north and east of the lake. The second can be seen in:

(15) Ruri c-amá-gur-a 'we bought (yesterday)'

which is present in all Suguti and also in Bukusu, the most northerly Luhya dialect, which is not adjacent to Suguti:

(16) Bukusu xw-ama xu-kula 'we just bought'

The Suguti and Bukusu forms refer to different times; they are very limited geographically; there is no obvious reason to think of them as inherited; they have a suspicious VCV shape, and the Bukusu version still has its infinitive showing. It seems to us likely that the Suguti and the Bukusu forms are separate and recent innovations.[22]

Other patterns are widely associated in Great Lakes with past references: *-ka-*, *-a-* (or maybe more than one *-a-*, varying tonally and lengthwise?), *a...ile*, and *ø...ile*.

The suffix *-ile* we have seen already, as the marker of Perfect. Since events which took place in the past and live on into the present are more

[20]Even these two are segmentally identical, but tonally different. Botne has pointed out to us that *ø...ile* also refers to (very near) past, but we interpret this as an extension of its present perfect function. Gusii also distinguishes tonally different degrees on segmentally identical structures.

[21]The exception is Mara. Our admittedly inadequate data suggests that this group splits into a northern (Kuria and Suba: and Gusii?) and a southern set, which behave rather differently.

[22]They probably derive from the *-a-* tense form of *-mala* 'finish', similar to Swahili *-me-*, which is the old-*ile* form of *-mala*, so *-mele,* with subsequent l-loss and vowel shortening. Hyman has pointed out to us that this *-ama-* is also used in Nande (Rwenzori).

likely to have happened recently, it would only require an emphasis on the event rather than the result for a semantic shift to occur. So, in its unmarked form (that is, *ø...ile*), Perfect could easily shade over into Near Past, as has happened widely elsewhere in Bantu (also Russian, Polish, etc. J. Hewson, p.c.). In fact, *ø...ile* is involved in past tense reference in all Great Lakes, except apparently Suguti and West Highlands.

This suffix also combines, in Great Lakes and elsewhere, with tense markers to refer to an event which occurred before the time of reference, thus giving forms meaning Past (various) or Future Perfect.

-Ka- is the most puzzling of the other three forms. While *-ka-* is widely enough distributed in Bantu to be assigned to proto-Bantu, its referent is unclear because its referents in today's Bantu languages, including Great Lakes, are several and various. In Haya, for example, we find it toneless and prestem in tense/aspect function (first three examples) but also hightoned and word initial in complementizer-like function (last three examples):

(17)	tú-*ka*-gura ébitabo	'we bought books (Far Past)'
	/-gura ébitabo/ → [-gurá ebitabo] → [-gurébitabo]	
	ti-tú-*ka*-guz-ire bitabo	'we have not yet bought books'
	orwó tw-a-ijá tú-*ka*-gura ébitabo...	'when we came and bought books...'
	ká-tu-gura ébitabo	'when(ever) we buy books..'
	ká-tu-raa-gya Torontó tú-ka-gura ébitabo turaabiguzá	'If we go to Toronto and buy books, we'll sell them'
	ká-tu-gur-é ebitabo	'Let's buy books'

We do not try to connect these contemporary forms, even within one language, but consider rather the Far Past form. Mould treats Far Past *-ka-* ambivalently: on one page (1981: 209) he selects it as an original marker of Far Past for his limited subset of languages but a few pages later (1981: 214) it does not appear in his list of TA reconstructions. Now Mould considered only seven languages/dialects, namely, Luhya, N. Nyanza, and one Rutara language, Nyoro-Tooro. As Far Past *-ka-* appears only in Nyoro-Tooɔ of these languages, it cannot have seemed important to him. But it occurs in all Rutara languages and in most (all?) southern Mara languages with that shape and meaning in MCAs (but not MCNs). Rutara and southern Mara are not adjacent. Unless it can be shown to be an independent innovation of that shape and meaning in these two sets of nonadjacent languages, we have to assume it is inherited (assuming Great Lakes is a valid grouping and Rutara and Mara belong to it). We see no way to explain it as independent innovation. Further it occurs also elsewhere in the system in at least Rutara languages, e.g., in negative perfects ((16) above), so is not likely to be a recent introduction. We think *-ka-* is a candidate for the original marker of Far Past in Great Lakes, kept in Rutara and parts of E.40, replaced elsewhere.

We are left with *-a-* [23] and *a...ile*. Both are widespread in Great Lakes. Even West Highlands has a universal past *a...ile*, with different tonal patterns for different past reference, and *-a-* with past reference in narratives and other patterns. In those languages where they cooccur as past tenses, *a...ile* usually refers to a more recent event than *-a-*.[24] In languages where *a...ile* and *ø...ile* cooccur, *a...ile* always refers to an event prior to that of *-ø-...-ile*. This also makes logical sense: *a...ile* is intermediate between, and combines the features of, Perfect *-ile*, suggesting most often recent events, and *-a-*, referring to events further in the past.

We are unwilling to reconstruct an unambiguous set of Past morphemes or categories on the basis of our current evidence. We find all the following six in current Great Lakes languages with past reference and a geographical distribution wider than a single language. We quote the typical meaning range in MCA forms:

- *-ka-* 'Far Past', in Rutara and southern Mara
- *-a-* 'Far Past, Middle Past', widespread. Also tonal variation - more than one -a?
- *a...ile* 'Middle Past', widespread
- *ø...ile* 'Middle Past, Near Past', widespread
- *-ama-* 'Middle Past' in Suguti, 'Just Past' in Luhya Bukusu and W.Highlands
- *-aka-* 'Just Past', in North Nyanza, Luhya, and a few adjacent languages

As no Great Lakes language nor any other Bantu language we know has a six-way past contrast, we do not assume that for a proto-Great Lakes. Therefore some of the above must be innovations within MCA forms for past reference. We incline to see *ø...ile* 'Near Past' as deriving from *ø...ile* 'Perfect' because it is easy to imagine a marker of Perfect shading over semantically into a marker of Near Past. At later stages, *ø...ile* could expand to 'Middle Past' and, as a suffix, *-ile* could co-occur with pre-stem markers, such as *-ka-* or *-a-*. Few languages show *ka...ile* but many show *a...ile*. This would fit the hypothesis that *-ile* originally represented Near Past, and *-a-* Middle Past, so *a...ile* would combine two semantically similar

---

[23]Our analysis would be improved if we knew the tonal characteristics of the various *-a-* in today's languages. Unfortunately we do not. Mould marks tone, but some of his remarks are contradicted by a later tonal study of at least one of his languages, Logooli (Leung 1991). In Gusii, Haya, (and Sukuma) high-toned (and maybe long-vowelled) *-a-* represents a nearer past than low-toned *-a-*, which is the reverse of the pattern in West Highlands.

[24]Exceptions are 1) Suguti, where *a...ire* represents Far Past/Perfect and *-a-* represents Near Past, 2) Rutara which has Near Past *-a(a)* but no independent *a...ile* past tense (it occurs as the second element of compounds). This *a...ire* appears in MCNs in Haya and Kerewe for Far Past.

categories. However, we are unwilling to say when these two hypothetical stages occurred in the evolution of Great Lakes languages. Once *-a-* and *-ile* fused as one pattern, it would have been available to spread across the existing TA systems or the early Great Lakes dialect continuum.

3.3. Present

Allowing for regular phonetic differences, and local morphological differences, nearly all Great Lakes languages have an unmarked form such as *tu-ø-gur-á* 'we buy' in the Simple, as mentioned in section (2.1) and exemplified in (1). The temporal range of this 'present' form varies from language to language: in W.Highlands for example, it covers the near future, as far as the end of the day. The only exceptions are in Mara, where the southern languages have *-ra-*, whose reference shades over into future and sometimes even past, and the northern languages Kuria and Suba seem to have *-(li)ku-*, although our data is poor for them here. Also as mentioned above in (2.2), other present forms, whatever their aspect, tend to be single word forms.

For Presents we therefore reconstruct Simple (see 2.1) *sp-ø-ROOT-a, Habitual *sp-ø-ROOT-a(n)ga, Perfect sp-ø-ROOT-ile, and Persistive *sp-kia-ROOT-a. Present Progressive is more problematic (see 2.2).

4. Unclear categories

Beside the major categories in sections 2 and 3, we found a number of other categories or markers. We assume some of these to be local and post-proto Great Lakes innovations. We mention here a few others about whose status we are unsure. They have a geographical distribution wider than one subgroup but less than the whole area.

4.1. Forms involving initial #ni-

Verbal forms involving initial [n] and a vowel[25] are quite widespread in Great Lakes languages. They can be generally categorized as follows:

(a) Rutara #ni- is a clitic associated with Progressive, in compounds and noncompounds. So Haya-Nyambo-Zinza (Haya form exemplified):

(18) tu-ø-gur-á 'we buy' vs. ni-tu-ø-gurá 'we are buying',
túkabá nitugurá 'we were buying', etc

This *ni-* shape is also used in at least one Suguti language (Regi) in Progressive compounds.

[25] In some dialects of Luhya, including Logooli, a Middle Future is expressed by initial *#na-* and suffixal *-e*. Whatever the etymology of this *#na-*, both its vowel ([a] for [i]) and its reference seem to us to suggest that it is not connected to the *#ni-* being discussed here. Also, we find no geographical overlap between this *#na-* and the [naa] variant of the other future *-laa-* (cf fn. 15).

(b) in a few nonadjacent languages (Shubi, Hangaza, in W.Highlands, and at least Isuukha and Saamia in Luhya), #ni- is a clitic and translates into English as "if" or "when", so:

(19)	Hangaza	ni-tu-ø-gura	'if we buy'
	Saamia	ni-hu-kul-ire	'if we bought'

We would emphasize that, while it translates as English 'if, when', its real meaning may be something else but our data does not allow us to expand on this.

(c) in Gusii, Kuria, and maybe Suba, #n(i)- can be cliticized to many tense and aspect forms. This makes it similar to #n(i)- in Chaga and Central Kenyan languages, where it marks focus. It is plausible to relate this to the preceding, especially to (a), because the shape and position are identical, and it is not too hard to see a semantic connection between focus and a Progressive marker. It should also be remembered that data from Gusii is suspect for reconstruction purposes, if it is the only evidence for a particular feature in Great Lakes languages: Gusii may have started life as a Central Kenyan language, brought this focus *ni-* with it, and passed it on to its smaller neighbours.

(d) Mould 1981 says a #ne- 'narrative' occurs in Nyoro-Tooro, Ganda, Soga, Saamia, Wanga, Bukusu, and Logooli. As he omits the intervening languages (Gwere, other Luhya dialects) it would seem reasonable to expect it to occur in them too. However, there are difficulties with the form and geographical distribution of Mould's claim. The shape [ne] is specific to Ganda: does this [ne] derive from a clitic [ni] or the conjunction [na] 'and, with'? Mould says the shape in all the other languages is also [ne], which is unlikely. Since we have little data on this we cannot decide between [ni] and [na] as phonological sources, so we cannot see whether it relates to the [ni] under discussion. Morphosyntactically, this [ne] is also opaque: the label 'narrative', implying '...and ...and ...' would link it to the conjunction *na,* but the discussion in Ashton et al (1954: 27) suggests another possibility: "common to all the contexts in which... NE... appears is the idea of association... expressed as a statement of facts having a logical connection or a logical sequence to what has gone before." Consider (18) and (19) and the statement above about Gusii and Kuria, following (19). The second part of the compound form in (18) and the examples in (19) are forms which have a logical connection to another event, and the focus function in Gusii and Kuria imply knowledge of what has gone before. These forms all have [n(i)], not [na].

Hyman (p.c.) thinks that the formal and tonal similarities between Ganda [ne] and the negative prefix [te] (ti- elsewhere in Great Lakes) support relating *ne-* to *ni-* rather than *na-*.

A summary of the foregoing examples (a-d) suggests this. Since the two [ni] of (a) and (b) have at least the same shape, they may have the same origin. While the [ni] in (c) has the same shape, the source language may be

Gusii, which makes it suspect. And we cannot be sure of the origin of the [ne] in (d), although it is most likely *ni-*.

In our present state of knowledge, we think it is likely that #ni- was a feature in the earlier stage of Great Lakes languages, but that its unitary meaning, if any, is unclear: our guess (see (2.2) is that indicated focus.

4.2. Forms involving -la-

Distinct from the (long-vowelled) Near Future *-laa-* there is some evidence for a *-la-*.

In Haya, and at least in some other Rutara languages, but our data is silent on the point, the use of *-ra-* in perfects pushes the time of the action farther back. Thus *tu-rá-guz-ire* and *tw-á-guz-ire* are both present perfects and translate as 'we have bought' but differ in that the buying was farther in the past in the first than in the second.[26] Something similar seems to be implied in W.Highlands, e.g., Rundi *tu-raa-bariira* 'Have we sewn *already*?'.

Second, in W.Highlands *-ra-* distinguishes verbal from postverbal focus forms,[27] thus;

(20) Postverbal focus tu-gur-a 'we buy (something, somewhere, sometime, etc)'

versus

Verbal focus tu-ra-gur-a 'we buy'

Third, in most Mara *-ra-* represents a combined Simple/progressive (*to-ra-gora* 'we buy, are buying') with the range of reference sometimes widening to cover near past or near future. Whiteley (1960) describes Gusii *-raa-* as not referring to time but to action sequence.

---

[26]Hyman and Byarushengo talk of the *-ra-* form as an 'experiental'. As the Perfect column in our Table shows, wherever the *-a-* Perfect can be used (Past, Present, Future), so also can the *-ra-* form. The difference is hard to pin down via an English translation. The *-ra-* form clearly refers to an earlier action. Thus, if asked 'How is your father?', two answers are possible, and both translate as 'He has already died': *y-áa-fiire* and *a-rá-fiire* (/-fá/). The first means it is a recent event, perhaps the body can still be seen, whereas the second means he is dead and buried. Both have present relevance, thus are 'perfects'. But obviously events that happened long ago generally have less immediacy or relevance. Thus *tu-rá-guz-ire émótoka* 'we once bought a car' might be termed experiental reference in that it is not an event which once took place and is over and now irrelevant—as a simple past would be—but it is less immediate than *tw-áa-guz-ire émótoka* 'we have already bought a car (and it is standing outside the house)'. We feel that calling them Near and Far Perfects covers both the relevance to the present ('Perfect') and the distance from the present (Near, Far).

[27]'Post verbal focus' forms require the explicit presence of a complement (Object, Adverbial, etc), while 'verbal focus' verb forms stand by themselves.

This is like the case of #ni-: a collection of forms similar in shape but functions so diverse that it is unclear how they might be reconciled to a single historical antecedent.

4.3. Focus?

Another issue only skirted so far is whether and how a proto-Great Lakes marked focus. W. Highlands indicates verbal focus by *-ra-*. Gusii and Kuria (see 4.1) mark some kind of focus with initial #ni-/ne-. Hyman and Byarushengo (1984) point out that one Haya tense, our Middle Past, distinguishes (singular, but not plural) forms like:

(21) y-a-bon-a Kató 'she saw Kato' (post verbal focus) from
y-á:bón-a 'she saw'

where a high tone and an extra mora ([a]) distinguish the prestem position in the verb focussed second form from the first. For other Great Lakes groups we do not have information. Thus, while the exponents of focus in W. Highlands, Haya, and Gusii/Kuria are quite different, the fact that they mark (postverbal) focus at all, plus the fact that it is widespread in Bantu languages in general, suggest the possibility that proto-Great Lakes probably had focus marking but they do not clearly suggest how it was marked. The W.Highlands languages in general have a reduced set of tense-aspect marking so it is possible they recycled some of their older morphology into focus marking.

4.4. A "vocalic mora with no features"?

A final issue is raised by example (12) and footnotes 15 and 18. In prestem position Haya and Ganda lengthen the vowels of certain morphemes, including subject prefixes and the *-ta-* negative:

(22) ti-*tuu*-gur-é 'we will not buy' (but *tu*-gur-á 'we buy')
tu-*táá*-ku-gur-a 'we should not buy (Near Future negative)' but
tu-*tá*-ri-gur-a 'we should never buy (Far Future negative)'

Hyman and Katamba (1997) suggest such forms might be analyzed as bimorphemic, where in a second prestem slot there is a morpheme which is a vocalic mora without features. The only apparently long-vowelled tense marker, the Near Future *-raa-*, can itself also be so analyzed:

(23) tu-*raa*-gur-á 'we will buy (NFuture)'
but
tu-*rá*-gur-a 'we should buy (NFuture)'

Finally, it will also be noticed that at various points in the text we mention unexplained length variation between languages (e.g., 4.2 *-laa-* vs *-la-*, and fns.15, 18). While some might be mistakes in phonetic notation, they might also be due to the presence or absence of this same vocalic mora.

Before assuming this phenomenon for earlier stages of Great Lakes, we need to know more of its meaning/function and geographical distribution.

5. Conclusions

The Introduction set out our three initial aims. Our first and principal was to examine how TA works in these languages. Our thinking on this is illustrated, mainly in sections 2 and 3, and the Table. These together offer an overview of Great Lakes TA systems by pulling together much data otherwise only available in individual monographs. Our second was to see how far this approach would produce better reconstructions of earlier TA systems, both for Great Lakes and for Bantu in general. Using the time-honored method—based on phonological and semantic identity—we have sketched at the end of each subsection the categories and structures we think can be reconstructed for a putative proto-Great Lakes. Along the way, we show how tricky this kind of reconstruction is, which explains why we have said little about proto-Bantu. As an experiment in methodology this is but a first step.

We had as a third and minor goal to see whether TA systems might be used as a tool for classification, and we do feel in a position to make limited remarks about this. As proto-Bantu slowly diversified and new dialects and languages emerged, the verbal system, with its constituent categories and structures, changed. Is there verbal evidence for the assumption of a proto-Great Lakes, intermediate between proto-Bantu and today's languages? Any intermediate proto is a combination of unchanged inherited parts, modified inherited parts, internal innovations, and innovations induced by contact with neighboring languages, and each intermediate proto is a unique combination. For a proto-Great Lakes the following could be assumed, and this combination is different from that assumable for neighboring languages, as far as we know:

- Aspects (cf sections 2.1-5): *-ø- Simple (Present), *-aga/-anga Habitual, *-ile Perfect, *-kiaa- Persistive. Also a Progressive, marking unclear.
- Tenses (cf 3.1-3): *-laa- Near Future; *-li- Far Future, *-e (1) subjunctive (2) associated in an undefined way with Near Future reference. Some combination of pasts (see 3.2). -0- Present.
- Tenses and aspects could co-occur in various combinations discussed in the text.
- Other possible categories and formants (cf 4, also various points in 2 and 3): *-liku-*, #ni-, *-la-*, focus.

This collection of features supports the idea of a proto-Great Lakes. Within Great Lakes, each of the six subgroups coheres well enough in terms of TA to support the idea that each had its own intermediate ancestor. The problem areas are W. Highlands, whose TA systems today are reduced and different from those in other Great Lakes languages, and the northern Mara languages, especially Gusii, which again are somewhat different from other Great Lakes languages.

Finally, since this is work in progress and, as can be easily seen, there are many questions and some answers, a conclusion should suggest directions for future work. They are:

- we need more good quality data on TA systems in Great Lakes languages in general. We found it hard to use or compare much of the existing data because the meaning and scope of forms, and especially the descriptive labels used, were unreliable or incomplete.
- we considered mainly data from positive, nonrelative, nonconditional, nonmood clauses, and we now need data on other clause types in particular, even for several of the languages for which we had good MCA data. This and the preceding include tonal information.
- it would be desirable to expand this to other Bantu languages/groups. By seeing what can be assumed as inherited from proto-Bantu we can isolate what appears to be innovation in Great Lakes, but we need comparative data to see how far the innovations extend outside Great Lakes.
- for the reasons set out in section 1.3, we need to know more about how change in TA comes about in general and to integrate this with the kinds of change suggested by Great Lakes data. Certain processes of change have been mentioned: aspects tend to become tenses but not vice versa; changes tend to occur in MCAs earlier than in other clause types; two-word forms can become single word forms but not vice versa; structures referring to "present" can expand their semantic range, especially into the future; subjunctives can come to refer to the future (both nonfactuals); and perfect morphemes can expand their meaning into past reference. These change suggestions need checking, and we need to add more plausible change types.
- this done, we can proceed to make better choices for proto status from among the various past tense forms.
- expanding our inventory of plausible changes will ultimately lead to a better overview of the categorial contrasts in the older system. All the TA contrasts and the minor features should fit together as parts of a system. Mould (1981: 208) accepts as a working hypothesis a certain number of past and future tense categories but does not justify this assumption. We posit two futures and think three pasts are likely: while the former are well borne out by the data, the latter are less solid and we have not discussed the underlying assumptions in depth.
- expanding our inventory of plausible changes will also enable us to show how each particular contemporary system derives from the older system.
- at a final stage we should be able to judge whether more deviant systems, such as those in Gusii/Northern Mara, and W. Highlands, can really be derived from a proto-Great Lakes.

References

Barreteau, Daniel (ed.). 1978. *Inventaire des études linguistiques sur les pays d'afrique noire d'expression francaise et sur madagascar*. Paris: CILF.

Bastin, Yves. 1978. Les langues bantoues, in: Daniel Barreteau (ed.), 123-185.

Botne, Robert. 1986. The temporal role of Eastern Bantu *-ba* and *-li*. *Studies in African Linguistics 17*,3: 303-317.

Botne, Robert. 1990. The origins of the Remote Future formatives in Kinyarwanda, Kirundi, Giha (J61), *Studies in African Linguistics* 21,2:189-210.

Bybee, Joan, Ronald Perkins & William Pagliuca. 1994. *The Evolution of Grammar, Tense, Aspect, and Modality in the Languages of the World.* Chicago: University of Chicago Press.

Clements, George N. & John Goldsmith (eds.). 1984. *Autosegmental Studies in Bantu Tone*. Dordrecht: Foris Publications.

Dahl, Oesten. 1985. *Tense and Aspect Systems*. Oxford: Basil Blackwell Ltd.

Dimmendaal, Gerrit J. Forthcoming. Language shift and morphological convergence in the Nilotic area. *Sprache und Geschichte in Afrika* 14.

Hinnebusch, Thomas. H., Derek Nurse & Martin Mould (eds.). 1981. *Studies in the Classification of Eastern Bantu Languages*. Hamburg: Buske Verlag.

Hyman, Larry. M. & Ernest R. Byarushengo. 1984. A Model of Haya Tonology, in Clements, G. N. & J. Goldsmith (eds.), 53-103.

Hyman, Larry M. & Francis X. Katamba. In press. The syllable in Luganda phonology and morphology. In Harry van der Hulst & Nancy Ritter (eds), *The Syllable: Views and Facts.* Berlin: Mouton de Gruyter.

Leung, Elizabeth. W-Y. 1991. The tonal phonology of llogoori: a study of Llogoori verbs. Ithaca. *Working Papers of the Cornell Phonetics Laboratory*, No. 6.

Mould, Martin. 1981. Greater Luyia, in: Hinnebusch, T.H., D. Nurse & M. Mould (eds.), 181-230.

Nurse, Derek & Franz Rottland. 1991-2. Sonjo: description, classification, history, *Sprache und Geschichte in Afrika* 12-13: 171-289.

Schoenbrun, David L. 1990. *Early History in Eastern Africa's Great Lakes Region*. [Unpubl. Ph.D thesis, University of California, Los Angeles.]

Whiteley, Wilfred H. 1960. *The Tense System of Gusii. Kampala*. Kampala: East African Institute of Social Research.

Appendix

Tense/aspect in Haya

TENSE/ASPECT	SIMPLE	PROGRESSIVE First verb 'be' + Second verb ni-..-ø-	HABITUAL -gá
FAR PAST Before yesterday -ka-	tú-ka-gur-a 'we bought' N ti-tú-á-guz-íre	tú-ka-bá ni-tu-ø-gur-á 'we were buying' N tú-ka-bá tu-tá-rí-ku-gur-a	tu-a-gur-a-gá 'we used to buy' N ti-tu-a-gur-a-ga
MIDDLE PAST Yesterday -ø-...-iré	tu-ø-guz-iré 'we bought' N ti-tú-ø-guziré	tu-ø-bá-iré nitu-ø-gur-a 'we were buying' N tubáiré tu-tá-rí-ku-gur-a	
NEAR PAST Today -áa-	tu-áa-gur-a 'we (just) bought' N ti-tú-áagur-a	tu-aa-bá ni-tu-ø-gúra 'we were buying' N tu-áa-ba tu-tá-rí-ku-gur-a	
PRESENT	tu-ø-gur-á 'we buy' N ti-tú-gur-a	ni-tu-ø-gur-á 'we are buying' N ti-tú-rí-ku-gur-a	
NEAR FUTURE Today, tomorrow -raa-	tu-raa-gur-á 'we will buy' N ti-tuu-gur-é	tu-raa-bá ni-tu-ø-gurá 'we will be buying' N tu-raa-bá tu-tá-rí-ku-gur-a	
FAR FUTURE After tomorrow -rí-	tu-rí-gur-á 'we will buy' N ti-tu-rí-gur-a	tu-rí-bá ni-tu-ø-gurá 'we will be buying' N tu-rí-bá tu-tá-rí-ku-gur-a	tu-raa-gur-a-gá 'we will buy regularly' N ti-tuu-gur-e-ga

TENSE/ASPECT	PERFECT First verb 'be' + Second verb -ire	PERSISTIVE First verb 'be' + Second verb -ki(áa)-
FAR PAST Before yesterday -ka-	1. túkabá tu-rá-guz-ire 'we had bought long before' N túkabá tutákagur-aga 2. túkabá tuáaguzire 'we had bought' N túkabá tutákaguzire	túkabá tu-kiáa-gur-a 'we were still buying' N túkabá tu-tá-kiáa-gur-a or N túkabá tutá-ki-gur-a
MIDDLE PAST Yesterday -ø-...-iré	tu-ø-báiré tuáaguzire 'we had bought' N tubáiré tutákaguzire	tu-ø-báiré tukiáagur-a 'we were still buying' N tubáiré tutakiáagur-a
NEAR PAST Today -áa-	tuáabá tuáaguzire 'we had bought' N tuáabá tutákaguzire	tuáabá tukiáagur-a 'we were still buying' N tuáabá tutákiáagur-a
PRESENT	1. tu-rá-guz-ire 'we (have) bought once/long ago' N ti-tú-ka-gur-a-ga 2. tu-áa-guz-ire 'we've already bought' N ti-túkaguzire	tu-kiáa-gur-a 'we are still buying' N ti-tukiáa-gur-a
NEAR FUTURE Today, tomorrow -raa-	turaabá tuáaguzire 'we will have bought' N turaabá tutákaguzire	turaabá tukiáagur-a 'we'll still be buying N turaabá tutákiáagur-a
FAR FUTURE After tomorrow -rí-	1. turíbá turáguzire 'we will have bought long before' N turíbá tutákagur-aga 2. turíbá tuáaguzire 'we will have bought' N turíbá tutákaguzire	turíbá tukiáagur-a 'we'll still be buying' N turíbá tutákiáagur-a

Notes on the Table

1. The table shows the interestion of tense and individual aspects. As in many languages (e.g., English we will have bought, will have been buying) tense co-occurs with more than one aspect, not shown above. So Haya *tw-a-bá-ga tw-áa-guz-ire*, where the first *-a-* refers to Far Past (in the Habitual), *-ga* refers to the Habitual, the second *-áa-* plus *-ire* refer to Perfect, and the unwieldly English translation would be 'We had always already bought it, (whenever..)'.
2. The table above shows 29 different positive forms, that is, a verb has at least 29 such forms. But many forms are not shown, see for example notes 4, 7, and 9 below. We would guess that a verb such as *-gura* could have at least 50 positive TA shapes. With negatives that number would more than double (see note 3 below). Dahl (1985) says that Bantu languages have some of the most elaborated TA systems in the world.
3. All Progressives, Perfects, and Persistives can be negated in more than one way, not shown. So for instance, in the Near Future either the second, lexical, verb can be negated or the first, auxiliary, part, thus *turaabá tu-<u>tá</u>-kaguzire* 'we won't have bought', or *<u>ti</u>-tuubé tuáaguzire* 'we won't have bought yet' (negative markers underlined). By negating the main verb, the focus is on denying the buying. When the first verb - which carries the time reference - is negated, the focus is on negating the time ('won't yet').
4. Aktionsart plays a role, not shown above. E.g., for the stative verb *-nágira* '(fall) asleep', there is a paradigm with *ø...ire* (not *a...ire*); tu-nagí-iré 'we are sleeping', Far Past *túkabá tú-nagiiré* 'we were sleeping', Near Past *tubáiré tú-nagiiré* 'we were sleeping', Near Future *turaabá túnagiiré* 'we'll be sleeping', etc.
5. In the Perfect, the alternative prestem marker *-ra-* (short vowel vs the long vowelled -raa- of the Near Future) pushes the action referred to further into the past. So -ra-, as -ga following, might be seen as a 'shifter'.
6. We label the Habitual marker as *-ga*, rather than *-aga*, because the first [a] can be replaced, e.g., *tugurêga* 'we should buy regularly'. For the future, it is the Near Future prestem marker that combines with *-ga* to give the Far Future Habitual forms, whereas the (short, toneless) prestem *-a-* of the Past Habitual is different from the (long, hightoned) *-aa-* of the Near Past. Besides its appearance above in the Simple column, *-ga* also appears in certain perfect negatives where it is associated with the meaning 'never', e.g., *tu-rá-guz-ire* 'we once bought', N *ti-tú-ka-gur-a-ga* 'we have never bought'. Why this should be is not clear to us.
7. Not shown above are forms expressing probability: so *tu-a-ku-guz-iré* 'we could have bought', N *ti-tu-á-ku-guz-ire*, and *tu-a-ku-gur-á* 'we might buy', N *ti-tu-á-ku-gur-a*.

8. Tone melodies will change, esp. in the Simple, depending on the phonological structure of the verb. In most cases, the Persistive/-kiaa-/can have two realizations, either [kyá:] or [ki], as in [*ti-tú-kyá:-gur-a*] 'we are not still buying' or [*ti-tú-ki-gur-a]* 'we will never buy any more'.
9. For some functions of *-ka-* in Haya, see (17).
10. Haya, as many Great Lakes languages, can use "Aux 'come' + infinitive" to render 'be about to = near future'. In Haya it is still clearly an auxiliary but it is more fully grammaticalized in other languages.
11. Details of TA in the neighboring languages Nyambo and Zinza are almost identical to those in Haya.

The Genesis of Verbal Negation in Bantu and its Dependency on Functional Features of Clause Types[1]

TOM GÜLDEMANN
University of Leipzig

1. Introduction

It is well-known that a number of Bantu languages distinguish at least two different ways of expressing verbal negation depending on the clause type the predicate occurs in. This observation has been recognized by various Bantuists in their reconstructions of an assumed Proto-Bantu. Apart from a possible critique associated with the very concept of such an ancestor language, a serious shortcoming of this approach is that in this frame no account has been taken of the important functional correlations of the phenomenon. Such an attempt, based mainly on research in grammaticalization and diachronic typology, will be made here. These theoretical tools provide an explanation of such a morphological alternation

[1]The present research, which resulted in my dissertation and of which this paper is one part, was sponsored by grants from the Federal State of Nordrhein-Westfalen and the German Service for Academic Exchange (DAAD), which are herewith gratefully acknowledged. Thanks to Larry Hyman for valuable comments on the paper and to Orin Gensler for helping to improve my English.

of negative predicates from various viewpoints and can readily relate it to crosslinguistically similar phenomena. This approach bears also on hypotheses regarding the historical emergence of the phenomenon within the family.

2. The morphotactic structure of finite predicates in Bantu and grammaticalization

To begin with, some remarks about the morphological structure of Bantu predicates and certain grammaticalization patterns associated with it are in order. A widely accepted outline of the different morpheme slots of the finite verb has been established since Meeussen (1967:108ff). A slightly modified version of this is presented below:[2]

SLOT	preinitial	initial	postinitial	preradical
FUNCTION	TAM/ *polarity*	subject	TAM/ *polarity*	object
SLOT	radical	prefinal	final	postfinal
FUNCTION	verbal root	derivation/ TAM	TAM	clause type/ object/*polarity*

Figure 1. Morphological structure of finite predicates in Bantu

As can be seen from my brief functional labels for each morpheme slot, the coding of negation (*polarity*) is achieved morphologically by three marker types, i.e., *preinitial, postinitial* and *postfinal.* Not all such markers can be assigned an etymology. However, as a grammeme class characterized by a fixed position with respect to other markers, each of these slots can with high probability be related to grammaticalization processes that are observable time and again in individual Bantu languages even today. Underlying this observation is the general thesis of grammaticalization research,[3] that syntactically complex expressions can and often do undergo

[2]There is no space here to motivate my adjustments to Meeussen's formulation. I will only note that I adhere more strictly to considerations that relate to the diachronic emergence of certain morphotactic positions, which will be explained below, and view, in keeping with general linguistic usage, all affixes purely with regard to their position vis-a-vis the verb root as pre- or suffixes. This leads to a merging of some of Meeussen's positions into a single slot, specifically as regards my postinitial and prefinal slots, and to renaming his infix as preradical. A more detailed discussion of this problem, as well as other ideas in section 2, can be found in Güldemann (1996, chapter 2.3).

[3]I will not go into this but refer to relevant treatments in (inter alia) Lehmann (1982), Heine-Reh (1984), Heine-Claudi-Hünnemeyer (1991), Traugott-Heine (eds., 1991) and Hopper-Traugott (1993).

phonetic contraction leading to the emergence of an inflected word form and transforming "ex-lexical" entities into grammemes of a certain morphotactically definable type.

This paper deals with the specific clause-type-induced relation between pre- and postinitial negative strategies. Hence I will confine my presentation just to these two morpheme types. The following schema lists the three most important grammaticalization patterns whereby a morphotactic slot is derivable from a certain morphosyntactic source constellation. These sources are binary, hierarchically organized structures that regularly consist of a constituent bearing the illocutionary force of the predicative expression and a second constituent conveying the central propositional information but deprived of its possible illocutivity. In syntactic terms, I call the former the nucleus, the latter the satellite:

	Illocutionary base as syntactic nucleus		*Propositional base as syntactic satellite*		
(1)	finite verb form	+	nonfinite verbal noun	>	postinitial
(2)	finite verb form	+	finite dependent verb form	>	preinitial
(3)	illocutionary particle	+	finite dependent verb form	>	preinitial

Figure 2. Grammaticalization in complex Bantu predicates and its morphotactic results[4]

The following examples, either representing cases reported within a language or else reconstructed by me on the basis of inter-language cognates, will illustrate each pattern:[5]

[4]This list does not claim to be exhaustive. Consider, e.g., another possible pattern, which will not be pursued in this paper: In some languages pronominal concords are used as a kind of predicative pivot in copular sentences. This could eventually yield a finite verb form if the subject concord is preposed to a verbal noun. Thus, one can imagine the grammaticalization path: (4) class concord + nonfinite satellite (verbal noun) > postinitial. This would explain the not infrequent existence of a verb structure *SC-ku-VS*, whereby the postinitial ku is derivable from the noun class prefix 15 for infinitives.

[5]Throughout this paper, the following abbreviations are used:

ABSTR abstract, ANT anteriority, COM comitative, COND conditional, COP copula(tive), D dependent clause, DEM demonstrative, FUT future, HAB habitual, IA inanimate, IMP imperative, INE inessive, INF infinitive, IPRFV imperfective, IR indirect relative clause, LOC locative, NEG negative, O object, P plural, PERF perfect, PF predication focus, POSS possessor, PRES present, PRFV perfective, PROG progressive, PROX proximal, PT past, R relative clause, REF anaphoric reference, REM remote (local or temporal), S subject or singular, SC subject concord, SIM simultaneity, STAT stative, SUB subordinator, SUBJ subjunctive, T.G. following all my own notes or comments, TAM tense-aspect-mode, V vowel, VN verbal noun, VS verb stem, Ø no TAM-function independent from another glossed morpheme, 1/2/3... noun class or personal category

Pattern (1) to postinitial in Mbundu (H.21):[6]

(1) ngal -a mu (ku) -bang -a
1S:be -PRES INE INF -do -Ø
'eu estou fazendo' [I am doing] (Chatelain 1888/1889:32)

becomes

ngolo -bang -a
1S:PROG -do -Ø
'eu estou fazendo' [I am doing] (Chatelain 1888/1889:32)

Pattern (2) in Mwera (P.22) vs. preinitial in Yao (P.21):

(2) a. tu -ci tu -jaŵul -e
1P -do 1P -go -SUBJ
'we are about to go' (Harries 1950:111)

versus

au mpini-u ci -tu -suumisy -e
thishandle FUT -1P -sell -Ø
'The handle we'll sell...' (Whiteley 1966:182)

Pattern (2) to preinitial in Zulu (S.42):[7]

(2) b. nga -ɓe ngi -thand -a
1S:REM.PT -be:STAT 1S:D[8] -love -SIM

becomes

nga:ngi -thand -a
1S:REM.PT.IPRFV -love -Ø
'I was loving' (Doke 1927:§425)

Alongside the name of a language I will also add its number within the established reference classification of Bantu according to the list in Bastin (1978:136-151).

[6]For this case, the two intermediate stages *ngala ubanga* and *ngalo banga* are also attested.

[7]This is a quite rare, but possible, instance of pattern (2) whereby the nucleus is reduced by dropping the auxiliary stem, thus yielding the marked phenomenon of a double initial.

[8]A gloss D or R indicates that the specific subordinate status of the predicate is signalled by a typical prosodic pattern of the word form, which usually has a regular reflex on the subject concord.

Pattern (3) in Kikuyu (E.51) vs. preinitial in Nkore-Kiga (J.11):[9]

(3)	ny	ma	-ryy	-ku	-aga
	PF	2:D	-PROX.FUT	-die	-HAB

'They will keep on dying' (Bennett et al. 1985:174)

versus

ni	-m	-many	-a
PROG	-1S	-know	-Ø

'I know' ('am knowing') (Taylor 1985:151)

3. Morphological strategies of verbal negation in Bantu

After outlining in brief the morphotactic structure of finite predicates and partially relating them to grammaticalization processes, I present in this section the major strategies of verbal negation.[10] It is advisable to classify these according to certain parameters in order to highlight structural and diachronic relations among them.

To begin with, one must distinguish differing *degrees of grammaticalization* that negative strategies may demonstrate. Although a linguistic expression may enter the functional domain of negation via very different grammaticalization paths,[11] it is of special importance here whether or not there exists an etymological relation between the negative morpheme and a lexical item in the given language. This criterion especially captures the phenomenon that a variety of Bantu languages, often correlating with a specific grammatical or pragmatic context, can express negation by way of a periphrastic construction, consisting of an inflected, inherently negative auxiliary and a frequently, though not universally, nonfinite complement. This leads to a simplified binary distinction of *grammaticalized* vs. *periphrastic* negatives.

Within the group of grammaticalized markers,[12] a second parameter refers to the distinction between *bound* and *unbound* negative markers, specifically whether they are morphological parts of the verbal constituent

[9]Cf. Güldemann (1996, chapters 4.3.1 and 4.5.1) for the relation between the two preinitials.

[10]This will exclude the encoding of negation by suprasegmental or by more than one segmental marker. Although the latter at least is a remarkably widespread phenomenon in Bantu, it does not enter into the present discussion. For a more comprehensive list of negative marking types see Westphal (1958) and, applying to all data in the following sections, Güldemann (1996, chapter 4.7).

[11]In addition to relevant data in Güldemann (1996:249), see already Meinhof (1948:183).

[12]In principle, the aforementioned and the following criterion can also pertain to less grammaticalized strategies. This will not, however, be further discussed here.

or not. Unbound elements are *particles* or *clitics*, bound elements are *affixes*. The latter correspond to already established morphotactic positions in an agglutinative verb form.

The third parameter captures *constituent* and *morpheme order*, as it is important to specify the position a certain marker has with respect to the verb. If a marker occurs at its margin I distinguish between *initial* and *final* elements. By definition, the *incorporation* of a negative into a verb form is only possible with affixes.

Using these three criteria, one arrives at the following classification of segmental, monomorphemic types of verbal negation in Bantu:[13]

I. periphrastic
II. grammaticalized
  1. function word
    a. initial particle/ proclitic
    c. final particle/ enclitic
  2. affix
    a. initial = preinitial
    b. incorporated = postinitial
    c. final = postfinal

Each negation type is illustrated by an example below:

Periphrastic negation (I) in Hungan (H.42):

(4)	beet	tu	-khoon	-aak	ku	-mon	ni	beet	tu	-biing
	we	1P	-fail	-PROG	INF	-see	that	we	1P	-win

'we don't think that we'll win' (Takizala 1972:274)

Negation by initial particle (II1a) in Mbala (K.51):

(5)	lo	i	-daad	-idi	giluungu
	NEG	1S	-see	-PT	calabash

'je n'ais pas vu la calebasse' [I didn't see the calabash]
(Ndolo 1972:78)

---

[13]It should be kept in mind, though, that distinctions between types within a parameter are often not differences of principle but ones of degree. This goes without saying with regard to differences of grammaticalization, as the theory starts from the assumption that change leading to grammemes is gradual. The level of fine-grained distinctions on such an evolutionary scale that one records for a given language will often depend largely on the particular reference one happens to be using. In the same way, the distinction between a function word and an affix, presented here as different categories, can be seen instead in continuous terms as expressing degrees of phonetic tightness or integration on a cline particle > clitic > affix. This, too, will often depend on the published source used. Nonetheless, as general classificatory devices, the above categories are convenient.

Negation by final particle (II1c) in Matumbi (P.13):

(6) u -yend -a lili
2S -go -PRES NEG
'du gehst nicht' [you don't go] (Krumm 1912:37)

Preinitial negation (II2a) in Standard Swahili (G.42d):

(7) ha -tu -tak -i
NEG -1P -want -PRES
'wir wollen nicht' [we don't want] (Brauner & Herms 1979:126)

Postinitial negation (II2b) in Shi (J.53):

(8) aa -rha -hiing -a
1 -NEG -cultivate -PRES
[(s)he] 'does not cultivate' (Polak-Bynon 1975:251)

Postfinal negation (II2c) in Nkoya (L62):

(9) ni -ku -mu -longesh -a -ha
1S/S -FUT -1/O -teach -Ø -NEG
'I will not teach him (today)' (Yukawa 1987:145)

Two of these negative marker-types are most salient within Bantu, both with regard to geographical extension in the family as a whole and to distributional frequency in a single language: Many Bantu varieties show a regular, syntactically conditioned distribution of pre- and postinitial negatives. This has been acknowledged by various Bantuists, who account for it by ascribing the distribution to a supposed proto-language. Here is a representative quotation from one of the most influential attempts at reconstructing common Bantu morphology and syntax by Meeussen (1967:114): "The use of a negative preinitial seems to be confined to «indicative» absolutive (=non-relative) tenses, whereas other tenses rather had a postinitial: infinitive, subjunctives, relatives (and conjunctives ? [= hypotactic verb forms T.G.])." However, this statement has to be formulated more precisely in order to capture the fact that a number of languages, even in indicatives, have only a postinitial negative at their disposal. I intend my following generalization to be a purely synchronic statement:

While the postinitial negation strategy is rarely subject to distributional restrictions with regard to major clause types, preinitial negation shows a strong tendency to be confined to unmarked main clauses.

With this statement we have arrived at the point where we can pose the problem for which I will try to provide an explanation that accounts for both its diachronic evolutionary and its synchronic functional aspects: Why do we find in many languages a regular formal alternation, in expressing one and the same function, between main predications and other clause contexts? How can we explain the obvious interaction of the two clearly distinct parameters verbal negation and clause type?

A first approach to these questions emerges by considering the morphotactic positions of the respective marker types and relating them to possible scenarios of their grammaticalizational genesis. I will argue that there exists strong evidence for the thesis that the postinitial negative is the result of grammaticalization according to pattern (1) in section 2 above. That is, its source is a negative periphrasis. For the preinitial negative I will demonstrate a close affinity to a binary predicate structure in which the syntactic and illocutionary nucleus, with scope over an affirmative, finite satellite, encodes the function of negation. Here, it is specifically grammaticalization pattern (3) that is relevant. These hypotheses will be treated in the next two sections.

4. The postinitial—result of the grammaticalization of a negative periphrasis?

Trying to demonstrate that negative postinitials[14] derive from former negative auxiliaries is a problematic undertaking from an etymological viewpoint. These markers regularly have too little phonetic substance to relate them to synchronically attested lexemes. Moreover, on the family level, the forms of individual languages obviously fall into a few clearly discernable cognate sets. These features indicate that their grammaticalization took place at a relatively early stage in the genesis of today's Bantu varieties. Even if Meinhof (1948:183) had already thought of deriving postinitial negatives from certain lexical items and other scholars later speculated on one or another language-specific morpheme in the same way, I consider such correlations in the majority of cases to be highly questionable.[15] Nonetheless, there exists a solid body of empirical facts that can serve to validate my general hypothesis.

The first phenomenon I will explore is the fact that in some languages postinitial negative elements show unmistakably verbal properties which clearly point to their origin in former inflected auxiliaries.

One such case is the postinitial negative *si* in Northern Swahili (G42). Here it is especially fortunate that we possess data from earlier chronolects of the language that can shed light on the historical processes which the element *si* has been subject to. The following two examples from Old Swahili poetry show that *si* could at this developmental stage still be

[14]See Guthrie (1967-71, 4:235f) and Kamba Muzenga (1981:167ff) for lists of both post- and preinitial negatives.

[15]This does not mean that searching for lexical cognates is bound to be useless. A comparison of reconstructed Narrow Bantu grammemes with verbal lexemes of related languages belonging to hierarchically higher genetic units, like Benue-Congo, could well yield interesting results.

inflected with a subject concord (10) and that it could function as a finite copula in relative and adverbial clauses (11):

(10) ku -si yuwa ku -si mwezi
17LOC -NEG.COP sun 17LOC -NEG.COP moon
'da gab es weder eine Sonne noch einen Mond' [There was neither a sun nor a moon.] (Miehe 1979:248)

(11) ni -ph -a karātasi n-djema i-si -yo kiasi
1S/O -give -IMP 9:paper 9-good 9-NEG.COP -9:R measure
'gib mir gutes Papier in unbegrenzter Menge' [Give me good paper (which is) without limit!] (Miehe 1979:248)

The latter function is still evident in modern Northern Swahili varieties as well as in Standard Swahili: In relative clauses, *si* serves as the base for copulative predicates (12b) in exactly the same way as its affirmative counterpart *li*, which is clearly a verbal lexeme (12a). Second, in the general negative form, *si* takes, at least from a diachronic point of view, a verbal noun as its complement as in (13b):

(12) a. waziri a-li -ye na uwezo mkubwa
1a:minister 1-COP -1:R COM ability great
'Der Minister, der ein großes Können besitzt, ...' [the minister who has great ability] (Brauner & Herms 1979:190)

versus

b. waziri a-si -ye na wizara maalum
1a:minister 1-NEG.COP -1:R COM ministry certain
'Minister ohne Portefeuille (eigtl.: Minister, der kein bestimmtes Ministeri-um hat)' [a minister who does not have a certain ministry] (Brauner & Herms 1979:190)

(13) a. mw -aka u-j -a -o
3 -year 3-come -PRES -3:R
'das kommende Jahr' [the year to come]
(Brauner & Herms 1979:174)

versus

b. m-tu a-si -ye -ku -j -a[16]
1-person 1-NEG -1:R -Ø -come -Ø
'Der Mann, der nicht kommt, ...' [the person who doesn't come] (Brauner & Herms 1979:181)

A very similar phenomenon is evidenced by the postinitial negative *sa* in Zigula (G.31). As the following example pairs show, *sa* behaves like a verbal stem in that it can take a verbal noun as its complement as in (14b) and (15b) and can itself even inflect for the subjunctive final suffix *e* as in (15b):

(14) a. a-ka -ung -a
1-D:SIM -want -Ø
'he wanting' [i.e., if/when he wants] (Woodward 1902:28)

versus

b. a-ka -sa ku -ung -a
1-D:SIM -?:Ø INF -want -Ø
'if/when he doesn't want' (Woodward 1902:28)

(15) a. a-ung -e
1-want -SUBJ
'he may want' (Woodward 1902:30)

versus

b. a-se -ku -ung -a
1-?:SUBJ -INF -want -Ø
'he may not want' (Woodward 1902:30)

Although the above data (from a geographically restricted area) indicates that one can sporadically come across clues toward identifying particular postinitial negatives as former verbal lexemes, and despite the fact that this general development can be shown to occur quite frequently,[17] it must be admitted that concrete evidence for reconstructing the earlier categorial status of postinitial negatives on a family-wide level remains sparse.

---

[16] Historically, this can be analyzed as a structure *SC-si-R+VN*, the first part equating to the still-existing general affirmative relative *SC-VS-R* shown in (13a). As (13b) shows, the old infinitive marker *ku* survives in the morphonologically marked contexts of monosyllabic and vowel-initial verb stems.

[17] Cf. a clear case in languages of Bantu zone C in Kamba Muzenga (1981:13f), example (4) above for Hungan (H.42) and some others to be given below.

In order to substantiate my hypothesis, I will turn to another argument, one which bears on the striking fact that periphrastic expressions and grammaticalized postinitial markers encoding negation have common functional characteristics. As will be shown below, both strategies are used predominantly in specific clause types; in the majority of languages, this is in fact so even if there exists an alternative, usually preinitial, negative which is regularly used in main clauses. The following prototypical domains for each, i.e., both the periphrastic and the postinitial, negation type have been identified:[18]

(1) verbal nouns[19]
(2) subjunctives[20]
(3) prohibitives[21]
(4) relative clauses
(5) hypotactic adverbial clauses[22]

In this respect, the periphrastic and postinitial strategy together stand in opposition to typical main-clause negatives and thus form a more abstract, but well-defined functional class, which I will call the *POSTINITIAL-*

---

[18]Cf. Meeussen's characterization of the function of the postinitial in section 3 above.

[19]I have intentionally chosen the more general term verbal noun and not infinitive, the latter bearing within Bantu terminology a strong connotation of noun class 15, as there are some languages which in this domain use a different class prefix (cf. (17) below).

[20]Here are included paradigms which are usually structurally relatable to a finite form based on a verb stem with the modal final morpheme *e*. They invariably function as irrealis verb forms including a strong performative component of directivity ranging from permission to obligation.

[21]This term is equivalent to negative imperative and comprises forms which are strongly and always performatively directive. However, this does not imply that the person who is obliged by the speaker to conform to a certain action/behavior must be coreferent with the addressee of the utterance. This allows for non-second person imperatives (cf. (21) below). Often a language has no grammaticalized prohibitive independent of the subjunctive. When it is explicitly stated in the source that the negative subjunctive comprises the imperative function, this is counted in the following table as a separate kind of prohibitive. The counts for such "quasi-prohibitives" are given there in brackets but not considered in the category total. Pre-stem negative markers in nonfinite imperatives, which lack an initial morpheme, cannot be easily characterized as pre- or postinitial. They will be subsumed in the table under the rubric "Other".

[22]The figures in the table below will include only verb forms whose subordinate status is unmistakably not encoded by any conjunctional segment—that is, predicates that are marked as subordinate either by a special word-internal marker, a grammaticalized suprasegmental pattern, or not at all, and which are thus linked to the main clause asyndetically. For lack of space, the reason for this analytic restriction cannot be fully laid out here, but it is more extensively treated in Güldemann (1996).

complex.[23] With regard to distributional frequency, it is in fact better to speak of a local markedness shift: Considering both the overall picture in Bantu and, where applicable, the situation within individual languages, the POSTINITIAL-complex is the marked strategy in the functional context of a finite declarative main clause. However, this situation is reversed in the above-listed contexts, i.e., nonfinite/ non-declarative/ non-main clauses, where the POSTINITIAL-complex is compared to other negatives clearly the most frequent strategy.

Before proceeding to show distributional frequencies of the different negative types, I will give one example each for periphrastic and postinitial negation in their typical clause contexts:

Negation in verbal nouns in Zaramo (G.33) and Masaba (J.31), respectively:

(16) ku -lem -a ku -lond -a
INF -refuse -Ø INF -love -Ø
'nicht zu lieben' [not to love] (Worms 1897:301)

(17) bu -ka -tek -a
14ABSTR -NEG -cook -Ø
'not cooking' (Purvis 1907:67)

Negation in subjunctives in Nilamba (F.31) and Zulu (S.42), respectively:

(18) wa -lek -e ku -mu -ku -a
1/S -leave -SUBJ INF -1/O -beat -Ø
'so that he may not beat him' (Yukawa 1989:443)

(19) si -nga -thand -i
1P -NEG -love -SUBJ
'we should not love' (Doke 1927:§454)

Negation in prohibitives in Tumbuka (N.21):

(20) rek -a ku -yowoy -a
leave -IMP.S INF -speak -Ø
'stop speaking; don't speak' (Young 1932:139)

[23]The term is justified insofar as the negative element in both the periphrastic and the postinitial strategy is positioned after the subject concord (or a noun class prefix) but before the propositionally salient verb stem. The capital letters serve to distinguish the functional class proper from the connotation postinitial in the narrow sense.

(21)

ngi	-nga	-timb	-anga
1S	-NEG	-beat	-IMP

'I must not strike.' (Young 1932:40)

Negation in relative clauses in Nkoya (L.62) and Zulu (S.42), respectively:

(22)

mu	-ntu	a	-bul	-ile	ku	-longesh	-a
1	-person	1:REM.PT:IR	-lack	-Ø	INF	-teach	-Ø

'the person whom he did not teach' (Yukawa 1987:161)

(23)

wena	o	-nga	-thand	-i	-yo
you	R:2S	-NEG	-like	-PRES	-R

'thou who likest not' (Doke 1927:§760)

Negation in adverbial clauses in Nyanja (N.31) and Shona (S.10), respectively:

(24)

ndi	-ka	-pand	-a	ku	-kond	-a
1S	-COND	-not to have	-Ø	INF	-love	-Ø

'se (eu) não amar' [if I don't love] (Missionários 1964:93)

(25)

waka	-uy	-a	ku	-no	ini
1:REM.PT	-come	-Ø	18LOC	-DEM	I

ndi	-si	-nga	-d	-e
1S:D	-NEG	-SIM	-want	-Ø

'He came here without my wish' [= I not wanting] (Fortune 1955:297)

Table 1 below presents statistics for the various negation types classified according to my typology. The survey is based on a sample of more than 100 Bantu varieties from the Savannah group.[24] Apart from category-specific criteria, which were given above, some remarks on general principles of counting and certain problems of representativity are in order here:

First, the figures are totals of all negative markers of a specific type which were found in the Bantu varieties considered. If in a language more

[24]This excludes the zones A, B, C and part of D and H. See Güldemann (1996, chapter 2.4) regarding the profile of the sample. I intentionally use the neutral term variety here, as the compared language units of Guthrie's reference classification are often not on the same level regarding linguistic distance. To give just one example, Ngazija (G.44a) and Nzwani (G.44b), which are treated by Guthrie as dialects, are conjugationally much more distinct from each other than are Xhosa (S.41) and Zulu (S.42), which qualify as languages.

than one marker, even if of the same type, is encountered within the same functional domain (which does occur, though not often),[25] each marker is counted separately. If the same negative marker occurs in different verb forms belonging to a functionally definable set, e.g. in all relatives, it only counts once.

Second, it goes without saying that the absolute figures must remain highly dependent on the descriptive standards of the individual sources, which treat the relevant functional domains to very different extents. This is shown clearly by the left column of totals, where the figures are consistently below the total number of relevant language varieties (100+) and, moreover, vary considerably among each other—even though one could safely start from the assumption that every Bantu language has, say, a strategy to negate a verbal noun at its disposal.

Moreover, a different counting schema has been used for the POSTINITIAL-strategies (2nd and 3rd column) and the non-POSTINITIAL's (last two columns). For the POSTINITIAL's, only those languages were considered where there actually exists a formal alternative to a POSTINITIAL; languages with POSTINITIAL's only were excluded. By contrast, all cases of non-POSTINITIAL's are counted regardless of whether they stand in opposition to a POSTINITIAL or not. The reason for this emerges from the purpose behind the table, which is to demonstrate the thesis that POSTINITIAL's are unmarked (i.e., the numerically most frequent types) in the given functional domains. My counting scheme has the effect (if anything) of undercounting the POSTINITIAL's and overcounting the non-POSTINITIAL's, thus deliberately biassing the numbers against the thesis I am trying to prove. If the thesis nonetheless holds true (as it does) even with this biassing, it can safely be considered valid.

Finally, it should not be forgotten that, because of shortcomings of the underlying reference classification of the family, weighting the data regarding the notorious distinction *language* vs. *dialect* is at the present state of knowledge a more or less hopeless endeavor.[26]

To sum up these introductory remarks: The figures as I have presented them bear only relative significance, with respect to their proportional relations, and not as absolute counts of conjugational items of languages in the survey.

---

[25] See (20) and (21) above, both representing prohibitives from Tumbuka.

[26] I have deviated from the reference classification in two cases by counting the identical negative markers found in the various Nguni (S.40) varieties only once, and similarly for the identical markers of the Shona (S.10) varieties. This again deliberately works counter to the thesis I am trying to prove: it in general will lower the scores for the POSTINITIAL-complex, as both Nguni and Shona (except with prohibitives) possess only postinitial markers in the relevant contexts.

	Total	*Postinitial*	*Periphrasis*	*Preinitial*	*Other*
Verbal noun	60	36	16	4	4
Subjunctive	88	46	18	16	8
Prohibitive	41	12 (+21)	17 (+11)	5	7
Relative clause	65	42	15	6	2
Adverbial hypotaxis	47	32	8	6	1

Table 1. Distribution of negation strategies in marked contexts in Bantu

What the table shows is the following: With the exception of prohibitives, postinitials always account for more than the half of all negatives. With prohibitives, periphrastic negatives outnumber postinitials; otherwise they are the second most common type. Except in the case of subjunctives, periphrases alone exceed all non-POSTINITIAL's taken together. United in my POSTINITIAL-complex, postinitials and periphrases make up at least O of each total, and in cases other than subjunctives and prohibitives more than I of it.

My generalization on prototypical contexts for the POSTINITIAL-complex is not intended as an absolute principle but instead has the status of a tendency. As such it is already firmly supported by the figures. However, it can be established still more strongly, if one additionally characterizes the profile of those cases which qualify as exceptions to my proposed tendency, i.e., those which underlie the figures in the two right columns.

First, one must concede that the figures for subjunctives apparently deviate from a generally clear picture. Even if some non-POSTINITIAL's can still be derived from a periphrasis,[27] preinitial negation is clearly a prominent and geographically evenly distributed alternative in its own right within the domain of subjunctives. The only general observation that might partially explain this fact is that preinitial subjunctives are invariably found in languages where preinitial negatives are generally prominent; one could think of their contextual expansion from this prototypical main-clause usage. However, such a phenomenon is in the end only explanatory if it can be founded on some functional feature of the subjunctive, an idea which at this point cannot be explored further.

Apart from the problematic morphotactic characterization of initial negatives in nonfinite prohibitives, another factor plays a role in accounting for some of the exceptions in this domain. Some markers, in spite of their predicate-initial position, are in fact akin to the POSTINITIAL-complex as regards their grammaticalizational genesis. They can have their source in the imperative form of a negative auxiliary, which has gradually become etymologically opaque. Compare, e.g., the specific case of the prohibitive

[27]See Horton (1949:131) on the initial particle negating a subjunctive in Lwena (K.14).

in Zulu (S.42), where this hypothesis is corroborated by the fact that the lexically non-transparent initial element *musa* is followed by a verbal noun and can, like affirmative verbal imperatives, be suffixed by the plural marker *ni*:[28]

(26) musa (-ni) uku -thand -a or contracted mus(an)ukuthanda
NEG:IMP -P INF -love -Ø
'don't (ye) love!' (Doke 1927:§417)

For non-POSTINITIAL's in the domain of relative clauses, a different factor must be taken into account, namely the type of linkage of the dependent clause to the main clause. Generally speaking, one can say that subordinate clauses introduced by function words or other conjunction-like elements show in their verbal morphology a much greater similarity to main clauses than do dependent clauses that lack such extra-predicate markers (which is a frequent phenomenon in Bantu, cf. Güldemann (1996, chapter 3)).[29] I cannot give all the empirical evidence for this statement, but will confine myself here to presenting as an example the representative and well-known case of Standard Swahili (G.42). Here, when the relative is constructed analytically on the basis of the subordinating element *amba*, the dependent-clause predicate has, apart from modal grammemes, no morphological restrictions. Thus, in addition to all the other TA-markers not found in synthetically constructed relative clauses, the preinitial main-clause negative *ha* also appears. Compare the following pair of examples for a synthetic and an analytic relative clause, respectively:

28That the element *musa* itself must have been originally a fully inflectable verb is, of course, also recognized by experts on Zulu, as it is considered to be a so-called deficient verb. According to Derek Gowlett (p.c.), it is etymologically related to a verb *-muka* 'go away', whose meaning would be a plausible source for such a negative marker.

29This consideration was also the main reason for excluding syndetically marked dependent verb forms within the domain of adverbial clauses.

(27) nchi zi -si -zo -pat -a uhuru
10:country 10 -NEG -10:R -receive -Ø liberty
'Länder, die die Freiheit nicht erhalten haben' [countries which did not receive their independence; also: do/will not receive...] (Brauner & Herms 1979:182)

(28) nchi ambazo ha -zi -ku -pat -a uhuru
10:country 10:R NEG -10 -PT -receive -Ø liberty
'Länder, die die Freiheit nicht erhalten haben' [countries which did not recieve their independence] (Brauner & Herms 1979:181)

A similar feature holds for the majority of counterexamples in the domain of adverbial dependent verb forms: Postposed clauses often controlled by complement-taking verbs are in some languages treated like main-clause predicates and accordingly can show non-POSTINITIAL negatives. Tonga (M.64) is a typical example for this phenomenon. Postposed asyndetic dependent clauses such as in (29) show verb morphology (i.e., the class 1 subject concord allomorph *u*, a marker for predication focus *li*, and the relevant preinitial negator *tV*) that is excluded from preposed dependent verb forms such as in (30):

(29) a. u -la -mu -jan -a u -li -kede
2S/S -FUT -1/O -find -Ø 1 -PF -sit:STAT
'You will find him sitting.'

b. ndaka -mu -jan -a ta -belek -i
1S/S:REM.PT -1/O -find -Ø NEG:1 -arbeit -PRES
'I found him idling (not working).' (Collins 1962:118)

(30) Timoti a -ta -bool -a ba -la -lil -a
Timothy 1:D.ANT -NEG -come -Ø 2 -PF -cry -PRES
'When Timothy does not arrive, they cry.' [= not having arrived] (Collins 1962:113)

Finally, I will mention a factor which, as an explanation, is not restricted to a specific functional domain but which accounts for a considerable number of exceptions. There are a few Bantu languages where postinitials or periphrases simply do not exist, or are very marginal in the language-specific morphological inventory in that they are confined to a few contexts, often only to a single verb form. Moreover, most such languages—listed in more detail in Güldemann (1996:267ff)—are found in two geographical clusters, each of which can be defined by genetic and/or contact relations. Hence, such extreme marginalization of POSTINITIAL's can be characterized as a local phenomenon within the family as a whole.

It will have become clear that the occurrence of non-POSTINITIAL's in the various clause domains is not only marginal but, where it does occur, can often be explained by other factors. In this respect, one can safely say that the generalization has the quality of a universal tendency within the family.

Now I will present further evidence for the unity of the POSTINITIAL-complex by showing that both of the relevant marker types, even when serving as an alternative strategy for negating main clauses, have similar functional characteristics. This has, until now, hardly been considered to be relevant for assessing the domain of negation in Bantu, let alone specifically associated with particular marking types.

For postinitial negatives, I illustrate this with the following examples:[30]

Chasu-Pare (G.22):

(31)	ha nini	tu	-tong	-a	n	-esi	-kund	-a
	why	NEG:2S	-go	-PRES	1S	-NEG	-love	-PRES

'warum gehst du nicht? Ich liebe es doch nicht.'
[Why don't you go? Because I don't like it!/ Oh, I don't like it, you know.]
(Kotz 1909:4)

Rwanda (J.61) doubt mood:

(32)	ba	-da	-som	-a
	2	-NEG	-read	-PRES

'don't they read?' (Kimenyi 1980:215)

Ziba (J.22):

(33)	n	-ta	-ri	muana
	1S	-NEG	-COP	child

'bin ich etwa ein Kind?' [Am I, after all, a child? > I'm not a child, am I?] (Rehse 1912/1913:226)

At first glance it might be difficult to discern a common denominator for the above negative utterances. In an English-language context, this problem is perhaps even more severe in the two examples taken from

[30]In all the languages concerned, postinitial negation also occurs in the prototypical contexts already discussed, while the unmarked strategy for main-clause negation is preinitial.

German sources, where the original translation conveys the functional features of the discourse context quite nicely, but only by virtue of German-specific modal particles. For the sake of brevity, I refer for the intra-linguistic details to the respective sources and, as regards the relevant discussion, to Güldemann (1996:279ff). Here, I will confine myself to giving a generalized account: What the negative alternatives in these languages have in common is that they show a kind of functional dissociation between the presentation of possibly new information in the predicate and the illocutionary type of the utterance as a whole. In fact, such expressions do not function as canonical speaker denials but appear to be contingent upon some other, contextually given illocution. The latter may be represented by a previous utterance as in (31); it can be condensed in a higher performative operator, like the quasi-interrogative in (32); or it can even be left totally implicit as in (33), where the actual pragmatic function seems to be the indirect speech act of denying something else. Connected with this characteristic is the fact that the negation, although itself possibly conveying new information, is never focussed upon as asserted; instead, the higher performative regularly has informational priority.

Similar functional effects can be connected with periphrastic negation as well. This will be demonstrated by the data given in Takizala (1972) for Hungan (H42). This language uses an initial particle *lo* in unmarked main-clause negation, while it regularly has recourse to a verbal periphrasis with *-khoona* 'to fail', 'to lack' in marked contexts:

Particle negation in main clause and periphrastic negation in dependent clause:

(34)	lo	i	-mween	kit	ki	a-khoon	-in	Kipes	ku	-suum
	NEG	1S	-see:PT	7:chair	7:IR	1-fail	-PT	Kipese	INF	-buy

'I didn't see the chair that Kipese... didn't buy' (Takizala 1972:264)

However, in a certain main-clause type called the tone-focus construction, the expected negative type does not appear. The defining characteristic of such utterances is that some constituent following the predicate is focussed upon, while the predicate itself is extra-focal. If these tone-focus constructions are to be negated, only the periphrastic alternative may be used. The following sentences illustrate the prosodic distinction between the unmarked and marked clause type (35) and the negation of the latter (36):

Neutral vs. tone-focus-construction:

(35)	a.	Kìpès	ká	-swíím	-ín	kìt	zòòn
		Kipese	1	-buy	-PT	chair	yesterday

'Kipese bought a chair yesterday'

versus

b.	Kìpès	ká	-swíím	-ín	kít	zóónó
	Kipese	1	-buy	-PT	chair	yesterday

'Kipese bought a *chair* yesterday' (Takizala 1972:262)

Negation in tone-focus-construction:

(36)	Kìpès	ká	-khóón	-ín	kù	-súúm	kít	zóónó
	Kipese	1	-fail	-PT	INF	-buy	chair	yesterday

'Kipese did not buy a *chair* yesterday' (Takizala 1972:265)

It can be concluded from these examples that, just as in the case of postinitials in marked main clauses, periphrastic negation in Hungan applies precisely when the negation is not part of the focal information in the utterance. Thus we see a further commonality uniting the two negation types with regard to their function.

Considering all these facts, it seems to be a valid generalization that both the postinitial and the periphrastic strategy are the unmarked cases in the specific negation contexts mentioned. This, in turn, confirms the argument that both marking types together form a functional class which stands in opposition to strategies that are typical for unmarked main clauses. An assessment of this more general phenomenon can only be given in section 6, after the discussion of preinitial negatives. At this point, it only serves as an argument for the assumed relatedness of the two marking types with regard to their diachronic evolution.

5. Preinitial negation—a complex predicate of an initial particle with a dependent verb form

In this section, I argue for the hypothesis that preinitial negation has evolved out of a complex predicate pattern in which the predicate can be analyzed as a binary structure wherein a negative nucleus bears the illocutionary force and a finite satellite conveys the propositional information of the predication.

The origin of the satellite can be correlated with an interesting syntactic device within the domain of clause linkage. Many Bantu languages can create complex sentences by the asyndetic linking of two clauses, one of which prototypically serves as the background for the information encoded in the main clause. The structural means for achieving this are quite economical in that a dependent finite predicate—often segmentally identical to though prosodically different from a main-clause verb form—is linked to the sentential matrix without any other segmental device signalling subordination.[31] It should be stressed that such dependent verb forms can

[31] Meeussen (1967:113) treats this subordination device briefly under the term "conjunctive tenses". Only in individual languages and certain sub-groups of Bantu (cf. Doke (1954) with regard to the participial mood in zone S), it has played a more prominent role in past analyses - if likewise only as a

serve a variety of functions: (usually indirect) relative clauses, adverbial clauses, and even others. Both on the family level and in individual languages, such verb forms are characterized by recurrent morphological features.[32]

According to grammaticalization patterns (2) and (3) (see Figure 2.), the "finite torso" of a preinitially negated predicate, i.e., the verb form stripped of its negative prefix, is to be viewed as the synchronic reflex of an erstwhile dependent verb form. Hence, the minimal empirical requirement on my hypothesis is that the conjugational make-up of such negative paradigms should indeed mirror the general characteristics of dependent verb forms. This is indeed corroborated by the linguistic data. Predicates with preinitials clearly demonstrate formal affinities to the verbal morphology of asyndetic background clauses.

A first parallel is evident in the form of the subject concord for class 1 referents. The morpheme in the relevant dependent predicates throughout the family is the verbal prefix *a*. In other contexts, however, one finds both the latter and an allomorph *u*, which I consider to belong to another concord series that Meeussen (1967:96f) terms *pronominal prefixes*. Preinitial negatives prefixed to initial subject concords form together a morpheme complex which, so far exceptionlessly, must be derived for class 1 from underlying NEG-*a*.

A second characteristic which is synchronically relevant for a variety of Bantu languages and considered by Meeussen (1967:97) to be a feature of Proto-Bantu is a tonal distinction between subject concords for *speech act participants* and for *noun classes* (i.e., 3rd persons) in indicative main clauses. This is regularly neutralized both in dependent and preinitially negated verb forms, where all initials have the same prosodic realization—a second parallel between the compared paradigm types.

A third phenomenon which at least strengthens the supposed formal affinity can be observed repeatedly in individual languages: The conjugational morphology of dependent and preinitially negated verb forms shows clear isomorphism, as opposed to that of affirmative main predicates. From the more extensive list in Güldemann (1996:287) I cite only two illustrative cases:

---

conjugational phenomenon. It surfaces across individual languages under various grammatical terms. In addition to Meeussen's "conjunctive"/ "conjonctif" and Doke's "participial", there are, i.a., further English terms like "participle" or "situative" and the Portuguese "gerúndio". Apart from Güldemann (1996), no family-wide analysis has been dedicated to this predicate class concerning its syntactic role on the level of clause linkage and discourse organization. Moreover, it has heretofore gone almost unrecognized as regards its high significance for inferring grammatical features of former chronolects of Bantu from syntactic and morphological features of today's languages.

[32]For further details regarding dependent verb forms, see Güldemann (1996, specifically part 3) and Güldemann (1997a, b).

Nkore-Kiga (J.11):

(37) a. a -rya -teer -a
1 -REM.FUT -beat -Ø
'he will strike'

versus

b. t -a -ri -teer -a
NEG -1 -REM.FUT -beat -Ø
'he will not strike'

and

a -ri -kor -a
1:R -REM.FUT -do -Ø
'who will do' (Taylor 1985:159,168)

Zigula (G.31):

(38) a. w -a -ung -a
2S -PRES -want -Ø
'you want'

versus

b. nk -u -ku -ung -a
NEG -2S -PRES -want -Ø
'you don't like'

and

u -ku -ung -a
2S -PRES:R -want -Ø
'you who like' (Woodward 1902:25,30)

After showing that the morphological characteristics of paradigms with preinitial negatives do not contradict the hypothesis of an origin from former dependent verb forms, I turn now to the relation between the preinitials themselves and free negative particles. What the following data will show is that in some languages we can reconstruct or even synchronically observe the genesis of preinitial negation: It is achieved by preposing a negative copula to a finite predicate, a process which, in turn, can be followed by the development of a phonetic junction between the two constituents.

First, I will present relevant data from Kuria (E.43). Apart from a final particle *he*, Sillery (1936) identifies a postinitial *ta* as the unmarked morphologized negation. However, the language has an alternative at its disposal which is characterized as follows: "Besides the negative forms given above [i.e., the postinitial T.G.], Kuria makes free use of a negative particle *nte*, which may be prefixed to nearly any positive tense and transforms it into a negative, with the addition of the negative suffix...

(39) ba -ta -mo he

2 -NEG -18INE:REF NEG

'They (persons) are not within'

versus

nte ba -mo he

NEG 2 -18INE:REF NEG

'They (persons) are not within'

The process is quite mechanical and may be applied to rebut an assertion such as

(40) chi -ŋgoko ni -na -cho

10 -fowl 1S -COM -10:REF

'"Chickens I have them"

nte chi -ŋgoko u -na -cho he

NEG 10 -fowl 2S -COM -10:REF NEG

"The chickens you have them not"'

It thus appears quite clear that *nte* means "it is not that," and is formed from "n-" (the invariable form of the indicative present of the verb "to be") and the negative particle te." (Sillery 1936:22f)

A similar constellation is encountered with the preinitial *si* in Nyanja (N.31a). This morpheme is both a negative copula and the preinitial negative—in the latter function contracting with vowel-initial subject concords:

(41) lelo si laciwili

today NEG.COP Tuesday

'Today isn't Tuesday.'

si	ku	-Chicago	kweni kweni
NEG.COP	LOC	-Chicago	exactly

'It's not exactly in Chicago'

(Stevick (ed.) 1965:66)

(42)

sa	-ma	-thandiz	-a
NEG:1	-HAB	-help	-PRES

'He/she doesn't help'

si	-ti	-dza	-pit	-a
NEG	-1P	-FUT	-go	-Ø

'We won't go.' (Stevick (ed.) 1965:174)

These two cases will suffice to illustrate the frequently encountered phenomenon (in certain Bantu zones) that a language's negative copula and preinitial negator are homophonous or at least phonetically similar.[33] This evidence fits my assumed source pattern for preinitial negatives.

Finally, the existence of languages where the negation of main clauses is not expressed by a preinitial morpheme but where the overall syntactic design is also a binary structure will substantiate the idea that a complex negation pattern of the type described above is a quite common feature in Bantu languages. I refer specifically to certain languages of zone K where negation is expressed by initial particles which, in turn, show clear sound resemblances (or identity) to copular elements.

This can be illustrated, e.g., in Mbukushu (K.38). The following examples represent a negative copula and its use as a verbal negator. As (44) shows, one also encounters the phenomenon of isomorphism between negative and dependent predicates (i.e., presence of the subjunctive marker *sho*):

(43)

peghundha	badi	mapeghu
tomorrow	NEG.COP	Saturday

'Morgen ist nicht Sonnabend.' [Tomorrow is not Saturday.]

(Fisch 1977:129)

---

[33]Other such languages are treated in Güldemann (1996, chapter 4.7.3.2). These more or less transparent cases are mainly associated with the preinitials listed in Kamba Muzenga (1981:167ff) under his types 2 and 3, reconstructed as *(n)tV* and *sV* respectively. These are especially widespread in zones J, N and parts of E and G. That his reconstructed preinitial *(n)kV* was once also a particle is today only marginally evidenced by copular constructions in some of the languages.

(44) a.

ni	-yend	-e
1S	-go	-SUBJ

'I may go'

versus

b.

badi	sho	ni	-yend	-e
NEG	SUBJ	1S	-go	-Ø

'I may not go'

and

yi	sho	gha	-tend	-e
8IA:IR	SUBJ	1	-do	-Ø

'what he should do'

(Fisch 1977:110,116)

An interesting case which sheds light on the possible origin of negative particles is found in Subiya (K.42). In this language we find relics of a preinitial negative *ka* as in (45):

(45)

ka	-ba	-nyw	-i	menzi
NEG	-2	-drink	-PRES	water

'They are not drinking water.' (Endresen 1983:46)

The unmarked negators, however, are initial particles. One of these, i.e., *kana/keena*, can with all probability be characterized as a paradigmatic reduction of an erstwhile fully inflected auxiliary verb *-ina* 'be', 'have' that took a subject concord of its own and was negated by the preinitial *ka*:[34]

(46)

keena	ni	-ba	-nyw	-i	menzi	izona
NEG	1S	-PT	-drink	-PRFV	water	yesterday

'I did not drink water yesterday' (Endresen 1983:45)

In this case, we observe an instance of my source pattern (2) given in Figure 2. above where, however, the negative finite nucleus did not result in a bound preinitial morpheme but developed, instead, into a phonologically independent function word. Nonetheless, the general parallelism to binary predicate structures, where the second finite constituent is syntactically dependent, is obvious.

[34]The original morphological structure must have been *ka-SC-ina*. For the existence and meaning of the verb in Subiya, see relevant examples in Endresen (1983:78f). A negation of this same pattern where the auxiliary still forms a complete personal paradigm is found, according to Yukawa (1992:318), in Luba-Lulua (L.31). This constitutes additional support for my internal reconstruction.

It must be stressed that all the empirical evidence presented so far supporting my hypothesis for the origin of preinitial negatives has related to a specific subdomain of negation: The two relevant source patterns (2) and (3), with all their concomitant morphological features, can be considered to be originally confined to the context of unmarked main clauses. With regard to this functional characteristic, one can speak—analogously to the POSTINITIAL-complex referred to throughout section 4—of a PREINITIAL-complex: namely, a more abstract function class consisting of preinitials proper, initial particles, and fully inflected preposed finite forms like the one mentioned in the last footnote for Luba (L31). The common denominator of these three subtypes is that in all of them the negative constituent, as the illocutionary nucleus, occurs before the initial subject concord of the finite form that conveys the main semantic content of the proposition. How these two formally, grammaticalizationally, and distributionally definable complexes can be related to each other will be demonstrated in the following section.

6. PREINITIAL- vs. POSTINITIAL-complex from a functional perspective

In the following discussion the theoretical concepts regarding negation are mainly taken from Horn (1989), the most extensive treatment to date. These can serve as a sound foundation for functionally assessing the relevant coding complexes in Bantu.

However, as a starting point, I will present a well-known theoretical approach that is based on the assumption that, compared to affirmation, negation appears in various ways as the marked member of an opposition pair. This asymmetrical analysis of negation has inter alia been repeatedly put forward by Givón, whose views provide a good basis for the discussion. I cite from Givón (1975:108f):

> Reports about negative events constitute valid information on two major types of backgrounds: (i) When the speaker believes that the hearer erroneously believes in the corresponding affirmative; and (ii) When the background expectation for the report was the affirmative action itself. On the first background, the *denial* constitutes a piece of *surprise* or new information for the hearer, given the background of his belief. On the second background, reporting a negative event constitutes a piece of genuine information, given the background of expectation of the affirmative. One way or another, negation is only appropriate if the corresponding event—or change in the inert state of the universe—has been made into *ground*, while normally it is the *figure*. ...
>
> (i) Negation in language has, in addition to its strictly logical aspect, a huge *pragmatic* component that cannot be predicted from the logic.
>
> (ii) Negatives constitute a different *speech act* than affirmatives. While the latter are used to convey new information on the presumption of *ignorance* of the hearer, negatives are used to correct misguided belief on the assumption of the hearer's *error*.

(iii) Negatives are consistently more *marked* in terms of discourse-pragmatic presuppositions, as compared to affirmatives. More specifically, negatives are uttered in a context where corresponding affirmatives have already been discussed, or else where the speaker assumes the hearer's belief in—and thus familiarity with—the corresponding affirmative. ...

This functional characterization of negation is certainly biassed, as will be discussed later. However, it becomes apparent that there exists here an obvious correlation with a specific marking type of Bantu discussed above, i.e., the PREINITIAL-complex.

First, negation is considered by Givón to be a speech act in its own right, where a pragmatically accessible proposition is the background for the negative utterance. This corresponds to the morphosyntactic structure of Bantu PREINITIAL-marking: The initial negative constituent in the form of a particle or a finite auxiliary bears, as the syntactic nucleus, the illocutionary force of the whole complex predicate construction. The following satellite is an affirmative finite verb form which is the presuppositional background and whose illocutionary potential is accordingly neutralized. The binary hierarchical structure within the complex predicate is the formal correlate of an ontologically underlying foreground-background distinction alluded to by Givón. As the function of negation is identified with the illocutionary force of the utterance itself, it follows that the relevant clause must occur in the kind of syntactic context that is, after all, capable of instantiating a speech act: namely, a main clause. And indeed in Bantu, this is precisely the predominant functional domain of the PREINITIAL-complex.

In addition to the relevant examples given above,[35] I will now give further evidence that prototypical main-clause negatives in Bantu do bear a certain degree of pragmatic load and can be structurally organized in a *figure-ground* schema.

In this respect, the following remarks by Horton (1949:179) on negation in Lwena (K.14) bring out the pragmatic distinction between preinitial and periphrastic negation: "The [preinitial T.G.] negative is frequently heard today with the relative clause, used by natives who are in close contact with Europeans, as in

(47)	vaze	ka	-v	-exi	na	-ma	-sevo
	2:DEM	NEG	-2	-be	COM	-6	-father

'Those who have no fathers; the fatherless'

Normally, however, there is no negative relative clause. In order to secure a negative idea the negative verbs *-zeneka* (be without), *-kana* (refuse), *-hona* (be unable, fail), and *-uci* (is not) are used. ...

[35]Cf. especially the case of Kuria (E.43), i.e. (39) and (40) above, where the preposed negative particle *nte* is explicitly said to "rebut an assertion".

(48) vaze va -zenek -a ma -sevo

2:DEM 2:R -lack -PRES 6 -father

'The fatherless'

...Natives who are good speakers say that the [preinitial T.G.] negative implies a statement..." It is not clear whether the "implied statement" alluded to by Horton for preinitial negation can be identified with Givón's "corresponding affirmative". What is evident, however, is that the preinitial negative was originally accompanied by syntactic restrictions. These can be readily explained by an apparent contradiction between the preinitial negative's pragmatic load and the non-illocutionary context of certain clause types, in this case a relative. With regard to these latter clause types, there clearly is a negative expression available in the form of verbal periphrases; what was originally lacking was a grammaticalized negative not associated with illocutionary force.

Another instructive case of main-clause negation can be found in Tumbuka (N.21). Consider first the following description given by Young (1932:137): "The straightforward negative method is to introduce into any affirmative statement the two words 'kuti' and 'chara'. There is no hard-and-fast rule as to how these words should stand in relation to the rest of the sentence, but speaking generally, 'kuti' should introduce and 'chara' should close the negative phrase." Thus:

(49) mw -ana uyu kuti wa -ku -khumb -a

1 -child 1:DEM NEG 1 -PROG -want -Ø

ku -ry -a chara

15INF -eat -Ø NEG

'this child does not wish to eat.' (Young 1932:137)

What is crucial for the analysis of this seemingly complicated negative structure is a semantic-functional assessment of the two function words involved. This is possible on the basis of both internal and comparative data. First, the final *chara* can easily be identified as one of the negative interjections that are used in Tumbuka to respond to a question:

(50) u -ku -ndi -pulik -a chara

2S/S -PROG -1S/O -hear -Ø No!

'do you hear me? no!' (Young 1932:140)

What the preposed element *kuti* does functionally is less transparent. Etymologically it can be related to the infinitive form of a defective auxiliary verb that is widespread in Bantu, the meaning of which, however, is to a certain extent elusive. Important in this context is the frequent grammaticalization of this auxiliary to a clause subordinator. While in postposed dependent clauses it generally serves as a complementizer similar to English *that*, in preposed contexts it has a quite different effect. Cf. a conditional clause from Shona (S10):

(51)	kuti	u	-ci	-many	-a	reg	-a	ku	-ceuk	-a
	SUB	2S	-D:SIM	-run	-Ø	leave	-IMP	15INF	-turn around	-Ø

'When you run, don't look round' (Fortune 1955:411)

In this predication complex *kuti* serves to introduce a preposed conditional protasis (and in fact it can do this only if the protasis is preposed), which is the background for the following sentential matrix. As the position of *kuti* in the negative (49) is parallel to the one found in the Shona complex sentence, i.e., in front of a finite clause which in turn is followed by an illocutionary constituent—in (51) a performative imperative and in (49) the interjection *chara*—I feel justified in carrying over the syntactic pattern of the Shona example to the Tumbuka negative construction: I consider the structure of the latter to be a complex of a topical background-clause conveying the propositional information and an illocutionary negative interjection. One could paraphrase the construction underlying (49) as follows: 'With regard to the state of affairs X(, I say): No!' This is, even from a structural viewpoint, a direct match to the illocutionarily based negation presented by Givón.

Although one cannot expect that language regularly reflects this ontological derivation of negation within its formal expression, typological evidence suggests that the assumed underlying structure for the PREINITIAL-complex in Bantu is not just an idiosyncrasy of this one family. There are geographically and genetically unrelated languages where a structure *illocutionary negative + non-illocutionary background clause* is discernable in main-clause negation, e.g., Rembarrnga (Australia), Nadëb (South America) and Squamish (North America).[36] A similar pattern is the frequent grammaticalization of complex main-clause predicates that demonstrate a source structure *negative existential + affirmative verb form*.[37] This also qualifies as a cross-linguistically attested parallel to the PREINITIAL-complex.

Another hint from a typological perspective is the phenomenon that negation in many languages appears to be an inherently focussed category, that is, it is closely related to the assertion of information within a clause. This idea emerges from the fact that in many languages utterances with a negative predicate but focussing on information other than negation are formally marked or even impossible, as this would amount to a kind of

[36]The sources are McKay (1988, section 5.3), Weir (1994) and Dahl (1979:80f) respectively.

[37]Cf. Horn (1989:450f) and especially Croft (1991) for extensive empirical data.

"double focus".[38] This can again be accounted for by the tendency to encode negation in illocutionary contexts by way of an intrasentential figure-ground organization whereby the focal information includes the negation.

In view of this typological data it will come as no surprise that a clause-context-induced alternation in the formal expression of negation, of the type seen in Bantu, is widespread crosslinguistically as well.[39]

Having outlined a conceptualization of negation which is based primarily on its pragmatic characteristics with regard to illocutionary aspects of an utterance and which emphasizes the asymmetry relation between affirmation and negation, and having shown a clear correlation between this theoretical account and the PREINITIAL-marking type of Bantu, it is necessary to stress that this approach must be seen in relative terms. There is no space here to repeat from the extensive literature all the arguments against such a one-sided analysis of negation. I will only alude to an obvious contradiction between viewing negation exclusively as a speech act and the existence of negation in linguistic contexts which, by definition, do not instantiate an illocution—that is, precisely the case of the POSTINITIAL-complex. By way of example, I append the following citation from Horn (1989), showing that this argument has also played a role in theoretical treatments:

> If my account of the markedness of negation is even generally correct, the asymmetry thesis... applies to the level of pragmatics. Negative propositions are typically, but not necessarily, less specific and less informative than positive propositions. ... however, the real asymmetry is located, not in the relation of negative to positive propositions, but in the relation of (speaker) denials to assertions.
>
> As Strawson stresses, 'the standard and primary *use*' of negatives is 'to correct and contradict' (emphasis mine)—but, pace Wittgenstein and Givón, use is not meaning. As a formal philosopher primarily concerned with meaning and truth, Frege (1919) focuses on the logical symmetry between positive and negative propositional content and correctly rejects the identification of negation with the speech act of denial; for one thing, as Frege teaches us, an embedded negative clause cannot be analyzed as asserting or denying anything. (Horn 1989:201f)

What both theoretical reasoning and linguistic facts concerning the purely pragmatically oriented approach to negation really call for, however, is not its total rejection but, instead, a search for a position, as Horn puts it, between the "radical asymmetricalists and the single-minded logical symmetricalists":

> Not every negation is a speaker denial, nor is every speaker denial a linguistic negation, but the prototypic use of negation is indeed as a

---

[38]Cf. Marchese (1983), Heine-Reh (1983) and Hyman-Watters (1984) for African languages.

[39]Cf. inter alia data in Heine-Reh (1983:23ff), Payne (1985:240f) and Horn (1989:447ff).

> denial of a proposition previously asserted, or subscribed to, or held as plausible by, or at least mentioned by, someone relevant in the discourse context.
>
> Thus, while affirmation not only can but standardly does function to introduce a proposition into the discourse model, negation—in its 'chief use'...—is directed at a proposition already in the discourse model. Further... we can isolate a METALINGUISTIC use of negation in English and other languages, specialized precisely for just this function of negative statements. But... not all instances of negation can be characterized in this way.
>
> Like Freud's dreamer... for whom *It is not my mother* really means 'It is my mother', the strong asymmetricalist thesis is literally false but psychologically true. (203)

The negation type termed by Horn *metalinguistic*, which apparently can be associated with Givón's *negative speech act*, is further described by Horn in the following way:

> Metalinguistic negation... is used to deny or object to any aspect of a previous utterance—from the conventional or conversational implicata that may be associated with it to its syntactic, morphological, or phonetic form. ... those aspects of the utterance which metalinguistic negation is used to focus on may have nothing to do with the proposition expressed by that utterance. (414f)

Having presented some necessary qualifications regarding a purely pragmatic approach to negation, I turn now to its other aspect, pertaining to the field of semantics. In such an analytical frame, negation appears as a semantic attribute standing in a symmetrical relation to its affirmative counterpart. Horn terms this type *descriptive* negation.

In some contexts this semantic symmetry between a descriptive negative and a positive expression is quite transparent, especially when the phenomenal space comprises only two members which are distinguished precisely by this parameter. Insofar as in the following pair of restrictive relative clauses the head noun is assigned a certain feature, with the negation an internal part of the embedded predicate, descriptive negation in such contexts can even be viewed as a positive statement about the attributional relation between an entity and a certain characteristic:

(52) people who work vs. people who don't work

Compare also:

(53) to have and to have not

In the sense that metalinguistic negation is inseparably linked to the illocutionary act of the utterance while descriptive negation is not, both negation types have to be kept apart functionally. And indeed, language shows a tendency to structurally reflect this ambivalent nature of negation. This leads us directly to the assessment of the second negation complex of Bantu, i.e., the POSTINITIAL type. If one reexamines its prototypical contexts treated in section 4 above, it becomes obvious that it is precisely the semantic aspect of negation that serves as a unifying common denominator. In all such contexts one observes a functional dissociation between the negation per se and the illocutionary force of the utterance. Either the relevant clause has no illocutionary force at all or the realized speech act does not coincide with negation as an illocutionary feature. The former case applies to the two backgrounded subordinate clause types, where the illocution is instantiated by the main clause, and to verbal nouns. The latter case holds for the two directive performatives prohibitive and subjunctive. Further, POSTINITIAL-strategies in marked main clauses seem to occur when the performative act is not directly conveyed by the predicate of which negation is an operator or when negation is, together with the predicate, extra-focal in that it is not part of the asserted information.

Even regarding morphosyntactic structure, the POSTINITIAL-complex appears in a way to correlate with descriptive negation: Especially in its nongrammaticalized form, i.e., the periphrastic type, a finite negative auxiliary may be considered to be a positive attribute of the predication base in that negation here is not an abstract morphologized operator of the predicate but in a very literal sense the predicate itself.

> Taking the previous considerations into account, the following extreme position by Givón (1984/1990:323) cannot be maintained: [The symmetrical, semantically based analysis of negation T.G.] has been sufficiently elaborated in the traditional logic-bound literature, and we will have relatively little to add to it. It pertains to a universe of propositions in an idealized system disembodied of speakers, hearers, discourse context, communicative intent or communicative function.

As the linguistic facts suggest, the semantic interpretation of negation can also be successfully incorporated in a functionally plausible way into a system with "speakers, hearers, discourse context, communicative intent or communicative function", because the complex organization of language provides contexts where clauses can lose their illocutionary potential and be reduced to their bare propositional content. It is not necessarily the linguist who pragmatically "disembodies" the system of language when he rightfully views negation as (inter alia) a purely semantic feature; it is the communicating speaker who, in particular clause contexts, strips a predicative expression of its illocutionary force.

7. Implications for Bantu reconstruction

Above, I have tried to functionally characterize the two main marking complexes of negation in Bantu: I have correlated them with different degrees of pragmatic relevance, i.e., PREINITIAL's in illocutive negation vs. POSTINITIAL's in semantic negation. Some clarifications in this respect are now in order.

Although the distributional features of these two types have long been acknowledged in Bantu philology and can easily be confirmed by statistical figures, it will have become clear that they only represent a strong tendency, not a one-to-one relation between a form and a function. I have already mentioned that there are, on the one hand, languages having only postinitials at their disposal, which means that this strategy is also capable of encoding metalinguistic negation as a speech-act. On the other hand, I have remarked on some languages where preinitials undoubtedly occur in non-illocutionary contexts, i.e., this strategy also can be used for descriptive negation. Hence it cannot be said that a specific negation type invariably covaries with the clause context.

Another more general qualification has to be made with regard to the relation between clause type and negation type: It must not be assumed that negation is in all illocutionary contexts of unmarked main clauses necessarily a rejection of an utterance that is in whatever sense pragmatically accessible. Discourse-based studies may well reveal that this even holds only for a minority of cases.

What does appear to be valid, however, is that the two basic marking complexes in Bantu have different functional biasses which stem from their specific grammaticalizational origins. What I have put forward in section 3 above, I would like to emphasize again here: The generalization which can be drawn from the data is not a simple pattern of complementary distribution of the two marking complexes but, instead, a relation of differing markedness.

In this regard, the POSTINITIAL's appear to be contextually more universal compared with PREINITIAL's and some other prototypical main-clause negatives, as they are not inherently subject to grammatical restrictions. This can be explained by the fact that their grammaticalizational origin is not necessarily tied to one particular pragmatic environment. A semantic feature negation that refers as such to the propositional content of an utterance is in principle open to any illocutionary type.

In contrast, this is not the case with PREINITIAL's, which evolve out of a construction that explicitly reflects, with regard to both form and function, the *correction* or *contradiction* of a previous utterance. Insofar as the negative constituent which is preposed to an affirmative finite verb is used by the speaker to perform the actual illocutionary act within the construction as a whole, the original linguistic contexts in which these negative constituent may finally undergo grammaticalization toward a PREINITIAL are severely constrained. This pragmatic feature of the least grammaticalized stages of PREINITIAL's is the reason for characterizing the resulting grammatical restrictions on their distribution as "inherent".

Such a difference in pragmatic markedness becomes especially obvious when markers of the two contrasting types are both compatible with main clauses. In this case, the PREINITIAL negative is invariably more marked compared with the POSTINITIAL alternative in that it always bears the above kind of pragmatic load in addition to its semantic feature. It condenses, so to speak, the negative meaning into the illocutionary act of the utterance.[40]

The regularly observable restrictions of PREINITIAL's with respect to clause-type distribution can be captured in terms of a common phenomenon in grammaticalization processes which is termed by Hopper (1991:28ff) *persistence*, i.e., the maintainance of structural and functional features which are associated with the source construction. That PREINITIAL's, after all, do occur as descriptive negatives does not represent a contradiction to my above arguments. Rather, it is in accordance with insights into grammaticalization: Linguistic structures with a high pragmatic load regularly are found at the beginning of grammaticalization processes. If these proceed further, the construction can be subject to gradual *context extension* which, in turn, can lead to the loosening of grammatical constraints associated with the original source pattern. Formerly prominent pragmatic functions can eventually be narrowed down to purely semantic features. What would be ruled out by my assumptions, however, is a PREINITIAL marker that was used in its grammaticalizational development as a descriptive negator before it had been used as a metalinguistic one. This is indeed corroborated by the empirical facts encountered so far.

The relation between the two marking types under discussion can also be discerned through their different patterning in single languages and the statistical representation of resulting language types in the family as a whole. This, in turn, will bear on possible conclusions regarding Bantu reconstruction. Four basic language-specific distribution patterns of POST- and PREINITIAL negation can be distinguished in this respect:[41]

(1) POSTINITIAL only
(2) POSTINITIAL in all clauses and a PREINITIAL alternative in main clauses
(3) POST- and PREINITIAL in the typical clause-type-dependent distribution
(4) PREINITIAL only (or at least predominantly)

Relating the grammaticalizational aspects of the two negation types to the above four patterns, one is tempted to establish a historical scenario for how languages change from one type to another. In a language of type (1),

---

[40]This is not to say that all utterances containing a PREINITIAL negative must be pragmatically more marked than those with a POSTINITIAL. Other functional features may intervene which can bear on the markedness assessment of the clause type as a whole (cf. inter alia the doubt mood of Rwanda (J.61) and the tone-focus constructions of Hungan (H.42) referred to above). An evaluation of these different constructions would require a functional classification of main clauses which is in principle independent of the semantic feature negation.

[41]This classification does not explicitly consider more complex cases where there is a negative alternation within main-clause indicatives according to TA-features. However, it is assumed that the classification could descriptively capture such phenomena.

the POSTINITIAL strategy serves to express negation in all clause types by virtue of its pragmatic neutrality. Although such a state of affairs is the second most frequent in my corpus, it is under certain conditions quite unstable. There exists an apparent tendency to use in a speech act of metalinguistic negation a structure whose expressiveness is more appropriate to the illocutionary force of such an act. As the PREINITIAL type is an adequate means to achieve this, a language of type (2) with two negations in illocutionary contexts would come into being. Although Kuria (E.43) could be cited as a relevant case in point, there are not many examples of type (2). The restriction of a PREINITIAL to express only speaker denials seems to be lost relatively early, thereby extending the formal strategy to other discourse contexts. In this process the POSTINITIAL becomes either restricted to marginal, sometimes highly marked main clause types or is, with the exception of directive performatives, lost completely from illocutionary contexts. In the latter case one arrives at a canonical language of type (3). As this is the most frequent type in Bantu, one can conclude that it is a fairly stable situation for languages of this family. If the PREINITIAL strategy is extended still further, intruding into non-illocutionary clause types, it will have been deprived of its original pragmatic characteristics and, in principle, will no longer be functionally distinct from a POSTINITIAL strategy. This move towards type (4) is found in relatively few languages and the change is completely achieved only in a very small number of them. Instead, most such languages show relics of POSTINITIAL's in their typical clause contexts, a nearly unmistakable sign that the synchronic situation has indeed evolved out of a type (3) pattern.[42]

Individual subgroups of the Bantu family appear to manifest at least parts of such a historical chronology.[43] Can one conclude from this, for the entire genetic unit Bantu, that POSTINITIAL's are generally older than PREINITIAL's?

---

[42]Moreover, it should be remembered that such a development is sometimes associated with other negation-independent factors. Some of these were briefly alluded to above in connection with the discussion of Table 1, especially as regards PREINITIAL's in dependent clauses—e.g., type of clause linkage, or position of dependent clause with respect to the matrix.

[43]Interlacustrine Bantu (i.e. languages of zones E and J) could be a case in point. There, the preinitial *(n)tV* apparently deriving from a negative copula seems to be historically younger than the postinitial *ta*. This can be concluded from the fact that we find languages of all intermediate stages of grammaticalization between pure types (1) and (3), while (4) is totally absent. We find in this group a considerable number of type (1) languages, the case of Kuria (E.43) belonging to type (2), a few languages with a situation intermediate between (2) and (3) like Rwanda (J.61) and Ziba (J.22), and finally the bulk of languages showing the Bantu-typical situation of type (3) (for more detailed information on the relevant languages and data sources see Güldemann 1996:288ff).

The facts derivable from comparative analyses on the family level do not yield much evidence in favour of such a hypothesis.[44] First, comparing the number of reconstructible cognate sets involving the post- and the preinitial marker class, respectively, one does not find any difference. On the assumption that postinitials have diachronic precedence one would have expected the synchronic situation in the family to reflect the processes of its genetic divergence by a higher etymological variation on the part of the presumably younger, i.e., the preinitial marker type. This is not the case. One arrives at a similar picture if the post- and preinitial negative affixes are compared with regard to possible differences in phonetic substance or morphophonological fusion with the predicate. Reconstructed preinitials are not remarkably longer or less fused with their adjacent morphemes; thus they do not show a lower degree of grammaticalization, which would be expected if they were at least tendentially younger than postinitials. These findings point, rather, to a fairly similar stratificational age for both negative prefix types.

A corresponding generalization for the relation between the two more abstract form classes POST- and PREINITIAL is even less tenable. This is evident from the existence of languages like the above-mentioned Lwena (K.14), which have a preinitial negative affix in main clauses and an apparently less grammaticalized verbal periphrasis encoding negation in relative clauses.

Another argument, which is a kind of necessary condition for the assumption of a same age for POST- and PREINITIAL's, can be put forward from a more general point of view: Both types of marking complexes are connected with one and the same morphosyntactic structure of the Bantu predicate. The fact that the formal preconditions for their genesis are similar—which also holds for the synchronic situation and provides for the still ongoing development of both marker types in individual languages—does not point to a different typological organization of Bantu at the periods when each type appeared for the first time in the family. To put it another way, the structural "grammaticalizability" of both POSTINITIAL and PREINITIAL markers pertains to one and the same language stratum.

In addition to these empirical findings, one can also argue against the above conclusion on theoretical grounds. It is necessary to distinguish between universal function types of negation and language-specific form classes that serve the linguistic expression of the former. The above scenario refers to the two morphosyntactically definable strategies PRE- and POSTINITIAL negation. However, what underlies the hypothesized developments are functional, form-independent considerations. These have all been mentioned above already, but will be recapitulated briefly here.

The first is the fact that negation has different functional characteristics depending on the discourse context in which it is to be expressed. Applying

[44]Cf. Kamba Muzenga (1981) as an extensive data source.

this to the concrete situation in the Bantu family and thus combining functional considerations with their language-specific instantiations, i.e., relating function to form, one can account for the different preferred patternings of the two marking types.

The second functional factor is the tendency toward structural innovation via pragmatic reinforcement, which plays an important role in the domain of negation. Such innovation of forms—and concurrent context-sensitive replacement of others—has obviously occurred in the Bantu family several times independently. This is demonstrated by the different morphological material involved and the varying degrees of its grammaticalization across individual languages. Because of the fact that this recurrent process starts and spreads out from the domain of metalinguistic, or more generally, pragmatically sensitive negation, one can explain why in this process certain family-specific form types are preferred over others.

Third and finally, the forces fostering a tendency toward different syntactic behavior of the two marking complexes pertain only to their initial evolutionary stages. This shows that form has also its function-independent aspects. Hence a PREINITIAL, although the prototype of metalinguistic negation in Bantu, can also stand at the beginning of the innovation cycle, i.e., whenever it has been extended into the domain of descriptive negation.

Taking all these considerations into account, two conclusions emerge. First, the above scenario is only one of several possible scenarios for how individual forms can be diachronically related to each other within the more general frame of a cyclic rise and fall of negative constructions. Second, there is, from both a formal and a functional point of view, no reason to believe that either the POST- or the PREINITIAL negation complex takes diachronic precedence over the other.

This should also be applied to the following statement by Kamba Muzenga (1981) regarding a Bantu-wide reconstruction of the form of the "indicatif negatif", which can be associated with the context of non-modal, syntactically independent main clauses. There, a general scenario for main clauses is proposed which runs directly counter to some of the considerations proposed in this paper:

> On constate que le morphème négatif figure en position préinitiale dans un très grand nombre de langues et en F, J, M, P et S. Deux hypothèses... peuvent expliquer cette répartition géographique. La première, qui ne résiste pas à la critique, supposerait que la position postinitiale est ancienne et que les langues à préinitiale, bien qu'elles soient beaucoup plus nombreuses, auraient innové; en effet, la position postinitiale est attestée au nord du domaine bantou et surtout dans des zones aussi éloignées géographiquement que les zones A, F, M et S... La seconde hypothèse, qui est plus plausible, considérerait la position préinitiale comme plus ancienne, car elle est largement attestée dans les langues bantoues. ...

> Nous sommes en présence d'une correspondance importante: le morphème négatif du protobantou aurait figuré en position préinitiale à l'indicatif absolutif. On peut dès lors supposer que, dans les langues qui attestent une postinitiale à l'indicatif, le morphème négatif était employé en position préinitiale à l'origine, mais est apparu, à une date plus ou moins récente, en position postinitiale, sans doute lorsque ces langues ont perdu l'usage de la préinitiale. D'ailleurs, le relatif objectif n'a plus de préinitiale dans ces langues. ...Nos conclusions confirment donc les thèses émises jusqu'à présent par les comparatistes concernant la position du morphème négatif à l'indicatif et qui ont été résumées par A.E. Meeussen dans ses *Bantu grammatical reconstructions*. (Kamba Muzenga 1981:17ff)

Kamba Muzenga's line of reasoning is mainly based on a single argument: With the implicit premise that all synchronically attested languages can be derived from one proto-form having only one negative expression in a particular context, he relies on the criteria of *frequency* and *geographical distribution* of the relevant strategies. If one considers only these criteria in the evaluation of the synchronically observable facts, one almost inevitably concludes—in view of the clear dominance of preinitials in main clauses—that these must have been the exclusive means in Proto-Bantu for expressing negation in this context and that postinitials only intruded at a later stage of development.

I will not again bring forward all the arguments which support the idea that in principle both marker types are today, and in the reachable time depth of Bantu presumably always have been, available in the domain of main clause negation. I also will not dwell on the consideration that the criteria of frequency and geographical distribution are often not very diagnostic for family-internal reconstruction. What the above analysis suffers from principally are the following points.

On the one hand, the very concept of his proto-language, regarding both its relation to the synchronic picture of variation within the family and its overall design as an instantiation of universal linguistic principles, appears to me highly questionable. With regard to the concept of the monogenetically oriented reconstructibility of a proto-language it will suffice to refer to the objections made by Bantuists like Möhlig (inter alia 1976, 1979), who views the factor of family-internal convergence as being just as important for the development of today's attested languages as divergence processes—a view which I share. Another problem arises when one considers the question of how many negation markers are to be reconstructed for a given grammatical context. First, from the situation in several Bantu languages it becomes clear that the traditional categorization of predicate classes or, on a higher linguistic level, of clause types into (to follow Kamba Muzenga) "indicatif", "subjonctif", "relatif", "infinitif", and "conjonctif" is not sufficient. In particular, what has been traditionally subsumed under the predicate category "indicatif" is far from being a homogeneous class. Rather, there exist functional parameters calling for a more fine-grained analysis—parameters such as *predication focus*, *event-*

central theticity, and even certain verbal features heretofore termed *aspects*, which operate especially in this "indicatif" predicate class and can further subdivide it.[45] Empirical data clearly shows that these functional features also interact intimately with the parameter of negation in that they often trigger a different negation strategy than do unmarked main clause contexts. Second, even if these cases were excluded, one would be left with others, where two negative markers coexist with no obvious motivation. Hence the question of whether some earlier chronolects of Bantu had one or more negation markers in the indicatif cannot be answered conclusively as long as this category is not defined more precisely. Thus, the presuppositions underlying Kamba Muzenga's analysis seem to me inappropriate.[46]

On the other hand, an analysis and reconstruction of form independent from relevant functional considerations has its effect on the results to be achieved. Although form cannot always be motivated straightforwardly by functional aspects of language, the ever-present possibility of a connection should not be neglected. Thus, in the particular case of negation in Bantu, it is not sufficient just to acknowledge the existence of different marking types in different contexts. One also should ask why that is the case—a question which, as I have tried to show above, can indeed be answered to a considerable degree. Kamba Muzenga's separate treatment of such established predicate classes as "indicatif", "subjonctif", "relatif", "infinitif", and "conjonctif" does not bring out the clear commonality of non-"indicatifs" vis-a-vis the "indicatif". This in particular obscures the specific interaction between certain clause-type features and the expression of negation. In my view, only a holistically oriented comparison of the various marking devices with regard to both formal and functional aspects can reveal the principles that govern family-internal regularities of frequency and distribution of negative markers and shed light on the historical emergence of these patterns.

References

Bastin, Yvonne. 1978. Les langues bantoues, in: Barreteau, Daniel (ed.), *Inventaire des études linguistiques sur les pays d'Afrique Noire d'expression française et sur Madagascar.* Paris: Conseil International de la Langue Française, 123-185.

[45]For the first two functional domains see Güldemann (1996, chapters 4.3 and 4.4).

[46]Kamba Muzenga cites an additional argument. Appealing inter alia to the analysis in the preliminary version of Nsuka Nkutsi (1982), where relative clause formation in Proto-Bantu is reconstructed, he refers to a language-specific correlation between the loss of a preinitial object relative marker and the loss of the preinitial negative. As the relative reconstruction relies on the same kind of premises as those criticized above, which must be questioned both theoretically and empirically (cf. Güldemann 1996, chapter 3.3., especially 116f), this evidence does not in fact bring any new argument to bear.

Bennett, Patrick R., Ann Biersteker, Waithira Gikonyo, Susan Hershberg, Joel Kamande, Carolyn Perez & Martha Swearingen. 1985. *Gĩkũyũ nĩ Kioigire: Essays, texts and glossaries.* Madison: The African Studies Program, University of Wisconsin.

Brauner, Siegmund & Irmtraud Herms. 1979. *Lehrbuch des modernen Swahili.* Leipzig: Enzyklopädie.

Chatelain, Heli. 1888/1889. *Grammática elementar do Kimbundu ou língua de Angola.* Genebra: Schuchardt.

Collins, B. 1962. *Tonga grammar.* London: Longmans and Green.

Croft, William. 1991. The evolution of negation, *Journal of Linguistics* 27:1-27.

Dahl, Östen. 1979. Typology of sentence negation, *Linguistics* 17:79-106.

Doke, Clement M. 1927. *Text-book of Zulu grammar.* London: Longmans and Green.

Doke, Clement M. 1954. *The Southern Bantu languages.* London: Oxford University Press.

Endresen, Rolf T. 1983. *Towards a grammar of Subiya.* Nittedal: manuscript.

Fisch, Maria. 1977. *Einführung in die Sprache der Mbukushu, Ost-Kavango, Namibia.* (Wissenschaftliche Forschung in Südwestafrika 15.) Windhoek: S.W.A. Wissenschaftliche Gesellschaft.

Fortune, George. 1955. *An analytical grammar of Shona.* London: Longmans and Green.

Givón, Talmy. 1975. Negation in language: Pragmatics, function, ontology, *Working Papers on Language Universals* 18:59-116.

Givón, Talmy. 1984/1990. *Syntax: A functional-typological introduction,* 2 vols. Amsterdam: Benjamins.

Güldemann, Tom. 1996. *Verbalmorphologie und Nebenprädikationen im Bantu: Eine Studie zur funktional motivierten Genese eines konjugationalen Subsystems.* (Bochum-Essener Beiträge zur Sprachwandelforschung 27.) Bochum: Universitätsverlag Dr. N. Brockmeyer.

Güldemann, Tom. 1997a. *Prosodisdic Markierung als sprachliche Strategie zur Hierarchisierung verknüpfter Prädikationen am Beispiel des Shona.* (University of Leipzig Papers on Africa, Languages and Literatures 2.) Leipzig: Institut für Afrikanistik, Universität Leipzig.

Güldemann, Tom. 1997b. Prosodic subordination as a strategyfor complex sentence construction in Shona: bantu moods revisited, in: Herbert, Robert K. (ed.), *African Linguistics of the Crossroads: Papers from Kwaluseni, First World Congres of African Linguistics, Swaziland, 18.-22.7.1994.* Köln: Rüdiger Köppe, 75-98.

Guthrie, Malcolm. 1967-1971. *Comparative Bantu.* 4 vols. Farnborough: Gregg Press.

Harries, Lyndon P. 1950. *A grammar of Mwera.* (Bantu Grammatical Archives 1.) Johannesburg: Witwatersrand University Press.

Heine, Bernd, Ulrike Claudi & Friederike Hünnemeyer. 1991. *Grammaticalization: A conceptual framework.* Chicago: Chicago University Press.

Heine, Bernd & Mechthild Reh. 1983. Diachronic observations on completive focus marking in some African languages, *Sprache und Geschichte in Afrika* 5:7-44.

Heine, Bernd & Mechthild Reh. 1984. *Grammaticalization and reanalysis in African languages.* Hamburg: Buske.

Hopper, Paul J. 1991. On some principles of grammaticization, in: Traugott, Elizabeth Closs & Bernd Heine (eds.), 1:17-35.

Hopper, Paul J. & Elizabeth Closs Traugott. 1993. *Grammaticalization.* Cambridge: Cambridge University Press.

Horn, Laurence R. 1989. *A natural history of negation.* Chicago: Chicago University Press.

Horton, A. E. 1949. *A grammar of Luvale.* Johannesburg: Witwatersrand University Press.

Hyman, Larry M. & John R. Watters. 1984. Auxiliary focus, *Studies in African Linguistics* 15,3:233-273.

Kamba Muzenga, J. G. 1981. *Les formes verbales négatives dans les langues bantoues.* (Annalen Menselijke Wetenschappen 106.) Tervuren: Koninklijk Museum voor Midden-Afrika.

Kimenyi, Alexandre. 1980. *A relational grammar of Kinyarwanda.* (University of California Publications in Linguistics 91.) Berkeley: University of California Press.

Kotz, Ernst. 1909. *Grammatik des Chasu.* (Archiv für das Studium deutscher Kolonialsprachen 10.) Berlin: Reimer.

Krumm, Bernhard. 1912. Grundriß einer Grammatik des Kimatumbi, *Mitteilungen des Seminars für Orientalische Sprachen zu Berlin,* 3. Abteilung: Afrikanische Studien 15:1-63.

Lehmann, Christian. 1982. *Thoughts on grammaticalization: A programmatic sketch.* (Arbeiten des Kölner Universalien-Projekts 48.) Köln: Institut für Sprachwissenschaft, Universität zu Köln.

Marchese, Lynell. 1983. On assertive focus and the inherent focus nature of negatives and imperatives: Evidence from Kru, *Journal of African Languages and Linguistics* 5,2:115-129.

McKay, Graham R. 1988. Figure and ground in Rembarrnga complex sentences, in: Austin, Peter (ed.), *Complex sentence constructions in Australian languages.* (Typological Studies in Language 15.) Amsterdam: Benjamins, 7-36.

Meeussen, Achille E. 1967. Bantu grammatical reconstructions, in: *Africana Linguistica 3.* (Annalen Wetenschappen van de Mens 61.) Tervuren: Koninklijk Museum voor Midden-Afrika, 79-121.

Meinhof, Carl. 1948. *Grundzüge einer vergleichenden Grammatik der Bantusprachen.* Berlin: Reimer.

Miehe, Gudrun. 1979. *Die Sprache der älteren Swahili-Dichtung (Phonologie und Morphologie).* (Marburger Studien zur Afrika- und Asienkunde, Serie A: Afrika 18.) Berlin: Reimer.

Missionários da Companhia de Jesus. 1964. *Elementos de gramática Cinyanja.* Lisboa: Junta de Investigações do Ultramar.

Möhlig, Wilhelm J. G. 1976. Guthries Beitrag zur Bantuistik aus heutiger Sicht, *Anthropos* 71:673-715.

Möhlig, Wilhelm J. G. 1979. The Bantu nucleus: Its conditional nature and its prehistorical significance, *Sprache und Geschichte in Afrika* 1:109-141.

Ndolo, Pius. 1972. *Essai sur la tonalite et la flexion verbale du gimbala.* (Archief voor Antropologie 19.) Tervuren: Koninklijk Museum voor Midden-Afrika.

Nsuka Nkutsi, F. 1982. *Les structures fondamentales du relatif dans les langues bantoues.* (Annalen Menselijke Wetenschappen 108.) Tervuren: Koninklijk Museum voor Midden-Afrika.

Payne, John R. 1985. Negation, in: Shopen, Timothy (ed.), *Language typology and syntactic description.* 2 vols. Cambridge: Cambridge University Press, 1:197-242.

Polak-Bynon, Louise. 1975. *A Shi grammar: Surface structures and generative phonology of a Bantu language.* (Annalen Menselijke Wetenschappen 86.) Tervuren: Koninklijk Museum voor Midden-Afrika.

Purvis, J. B. 1907. *A manual of Lumasaba grammar.* London: Society for Promoting Christian Knowledge.

Rehse, Hermann. 1912/1913. Die Sprache der Baziba in Deutsch-Ost-Afrika, *Zeitschrift für Kolonialsprachen* 3,1:1-33/3,2:81-123/3,3:201-229.

Sillery, A. 1936. Notes for a grammar of the Kuria language, *Bantu Studies* 10:9-29.

Stevick, Earl W. (ed.). 1965. *Chinyanja basic course.* Washington, D.C.: Foreign Service Institute, Department of State.

Takizala, Alexis. 1972. Focus and relativization: The case of Kihung'an, *Studies in African Linguistics* 3,2:259-284.

Taylor, Charles. 1985. *Nkore-Kiga.* London-Sydney-Dover, New Hampshire: Croom Helm.

Traugott, Elizabeth Closs & Bernd Heine (eds.). 1991. *Approaches to grammticalization.* 2 vols. (Typological Studies in Language 19.) Amsterdam: Benjamins.

Weir, E. M. Helen. 1994. Nadëb, in: Kahrel, Peter-René van den Berg (eds.), *Typological studies in negation.* (Typological Studies in Language 29.) Amsterdam: Benjamins, 291-323.

Westphal, Ernst O. J. 1958. An introductory comparative study of negation in Bantu, *Mitteilungen des Insituts für Orientforschung* 6,2:284-320.

Whiteley, Wilfred H. 1966. *A study of Yao sentences.* Oxford: Clarendon Press.

Woodward, H. W. 1902. *Collections for a handbook of the Zigula language.* Msalabani: Universities' Mission, Magila Deutsch-Ostafrika.

Worms, A. 1897. Grundzüge der Grammatik des Ki-Zaramo in Deutsch-Ostafrika, *Zeitschrift für afrikanische und oceanische Sprachen* 3:289-310.

Young, T. Cullen. 1932. *Notes on the speech of the Tumbuka-Kamanga peoples in the northern province of Nyasaland.* London: The Religious Tract Society.

Yukawa, Yasutoshi. 1987. A tonological study of Nkoya verbs, in: *Studies in Zambian languages.* (Bantu Linguistics (ILCAA) 1.) Tokyo: Institute for the Study of Languages and Cultures of Asia and Africa, Tokyo University of Foreign Studies, 129-184.

Yukawa, Yasutoshi. 1989. A tonological study of Nilamba verbs, in: *Studies in Tanzanian languages.* (Bantu Linguistics (ILCAA) 2.) Tokyo: Institute for the Study of Languages and Cultures of Asia and Africa, Tokyo University of Foreign Studies, 405-450.

Yukawa, Yasutoshi. 1992. A tonological study of Luba verbs, in: *Studies in Cameroonian and Zairean languages.* (Bantu Linguistics (ILCAA) 3.) Tokyo: Institute for the Study of Languages and Cultures of Asia and Africa, Tokyo University of Foreign Studies, 303-362.

Language Index

In this index, Bantu language names are generally listed without their prefix: hence, Bemba instead of Cibemba, Ganda instead of Luganda, etc. In certain cases where a language is frequently referred to in the literature with its prefix (e.g. in the papers in this collection), a cross-reference is given. In addition to languages, names of several of the proposed language groupings are also included, e.g. Rutara, Sabaki etc.